ROUTLEDGE COMPANION TO INTELLIGENCE STUDIES

The *Routledge Companion to Intelligence Studies* provides a broad overview of the growing field of intelligence studies.

The recent growth of interest in intelligence and security studies has led to an increased demand for popular depictions of intelligence and reference works to explain the architecture and underpinnings of intelligence activity. Divided into five comprehensive sections, this Companion provides a strong survey of the cutting-edge research in the field of intelligence studies:

- **Part I:** The evolution of intelligence studies;
- **Part II:** Abstract approaches to intelligence;
- **Part III:** Historical approaches to intelligence;
- **Part IV:** Systems of intelligence;
- **Part V:** Contemporary challenges.

With a broad focus on the origins, practices and nature of intelligence, the book not only addresses classical issues, but also examines topics of recent interest in security studies. The overarching aim is to reveal the rich tapestry of intelligence studies in both a sophisticated and accessible way.

This Companion will be essential reading for students of intelligence studies and strategic studies, and highly recommended for students of defence studies, foreign policy, Cold War studies, diplomacy and international relations in general.

Robert Dover is Senior Lecturer in International Relations and Director of Taught Postgraduate Programmes at Loughborough University. He is author of *The Europeanization of British Defence Policy 1997–2005* (2007) and co-author, with Michael S. Goodman, of *Spinning Intelligence: Why Intelligence Needs the Media, Why the Media Needs Intelligence* (2009).

Michael S. Goodman is Reader in the Department of War Studies at King's College London. He is author of *Spying on the Nuclear Bear: Anglo-American Intelligence and the Soviet Bomb* (2008), and co-author of *Spinning Intelligence: Why Intelligence Needs the Media, Why the Media Needs Intelligence* (2009).

Claudia Hillebrand is Lecturer in the Department of International Politics at Aberystwyth University. She is author of *Counter-Terrorism Networks in the European Union: Maintaining Democratic Legitimacy after 9/11* (2012).

ROUTLEDGE COMPANION TO INTELLIGENCE STUDIES

Edited by
Robert Dover, Michael S. Goodman
and Claudia Hillebrand

Routledge
Taylor & Francis Group

LONDON AND NEW YORK

First published 2014
by Routledge
2 Park Square, Milton Park, Abingdon, Oxfordshire OX14 4RN

and by Routledge
711 Third Avenue, New York, NY 10017

First issued in paperback 2015

Routledge is an imprint of the Taylor & Francis Group, an informa business

British Library Cataloguing in Publication Data
A catalogue record for this book is available from the British Library

Library of Congress Cataloging in Publication Data
Routledge companion to intelligence studies / edited by Rob Dover, Michael Goodman and Claudia Hillebrand.
pages cm.
Includes bibliographical references and index.
1. Intelligence service—Cross-cultural studies. I. Dover, Robert, 1977–
JF1525.I6R68 2013
327.12—dc23
2013008152

ISBN 13: 978-1-138-95196-9 (pbk)
ISBN 13: 978-0-415-50752-3 (hbk)

Typeset in Bembo
by Swales & Willis Ltd, Exeter, Devon

CONTENTS

List of illustrations   *viii*
Notes on contributors   *ix*
Preface   *xvi*

PART I
The evolution of intelligence studies   **1**

  1 The development of intelligence studies   3
     Loch K. Johnson

PART II
Abstract approaches to intelligence   **23**

  2 Theories of intelligence: the state of play   25
     Michael Warner

  3 Cultures of national intelligence   33
     Mark Phythian

  4 The theory and philosophy of intelligence   42
     Jennifer Sims

  5 Strategists and intelligence   50
     R. Gerald Hughes

  6 The cycle of intelligence   59
     David Omand

  7 The evolving craft of intelligence   71
     Robert David Steele

PART III
Historical approaches to intelligence   **85**

  8 Signals intelligence   87
     Julian Richards

  9 Human intelligence   96
     Len Scott

 10 Economic intelligence   105
     Peter Davies

 11 Measurement and signature intelligence   114
     Matthew M. Aid

 12 Open source intelligence   123
     Stevyn D. Gibson

PART IV
Systems of intelligence   **133**

 13 The United Kingdom   135
     Michael S. Goodman

 14 The United States   145
     Stephen Marrin

 15 Canada   154
     Andrew Brunatti

 16 Australia   161
     Frank Cain

 17 France   171
     Pierre Lethier

 18 India   182
     Rudra Chaudhuri

 19 China   191
     Nicholas Eftimiades

 20 Japan   201
     Ken Kotani

21 Israel   209
    Uri Bar-Joseph

22 Germany   218
    Anna Daun

23 Russia   227
    Reginald Brope

24 Spain   235
    Rubén Arcos

PART V
Contemporary challenges   **243**

25 Counterterrorism and intelligence   245
    Neal A. Pollard and Lt John P. Sullivan

26 Cybersecurity   256
    Dave Clemente

27 Globalisation and borders   264
    Zakia Shiraz and Richard J. Aldrich

28 Weapons of mass destruction   274
    James J. Wirtz

29 Energy and food security   283
    Petra Dolata

30 Intelligence sharing   290
    James Igoe Walsh

31 Communications, privacy and identity   297
    Robert Dover

32 Intelligence oversight and accountability   305
    Claudia Hillebrand

33 Organised crime   313
    Peter Gill

References   *321*
Index   *358*

ILLUSTRATIONS

Figures

3.1	The comparative analysis of national cultures of intelligence: levels of analysis	35
6.1	The CIA version of the intelligence cycle	59
6.2	British Army version of the intelligence cycle	60
6.3	FBI Intelligence Directorate version of the intelligence cycle	61
6.4	An early intelligence cycle	62
6.5	A 'national security' all-risks intelligence cycle	67
7.1	Changing dynamics	74
7.2	The craft of intelligence, from infancy to maturity	74
7.3	Strategic analytic model	76
7.4	Information cube	77
7.5	Four quadrants of information to intelligence	77
7.6	Towards the unity of knowledge	80
7.7	Autonomous internet	80
7.8	Comprehensive architecture for global intelligence	81
7.9	Open source everything and the autonomous internet	81
7.10	Strategy for creating a prosperous world at peace	82
22.1	The German intelligence community	226

Tables

1.1	Articles in the journal *Intelligence and National Security*, by topic	10
1.2	Articles related to intelligence collection in the journal *Intelligence and National Security*	11
1.3	Number of authors appearing in *Intelligence and National Security*, by nationality	14
1.4	Author nationalities in *Intelligence and National Security*, US/UK versus Other	14
1.5	Author nationalities in *Intelligence and National Security*, by per capita ranking	15
1.6	Authors in *Intelligence and National Security*, by gender	16
1.7	Intelligence articles in *Intelligence and National Security* and the *New York Times* (2006–11), by topic	17
1.8	The chief differences in focus for academic and media articles on intelligence, 2006–11	18
25.1	Intelligence requirements	248
32.1	Democratic values and intelligence practice	306

CONTRIBUTORS

Matthew M. Aid is the author of *Intel Wars: The Secret History of the Fight Against Terror* (Bloomsbury 2012) and *The Secret Sentry* (Bloomsbury 2009), the definitive history of the National Security Agency. He is a leading intelligence historian and expert on the NSA, and a regular commentator on intelligence matters for the *New York Times*, the *Financial Times*, the *National Journal*, the Associated Press, CBS News, National Public Radio (NPR) and many others. He lives in Washington, DC.

Richard J. Aldrich is Professor of International Security in the Department of Politics and International Studies, University of Warwick, and is the author of several books, including *The Hidden Hand: Britain, America and Cold War Secret Intelligence* (John Murray 2001) and *GCHQ: The Uncensored Story of Britain's Most Secret Intelligence Agency* (HarperPress 2010). He has recently spent time in Canberra and Ottawa as a Leverhulme Fellow while working on a study of the impact of globalisation upon intelligence services. Since 2008, he has been leading a project funded by the AHRC entitled: 'Landscapes of Secrecy: The Central Intelligence Agency and the Contested Record of US Foreign Policy, 1947–2001'.

Rubén Arcos is Visiting Professor of Communication Sciences at Rey Juan Carlos University. He is coordinator of programmes of the Intelligence Services and Democratic Systems Chair, Professor and coordinator of the MA in Intelligence Analysis. His current research is focused on intelligence, analytic outreach and strategic communications. Among other works, he is co-editor of *Cultura de Inteligencia* (*Intelligence Culture*, Plaza y Valdés 2012), *La Inteligencia como disciplina científica* (*Intelligence as a Scientific Discipline*, Ministry of Defense, Plaza y Valdés 2010), author of the chapter on communication, culture and intelligence reserves in the handbook *Inteligencia* (*Intelligence*, Tirant lo Blanch 2012), and of the book *La lógica de la excepción cultural* (*The Logic of Cultural Exception*, Cátedra 2010). He is member of the board of the Spanish intelligence journal *Inteligencia y seguridad: Revista de análisis y prospectiva*.

Uri Bar-Joseph is Professor in the International Relations Division at Haifa University, Israel. He concentrates on strategic and intelligence studies, especially focusing on the Arab–Israeli conflict and Israeli security policy. In addition to close to 70 book chapters and refereed journal articles in journals such as *Political Science Quarterly*, the *Journal of Conflict Resolution*, *Security*

Studies, Political Psychology and *Armed Forces and Society*, he has written five books, the most recent of which is *The Angel: Ashraf Marwan, the Mossad, and the War of Yom Kippur* (Hebrew 2011).

Reginald Brope's research interests focus on the domestic politics and power networks in post-Soviet states, particularly in Russia. He holds a PhD from the University of London in International Affairs, and has extensive experience of working in governmental and intergovernmental institutions and academia.

Andrew Brunatti is a PhD candidate at the Brunel Centre for Intelligence and Security Studies (BCISS) at Brunel University. He is also a graduate of the Norman Paterson School of International Affairs at Carleton University, and a former Canadian intelligence analyst. His doctoral research comparatively examines intelligence community management architecture in Canada, Australia and New Zealand.

Frank Cain is Visiting Fellow in the School of Humanities and Social Sciences at the University of New South Wales in Canberra, Australia, where he taught Australian history until recently. His main research interests are in Australian political history, the Cold War, the history of intelligence organisations and the Vietnam War. His book *Economic Statecraft During the Cold War: European Responses to the US Trade Embargo* (Routledge 2007) has been published in paperback. His most recent book is *Terrorism and Intelligence in Australia: A History of ASIO and National Surveillance* (Scholarly Publishing 2008).

Rudra Chaudhuri joined the Department of War Studies, King's College London, in September 2009. He previously taught at the UK Joint Services Command and Staff College. His doctoral thesis looked at the importance of strategic culture in India's historical and contemporary relationship with the United States and will shortly be published by OUP. He completed his BA at St Stephen's College, Delhi University, MA at Exeter and PhD at King's College London.

Dave Clemente is a Research Associate with International Security at Chatham House. His areas of research include cybersecurity policy, and US and UK security and defence policy. He was educated at the Ohio State University, the University of Damascus and the School of Oriental and African Studies, University of London, and has worked at the International Institute for Strategic Studies and the Overseas Development Institute. He is author of *Cyber Security and Global Interdependence: What is Critical?* (Chatham House 2012) and co-author of *Cyber Security and the UK's Critical National Infrastructure* (Chatham House 2011) and *On Cyber Warfare* (Chatham House 2010).

Anna Daun is a Researcher at the Institute for Political Science at the University of Cologne. Intelligence is one of her major research interests. She has published two books and several articles about intelligence in the EU, Germany and within the transatlantic relationship. Her dissertation was on the topic of German–American intelligence relations. Other research areas include fragile states and political psychology.

Peter Davies specialised in economic intelligence during a career of 30 years at the Ministry of Defence, Cabinet Office and other government departments involved with the intelligence cycle. He is currently associated with the Mile End Group at Queen Mary, University of London, and is writing a history of the British economic intelligence capability from its emergence as a distinctive intelligence field in the early 1930s to the collapse of the Soviet Union in 1991.

Petra Dolata is Lecturer in International Politics in the Department of Political Economy at King's College London, and Research Director of King's European Centre for Energy and Resource Security (EUCERS) in the Department of War Studies. She has published research on Canadian foreign and Arctic policies, as well as energy and geopolitics, specifically energy security in a North American and transatlantic context.

Robert Dover is Senior Lecturer in International Relations at Loughborough University, specialising in issues of international security and intelligence. Along with Michael S. Goodman, he holds a Research Council grant on 'Learning Lessons from Intelligence History', and together they have edited two books on intelligence matters, *Spinning Intelligence: Why Intelligence Needs the Media, Why the Media Needs Intelligence* (Hurst 2009) and *Learning from the Secret Past: Cases in British Intelligence History* (Georgetown University Press 2011). In addition to these, he has written articles on European security, British defence policy and arms trade intelligence.

Nicholas Eftimiades is Visiting Fellow at King's College London. His 27-year government career includes seven years at the US National Security Space Office leading engineering teams designing 'generation after next' national security space capabilities. He was also Senior Technical Officer in Defense Intelligence Agency, Future's Division, and Chief of DIA's Space Division. He served as DIA's lead for national space policy and strategy development. He has authored books and a number of scholarly articles on national security, technology and outer space issues. His book *Chinese Intelligence Operations* (1994) is an examination of the structure, operations and methodology of the intelligence services of the People's Republic of China. His research focuses on China's intelligence operations, economic espionage and future technology, and implications for global and nation state security

Stevyn D. Gibson lectures and writes on concepts of intelligence, security, resilience and risk at the UK Defence Academy, and more widely for Cranfield University. His intelligence experience includes: collection behind enemy lines with the British Military Commanders'-in-Chief Mission (BRIXMIS); analysis for hostage rescue; and intelligence briefing to war headquarters. His PhD examines the contribution of open source exploitation to the national intelligence function. He is on the steering committee of the Oxford Intelligence Group. He is author of *The Last Mission* (Sutton 1997) and *Live and Let Spy* (The History Press 2012).

Peter Gill is Honorary Senior Research Fellow at the University of Liverpool, UK; previously Research Professor in Intelligence Studies at the University of Salford. He is the author of *Policing Politics* (Cass 1994) and *Rounding Up the Usual Suspects?* (Ashgate 2000), and co-author of *Intelligence in an Insecure World* (Polity Press, 2nd edn, 2012). He is co-editor of the *PSI Handbook of Global Security and Intelligence: National Approaches*, two volumes (Praeger 2008) and *Intelligence Theory: Key Questions and Debates* (Routledge 2009). His current research is into the democratisation of intelligence in former authoritarian regimes, for which he was awarded a Leverhulme Emeritus Fellowship in 2010.

Michael S. Goodman is Reader in the Department of War Studies at King's College London. He has published widely in the field of intelligence history and scientific intelligence, including *Spying on the Nuclear Bear: Anglo-American Intelligence and the Soviet Bomb* (Stanford University Press 2008), *Spinning Intelligence: Why Intelligence Needs the Media, Why the Media Needs*

Intelligence (Columbia University Press 2009) and *Learning from the Secret Past: Cases in British Intelligence History* (Georgetown University Press 2011). His next two books – *Spying on the World: The Joint Intelligence Committee and Events Which Shaped History* (Edinburgh University Press) and *The Official History of the Joint Intelligence Committee* (Routledge) – will be published in 2013. He is Series Editor for 'Intelligence and Security' for Hurst/Columbia University Press, and is a member of the editorial boards for *Intelligence and National Security*, *International Journal of Intelligence and Counterintelligence*, *Inteligencia y Seguridad: Revista de análisis y prospective* and *Contemporary British History*. He is a member of the International Advisory Forum for the Italian Institute of Strategic Studies. He is currently on secondment to the Cabinet Office, where he is the Official Historian of the Joint Intelligence Committee.

Claudia Hillebrand is Lecturer in Intelligence and Counter-Terrorism at the Department of International Politics at Aberystwyth University. She is the author of *Counter-terrorism Networks in the European Union: Maintaining Democratic Legitimacy after 9/11* (Oxford University Press 2012). The research project was supported by a Marie Curie Early Stage Research Fellowship of the European Community. Previously, she was a Post-Doctoral Research Fellow at the Department of War Studies, King's College London. She has published widely on intelligence oversight and intelligence and police cooperation.

R. Gerald Hughes (FRHistS) is Director of the Centre for Intelligence and International Security Studies (CIISS) at Aberystwyth University. He is the author of *Britain, Germany and the Cold War: The Search for a European Détente, 1949–1967* (Routledge 2007). He is an assistant editor of the journal *Intelligence and National Security* and the co-editor of three books: *Intelligence, Crises and Security: Prospects and Retrospects* (Routledge 2008), *Exploring Intelligence Archives: Enquiries into the Secret State* (Routledge 2008) and *Intelligence and International Security: New Perspectives and Agendas* (Routledge 2011). He is a Fellow of the Royal Historical Society.

Loch K. Johnson is Regents Professor of International Affairs at the University of Georgia and Senior Editor of the international journal *Intelligence and National Security*. His latest book is entitled *National Security Intelligence* (Polity 2012). He was named the inaugural Southeast Conference Professor of the Year in 2012.

Ken Kotani is Senior Research Fellow of the National Institute for Defense Studies, Ministry of Defense, Japan, and Lecturer at the National Defense Academy. He obtained his MA from King's College London and PhD from Kyoto University. He is the author of *Japanese Intelligence in World War II* (Osprey Publishing 2009).

Pierre Lethier was a former senior intelligence officer with France's foreign branch. He is a Fellow of Buckingham University (BUCSIS).

Stephen Marrin is Associate Professor in the Department of Integrated Science and Technology at James Madison University. He has also held positions with Brunel University's Centre for Intelligence and Security Studies and Mercyhurst University's Intelligence Studies Department. Before that he was an analyst with the Central Intelligence Agency and then the US Government Accountability Office (GAO). Holder of a PhD from the University of Virginia, he is Chair of the Intelligence Studies Section of the International Studies Association. A prolific author on aspects of intelligence analysis, the *National Journal* in 2004 profiled him as one of the ten leading experts on the subject of intelligence reform.

Sir David Omand GCB is Visiting Professor in the Department of War Studies at King's College London. He was appointed in 2002 the first UK Security and Intelligence Coordinator, and Permanent Secretary in the Cabinet Office responsible to the Prime Minister for the professional health of the intelligence community, national counterterrorism strategy, 'homeland security' and domestic crisis management. He served for seven years on the Joint Intelligence Committee. He was Permanent Secretary of the Home Office from 1997 to 2000, and before that Director of the UK signals intelligence agency, GCHQ. Previously, in the Ministry of Defence he served as Deputy Under Secretary of State for Policy. His book *Securing the State* was published by C. Hurst (Publishers) Ltd and Columbia University Press in 2010.

Mark Phythian is Professor of Politics in the Department of Politics and International Relations at the University of Leicester, UK. His research interests are in the areas of intelligence, national security and foreign policy. He is the author or editor/co-editor of 13 books – most recently *Intelligence in an Insecure World* (with Peter Gill, 2nd edn, Polity Press 2012) and (as editor) *Understanding the Intelligence Cycle* (Routledge 2013) – as well as numerous journal articles and book chapters.

Neal A. Pollard is Director in PricewaterhouseCooper's Forensic Technology Solutions practice. Prior to joining PwC, he was a senior officer in the US intelligence community, where he served multiple managerial and operational assignments in the Office of the Director of National Intelligence, the National Counterterrorism Center and the Central Intelligence Agency. He was also Director for Counterterrorism on the staff of the Commission on the Prevention of WMD Proliferation and Terrorism (Graham-Talent Commission). He is also Adjunct Professor at Georgetown University. He is a member of the Council on Foreign Relations Independent Task Force on US Policy in the Digital Age, and was a member of the United Nation's Expert Working Group on use of the internet for terrorist purposes. He also holds many other academic affiliations, including Board Director of the Cyber Conflict Studies Association, Senior Associate of the Homeland Security and Counterterrorism Program at the Center for Strategic and International Studies, and Senior Fellow of the Cyber Statecraft Initiative of the Atlantic Council of the United States. He is a member of the Council on Foreign Relations.

Julian Richards successfully completed a PhD in Political Violence in Pakistan at the University of Cambridge in 1993. He then spent nearly 20 years working in intelligence and security for the British government. In 2008, he co-founded the Centre for Security and Intelligence Studies (BUCSIS) at the University of Buckingham. His affiliations include Associate of the Pakistan Security Research Unit in Bradford University, an Advisory Board member of the European *Observatoire des Think-Tanks*, and the editorial board of the Spanish journal *Intelligencia y seguridad*. He is the author of two books, *The Art and Science of Intelligence Analysis* (Oxford University Press 2010) and *A Guide to National Security: Threats, Responses and Strategies* (Oxford University Press 2012), in addition to a number of papers on a range of security and intelligence issues.

Len Scott is Professor of International Politics at Aberystwyth University, where he is Dean of Social Sciences. His recent publications include: *Intelligence and International Security: New Perspectives and Agendas* (Routledge 2011), co-edited with R. Gerald Hughes and Martin S. Alexander; *The Cuban Missile Crisis and the Threat of Nuclear War: Lessons from History* (Continuum

Books 2007); and *Exploring Intelligence Archives: Enquiries into the Secret State* (Routledge 2008), co-edited with R. Gerald Hughes and Peter Jackson.

Zakia Shiraz was a Research Fellow at CERAC (Conflict Analysis Resource Centre) in Bogota in 2011 and is re-examining the long-standing Colombian conflict by focusing on the internal dynamics of the violence and drawing on the 'New Wars' literature. She is completing a doctorate in the Department of Politics and International Security at the University of Warwick, where she teaches American foreign policy. Her most recent article is 'CIA Intervention in Chile and the Fall of the Allende Government in 1973', which appeared in the *Journal of American Studies* in 2011.

Jennifer Sims is currently Senior Fellow with the Chicago Council on Global Affairs. Prior to this she served as Director of Intelligence Studies and Visiting Professor in the Security Studies Program at Georgetown University's Walsh School of Foreign Service. In 2010, the Director of National Intelligence appointed her to his Senior Advisory Group, which advises on matters of intelligence policy. She has served as Deputy Assistant Secretary of State for Intelligence Coordination (1994–98) and Intelligence Advisor to the Under Secretary for Management and Coordinator for Intelligence Resources and Planning at the US Department of State (1998–2001). She has also been a Professional Staff Member of the Senate Select Committee on Intelligence (1991–94), and a legislative assistant to Senator John Danforth on foreign and defence policy (1990–93). She has co-edited with Burton Gerber, *Vaults, Mirrors and Masks: Rediscovering US Counterintelligence* (Georgetown University Press 2009) and *Transforming US Intelligence* (Georgetown University Press 2005).

Robert David Steele is CEO of Earth Intelligence Network, a 501c3 organisation. He served for nine years as a spy with additional responsibilities in advanced analytics, counterintelligence, information technology and overhead system program management. An honorary hacker since 1994, he was among the first to call for cyber-security standards and education, and also the first to conceptualise a 'Smart Nation' in which education, intelligence and research are seamlessly integrated. He served in addition four years' active duty as a Marine Corps infantry officer and S-1/Adjutant, 16 years as a Reserve intelligence officer, and five years as the second-ranking civilian for Marine Corps Intelligence, where he was the senior civilian responsible for creating the Marine Corps Intelligence Center in 1988, and the Study Director for the first global intelligence study to create strategic acquisition generalisations, *Planning and Programming Factors for Expeditionary Operations in the Third World* (MCCDC 1990). Author of many books, articles and chapters, he is also the number-one Amazon reviewer for non-fiction, reading and reviewing in 98 categories accessible at Phi Beta Iota, the Public Intelligence Blog.

Lt John P. Sullivan is a career police officer. He currently serves as a lieutenant with the Los Angeles Sheriff's Department. He is also Adjunct Researcher at the Vortex Foundation, Bogotá, Colombia; Senior Research Fellow at the Center for Advanced Studies on Terrorism (CAST); and Senior Fellow at *Small Wars Journal – El Centro*. He is co-editor of *Countering Terrorism and WMD: Creating a Global Counter-Terrorism Network* (Routledge 2006) and *Global Biosecurity: Threats and Responses* (Routledge 2010). He is co-author of *Mexico's Criminal Insurgency: A Small Wars Journal – El Centro Anthology* (iUniverse 2011). His current research focus is the impact of transnational organised crime on sovereignty in Mexico and other countries.

James Igoe Walsh is Professor of Political Science at the University of North Carolina at Charlotte. He holds a PhD in International Relations from American University. His research interests include political violence and terrorism, human rights violations, and intelligence and national security. His book *The International Politics of Intelligence Sharing* (2009) was published by Columbia University Press and was named an Outstanding Title by Choice. He is the author of another book, as well as articles in *Comparative Political Studies*, *International Studies Quarterly*, *Terrorism and Political Violence* and other journals. In recent years, his work has been supported by the Army Corps of Engineers, the Department of Homeland Security, the National Science Foundation's Time-Sharing Experiments in the Social Sciences, and the Institute for Homeland Security Solutions.

Michael Warner serves as Command Historian in the US Department of Defense, and has written and lectured on intelligence history, theory and reform. He is also Adjunct Professor at American University's School of International Service in Washington, DC. His new book, *The Rise and Fall of Intelligence: A History*, will be published by Georgetown University Press.

James J. Wirtz is Dean of the School of International Graduate Studies, and Professor in the Department of National Security Affairs at the Naval Postgraduate School, Monterey, California. He is the co-editor of *Complex Deterrence: Strategy in the Global Age* (University of Chicago Press 2009). He received his PhD from Columbia University.

PREFACE

Robert Dover, Michael S. Goodman and Claudia Hillebrand

Intelligence studies is one of the most dynamic areas of academic study today. Traditionally it sits as a sub-field of international relations and diplomatic history, but during the last 20 years it has undergone significant changes. The work of intelligence agencies against rogue states, global Jihadists and organised crime has been at the forefront of media and public attention, and the increased demand for oversight following controversial, intelligence-based, decisions has thrown greater spotlights on the culture and governance of the various agencies. Worldwide, there are more undergraduate and graduate students studying intelligence and related fields than ever before.

This recent growth of interest in intelligence and security studies has led to an increased demand for popular depictions of intelligence, and reference works to explain the architecture and underpinnings of intelligence activity. The *Routledge Companion to Intelligence Studies* provides a strong survey of the cutting-edge research in the field of intelligence studies, and is essential reading for anyone interested in the subject. It focuses broadly on the origins, practices and nature of intelligence, and includes not only the classical issues but also more wide-ranging ones that address topics of recent interest in security studies. The *Companion* explicitly embraces the disparate approaches to intelligence studies. The approach varies across the main sections of the book, encompassing bureaucratic politics, diplomatic history, area studies, comparative politics and mainstream international relations thought. Our overarching aim is to reveal the rich tapestry of intelligence studies in both a sophisticated and an accessible way.

Intelligence is a means for public policy to ensure security (Omand 2010a). More precisely, as Michael Warner (2007: 17) suggested, the term intelligence comprises 'that which states do in secret to support their efforts to mitigate, influence, or merely understand other nations (or various enemies) that could harm them'. Studying such secret activities poses considerable challenges for students and scholars. Limited access to primary sources and a general lack of information in this field mean that researchers – just like policy-makers and intelligence overseers – are often faced with the challenge of incompleteness. Indeed, as Lord Butler found in his review of intelligence on Iraqi weapons of mass destruction, 'much ingenuity and effort is spent making secret information difficult to acquire and hard to analyse' (Committee of Privy Counsellors 2004: 14). Nevertheless, as the compilation in this volume demonstrates, it is not only possible, but illuminating and fascinating, to study aspects of intelligence, both in historical and contemporary contexts. Openness towards, and willingness to learn from, the various disciplinary and methodological approaches to the study of the phenomenon, as promoted in this volume, helps to overcome the lack of transparency in the intelligence realm.

While some intelligence practices, such as espionage, are known to have been used in the ancient world, counterterrorism campaigns and related inquiries during the post-9/11 era have illuminated in unprecedented detail some of the ways in which intelligence is used in policy-making, and its overall significance for ensuring (inter-)national security. Overall, intelligence efforts have deepened and broadened since the end of the Cold War, and in the previous decade in particular. They have been deepened in the sense that, for example, more resources and efforts have been allocated to intelligence services, and the intelligence input into daily policy-making has increased. And they have been broadened through the widening of mandates – including intelligence contributions to areas such as tackling organised crime or ensuring energy security – and the proliferation of intelligence, or intelligence-led, institutions. Today, intelligence is being used by an unprecedented group of policy-shaping institutions. Yet, the increased efforts at information gathering and, in particular, the renewed emphasis on human source intelligence (HUMINT) during the post-9/11 era also caused concerns and debates with respect to human rights abuses. This development of intelligence at the beginning of the twenty-first century raises a number of questions, which this *Companion* addresses: what is the purpose of intelligence; what are the new fields in which intelligence has a role to play; what can we learn from historical studies of intelligence for current intelligence efforts; what are current challenges that intelligence systems face; and what does a legitimate, proportionate and necessary conduct of intelligence services look like?

The scope of the book and our approach to it are straightforward. The *Companion* explains the main lessons of intelligence – what it is, how it is collected, how it is processed and then how it is disseminated to those who need to act upon it. It is divided into five major sections, covering the evolution of intelligence, abstract approaches to intelligence, historical approaches to intelligence, national intelligence systems, and contemporary challenges. The importance of the first three sections is to highlight how our understanding of intelligence has been shaped by the nature of the 'threat'. The fourth section – on systems of intelligence – grounds the book in an international context as it comprises studies of 12 intelligence systems, some of which have seldom been explored before now. The final section examines some of the challenges with which intelligence services are currently confronted.

The *Companion* should be of particular interest to those studying security studies and strategic studies, as well as more general international relations, history and politics courses. While it naturally covers aspects of national and global security, surveillance, espionage and defence issues, the study of intelligence also has a lot to say about the making of foreign policy, 'cheating' in the international system, the global system in the post-9/11 era, and human rights and individual liberties and freedoms. The volume aims to provide a solid and interesting introduction to the subject, contexts within which students should view the machinery of intelligence, a launching pad for advanced study and a tool for tutors. It is also accessible to intelligence practitioners and policy-makers as well as those who are generally interested in the subject and wish to gain a comprehensive overview of the status quo of intelligence studies.

| *Robert Dover* | *Michael S. Goodman* | *Claudia Hillebrand* |
| *Loughborough* | *London* | *Aberystwyth* |

PART I

The evolution of intelligence studies

1

THE DEVELOPMENT OF INTELLIGENCE STUDIES

Loch K. Johnson

Introduction

The topic of national security intelligence – which at its core encompasses the collection and analysis of information, covert action and counterintelligence – has long exercised a fascination on society, as the popularity of spy movies and novels attests. The reason for this widespread interest is easy to understand, for the motivations that lead to intelligence operations reside at the heart of the human psyche. Human beings, like other living species, seek security from threats; moreover, they hope to improve their station in life. Fear and ambition – here are powerful, primordial instincts that have driven kings, tyrants, prime ministers and presidents, while providing fodder for Shakespeare and countless other scribblers down through the ages.

Central to the safety of a nation is the possession of information about what threats may lurk in the byways that lie ahead; and, for advancement, a nation seeks an understanding of opportunities that may present themselves. Whether the goal is protection or prosperity, the collection and analysis (assessment) of information about the global setting is vital for effective decision-making by a nation's leaders. 'Creating Decision Advantage' is the motto inscribed on the wall at the headquarters of America's Director of National Intelligence (DNI), located at Liberty Crossing ('LX') in northern Virginia.

Critical to a nation's success, as well, may be a more aggressive use of intelligence agencies known as covert action – that is, efforts to intervene with a hidden hand in events aboard with the hope of nudging history in a more favourable direction. In this mode, a nation's intelligence agencies become secret weapons for propaganda, political, economic and paramilitary operations. Finally, with the mission of counterintelligence, a nation's secret agencies are called upon to act as a shield against the clandestine machinations of foreign intelligence services, terrorist organisations and internal subversives.

From Sun-Tzu and Machiavelli to the laptop-toting counsels of the modern era, the goals of war planners and political advisers alike have been to help their masters maintain a secure defence, achieve success on distant battlefields, and advance their strategic, political and economic objectives. The prescriptions offered by these advisers have inevitably included reliance on an effective intelligence capability, although with the caveat that an existential uncertainty about world affairs will forever haunt the best-laid plans of strategists. Not until recently, though, has the topic of national security intelligence moved from episodic treatment by a few insightful thinkers to become an academic discipline worthy of entry into university curricula and subject to the rigours of scholarly inquiry. While precise definitions of this new discipline known as 'intelligence studies' remain disputatious, British intelligence scholar Michael Herman offers a reasonable suggestion: 'Think of the subject as a mixture of history and the study of intelligence institutions, and what they do, and not worry further about boundaries' (2011: 1). One might only underscore that the intelligence missions of collection-and-analysis, covert action and counterintelligence are the core subjects of the field, along with the question of accountability (at least within the world's democracies).

The emergence of intelligence studies as an academic discipline

In the middle years of the twentieth century, only a few prominent scholarly works dotted the landscape of intelligence studies: the trail-blazing *Strategic Intelligence for American World Policy* by Sherman Kent (1949), a leading analyst at the Central Intelligence Agency (CIA) in its early days and a former Yale University history professor; *Strategic Intelligence and National Decisions* by Roger Hilsman (1956), a former director of the Intelligence and Research (INR) Bureau in the Department of State; *Central Intelligence and National Security* and *The Intelligence Establishment*, both by political scientist Harry Howe Ransom (1958 and 1970, respectively), who began teaching courses on this subject at Harvard University in the 1960s; *The Quiet Canadian*, a study of Sir William Stephenson, Britain's spy chief in the United States during the Second World War, written by H. Montgomery Hyde (1962), a veteran of British intelligence (MI6 – the Secret Intelligence Service, or SIS); *Pearl Harbor: Warning and Decision* by Roberta Wohlsetter of RAND (1962); *The Invisible Government* by journalists David Wise and Thomas Ross (1964); *SOE in France: An Account of the Work of the British Special Operations Executive in France, 1940–1944*, a path-breaking experiment in official British intelligence history, written by M.R.D. Foot (1966); *The Codebreakers* by David Kahn (1967), an American journalist and historian; and *The Double-Cross System in the War of 1939 to 1945* by J.C. Masterman (1972), a senior British counterintelligence officer during the Second World War and later Provost of Worcester College, Oxford University.[1] Stirring early interest, too, was an insider exposé, *The CIA and the Cult of Intelligence*, written by two former American intelligence officers, Marchetti and Marks (1974).

These gems aside, the distinguished historian and intelligence scholar Professor Ernst R. May of Harvard University observed that 'the literature on intelligence was at or below the level of literature on business before the arrival of modern business history and business education' (May 1995: 1).[2] Ransom similarly lamented the thinness of scholarly research on espionage and related activities during these years and earlier. The barren landscape was, however, about to change dramatically. In the wake of the Watergate scandal and allegations of CIA domestic spying, government investigators in the United States uncovered for public view a mountain of formerly classified documents about America's secret agencies and their operations. Professor Ransom recalls using a 'pick and shovel' to mine a few intelligence nuggets here and there; then, in 1975, the Church, Pike and Rockefeller panels of government inquiry deployed their 'bulldozers'.[3]

Practically overnight, the subject of intelligence suddenly seemed amenable to systematic study by academic researchers. Across the United States, Canada, and the United Kingdom, universities and colleges established full-blown courses on intelligence, or at least integrated this subject more explicitly into existing courses on foreign and security policy, as well as international affairs. In the place of a handful of such courses before 1975, more than 250 were up and running in the United States by the 1980s, and that number has steadily increased. Degrees hinged to intelligence studies began to appear. For example, the National Intelligence University, founded in 1962 and sponsored by the Defense Intelligence Agency, now offers a Bachelor of Science in Intelligence (BSI), and a Master of Science and Technology Intelligence (MSTI). Further, PhD concentrations in intelligence have been established at several American and British universities, leading to thoughtful dissertations on the subject.

Path-breaking research during these early days came from scholars across the United States, Canada and the United Kingdom.[4] Among the leaders in the United States were Matthew M. Aid and James Bamford, Washington, DC; David M. Barrett (2005), Villanova University; Richard A. Best, Jr, Al Cumming and Fred Kaiser, Library of Congress; Richard K. Betts (2007) and Robert Jervis (2010), Columbia University; Adda Bozeman, Sarah Lawrence College; Roy Godson, Georgetown University; Michael I. Handel (1983), Navy War College and a co-founder (with Christopher Andrew of Cambridge University) of the journal *Intelligence and National Security* in 1986;[5] Glenn P. Hastedt (1991a), James Madison University; Loch K. Johnson (1980), University of Georgia; David Kahn, New York; Walter Laqueur (1985), Georgetown University; Anthony G. Oettinger, Harvard University; John Prados (2006), Maryland; Jeffrey T. Richelson (2012), California; Stan A. Taylor, Brigham Young University; Athan Theoharis, Marquette University; Gregory F. Treverton (1987, 2009), RAND; and Robin Wink (1987), Yale University.

The discipline was further advanced by the insider experience of former CIA intelligence officers who retired to academic positions and took up pens, including Bruce D. Berkowitz, Carnegie Mellon; William J. Daugherty, Armstrong Atlantic State University; Allan E. Goodman, Georgetown University; Frederick P. Hitz, Princeton University; Arthur S. Hulnick (1999), Boston University; Paul R. Pillar and Richard L. Russell, Georgetown University; and Michael A. Turner, San Diego University. Some insiders came to academe from other intelligence agencies, such as William Nolte of the National Security Agency (University of Maryland). Some wrote in their retirement years, as in the case of the CIA's Ray S. Cline, Cord Meyer, Harry A. Rositzke, Kermit Roosevelt and David Atlee Phillips, as well as former Marine Corps Intelligence officers William R. Corson and Robert David Steele. Others produced notable studies while still serving inside the intelligence community, such as CIA officers Arthur B. Darling, Jack Davis, John Hollister Hedley, John L. Helgerson, Fred Manget, Hayden B. Peake, David H. Sharp and Thomas F. Troy, as well as Michael Warner, who has been a historian in the intelligence community. Finally, a few scholars wrote on intelligence while employed in government agencies other than the intelligence community, as was true with Abram N. Shulsky of the Defense Department.

Professor Godson set up an influential Intelligence Consortium in the 1980s that held conferences, published monographs and ran a summer training programme for young scholars interested in intelligence studies. Mark M. Lowenthal, a scholar with extensive experience in academe and the intelligence community, authored *Intelligence: From Secrets to Policy*, which became the basic text for many of the intelligence courses taught in the United States and elsewhere.[6] In addition, the memoirs of former Directors of Central Intelligence (DCIs) provided insights into intelligence from the highest level of America's secret agencies.[7] Recently, a former intelligence officer and now academic, Mark Stout (Johns Hopkins University), led the establishment of H-INTEL, an online channel of scholarly discourse for intelligence researchers (http://www.h-net.org/~intel/), in the manner of the well-established H-DIPLO for diplomatic historians. The site went live in June 2012, starting with an excellent essay by John Ferris (University of Calgary) on US drone attacks in Southwest Asia.

The United Kingdom displayed a similar evolution. As early as 1963, a government inquiry headed by Lord Alfred Thompson Denning into a Cabinet scandal (the Profumo affair) led to a declassification of secret documents that stimulated academic interest in intelligence. By 1972, Masterman's book on British counterintelligence was in print, soon joined by Winterbotham's pioneering study of ULTRA (1975) and a masterful five-volume official history of British intelligence in the Second World War (Hinsley, Thomas and Howard 1979). Sir F.H. Hinsley, a veteran of the British signals organisation GCHG (Government Communications Headquarters) and later a Master of St John's College, Cambridge University, led the five-volume history project, for which the research and writing had been long under way before the Masterman and Winterbotham volumes appeared.

Academic studies on intelligence soon took flight in the United Kingdom, with leadership coming chiefly from university historians. Their dominance continues today in what is sometimes referred to as 'the British school of intelligence studies', although Ken Robertson (1982, 1987) and Peter Gill (1994) provide early examples of an important social science tributary in this wider stream of historical research. Robertson also organised the Security Intelligence Studies Group, or SISG, a valuable forum that encouraged the academic study of intelligence. In contrast, the scholarship in the United States has been driven by a broader mix of political scientists, historians, sociologists and scholars from other disciplines engaged in intelligence research.

Among the early British scholars in this field, none become more prominent than Christopher Andrew, whose study of the British Secret Service (1985) demonstrated that serious, deep scholarship could be achieved on the hidden side of government in the United Kingdom. His co-edited volume with David Dilks, entitled *The Missing Dimension: Governments and Intelligence Communities in the Twentieth Century* (Andrew and Dilks 1984), was also influential in these early days.[8] That same year a US–British academic conference on intelligence, held in London and supported by the Intelligence Consortium established by Professor Godson at Georgetown University, helped to signal the arrival of a new academic discipline in the British Isles. Subsequently, British government reports on intelligence have periodically stimulated academic research that drew upon their findings (Hughes, Jackson and Scott 2008), such as Prime Minister John Major's 'Open Government' initiative begun in 1993; the creation in 1994 of the Intelligence and Security Committee (ISC) in Parliament, which has published 'a rich vein of annual and special reports' (Davies 2004b); the Scott inquiry of 1996 into the export of defence and dual-use goods to Iraq; and a spate of post-9/11 government inquires, including a Commons Foreign Affairs Committee report on Iraq, another report on Iraqi weapons of mass destruction (WMD) from the ISC, the Hutton inquiry into the death of David Kelly (a UK WMD inspector), Lord Butler's review of Iraqi WMD, the Scott Baker inquest into the death of Princess Diana, and Sir John Chilcot's Iraq inquiry – a combined release into the public domain of an unprecedented volume of once-secret documentation.

At the beginning of the twenty-first century, 16 British universities were offering full or partial courses on intelligence. In 1999, Michael Herman led a well-subscribed intelligence seminar at St Anthony's College, Oxford University, which resulted in the publication of an influential book on espionage (Shukman 2001). Herman's seminar led to the creation of an intelligence studies group at the College. When the funding for this venture ran out, he formed an Oxford Intelligence Group (OIG) at Nuffield College, also at Oxford University, that offers seminars and conferences on a 'variable' basis (according to the Nuffield website). This outstanding programme has endured, although Oxford has yet to establish a permanent course on intelligence.

At Aberystwyth University in Wales, R. Gerald Hughes, Peter Jackson and Len Scott (2008) created a centre of excellence for intelligence research and published a raft of noteworthy articles and book reviews on intelligence (among them, Scott and Jackson 2004a), as did Lawrence Freedman (1986), Michael S. Goodman (2007) and Joe Maiolo at King's College London. Throughout the British Isles insightful studies emerged from a host of scholars at other universities, among them: Richard J. Aldrich (2001), Warwick; Rhodi Jeffreys-Jones (1989), Glasgow; David Stafford, Edinburgh; Anthony Glees (2003), University of Buckingham; Philip H.J. Davies (2012a), Kristian Gustafson and Stephen Marrin at Brunel, which has emphasised the policy side of intelligence studies; Keith Jeffery, Queen's University (Belfast); Laurence Lustgarten and Ian Leigh (1994), Durham; Peter Gill of Liverpool Polytechnic and Mark Phythian of Leicester (2006); and the prolific writings on military affairs by historian Sir John Keegan (2003). Former Member of Parliament and historian Rupert Allason, writing as Nigel West, contributed knowledgeable works on counterintelligence. Recently, the British government has commissioned prominent historians to write official histories of various UK intelligence agencies (see Gibbs 2005), including a work on MI5 by Andrew (2009).

As in the United States, former British intelligence officers also joined the intelligence studies effort. The best known in the academic world are the late Sir Percy Cradock, former chairman of the British Joint Intelligence Committee, who offered an elegant overview of British intelligence (2002); Sir Richard Dearlove (2010), former MI6 chief; Michael Herman (2001), another veteran of GCHQ; John N.L. Morrison, former head of the Defence Intelligence Analysis Staff; and Sir David Omand (2010a), erstwhile Director of GCHQ and now associated with King's College London.

Intelligence studies ignited in Canada as well in the late 1970s, and again with historians at the forefront. Spearheading the movement were scholars David Charters, University of New Brunswick; A. Stuart Farson, the House of Commons staff (now with Simon Fraser University); John Ferris, University of Calgary; Martin Rudner, University of Ottawa; Wesley K. Wark (1993), Universities of Ottawa and Toronto; and Reg Whitaker, York University and the University of Victoria.

The discipline was on the march, although some countries proved less hospitable territory for intelligence research. French attention to this subject, for example, remained largely dormant in the 1970s and 1980s, although Admiral Pierre Lacoste was an early, energetic advocate. In the mid-1990s, however, intelligence research in France 'dramatically expanded around three main disciplines: management, history, and political science' (Denécé and Arboit 2012: 51). An independent think-tank, the Center for Intelligence Studies established in 1999, provided an important focal point for advanced French intelligence studies, as did the work of Sébastien Laurent at the Université Michel de Montaigne in Bordeaux. In Germany, one of the leading researchers in the field, Wolfgang Krieger, has reported 'scant' interest in this scholarly pursuit within his country (2004: 185); nevertheless, some important studies have been published by German scholars, including the work of Professors Krieger (Philipps University in Marburg), Klaus-Jügen Müller (Hamburg) and Jürgen Rohwer (Stuttgart).

Elsewhere on the European continent, academic attention to intelligence similarly remained at a low level of interest. Still, several nations produced worthy research, including the findings of Hans Born (Born, Johnson and Leigh 2005) at the Centre for the Democratic Control of Armed Forces in Geneva; Siegried Beer in Austria; Prof. Jean Stengers, Université Libre de Bruxelles; and Cees Wiebes of the Netherlands. The insightful writings of Desmond Ball at the Australian National University in Canberra and David Martin Jones at University of Queensland; researchers at the Italian Institute of Strategic Studies in Rome, as well as with the Mediterranean Council of Intelligence Studies (MCIS) in Greece; the Institute of National Remembrance in Poland; and Uri Bar-Joseph, Shlomo Gazit, Ephraim Kahana, Ephraim Kam and Shlomo Shpiro in Israel, further demonstrated that pockets of serious research on intelligence could be found around the globe (in 2009, Adelaide University in Australia and Nuffield College at Oxford established Project GOA, a web-based think-tank on intelligence); so does the participation of government personnel from Romania, Georgia and Slovakia on intelligence studies panels, as occurred at the 2012 International Studies Association (ISA) meeting in San Diego. Further, the research of young scholars in the developing world is attracting attention, including the work of Prem Mahadevan of India and Joanisval Brito Gonçalves of Brazil.

Two key academic journals emerged as part of the surge in intelligence research: *Intelligence and National Security* (*INS*), published six times a year, and the *International Journal of Intelligence and Counterintelligence* (*IJICI*), a quarterly. Both bear Taylor & Francis imprints (a British publishing house under the umbrella of the Informa Corporation, London) and first appeared in 1986 and 1987, respectively. Arriving soon afterwards was a more specialised periodical entitled *Journal of Cryptology*, which has been published quarterly since its founding in 1988 by the International Association of Cryptological Research (IACR) under the Taylor & Francis imprint. This journal is devoted to the subject of information security, as well as the study of ciphers and codes often used in espionage and diplomatic communications. However limited German interest may be for the time being when it comes to intelligence scholarship, a cluster of historians in that nation began the *Journal of Intelligence History* (*JIH*) in 2001, and have followed up with a series of monographs and annual conferences sponsored by the International Intelligence History Association, or IIHA. (The IIHA held its 18th annual conference in Paris in 2012.) A more recent arrival to the periodical scene is the *Journal for Intelligence Propaganda and Security Studies*, with Siegfried Beer at the helm. The *JIPSS* has been published semi-annually since 2005 by the Austrian Center for Intelligence, Propaganda and Security Studies in Graz, with a variety of articles in German and English. The latest entry into the field is the *International Journal of Intelligence Ethics* (*IJIE*), issued semi-annually since 2010 by Scarecrow Press (Rowan & Littlefield) on behalf of the International Intelligence Ethics Association.

These journals joined two already established publications on intelligence in the United States. The better known is sponsored by the Center for the Study of Intelligence at the CIA and entitled *Studies in Intelligence* (*SI*, the 'Journal of the American Intelligence Profession', according to the masthead). Its lineage dates back to 1955 and it is printed in both a classified form for intelligence officers and an unclassified form for public consumption.[9] The other journal is sponsored by the National Military Intelligence Association and entitled *American Intelligence Journal*. It dates back to 1982, is published on a semi-annual basis and is billed as 'the Magazine for Intelligence Professionals'. Both are valuable sources of intelligence insights provided by inside practitioners and sometimes by invited outside researchers.

The CIA's Center for the Study of Intelligence has also sponsored many intelligence conferences since the late 1970s, bringing together scholars and practitioners for lively discussions. While friendly on these occasions, the relationship between the two groups has sometimes been uneasy. The intelligence agencies are reluctant to release secret archives at the rate scholars would wish, on the one hand, and scholars are wary of being manipulated by intelligence officials, on the other. On another front, governments tend to be unhappy about the idea of former intelligence officers writing books and articles on their experiences and, as a result, disputes over official pre-publication clearance of such works have become a regular event in the United States and periodically in the United Kingdom as well.

Despite these riches of specialised publication outlets, interest in intelligence all but disappears when one enters the mainstream journals of history and political science. Academic periodicals that examine matters of foreign policy and national security will publish an intelligence article now and then, as attested to by a survey of such journals as *Comparative Strategy*, *Conflict Resolution*, *Diplomatic History*, *Foreign Affairs*, *International Security*, *International Studies Quarterly*, *Political Science Quarterly*, *Polity*, the *Journal of Military History*, and *World Politics*. Intelligence articles are rare, however, in these and other mainstream academic journals. A check through the index of the *American Political Science Review*, for example, yields only one article on intelligence throughout its long history, stretching back to 1906. Rare, too, are scholarly blogs on intelligence. Some good ones do exist, though, such as 'Secrecy News', the widely consulted electronic newsletter of the Federation of American Scientists (FAS) Project on Government Secrecy (www.fas.org/blog/secrecy, with a mailing list of some 13,000 subscribers), and another useful site run by the Canadian intelligence scholar Martin Rudner (mrudner@magma.ca).

An exception to this rule of omission in mainstream journals is *Foreign Policy*, which has gravitated from being a scholarly quarterly founded in 1970 to a glossy, bimonthly newsrack magazine – although it continues to publish thoughtful pieces by prominent academicians. It has displayed a steady interest in the subject of intelligence, and a former DCI, John Deutch, serves on its editorial board. Mainstream law journals are more apt than history and social science journals to have articles on intelligence, although the primary intelligence interest in the legal profession has been on questions of privacy and accountability (see, for example, O'Connell 2006; Clark 2010).

Political scientist Amy Zegart (2005, 2007) has commented on this intelligence void in the mainstream scholarly literature, attributing it to the dominant emphasis in academic circles on theoretical (as opposed to policy) topics, and to the difficulty of conducting research on secret intelligence organisations – at least quickly enough in time to gain tenure. Some members of the academy also seem to think that intelligence is unimportant in the study of international affairs – an argument advanced primarily by those who have failed to explore the subject in any serious way; after all, if policy decisions are based on information, and intelligence agencies provide much of the information that enters into the deliberations of national decision councils, it is difficult to conclude that intelligence is unimportant.[10] McDermott (2012) suggests that many liberal academics associate intelligence studies with political conservatism and, therefore, they shy away. Further, others have noted (Andrew and Dilks 1984, for example) that some academics have been turned off the subject because intelligence agents have periodically engaged in operations they find unsavoury.

A profile of the scholarly interests of intelligence researchers

Despite the lack of interest in intelligence studies displayed by many prominent scholarly journals, the ranks of researchers who study this subject have continued to swell since 1975, with their work appearing chiefly in specialised intelligence journals. A wide range of topics have drawn the attention of researchers and this work may be sorted into a number of categories: collection, analysis and dissemination (key elements in the 'intelligence cycle', a theoretical construct that traces the pathway of intelligence from its gathering in the field to its final reporting to policy-makers); organisation, leadership and management; military intelligence; covert action; counterintelligence; accountability; historical case studies; theory and methods; biography; foreign intelligence services; and critiques of spy fiction. A sense of this research diversity can be gleaned from an examination of articles published in the journal *Intelligence and National Security* since its inception in 1986, as shown in Table 1.1 (where the categories are organised in descending order of publication frequency).[11]

The most popular research category in this journal was 'intelligence collection' – the methods by which a nation's secret agencies gather information. The *modus operandi*, or 'tradecraft', used in this gathering includes, primarily, technical means (technical intelligence, or 'TECHINT'); classic human espionage (human intelligence, or 'HUMINT'); a search through public sources, such as the Library of Congress or the internet (open source intelligence, or 'OSINT'); and the exchange of intelligence between nations (foreign intelligence liaison, sometimes referred

Table 1.1 Articles in the journal *Intelligence and National Security*, by topic

Topic*	Time period					
	1986–90	*1991–95*	*1996–2000*	*2001–05*	*2006–11*	*Total*
Intel collection	39	22	51	31	25	168 (19%)
History	29	27	26	25	38	145 (16%)
CI	32	12	16	18	22	100 (11%)
Analysis	17	12	10	16	30	85 (9%)
Theory/methods	11	14	11	15	25	76 (8%)
CA	2	4	16	28	18	68 (7%)
Biographical	14	11	12	8	14	59 (6%)
Accountability	7	2	9	13	21	52 (6%)
Organisation	5	8	6	4	15	38 (4%)
Non–US/UK agencies	8	9	10	5	6	38 (4%)
Military intel	12	7	7	4	2	32 (4%)
Dissemination	4	9	4	3	7	27 (3%)
Fiction	13	1	2	2	8	26 (3%)
						N = 914

* The 'intelligence collection' category includes technical intelligence, human intelligence, open-source intelligence and foreign liaison relationships (see Table 1.2); 'history' refers to studies into the role of intelligence in major events of the past, most often case studies with a pre-1946 focus; 'CI', counterintelligence (including counterterrorism and domestic security operations); 'CA', covert action; 'biographical', articles on specific intelligence officers and policy-makers; 'accountability' includes oversight, reform and ethics; 'theory and methods', articles explicitly directed at these research concerns; 'analysis', anything to do with preparing assessments, as well as commentary on intelligence failures; 'non-US/UK services', articles that look at other intelligence services besides these two (which dominate the 'organisation' category); 'organisation' includes intelligence management and leadership articles; 'military intelligence', articles with a narrow focus on some aspect of this form of intelligence, 'dissemination', articles about the relationship between policy-makers and intelligence officers, including the politics of intelligence; and 'fiction', which encompasses non-fictional critiques of spy fiction.

to as 'burden sharing'). Articles on collection accounted for almost a fifth (19 per cent) of the total number of accepted submissions in *INS* from 1986 through 2011 (n = 914). Within this category, TECHINT accounted for a majority of articles, followed by studies on foreign liaison and then a blend of HUMINT (chiefly) and OSINT (see Table 1.2).

No intelligence topic is easy for the outside scholar to research, but liaison and HUMINT are particularly difficult; few intelligence activities are more closely held within a nation's secret

Table 1.2 Articles related to intelligence collection in the journal *Intelligence and National Security*

Topic*	Time period					
	1986–90	*1991–95*	*1996–2000*	*2001–05*	*2006–11*	*Total*
TECHINT	35	10	23	15	5	88 (52%)
Liaison	2	4	19	10	12	47 (28%)
HUMINT/OSINT	2	8	9	6	8	33 (20%) N = 168

TECHINT = technical intelligence
Liaison = the sharing of intelligence between or among foreign intelligence services
HUMINT/OSINT = human intelligence/open-source intelligence

agencies than the activities of their agents ('assets'), as well as institutional ties with foreign intelligence services. In contrast, some information about technical collection systems has seeped into the public domain, as in the case of drone technology. Moreover, controversies during the second Bush administration over wiretap authority have made electronic surveillance a TECHINT topic of widespread public and academic interest. Overall, since intelligence agencies with an international mission exist above all to gather information for their national leaders about threats and opportunities around the world, perhaps it should be no surprise that researchers have given 'collection' so much attention.

Second on the list of the topics most researched by scholars contributing to *Intelligence and National Security* are historical case studies, especially from the Second World War and earlier. Most of the *INS* editors have been academic historians, and this fact may have encouraged other historians to write for its pages, although a political scientist has been senior editor in recent years and the accepted articles with a historical focus have continued at a high rate. Another explanation is that, often, decades must pass before intelligence archives are released to the public (if ever); as a result, fewer scholars have attempted to engage in research on contemporary issues, for which most of the relevant documentation remains under lock and key. Despite this research obstacle, though, much of the research published in *INS* has been on matters of recent vintage.

Counterintelligence (CI) is the only other topic to reach the threshold of 100 or more articles published in the journal. As with spy novelists and the general public, scholars have been drawn to the subject of 'moles'. These are traitors within a nation's secret service, recruited by foreign intelligence agencies to spy against their own country. They are usually motivated by a desire for personal enrichment; but sometimes, especially in the early days of the Cold War, they have been driven by ideological convictions. Today, ethnic ties to foreign nations have been a motivator.

Analysis is fourth on the list, even though it is often considered by insiders as the heart and soul of intelligence. If the data gathered by machines and human agents are inadequately assessed by analysts to provide useful insight for policy-makers, collection is for naught. When the categories of 'collection', 'analysis' and 'dissemination' – the three essential phases of the intelligence cycle – are combined, they account for 29 per cent of the total number of articles published in *INS*. This sum underscores the fact that, in *INS* at least, most scholarship has been devoted to the question of how the secret agencies collect and attempt to understand data about foreign threats and opportunities, and how they communicate these findings to decision-makers. No great surprises here, since these topics are the essence of intelligence.

As one might expect in a scholarly journal, the topic of theory and methods attracted attention as well – everything from how well the 'ideal' construct of the intelligence cycle matches reality ('only approximately' is the answer) to descriptions of newly opened intelligence archives. Some researchers in the field believe that intelligence studies must go beyond its usual concentration on case studies and descriptive narratives to develop testable hypotheses and models of intelligence behaviour, just as the social sciences have done in other fields (led by political science electoral studies in the 1960s). While many of the social sciences have become dominated by statistical analyses – the quantification of research – this approach, for better or for worse, has yet to take root in the field of intelligence studies. It is apt to arrive one day, though, and certainly the emphasis of this mathematical approach on rigour and replicable research findings is laudable, so long as regression equations don't replace clear English sentences or turn important subjects into pedantic exercises in methodology nuance. Just as the healthcare sciences and the practice of medicine have benefited significantly from Evidence-Based Medicine (Timmermans and Mauck 2005), so can intelligence scholars benefit from Evidence-Based Intelligence Studies (EBIS); more empirically based researched will greatly benefit the field.

Covert action has been of interest, too, with 68 articles (7 per cent of the total); but, as with HUMINT and foreign liaison, this subject is highly sensitive and closely held by governments, making it difficult for scholars to uncover fresh findings. Many of these studies have had to await the slow release of government archives, such as the piece by Stephen R. Weissman (2010) on the assassination of Congo President Patrice Lumumba in 1961 (which won the *INS* award for the 'Best Article of 2010'). Next on the list, one of the attractions of the 'biographical' category (which also includes a few autobiographical pieces) is the existence of more readily available papers on leading intelligence personalities, perhaps even an opportunity to interview these individuals.

Accountability – that is, the attempt to maintain proper supervision over secret intelligence agencies in democratic societies – has been of keen interest to some researchers, as have questions about organisation, leadership and management. In light of the spy scandals that erupt now and then in almost every society, as well as the daunting bureaucratic barriers that have prevented the integration of intelligence findings ('all source fusion') among services within the same nation, it is remarkable that these two categories ('accountability' and 'organisation') have not yielded more studies. After all, it was the scandal of CIA domestic spying in the United States that triggered the explosion of intelligence research in 1975 in America, as did America's Iran-*contra* scandal in the 1980s; and the organisational mistakes associated with the 9/11 surprise attacks and the faulty analysis of WMD in Iraq in 2002 produced a raft of intelligence reform efforts in the United States and the United Kingdom, accompanied by a further surge in intelligence studies research. In the United States, practically every commission and investigative committee on intelligence since 1948 has called for the better organisational integration of America's secret agencies. These investigators have pointed to the problem of 'stovepipes' in the intelligence community and the pressing need for a national spymaster with budget and personal authority over all the spy entities in the government (Johnson 2011b). This prescription has yet to be adopted, however, mainly because of resistance from the Pentagon.

Some scholars have attempted to understand the inner workings and outward effects of foreign intelligence services, such as the Soviet KGB during the Cold War or the contemporary Chinese approach to espionage. The number of these articles has been limited, though, because foreign intelligence services are not in the habit of revealing their objectives, or even their structure, to academic researchers. Nonetheless, attempts at comparative analysis remain vital (see Davies 2012b, for example), for the same reason that comparative studies in international affairs generally have been so important – not least for helping scholars understand the strengths and weaknesses of approaches to governance in the West.

Near the bottom of the research hierarchy depicted in Table 1.1 are specific studies on military intelligence, the pitfalls of intelligence dissemination, and critiques of spy fiction. Most intelligence scholars have been interested in the strategic level of study: the role of intelligence in national decision councils where sweeping global objectives are at play. Yet much intelligence funding by governments is dedicated to SMO: support to military operations in the field – meeting the information needs of uniformed war-fighters at the tactical level. Journalists have become more adept at 'embedding' themselves into combat units for reporting on foreign conflicts; scholars have yet to adopt this methodology, which would provide first-hand observations of intelligence-at-work at the tactical level. Nor have scholars conducted many interviews with returned combatants to probe their intelligence experiences in the field.

Dissemination is an intelligence step of great significance, yet accounts for only 3 per cent of all the articles examined here. Politicisation, cherry-picking, 'intelligence to please', intelligence as a political football – all of these topics fall into this category and represent distortions that can ruin the best of intelligence reports as they make their way from analysts to policy-makers. The cardinal sin of intelligence is to twist intelligence for political purposes. The influences that lead to these distortions have been well plumbed by some scholars in the discipline (for instance, Lowenthal 1992), but such an important topic warrants wider attention.

Finally, the caboose in this train of subjects is the 'fiction' category, although on two occasions *INS* published special issues on spy fiction. A dominant theme in these issues was that Hollywood and most spy novels fail to capture the reality of espionage. Nonetheless, a few do, such as film-maker Tomas Alfredson (*Tinker Tailor Soldier Spy*), and novelists John le Carré and Charles McCarry. Here is one reason for scholars to pay attention to spy fiction: these works are written now and then by former intelligence officers who can get away with discussing their trade in a fictional format, whereas government censurers would red-line comparable revelations in a non-fictional account.

The book literature

Just as the periodical literature on intelligence studies has burgeoned since the 1975, the rate of book-length publishing on the subject has been nothing less than astounding (see, for example, the large number of book-length works cited in the References section of this volume). In the past three years alone, four major 'handbooks' on intelligence have appeared (including this book), one consisting of five volumes (Johnson 2005b, 2007b, 2010). Further, two general readers on intelligence are widely used in university courses (Andrew, Aldrich and Wark 2009; Johnson and Wirtz 2011), along with a specialised reader on intelligence ethics (Goldman 2006) and a four-volume set of classic articles on intelligence (Johnson 2011).[12] Not a single week seems to pass without the release of another new book on this subject; and, unlike the pre-1970s era, a large number of them are credible, carefully researched studies.[13] The intelligence journals are sorely pressed to keep up with the reviewing of this literature and some are moving to online book reviews as a means of publishing critiques in a more timely fashion.

The demographics of intelligence scholarship

A further look at the articles published in the journal *Intelligence and National Security* offers some insights into the demographics of intelligence scholarship. One aspect is the home base of the researchers.[14]

Country of origin

The percentages in Table 1.3 display the total number of articles accepted by *INS* from around the world. This ranking indicates a geographic hierarchy of successful submissions, with the United Kingdom at the top (41 per cent), followed by the United States (38 per cent), Canada (9 per cent), non-UK Europe (6 per cent), Australia and Israel (tied at 3 per cent), and Asia (1 per cent). These percentages have fluctuated only slightly over the years.

In the aggregate count of articles published in *INS*, researchers in the United Kingdom and the United States have been predominant (see Table 1.4). Even though the journal encourages submissions from around the world, almost 80 per cent of the articles came from just these two places. This trend has been persistent throughout the entire period since the founding of the journal in 1986, and from 2006–11 the total rose to 83 per cent. In terms of the sheer volume of scholarly production, the field of intelligence studies (at least as reflected in the pages of *INS*) has been primarily a British–American pursuit.

The top ranking for the United Kingdom in Table 1.3 is no doubt a result stemming in part from the fact that the journal is published in London and has an especially high visibility in the British Isles. Moreover, the senior editors for the journal have often been based in the

Table 1.3 Number of authors appearing in *Intelligence and National Security*, by nationality

Nationality	Time period					
	1986–90	*1991–95*	*1996–2000*	*2001–05*	*2006–11*	*Total*
UK	90	60	75	80	117	422
	(49%)	(36%)	(37%)	(43%)	(41%)	(41%)
US	54	66	85	66	119	390
	(30%)	(40%)	(42%)	(35%)	(42%)	(38%)
Canada	19	20	21	16	11	87
	(10%)	(12%)	(10%)	(9%)	(4%)	(9%)
Other Europe	7	8	9	16	21	61
	(4%)	(5%)	(4%)	(9%)	(8%)	(6%)
Australia	6	7	4	6	6	29
	(3%)	(4%)	(2%)	(3%)	(2%)	(3%)
Israel	8	3	6	2	9	28
	(4%)	(2%)	(3%)	(1%)	(3%)	(3%)
Asia	0	1	4	1	0	6
	(0%)	(1%)	(2%)	(1%)	(0%)	(1%)
						N = 1,023

Table 1.4 Author nationalities in *Intelligence and National Security*, US/UK versus Other

Nationality	Time period					
	1986–90	*1991–95*	*1996–2000*	*2001–05*	*2006–11*	*Total*
US/UK	144	126	160	146	236	812
	(78%)	(76%)	(78%)	(78%)	(83%)	(79%)
Other	40	39	44	41	47	211
	(22%)	(24%)	(22%)	(22%)	(17%)	(21%)
						N = 1,023

United Kingdom, although roughly half of the time this position has been filled by a Canadian or American. Of course, a language barrier plays a heavy role in these statistics. Intelligence scholars in non-English-speaking countries may feel uncomfortable in their ability to write well enough in English for their pieces to be accepted by *INS*, or the other English-prose journals on this subject. Surely in China, the Arab world, in continental Europe and elsewhere there is reputable scholarly research on intelligence that never comes to the attention of most English-speaking scholars because of the language barrier. The readers of *INS*, *IJICI*, *IS* and *AJI* could benefit enormously from the publication in their pages of key foreign-language pieces on intelligence translated into English, a step currently prohibited chiefly by the costs of translation.

A per capita perspective on country origin

The more populous nations are likely to have a larger number of scholars involved in almost any academic pursuit, including intelligence studies, so it is useful to consider national scholarly production within a field on a per capita basis. From this vantage point, the portraits displayed in the earlier aggregate figures take on a different hue. Even on a per capita basis, the United Kingdom retains its first-place position in all but the first few years (1986–90) since *Intelligence and National Security* began publication; however, as the findings in Table 1.5 illustrate, some less populous nations have conducted research on intelligence at higher rates than the aggregate data suggest. Based on this per capita reckoning, Israel stood in first place at the beginning of the journal's existence and has come in second on two other occasions during the periods of publication displayed in the table. From this vantage point, Israeli scholars have been strikingly active in intelligence studies. So have Canadian scholars, who recorded second-place finishes during two of the time periods.

Author gender

As the percentages presented in Table 1.6 underline, male researchers have dominated the field of intelligence studies as captured in the pages of *INS*. This result seems to be true for researchers who write on national security matters across the board, in a wide variety of journals. Moreover, positions in the national security apparatus of all governments around the world have

Table 1.5 Author nationalities in *Intelligence and National Security*, by per capita ranking

Nationality	Time period					
	1986–90	*1991–95*	*1996–2000*	*2001–05*	*2006–11*	*Overall*
UK	2nd	1st	1st	1st	1st	1st
Israel	1st	3rd	2nd	3rd	2nd	2nd
Canada	3rd	2nd	3rd	2nd	4th	3rd
Australia	4th	4th	5th	4th	5th	4th★
US	5th	5th	4th	5th	3rd	4th★
Other Europe	6th	6th	6th	6th	6th	6th
Asia	7th	7th	7th	7th	7th	7th

★ Tied

The population data upon which these rankings are calculated are for the beginning year of each time period, based on the Correlates of War National Material Capabilities Dataset (Singer, Bremer and Stuckey, 1972: 19–43).

Table 1.6 Authors in *Intelligence and National Security*, by gender

Gender	Time period					
	1986–90	*1991–95*	*1996–2000*	*2001–05*	*2006–11*	*Total*
Male	178	160	181	169	248	936
	(97%)	(97%)	(89%)	(90%)	(88%)	(92%)
Female	6	5	23	18	35	87
	(3%)	(3%)	(11%)	(10%)	(12%)	(8%)
						N = 1,023

been filled chiefly by males. The United Kingdom has had women in key intelligence offices, though. They have led MI5, for example; and indeed, today, more than half of the personnel in this British internal security organisation are female (Burns 2009: A14). The photographs of heroes from the Second World War that adorn the walls of the Special Operations Executive (SOE) Club in London include many women who excelled in espionage activities against the Nazis. In contrast, only one woman directs a major intelligence agency in the United States today and few have served in that capacity in the past – including none in the most prominent agencies: the CIA, the National Security Agency, the National Reconnaissance Office, the National Geospatial-Intelligence Agency and the FBI. Of all the publications in the journal *Intelligence and National Security*, 93 per cent have been authored by males. In recent issues, however, female authorships reached 12 per cent – a four-fold increase since the journal's beginning years.

Another medium of intelligence studies: the media

Intelligence scholars in the universities and think-tanks are not the only outsiders interested in taking a serious look at the operations of spy agencies. Several media reporters also have an intelligence beat, and some of them have produced significant works in article and book form.[15] Intelligence reporters and scholars both have an interest in international affairs, in the role of information in foreign policy decisions and in the question of maintaining accountability over secret agencies in a democracy. There is some degree of interaction between the two as well. Professors and other outside experts are occasionally tapped as sources for media reporting on intelligence, especially for the purpose of placing current espionage activities into historical context; and scholars scour media reporting for information about secret operations, as well as for quotes from intelligence officers that might shed light on their own research.

Reporting in the media is important to the discipline of intelligence studies; and this reporting is also the source of most public knowledge about the activities of a nation's secret agencies – at least in those countries that enjoy a free and active press. For this reason, it is worth exploring what topics the media finds significant when it comes to intelligence. The interests of scholars and reporters can be quite different from one another, as indicated by the data in Table 1.7 (which is based on articles published in the *New York Times* from 2006–11).[16]

As shown earlier (Table 1.1), authors who published in *Intelligence and National Security* during the time period from 2006 to 2011 concentrated mainly on historical case studies, along with attention to the problems of collection and analysis. Reporters for the *New York Times* on the intelligence beat were interested in collection issues, too, but showed a greater attraction to the topics of accountability and counterintelligence. The primary objective of the newspaper business is to sell newspapers; scandals and disastrous intelligence failures – the central concerns

Table 1.7 Intelligence articles in *Intelligence and National Security* and the *New York Times* (2006–11), by topic

Topic	Intelligence and National Security	New York Times
History	38	61
	(16%)	(5%)
Analysis	30	65
	(13%)	(5%)
Intel collection	25	139★
	(11%)	(11%)
Theory/methods	25	13
	(11%)	(1%)
CI	22	220
	(10%)	(17%)
Accountability	21	352
	(9%)	(28%)
CA	18	74
	(8%)	(6%)
Organisation	15	102
	(7%)	(8%)
Biographical	14	90
	(6%)	(7%)
Fiction	8	8
	(4%)	(>1%)
Dissemination	7	16
	(3%)	(1%)
Non-US/UK services	6	114
	(2%)	(9%)
Military intel	2	16
	(1%)	(1%)
Total	231	1,270

★ Within the 'Collection' category for the *New York Times* were these subsets:
Technical intelligence = 74 (53%)
Human/open-source intelligence = 39 (28%)
Liaison relationships = 26 (19%)

of accountability – are red meat for the hungry lions of the print and television media. So, too, are such matters as moles, waterboarding and other forms of torture, secret CIA prisons, and extraordinary renditions – all of which lie within the counterintelligence domain. Here are subjects that produce congressional inquiries, presidential commissions, newspaper headlines and Pulitzer prizes. They also happen to be important subjects in their own right. Scholars in democratic societies would do well to pay more attention, for example, to the dynamics of accountability, in hopes of knowing more about – and thereby reducing – the incidents of scandal and failure by a nation's secret agencies. As for the high levels of *New York Times* reporting on intelligence collection, warrantless wiretaps, drones of all shapes and sizes, and sophisticated satellites make for interesting reading, too, and thus gained space in the newspaper's pages.

Given less attention by *New York Times* reporters (or their editors, at any rate) were stories based on covert action (6 per cent of the total), except for a recent focus on the use of Predator and Reaper drones as instruments for assassinating Al Qaeda and extremist Taliban targets; on an historical analysis of intelligence case studies (5 per cent); on analysis (5 per cent, perhaps too dry a topic for the media); on the politics of intelligence dissemination (1 per cent); on military intelligence (1 per cent, despite reporter embedding); and on theory-and-methods (1 per cent) with its graduate seminar flavour. Once in a while, though, the *Times* has had articles on newly opened intelligence archives, or on the complaints of scholars about access to intelligence documents. Doubtless the *Times* would like to report more on covert action but reporters, like scholars, have trouble finding out about these operations, as is likely the case for military intelligence even if reporters are embedded in some operations.

Where reporters could especially make a valuable contribution to public and scholarly understanding of intelligence, but fail to, is on the subject of dissemination – especially how information and analysis is distorted by policy-makers in support of their political objectives. Indeed, the *Times* became part and parcel of this distortion when its reporters accepted too readily the political posturing of the Bush White House over alleged Iraqi WMD in 2002, paying little attention to dissenting views from intelligence units in the Air Force, the State Department and the Energy Department. The divergent interests of academic and journalistic intelligence researchers are summarised in Table 1.8.

Intelligence studies organisations

Another dimension of intelligence studies is the existence of scholarly organisations dedicated to this pursuit. In addition to the various groups referred to earlier, others have cropped up in recent years. In 2006, an Intelligence Studies Group (ISG) came to life within the framework of the American Political Science Association (APSA). This status permits intelligence scholars to have a panel at the APSA's annual meeting. If enough people attend the panel, the number of ISG panels may then rise in the following year to two or more. The ISG, which had to be established by a petition and the signatures of 50 political scientists, is one of many specialised groups within the framework of the APSA. The median number of attendees at all of the APSA special group panels has been 17 in recent years, with the ISG recording a score of 23 – 15th out of the 62 groups. This result augers well for the growth of intelligence panels within the APSA, although so far the number has remained stuck at only one panel for each convention. The prospects have been hindered by the scheduling given to the group: usually a Sunday morning or some other undesirable time slot.

Greater success has been achieved by the Intelligence Studies (IS) Section of the International Studies Association. At ISA's annual meetings, the IS Section has enjoyed the scheduling of anywhere from 12 to 18 panels in recent years, with robust participation at many of them. Active, too, has been CASIS, the Canadian Association for Security and Intelligence Studies,

Table 1.8 The chief differences in focus for academic and media articles on intelligence, 2006–11

	Intelligence and National Security	*New York Times*
Highest interest	History	Accountability
	Analysis	Counterintelligence
	Collection	Collection
Lowest interest	Dissemination	Dissemination/Mil intel (tied)
	Non-US/UK services	Theory and methods
	Military intel	Fiction

which holds a first-rate conference each year in Ottawa that includes hundreds of partici-pants – mainly from Canada, but with paper-presenters from several other countries as well. In the United Kingdom, the British International Studies Association and the Political Studies Association have both offered intelligence panels since the 1980s.

Other intelligence studies groups have arisen. In the United States, for example, one of the most influential has been the CIA's Center for the Study of Intelligence, staffed by in-house historians who periodically release solid studies and documents related to CIA activities since the Agency's establishment in 1947 (see, for example, Pedlow and Welzenbach 1998; Robarge 2007). Important, as well, is the National Security Archive at George Washington Univer-sity, which has had remarkable success in pressing the government for the release of classified documents. Another group with an interest in intelligence scholarship is the Intelligence and National Security Alliance (INSA), an umbrella organisation that counts among its members more than 100 corporations and scores of intelligence experts. Prominent, too, is the Associa-tion of Retired Former Officers (ARFO), which sponsors forums on intelligence through its regional chapters; and the International Association for Intelligence Education (IAFIE), which holds an annual conference in the United States. Further, an intelligence salon has been estab-lished in the District of Columbia, associated with scholars Jennifer Sims (Georgetown Univer-sity) and William Nolte (University of Maryland). One organisation with a mandate to advance professional knowledge about intelligence and related matters is the granddaddy of them all: the Armed Forces Communications and Electronics Association (AFCEA), founded in 1946. Looking into the future, Marrin (2012: 420) recommends the establishment of Intelligence Studies Centers – intelligence-related think-tanks that could 'supplement knowledge creation in both traditional academic departments and the newer public policy-orientated intelligence schools'.

The road ahead

In sum, the field of intelligence studies is alive and progressing well in several nations. A heart-ening indicator of this vibrancy is the large number of young professionals joining the discipline, as reflected in their attendance at APSA, CASIS and ISA meetings (among other forums) and their growing ranks among published authors in the leading intelligence journals.

What does the future hold for intelligence research? Scholars in the field know better than to predict the future with any sense of certitude, but some educated guesses may be allowed. It is likely that the research directions proposed by Professor May almost two decades ago will continue to be part of the scholarly agenda (May 1995). One of his suggestions dealt with the matter of whether or not intelligence plays a significant role in the making of government decisions. In this vein, Betts (2012) believes that the most under-researched intelligence topic is 'what effects on policy can really be attributed to intelligence'. Jervis (2012) agrees, as well, that 'the influence of intelligence on policy' may be the most under-studied central topic in the field. A recent work by Pillar (2011), a senior CIA analyst, exhibits a profound scepticism that intelligence has any importance at all on policy choices. His judgement seems overly harsh, perhaps born of his frustrations with the dismissive handling of intelligence estimates by the second Bush administration. Clearly, much more research needs to be done on this topic. Further, Treverton (2012) urges more attention to counterintelligence and more research on US signals intelligence. For Sir David Omand (2012b) at least, British signals intelligence may be an overworked topic; he thinks that least cultivated is 'the relationship between intelligence analysts and intelligence officers involved in collection and the senior managers of both groups (as against the well-research analyst/policymaker interaction)'.

May suggested, as well, that intelligence scholars try to evaluate whether the democracies are getting their money's worth from spending on intelligence activities – some $80 billion per annum in the United States. Reliable answers will require more sophisticated metrics than currently available. Further, May urged attention to the interplay between intelligence and policy, along with deeper probes into the organisational cultures that make up intelligence 'communities'. Christopher Andrew's research (1995) points to the value of studies on the influence of intelligence in high decision councils; and he has also been a leader in scholarly counterintelligence inquiries (2009, for example). Further, he emphasises that 'much more research still remains to be done on all stages of the intelligence cycle . . . ', and he notes that basic questions about the attitude of most world leaders towards intelligence 'have yet to be asked, let alone answered' (2004: 72). David M. Barrett (2012) reminds us, moreover, that 'a lot of intel history remains mostly untold, despite all the historical literature'.

In addition, Herman (2012) points to the need for a typology of intelligence systems worldwide, along with research that sets intelligence properly into the context of a government information service. He recommends, too, greater focus on those findings from economics and management studies that are likely to be applicable to intelligence organisations (see Herman 1996). The American intelligence scholar and former National Security Agency official William Nolte (2012) suggests that academicians grapple more with the question of 'where intelligence studies fits' into the broader scope of the international relations research. Along with Betts and Jervis, he asks further: 'When does [intelligence] work? How would we know?' And, with May, 'What is it worth?' Canadian researcher A. Walter Dorn (2012) recommends more attention to intelligence as used by international organisations, such as the United Nations, especially since national security may well depend on the degree of international security.

As the field continues to mature, scholars are apt to undertake more hypothesis testing and theory building. McDermott (2012) notes that 'sometimes being able to see repetitions across time and space can help identify places where improvements can be made or successes can be built upon'. Betts (2012) poses an appropriate and vexing question, though: how can one 'do systematic social science analyses when [a] big portion of relevant data is secret?' Omand (2012b) adds: 'What works for economics with the "law of large numbers" to underpin statistics is unlikely to be meaningful in the small domains of intelligence where non-quantitative factors dominate.' Certainly, though, Herman (2012) is on target with his suggestion that more interdisciplinary research will be useful, with the disciplines of psychology, organisational theory and management, cultural anthropology, economic theories on uncertainty and imperfect information, and decision theory all providing fertile ground for mining hypotheses that may apply to the behaviour of intelligence agencies and their officers. Moreover, Glees (2012) advocates a stronger research concentration on the question of why the British government is unwilling to provide more data and documentation for scholars in the intelligence field; and he joins a host of other scholars in advocating more digging into the organisation and practices of secret agencies beyond the usual Anglo-Saxon suspects, especially in Asia and Africa.

The data presented in the tables of this chapter indicate the need, as well, for more studies on intelligence consumer–producer relations (see 'Dissemination' in Table 1.1). Limited existing research indicates a troubling dislocation at this nexus that can undermine all the earlier phases of the intelligence cycle.[17] One would also expect to see more intelligence scholarship from outside the Anglo-Saxon nations, as well as more women entering the field. Finally, one can hope for increased cooperation by intelligence services and their government managers in providing archival access to research scholars. In far too many instances, cases that are over 25 years old still languish in the dusty files of secret agencies or national archives, when they could be used by researchers to bring greater understanding to this vital government domain.

'The subject [intelligence studies] has come a long way in the last twenty or so years,' writes Mark Phythian (2012), 'but relative to other areas of the social sciences there is still enormous scope for further development.' That is exactly right – and how exciting for all of us interested in this field to help chart the future course.

Notes

The author would like to express his appreciation to Philip H.J. Davies and Michael Herman for suggestions regarding the current state of intelligence studies; to David M. Barrett, Richard K. Betts, A. Walter Dorn, Anthony Glees, Robert Jervis, Rose McDermott, William Nolte, Mark Phythian, and Gregory F. Treverton for sharing their thoughts in the context of a survey about the field mailed to them by the author; and to Allison Shelton, a PhD candidate in the Department of International Affairs at the University of Georgia, for her assistance with the survey, and with the data collection and analysis throughout this chapter.

1 Ransom also reached a wide audience in the early 1960s with two articles on the CIA in the *New York Times Magazine* (1960) and (1961). On Ransom's early influence in the field, see Johnson (2007a).
2 See May's seminal study on French intelligence during the Second World War (May 2000).
3 In 1975, the US House of Representatives launched an inquiry into allegations printed in the *New York Times* that the CIA had spied on American citizens; Representative Otis Pike (D, New York) led that inquiry, which ended up focusing on the Agency's analytic mistakes ('intelligence failures'). A similar, though far more extensive, inquiry took place in the Senate, led by Senator Frank Church (D, Idaho). It concentrated on the original charges of domestic spying, but went on as well to examine CIA covert actions (including assassination plots). Not to be left behind, the White House under President Gerald R. Ford (R, Michigan) established a presidential commission to probe the *Times* spying allegations and named his Vice President, Nelson Rockefeller (R, New York), to guide the inquiry. These three panels produced a vast quantity of public reporting. The documents (hearings and reports) released by the Church Committee alone stood some six feet high. The Rockefeller Commission released only a single report, but it was a thorough and biting criticism of domestic intelligence abuses traced to the CIA and several of its companion agencies. Members of the Pike panel voted to keep their highly classified report bottled up in committee, but it leaked to the *Village Voice* (a newspaper in New York City) and revealed to the public strong criticism of the Agency's intelligence failures. Whether the leak came from the Committee or from a whistleblower in the intelligence community was a matter never resolved, despite extensive investigations by the FBI and other agencies. For the main findings of these panels, see: Pike Committee (1976); Church Committee (1975a, 1975b, 1976); and the Rockefeller Commission (1975). For accounts of these watershed investigations, see Johnson (1985, 2004); Schwarz and Huq (2007); and Smist (1994).
4 Owing to space limitations, I have been able to cite only a few works by just some of the leading scholars mentioned in this essay. These citations serve as a useful starting place for new scholars entering the field and seeking an orientation, but the reader is encouraged to explore the more complete bibliographies in Gibbs (2005), Johnson (2005, 2012) and Wirtz (2007), and to conduct an internet search on particular authors referred to in this chapter.
5 Serving on the editorial advisory board for *Intelligence and National Security* during these formative years were such academic luminaries as Samuel P. Huntington, Ernest May and future Nobel Laureate Thomas C. Schelling, all on the faculty at Harvard University (with Schelling now at University of Maryland); Harry Howe Ransom of Harvard and later at Vanderbilt; Sir F.H. Hinsley, Cameron Watt and Prof. Sir D.G.T. Williams, Cambridge University; and Aharon Yariv, University of Tel Aviv.
6 Now in its 5th edn (2012).
7 Colby and Forbath (1978); Dulles (1977); Gates (1996); Helms, with Hood (2003); Turner (1985); and Tenet, with Harlow (2007); and the remarks of James R. Clapper, Jr (2010), DNI in the United States.
8 See, also, Andrew (1985).
9 For an anthology of outstanding articles drawn from *SI*, see Westerfield (1995). A distinguished professor of political science at Yale University for decades, Westerfield stands among the early pioneers of intelligence studies in the United States and taught a popular course on the subject for decades at Yale.

10 Echoing several of his predecessors, President Bill Clinton once said that 'every morning I start my day with an intelligence report. The intelligence I receive informs just about every foreign policy decision we make' (author's notes, President Clinton's remarks to the CIA, Langley, VA, 14 July 1996).

11 Included in this analysis are all the peer-reviewed articles that were published, along with extended book-review essays and roundtables, but not research notes and single book reviews. Many of these publications touched upon several aspects of national security intelligence; however, they were placed in only one of the categories in Table 1.1, based on the predominant subject focus in the publication.

12 In addition, Polmar and Allen (1997) prepared a helpful compendium of intelligence terms.

13 A good way to keep up with this literature is by reading Hayden Peake's bibliographic column that appears regularly in *Studies in Intelligence*.

14 In the analysis presented here, there are more authors than articles published in *INS*, owing to the co-authorships of some articles.

15 Examples include, in the United Kingdom, the reporting over the years of Gordon Corera with the BBC; Peter Hennessy (2002) with *The Times* and BBC Radio; and Richard Norton-Taylor with the *Guardian*. Further, Anthony Cave Brown (1975) published a tome about British intelligence during the Second World War; Tom Mangold (1991) advanced the field's understanding of counterintel-ligence; and John Ranelagh (1986) weighed in with a hefty volume on the CIA. In the United States, examples include Seymour Hersh, Nicholas M. Horrock, Eric Lichtblau, James Risen (2006), Scott Shane, Tim Weiner (2008) and Tom Wicker with the *New York Times*; George Lardner, Jr, Walter Pincus and Bob Woodward (1987) with the *Washington Post*; David C. Martin (1980) of CBS Televi-sion; and freelance journalists Thomas Powers (1979) and David Wise (1988, 1992) in Washington, DC.

16 The author clipped each article on intelligence published by the *New York Times* from January 2006 through December 2011, then sorted them into the same categories used above in the examination of articles published by *Intelligence and National Security*. Earlier, the author had carried out this same exercise from 1975–2005. At first, it was unusual to find more than one article every few weeks, with the exception of a some years when Congress was busy investigating intelligence agencies for scandals (1975–76, 1987, 2004) or when there was a highly visible intelligence failure (2001, 2003). Since the 9/11 attacks, however, one or more articles on intelligence have appeared practically every week in the *Times*, even when there were no investigations under way or intelligence failures at hand.

17 This is a central finding in Johnson (2011).

PART II

Abstract approaches to intelligence

2

THEORIES OF INTELLIGENCE

The state of play

Michael Warner[1]

What is intelligence? What does it do? And what should it do? The field of intelligence studies has turned more explicitly towards these questions since the Cold War. Discussions over the possible answers to these and related questions have included professors, students, independent scholars and intelligence practitioners, both active and former. They have informed a growing number of articles, conference panels and anthologies. These debates have indirectly influenced policy. Indeed, a workshop at the RAND Corporation sponsored by the United States' new Office of the Director of National Intelligence in the summer of 2005 assembled participants in this debate from both sides of the Atlantic; that workshop affected the drafting of the Director's first *National Intelligence Strategy* a few months later (Treverton *et al.* 2005; Warner 2012a: 168). The concept of 'decision advantage' in the Director of National Intelligence J. Michael McConnell's 2008 white paper, Vision 2015 (US Director of National Intelligence 2008: 8), came from an essay on intelligence theory by Jennifer E. Sims of Georgetown University. Doubtless other examples as well will emerge in time.

The course of such discussions, of course, begs a larger question: why look for theory at all where intelligence is concerned? Espionage has got along just fine for thousands of years without much scholarly reflection. But longevity does not automatically mean understanding. Indeed, as reliable accounts of intelligence operations and then their actual documentation became available to scholars over the course of the last century, the lack of an intellectual context for these revelations hampered scholarship, both on intelligence itself and on the events it had affected. Christopher Andrew and David Dilks (1984) noticed a 'missing dimension' in historical comprehension in 1984; what they could well have added was that a better understanding of what intelligence is and does might have helped the gap from opening in the first place.

Before surveying the state of theory in intelligence studies, a quick definition might help clarify the discussion. 'Theory' is our label for the notion that we can explain events in terms of replicable causes and effects – replicable, that is, by different observers in various times and places, so long as the observable factors behind the result are held the same. We hypothesise that A and B cause C in such a way that when we see A and B we expect to see C. Theory thus links hypotheses into the beginning of an explanation of what underlies the phenomena that we have become able to foresee. Intelligence activities and institutions, of course, can hardly be replicated in laboratories and subjected to experiments. But neither can political systems, societies or economics – all of which have yielded to methodologies designed to result in theoretical conclusions.

Theory for intelligence seemed for a time out of reach given this imprecision in the very meaning of the term. '[A]ll attempts to develop ambitious theories of intelligence have failed,' noted Walter Laqueur (1985: 8). Adda Bozeman (1988: 149) metaphorically despaired after surveying non-Western intelligence systems in 1988. Noting that intelligence practices are organically linked to a regime's norms and values, and then reflecting on the global diversity of political systems, she judged it 'unlikely that there *can* be one theory that would do justice to the world's varieties of intelligence' (emphasis added). Ironically, however, Bozeman's research had itself shown a way forward. A critic might say her idea that intelligence is too diverse to be categorised because it is something unique to each political system was itself a theory of intelligence by default. More to the point, Bozeman's essay offered some thoughtful generalisations about the way intelligence works in traditional and non-Western societies, and hinted at hypotheses that might be built into theories of the utility of intelligence to various regimes and the influences of regime type on intelligence itself.

The end of the Cold War coincided with heightened interest in the possibility of intelligence theory. The timing was no accident. The 1980s saw considerable declassification of intelligence files from the Second World War in both Britain and the United States, including documents relating to wartime signals intelligence and the mostly complete records of the Office of Strategic Services. Scholars suddenly had more evidence to work with on both sides of the Atlantic, and practitioners could point to earlier examples of intelligence activities and structures to illustrate general points about the discipline. That missing dimension that Andrew and Dilks had sought has begun to be reconstructed in no small part because of the efforts of scholars and practitioners interested in reaching conclusions about intelligence that transcend times and cultures. Such conclusions can embrace not only empirical ('what is') assessments but also normative ('what ought to be') judgements.

What follows is a horseback tour of the new understandings that have not only been debated but seem also to have some explanatory power to guide future research. It reveals not only instances of 'how the social sciences have sought to explain intelligence phenomena – its structures and processes', in Peter Gill's words (2010: 43), but also how scholars of intelligence have inductively sought to build, from some unique data sets, knowledge that might be of use to social science writ large. The discussions about intelligence theory are herein grouped in four sub-fields: debates over the definition of intelligence (i.e. what is the proper subject matter of intelligence theory?); attempts to place intelligence in context as a tool of state power; attempts to examine intelligence as a means of mitigating risk and uncertainty; and proposed methods for comparing intelligence systems and services.

What is intelligence?

Debates over intelligence theory began with the very definition of intelligence, specifically with discussions over what to include and what to exclude from the term. The most oft-cited definition is that intelligence is simply information for decision-makers. In the United States, for instance, the Joint Chiefs of Staff have long followed this formula, basing their usage of the term on a consistent line of definitions that grew from one originally tailored to denote military intelligence for US Army field commanders in the 1920s (Warner 2008). The latest (2012) edition of the Joint Chiefs' *Dictionary of Military and Associated Terms* continues this tradition, calling intelligence

> [t]he product resulting from the collection, processing, integration, evaluation, analysis, and interpretation of available information concerning foreign nations, hostile or potentially hostile forces or elements, or areas of actual or potential operations. The term is also applied to the activity which results in the product and to the organizations engaged in such activity.

While this military-centric definition of intelligence as information for commanders has gained wide currency, an older notion of intelligence as espionage had never disappeared. In the popular mind that notion still reigns, personified by James Bond or George Smiley. Most people casually employ the word 'intelligence' to mean any sort of privileged information useful in making personal or business decisions, from football wagers to corporate mergers. The present author (Warner 2002) sought to summarise this debate in a 2002 article which argued that both the traditional and modern military definitions of intelligence possess independent validity – in short, that they cannot be collapsed into one another. Intelligence is information for decisions if one is a decision-maker, but if one is a national leader intelligence is something more. It is 'secret, state activity to understand or influence foreign entities'.

The article in which I offered this definition has since been reprinted in several anthologies, and inspired a cottage industry of refutations and suggested revisions. Indeed, I have amended the definition of national intelligence to add violent internal threats from 'foreign entities' as the subjects of intelligence activities (Warner 2012b: 230). Kristan J. Wheaton and Michael T. Beerbower (2006: 327, 329) argued that intelligence does not act – that is the decision-maker's job. Intelligence is not operations, and 'it makes sense to separate the activities of knowing, understanding, analyzing, and synthesizing information about a foreign entity – activities largely conducted by government employees – from the conscious act of attempting to influence foreign entities'. Alan Breakspear (2011) has recently made a similar point, defining intelligence as 'a corporate capability to forecast change in time to do something about it'. He also cautions readers against the 'flawed and dangerous' reasoning that intelligence professionals are better able than other officials to understand the 'action domains' of overt operations and counterintelligence, which are 'informed by intelligence rather than integral to it'.

Although we lack space here to review the debate over intelligence definitions in detail, one recent contribution to the discourse merits attention. Milton Diaz (2010), a retired US Air Force officer, interviewed 66 'intelligence professionals, military theorists, and academicians' in the United States using a methodology borrowed from social science for dispelling 'the subjectivity surrounding controversial subjects'. He also took care to distinguish three levels of certainty in deriving a definition of intelligence from the results of the interviews. At the base, or 'lexical' level, participants loosely used the word intelligence to describe 'any process producing knowledge for the purpose of making a decision'. The next, or 'precising', level incorporated limiting factors (i.e. intelligence informs national policy decisions in competitive situations) to bound what lies within and without the purview of intelligence. These considerations led Diaz to posit a third, or theoretical-level, definition of intelligence 'upon which to form intelligence theory' and construct future research:

> Intelligence is any process producing knowledge that might be used in making a decision OR influencing the processes, knowledge, or decisions of competitors AND in the face of competitors' efforts – real or imagined – to affect one's own processes, knowledge, or decisions in matters of national policy.
>
> *(original emphases)*

Intelligence as a tool of state power

Espionage has always evoked strong emotions. Dante consigned traitors to the Inferno's deepest pit, with the most infamous of their lot (Judas, Cassius and Brutus) being gnawed for all eternity by the Arch-Traitor himself. It should not surprise anyone that normative theories of what intelligence should be and do have a very long pedigree. The excuse that 'might makes right' has never quite satisfied; even Sun Tzu felt compelled to provide a reason why spying not only was done but should be done. He gave a subtle retort to those who regarded such work as too disreputable to be studied. War is a perilous and expensive business, he noted: who is more humane, the ruler who puts his kingdom and subjects in harm's way without a thorough understanding of the risks, or he who does all he can to ensure victory (XIII: 1–3)? A growing cast of writers in recent decades have sought to lend logical rigour to analyses of intelligence and its place in statecraft. One of the first was John Barry (1993), who in 1993 situated covert action within the frame of the 'Just War' theory that had recently swayed political debates over the use of force in national policy. His was but an early sally; authors applying Just War principles to intelligence methods in recent years include Michael Quinlan (2007), David Omand (2010a: 286) and Ross Bellaby (2012). Although these attempts seem plausible, this branch of the literature has not yet inspired internal debates, a fact which suggests the notion of intelligence as an extension of Just War principles is still novel and likely to come under scrutiny when it attracts the attention of critics of the Just War approach to state policy. This normative school in intelligence theory is also related to the emerging field of intelligence and ethics, which goes beyond the scope of this essay (Goldman 2006).

The major work of theorisation for intelligence has taken place in a more avowedly empirical vein of explaining what it *is* independently of changing times and mores. Authors in the 1990s began exploring intelligence as a function that constitutes something larger than a product for decision-makers; indeed, it is in effect a 'force multiplier' for nations and their commanders. This exploration took two paths over the next decade or so.

On the one hand, some researchers eschewed the idea that intelligence is mere information and emphasised its operational aspects. In Washington, independent scholars Abram Shulsky and Gary Schmitt (2002) had argued for such an emphasis in their *Silent Warfare: Understanding the World of Intelligence*. Even in its informational side, they explained, intelligence 'as an activity may be defined as the component of the struggle between adversaries that deals primarily with information'. James Der Derian (1994), now at Brown University, around the same time hinted that the operational side of intelligence was all there was. He called intelligence 'the continuation of war by the clandestine interference of one power into the affairs of another'.

Simultaneously, other scholars concentrated on the ways in which intelligence as a provider of information helps to focus and enhance state power. Michael Herman (1996), a veteran of British signals intelligence and the Joint intelligence Committee, led the way with his work *Intelligence Power in Peace and War*. The historian David Kahn (2001) described the ways in which intelligence, in war, is a tool that optimises a commander's resources (and also benefits the defence more than the offence). Jennifer E. Sims (2008: 151, 159) of Georgetown University cast a wider net, offering intelligence and specifically the concept of 'decision advantage' to international relations theory (specifically Neo-Realism) as an inevitable facet of interstate competition. Intelligence, it seemed, had largely been ignored by international relations theorists, who potentially could profit by studying the ways in which secret activities (if done well) enhanced the power of even lesser states. Sims emphasised that intelligence enhances the effectiveness of decisions made by actors who are working in opposition to other actors (who may well be employing their own intelligence assets). Thus it should be studied in a modified Realist paradigm of semi-anarchic interstate relationships. 'If politics involves the competition for power, "intelligence" may be best understood as a process by which competitors improve their decision-making relative to their opponents' (Sims 2007). It provides 'decision advantage', either by making our decisions better, or theirs worse. 'Success is not getting everything right, it is getting enough right to beat the other side.' Intelligence methods can foster decision advantage by stealing opponents' secrets or adulterating the information available to rivals – or both (US Office of the Director of National Intelligence 2006: 19).

Peter Gill (now at the University of Liverpool) and Mark Phythian (University of Leicester) built upon the concept of intelligence as a force multiplier but also sought to account for its operational as well as its informational utility. What Gill and Phythian (2006) added was a theoretical base for this link – i.e. an explanation of why regimes the world over have consistently linked secret informational and operational activities. As James Der Derian had before them, they found this link in the context of critical social theory, specifically Michel Foucault's concept of *surveillance* as the state's manifestation of knowledge and power over its subjects. *Surveillance*, after the French term (rather than its English cognate), is used 'not in the narrow sense of "spying"', explains Christopher Dandeker (1991: vii), but more broadly 'to refer to the gathering of information about and the supervision of subject populations in organizations'. Gill and Phythian saw states as pursuing power and knowledge to protect and advance their interests, however defined; the notion of *surveillance* sets aside questions of whether leaders have properly understood those interests.

For states, intelligence is that special mode of *surveillance* that deals with security, secrecy and resistance. It comprises 'the range of activities – from planning to information collection to analysis and dissemination – conducted in secret, and aimed at maintaining or enhancing relative security by providing forewarning of threats in a manner that allows for the timely implementation of a preventive policy or strategy, including, where deemed desirable, covert activities'. Intelligence thus does more than provide forewarning; often it serves to establish conditions in which threats are eliminated or kept at a distance. Gill and Phythian (2006: 7, 29, 34) argued that secrecy is perhaps the salient feature that delineates intelligence from related fields, like diplomacy and security. In addition, they insist that intelligence always encounters resistance, as 'the relationship between surveillance and its subjects is always dialectical'. That resistance might be peaceful or violent, but it is a constant of intelligence, which thus should be seen as a continuing effort to overcome adversaries' efforts to overcome it.

Intelligence and risk

Intelligence has been widely viewed as a tool for managing risk – indeed, any number of authors have remarked that intelligence is a means of reducing uncertainty for decision-makers. Kristan J. Wheaton and Michael T. Beerbower, for example, defined intelligence as 'a process, focused externally and using information from all available sources, that is designed to reduce the level of uncertainty for a decision maker'. For Wheaton and Beerbower, 'intelligence is more than information'. It is 'something that happens, not something that just is'; intelligence is made to happen for the benefit of decision-makers, who want assurance or 'certainty regarding the future', but who often have to accept 'something [else] that is based in fact but allows them to plan'.

Just how does intelligence reduce uncertainty for decision-makers? This author (2008) teamed with Gill and Phythian to explore the notion that intelligence not only mitigates risk but actively shifts it to witting and unwitting recipients. Such shifting meets resistance, of course, and thus intelligence activities can be seen not as a set of organisations and processes, but instead can be studied more like astronomers view the solar system – as a set of entities in motion that constantly influence one another. Those entities, moreover, are intentional actors – very complex ones at that. Thus intelligence should be viewed as a reflexive activity, for intelligence operatives and agencies are under scrutiny by competitors and they always interact with other operatives and agencies (and with the world around them). The people involved in intelligence and the regimes that employ them might be professional but still possess tendencies to biases, habits and non-linear reactions to events. Gill and Phythian did not, however, follow Der Derian towards a 'poststructuralist' approach which would argue that intelligence, being shadowy and apt to project and magnify 'threats', should best be studied at the level of discourses and texts. Such a method, argued Phythian (2008: 55, 60–63), had a certain merit but might obscure the real existence of threats and at any rate would likely prove unconvincing to policy-makers who oversee intelligence.[2]

This approach recently gave rise to a series of conference papers and articles on intelligence and 'reflexivity'. Phythian (2012) has shown how intelligence goes beyond mitigating risk to understanding and narrowing uncertainty, defined in the more narrow economic sense as a situation in which (unlike risk, properly speaking) the probability of a negative event or of its potential impact cannot be determined. The more this form of uncertainty accrues around the subjects intelligence seeks to observe and influence, the more intelligence becomes like modern science in certain ways, especially in that science is entering a 'post-normal' phase where so many of its findings now seem to have far-reaching policy ramifications. Intelligence was always in this sense 'post-normal', and it still is. Gill (2012) examines the ways in which uncertainty can give rise through reflexivity to efforts to pre-empt threats, which in turn create new threats. My own contribution to this approach (Warner 2012b) has been to explain the secrecy that shrouds intelligence as a consequence of the reflexive nature of intelligence practices, and to speculate on an 'economy of secrecy' that might explain why regimes perform some actions under a cloak of secrecy while others conduct the same activities in public.

Comparative systems and services

The idea of creating systematic ideas for comparisons of intelligence structures, and hence laying the ground for theorising about them, dated to the end of the Cold War as scholars gained access to newly declassified (or at least public) sources. Glenn Hastedt (1991a: 60–64), of James Madison University, in 1992 noted two principal ways in which intelligence activities had previously been compared: by the characteristics of agencies employed by several countries and/or by how those agencies approached certain types of events or activities (such as the perennial problem of surprise). He also proposed additional planes of comparison that he believed could encourage the development of testable hypotheses and theories of intelligence. Hastedt in essence stepped to the verge of offering a theory of intelligence and a framework for testing it through comparative observations.

Subsequent work brought us closer to defining the independent variables essential to the comparisons that Hastedt had suggested. Loch Johnson (2003a: 657), for instance, listed a set of factors affecting the amount or scope of resources that states expend on strategic intelligence; he identified the chief factors in this equation as 'a nation's foreign policy objectives, its sense of danger at home and abroad, and its affluence'. In a second essay published almost concurrently, Johnson offered 37 propositions about the factors affecting the efficacy of national intelligence efforts. Effective intelligence, he argued, is largely a function of national wealth, though other factors also play their roles in determining the relative effectiveness of a nation's specific intelligence functions (2003b: 22–23). Kevin O'Connell (2004: 193–197) proposed comparing national intelligence services or 'systems'. He posed a series of questions relating to intelligence establishments under study, and suggested that answering such questions systematically could allow categorisation of a nation's political, diplomatic and military contexts, as well as the organisational factors affecting its intelligence organs, and even the varied emphases on security and cooperation within the services under scrutiny:

It is clear that there are overarching similarities in the demands and structures of intelligence systems across the world. However, it is the differences that require our close attention, as they reveal different possibilities for various intelligence services. The data collected and sorted according to this framework could provide 'some basis within which to assess performance, relevance, patterns of innovation, and variation within norms and standards.

O'Connell's insight suggested how to compare intelligence systems across national and temporal boundaries. If followed, it could open a way for more policy prescriptive comparisons like those proposed by Loch Johnson.

Perhaps the most ambitious effort came in the form of a two-volume study edited by Stuart Farson, Peter Gill, Mark Phythian and Shlomo Shpiro (2008) that compared the intelligence establishments of two dozen-odd states. The editors of this *Handbook of Global Security and Intelligence: National Approaches* asked their contributing authors to concentrate on the effects of some common factors that presumably influence all intelligence systems. The *Handbook* explained that intelligence systems vary across national contexts according to two variables: strategic environment and regime type. The former was a proxy for a nation's 'grand strategy' per se – its posture towards countries that can help or harm it, both in its immediate neighbourhood and more distant. The *Handbook*'s employment of regime type as an independent variable, moreover, was overdue among works of intelligence theory. The *Handbook* omitted to pay sustained attention to how technology factors into different intelligence systems, but at roughly the same time, however, this author (Warner 2009b) separately sought to fill this gap, adding a technology variable to the strategy and regime factors in hopes of giving the comparisons greater explanatory power not only across cultures and nations but over time as well.

John Ehrman (2009) of the Central Intelligence Agency has recently built upon these approaches in comparing intelligence services, specifically those performing counterintelligence tasks. While speculation about the differences between security agencies and denizens is not novel (indeed, Glenn Hasdedt had alluded to it), Ehrman approached the problem in an explicitly theoretical manner, beginning with a definition of counterintelligence ('the study of the organization and behavior of the intelligence services of foreign states and entities, and the application of the resulting knowledge') and then proceeded to elucidate a taxonomy of intelligence services and the factors that influence their behaviour. Ehrman did not offer a theory of how the independent variables identified in his taxonomy related to one another, but his essay prepared the way for just that step in the future.

Conclusion

Sun Tzu and Kautilya suggested long ago that espionage has divine efficacy; that its practitioners, while hardly supernatural, can cause effects that most people would understandably attribute to the interventions of gods. Colonel George Furse (1895) of the British Army argued (in an uncanny echo of Sun Tzu) that understanding espionage – however unchivalrous its activities – was essential to victory in modern war. He also implied that a commander's need for information far exceeds that which is possible for spies to provide, insisting that an army needs a trained and dedicated information service in peace as well as in war. Spying had thus been transformed into intelligence, and perhaps inevitably debates arose over the similarities and differences between the two. Sporadic reflections under this heading over the intervening decades down to the end of the Cold War did not make much progress, but with the partial opening of intelligence files over the last two decades, prospective theorists have finally gained the raw material of hypotheses. Perhaps as important, scholars engaged in this enterprise began to compare findings, debate results and build on one another's insights. The growth of intelligence theory had become self-sustaining.

Where will that progress lead? Good theory, as Loch Johnson (2008: 33) reminds us, must have 'explanatory power, parsimony, and the attribute of falsifiability'. Few of the statements related above about causal relationships in the field of intelligence can be said to have attained these goals. The fact that some have, particularly in the emerging of a consensus over definitions as well as in comparative studies of intelligence systems and services, provides grounds for optimism. Intelligence theory is still something of a novelty, and thus we can expect at least two developments in this area. First, the theories themselves should become both fuller and more rigorous in their articulation (as scholars grow accustomed to framing true hypotheses) and in their coverage of the range of intelligence activities and structures. Second, more intelligence scholars will begin to read the historical documentation and current events as either verifying or challenging the hypotheses and the theories they accompany. In these ways the flashes of insight and consensus we glimpse in the kaleidoscope of opinions and debates over intelligence theory could one day focus into true knowledge of cause and effect.

Notes

1 Michael Warner serves as an historian in the US Department of Defense. The opinions expressed in this article are his alone and no way represent official positions of the Department or any US government entity.
2 See also Gill and Phythian (2012: 24); also Der Derian (1994: 38, 42–43).

3

CULTURES OF NATIONAL INTELLIGENCE

Mark Phythian

Introduction

As a social science project, intelligence studies has its origins in the United States. US scholarship has done much to shape this project, and continues to do so. The focus of much of this scholarship, however, has been on US intelligence structures and practices, and it has not always been clear how far the conclusions of some of this scholarship are transferable beyond the confines of the US intelligence system. Increasingly, a number of intelligence scholars – both in the US and beyond – have identified the paucity of comparative analysis of intelligence as a challenge that intelligence studies must confront if it is to advance further as a social science project. This is rooted in the understanding that to 'be effective in developing theory, and in being able to make statements about structures larger than an individual or the small group, the social sciences must be comparative' (Peters 1998: 25). In turn, this reflects the fact that while the core responsibility of all states is to provide for the security of their citizens, the ways in which states seek to achieve this goal differs; all states 'do' intelligence, but there is marked variation in the extent to which they invest in it, the roles, reach and intrusiveness of intelligence bodies, and the nature and extent of their oversight.[1] Comparative analysis is needed to facilitate awareness of the extent of similarities and differences, and allow for the generation of hypotheses to explain these.[2] However, recognition of the comparative challenge has not resulted in a scholarly stampede to meet it, a situation at least in part attributable to the problem identified by Michael Warner; 'the lack of agreement, among both scholars and practitioners, of just what would be compared in a comparative approach to intelligence studies' (Warner 2009a: 11).

What to compare?

This chapter proposes that, equipped with a clear understanding of our terms, national intelligence cultures can provide a fruitful frame for comparative analysis. At the outset, it is important to define what we mean by both 'culture' and 'intelligence culture'. In doing this we need to recognise that culture is a slippery concept, and in abstract discussion of it we run the same risk as that identified by Wilhelm Agrell with regard to the study of intelligence itself – 'if everything is intelligence, then nothing is intelligence' (Agrell 2002). The *Oxford English Dictionary* defines culture as the 'philosophy, practices, and attitudes of an institution, business, or other organization'. For Raymond Williams, one of the most influential commentators on culture, the term had three meanings: as an 'ideal', as the 'documentary' and as the 'social' (Williams 2009: 32).

The latter of these sees culture as 'a description of a particular way of life, which expresses certain meanings and values not only in art and learning but also in institutions and ordinary behaviour'. In this context, the study of culture involves 'the clarification of the meanings and values implicit and explicit in a particular way of life, a particular culture' (Williams 2009: 32). Both of these are useful starting points for thinking about what we mean by 'culture' in the context of intelligence. While the OED definition might suggest a relatively narrow focus on organisational culture, Williams' inclusion of the 'social' dimension demands a broader focus that encompasses the links between intelligence culture and the wider political culture within which intelligence is inescapably situated. This is because the 'meanings' and 'values' to which Williams refers are rooted in this wider political culture, and while this political culture might appear fixed at the macro-level, at the micro-level it is dynamic, a product of contestation and consequent evolution. It is this broader focus that this chapter proposes.

Given that intelligence studies and strategic studies have concerns in common, and that the idea of culture is recognised now as being central to the study of strategy, strategic studies seems an obvious starting point when considering what the comparative study of intelligence cultures should include. The focus on strategic culture within strategic studies arose from the insight that, during the Cold War, Soviet approaches to nuclear strategy differed from Western approaches for reasons attributable to culture; that there was 'a "Russian way" both of thinking about the threat or use of force for political purposes, and of acting strategically' (Gray 2009: 225). By extension, this means that 'different security communities think and behave somewhat differently when it comes to strategic matters', and that those differences 'stem from communities' distinctive histories and geographies' (226). Hence, just as there might be said to be an identifiable American, British, Russian or French 'way of war', we might also be able to identify distinctive (or, at least, distinguishable) American, British, Russian and French 'ways of intelligence'. Whereas strategic culture can be regarded as the product of 'the sum total of ideas, conditioned emotional responses, and patterns of habitual behaviour that members of a national strategic community have acquired through instruction or imitation' (Snyder 1977: 8), so intelligence culture may be regarded as the ideas, responses and behaviours acquired by intelligence communities and conditioned by history and geography.[3]

However, as suggested earlier, intelligence culture also needs to be considered more broadly. While there are important studies that focus on organisational cultures and different understandings within these of what is meant by 'intelligence' (for example, Davies 2002, 2004a; Bean 2009), what is required for comparative analysis is a broader study of intelligence *systems* rather than a more specific focus on intelligence communities and the production of intelligence. What is meant by an 'intelligence system'? We could do worse than adopt Michael Warner's definition of an intelligence system as comprising 'the collective authorities, resources, oversight, and missions assigned to parties officially assembled to perform intelligence duties' (Warner 2009a: 15–16). This definition has the advantage of incorporating the 'social', or societal, via the inclusion of oversight.

Adopting this broader approach helps distinguish analysis of intelligence cultures from that of strategic cultures. While there is some recognition within strategic studies that the question of strategic culture needs to be capable of distinguishing between three distinct elements – public culture, strategic culture and military (organisational) culture (Gray 2009: 227) – the study of public culture and understanding of its significance within overall strategic culture remains underdeveloped. The focus of strategic culture is overwhelmingly at the level of professionals and political elites. However, the simultaneously inward- and outward-facing nature of intelligence means that it impacts more directly on the political culture – 'the predispositions which give shape and meaning to political acts' (Kavanagh 1972: 13) – and that the nature of intelligence – the nature and clarity of the intelligence mandate, the degree of secrecy that attaches to intelligence, the extent and efficacy of oversight, the scale and reach of intelligence organisations, and the frequency of recourse to and nature of covert actions – does much to shape the broader political culture, to the extent that it can be considered a key element of political culture. The emergence of oversight as a norm means that the professional group is not beyond the reach of the wider political culture. It provides an opening via which overseers and inquiries, and those who take up their conclusions and recommendations, can impact on intelligence culture. This makes intelligence culture a more open culture than previously. Moreover, intelligence agencies' increased tendency to respond to criticisms and perceived criticisms, if only for reasons of continued legitimacy and budget protection, has itself resulted in a general trend towards greater public engagement – for example, through public speeches, the development of websites and even the sanctioning of official histories – which has encouraged greater public awareness and debate. This is not to say that intelligence agencies have not engaged in acts of resistance, or that overseers always demonstrate the necessary political will, but this is the essence of the contestation and evolution mentioned earlier.

The importance of the inclusion of a societal dimension has also been recognised by other writers on intelligence. Glenn Hastedt, one of the first to call for the comparative study of intelligence, suggested a framework based on four levels of analysis: the individual, the institutional, the societal (that is, the impact of values, norms and political structure), and the influence of the international system (Hastedt 1991). Michael Turner adopted a wide range of variables to explain the emergence of a unique US intelligence identity (Turner 2004). Although Turner describes this as a 'unique' identity, several of the norms he identifies clearly apply in other national intelligence contexts. For example, ideas of secrecy and the provision of accurate, timely and relevant intelligence are central to a number of definitions of intelligence (for example, Gill and Phythian 2012: 19). Similarly, the idea of 'intelligence exceptionalism' extends beyond the US. A more recent study of national approaches to intelligence employed strategic environment (i.e. the impact of geography and history on threat perception), regime type, organisation and control, and oversight as key variables (Farson *et al.* 2008). This approach has much in common with the variables embedded within Warner's definition of an intelligence system. Both are rooted in a broad understanding of 'intelligence', one that goes beyond the confines of the traditional model of the intelligence cycle. Both recognise that covert actions can be part of intelligence, and that oversight is a core component of intelligence *systems* in liberal democratic contexts.

By drawing together elements of these approaches, it is possible to suggest key variables that can provide a basis for the comparative analysis of national cultures of intelligence, organised around different levels of analysis (Figure 3.1).

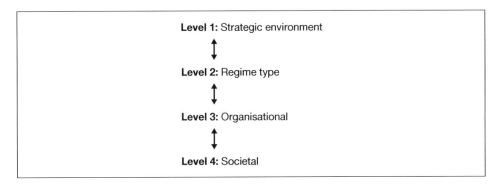

Level 1: Strategic environment

↕

Level 2: Regime type

↕

Level 3: Organisational

↕

Level 4: Societal

Figure 3.1 The comparative analysis of national cultures of intelligence: levels of analysis

In practice, these levels of analysis are highly permeable, as indicated by the arrows (e.g. Level 1 can impact on Level 2, Level 2 impacts on Levels 3 and 4, Level 3 impacts on Level 4, etc.), and are isolated in this way for the purposes of analysis. Considerations of strategic environment are in essence those that underpin approaches to strategic culture within strategic studies. Having already discussed this area of commonality, and argued that the notion of 'culture' with regard to intelligence needs to go beyond that most usually involved in understandings of strategic culture, it makes sense to now focus on the other three levels.

Regime type

The distinction between Level 2 and Level 4 is based on the Weberian distinction between state and society. As a basis for comparative research, distinguishing between established democratic, transitional democratic and non-democratic regimes is a sufficient starting point; given that cultures of intelligence play a role in determining the complexion of the state, distinctions within each of these broad categories can be expected to emerge from comparative analysis. As a starting point, each of these categories contains certain a priori assumptions that further inquiry may require to be qualified. For example, in the case of non-democratic states it might be expected that: intelligence organisations would exhibit significant degrees of autonomy; national security would rank at or near the top of the policy agenda, with threat definition pointing to both internal and external threats, but with intelligence more orientated towards addressing the former; intelligence autonomy may create a not insignificant space for official corruption to flourish; human rights norms would not represent a significant impediment to the pursuit of internal or external 'enemies'; and that international intelligence cooperation would be more limited. However, environmental factors may produce marked differences in some of these cases. At the same time, the formal appearance of democracy (the existence of a range of political parties, the holding of regular elections, etc.) may conceal degrees of intelligence autonomy and/or corruption that qualify the very notion of 'democracy' – for example, as in Peru under the premiership of Alberto Fujimori and Russia under Vladimir Putin. Cross-temporal analysis of intelligence cultures in different forms of regime that share the same broad classification can also generate important insights – for example, the role of the Gestapo and Stasi in Nazi Germany and the GDR (Dennis 2003: 4–6).

An alternative approach would be to simply distinguish between 'strong' and 'weak' states, where 'weak states either do not have, or have failed to create, a domestic political and societal consensus of sufficient strength to eliminate the large-scale use of force as a major and continuing element in the domestic political life of the nation' (Buzan 1991: 99). The paradox here is that the 'weaker' the state the more pronounced and interventionist are the organs of state intelligence (as the unofficial Stasi motto put it, 'trust is good but surveillance is better'), giving the appearance of state strength.

This strong state–weak state dichotomy raises the question of what might be termed the 'two states problem' in intelligence studies. One of the advantages of a focus on national cultures of intelligence is that it offers a means of addressing this problem. It arises from the dual focus of intelligence studies. On the one hand, this focus is on the international, on the other it is on domestic security intelligence. The international focus tends to take its underlying assumptions from realist and neo-realist theories of international politics. The state here is assumed to be a unitary actor on the world stage, encompassing all national territory and all those who live within it. The state is either a status quo or a revisionist power. There is no need to delve any more deeply, because foreign and security policies are determined by the nature of the international system rather than internal political factors, such as regime type. Hence, neo-realism (particularly offensive realism) explicitly excludes consideration of internal political factors from its analysis.

At the level of domestic security intelligence, notions of the state are much more nuanced. Arguably, the most useful way of approaching the state from an intelligence studies perspective is via the Weberian notion of the state as an institution that claims a monopoly on the legitimate use of force within a territory.[4] John Hoffman has highlighted the fundamental tension that arises from this approach, one that generates the requirement for domestic security intelligence:

> The very need to exercise a monopoly of legitimate force arises only because states are challenged by rebels and criminals who themselves resort to force, and who (either implicitly or explicitly) *contest* the legitimacy of the laws they break . . . The state which actually *succeeds* in imposing a monopoly of legitimate force thereby makes itself redundant since a gulf between ideals and reality is essential to the state's very *raison d'être*.
>
> *(Hoffman 1995: 5)*

Hence, by definition, the state can only ever be partially successful in asserting its claim to this monopoly. Nevertheless, different states experience this dilemma to differing extents, depending on strategic environment and regime type variables. Some operate in environments where their legitimacy in at least parts of the geographic area they formally cover is severely contested – for example, the UK and Northern Ireland, the Colombian state by the FARC (and other guerrilla groups) and drug traffickers (see Boraz 2008). This can also be true of new states that emerge from secessionist processes and/or wars – recently, for example, Bosnia, Kosovo, Iraq and Libya (see, for example, Hauslohner 2012). The strategic environment into which these states emerge can require them to deal with land and maritime borders that invite forms of trafficking and criminality unless effectively policed, or can require them to address the hostility of neighbouring states or other states in the international system if they are to survive. This, then, is an area where the proposed approach to cultures of intelligence, with its four levels of analysis, can be beneficial by drawing attention to the impact of the international on the national. The key point is that cultures of intelligence do not develop in isolation; their development is influenced by the strategic environment in which they exist. This environment plays a part in determining, for example, the values held by state intelligence personnel, the scale of investment in intelligence, and the relative size, influence and reach of security intelligence organisations.

This also suggests a related variable that could be considered within discussion of regime type in assessing cultures of intelligence – the nature of state formation. For example, we can extend the logic of the preceding discussion to revolutionary states – states that come into existence or are transformed via successful socio-political revolution, as with the Soviet Union in 1917, Cuba in 1959 and Iran in 1979. This also has the capacity to address an important question posed by Michael Warner: 'While many national leaders may feel themselves swept along by historical tides, there have been some important ones who saw their nations as shapers of history. How did they wish intelligence to serve them in their projects?' (Warner 2009c). In short, revolutionary states have tended to combine defensive concerns with expansive agendas designed to spread revolution, giving intelligence a distinctive role and giving rise to distinctive intelligence cultures.

Moreover, as Fred Halliday observed, with regard to revolutionary states, 'the survival of the state is uncertain from month to month, the practicalities of ensuring security against invasion and subversion take an enormous toll on the allocation of resources, and on the time, nerves and concentration of those in power, as well as affecting the conception of what is licit dissent' (Halliday 1994: 86). Particularly high degrees of secrecy attach to intelligence in these contexts, over which there is either limited or only formal (ministerial) oversight. The legislative oversight norm that has come to apply in established democracies, and that constitutes a link between state, government and society with regard to intelligence, is absent here. Instead, the only links between state and society that exist in respect of intelligence are via networks of local informers, equivalents of Cuba's Comité de Defensa de la Revolución network or the GDR's network of IMs (Inoffizielle Mitarbeiter – informal collaborators), these latter coming to number around 170–180,000 (around one informer for approximately every 60 citizens), and testimony to the GDR's siege mentality and sensitivity to the possibility of internal subversion.

This absence of oversight, distance between state intelligence and society, and centrality of security intelligence give rise to the potential for intelligence agencies to operate as a 'state within a state' – an analysis regularly offered with regard to the Stasi in the GDR, but also the Dirección General de Inteligencia (DGI) in Cuba, General Department II of the Ministry of National Defence (Bo Quoc Phong) in Vietnam (see Thayer 2008), and Iran's Ministry of Intelligence and National Security (VEVAK) – with the attendant capacity for corruption to flourish. In any case, their separation from society means that their officers constitute a privileged class in national contexts where either the causes of revolution or process of revolutionary state-building were to be found in, or gave rise to, shortages and suffering among the general public.

While revolutionary regimes need to develop intelligence capabilities quickly, they are rarely required to establish these on their own and usually receive assistance from sympathetic states – in the twentieth century this mostly meant the Soviet Union and its Eastern European allies, often the GDR. Hence, *national* intelligence systems in revolutionary states have historically contained a significant *international* dimension – whether Cuba after the Bay of Pigs invasion of 1961 (see Klepak 2008), Iran after 1979 or Iraq after 2003. Hence, national intelligence cultures in these states can contain a foreign imprint at times at odds with elements of the broader national culture. These factors together help explain Fred Halliday's observation that, 'within [revolutionary] states, an initial overthrow of the pre-revolutionary state, and utopian statements about new, spontaneous, forms of political order, are immediately replaced by the formation of recast, authoritarian and coercive institutions' (Halliday 1999: 12).

The question of ideology

There is a risk that this focus (in essence, rooted in historical sociology) could result in the role of ideology being understated. The role of ideology and extent of variation in this are questions that require further comparative analysis if they are to be answered. For example, while accepting that the 'export' of revolution involves some combination of ideology and pragmatism, Theda Skocpol's emphasis on the impact of the international on post-revolutionary development suggests that ideology itself does not determine the emphasis on, or form of, security intelligence in revolutionary states (Skocpol 1979). That it does has been a staple of a number of analyses, such as that of John Dziak with regard to the Soviet Union (Dziak 1988a, 1988b). In place of this, Skocpol places greater emphasis on the fact that 'states also exist in determinant geopolitical environments, in interaction with other actual or potential states. An existing economy and class structure condition and influence a given state structure and the activities of the rulers. So, too, do geopolitical environments create tasks and opportunities for states and place limits on their capacities to cope with either external or internal tasks or crises' (Skocpol 1979: 30). Hence, Skocpol's explanation for the nature of the evolving Soviet state and prominent coercive role of the Cheka within this emphasises the environment of counter-revolutionary subversion that existed in 1917 (Skocpol 1979: 215), rather than suggest that the emergence of the Cheka was a natural outgrowth of Bolshevism (see Dziak 1988b: 74).

However, ideology clearly has a role to play, particularly in states formally organised around an official ideology. For example, Beatrice de Graaf has shown how the Stasi's foreign operations were hampered by adherence to an official ideology that determined information requirements independently of international developments. It also restricted the pool in which the Stasi could fish for potential foreign IMs – already limited to left-wing political *milieux* – by excluding all Trotskyist and related groups on the grounds that they were deviationists and enemies of the GDR. Moreover, ideological assumptions affected and distorted analysis, while dissemination was affected by a tendency to avoid forwarding reports that might point to economic or administrative failure for which the ruling party, the SED (Socialist Unity Party of Germany), was responsible, thereby leaving policy-makers without a full picture of the nature and scale of internal dissatisfaction with SED rule (de Graaf 2010). In short, ideology compromised every stage of the intelligence cycle.

Organisational level

This is the level at which most existing approaches to intelligence culture have focused. Here, organisational culture can refer narrowly to the form of intelligence organisation, which can itself be seen to be a product of environmental factors. For example, it is possible to view the fragmented nature of the US intelligence community as being a product of a political culture within which suspicion of strong central government has been a core feature. Alternatively, it can be seen to be the product of bureaucratic infighting. Either way, its 'flawed by design' nature provides one source of explanation for intelligence failures (Zegart 1999).

It can also embrace consideration of the relative openness of intelligence. Notwithstanding the centrality of secrecy to the practice of intelligence, different states have exhibited differing degrees of openness. Some have embraced the need for a degree of openness as a by-product of the introduction of oversight, or as arising from the need to justify increased expenditure to taxpayers who want to understand more about this need, or as a consequence of past intelligence failures or scandals draining public confidence, or as a combination of all of these. For others, it is more a reflection of the extent to which notions of openness are embedded in the broader political culture. Hence, the US is usually recognised as being distinctive in the degree of openness that characterises discussion of intelligence, including via media briefings (see, for example, Wirtz 2007: 28–38). However, even in contexts where openness about intelligence derives from a wider norm, it can be subject to temporal shifts and reined in if it is held to have gone too far in relation to the wider environmental context (see, for example, Shane 2012).

Additional factors can also be considered here, such as the 'reach' of national intelligence organisations – i.e. the extent, frequency and nature of interventions, domestically and internationally. Similarly, the nature and extent of international intelligence cooperation can be considered. This tends to be greater among democratic states, but generates the paradox that it lies largely beyond the reach of national intelligence oversight – or, at the very least, is much more challenging for national overseers to capture (see Born, Leigh and Wills 2011). For all these reasons, I would suggest that organisational culture should not be considered in isolation from the other levels proposed here.

Societal level

This question of the reach of national oversight bodies leads to the final level of analysis; that concerned with the reception of intelligence in the wider political culture and the impact of this on intelligence organisations and practices. This, then, is the site of intersection between political culture and intelligence culture. In a liberal democratic context, intelligence practice can, at times, exist in tension with principles held to be core to the broader political culture. This can generate a scepticism towards national intelligence bodies on the part of those they are intended to protect (although on the Weberian reading offered above, there will always be some groups in society who are more targets of intelligence than beneficiaries of it). This is true to a greater or lesser extent across all liberal democracies. For example, Eric Denécé and Gérald Arboit have written of the French public's 'longstanding contempt' towards French intelligence agencies arising from their domestic role (Denécé and Arboit 2010: 726). The tension between intelligence and society that exists in New Zealand has been well captured by Willem de Lint (de Lint 2008), while a number of commentators have identified a tension between society and intelligence in the US, one expression of which is the almost uniformly critical nature of histories of the CIA (for example, Weiner 2008).

At the intersection of political and intelligence cultures, discussion is often framed in terms of a 'trade-off' between security and liberty. Where different societies collectively draw the line here will be also influenced by environmental factors. At the same time, notions of a 'trade-off' can introduce a false dichotomy, and intelligence professionals contest them because they imply that, by definition, they are 'against' liberty because they are 'for' security (see, for example, Manningham-Buller 2012: 36–37). The key point here is that, in liberal democratic contexts, national intelligence cultures are not simply the product of currents within policy and professional elites, they are also influenced by pressures applied on policy and professional elites from without. In the terms of Almond and Verba's classic study, these are *participant* political cultures in which intelligence was previously a closed-off sphere, but has now been opened up by the establishment of the oversight norm and the progressively greater openness this has brought, as opposed to the *subject* political cultures of non-democratic states, such as the former GDR (Almond and Verba 1963). This is not to make exaggerated claims for the effectiveness of oversight arrangements, or to suggest that there is no need to press for more extensive oversight (in a UK context, the revelations of the last decade strongly suggest that there is), but simply to recognise that intelligence is no longer separate from, and so immune to, the wider political culture. Oversight has created an *apertura* linking intelligence to society. Some of the exceptionalism surrounding intelligence has been lifted as a result of this process – or, at least, sweeping claims as to the extent of this exceptionalism do not command the same support as in the past.

This does, however, raise the problem of secrecy, the other side of the openness coin. For oversight or the public to apply pressure from without, it must have some knowledge of what is going on within. While secrecy is a key element of intelligence, being fundamental to the comparative advantage that investment in intelligence seeks to secure, national security can also be invoked as a convenient blanket to conceal awkward, damaging or otherwise embarrassing facts about intelligence practices. The existence of struggles over secrecy and the extent to which public, media, overseers and legislators are prepared to contest secrecy, and expose practices that diminish the broader political culture, is a key element of the broader conception of intelligence culture that I have proposed here. Liberal democratic contexts provide an implicit 'invitation to struggle' over specific intelligence policies and practices, and the application of excessive secrecy to avoid political inconvenience or embarrassment. Approaches that radically depart from the expectations of the broader political culture are, in these contexts, unlikely to be sustainable if the ring of secrecy in which they are developed and enveloped is broken. This is the essence of participant political cultures.

Conclusions

If viewed from the (macro) level of the state, parallels in intelligence logic and practice are easily discernible. After all, the need for intelligence arises from concerns common to all states to varying degrees, rooted in the nature of the international system and the domestic context of the state, which mean that, by definition, all states are likely to face challenges to their claims. However, comparative analysis of national intelligence cultures can highlight the nature and extent of key differences across states by prompting questions about: the significance of different historical experiences and geographical contexts; the impact of these on elite and popular perceptions; the significance of regime type on, for instance, the reach and intrusiveness of (foreign and domestic) intelligence and frequency of resort to covert actions; and on the related question of the importance of the circumstances of state formation. Such a focus also concentrates our attention on the organisation, control and oversight of intelligence agencies. In short, it alerts us to the fact that not all states are alike, and that the practice of intelligence at the national level is conditioned by the interaction of a complex set of factors and considerations, operating at different, albeit permeable, levels that collectively constitute the national intelligence culture.

Notes

1   The focus of this chapter is national intelligence, although the comparative analysis of intelligence can take place at the different levels at which intelligence activity occurs (see Gill and Phythian 2012: Ch. 2, esp. the map for theorising and researching intelligence, p. 51).

2   As Macridis advised: 'Comparative analysis has one purpose that is central to the development of political science: the identification and explanation of uniformities and differences in political behaviour' (Macridis 1961: 39).

3   Snyder's is one of the foundational definitions of strategic culture. Similarly, Colin Gray defines strategic culture as comprising 'the persisting socially transmitted ideas, attitudes, traditions, habits of mind, and preferred methods of operation that are more or less specific to a particular geographically based security community that has had a unique historical experience' (Gray 1999: 131).

4   Weber's original 1919 definition was that a state could be considered to exist, 'if and insofar as its administrative staff successfully upholds a claim on the monopoly of the legitimate use of violence (*das Monopol legitimen physischen Zwanges*) in the enforcement of its order' (Max Weber, 'The Profession and Vocation of Politics', in Lassman and Speirs 1994: 309–369).

4

THE THEORY AND PHILOSOPHY OF INTELLIGENCE

Jennifer Sims

The importance of theory

What is the essence of intelligence? Unless the essence is understood, the practice will fail. Getting to the essence of social practice is what philosophers and theorists do, and unfortunately, they have not agreed on much about intelligence. As Michael Warner's chapter in this volume discusses, theories of intelligence exist, but most are underdeveloped and therefore add little predictive power to theories of international relations or practical power for diplomacy and war.

Unfortunately, the conceptual fuzziness of the field brings serious real-world consequences. One effect of squishy thinking has to do with institutional reform: if, in the aftermath of surprise, reformers focus on looking backwards to fix only what seems to have gone wrong, they risk all that went right on other days and against different adversaries. If, believing intelligence is essentially about secrets, reformers look only at secret agencies for failures, they may miss the serious costs that neglect of open source intelligence can levy. In the absence of sound theory, underappreciated excellence is always at risk of getting lost, but it is especially at risk after failure. Good theory should help us avoid deleterious cognitive biases, including the 'availability bias' that, induced by crisis, often shapes reform of intelligence institutions.

This chapter will show that many of our traditional notions about intelligence may not be correct. It begins by exploring these notions, then proposes a new theory of intelligence and relates it to international politics. In so doing it makes the case that improving intelligence is not just a way to empower statesmen, but may offer a path to a more peaceful world.

Intelligence and secrecy

Many experts argue that the essence of intelligence is stealing and keeping secrets (Shulsky 1995; Gill 2009). This proposition would, at first blush, seem self-evident. If the purpose of intelligence is to deliver an information edge to one side, then hiding that edge should be integral to the enterprise. Secrecy would also seem essential to good intelligence practice; collectors know that intelligence is often most productive when the target does not know it is being watched.

Yet, if a capacity for secrecy is usually critical to success, it is not in all cases. Sometimes speed in decision-making trumps the benefits of secrecy. Sometimes an opponent is wrong about what is needed to win, so stealing his secret information would be worthless. One of the sixteenth century's better pirates, Sir Francis Drake, collected intelligence on the Spanish empire's treasure shipments simply by watching Philip II's ships and mule trains, and then interdicting them (Parker 1998). Or consider the fine intelligence to be gained by watching an adversary's response to overt collection against him. During the Cold War, for example, US reconnaissance aircraft deliberately threatened Soviet air space to trigger radar systems and thus locate Soviet surface-to-air missile batteries. And of course sometimes it is impossible to keep secret the intelligence others need to win; Al Qaeda did not need to steal US classified information to collect sufficient intelligence for its attack on 11 September 2001. They used their own names and allowed themselves to be video-taped by security cameras.

The foregoing examples suggest that exclusive focus on keeping or stealing secrets may lead to intelligence failure if protecting the source or method imperils advantage, or an opponent classifies worthless facts, builds strategies that capitalise on open information or 'hides' information to deceive the other side into believing it is valuable when it is not.[1] Tailoring collection to secrets would, in these cases, provide little gain for the cost and risk. In fact, the idea that stealing secrets is the essence of intelligence rests on a fundamentally flawed premise: that competitors know best what is needed to win and that they unfailingly hide it.

Intelligence as truth

If experts seem to agree about anything, it is that intelligence should embody objective truth, such as whether Saddam Hussein had weapons of mass destruction, where Osama Bin Laden hid, or precisely where and how drug-runners cross borders. Catching terrorists or interdicting drug-running requires knowing where people or shipments truly are. So it would seem that good intelligence must always capture truth.

The idea that truth-seeking is the essence of intelligence has, however, rather serious flaws. For one thing, if decision-makers do not need truth to take decisive action, then pursuing perfect knowledge can cause delays or overwhelm them with information they do not need. Sometimes 'just enough' or 'good enough' intelligence will not only do, but do better than truth. One case in point involves Jedediah Hotchkiss, Stonewall Jackson's map-maker during the US Civil War. This school teacher and amateur geologist sketched relatively crude battlefield maps that relayed essentials for Jackson's fast-moving 'foot cavalry' during the Shenandoah Valley campaign in 1862. His competition, West Point engineers who worked for the Union generals, created 'truer' maps that conveyed far more precise details for the generals they served. Yet, Jackson won the Valley campaign. When asked to what he owed his victory, Jackson credited Hotchkiss's maps. These relatively sparse and not entirely accurate maps told him all that he needed to know, in a timely way (Hotchkiss 1973). They constituted successful intelligence *because* they weren't perfect; they simply lubricated choice.

Truths can also be dangerously misleading when estimating probabilities. Consider the Cuban Missile Crisis of 1962. In the midst of the crisis, when Soviet purposes were unknown, intelligence analysts identified several incontrovertible, objective truths: strategic nuclear war was unwinnable and therefore in neither superpower's interest; Soviet emplacement of nuclear missiles in Cuba would almost certainly be destabilising; and Soviet leaders were rational and demonstrably conservative, having *never* deployed nuclear weapons outside territories under their direct control. Based on these solid truths, the US Board of National Estimates (BNE) concluded that Moscow was highly unlikely to deploy nuclear missiles in Cuba. The BNE was wrong. Moscow's surprising hubris almost triggered a nuclear exchange between the superpowers. Though Sherman Kent, the head of the Board of National Estimates at the time, famously claimed that history had proved US intelligence more 'right' than the Soviet leader was, policy-makers were not amused by this proximity to total war. Objective, factual analysis had missed the passions, misperceptions and insecurities driving Khrushchev's choices.

What about objectivity and relevance?

This point about Sherman Kent's difficulties during the Cuban Missile Crisis raises the thorny issue of objectivity. How can analysts derive subjective meaning from events while also remaining objective? Conventional wisdom has it that intelligence is bad if the information it delivers is twisted to support the preferences and biases of the decision-makers it serves. Instead, it should be impartial and 'unvarnished'. Delivering bad news is essential if, for example, intelligence officers are to prevent surprise. This precept seems incontrovertible as far as it goes.

Yet, intelligence professionals who are not biased to some degree also risk failure. Some kinds of bias are necessary when assessing facts (Russell). This is so because, as explained above, it is impossible to discuss the meaning of facts without reference to the strategies and purposes of the decision-makers involved. Having this kind of sensitivity cannot, of course, be allowed to interfere with the mission to warn when evidence suggests strategies are not working; intelligence must seek and deliver such news. But intelligence is wasteful and even disabling if, harbouring a disinterested orientation in the name of objectivity, analysts seek to be a 'check' on policy because they believe policy-makers are dealing poorly with uncertainty or have an unwise strategy all together. Certainly in democracies, *rejecting* the values, 'frames' or risk propensities that policy-makers use to cope with uncertainty (that is, the absence of knowledge) is a matter for the electoral process, not intelligence. Intelligence can only hope to *adjust* these values and propensities at the margins, and does so solely for the purpose of helping such leaders gain advantages and, thereby, succeed in their larger purposes. Similarly, decision-makers who view intelligence as an encyclopaedic reference service that deals only with objective facts – so has no need to be fully integrated into the policy process or be privy to strategy – are likely to be disappointed in the support they receive.

In this regard it is instructive to recall the Clinton administration's secret decision to look the other way as Iran shipped weapons to Bosnian Muslims during the US-led international arms embargo, which was intended to result in a de-escalation of hostilities in the Balkans. Failing to tell the Director of Central Intelligence or alert the intelligence community to its plan, the State Department and its ambassador became subject to crimes reporting by a CIA station convinced it was observing unauthorised covert action run by the US embassy in Prague. The tortuous war inside the embassy walls almost hobbled US efforts to stop the one going on outside of them. Policy and intelligence must embrace each other to work, and intelligence must know its own side's capabilities and intentions as well as the adversary's.

Policy-makers and intelligence briefers dedicated to doing their best can nonetheless cause this kind of disconnect; it happens when perseverating on 'objective truth' interferes with decisive action. During negotiations over North Korea's nuclear programmes in the 1990s, senior-level interagency meetings often began with a briefing from the Director of Central Intelligence. According to participants at the time, the DCI usually focused on the threat posed by the Kim Jung Il regime, including that it would deceive and cheat in any negotiation. His repetitive assessments that the North Koreans were hostile and duplicitous – objective 'truths' that everyone knew and shared – were not helpful; the decision policy-makers faced was not whether to befriend Kim Jung Il, but how to bargain for delays or termination of his regime's nuclear programme. The negotiators did not trust the North Koreans either, but they wanted to see if they could make a deal that might influence Pyongyang's incentives or buy time. In this context, the DCI's focus on the threat of being duped seemed an attempt to discredit the effort and, implicitly, the skills of the negotiators (Gallucci 2012). Although the North Koreans did cheat and the Agreed Framework did break down, the negotiators believed they had succeeded in delaying the North Korean programme for a decade (Witt, Poneman and Gallucci 2005).

In this circumstance, 'objectivity' in intelligence analysis was, in the eyes of policy-makers, the DCI's vehicle for artful delivery of a clear but unhelpful policy preference.

Unmitigated objectivity can also have unintended political effects as dangerous as are those of purposeful politicisation. For example, before the first Gulf War in 1991, the Defense Intelligence Agency's briefings for Congress were accurate, objective and 'true'. Yet, absent good information on US capabilities, they also misled many members into believing the war would be a bloodbath for American troops and their allies. Support for the war nonetheless crystallised after one influential senator asked individuals at the National War College to provide an informal *net assessment* of Iraqi and US capabilities. His thorough discussion with senior military officials convinced him that the threat was not as great as DIA's objective yet one-sided analysis had suggested and that the war was quite winnable.[2] A respected moderate, he was able to persuade a number of his Republican colleagues to put DIA's intelligence in context and support the authorisation to use force. Other senators, such as Senator David Boren, Democrat and Chairman of the Senate Select Committee on Intelligence, were equally committed to making the right choice for the country but were privy only to the best 'objective' intelligence on the adversary so chose otherwise. Boren later blamed intelligence, and the DIA briefings in particular, for his failure to foresee that the war could be quickly won.

These examples suggest a dangerous corollary to overindulgent objectivity: intelligence organisations are likely to miscalibrate threats and opportunities. This danger may be greatest when intelligence analysts believe or are told that objective appraisal of the adversary is their sole business and that knowledge of their own side's strategy, vulnerabilities or capabilities is out of bounds. Similarly, policy-makers are likely to suspect that intelligence officers, trying to remain objective, are actually hiding policy preference behind fact checking exercises and one-sided analyses. Yet few take the necessary corrective action by ensuring intelligence is always in the room when critical decisions are made. Both sides are deterred from sorting out such differences because of fears of 'politicisation' of intelligence. Even if both sides try their best, a fixation on a 'red line' between policy and intelligence results. Over time, intelligence analysts and collectors thus become more expert on foreign threats than they are on their own side's strategic capabilities. Intelligence becomes ever more expensive as it lacks insights on which threats matter least given the capabilities and intentions on their own side. Policy-makers, bored by threat assessments they have discounted because of suspected bias or irrelevance to strategic plans, begin to ignore or resent intelligence products that suggest danger where they see none. In this context, the most important intelligence function, warning, atrophies.

In sum, the divide that emerges from ill-defined 'objectivity' can easily become both dangerous and wasteful. Intelligence cannot be reduced to a fact-checking service and still succeed at enabling competitive wins. It is also not healthy when divorced from its own team. Absence of good knowledge of one's own side can lead an intelligence service to over-inflate threats, take too many risks chasing irrelevant ones and spend too much money collecting against them. The critical function of net assessment must be done somewhere, and if not in intelligence agencies, then those agencies need access to it if they are to get their jobs right at reasonable cost and risk. In at least this sense, it would seem the 'red line' between policy and intelligence needs reconsideration.

The nature of intelligence

So, how should intelligence work? Few intelligence theorists measure intelligence capacity in terms of its ability to lubricate choice for competitors. Yet, this is the essence of the function. To lubricate choice, intelligence must deliver leverage or winning knowledge of some kind. Good intelligence involves reducing uncertainty *relative to* adversaries and in the context of conflict at hand. Its essence therefore encumbers both collectors and users. In some cases, though not all, intelligence can be wrong (not perfectly true) so long as it enables superior decision-making, as Jed Hotchkiss did in Stonewall Jackson's Valley Campaign. Superior decision-making is achieved both by superior collection and analysis (the derivation of the meaning of what is collected) and by disabling intelligence flowing to the decision-makers on the other side.

Seen in this light, intelligence would seem hard to measure. How, absent historical knowledge of the matching of wits, does an intelligence service determine its inferiority or superiority in lubricating choice? After all, US intelligence capabilities prior to the terrorist attacks of 9/11 seemed unmatched by any other state, let alone the capabilities of a band of jihadists with no imagery or signals intelligence satellites to aid them.

Here, of course, is where strategy plays a crucial role. For relative capabilities in intelligence performance are mediated by the strategies both sides employ. If the jihadists had sought to invade the US in the traditional way, using ships, planes and the like, their intelligence would have been unable to meet the demands for good information on how to do so and the US would have easily seen them coming. But in support of a strategy that delayed blatantly hostile engagement until the last moment – the hijacking of aircraft already in the air – winning intelligence was not hard for the terrorists to acquire. Prior to the moment of attack on 9/11, US intelligence was monitoring terrorist activity more than enabling decisions focused on stopping or interdicting an attack on the homeland. Distracted US policy-makers had no combined strategy for domestic interdiction because they did not imagine the terrorists' strategy for attack – it was literally unbelievable. Yet this was the perfect strategy to fit the terrorists, who used US openness to their intelligence advantage in collecting information on how and when to fly. Al Qaeda built an attack strategy that enabled a winning intelligence capability, and vice versa. How did they do this? And how do we measure relative intelligence capabilities if competing strategies make a difference?

Measures of success

There would seem to be four critical components of a high-quality intelligence service, and each of these builds on the preceding one. An intelligence service that optimises all four will enable the side it supports to prevail. Since these capabilities must vary depending on the strategy employed, the capacity to adapt to the competition by altering the weights given each is a critical element of decision-advantage. If intelligence is not flexible, the side that can best alter strategy to optimise its own intelligence capacity is most likely to win. These four components are collection, anticipation, transmission and selective secrecy, the last of which enables the capacity for misdirection or denial of information to an adversary. Analysis, an ingredient of each of these four capacities, is only indirectly measurable as a component of intelligence power.

1. Intelligence *collection* is the capacity to gather competitively relevant information. Collection capacity is measured by the number of collection systems available; the degree to which their components, such as sensors and platforms, are tightly integrated and controlled; and the extent to which these systems can cover the entire domain of competition.
2. *Transmission* is the capacity to freely exchange information across the intelligence–policy-making functions. It is measured by the degree to which policy-makers share their strategies with their intelligence colleagues, and those colleagues share their sources and methods with policy-makers. Indirect measures include the degree to which decision-makers adjust

strategies to fit intelligence capabilities and intelligence methods take policy risks into account.

3. *Anticipation* is the capacity to warn, which of course depends on having collection systems in place and having engaged policy-makers – the two capacities described above. Success entails timely alerts of surprising moves by known adversaries and surprising moves by unknown adversaries. The first might involve warning of the abrogation of treaties or a border crossing by a known terrorist. It turns on the same kind of collection capabilities outlined above for known targets. The second type of warning is, however, both the greater challenge and uniquely demanding because it requires that collection cover domains *that are not part of any accepted competition or conflict appreciated by one's own side*. The best indicators of good anticipatory intelligence are independence for the service and, ironically, effective oversight. The latter should build trust and, thus, sufficient independence for the service to explore threats and opportunities unrelated to current policies and that may, in fact, put them at risk.

4. *Denial and deception* builds on the first three capabilities, but adds a crucial piece: selective secrecy. The higher the stakes, the more vital secrets will generally be. But retaining them must always be selective since stopping up information is both costly and dangerous; it gets in the way of net assessment on one's own side, increases the entry hurdles for new customers and slows the movement of information as threats and opportunities become layered and increasingly complex (Steele *passim*). Deception is also highly dependent on engagement with policy-makers because its purpose is to alter the decisions of opponents by twisting what they think they know. Twisted the right way and one's own side can win victories at lower cost; twisted the wrong way and one's own side may face worse challenges than it had before, or lose.

Although the four measures of intelligence capability can be described in greater detail, this discussion is enough to outline both the importance of intelligence to strategy and the way intelligence can be measured for each competitor: number, integration and range of collectors combined with centralised management of them; proximity of intelligence and strategy, including intelligence access and policy-makers' oversight; independence of action, including diversity of recruitment; and selective secrecy, including an agile and easily laundered classification system. Since differing conflicts will generate differing strategies that place greater or lesser demands on each of the above four measures, to generalise from this discussion requires a simplification: the best intelligence service should optimise all four capabilities to provide the greatest strategic flexibility possible. This generalisation cannot ensure, however, that in any particular competition, which may entail strategic surprise, for example, the most capable service *overall* will prevail, since opposing strategies will exploit relative intelligence weaknesses where they find them. Depending on the competition and stakes, a lesser service can, in any given instance, gain decision advantage provided it employs a strategy that optimises its relative intelligence power. This is how Al Qaeda achieved its temporary advantage on 9/11: it exploited US weaknesses in coordinating intelligence support to key domestic decision-makers (in domestic airlines, local governments and law enforcement) and in collecting against adversaries operating within the homeland.

Intelligence power and international politics

What might this theory of intelligence mean for international politics? Theories of international politics aim to explain the workings of the international system and the causes of war and peace. Although the intricacies of these formal theories matter mostly to academics, the underlying notions and broad outlines of them colour how policy-makers see the world and understand their choices. To act with a purpose requires theory, after all. Without understanding causation, problems are unfixable, whether they relate to a rattle in an engine, a child's temperature or a terrorist attack.

Realism and Liberal Institutionalism are the two dominant theories of international politics, and the latter builds off many of the Realists' premises and assumptions about how the world works. For Realists, war is caused by an irreducible insecurity among states, which must fend for themselves in an anarchic world where survival cannot be guaranteed and uncertainty is endemic. Self-help includes building one's own capabilities to protect one's interests and allying with others to balance the power of common adversaries. A central problem is what Realists call the security dilemma: states building power for self-preservation inevitably raise fears among others who will respond by building power too, thus reinforcing the first state's initial fears. In this way, safety constantly escapes those who grasp for it. The gap, however, is two-fold: how do states know about these build-ups and why assume, if they can know this much, they cannot know (or learn) more?

The idea that states 'learn' is obviously not foreign to Realist thought: the theory argues that the effects of changes in the distribution of power play out through the agency of states as they somehow come to know the relative capabilities of their adversaries. But the assumption seems to be that intelligence is universally poor, so states end up, tragically, trapped in the security dilemma. Little thought has been given to how varying capacities to discern relative strength might affect outcomes or whether the capacity to learn about power might work equally well for learning about decisions to use it. Such decisions can be recorded and observable in the form of action; learning about them and what they mean for what an opponent intends to do next need not entail divination or foreknowledge. If intelligence is the instrument by which states learn, adjusting and adapting to the power of others, then attempts to perfect it could lead to fewer wars of misperception and folly. Improving intelligence could be seen as a self-interested route to a less violent world. And in those circumstances where war is unavoidable, then good intelligence could help expedite the resolution of it for all parties, thus limiting its cost in both blood and treasure.[3]

The conception of intelligence presented above would thus appear to fit the 'Realist' frame rather well and even fix some its most glaring defects. This is true, though most academic theorists of this school resist the association.[4] Such neglect or misunderstanding of intelligence is not, however, confined to Realists alone. IR theorists interested in the impact of trade, democracy and institutions, such as the UN or NATO, on the likelihood of war, find improved information flows to have significant effects, but do not usually consider intelligence as a means to these same ends. Constructivism, the third most prominent IR theory, steers clear of defining national interest in terms of power; but in emphasising the role of identities, norms and taboos in the systemisation of international relations, it ignores the methods by which international actors derive meaning and identity from their interactions – precisely what intelligence works at doing. Even if states are not fundamental to the organisation of international politics, but only representative of an idea that crystallised in counterpoint to the identity politics of Catholicism and the Reformation in Western tradition, the anchoring of the idea of the state may have a great deal to do with the superior capabilities monarchs had to know threats and thus how to make their people secure. They could thus sell the concept of state over religion. Constructivists fail to explore the mechanisms through which such norms come to be, one of which surely could be intelligence in service to humans in conflict, whether organised as states, businesses or religions. For most Constructivists, intelligence seems to be uninteresting except, perhaps, in its role as a magnifier of current conceptions of 'us' versus 'them'. They might do well to give it another look.

Conclusion

If knowledgeable states are less likely to misperceive one another, and if intelligence capabilities can be measured, then we are back to the Realists' argument: states able to understand the distribution of power in the competitive state system will be positioned to optimise their security at the lowest possible costs. A world full of such states should be more predictable and more stable than one full of ignorant ones, not least because their ability to learn allows escape from the cycle of threat, fear, arming and militarism that theorists have termed the 'security dilemma'. The structure of power matters to the behaviour of states in international politics, but only to the extent that states know and appreciate that structure. Governments are wise to invest in intelligence, which is a craft honed over centuries to appraise the power and decisions of others.

Such an appreciation of the role of intelligence should place it at the centre of theories of war and peace. As long as states are the dominant power information aggregators in the international system, what governments are equipped to know will affect the likelihood of war and peace. Intelligence at the systems level is about the gains that come from this appreciation of the distribution of power – nothing more or less. A theory of intelligence or competitive learning in international politics should allow Realists to better make their case, Liberal-Institutionalists to correctly identify the real cause of their findings, and Constructivists to describe how norms and the idea of 'other' become learned and institutionalised, thus contributing to learning failures – i.e. intelligence failures – and war. The dominant theories of international politics speak to different questions; intelligence theory can inform them all.

Good theory thus enables intelligence policies, their oversight and their reform. The theory presented here does so by offering measures for success. It rests on a philosophy of intelligence that is epistemological, not political[5] and holds that the essence of intelligence is not secrecy, truth or objectivity but rather 'decision-advantage'. Important as truth and secrecy may be from time to time, the point of intelligence is competitively lubricated choice, which *always* matters, Decision-makers are therefore – in theory at least – at the centre of the business: they share credit for intelligence successes and are often culpable for intelligence failures. After all, a competitor's ability to gain advantages depends on the fit of his intelligence capabilities to his strategy. Uncertainty may be a given of international politics, but it is unevenly distributed and malleable by those who ensure they are properly equipped.

Notes

1 This latter deceit is a type of offensive counterintelligence.
2 The author was this senator's intelligence and defence policy adviser at the time.
3 Liberal-Institutionalists build on these broad Realist precepts, but argue that institutions such as the United Nations or NATO, and economic or political conditions, such as trade and the democratic structure of states, can moderate the chances of war by introducing new or shared vital interests and a measure of transparency among states. The third prominent IR school, Constructivism, explains how global discourse creates norms, such as freedom of the sea, sovereignty and the non-use of nuclear weapons (Wendt 1992). Finding the 'stuff' of global politics resident in the evolution of norms rather than in the triumph of any one, such as the idea of the sovereign state so embedded in Realist thinking, Constructivists nonetheless struggle to account for how ideas and identities propagate and take root.
4 For an exception, see Robert Jervis's works (especially Jervis 1968).
5 Not, in other words, defining intelligence as any secret activity of the state, such as covert action. Covert action is best understood as secret policy often conducted by intelligence agencies, but analytically distinct from competitive learning.

5

STRATEGISTS AND INTELLIGENCE

R. Gerald Hughes

One should know one's enemies, their alliances, their resources and nature of their country, in order to plan a campaign.

> *Frederick II of Prussia (r. 1740–86)*, Instructions for His Generals
> *(Frederick the Great 1944: 24)*

Although our intellect always longs for clarity and certainty, our nature often finds uncertainty fascinating.

> *Carl von Clausewitz (1780–1831)*, On War, *Book One (Clausewitz 1976: 86)*

The trouble with the world is not that people know too little, but that they know so many things that ain't so.

> *Mark Twain (1835–1910)*

An understanding of the place of intelligence in the evolution of strategic thought is an important facet in the study of war. In seeking to gain some insight into these matters, this chapter will focus primarily on three great strategists: Sun Tzu, Clausewitz and Jomini.[1] One of the major problems in the contemporary study of strategists, strategy and intelligence lies in the modern corruption of the word 'strategy' itself. As Hew Strachan has noted, 'The word "strategy" has acquired a universality which has robbed it of meaning, and left it only with banalities' (Strachan 2005: 34). Elsewhere Strachan has written that 'Today the word "strategy", used by governments to describe peacetime policies more than by armies to shape wars, has gained in breadth but has forfeited conceptual clarity' (Strachan 2007: 106). Hannah Arendt (1906–75) also despaired of the manner in which the misuse, and deterioration, of language often seemed to inhibit thought. She believed that it was important to help people think in conceptual terms, to 'discover the real origins of original concepts in order to distil from them anew their original spirit which has so sadly evaporated from the very keywords of political language – such as freedom and justice, authority and reason, responsibility and virtue, power and glory – leaving behind with which to settle almost all accounts, regardless of their underlying phenomenal reality' (Arendt 1968: 14–15). This reasoning goes for strategy as much as any other field of human endeavour. In these circumstances Strachan advises that we turn to Clausewitz (Strachan 2007: 106).

Clausewitz defined strategy as 'the use of the engagement for the object of the war' (Clausewitz 1976: 177). Antonie-Henri Jomini wrote that 'strategy is the art of making war upon the map, and comprehends the whole theatre of operations' (Jomini 1862: 69). For Jomini it was obvious 'That strategy is the key to warfare' (Shy 1986: 146). Basil Liddell Hart (1895–1970) defined strategy as 'the art of distributing and applying military means to fulfil the ends of policy' while 'grand strategy' should coordinate and direct all the resources of a nation, or band of nations, towards the attainment of the political object of the war – the goal defined by fundamental policy' (Liddell Hart 1967: 321, 322). This fits with the consensus, stretching back to Sun Tzu, which posits that the grand strategy of any political entity must be under political control (Sun Tzu 1971: 11). Clausewitz famously phrased matters thus: 'war is not merely an act of policy but a true political instrument, a continuation of political intercourse carried on with other means. What remains peculiar to war is simply the peculiar nature of its means' (Clausewitz 1976: 87).

In examining the strategy-intelligence nexus it is important to note that, as an American consultant to the Intelligence Community (IC) and the Department of Defense (DoD) recently observed, 'A strategy is not really a plan but the logic driving a plan' (Heidenrich 2007). And intelligence and information are essential elements in *any* decision to use force (Smith 2005: 323). The interaction of strategists and intelligence is often reduced to the notion of strategic intelligence. The latter is concerned with issues such as the political developments and intentions, economic factors, military assessments, alliance links of certain foreign states (and, on occasion, of sub-state actors). Such intelligence may be technical, political, diplomatic or military in nature. Developments in these areas are then placed under analysis in combination with certain knowledge about the state, area or faction under scrutiny. The US Department of Defense defines strategic intelligence as 'Intelligence that is required for the formulation of strategy, policy, and military plans and operations at national and theater levels' (Department of Defense 2001: 509). In the modern world the combination of the word 'strategy' with 'intelligence' is often related to modern management techniques that usually employ metaphors predicated upon the idea of 'business as war' (Leibowitz 2006; McDowell 2009).

Unsurprisingly, given its centrality to the history of war, strategy has ancient roots. Indeed it is from Ancient Greece that the word *stratēgos* (Στράτηγος), meaning 'general', is derived. One of the most notable studies of strategy in the ancient era is the history of the Peloponnesian War, fought between Athens and Sparta (Thucydides 1974). Thucydides wrote that 'I have written my work, not as an essay which is to win the applause of the moment, but as a possession for all time' (Schiffman 2011: 50). In this he succeeded and Thucydides can be regarded as a thinker in a philosophical tradition of strategy that stretches to the present day (Murray 1997a). In Ancient China, military thought was recorded and developed by Sun Tzu in *The Art of War* (*Sunzi bingfa*, written *c*.500 BC), which famously advised that 'all warfare is based on deception' (Sun Tzu 1971: 41). It is important to remember that intelligence is, at base level, information. Hence the compelling simplicity of Sun Tzu's advice: 'Know the enemy, your victory will never be endangered' (Sun Tzu 1971: 129). In India, the *Arthashastra*, a treatise on government and princely arts written by Kautilya (or Chanakya),[2] also advocated the use of spies and espionage – in almost every conceivable situation (Kautilya 1992). Its Western equivalent hails from the sixteenth century: Niccolò Machiavelli (1469–1527), most notably in the guise of his *The Prince* (Machiavelli 2008 [1532]) and his *The Art of War* (Machiavelli 2001 [1521]). Machiavelli, like Sun Tzu, pitched his arguments at an audience that was essentially composed of the governing elite (Warner 2006: 487). And that elite was advised that 'Nothing is more worthy of the attention of a good general than the endeavour to penetrate the designs of the enemy' (Machiavelli 1998: 160).

Certain theories of war, as developed long ago by the likes of Thucydides and Sun Tzu, have continuing contemporary relevance. The late Michael Handel argued that 'the logic of strategy and waging war is universal rather than parochial, cultural, or regional' (Handel 2001: xxiv). By the latter part of the nineteenth century, what Handel terms a 'classical strategic paradigm for the understanding and direction of war' had emerged out of the works of Sun Tzu, Machiavelli, Clausewitz and Jomini. These Handel summarised in six points. First, since they are fought in pursuit of political goals, the political elite must always control wars. Clausewitz thus stressed the inherent link between war and politics remarking that King Charles XII of Sweden (r.1697–1718), 'is not thought of as a great genius, for he could never subordinate his military gifts to superior insights and wisdom, and could never achieve a great goal with them' (Clausewitz 1976: 111). Second, Handel notes that war should not be the first or the last resort of any political community. As General Sir Gerald Templer noted of the Malayan Emergency (1948–60): 'The shooting side of the business is only 25% of the trouble and the other 75% lies in getting the people of this country behind us' (Cloake 1985: 262). Third, Handel states that wars should be fought with clear goals while employing a cost–benefit analysis. Ideally, they should thus be won as quickly as possible for the lowest possible material outlay. Fourth, there are limitations on the rationality that can be brought to bear in terms of the analysis of the conduct of wars. Indeed, given factors like emotion and ideology, wars can even be fought rationally for non-rational ends (or vice versa). Fifth, wars cannot be won simply in military terms: political and diplomatic factors must continue to play a role even after the onset of hostilities. And, finally, Handel's paradigm is based upon his observations of human nature and a reading of human history. It is fatalistic, accepting that war can never be abolished (although some wars can be prevented) and that violence is an integral part of the relationships between nations (Handel 2001: xviii–xix).

In traditional terms it is often asserted that while Sun Tzu venerated intelligence, Clausewitz was sceptical, and Jomini's views fell somewhere between the two. British General Sir Rupert Smith opines that 'Sun Tzu's *Art of War* is in many ways one long treatise about the use of information and spies, preferably to achieve one's aim without the use of force, or else to enable force to be used most effectively' (Smith 2005: 326). Sun Tzu himself advised that 'only the enlightened sovereign and the worthy general who are able to use the most intelligent people as agents are certain to achieve great things. Secret operations are essential in war; upon them the army relies to make its every move' (Sun Tzu 1971: 149). Jomini was less enthusiastic about intelligence than was Sun Tzu, because of his opinion that war was a *science* and not an *art* (Mertsalov 2004: 14). It was this view that caused Jomini to constantly lobby for the creation of a Russian staff college, which was opened in 1832 as the Nicholas Academy (Hittle 1961: 246). Although Jomini had retired in 1829, the college – which soon achieved notoriety – was an enduring monument to his work.

Although many modern scholars of intelligence and war dismiss Clausewitz (e.g. Keegan 1994, 2003), his negative impulses towards intelligence are immensely useful. It is nonsensical to say that Clausewitz has nothing interesting to say about intelligence given his observation that 'Although our intellect always longs for clarity and certainty, our nature often finds uncertainty fascinating' (Clausewitz 1976: 86). In any case, it should also be noted that the decades after Clausewitz's death saw significant technological advances that rendered intelligence of greater utility in war (Andrew, Aldrich and Wark 2009: 1). And it is certainly true that the twentieth century saw a shift in the nature of intelligence that, it has been suggested, amounted to a 'Revolution in Military Affairs' (RMA) on the 'conceptual, political and ideological' levels (Murray 1997b: 70). This has been evidenced by historical scholarship. In a seminal 1984 volume, edited by Ernest May, the extensive use of intelligence made by the Great Powers before the two world wars was revealed in luxuriant detail (May 1984). Hew Strachan notes how, in recent years, many observers have argued 'that developments in information technology would remove the fog and uncertainty that surrounded the battlefield – what Clausewitz had called friction' (Strachan 2007: 5). At the risk of engaging in idle speculation, Clausewitz would surely have acknowledged these had he been alive. In actual fact, there is now a consensus that Clausewitz *did* acknowledge the utility of intelligence, although he was insistent that commanders did not *always* have access to it (Kahn 1986: 125). These limitations are obviously more evident *after* intelligence has failed in any given mission. And such failures are often rendered all the more dramatic by virtue of the faith invested in intelligence as a universal panacea for the modern national security state. Such high expectations have persisted in spite of the perceptive work of Richard K. Betts on the inevitability of intelligence failure and the limitations of intelligence generally (Betts 1978, 1980–81, 1998, 2007). In the wake of the adventurism in Iraq since 2003, we can see the value in Clausewitz's observation that: 'Many intelligence reports in war are contradictory; even more agree false, and most are uncertain' (Clausewitz 1976: 117). Although enthusiasts of intelligence often use this phrase against Clausewitz, Robert Jervis rightly opines that: 'the only fault with Clausewitz's view is that he restricts it to wartime' (Jervis 2006: 11). The farcical saga over Western intelligence and Saddam Hussein's WMD programme (Jervis 2006), granted even more contemporary resonance in view that 'Men are always more inclined to pitch their estimate too high [rather] than too low, such is human nature' (Clausewitz 1976: 85). It would be useful if more people were familiar with the opinion of General Michael Hayden (a former head of both the National Security Agency, NSA, and the Central Intelligence Agency, CIA), who once observed: 'If it were a fact, it wouldn't be intelligence' (Woodward 2004: 132).

In common with Clausewitz, Jomini was alert to the disadvantages of intelligence in a way that Sun Tzu simply was not. Jomini reinforced Clausewitz's insistence upon the distinction between war in theory and war in practice (a difference that Clausewitz held was derived from 'friction'). Indeed, it was the near impossibility of obtaining good intelligence that was 'one of the chief causes of the great difference between the theory and practice of war' (Jomini 1977: 268–269). Thus, while others have often stressed the advantages to be accrued from intelligence, and simultaneously belittled Clausewitz, such things should be placed in their proper perspective. We should understand that Clausewitz was talking about *tactical* intelligence – which suffered from very real limitations in his day – in *On War*. Indeed, Clausewitz had the greatest respect for the utility and capabilities of *strategic* intelligence (Probst 2006: 3). Further, as Colin Gray notes, Clausewitz might well have made less of the negative aspects of intelligence had he had the foresight to have identified certain of the technological developments that have greatly enhanced capability in these areas (Gray 1999: 96). Indeed, it was the relative technological primitivism of his era which led Clausewitz to assert that intelligence was less reliable of the tactical (or operational) level than at the strategic one (Handel 2001: 8). Michael Handel cautions that 'Clausewitz's frequent pessimistic comments regarding the value of intelligence should not be understood as a blanket dismissal of all intelligence gathered in wartime . . . Since real-time communication in combat was rarely possible in his day, Clausewitz was simply giving an accurate picture of reality' (Handel 2001: 228). Indeed, Clausewitz himself defined intelligence in terms that were far from wholly negative: 'By "Intelligence",' he wrote, 'we mean every sort of information about the enemy and his country – the basis, in short, of our own plans and operations' (Clausewitz 1976: 117). In 1995 John Ferris and Michael Handel produced an intelligent discussion of the impact that developments in intelligence had made upon the art of war since Clausewitz's time (Ferris and Handel 1995). Clausewitz's stress upon the unreliability of intelligence at the operational level had been derived, not least, from his concept of 'friction' (Ferris 2005: 241). There are qualitative aspects of enemy forces that will always resist quantification by intelligence assessments. Chief of these intangibles (or 'moral' factors)[3] was what Clausewitz termed *will*:

If you want to overcome your enemy you must match your effort against the power of his resistance, which can be explained as the product of *two inseparable* factors, viz. *the total means at his disposal and the strength of his will.* The extent of the means at his disposal is a matter – though not exclusively – of figures, and should be measurable. But the strength of his will is much less easy to determine and can only be gauged approximately by the strength if the motive animating it.

(Clausewitz 1976: 77)

Clausewitz had no time for those who believed that war could be fought by anyone with a reasonable grasp of elementary mathematics:

It is even more ridiculous when we consider that these very critics usually exclude all moral qualities from strategic theory, and only examine material factors. They reduce everything to a few mathematical formulas of equilibrium and superiority, of time and space limited by a few angles and lines. If that were really all, it would hardly provide a scientific problem for a schoolboy.

(Clausewitz 1976: 178)

The misleading nature of moral qualities and raw statistics in assessing opposing forces in war was rarely as evident as during the lead up to the First Gulf War of 1991. At this time the global media was packed with alarmist stories about the supposedly vast size and impressive capabilities of the Iraqi armed forces. Nonsensical prophecies of an impending war akin in duration and casualties to the First World War were legion.[4] Yet, while it was true that the Iraqi armed forces were – nominally – very large, the war was ended very quickly by the overwhelming qualitative superiority of the Allied coalition. Nevertheless, the cautionary approach of the Allies in the 1991 war was well grounded in many hundreds of years of evolution in strategic thought. In November 1990 General Sir Rupert Smith reminded his commanders in the Gulf that: 'Command in war rarely involves the rehearsal of a carefully laid plan. The enemy, who is missing in peace, is taking every step he can to destroy the coherence of our organization and plans. It is the will and the method of overcoming the enemy that decodes the outcome' (Smith 2005: 13). This resonates with Sun Tzu's advice to the general that 'what is of supreme importance in war is to attack the enemy's strategy' (Sun Tzu 1971: 77). The opportunities in this regard are now greater than ever, although they are not always fully exploited. John R. Schindler, a former NSA analyst, laments the use of counterintelligence in the 'War on Terror':

Our spies are too narrowly focused to be able to see counterintelligence for what it is: potentially one of the most effective weapons in the war on terrorism. The strategic purpose of counterintelligence is not preventing moles, but using offensive counter-espionage to gain control of the enemy's intelligence apparatus. This fact is clearly understood by others – not least the Russians, who perfected the art.

(Schindler 2009: 255)

Sun Tzu *did* unambiguously stress the importance of intelligence in strategy (alongside manoeuvre, morale, political–military demarcation and national unity). The differences between Clausewitz and Sun Tzu on strategy and intelligence are plainly obvious. Sun Tzu advised the general to 'Attack where he is unprepared; sally out when he does not expect you (Sun Tzu 1971: 69). For Clausewitz that was obvious, if entirely laudable, advice. The problem was that 'It is very rare . . . that one state surprises another, either by attack or by preparations for war' (Clausewitz 1976: 199). In comparison to Sun Tzu, Clausewitz takes an altogether more sophisticated approach to strategy and much of his advice requires significant reflection on the part of the reader. As Michael Handel notes, 'In his more limited expectations of the benefits flowing from rational calculations, Clausewitz is in many ways more realistic than Sun Tzu' (Handel 2001: 79). Sun Tzu was, nevertheless, an acute observer of society and he advocated the limitation of the duration of wars and, if at all possible, of coercing an enemy without actually having to fight at all (Sun Tzu 1971: 87). With his stress on avoiding fighting if at all possible, allied with an insistence on good intelligence, Sun Tzu is often invoked by finger wagging strategists. Of the US war in Afghanistan, launched in 2001, one US Army colonel and author wrote:

> American strategy has flunked Sun Tzu. America's core policy goal from the start of the war in 2001 up to the present – remembering that policy gives war its overall direction and purpose – is focused on disrupting, disabling and eventually defeating al-Qaeda. It is actually a quite limited core policy goal that makes infinite sense since it was al-Qaeda that attacked America on 9/11. But in order to achieve that core policy objective, American strategy has sought to use a maximalist operational method of counterinsurgency – armed nation-building – to achieve it. It is like using a sledgehammer to drive a nail through a soft piece of pinewood when a carpenter's hammer would do the trick.
>
> *(Gentile 2007)*

Integral to Sun Tzu's philosophy of war was the use of human intelligence (HUMINT) assets. Sun Tzu's advice on the 'Employment of Secret Agents' even broke such individuals down by category.

> [vii] Native agents are those of the enemy's country people whom we employ.
> [viii] Inside agents are enemy officials whom we employ.
> [ix] Doubled agents are enemy spies whom we employ.
> [x] Expendable agents are those of our own spies who are deliberately given fabricated information.
> [xi] Living agents are those who return with information.
>
> *(Sun Tzu 1971: 145–146)*

In the eighteenth century Frederick II of Prussia advised: 'in general it is necessary to pay spies well and not be miserly in that respect. A man who risks being hanged in your service merits being well paid' (Frederick the Great 1944: 60). On occasion, HUMINT has yielded information that has benefited nations to an extraordinary degree, even allowing for adjustments in national policy and serving up startling benefits. Among the most notable of these cases is that of Richard Sorge, the Soviet spy who accurately predicted that Japan was planning to strike south in 1941. This vital intelligence allowed the USSR to transfer substantial forces west for the defence of Moscow against Hitler (Whymat 2006). In the era of a globalised media, revelations about the achievements of the likes of Sorge have contributed to a widespread belief in the abilities afforded by intelligence. Thomas Schelling highlighted what he termed the 'intelligence value' accrued by states when rivals demonstrate 'what can be done'.

> The Soviet Sputnik and some other Soviet space performances may have had some genuine value in persuading Americans that certain capabilities were within reach. The United States' detonation of nuclear weapons in 1945 may have been comparably important in making clear to the Soviets, as to everyone else, that nuclear weapons

were more than a theoretical possibility and that it was perfectly feasible to build a weapon that could be transported by airplane.

(Schelling 1966: 275)

Since 1945 Sun Tzu's reputation, not least as an ancient advocate of espionage, has soared to ever-greater heights. In 1963 Liddell Hart opined that:

> Sun Tzu's essays on 'The Art of War' form the earliest of known treatises on the subject, but have never been surpassed in comprehensiveness and depth of understanding. They might be termed the concentrated essence of wisdom on the conduct of war. Among all the military thinkers of the past, only Clausewitz is comparable, and even he is more 'dated' than Sun Tzu, and in part antiquated, although he was writing more than two thousand years later. Sun Tzu has clearer vision, more profound insight, and eternal freshness.
>
> *(Meyer and Wilson 2003: 99)*

The Soviet KGB favoured *The Art of War* as an instructor text (Albats 1995: 170). And in their post-1945 wars against the French and, subsequently, the Americans, the Vietnamese communist leadership repeatedly invoked Sun Tzu. The Viet Minh certainly had the advantage of a foreknowledge of enemy movements that their opponents lacked. Bernard Fall pointed out that, in the first Indochina War, the French laboured under the severe handicap of having all their troop movements taking place in a 'fish bowl' (Fall 1961: 73). Both Clausewitz and Jomini reflected on such 'national wars' although Jomini added a discussion on the advantages of intelligence.

> Each armed inhabitant knows the smallest paths and their connections; he finds everywhere a relative or friend who aids him; the commanders also know the country, and, learning immediately the slightest movement on the part of the invader . . . while the [invader] . . . is like a blind man . . . he finds no sign of the enemy but his campfires: so that while, like don Quixote, he is attacking windmills, his adversary is on his line of communications, destroys the detachments left to guard it, surprises his convoys, his depots, and carries on a war so disastrous for the invader that he must inevitably yield after a time.
>
> *(Jomini 1977: 31)*

Sun Tzu's maxim that one should 'know your enemy' remains at the heart of the intelligence mission. Yet, things are rather less straightforward than this not least because, for the majority of modern states, today's wars are rarely – if ever – fought unilaterally. This is certainly the case for medium-sized powers such as the United Kingdom. In such circumstances it is now very important to obtain intelligence on the intentions and reliability of friends and partners (Alexander 1998). Thus, for example, it was important that the United States be aware of the exact level of French recalcitrance vis-à-vis the proposed invasion of Saddam's Iraq in 2003 as early as possible. And, in another case, those states involved in peacekeeping in Bosnia in 1995 came to regret their lack of foreknowledge of the weakness and irresolution of the Dutch military prior to the Srebrenica massacres. Of course, spying on one's friends is even more problematic than spying on one's enemies. It remains an essential component of the intelligence mission nevertheless.

In recent times, the lack of US HUMINT assets in the targeting of Al Qaeda attracted significant critical comment, especially after the terrorist attacks of 11 September 2001 (Aid

2009: 47, 56–57). And shortcomings in US HUMINT contributed directly to the difficulties experienced in Iraq after the invasion of that country in 2003. Donald Rumsfeld, the former US Secretary of Defense, reflected on the consequences of this in his memoirs:

> It soon became clear that the gaps in our intelligence about the Fadayeen Saddam [paramilitaries] were signs of a broader problem. For years there had been an overreliance on reconnaissance from aircraft and satellites rather than on-the-ground human intelligence . . . While the attraction of foreign jihadists to the conflict in Iraq was possible given their hatred of America, the fact is that our intelligence agencies failed to warn of the possibility, and as a result, our forces were not prepared for it.
>
> *(Rumsfeld 2011: 463–464)*

The fact that the immediate aftermath of 11 September 2001 revealed flaws in US HUMINT capabilities – especially in the Middle East and in South Asia (Scheuer 2005: 29–30) – and led to a period of self-flagellation is not, in itself, anything new. The end of US involvement in the war in Vietnam, a war in which technology and firepower had been allowed to substitute for sound strategy, gave a pause for thought (Handel 1993: 10). It was in this period that Sun Tzu – whose maxims were venerated by the Viet Cong – and Clausewitz (Handel 1993: 10–11; McCready 2003) came to increasing prominence in US military circles. The Department of the Army in the United States, through its Command and General Staff College, has long directed all units to maintain libraries within their respective headquarters for the continuing education of personnel in the art of war (US Army 1985). The soaring influence of such figures in the United States, reminds one of Alexis de Tocqueville's warning that 'When the past no longer illuminates the future, the spirit walks in darkness' (Weinstein 2007). Colonel (as he was then) Colin Powell[5] discovered Clausewitz at US National War College in the 1970s. According to Powell, *On War* was a 'beam of light from the past, still illuminating present-day military quandaries' (Powell, with Persico 1995: 207). Today Clausewitz is deemed essential reading by every military across the globe. The Australian Army, for instance, advises its soldiers that:

> *On War* is one of the classical theoretical works on the nature of war, arguably the greatest. Clausewitz . . . sought to understand both the internal dynamics of his calling and the function of war as an instrument of policy. . . . *On War* is essential reading for officers desiring high command. It should not be read in a single sitting but thoughtfully considered over the course of a career.
>
> *(Grey 2012: 45)*

Sun Tzu, meanwhile, remains an iconic figure among soldiers, statesmen and others (McNeilly 2001, 2011): his wisdom boundless, his relevance enduring. Senator Joseph Lieberman (D-CT) invoked Sun Tzu in the Congressional debates over the Intelligence Reform and Terrorism Prevention Act of 2004 stating:

> It never hurts to quote Sun Tzu, the classic Chinese strategist of war, who said:
>
> > If you know yourself but not the enemy, for every victory gained you will also suffer a defeat. If you know neither the enemy nor yourself, you will succumb in every battle . . . but if you know the enemy and know yourself, you need not fear the result of a hundred battles.

> The American people know themselves. We know our strengths. We know
> our purpose. We know our principles. As a result of this bill, I am confident we
> will better know our enemy and, therefore, have much less cause for fear.
>
> *(Congressional Record 2004: S12009)*

Sun Tzu is also the darling of management consultancy and business studies (Michaelson and
Michaelson 2010; McNeilly 2011), and was quoted approvingly by Gordon Gekko, the fictional
corporate 'raider' and insider trader in Oliver Stone's film *Wall Street* (1987). But Sun Tzu's
appeal is far from limited to the capitalist world. Today's communist rulers of China remain as
proud of Sun Tzu as was any mandarin of the old imperial order: 'As we have entered the 21st
century, the influence of Sun Tzu's *Art of War* has not declined; rather, it has taken another step
towards surpassing the constraints of regional and language barriers, gaining the respect of more
and more people of every color' (Ministry of National Defense of People's Republic of China
2011). This is no mere hyperbole. In the contemporary world intelligence is a key component
in formulating national policy, a state of affairs that is unlikely to change in the foreseeable
future. One should not, however, exaggerate the (undoubted) opportunities afforded by intelligence. In the conclusion to his *Knowing One's Enemies*, Ernest May reflected that 'If just one
exhortation were to be pulled from this body of experience, it would be, to borrow Oliver
Cromwell's words to the Scottish Kirk: "I beseech you in the bowels of Christ think it possible
you may be mistaken"' (May 1984: 542). There are very sound reasons for this constant need
for reflection and self-enquiry. Richard H. Immerman recently argued that omnipresent cognitive bias had blunted the impact of intelligence since the initiation of the National Security Act
of 1947. The main reason for this is very straightforward: the highly politicised attitude of the
chief of the executive branch. This, Immerman asserts, has been the case for every holder of that
office, from President Harry S. Truman to President George W. Bush (Immerman 2008). This
is but one of the obstacles to the effective use of intelligence derived from its intimacy with the
political process. Nevertheless, while the result of the ascendancy of the political component
may be anathema to the intelligence community one should recall that, whatever its drawbacks,
Clausewitz identified such a state of affairs as being an essential precondition for the success
of *any* strategy. Even in the twenty-first century, it doesn't do to underestimate the Prussian
'Master of War'.

Notes

1   Sun Tzu (*c*.544 BC–*c*.496 BC) was an ancient Chinese general, strategist and philosopher. Antoine-
    Henri, Baron Jomini (1779–1869) was of Swiss birth and served in the Swiss army before transferring
    to the French army of Napoleon. He later served in the Russian army and became a celebrated writer
    on the Napoleonic art of war. Carl von Clausewitz (1780–1831) was a career officer in the Prussian
    army and became one of the most celebrated philosophers of war in history.
2   Kautilya was an adviser to the Emperor Chandragupta Maurya (*c*.340 BC–298 BC).
3   This often leads English-speaking authors wrongly to equate the meaning of the word '*moralisch*',
    which Clausewitz uses regularly, with morale (Strachan 2007: 123–124).
4   Certain of these prophecies cited the recently ended Iran–Iraq War (1980–88) to evidence such pes-
    simism. In fact, Iraq had managed to avoid defeat in that conflict only by massive (direct and indirect)
    external aid from the Gulf Arab states, the Soviet Union and the West (Bulloch and Morris 1989: 119,
    182–183).
5   Powell was later US Chief of Staff and Secretary of State.

6

THE CYCLE OF INTELLIGENCE

David Omand

Introduction: modelling the functions involved in secret intelligence

The traditional intelligence cycle is a simple, easy to remember visual representation, in the words of the CIA, of 'the process by which information is acquired, converted into intelligence, and made available to policymakers' (CIA 1983: 17) originally aimed at helping the understanding of all those involved, be they producers or consumers of intelligence, but in recent years also widely used in the commercial world and as a public information tool (Wark 2003: 1–14). In the words of the FBI website, 'the intelligence cycle is the process of developing unrefined data into polished intelligence for the use of policymakers' (FBI 2012). Policy-makers in this context should be interpreted widely to include all those in government or in public service, including the armed services and the police, for whom intelligence can help improve the quality of decision-making.

The cycle is represented as a feedback loop: a repeating process of steps arranged in a circular pattern, modelled as a production process in which the requirements for intelligence on the part of customers generate intelligence community activity that results in the customer receiving finished intelligence on the topic, and that in turn allows the requirements to be refined or adjusted so the cycle can start again. The most common version of the cycle, as used by the US Intelligence Agencies (Figure 6.1), has the following five steps: planning and direction (includ-

Figure 6.1   The CIA version of the intelligence cycle

Source: adapted from https://www.cia.gov/library/publications/additional-publications/the-work-of-a-nation/work-of-the-cia.html

ing statements of requirement for intelligence on the part of customers, sometimes called intelligence needs that are then turned into detailed and prioritised tasking for the collecting agencies); collection of raw information or data that may be relevant to the requirements; processing of the data into a form that intelligence analysts can exploit; analysis involving evaluation of the data for reliability, validity, relevance and context leading to production of intelligence reporting; and, finally, dissemination of the products (in the form of oral briefings, written products, photographs, maps and graphics or entries in databases) to those who need them, resulting in customer feedback into the next iteration of planning and direction.

In some variants of the cycle (Figure 6.2), for example as found in British military doctrine (MODUK 2011: 3–5), there are four basic steps: direction; collection; processing and dissemination (DCPD). In British intelligence community practice, a further distinction is drawn between 'analysis' of intelligence in its own right as 'the process required to convert complex technical evidence into descriptions of real world objects or events' (Butler 2004: 10) and 'assessment' of intelligence in order to make estimative judgements about its meaning and what it might imply for the future course of events. It is usual too to distinguish reporting based on a single type of intelligence (human, technical, communications, etc.) from that based on assessment of all the available intelligence on a topic (from both secret and open sources) to produce what is known as assessed, finished or all-source intelligence products. Examples include the US National Intelligence Estimates (NIE) and intelligence assessments from the UK Joint Intelligence Committee (JIC).

The cycle is globally ubiquitous: examples that could be cited range from Canada[1] to Austria[2] to Kenya,[3] and are also widely used in the commercial sector to represent the acquisition and exploitation of marketing intelligence as a specialised form of support to decision-making

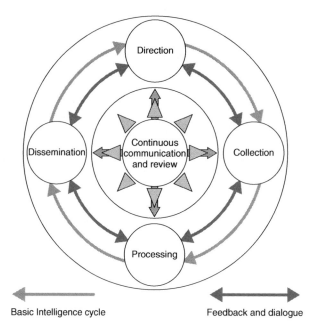

Figure 6.2 British Army version of the intelligence cycle

Source: adapted from MODUK (2011) JDP2-00: *Understanding and Intelligence Support to Joint Operations.* Shrivenham, UK: Defence Concepts and Doctrine Centre

during some form of competitive or adversarial contest, although it also assists cooperative situations where both sides care more about securing relative gains than defeating each other (Sims 2009).

A modern example of the use of the cycle to describe intelligence work is the description by the FBI Intelligence Division of their domestic security activity as seen after 9/11 (Figure 6.3).

History of the intelligence cycle

As early as the Boer War, Lord Wolseley's Pocket-Book for Army Field Service in 1886 provided detailed instructions for the field commander and his staff on how to choose an intelligence officer and how to set up a field intelligence organisation. Three phases of intelligence work were covered: collection, analysis and reporting. Such systematic description of what is involved in the production and use of intelligence was developed by the pioneers of military intelligence before the First World War, distinguishing between what is involved at the acquisition stage from that of the tasks of classifying and disseminating the product to field units (Henderson 1904). British Admiralty intelligence in Room 40 during the First World War introduced analysis as a separate function to collection and processing. US Army regulations published during the First World War identify collection, collation and dissemination of military intelligence as essential duties of what was then called the Military Intelligence Division. By 1926, US military intelligence officers were recommending four distinct functions for tactical combat intelligence: requirements, collection, 'utilisation' (i.e. processing and analysis), and dissemination, although, again, there was no explicit mention of an intelligence cycle (Wheaton 2012). And Wilhelm Agrell has drawn my attention to an early use of visualisation of a structured reporting system based on military field experience in Max Ronge's 'Kriegs und Industrispionage', printed in Vienna in 1930 with an illustration of a complete intelligence system, with sources and their employment in war, and with all-source analysis at the centre (called 'Feind-Evidenz'). Ronge

Figure 6.3 FBI Intelligence Directorate version of the intelligence cycle

Source: adapted from http://www.fbi.gov/about-us/intelligence/intelligence-cycle

was the last director of the intelligence department of the Austrian-Hungarian general staff in the First World War. By 1940, US military doctrine (US Army Air Corps 1940) was specifying the responsibilities of an intelligence officer in the following terms:

(1) specify the information to be gathered;
(2) initiate and maintain a systematic and coordinated search for required information by all available collecting agencies;
(3) collate, evaluate, and interpret all information collected;
(4) reduce the resulting intelligence to a systematic and concise form and disseminate it to all concerned in time to be of value to the recipients;
(5) insure that intelligence is given due consideration in the preparation of plans and that orders are checked to see that this is done.

It appears that the visual representation of an intelligence cycle entered into general use in intelligence teaching in the US during the Second World War, probably at Fort Leavenworth, and may have drawn on the applied psychology of the learning process (Warner 2012d; Wheaton 2012). The US Command and General Staff College in 1948 was teaching on the basis (Glass and Davidson 1948) of a diagram that showed the mission being supported by a cycle of four functions: direction of the collection effort; collection of information; processing of information; and use of intelligence (Figure 6.4).

This concept was developed by NATO intelligence staffs to help commonality of thinking in the Alliance using the term intelligence cycle/cycle du renseignement to describe 'the steps

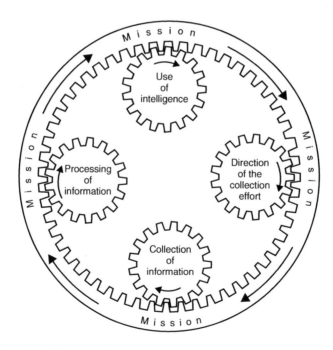

Figure 6.4 An early intelligence cycle

Source: adapted from Davidson, P.B. and Glass R.R. (1948) *Intelligence is for Commanders*, US Army Military Service Publishing Company

by which information is assembled, converted into intelligence, and made available to users' (NATO 1975: 134).

The utility of the intelligence cycle as a teaching tool was also developed in the same period by Sherman Kent and his colleagues in the newly formed CIA (Kent 1949). In his teachings, however, he split the 'processing' function identified in the military version of the cycle into further separate steps in order to highlight the importance of intelligence analysis as a professional function in its own right. That practice, of having analysis as a separate function, is followed to this day by the US Agencies.

In the UK intelligence community the cycle metaphor does not seem to have caught the imagination in the same way in the 1940s and 1950s, although the logical relationship between the intelligence functions was well understood. Hinsley, in his monumental official history of British intelligence during the Second World War (Hinsley, Thomas and Howard 1979: 5–11), described the forced evolution of intelligence under the pressures of war and the complexity caused by all the new bodies and committees created with some part in intelligence work. Abstracting from their organisational acronyms to basic intelligence functions to explain what was going on made sense. A British wartime metaphor was to see intelligence as a chain (rather than a cycle), with each link in the chain representing one of the functions, from requirements through collection, processing, analysis and dissemination, a description used by Professor R.V. Jones in his 1942 report on the organisational problems of Hut 3 at Bletchley Park (Jones 1994: 1–11).

While the formal intelligence cycle was increasingly entering American usage, the British practice was to describe the many contributing organisations in secret intelligence as together making work an 'Intelligence Machine' (CID 1936). The Secretary and Assistant Secretary of the wartime Joint Intelligence Committee produced in January 1945 proposals for post-war British intelligence (Cavendish-Bentinck and Capel-Dunn 1945):

> To sum up, the machine that it is our task to devise should, we suggest, have the following characteristics. It should ensure that the agency best fitted for the collection of a particular type of intelligence continues to collect it. It should ensure that, as far as possible, no other agency should collect the same material from the same source. It should ensure that the material collected is collated with other material bearing on the same subject, so that the best possible evaluation may be made. It should ensure that the information, when received and collated, is made available to all those with a legitimate interest in it and whose work will profit from its receipt. It should be controlled at the top by a strong inter-service and inter-departmental body, representing the needs of producers and consumers of intelligence.

The machine metaphor survived into contemporary times with the official Cabinet Office booklet describing British intelligence as the Central Machinery for Intelligence (Cabinet Office 1993).

Challenges to the concept

Critics have been pointing out for many years that the intelligence cycle oversimplifies what happens within the intelligence community and in its interactions with its customers, and should not be taken as a process map (Marrin 2009; Quarmby and Young 2010: 12). As a CIA sponsored study concluded (Johnston and Johnston 2005) on the pedagogic use of the intelligence cycle: 'Teaching with an inaccurate aid merely leads to misconceptions that can result in poor performance, confusion and a need for unlearning and re-teaching'. Criticisms have taken two main forms.

A first challenge is to the accuracy of the cycle as a description of how intelligence is actually produced (Lowenthal 2006: 65–67), implying that the steps follow each other in the prescribed order round a circle with a feedback loop at the end thus continuously refining the intelligence product (George and Bruce 2008: 2). The cyclical process has also been criticised as a model of intellectual activity that limits and perhaps even renders impossible imaginative analysis of observations and data that do not correspond to the prevailing theory (Agrell 2009: 106–108).

By contrast, the CIA's Arthur S. Hulnick noted in 1986 how much collection and analysis work is performed in parallel, with interaction between producers and consumers of intelligence with many opportunities for mutual feedback (Hulnick 1986: 212–233).

Technical developments, especially in support of military and paramilitary operations, have also reduced the need for steps in the cycle to be followed strictly sequentially. Modern communications allows fast interaction: military targets geo-located by intelligence and identified as hostile by intelligence analysts can have their coordinates uploaded onto precision guided missiles already airborne under the wings of combat aircraft or drones already in orbit. Miniaturisation of electronic components, reducing weight and power requirements, also allows processing onboard collection platforms closer to users rather than requiring forwarding back to national headquarters. In cyberspace the gap between a hostile decision to attack and its impact on the commander can be milliseconds: cyberintelligence is unlikely to follow the classic intelligence cycle.

Digital communications also enable electronic dissemination of intelligence, changing the relationship between the intelligence analyst and the military staff or policy customer. The technologies of the internet and secure broadband communication are being used to allow databases of intelligence product (written reports, indexes, watch lists, multi-spectral images, annotated digitised mapping, equipment schematics and the like) to be maintained to be searched securely online and then pulled as required by the user. This replacement of the traditional intelligence cycle's 'push' architecture by a modern 'pull' from the user sitting at the centre of the cycle is a major conceptual development in understanding how modern intelligence works (Sharfman 1995: 201–211).

The detailed form of the cycle would look different, for example, in imagery, signals intelligence and human intelligence. Differing national organisational structures, as well as historical differences in working cultures, also mean that the standard cycle is unlikely to capture precisely any given nation's intelligence production processes (Berkowitz and Goodman 1989: 30–39).

Nor do the responsibilities for each step in the standard cycle line up neatly with the boundaries of professional skill groupings such as 'analysts' or 'operational intelligence officers'. Some analysts may work within collection agencies and be responsible for the validation and interpretation of single source reporting; other analysts may be part of central all-source assessment organisations; yet others may be also carrying out operational duties in investigative teams or multi-agency fusion centres.

Oversimplifying, the intelligence cycle seems best to fit circumstances where the target is stable and operational urgency is not the driver. The Cold War model of intelligence on Soviet military order of battle and scientific and technical weapons developments provides an example in which dissemination of intelligence findings was principally by way of detailed written reports that were not highly time sensitive adding pieces to the users' understanding of the adversary, and where feedback on gaps and ambiguities in the evidence would have resulted in additional collection effort.

A second challenge that has been raised to the use of the cycle in intelligence training and public education (Hulnick 2006) is that it only captures certain parts of the work of intelligence agencies, and excludes such important activities as security and counterintelligence and covert actions that during the Cold War occupied a significant part of the Western intelligence effort. In US military doctrine the cycle is therefore described as 'the intelligence analytical cycle' (Joint Staff 2012: Appendix D). A comparable point has been made (Cormac 2010: 800–822) about the work of the British intelligence community over much of the twentieth century in supporting the civil power in British colonies and dependencies. Colonial intelligence was more active, going beyond traditional conceptualisation of the intelligence cycle to perform a dual role of anticipating, and then policing, unrest, and the same could be said for the intelligence support in the British counterterrorist campaigns in Northern Ireland or the French in Algeria. The speed with which intelligence can be made available for use today also considerably expands the scope for police and border security forces making operational use of intelligence, for example to prevent terrorist suspects from boarding airliners.

The Al Qaeda attacks on 9/11 dramatically reinforced the trend towards making counterterrorism the dominant mission for Western intelligence (Herman 2003). Counterterrorism has been accepted as a distinct and important intelligence category, akin to the older political, military and economic subsets, and subsuming much of what has previously been labelled as 'security intelligence'. The analysts – like detectives on a murder case – have to be proactive in order to populate their models by seeking out information from informants, witnesses, databases, from open sources and from secret sources, identifying gaps and tasking fresh sources. Intelligence officers become hunters as well as gathers of information (Hayden 2002: 8).

Variants on the cycle

Current British military doctrine (JDN-1/10 2010: 2–4) provides a good example of updating to modern conditions the DCPD version of the cycle based on rethinking and revalidating the core intelligence functions (Davies 2012a: 2):

- Direction: having received the Commander's direction the intelligence staffs generate intelligence requirements (IRs) and supporting indicators or Essential Elements of Information (EEIs) from which come Requests for Information (RFIs).
- Collection: to answer the RFIs the staff will plan, coordinate and employ Intelligence, Surveillance, Target Acquisition and Reconnaissance (ISTAR) assets.
- Processing: involves collation, evaluation, analysis, integration and interpretation of the material, normally by an Operational Intelligence Support Group (OISG) complementing an All-Sources Analysis Cell within the headquarters.
- Dissemination: the timely conveyance of the intelligence in an appropriate form, with appropriate security, to those that need it as a written brief, an urgent signal, a routine intelligence summary, or, more usually in urgent cases, a verbal brief to the commander.

(Hughes-Wilson 1999: 12–15)

The impact of modern ISTAR on military operations has also led to alternatives to the DCPD model in the form of a 'hub-and-spoke' diagram in which the need for the continuous assessment of the operational environment and commander's intent is placed centrally to highlight the need for processes to ensure close mutual understanding between intelligence and command staffs (Evans 2009: 22–46). In the view of an experienced military intelligence officer, interpretation is the key function of intelligence staffs, emphasising the value of interaction with the commander including verbal briefs in cases of urgency (Hughes-Wilson 1999: 12–15).

A so-called 'Real Intelligence Cycle' (Treverton 2001) has been developed with five components in the basic cycle:

1. intelligence community 'infers' the needs of policy-makers;
2. tasking and collection;
3 'raw' intelligence;
4. processing and analysis;
5. policy-makers receiving and reacting to intelligence.

Treverton thus takes into account that in reality policy-makers are too busy – and often not sufficiently expert – to articulate their 'needs'. Instead their needs are inferred by members of the collecting agencies (or in some cases collective mission managers) who know sufficient of the world of the policy-maker to know what will make a difference to the quality and timeliness of their decisions and judgements.

Treverton also highlights the US, UK and allied practice of encouraging the direct distribution of 'raw' intelligence to the policy-makers, reflecting the real-world practice (at least in the Anglo-Saxon intelligence world) of intelligence agencies being authorised to distribute their single-source unassessed (but validated) intelligence reporting to selected expert customers and the direct feedback from those customers who will have a direct relationship with Agency requirements or liaison staff. High-value or operationally urgent material may be sent direct to ministers and senior policy-makers. Direct connections between the policy-makers and the tasking process are also included, for example to allow the highlighting of specific requirements and timeframes, and direct connection between the analysts and the tasking and collection process, for example to refine search parameters or provide names of individuals of intelligence interest.

An alternative model (Lowenthal 2012: 49) emphasises the complex iterations between analysts and their managers, and often between the latter and policy-makers, leading to revisions before a major finished piece of intelligence such as an NIE emerges. The customer can use the intelligence in formulating policy or operations and thus has the capacity to alter the very environment in which the information was collected and analysis undertaken, leading to the need for another type of feedback loop in the diagram (Gill and Phythian 2006: 4).

What no simple version of the cycle can easily reproduce is the cumulative value of assessed intelligence in providing situational awareness, understanding and prediction, representing more than the impact of individual intelligence reports that may well be fragmentary and incomplete as read by the customer. This drawback is at least partially overcome by the stocks and flows approach of systems analysis. Judith Meister Johnston and Rob Johnston have proposed (Johnston and Johnston 2005) a closed feedback loop systems analytic approach in which the elements of the intelligence cycle are identified in terms of their relationship with each other, the flow of the process, the stocks of knowledge that are built, and the phenomena that influence the elements and the flow in terms of world events or other triggers for changes in customer needs or in timescales for the delivery of intelligence. Thinking in that way highlights, for example, the importance of the stock of useable intelligence available to the analyst in seeking to answer a question from the policy-maker, and the serious problems that can arise if the analyst is pushed to reach conclusions on the basis of inadequate information, or the terrorist suspect has not been previously identified and is thus not included in the 'no fly' watch list. Such attempts to study the total intelligence process as a system of systems suffer, however, from the inevitable complexity of the model that results from trying to capture more of the reality of intelligence work.

In order to reflect the increasing pressure on intelligence agencies to develop exploitable intelligence, a variant of the intelligence cycle has been developed under the general heading of 'target centric analysis' (Clark 2003), where the components of the cycle connect together in a network, with the participants collaborating to produce a shared picture of the target. The function of the analyst is central in this model (although the analyst as an individual may well be located inside an Agency or a multi-agency specialised centre). Under this approach the 'requirements' of the policy-makers can be stated in general terms (such as the priority to be given to supporting deployed military forces, or protecting the population by identifying terrorist networks, identifying nuclear proliferation networks and so on) leaving the intelligence community to turned them into detailed tasking and collection plans.

An alternative British rendering of the intelligence cycle (Figure 6.5) (Omand 2010b) adds taking 'action on' intelligence as a function worth depicting in its own right, thus recognising that, for the present at least, the demands of modern national security strategy are for pre-emptive intelligence for the purpose of public protection and the protection of deployed military forces. User interaction is placed centrally inside the cycle, connecting to each function in a network of feedback. This depiction of the cycle also represents the access (collection) and elucidation (analysis and assessment) functions as overlapping, reflecting the increasing exploitation of digital sources of information. Such a Venn diagram has also been explored in British defence doctrine, with the activities of validation, interpretation and evaluation lying in the intersection of the core DCPD functions of Collection and Processing, and similarly collection management shared between Direction and Collection and analytic drafting between Processing and Dissemination (MODUK 2010).

Praxis: understanding the modern intelligence cycle in practice

Debate about the intelligence cycle has largely been between 'conceptualists', who see the cycle simply as a framework of intelligence functions, and the 'proceduralists', who seek a model of how intelligence is actually carried out (Davies 2012a: 5). Pedagogic use of the intelligence

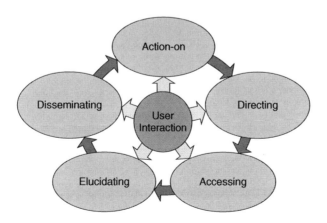

Figure 6.5 A 'national security' all-risks intelligence cycle

Source: adapted from Omand, D. (2010a) *Securing the State*, London: Hurst and New York: Columbia University Press, p. 119

cycle will certainly continue to provide an understanding of the complexity of what usually lies behind a finished intelligence report such as a UK JIC paper or a US NIE, despite the objections raised in previous sections. In which case, it becomes even more important that the functions represented in the cycle are understood in their modern context.

Planning and direction

Most nations have developed formal processes to capture the requirements and priorities of customers. CIA Director William E. Colby introduced Key Intelligence Questions (KIQs) to which policy-makers were interested in having answers, later replaced by a larger number of National Intelligence Topics (NITs). In the UK, the JIC annually surveys departments to collate a list of topics on which intelligence would be of value, and undertakes a prioritisation exercise in which departmental customers are forced to rank their ambitions for intelligence reporting. The result – at least in summary terms – will be endorsed by the relevant supervising ministers, an important step in establishing legitimacy for the overall intelligence effort. Policy-makers' priorities ought to include a general authorisation to the intelligence community to provide intelligence to forewarn government of the unexpected. President Carter is reported (Johnson 1986) as being concerned that 'quite often the intelligence community, itself, set its own priorities as a supplier of information. I felt that the customers – the ones who receive the intelligence information, including the Defense Department, myself and others – ought to be the ones to say this is what we consider to be most important'. The risk of policy-makers directing collectors to seek evidence to support predetermined policies (Andrew, Aldrich and Wark 2009: 21) also has to be avoided.

As already noted, however, the end user, especially at a senior level, may not be able to make their needs clear or at a sufficiently detailed level (Johnson 1986: 1–23). Nor may the customers' prioritised wish-list be achievable within the limited technical, human and budgetary resources available. Dialogue is needed to address whether it is better to have high probability of good coverage of second-order targets or place all the bets on the key priority questions, with only a low probability of success.

Collection and processing

The centre of gravity of intelligence work since the Cold War has shifted significantly towards the protection of the public from the malign activities of so-called non-state actors, terrorists, proliferators, narco-traffickers, cyber and other serious criminals (Omand 2010b). Intelligence has therefore less of the appearance of a zero-sum interstate competition and more of a cooperative enterprise in which intelligence on suspect individuals and networks provided by liaison services has become a vital source.

Collecting counterterrorist intelligence has created significant challenges for traditional SIGINT agencies (Aid 2009: 40–77). The increased demand has, however, been matched by remarkable advances in the technical ability of the intelligence community to supply it. To the collection of the traditional 'ints' of HUMINT, SIGINT, IMINT, GEOINT, MASINT, etc. must increasingly be added open source information, including that derived from the examination of overseas media broadcasting, for example by the BBC Monitoring Service or by the US FBIS. A further 'int' has been suggested (Omand, Bartlett and Miller 2012: 11) to cover the exploitation of social media such as Twitter and Facebook. Social media intelligence – 'SOCMINT' – can contribute decisively to public safety: identifying criminal activity; giving early warning of disorder and threats to the public; or building situational awareness in rapidly changing situations. As society develops and adopts new ways to communicate and organise, it is vital that public bodies, including law enforcement and the intelligence community, keep up with these changes.

In addition, a further category of intelligence collection can be identified as having greatly increased in importance since 9/11. This new type of source has been described by this author (Omand 2010b) as access to 'PROTINT', data-protected information about individuals held on government or private-sector digital databases. Such data can be exploited to reveal clues to the identities, location, movements, finance and associations of suspects.

The term 'access' rather than 'collection' better describes what the modern counterterrorism analyst acting as detective does in respect of such digital data, carrying as it does the double meaning of 'that which is capable of being reached' and 'that which is approachable in different senses'.

One result of these technical developments is that managing and moving data efficiently within intelligence agencies has become a preoccupation, searching for the ability to integrate and fuse all elements of the process (Dupont 2003: 34). Intelligence agencies are now knowledge management industries coming to terms with the cultural and structural transformations of the postmodern world (Rathmell 2002: 99).

Analysis, assessment and production

Analysis can increasingly be described as a process of elucidation, shedding light into hidden corners and explaining that which is in shadow. There are two types of demand, pulling in different directions. On the one hand, after 9/11 the pressure on the analyst is for intelligence for immediate action, whether to protect deployed military forces or identify and locate terrorists, as well as to interdict embargo breaking or proliferation activities, interrupt narcotics supply or other forms of operational military, police or border security activity. On the other hand, following the inquests on intelligence leading up to the Iraq war, there is understandable pressure on intelligence communities to provide better understanding of international events that could affect national interests. That task is to generate and test hypotheses in order to provide the best possible explanation consistent with the available evidence, and with a deep understanding of the individuals, groups, regions and countries concerned, and thereby be able to provide policy-makers with current, predictive and research intelligence assessments. To achieve this the challenge is to become a more strategic analytic organisation, engaging more with outside experts, and developing a more rigorous intelligence community training programme – identifiable, but not necessarily organisationally easy, measures (George 2011: 72–81).

Dissemination and the interaction with the policy-maker

Dissemination now includes liaison with customers to help the non-specialists working in policy or in executive agencies providing homeland security know what intelligence products are available and how far modern intelligence methods (fast advancing in reach thanks to applying advanced technology) might assist in their mission. Different models have been proposed, including 'intelligence brokers' (Gardiner 1991) who would sit in the policy departments and simultaneously interpret the policy-makers' needs, guide the analysts in the most effective way to respond, would deliver the product directly, and provide feedback from one to the other. A key element of feedback is the appreciation of just how little time senior policy-makers have to read intelligence. The UK SIGINT and HUMINT agencies have both developed customer liaison staffs that in a commercial setting would include marketing as part of their function.

Marketing is not, however, the same as sales and it remains important that those in contact with customers do not fall into the trap of making a case for the conclusions of their intelligence.

A significant literature has developed on the different cultures of policy-makers and analysts (Betts 1988; Gardiner 1991) and on patterns of tension between them (Davis 1986: 999–1021). The 2003 Iraq experience reignited old debates within and outside the US and UK intelligence communities about the dangers of politicisation of intelligence reporting if analysts and their customers get too comfortable in their relationship, a danger originally highlighted by Sherman Kent. As a greatly respected chairman of the UK JIC put it: 'The best arrangement is for intelligence and policy to be in separate but adjoining rooms, with communicating doors and thin partition walls, as in cheap hotels' (Cradock 2002). Often elected politicians prefer oral briefings to studying papers, with the danger that 'mediocre analysis appears better when dressed up with pictures and a confident voice' (Betts 1988), and with the inclusion of intelligence highlights to grab attention or as 'local colour' to illustrate otherwise abstract and dry reporting (Omand 2010a). The 9/11 experience and the subsequent creation in the UK of the Joint Terrorism Analysis Centre and in the US of the National Counter Terrorism Centre reinforces the view that analysts and those acting on their intelligence including domestic law enforcement must be partners in a joint enterprise to protect the public.

Breakdowns leading to failure of policy (or military operations) can take place in each function represented in the intelligence cycle (Wirtz 1989), and where failure can also arise from imperfections in the transitions between the functions. That includes the customers for intelligence understanding and accepting the significance of what they are being told – the paradox of rejection (Johnson 1996: 665) – a welcome cannot be guaranteed for the bearer of bad tidings: the Cassandra complex (Kahn 2001: 88). Finally the customers have to make the right judgement calls on what actually should be done (and have the means to do something about it) – an under-researched area (Kovacs 1997: 145–164). Intelligence studies literature is full of discussion of cognitive failures (Kam 1988) including groupthink, mirror imaging, transferred judgements, perseveration and confirmation bias. In considering their impact on the intelligence cycle it should always be borne in mind that these weaknesses apply as much to their customers as to the intelligence analysts.

Notes

1   Canadian Security Intelligence Service and the Intelligence Cycle, CSIS website (http://www.csis. gc.ca/bts/ccl-eng.asp, accessed 19 June 2013). The Canadian version of the cycle emphasises that it is a security intelligence process, starting with government direction, from the Minister for Public Safety. An earlier version of the Canadian cycle (2004) emphasised that this government direction under the CSIS Act is what distinguished security intelligence from the work of the police service.

2   The Austrian Armed Forces use a simplified cycle in which 'direction' sits at the centre of the cycle, with information inputs entering the cycle, passing through collation, evaluation, and dissemination before leaving the cycle as intelligence outputs (http://www.bmlv.gv.at/organisation/beitraege/n_dienste/index.shtml, accessed 19 June 2013).

3   The Kenyan Security Intelligence Service uses a traditional cycle, with the customers outside the cycle, connecting dissemination to planning. The Kenyan version also highlights that 'collection' can be of signals, imagery, human and technical intelligence, as well as open sources (http://www.nsis.go.ke/whatwedo.php, accessed 19 June 2013).

7

THE EVOLVING CRAFT OF INTELLIGENCE

Robert David Steele

There is little desire in the developed intelligence nations to see the craft of intelligence evolve in line with the revolutions in information technology and globalisation. Indeed, it can safely be said that most leaders with access to intelligence services do not value them – they are much more influenced by networks of influence and ideology that demands the status quo. Where intelligence is used at all it is generally to confirm pre-existing policy positions rather than what governing elites need to know (Davis 1986; Treverton 1986; Pillar 2011; Garland 2012). Ada Bozeman has written:

> [There is a need] to recognize that just as the essence of knowledge is not as split up into academic disciplines as it is in our academic universe, so can intelligence not be set apart from statecraft and society, or subdivided into elements . . . such as analysis and estimates, counterintelligence, clandestine collection, covert action, and so forth. Rather . . . intelligence is a scheme of things entire.
>
> *(Bozeman 1998: 177)*[1]

What can be observed within both the closed intelligence communities and open academic, civil society, commerce, government at all levels, law enforcement, media, military and non-governmental/non-profit (hereafter the 'eight communities') is a failure to comprehend the shift in the nature and reliability of their unwittingly shared sources and methods; the Earth (reality), and the mix of humanity, culture and technology.

Intelligence – the art of forecasting, warning, and holistic evaluation of cause and effect – has generally focused in the past on the identification and evaluation of grave threats and in supporting the judgement of executive agencies and political leaders with respect to those threats (Iraq and Afghanistan are two such recent incidents, and Iran is likely to become the next incident of its type).

Since 1988 I have sought to generate a paradigmatic shift in the understanding of intelligence to refocus it on holistic analytics and opportunities as well as the expansion of the craft of intelligence to embrace all human minds, all information in all languages, all the time. This approach – which approaches the social world as an ecology – is the only one capable to dealing with the complexity present in a fluid international system typified by revolutions in the production and dissemination of knowledge, and in the character and dynamics of social relations.

The intelligence community (and the accompanying political apparatus) as one of the eight information-processing communities is – as a result of the failure to understand and adapt to these changes – so isolated that on its own terms it has become an irrelevance. More worryingly, it has become an expensive and unethical irrelevance that is undermining the craft of intelligence as a whole. I wish to restore the relevance of what I term the secret world – in the US it now provides less than 4 per cent of what national-level leaders need – but only in the context of a renaissance of intelligence that creates a *Smart Nation* and a *World Brain* focused on creating a prosperous world at peace by eradicating corruption, fraud, waste and abuse.[2]

Intelligence should be an inherent responsibility of and benefit for all citizens, not just of leaders – 80 per cent of whom do not get intelligence support now.[3] We must migrate from secrets for the few to public intelligence for all.

Intelligence is decision support

What I present here represents the shift in my own scholarly focus from one that centred on a traditional perspective of nationally bounded intelligence activity to one in which the world's population is taken as one informational ecology. Thus the craft of intelligence presented here is not for the benefit of one set of government actors, but is one which seeks to bring coherence within, between, and among the 'eight communities'.

While it might be desirable to include several pages of definition here, I will simply point out a distinction between *data* (any raw single piece of information), *information* (integrated data with a narrative, generic in nature) and *intelligence* (both a process,[4] and a tailored answer to a given question – *decision support*). *Intelligence is defined by the outputs, not the inputs.*

In other words, data need to be separated from noise and collated to create information, from which intelligence directly responsive to a need can be created. *Information is the input, intelligence is the output.*

The process of intelligence is a good one that should be understood, valued and practised by every citizen and demanded of every 'leader'. Secret collection that is not processed is a symptom of failure, as is the neglect of open sources in 183 languages we do not speak (Olcott 2012). The cost to us – in tolerating local to global decision-making and investment that is at best incompetent and at worst a betrayal of the public trust – is now potentially catastrophic (Perrow 2011). What we do to ourselves every day out of ignorance is vastly more threatening than any possible combination of external threats being realised.

Past critiques of the secret world that remain valid today are represented in one paragraph from a senior serving officer that bears on this chapter:[5]

> The intelligence institutions have neglected support of judgment. This is partly due to being disinvited to help shape the sovereign's judgment, but also partly due to mistaking who the sovereign has become. The people's judgment is now being poisoned by ideologues who have filled the void. The situation is not honestly and soberly appreciated. Societal sense-making suffers due to the failure of the intelligence function and the craft to support it.

Three eras of intelligence

The craft of intelligence has gone through two eras and is now entering a third new era. The first era, running from the first days of recorded history and still to date, is the era of secret war, surreptitious entry and theft, and bribery to achieve ends inconsistent with those of the host country or target organisation. In this tradition, intelligence is generally the province of governments, mixing dark side diplomacy and military spies, augmented by a separate track of agricultural and industrial espionage and bribery among multinational banks and corporations for whom practices that verge on the sharp and questionably ethical are a means towards illicit profit.[6] This remains – and wrongly so – the public perception of what 'intelligence' is and should be.

The second era of intelligence, at least among the prominent Western nations and the US in particular, was defined by Sherman Kent with his emphasis on strategic analytics (Kent 1949) but was immediately diminished by the unchecked expansion of clandestine and covert action operations, something never intended by President Harry Truman when he first authorised the Central Intelligence Agency (CIA) (Truman 1963).

The second era of intelligence also saw the emergence of very large commercial educational research programmes as well as government and commercial research programmes; and also business intelligence (data-mining dashboards), competitive intelligence (narrow), and commercial intelligence (e.g. 360°). All of these failed to share data or evolve together. A modest literature on how the academy has failed to maintain its position as providing critical thinking skills to generations of students and in diminishing its place in providing original thought to the narrow and short-term ends of commercial and government contracts exists, as does a varied literature on bespoke research for the marketplace.

The second era also ushered in the use of technology, with collection displacing analysis. Coupled with the lack of outreach and the narrowness of external research efforts, the second era has failed to understand the world, including cause and effect. Ignorance has been the result.

The third era: collective intelligence

The third era is the era of the Smart Nation leading towards the World Brain and Global Game (the first is the content, the second the method), focusing on uniting the 'eight communities' of intelligence, creating a Multinational, Multiagency, Multidisciplinary, Multidomain Information-Sharing and Sense-Making (M4IS2) network with call centre nodes in each region, and ideally underpinning that with either an Open Source Agency under diplomatic auspices in the US, or a privately funded venture that upholds stated principles of integrity such as my mooted 'Virgin Truth'.[7]

Collective intelligence is in its infancy. The craft of intelligence must – will – eventually turn every citizen into a collector, producer and consumer of intelligence (decision-support) in a pervasive manner not yet accepted by governments or corporations. Intelligence – decision-support – is an inherent responsibility of every citizen who wishes to foster democratic government, just society and moral commerce.

The changing dynamics between the first two eras and the third are illustrated in Figure 7.1.

Context for old versus indigenous/new intelligence

Corruption, market distortions and crime – especially financial crime – are 'sand in the gears' of any economy or society. Intelligence – when properly led – is the lubricant of progress and of empowering the majority in society to drive individual and then economic growth. A reworked understanding of intelligence can use 'truth' as a lever and 'trust' as a source of intangible wealth. This is the diametric opposite of the prevailing culture of intelligence, which permits the hijacking of national and business power by selfish individuals. But to bolster this aspirational larger end, of a global open source intelligence, the secret intelligence capacity of all nations should be

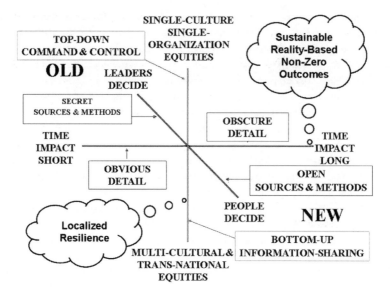

Figure 7.1   Changing dynamics

deployed as counterintelligence to protect the whole from internal corruption. With the one exception of counterintelligence, the third era is the era of 'Open Everything', emphasising transparency and truth so as to provide decision-support to everyone from the citizen to the executive, building trust along the way. Vital to all of this is holistic analytics.

Figure 7.2 provides a visualisation of where we have been and where we might go if we wish to respect reality – the top ten high-level threats to humanity – while also rapidly evolving our sources and methods to the fullest possible extent so as to serve all of humanity.

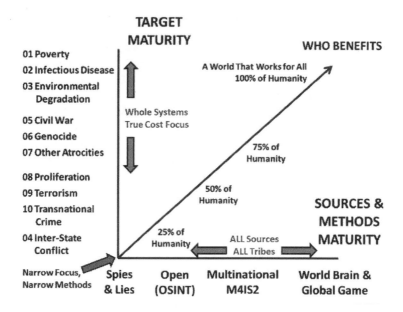

Figure 7.2   The craft of intelligence, from infancy to maturity

The ten high-level threats to humanity as depicted in Figure 7.2 are as identified and prioritised by Lt Gen Dr Brent Scowcroft, USAF (Ret.) and other members of the United Nations High Level Panel on Threats, Challenge, and Change (United Nations 2004).[8]

Poverty appears to do more damage to local, national and global security in terms of survival and sustainability than all of the corporations put together – or the proliferating nations. The conventionally ignored five billion poor are also an infinite resource for changing how we do things, for creating infinite wealth with their most precious resource: their brains, knowledge and skill-sets human brain (Prahalad 2009).

Infectious disease and environmental degradation (including climate change), threats two and three respectively, are absolutes. Today's elite appear to have forgotten the lesson learned by the elite in New York City in the 1920s, when public health for the poor was established precisely because infectious disease takes the rich as easily as it does the poor.

There are (at least) 12 core policy areas where the information must be shared and made sense of across all boundaries. These are:

1. agriculture
2. diplomacy
3. economy
4. education
5. energy
6. family
7. health
8. immigration
9. justice
10. security
11. society
12. water.

Combining these with the ten high-level threats results in a Strategic Analytic Model (EIN 2006) that frames the ten high-level threats across the vertical axis, and the twelve core policies across the horizontal axis, deepening the model by focusing particularly on the eight demographic challengers that are defining the future of Earth: Brazil, China, India, Indonesia, Iran, Russia, Venezuela, and 'wild cards' such as Congo, Nigeria and Turkey.

The two dots in the figure, red when depicted in colour, show where the secret world continues to focus: interstate conflict and terrorism. All others (across the 'eight communities') tend to focus on one issue area in isolation or provide piecemeal linkages between issues. Except for myself, no one I know of is devising a comprehensive architecture for doing holistic reflexive analytics or focusing on doing the right thing instead of the wrong thing righter (Fuller 1969; Ackoff 2004; Myers 2010).

This is a sense-making model for local to global multinational information-sharing and sense-making. This is a model that seeks to unify the 'eight communities' and what should be, but is not – a robust national, regional and global information commons. Only a global network – a near-real-time global network, will do. As David Weinberger puts it, in a room full of experts the only true expert is the room itself (Weinberger 2012). It is the network, the World Brain and Global Game connecting all minds to all relevant information – the 'whole' – that is smart, not the nodes.

In reflecting on 'whither [conventional] intelligence', it is helpful to contemplate the purpose of government and the role that intelligence could or should play in achieving that role.

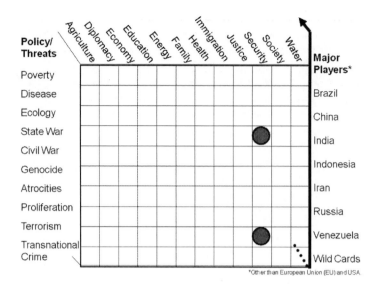

Figure 7.3 Strategic analytic model

The Preamble of the US Constitution is a generic model:

> We the People of the United States, in Order to form a more perfect Union, establish Justice, insure domestic Tranquility, provide for the common defence, promote the general Welfare, and secure the Blessings of Liberty to ourselves and our Posterity, do ordain and establish this Constitution for the United States of America.

Two of these four goals (establish justice, secure the blessing of liberty) should be considered to be counterintelligence challenges. Corruption in all its forms is a major target for the new global form of intelligence outlined here. The other two (domestic tranquillity, promote the general welfare) are intelligence/decision-support challenges that are best served by open sources and methods. In all four areas, *domestic* enemies are central actors (North 2012; Taibbi 2010).

Most governments, less Iceland specifically and the Nordics generally, are not actually working in the best interests of the 99 per cent – their larger publics. Western governments have been captured by banks and corporations (Taibbi 2010).

Information costs money, intelligence *makes* money

I first recognised the market distortions inherent in the information industry in the 1990s, when I understood that the emphasis was misplaced – on selling and buying massive amounts of information without being able to make sense of it, never offering a precise answer for a precise price.

At the same time, I began to recognise the fragmentation of knowledge and the fragmentation of the marketplace of knowledge. Below, in Figure 7.4, is my first attempt to get a grip on the generic structure of knowledge that must be integrated.

In Figure 7.5 is another depiction of the information topography; various communities continue to resist maturation towards holistic information ingestion and exploitation culminating in organisational intelligence.

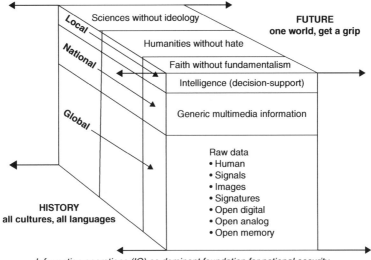

Figure 7.4   Information cube

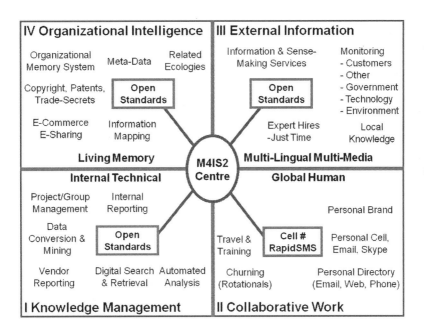

Figure 7.5   Four quadrants of information to intelligence

Most of the world, including most of the major governments and corporations, are in Quadrant I, leveraging current internal knowledge (but forgetting much of what they know from year to year). A major impediment to maturing on the information side is the continued retardation of the inherently closed, selfish, and often dangerously insecure and misleading information technology (IT) marketplace.

Emerging information networks including many civil advocacy groups are in Quadrant II, utilising the internet as a host and social productivity as a mind-set for sharing information, but with a very troubling lack of structure, historical and cross-disciplinary coherence, or the ability to produce actionable intelligence that can mobilise voices outside of one isolated issue at a time. None seem to understand that it is not social media that matters, but rather the social operating system that uses social media (Rheingold 2012).

Few are able to master Quadrant III, not for lack of access or money, but for lack of mindset and appreciation for the new craft of intelligence. Most of the deep knowledge needed has not been published. Indeed, the acme of skill for the modern analyst is to know who knows, to bring the consumer and the individual external producer together so as to shepherd the creation of new tailored intelligence precisely suited to the need in real-time. This is not something that can be done by young people oppressed by 1950s security mind-sets, deprived of access to twenty-first-century technology and limited in their ability to find, much less exploit, humans who do not have the citizenship, clearances or other burdensome access 'qualifications' imposed on analysts by security mandarins.

Then we have Quadrant IV, visualised and documented in the 1960s (Wilensky 1967) and never heard from again. Today's governments and corporations continue to suffer from lost knowledge due to high turnover and inadequate tools and practices for retaining all knowledge once acquired.

Time and transparency

When taking the long view, it is most difficult to justify secrecy (Herman 1996). At the same time transparency has a value so great that any effort to impose secrecy beyond a short tactical timeframe is deleterious to the broader interests of the society affected (Brin 1999).

Despite the fact that open intelligence appears more urgently needed for all elements of government and society than secret intelligence against non-existent conventional power threats or dubious terrorism threats, all 'eight communities' persist in embracing secrecy (or proprietary) and hoarding over transparency and sharing, serving the few over the many. The inherent good in open society has been subverted by closed corruption.

The (new) craft of intelligence, in my view, must seamlessly integrate education, intelligence and research, on a foundation of 'open everything'.

Geospatial dimension

In 1988 I pointed out to the General Defense Intelligence Program (GDIP) annual meeting that geospatial attributes were essential if we were to get to machine-speed all-source fusion. Still today the secret world refuses to be serious about this fundamental prerequisite and foundation for being able to do machine-speed all-source fusion.

There is however very good news, and here I single out Dr Patrick Meier, whose blog *iRevolution* provides regular updates about the intersection of geospatial information, open source software and crowdsourcing: where diasporas not only plot events and observations on a digital map, but also translate short message service (SMS) texts from 183 languages into English.

Human dimension

Human intelligence is central to the craft of intelligence – technology is not a substitute for thinking – to which I would add James Bamford's point that no one has yet built a computer equal to the human brain (Bamford 2001). My monograph, *Human Intelligence: All Humans, All Minds, All the Time*, is easily found online, as is the graphic with Jim Bamford's full quote.[9]

Information pathologies

Across current knowledge production industries there are a disturbing number of persistent information pathologies that enable those who wish to prey on the uninformed to do so at will. Such pathologies include: a culture of cheating, propaganda and PR, forbidden knowledge, missing history, manufactured consent, false science, secrecy, false instruction, and outright lies. The secret world distinguishes between 'denied areas' and 'hard targets' at the same time that it rejects doing what it calls 'global coverage' (Sutton 2006). What no one in the secret world appears willing to acknowledge is that, without global coverage, and without a full and complete understanding of what is available from legal and ethical open sources of information (including direct local knowledge not published), it is, as one author has put it, 'spying blind' (Zegart 2007). Everyone else neglects history, to their detriment (Gaddis 2004), as well as foreign language and foreign cultural studies including foreign literature (Hill 2011; Olcott 2012).

The craft of intelligence as practised today also refuses to acknowledge the importance of steady-state and 'true cost' economics (Daly 1991, 1993, 1994, 2010), called by some the triple-bottom line (ecological and social as well as financial costs). As the world begins to recognise that, beyond peak oil we face peak water, that chlorine and other toxins are externalised costs that cause current illness while imposing future social and ecological costs on future generations, one has to ask:

> What is the point of a 'secret' intelligence community that produces so very little for the top leaders and nothing for everyone else?

A single cotton undershirt 'costs' 570 gallons of water, 45 per cent of that in irrigation; 11–29 gallons of fuel; child labour at 50 cents a day across any of 17 countries; and it emits a number of volatile compounds including Nox, SO_2, CO, CO_2 and N_2O (Liszkiewicz 2010). Within a single country, the US, there is no 'national' grasp of our vulnerability to breaking levees across nearly every county in the land, many built to the lowest engineering and financial standards possible (Boyd 2009); there is no 'national' grasp of the nationwide vulnerability to industrial-based biological, chemical and radiological catastrophes all too possible (Denninger 2011; Perrow 2011).

Meanwhile, false US government statistics misrepresent the unemployment rate (it is 22.4 per cent, not 8 or 9 per cent) and falsely claim new jobs rather than job losses (Roberts 2012). Other countries appear to have similar issues:

> How is one to cope with a government that does not tell the truth, corporations that do not tell the truth, media that do not tell the truth, even schools that do not teach the truth nor how to grasp the truth?

This is the challenge of our times, and this is the challenge towards which I seek to direct the craft of intelligence in the twenty-first century.

What is to be done?

With that exception of robust counterintelligence against domestic threats, I champion 'Open Source Everything'. Figure 7.6 illustrates both our challenge and our objective.

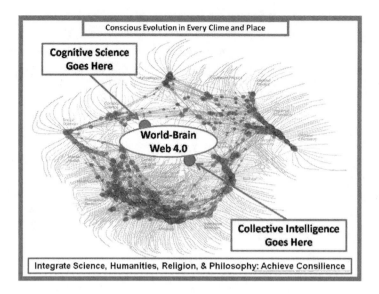

Figure 7.6 Towards the unity of knowledge

Figure 7.6 depicts the fragmentation of academic disciplines and sub-disciplines.[10] Similar divisions also characterise the other seven communities of information and intelligence. The developed world has achieved a modern variant of the proverbial Tower of Babel, creating a system that seems incapable of holistic coherent sustainable analytics!

If we cannot create a craft of public intelligence that achieves both intercommunity and multinational information-sharing and sense-making, then the ethical and environmental challenges we face as a species may well overwhelm us. There must be a 'priority of effort' towards first creating an 'autonomous internet' (one that cannot be shut down by any government or corporation) that delivers the 'six bubbles' shown in Figure 7.7 to the affluent one billion; and then is rapidly expanded towards embracing and empowering the five billion poor with free cellphones and cellphone service for at least three years, along with access to multilingual call centres that educate each poor person – many illiterate but not stupid – 'one cell call at a time'.[11]

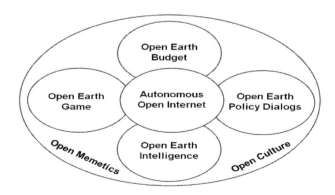

Figure 7.7 Autonomous internet

Figure 7.8 shows my comprehensive architecture for connecting all humans to all information in a manner that produces pervasive intelligence for all.

It is not possible here to address the emerging disciplines of cognitive science and collective intelligence; both are severely constrained by the generally isolated and insular nature of each of the 'eight communities', but some intellectual progress is being made (Atlee 2002, 2009, 2012; Tovey 2008).

The two preceding objectives cannot be accomplished without a radical change in how we conceptualise and implement security within networks.[12] To be scalable at an affordable price, and to avoid the pathologies associated with proprietary software and hardware, the craft of intelligence must demand and embrace an 'open source everything' approach as illustrated in Figure 7.9. Robert Garigue's lasting contribution to this field is this: security is about creating and maintaining trust among individuals.[13]

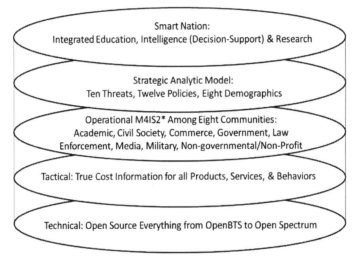

* Multinational, Multiagency, Multidisciplinary, Multidomain Information-Sharing & Sense-Making (M4IS2)

Figure 7.8   Comprehensive architecture for global intelligence

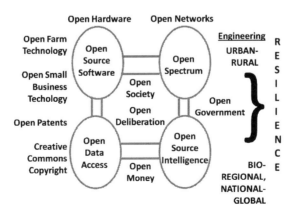

Figure 7.9   Open source everything and the autonomous internet

We all need to discuss the open source everything approach, and the transparency, truth and trust that it seeks to foster worldwide, at every level from neighbourhood to regional water authorities and more, elsewhere – this is particularly so with respect to shared information and the shared burden of sense-making from local to global (Olcott 2012). No other approach is affordable and therefore scalable. No other approach yields a good outcome.

There is so much more to be integrated into the craft of intelligence as we go forward together, but it is important to bring this chapter to a close and do so with one word and one final graphic.

The word is INTEGRITY. We have lost our integrity across all 'eight communities', and become cheating cultures with little accountability within governments, banks, corporations, even universities, trades unions and religions. If we can share one word as an operational principle going forward, that word is INTEGRITY.

A reworked understanding of intelligence that is based on open everything, an open source principle that is premised on transparency, integrity and global commons. There are clearly considerable barriers to entry for this revised system of intelligence: vested commercial and intelligence interests have profited from the closed and fragmented system that is currently in place. It would also seem unlikely – therefore – that they would be prepared to step aside for an open source system readily. However, it seems clear to me that the open source everything transformation could begin as a start-up funding via philanthropic sources, and then take on crowdsourced funding as its value became demonstrated. The open source revolution described here is potentially very profitable, in keeping with the concepts developed by C.K. Prahalad with respect to 'the fortune at the bottom of the pyramid' (Prahalad 2009). And thus the principle of open source intelligence could be used as an alternative and empowering form of economic development in the developing world, and within developed societies, too. Such a system would also radically reorientate the international system away from a narrow and aggressive competition between self-seeking states and corporations, and towards greater cooperation (Wright 2001).

I wish to conclude, most humbly, with an illustration (Figure 7.10) of a strategy for creating a prosperous world at peace, a strategy that requires only that the public pay attention and demand 'open everything'.

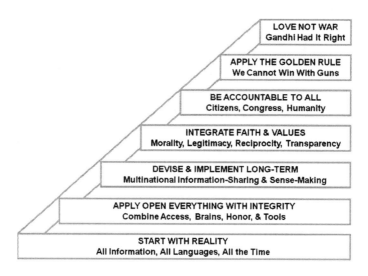

Figure 7.10 Strategy for creating a prosperous world at peace

Notes

1 See also Wilson (1999) and Weinberger (2012).

2 General Tony Zinni is cited with respect to 4 per cent, in my chapter on 'Open Source Intelligence' in Loch Johnson (ed.) *Strategic Intelligence* (Vol. 2, Ch. 6), Santa Barbara, CA: Praeger: 95–122

3 The secret world is focused on 'hard targets' (a very few) instead of 'global coverage' (everything always), and also focused on impressing the top political leader(s) rather than providing balanced support to all elements of the government or to society at larger. Cf. 'Intelligence for the President – and Everyone Else', *Counterpunch*, Weekend Edition, 29 February–2 March 2009.

4 Requirements definition, collection management, source discovery and validation, multisource fusion with machine and human processing, machine and human analytics, and timely actionable presentation to a decision-maker in a form that is useful and portable.

5 Anonymous. A still valid statement from the 1990s, by Ellen Seidman, then Special Assistant to the President on the National Economic Council (Steele 2002: 124): *CIA reports only focus on foreign economic conditions. They don't do domestic economic conditions and so I cannot get a strategic analysis that compares and contrasts strengths and weaknesses of the industries I am responsible for. On the other hand, Treasury, Commerce, and the Fed are terrible at the business of intelligence – they don't know how to produce intelligence.*

   Ralph Peters has described to me the challenge of 10,000 elephants each being examined by a 100,000 blind men, none of whom talk to each other.

6 See http://tinyurl.com/Steele-Craft-Refs. Relevant here are Esiemokhai (2011), Kahn (2001), Marchetti and Marks (1974), Mitelman (1974) and Taplin (1989).

7 'Open Source Agency Executive Access Point', online at: http://tinyurl.com/OSA2011 (accessed 19 June 2013). My one-pager to Sir Richard Branson never reached him. It can be viewed online at: http://tinyurl.com/Steele4Branson (accessed 19 June 2013).

8 An earlier and complementary view is provided by J.F. Rischard (2003), who distinguishes among three groups of challenges associated with sharing our planet, sharing our humanity, and devising a shared 'rules of the road' helpful to all.

9 See http://tinyurl.com/NSA-BRAIN.

10 The foundation image above came from Dick Klavans, long a pioneer of citation analytics, and more recently a founder of Maps of Science (cf. Maps of Science at http:mapsofscience.com; see also Wilson (1999).

11 Earth Intelligence Network (2006).

12 For a more nuanced discussion of old versus new cybersecurity mind-sets, see 'Who's Who in Cyber-Intelligence: Robert Garigue', online at: http://tinyurl.com/RIP-Garigue (accessed 19 June 2013).

13 Ibid.

PART III

Historical approaches to intelligence

8

SIGNALS INTELLIGENCE

Julian Richards

Introduction

In considering the history of signals intelligence (SIGINT), it quickly becomes apparent that this particular element of the modern intelligence-gathering capability is intimately connected with another, much older science, in the shape of cryptography. In one sense, the history of modern SIGINT as we know it today can only have begun with the emergence of the first electronic methods for transmitting signals from one place to another. In 1838, Samuel Morse demonstrated the method for sending a series of pulses down a cable (these formed the basis of the Morse Code); five years later, work began on the first experimental telegraphic line, between Washington, DC, and Baltimore in the US. Thus began the method for sending messages over long distances, and the birth of cable telegraphy. As with many advances in science, the intelligence implications of this development were born almost simultaneously, as governments considered how to eavesdrop of their adversaries' telegraphic messages.

Whenever a message is transmitted over a distance, the sender immediately loses some degree of control over the journey, destination and integrity of the message. For this reason, people have realised from the birth of time that the damage caused by the interception of a sensitive message can be mitigated by protecting or obscuring that message in some complex way. In the world of human intelligence (HUMINT), deception and misinformation have been the methods to do so. In SIGINT, cryptography provided a method whereby only the sender and intended recipient could make use of a sensitive message. The history of this element of SIGINT is, of course, much older than that of electronic communications, and probably dates back almost to the beginning of the transmitted written word.

Early history of cryptography

Kahn (1968: 69) places the oldest-known example of cryptography in text with the regime of the ancient Egyptian pharaoh, Amenemhet III, in approximately 1900 BC. On the military front, we know that the great Chinese military strategist, Sun Tzu, wrote in his sixth-century BC tome, *The Art of War*, that foreknowledge of the enemy's plans and intentions was important, as was concealment of one's owns plans and intentions from the enemy (Sun Tzu, trans. Griffith 1963: 1440). The Romans clearly employed cryptography, as Julius Caesar's basic substitution code – still known as the Caesar Cipher – attests. By the time of the Renaissance in Europe, separate units called Black Chambers (*cabinets noirs*), in which skilled linguists and cryptanalysts were employed, had been widely established within the postal services to intercept and decode the letters to and from foreign diplomats (De Leeuw 1999: 133). De Leeuw links this development with that of the European state system in general, beginning with the Italian states from the late fifteenth century, and gathering pace in the post-Westphalian period after 1648 (De Leeuw 1999: 134). In England, by the seventeenth century, the Stuart regime saw the interception of letters as justified, if not entirely morally sound, for 'reasons of state' (Marshall 1994: 82). By this time, approximately 50 people were employed in such covert activities within the General Letter Office, skilfully steaming open, then resealing letters (Marshall 1994: 80).

Electronic communications

By the time telegraphic systems started to be installed in the nineteenth century, the existing culture and process of intercepting diplomatic communications for reasons of state allowed for telegrams to be incorporated readily into the business of espionage. Andrew and Neilson estimate that, by the beginning of the twentieth century, the French and Russian *cabinets noirs* had become the most effective in Europe (Andrew and Neilson 1986: 6). Much of the traffic analysed in these offices were telegraphic cables to and from foreign embassies in their respective capital cities. The Tsarist regime in Russia had ensured that its cryptanalytical capabilities were developed from a poor start to become highly effective against virtually all of Russia's diplomatic contemporaries, particularly under the Westernising rule of Tsar Peter the Great (Van der Oye 1998: 345). Recently opened archives in Russia have revealed how The Tsar himself received hundreds of decrypted diplomatic telegrams for perusal, covering the foreign ministries of most of his European neighbours with the one exception of the Austro-Hungarians, who seemed to have been able to keep their encryption unbreakable (Van der Oye 1998: 350).

In Britain, the *cabinet noir* was disbanded in 1844, and SIGINT operations did not resume in any dedicated way until the run-up to the First World War (Andrew and Gordievsky 1991: 26–27). The rationale here could have been a Victorian belief that Britain's imperial and diplomatic penetration of the world was enough to give it all the information it needed. In other countries, notably Tsarist Russia, the world-view was somewhat different and SIGINT activities continued to develop apace.

At the end of the nineteenth century, a further major development occurred in telecommunications in the shape of the radio. In 1901, Gugliemo Marconi successfully transmitted a radio message from Newfoundland to Cornwall in England. The age of long-distance radio communication had begun, and quickly developed.

Radio offered tremendous benefits to the expansion of communications, in that it allowed for distributed communications networks to be set up quickly and easily with no major infrastructural development on the ground. It also allowed for long-distance communications to begin spanning the globe, and for land-to-sea networks to be set up readily, giving a boost to naval activities. From an espionage point of view, however, there were obvious vulnerabilities, in that radio could not be directed exclusively to a single recipient. Again, this emphasised the importance of encrypting the more sensitive messages. There is some evidence that, during the First World War, the high echelons of the military were reluctant to use radio for fear of interception, relying on cable telephony (such as field telephones) and telegraphy. This fed into a belief in the run-up to the Second World War that radio would not feature greatly for sensitive communications (Stubbington 2010: 33). In practice, however, faith in complex systems of encryption, and particularly the Enigma system on the part of the Germans, meant that radio was used extensively in the military realm.

SIGINT in the World Wars

In terms of the historiography of conflict, the two World Wars that dominated the first half of the twentieth century were the first that could be described as 'modern warfare'. As Gray (2007: 91) describes: 'World War I was a protracted learning experience about the mysteries of modern warfare and how those mysteries could be penetrated and overcome.' The history of intelligence is intertwined with that of conflict, and in this respect, the First World War was also a testing ground for new forms of 'technical' intelligence gathering, alongside more traditional forms of intelligence such as HUMINT. Much as the First World War marked the beginning of modern warfare, it also represented the beginning of the 'modern age of intelligence' (Ferris 2002: 65). The two areas in which this was particularly the case were in SIGINT, and the collection of imagery intelligence (IMINT), particularly from airborne platforms. In Britain, the Admiralty was initially in the forefront of SIGINT exploitation through the 'Room 40' department, while the War Office housed a code-breaking unit called MI1(b). Both transitioned into the Government Codes and Ciphers School (GCCS) in 1919, which became resubordinated under the Foreign Secretary in 1921/22 (Freeman 2007: 207).

Ferris argues that Britain won the SIGINT war in the 1914–18 period, and that code-breaking was operationally essential to the army in particular (Ferris 2002: 53, 60). This was not just the case in Europe, but also in Iraq and Palestine, where British SIGINT units derived particular benefit from intercepting and decrypting German and Turkish tactical radio traffic (Ferris 2002: 61). In other parts of the British Empire also, SIGINT collection grew rapidly to become an important source of intelligence. In India, radio intercept stations were located around the northern and western borders, with particular attention paid to traffic emanating from Afghanistan, Persia and Russia (Ball 1996). Many of these capabilities were inherited by Pakistan on the partition of the subcontinent in 1947.

Howard notes that the most successful military generals in the early twentieth century were those that made best use of their radio intercept capabilities (Howard 1976: 134). As discussed, however, this was not just about collecting signals, but also about protecting one's own communications. In this area, SIGINT often relied on an important interplay with other forms of intelligence-gathering, particularly in the area of finding supplementary information on codes and ciphers. The Allies' successes in tactical radio exploitation in the First World War were heavily influenced by some fortuitous early captures of German naval codebooks (Herman 1996: 67). Conversely, episodes such as the much-documented Battle of Tannenberg in 1914, in which the Germans completely outflanked the Russian army by exploiting their unencrypted tactical radio communications, served to illustrate the enormous risks to be derived from poor information assurance. Also much documented is the SIGINT success scored towards the end of the war, in which the British intercepted and decoded the 'Zimmermann telegram', which represented an attempt by the Germans to persuade Mexico to ally itself with Germany and attack the US. This piece of intelligence finally brought the US into the war in Europe and hastened its conclusion. Kahn somewhat boldly estimates that this single piece of SIGINT was 'the most important intelligence success in history' (Kahn 2001: 82).

The interwar period was one in which idealism tried to play a small part, epitomised by the decision of the US Secretary of State, Henry Stimson, to close the American *cabinet noir* in 1929 on his appointment under President Hoover, on the infamous grounds that 'gentlemen do not read each other's mail' (Schulsky and Schmitt 2002: 169). Like the League of Nations of the same era, however, the idealism proved to be misplaced and relatively short-lived. In Europe, the Bolshevik revolution in Russia and the emergence of the Comintern movement had caused many European governments to continue their work on diplomat traffic and ciphers. In the

UK, the Liberal Prime Minister, David Lloyd George, purportedly made extensive use of SIGINT against the Russian delegation during the Anglo-Soviet trade talks in 1920 (Andrew 2010: 144). Within the US system, the head of the Research Division of the army's Signal Intelligence Service (which later transitioned into the National Security Agency (NSA)), William Friedman, noted how Henry Stimson's outrage on discovery of the Black Chamber presented a delicate challenge for those within the bureaucracy, and that the outcome was merely to transfer the cryptanalytic work against diplomatic telegrams to the Signals Corps, where it supplemented some new work being launched at the time on covert radio intercept. The Secretary of State's outrage had been anticipated to some degree, since 'it was with some trepidation that a few translations of Japanese code messages were placed on Mr Stimson's desk' when he took office (Friedman 1991: 268).

The story of SIGINT during the Second World War is much documented and analysed, even if there is not complete consensus on the centrality of its importance to the ending of the war. The emergence of new weapons systems in addition to the development of aircraft, ships and submarines, meant that SIGINT was no longer just about the exploitation of human communications (COMINT) but also about electronic signals associated with modern weapons systems, such as radar, sonar, guidance systems and direction-finding (collectively referred to as electronic intelligence, or ELINT). The complex and wide variety of signals under the ELINT umbrella proved to be as important as COMINT in the ensuing Cold War, as the primary intelligence questions were usually about the nature and capabilities of the opposing side's weapons systems, and about how to protect one's own weapons systems from surveillance and jamming. (High-level COMINT on leadership intentions was also required, but invariably much harder to obtain.)

During the Second World War, the importance of ELINT was underscored by a number of episodes, including the successful diversion of electronic beams used to guide German bombers on their raids into the UK, and the activities of the 'ferret' ELINT-equipped aircraft in South-East Asia, which would patrol around Rangoon during the night to activate Japanese radar and listen to its characteristics (Aldrich 2010: 110).

In the popular imagination, such activities have tended to be eclipsed by the story of the German 'Enigma' encryption system, and its exploitation by GCCS in Bletchley Park following some initial pioneering work by Polish code-breakers. (The traffic that resulted was codenamed 'Ultra'.) The traditional view is that the success against the German codes, achieved in part through the innovative use of brilliant mathematicians such as Alan Turing, probably shortened the Battle of the Atlantic by some months (Kahn 2001: 83). The Bletchley Park veteran, Harry Hinsley, suggests that the impact in terms of shortening the war was much greater, at two to four years (Hinsley 1996). As important were American cryptanalytic successes against Japanese naval ciphers (codenamed 'Purple'), which helped to turn the tide in the Pacific War, particularly in the period following the Battle of Midway in 1942 (Kahn 2001: 83). Some observers are slightly more circumspect about the impact of the SIGINT successes. Ferris, for example, notes that Germany was very much winning the 'wireless war' in the early part of the Second World War, and that SIGINT only became significant to Allied success after 1942, when the military tide was already turning against Germany and Japan (Ferris 2002: 71, 81).

The Cold War

Bletchley Park's role in the Enigma story only became fully public with the publication of F.W. Winterbotham's book, *The Ultra Secret*, in 1974. Whatever the truth of the impact of the wartime activities at Bletchley Park and elsewhere, the Cold War that followed Allied victory in Germany was a period in which large-scale SIGINT became firmly established at the centre of the intelligence effort on all sides. In the US, Friedman's wartime recommendation that the SIGINT effort be placed on a permanent and established footing was heeded, and the NSA commenced operations at Fort Meade, Maryland, in 1952. The US SIGINT effort was still headed by the Department of Defense and staffed by a number of military Siginters, but they were now joined by civilian analysts and administrators. Reflecting the new age of mass computing against the cryptologic effort, which had seen its early beginnings in the wartime code-breaking operations, NSA already boasted the single largest computer complex in the world at its launch (Andrew and Gordievsky 1991: 451). On the other side of the Iron Curtain, the Soviets may have had access to less sophisticated computing power, but they had invested a great deal of resource into the SIGINT effort and supplemented it with a superior effort on HUMINT access to codes and ciphers, focused particularly on foreign embassies (Andrew and Gordievsky 1991: 451).

In the UK, GCCS was renamed Government Communications Headquarters (GCHQ) in 1948, and began moving to new premises in Cheltenham in 1952. Unlike the NSA, GCHQ remained under the command of the Foreign Secretary, alongside the Secret Intelligence Service (SIS). One of the most significant elements of the post-war history of SIGINT is the formal relationship established on SIGINT collaboration between the UK and US, following the success of the wartime operations and the joint interest in combating the new Soviet threat. In 1943, a series of agreements were signed between Britain and the US on SIGINT cooperation, called the BRUSA agreements, and these were updated as the UKUSA Communications Intelligence Agreement in 1946. This agreement brought Canada, Australia and New Zealand into the SIGINT relationship. As Aldrich points out, critics lambast this arrangement as a 'cosy Anglo-Saxon club sharing everything in the super-secret realm of SIGINT', and marking the creation of a 'secretive leviathan . . . to command almost unlimited intelligence power' (Aldrich 2010: 89). Whatever the merits of such observations, it is certainly true that the post-war cooperation on SIGINT and information assurance that the UKUSA alliance represents has been historically unprecedented in terms of its depth and breadth, and continues to be strong to the present day.

In the early years of the Cold War, military manoeuvres, exercises and tests of capabilities such as ballistic missiles were particularly high-priority targets for SIGINT collectors. In parallel with the security dilemma between the superpowers that led to spiralling investments in newer and more numerous military capabilities, investment in SIGINT and information assurance grew steadily. Activities included cable tapping wherever this was possible, whether it was the audacious joint CIA and SIS 'Operation Gold' in Berlin in 1955 to dig a tunnel and tap into Soviet diplomatic cables, or equally daring and dangerous submarine cable-tapping operations, conducted by the US in the north Pacific and the Barents Sea from the 1960s onwards. Meanwhile, a number of land-based intercept stations were established throughout the Cold War, to intercept the full range of COMINT and ELINT signals across the radio spectrum. In the case of the UK alone, Aldrich identifies 34 separate locations for SIGINT and Communications Security (Comsec) establishments, and 48 overseas SIGINT stations and facilities, which were operational at various stages during the post-war period (Aldrich 2010). Many of these were located on military bases, such as Cyprus and Aden, and many are still functioning today, even after the budget reductions that followed the end of the Cold War (Aid 2003: 73).

As the need to establish intelligence on the enemy's capabilities grew, the number of platforms from which SIGINT was conducted proliferated. The early days of radio exploitation had already seen interception conducted from both land-based and ship-based platforms, with airborne interception, particularly of ELINT signals, starting to be conducted in earnest during the Second World War. During the Cold War, all of these platforms were used extensively, and were supplemented by more extensive use of others, such as submarine, and, from the 1960s onwards, satellite-based platforms. In the case of the latter, Day notes from recently declassified information that the first successful SIGINT satellite was launched by the US Navy in 1960, in the wake of the panic engendered by the Soviets' launch of their Sputnik satellite (Day 2004: 449). As intelligence on military capabilities hidden deep within continental territories became a pressing requirement, satellites offered a unique new capability to capture on-air signals which leaked beyond national boundaries, and to do so in a way that was less risky and observable than was the case with high-altitude aircraft such as the U-2. In particular, satellites were perceived to be a good way of capturing microwave telecommunications passing East–West across the Soviet Union between microwave relay towers, some of the emanations of which would leak out into space (Day 2004: 458). Satellites were also able to capture various ELINT signals across the radio spectrum emanating from weapons systems and military units, and to offer new possibilities for remote imagery collection on weapons installations and dispositions deep within foreign territory. The Cuban Missile Crisis of 1962 was the first, and perhaps most dramatic example of where such technologies could become pivotal capabilities in the Cold War confrontation.

While the US and the Soviet Union moved into the space realm, the latter is thought to have developed a SIGINT capability five times larger than that of its Western foe by the end of the Cold War (Herman 1996: 68). Ball notes that, in addition to more than 500 ground stations within the Soviet Union itself and overseas, this capability comprised clandestine SIGINT operations in embassy premises in 62 countries, 63 dedicated SIGINT ships, 20 SIGINT-equipped aircraft of various types, 'several' types of SIGINT satellites, and numerous trucks and other vehicles that could conduct tactical, close-range SIGINT operations in the field (Ball 1989: 136).

Significantly, such was the awareness by this time of the need to fiercely protect sensitive communications with cryptography, it is probably the case that much of the Cold War exploitation of SIGINT remained largely in the realm of 'traffic analysis' (i.e. examination of who was speaking to whom, and when) rather than the actual content of communications (Schulsky and Schmitt 2002: 23). There were occasional exceptions, such as the initial intelligence bonanza that the US enjoyed when first conducting a clandestine submarine tapping of a Russian military cable under the sea off Okhotsk, in the north Pacific (Sontag, Drew and Drew 2000: 174).

Many of the most significant SIGINT successes were achieved with the help of HUMINT agents. The Soviet Union scored some notable hits in this area, most strikingly with the recruitment of Geoffrey Prime, a British military linguist who worked briefly at GCHQ in the late 1960s and early 1970s, and John Anthony Walker, a naval officer who worked on the staff of the US submarine forces in the Atlantic at around the same time (Andrew and Gordievsky 1991: 524–525). Both provided the Soviet Union with very significant information on SIGINT capabilities and cryptographic systems, and both remained undiscovered for some years afterwards. Once the Cold War had ended, the balance sheet of effectiveness across the different forms of intelligence gathering is difficult to assess. Aid and Wiebes (2001: 7) suggest that, at least on the US side, SIGINT was considered 'the premier source of information for national security officials and foreign policymakers during the Cold War', in large part due to the extreme difficulty of gathering any intelligence on the ground. On the Soviet side, it is arguably the case that HUMINT provided the more significant breakthroughs, but much key information is still very much shrouded in mystery. To a large extent, the true story of SIGINT's contribution in the Cold War remains something of 'an inventory of ignorance' (Aid and Wiebes 2001: 1).

The contemporary era

As the twentieth century progressed, SIGINT, and intelligence generally, increasingly turned their hands towards non-military targets related to the 'underside of globalisation' (Aldrich 2009a: 29). State-sponsored, domestic and international terrorism became key intelligence issues through the latter part of the twentieth century, involving targets ranging from Palestinian movements to Irish Republicanism, and latterly, Al Qaeda. Aid notes that SIGINT was at least partially instrumental in a number of high-profile operations in this era, including the arrest of the infamous terrorist, 'Carlos the Jackal', in 1994 (Aid 2003: 74).

One of the consequences of this move by intelligence collectors beyond merely traditional military and diplomatic targets is a steadily growing anxiety among sections of the public over the breadth and penetration of the state's surveillance capabilities. It may be the case that SIGINT offers particularly complex challenges in this area. It is, at once, particularly sensitive and subject to fierce secrecy, given the ease of neutering its effectiveness when compromised. At the same time, despite the intense secrecy surrounding SIGINT, there is something starkly visible and sinister about intercept stations, as characterised by futuristic radomes surrounded by high fences and intense security. Such anxiety was typified by debate around the 'Echelon' arrangement of shared satellite-intercept capabilities between the UKUSA partners, which Aldrich tellingly describes as a 'mysterious international network', and 'the world's largest "vacuum cleaner", drawing in huge amounts of communications – an estimated five billion intercepts every day' (Aldrich 2010: 7). Such sentiments have led to ground stations such as Menwith Hill, on the Yorkshire Moors in England, becoming the scene of demonstrations and peace vigils protesting at what were claimed to be near-ubiquitous intelligence capabilities.

With the rise of the internet, a new set of challenges is added to the picture. As the proposed new Data Communications Bill in the UK attempts to convey (Home Office 2012b: 2), the changes in public modes of communication, whereby an increasing amount is conducted using internet-based functionality such as social networking, mean that SIGINT has to move beyond the traditional concept of intercepting communications moving from one place to another. It now has to encompass monitoring of communications and other activity on the internet, moving resolutely into the cyber realm. This, in many ways, poses some very different questions from those of traditional SIGINT. There are considerable technological challenges in terms of the volume and complexity of data – and the rates at which both are now expanding – not to mention the accessibility of them (the Communications Bill proposes that some data are made available to the government by the network providers themselves). As Bamford noted in 2008, the internet 'doubles in size every one hundred days', meaning that the scale and pace of increase in global communications from which SIGINT agencies such as the NSA have to derive intelligence is unprecedented (Bamford 2008: 463).

At the same time, new opportunities are opening up for 'cyber operations' of both a defensive and offensive nature. Advanced nations such as the US are clearly investing a great deal into such capabilities, as evidenced by the creation of Cyber Command (CYBERCOM) under the Department of Defense. Meanwhile, emerging nations such as China are also taking this new capability very seriously and are adding it to their SIGINT arsenal, as demonstrated by the announcement in 2010 of the People's Liberation Army's new 'Information Assurance Base'. Observers estimate that China's capabilities in cyber-operations are growing rapidly to become potentially very significant (Stokes, Lin and Hsiao 2011).

Aside from the technical aspects, there are considerable philosophical and ethical challenges around whether the monitoring of people's behaviour on the internet (or indeed the active manipulation of it) crosses red lines in terms of proportionality and privacy. It is for this reason that many sections of the media in the UK dubbed reports of an Intercept Modernisation Pro-gramme (IMP) at GCHQ as the emergence of a 'Big Brother database' (Verkaik and Morris 2008). It is also the reason that GCHQ took the very unusual step of issuing a press release in 2009, in which it stressed that all of its activities are 'meticulously' in accordance with ministe-rial approval. 'GCHQ does not target anyone indiscriminately,' said the statement, and 'does not spy at will'.[1] Such political and ethical issues are now ones with which SIGINT, and intel-ligence generally, must grapple in the twenty-first century, at least in liberal democracies.

Conclusions

Herbert Yardley, the founder and head of the US Black Chamber until its closure in 1929, predicted that the profession of code-breaking would eventually die, as all governments would naturally adopt unbreakable one-time ciphers (Yardley 1931: 365). Similarly, after the well-publicised SIGINT successes against radio communications during the First World War, many predicted in the run-up to the Second World War that radio would not feature much at all in the SIGINT realm, as governments and militaries would be anxious to keep their sensitive communications off the air. To a certain extent, both predictions have yet to be proven right, and the business of SIGINT has continued into the twenty-first century, perhaps somewhat against the odds.

One of the factors that has ensured continued exploitation of signals is the changing nature of targets and their patterns of communication. At the top level of diplomatic communications, and particularly those relating to more sophisticated governments with a good understanding of information assurance, Yardley's prediction probably has come to pass to a large extent. However, with the shift towards such targets as international terrorism in the latter part of the twentieth century, the SIGINT challenges changed. Terrorists, criminals and similar targets who are not directly state sponsored, will use ordinary public communications and not highly encrypted diplomatic or military networks.

Unfortunately, this does not mean that all the former problems are absent, just that there are new ones. The early experience of exploiting international terrorism of the Al Qaeda variety has thrown up issues of lacking linguistic resources, and problems with cultural awareness. A very unusual dialect or cultural code can be just as difficult to crack as the most sophisticated cipher.

SIGINT historically could not, and probably never can be understood in isolation from other forms of intelligence-gathering. Berkowitz pondered the accusation levelled by some at the US intelligence machinery in particular, that a growing Cold War infatuation with sophis-ticated technical intelligence gathering, particularly in the areas of SIGINT and IMINT, had led to a parallel neglect and reduction of traditional HUMINT capabilities (Berkowitz 2002: 294–295). If such a neglect had occurred, it proved very problematic in the post-Cold War era, when new, more dynamic and less state-centred targets emerged on the scene, and the some-what 'Fordist' intelligence production line found itself poorly equipped to cope. At the same time, Aid (2003: 81) suggests that, given the extreme difficulty of penetrating an organisation such as Al Qaeda with human agents, SIGINT from NSA was 'by far the most important source of intelligence about Bin Laden and Al Qaeda within the US intelligence community' during the mid-1990s.

Despite many predictions of disaster through history, therefore, SIGINT appears to have remained an essential and integral component of the intelligence machinery, even in the new world of globalised threats. Every self-respecting modern state now has a SIGINT capability, both individually and, frequently, in close collaboration with major SIGINT partners, such as the UKUSA member countries. As it moves into the cyber realm, SIGINT may be mutating and developing in such a way that its traditional definition needs to change, but it remains a core element of intelligence activity as we move into the twenty-first century. At the same time, many of the problems that today's SIGINT analysts face are probably little different in their fundamental essence from those that their forebears have faced since the beginning of the last century.

Note

1   GCHQ press release, at http://www.gchq.gov.uk/prelease.html (accessed 15 August 2009).

9

HUMAN INTELLIGENCE

Len Scott

When most people think about intelligence they think about espionage (or spying). Espionage pre-dates modern ideas of intelligence and indeed modernity itself. Sun Tzu wrote in the fifth century BC that, 'an army without spies is like a man without ears or eyes' (Tzu 1987: 95). HUMINT (or human intelligence) is usually seen as a synonym for espionage, though some human sources are not run as agents. The term 'agent' is also sometimes applied to intelligence officers. Within the CIA spies are called assets. Further semantic confusion arises when the term 'spying' is used to cover other forms of intelligence-gathering, such as in reference to 'spy planes' or descriptions of signals intelligence. Indeed GCHQ, in a rare public utterance, made use of the term 'spy' when describing its activities (Richards 2012: xx). For the purpose of this chapter, HUMINT will be taken as a broader term than espionage, though discussion will primarily focus on spies or agents.

Public attitudes towards, and understanding of, espionage may well reflect representations provided in books and films. Much of this is sensationalist, though many real-world examples bear out the axiom that truth is stranger than fiction, and many of those who write espionage fiction are former practitioners. HUMINT in the broader sense attracts less opprobrium. Since the nineteenth century military attachés have been officially accredited members of diplomatic missions who often provided valuable military intelligence. During the early Cold War, Western intelligence services sought to glean information about the USSR from tourists and visiting businesspeople, and more systematically, from returning German prisoners of war who had been conscripted into Soviet military-industrial organisations (Maddrell 2006). HUMINT can also be traced back into antiquity and scripture.

According to the Old Testament, divine instruction was given to Moses to send leaders of the tribes of Israel into the land of Canaan, 'to go spy out the land'. The intelligence sought covered economic and topographical information, though some military intelligence (about the strength of Canaan's defenders) was also acquired. None of the information seems to have involved clandestine agent running, and thus comes within a broader definition of HUMINT rather than espionage. The biblical narrative further provides probably the first example of democratic accountability of intelligence, when the reports of Canaan, and assessments of the military capabilities of its defenders, were presented to the congregation of the children of Israel. The ensuing debate precipitated a political crisis for Moses and a more disastrous loss of the divinity's confidence in the people of Israel, resulting in them being cast into the wilderness – an early account of an intelligence failure.

The state does not have a monopoly on the activity of spying. Private companies conduct industrial espionage against other private companies, although some states themselves spy on the industries of others. In the mid-1990s France and America accused each other of conducting such operations. Individual citizens also spy on other citizens, often using private detectives, often as a result of suspicion that partners or lovers may be engaged in betrayal. And in the age of the internet, WikiLeaks and cyberwarfare there are opportunities for individual citizens to target the state.

Possibly the most remarkable story in the history of espionage and deception concerned a man who set out to wage his own war on Nazi Germany. A Catalan businessman, Juan Pujol, walked into the British embassy in Madrid in January 1941 to offer his services. When this was rejected he approached German Military Intelligence, the *Abwehr*, who accepted his offer to spy for them. He told the Germans he would travel to Britain, where he supplied them with information from a network of agents he began to establish. In fact, he went to Portugal, where he supplied the *Abwehr* with fictitious intelligence from his imaginary spies.

The Germans took his reports seriously, even despite his unfamiliarity with aspects of British culture that at one point led him to concoct a report that, 'Glasgow dock workers would do anything for a litre of wine' (Andrew 2009: 254). Having succeeded in working for the Germans, Juan Pujol then went to the British embassy in Lisbon where SIS again turned him away. However, his activities were soon detected through signal intelligence and in April 1942 he was brought to Britain where he worked with MI5 and, as Agent Garbo, played a vital role in the most significant strategic deception of the Second World War in support of the allied invasion of Normandy (Howard 1990).

Intentions and capabilities

One important distinction in the study of intelligence is between intentions and capabilities. During the Cold War, for example, nuclear weapons were principal concerns for the major protagonists. Proliferation of weapons of mass destruction, particularly in areas of regional instability, remains a continuing anxiety. Espionage is often equated with reaching the parts that technical capabilities cannot reach. Photographic intelligence can help count bombers or missiles, but cannot reveal what the adversary wishes to use them for or when. In July 1990, for example, American satellites identified Iraqi troops moving towards Kuwait, but the CIA could not determine whether this was military sabre-rattling, preparations for an invasion or the initial phase of a campaign against Saudi Arabia. Unlike satellites, spies can (sometimes) tell us what the enemy intends.

There are certainly important examples of where espionage discovered such intentions. One of the most celebrated spies of the twentieth century, Richard Sorge, working under cover as a journalist in Tokyo, was a Soviet agent posing as a Nazi sympathiser. Sorge had extraordinary success in discovering the military intentions of Japan and its allies. He reported to Moscow on Hitler's preparations to invade the USSR in 1941, which Stalin ignored (along with over 80 other warnings he received). Later that year, though, Sorge told Soviet Military Intelligence (GRU) that Japan intended to strike South and East at the Americans, British and Dutch, and would not attack the Soviet Far East. This enabled Stalin to move troops to reinforce the defence of Moscow in the winter of 1941.

Correlation between HUMINT and intention, and between technical intelligence and capability, should not be overdrawn. Ultra, the triumph of British signals intelligence in the Second World War, provides many examples of how German intentions were determined by the interception and decryption of their communications. Conversely, spies can provide vital details of capabilities. Oleg Penkovsky, who spied for SIS and CIA from within the GRU, for example, supplied Western intelligence with the field manual for the Soviet nuclear missiles deployed in Cuba in 1962. This enabled assessments to be made of their readiness state, which in the opinion of some officials and historians contributed to the view of Penkovsky as *The Spy Who Saved the World* (Schecter and Deriabin 1992).

Why do they spy?

Examining why people spy involves exploration of treachery (and in the legal context treason) (Hitz 2008). Treachery is invariably used as a pejorative, though one side's villain is often the other side's hero. Political theorists have long debated the obligations owed by the individual to the state, and historically, loyalty to country was a motivating force in human affairs. Belonging and identity are often crucial in exploring loyalty and betrayal. Kim Philby, one of the most successful Soviet agents during the Cold War, declared: 'To betray, you must first belong. I never belonged' (Knightley 1986: 271).

In some cases identities and loyalties may be divided. Jonathan Pollard was a US naval intelligence analyst, who as a Jewish-American professed loyalty to both states, but who betrayed America and provided Israel with extensive secret intelligence. Yet in espionage, betrayal is not simply an act of apostasy. It is the betrayal of professional relationships and personal friendships. In battles, soldiers usually fight for their comrades rather than ideals. So betrayal of the service excites deep bitterness and in some organisations, such as the Soviet intelligence services, the desire and determination for retribution.

The history of espionage suggests that people betray their country for different reasons (and may have mixed reasons), though the more venal the motive, the less complex the explanation. Many of those who spy for money express contempt for the organisations they betray and resentment that their own abilities have not merited adequate recognition. Some, such as Robert Hanssen, a Soviet agent in the FBI, appear to have been driven by a desire to play the Great Game for its own sake – certainly, Hanssen's tradecraft stood in contrast to that of Aldrich Ames (see below) and Oleg Penkovsky. He communicated entirely through 'dead drops' (prearranged hiding places for messages and material) without ever meeting his KGB and GRU case officers.

Moles and mirrors

It is also worth distinguishing between those who, when recruited, are already working for intelligence services (referred to as double-agents) and those who are government officials, soldiers, scientists, etc. There are also those who, having been recruited are then tasked to join (or penetrate) a secret service, government department or weapons laboratory. These 'deep penetration agents' are often known as moles. Moles also inhabit the field of counterintelligence, where efforts to identify enemy agents are frequently described as 'molehunts'. Molehunts in counterespionage can occur on the mistaken suspicion that moles are present. The damage can then be just as bad as if the moles existed.

The molehunts in British intelligence in the 1960s pursued Soviet agents within the government (the 'Cambridge moles' discussed below) who had already been compromised, so most historians now believe (Andrew 2009: 420–441). When these molehunts became public there was considerable embarrassment for British intelligence, not least at the suggestion that a former Director-General of the Security Service, Sir Roger Hollis, had been suspected (wrongly) to have been working for Moscow. The CIA's search for Soviet moles around this time effectively stymied its espionage capabilities against the USSR, as senior officials came to believe that it was penetrated by the KGB and its agents were feeding back Soviet disinformation (Mangold 1991).

One useful concept in understanding the relationship between espionage and counterespionage is the term 'wilderness of mirrors': what seems true one moment becomes false the next – a triumph of espionage can be instantly transformed into the disaster of deception. The best – and best documented – example of how espionage can be turned against itself is the success of the British double-cross system in the Second World War, where agents of the *Abwehr* were 'turned' and fed back disinformation, becoming conduits for highly successful deceptions run by British intelligence.

Twenty pieces of silver

Few forms of human activity can be readily understood in mono-causal terms. Categorising betrayal inevitably risks oversimplification. Yet understanding why people betray is not simply of historical interest – it can be operationally important. 'If we trust the motive, we trust the man. Then we trust his material', one of John Le Carré's British intelligence officers tells us in *The Russia House* (Le Carré 1989: 110). Money and ideology loom large as explanations. A study of American cases of treason over five decades, by Stan Taylor and Daniel Snow, concludes that money is the most prevalent (and growing) motive in recent American history (Taylor and Snow 1997: 302–311). A later study suggested that nearly a half of cases of treason in the period 1947–2008 were motivated by money and nearly a third by ideology (Taylor and Buchanan 2010: 526).

Conversely, the KGB's Victor Cherkashin (case officer for both Aldrich Ames and Robert Hanssen) is sceptical of claims about ideology: 'ideology very rarely, if ever, motivates treason', he argues (Cherkashin 2005: 63). Cherkashin attaches crucial importance to, 'more private and immediate motivations', including grievances and thwarted ambitions. He suggests, for example, that the GRU's General Dmitri Polyakov spied for American intelligence for eighteen years as the consequence of the death of his son for which he blamed the Soviet authorities (Cherkashin 2005: 114).

The most lucrative case of espionage (that we know of) was that of Aldrich 'Ric' Ames, who spied for the KGB (and then the SVR) from within the CIA from 1985 to 1994, and who was paid $2.7 million dollars (Cherkashin 2005: 4). Although he expressed disillusionment with the CIA, his motives are almost universally seen as financial. Of interest was his claim that the material he initially handed over was designed not to seriously damage the CIA. Subsequently, it was estimated that Ames compromised more than 20 agents (around ten of whom were apparently executed) though it was later believed some of these were betrayed by Robert Hanssen.

Ideology

A second principal factor associated with spying is ideological commitment. The Cold War provided examples on both sides of those who secretly embraced the ideology of their opponents while rejecting that of their own state. In many cases this led to their defection. Others remained to spy (sometimes called 'defectors in place'). Oleg Penkovsky spied for the West from within the GRU in 1961–62, while Oleg Gordievsky spied for the British from within the KGB for a decade until 1985. Some of the most notable and fascinating examples in the history of espionage are the Cambridge moles, the Cambridge University graduates, recruited in the 1930s, who acted as Soviet deep penetration agents in the British government: Guy Burgess, Donald Maclean, Kim Philby, Anthony Blunt and John Cairncross.

Their treachery has excited enormous interest over the years among journalists, academics, playwrights and novelists. Alan Bennett's televised plays, *An Englishman Abroad* and *A Question of*

Attribution, and John Le Carré's Smiley novels, including *Tinker Tailor Soldier Spy*, were inspired by the Cambridge moles, and are themselves interesting sources for reflection on treachery and betrayal (Le Carré 1974; Bennett 1983; Bennett 1991).

Why did members of the 'British establishment' choose to work for the Soviet Union (and why did they maintain their allegiance even after the crimes of Stalin against the Soviet peoples were apparent)? Part of the answer lies in the ideological and political appeal of communism in the 1930s which contrasted with the failings of capitalism, manifest in the depression, mass unemployment and poverty. Communism, moreover, was not only a social and economic alternative; the USSR appeared the only bulwark against fascism. Kim Philby witnessed at first hand the overthrow of democracy and the defeat of social democrats at the hands of the fascists in Vienna in 1934. He later reflected: 'I have followed exactly the same line the whole of my adult life. The fight against fascism and the fight against imperialism were, fundamentally, the same fight' (Knightley 1986: 271).

The Cambridge moles were intellectually impressive: Blunt became a Cambridge don, a London University professor and later Surveyor of the Queen's Pictures; Maclean and Cairncross entered the Foreign Office as high-fliers; Philby took many years to work his way into SIS, where his successful wartime career paved the way for later promotion to SIS liaison officer in Washington. There was speculation that if his treachery had not been uncovered he might well have gone all the way to the top of SIS. Not all spies are high-minded high-flyers, and many effective and productive agents occupy clerical and secretarial positions. The East German *Stasi* acquired a reputation for successfully targeting emotionally vulnerable secretaries in the West German government and in NATO (see below).

In the early years of the Cold War, the Soviet Union was able to recruit able and idealistic people to spy and betray. Among the most successful were the agents who supplied details of the allied development of atomic weapons. The 'atom bomb spies' included Allan Nunn May, Klaus Fuchs and, it is now clear, John Cairncross. In his written confession to MI5, Nunn May said of his espionage, 'The whole affair was extremely painful to me and I only embarked upon it because I felt this was a contribution I could make to the safety of mankind. I certainly did not do it for gain' (Hyde 1982: 56). The idea that the safety of mankind would be served by early Soviet acquisition of the atomic bomb was a view not widely shared in the West. Two others convicted of atomic espionage, Julius and Ethel Rosenberg, were sent to the electric chair in America by a judge who claimed their spying, and the resulting Soviet acquisition of the atomic bomb, had brought about the Korean War in which thousands of American servicemen were killed.

Klaus Fuchs is seen as the most significant atom bomb spy. In December 1943 he travelled to America to join the Manhattan Project and was later posted to Los Alamos in New Mexico where the bomb was being assembled. His intelligence on the manufacture of the weapon was of considerable importance. Another Soviet agent, David Greenglass, Julius Rosenberg's brother-in-law, provided material on the engineering side. Both Fuchs and Greenglass were uncovered when Soviet enciphered communications were decrypted (under the US *Venona* project), and Fuchs confessed to MI5 in January 1950 having left Los Alamos for the UK atomic energy research centre at Harwell. He was sentenced to 14 years in prison.

Stalin was officially told of the atomic bomb by Harry Truman at the Potsdam conference in July 1945. Before then, Moscow's only evidence of its existence came from its spies. Building atomic weapons meant a huge commitment of resources and scientific genius and Moscow knew of allied strategic deception against the Germans through NKVD penetration of MI5. So what the atom bomb spies were telling Moscow had to be evaluated with great care. Lavrentii Beria, the feared head of the NKVD, was put in charge of the Soviet project and told his officers that if they were being fed disinformation, they would be for the 'cellar' – a reference to the torture and execution chambers deep in Lubyanka, NKVD headquarters (Holloway 1994: 115).

Beria's doubts about his networks were dispelled with the destruction of Hiroshima. There remains dispute about the relative importance of Soviet scientists and Soviet intelligence in developing the atomic bomb. In the most authoritative study, David Holloway concludes that the, 'first Soviet atomic bomb was a copy of the American plutonium bomb tested at Alamogordo in July 1945. Espionage played a key role in the atomic Soviet project, and its role would have been even greater if the Soviet leaders had paid more heed to the intelligence they received during the war' (Holloway 1994: 366).

Shifting ideological paradigms

As the failings of Soviet communism became ever more apparent, the attractions of Marxism–Leninism faded, while in the USSR, those such as Oleg Gordievsky became increasingly repulsed by the Soviet system. Moscow's intervention in Czechoslovakia in 1968 marked a turning point for Gordievsky, who spied for SIS for a decade from the mid-1970s. In the early 1980s, Soviet-American tension reached new heights, in what became known as the Second Cold War. In 1981, the KGB and the GRU were tasked to provide strategic warning of nuclear attack from the West. This joint operation was code-named Operation RYAN, details of which were supplied to British intelligence by Gordievsky, whose espionage provided significant insights into how the Soviet leadership saw the threat from the Reagan administration. Moscow's rhetoric reflected genuine anxiety about the prospect of a nuclear confrontation. In short, it became clear that the Soviet leadership believed much of its own propaganda.

Some agents and defectors looked to the West as ideologically (as well as economically) superior. One aspect of Immanuel Kant's criticisms of espionage was the assertion that it, 'exploits only the dishonesty of others' (Herman 2004: 180). While dishonesty is inevitable in espionage, other (and higher) motives may loom much larger. Comparing his actions with those of Aldrich Ames, Gordievsky argues,

> Ames's motives in changing sides were purely financial: mine were ideological and philosophical . . . one of my conditions for starting to work with the British was that I should not be paid; and although the British government has been kind and good to me since I escaped to live in England, financial gain was never my incentive. Rather, I was driven by contempt for Communist tyranny – and now history has endorsed my opinion that the system was one under which it was it was impossible for humans to live happily.
>
> *(Gordievsky 1995: 388)*

Non-spiritual enticements

Some traitors are created through entrapment or blackmail, often involving sex. 'Honey traps' – both heterosexual and gay – have been used over the centuries, and also pervade the espionage literature (Hitz 2004: 99–106). John Vassal, an Admiralty civil servant, was blackmailed into spying for the KGB after they photographed him in Moscow, having (in his own words) 'oral, anal or a complicated series of sexual activities with a number of different men' (Andrew 2009: 398). The KGB acquired a reputation for honey traps and 'swallows' (female operatives trained in the arts of seduction). In the 1980s an American Marine Corps sergeant, Clayton Lonetree, became the target of such an operation. His ensuing treachery compromised the security of the American Embassy in Moscow where he was a guard (Hitz 2004: 102–105). It is clear that other intelligence services developed expertise in exploiting sex for espionage purposes. Markus Wolf, the famed head of the German *Stasi* describes how, 'My Romeo spies gained notoriety across the world by winning women's hearts in order to obtain the state and political secrets to which their targets had access' (Wolf 1997: 123).

Intelligence services invest great energy (and resources) seeking to recruit people in key positions. The CIA, for example, expended considerable effort unsuccessfully trying to develop agents with knowledge of Iraq's weapons of mass destruction before 2003. Yet many of the most effective spies were not actively recruited but volunteered their services. Known as 'walk-ins', they include some of the more celebrated cases, such as Oleg Penkovsky, Aldrich Ames and Juan Pujol Garcia. Understanding the opportunities afforded by walk-ins has important implications for the conduct of operations. Actively recruiting agents can expose the 'talent-spotter' or whoever is tasked with the approach (or 'pitch' in the American lexicon). Both Anthony Blunt and Kim Philby were eventually uncovered by statements from those they had attempted to recruit many years before.

Some walk-ins may be deliberate provocations (known as 'dangles') designed to embarrass or expose the intelligence officers. Others may be carefully prepared double-agents designed to sow disinformation. In the United States, one of the most controversial cases concerned Yuri Nosenko who defected from the Second Chief Directorate of the KGB in 1964 and who was investigated for a decade while the CIA struggled to determine his *bona fides*. Yet walk-ins can also bring treasure, as in the case of KGB archivist Vasili Mitrokhin, who walked into the British embassy in Latvia and whose offer to provide a vast amount of documentation was successfully exploited (Andrew and Mitrokhin 1999: 17–19). The ability to respond to serendipity can be a valuable part of the espionage war.

Lessons from espionage history?

Intelligence services have been criticised for retaining a Cold War mentality in the conduct of their operations. The espionage war against Al Qaeda has generated some pessimism at the prospect of penetrating an organisation that is not an organisation. In August 2001, shortly before 9/11, a former member of the CIA's Directorate of Operations, Reuel Marc Gerecht, published an article attacking the agency's approach to espionage (Gerecht 2001). He explained that the CIA relied on officers working under official cover, as diplomats with diplomatic immunity. Gerecht argued that, 'the only effective way to run offensive counterterrorist operations against Islamic radicals in more or less hostile territory is with "non-official-cover" [NOC] officers'. One CIA officer claimed, 'The CIA probably doesn't have a single truly qualified Arabic-speaking officer of Middle East background who can play a believable Muslim fundamentalist who would volunteer to spend years of his life with shitty food and no women in the mountains of Afghanistan.'

The Director of Central Intelligence, George Tenet, provides a rather different picture of CIA activity in this period (Tenet 2007: 179 *et seq.*). Yet Al Qaeda remains a formidable challenge to Western security and intelligence services, not least where the threat is from indigenous groups (or even individuals) inspired by, but not controlled from, abroad. The history of counterinsurgency and counterterrorism, however, suggests that cell-like structures of organisations like the Provisional Irish Republican Army are not immune to penetration. Western democracies are also multicultural societies. If Al Qaeda can recruit and inspire people to commit acts of terrorism, then Western societies ought to be able to recruit and inspire those willing to demonstrate the same tenacity and self-sacrifice. Recent examples suggest that Western intelligence services and their allies are capable of mounting effective operations against Al Qaeda and their affiliates (MacAskill and Norton-Taylor 2012). Some aspects of Al Qaeda, including its religious character, may provide very different challenges than in Cold War and post-colonial conflicts. The prospect of ideological conflict over generations may nevertheless suggest that Cold War espionage has some relevance today.

How do we know about spies?

The world of secret intelligence inextricably involves secrecy. So how do we know about spies? We learn through authorised and unauthorised disclosure, through memoirs and accounts of whistleblowers, and from where cases end in trials and convictions. Different organisations have different attitudes to disclosure. The authorised history of SIS avoids identification of agents run many generations ago, in part to safeguard their families and in part to safeguard a principle (Jeffery 2010). The CIA has a different attitude to declassification, though it retains a necessary professional interest in protecting sources and methods. Its web pages, for example, provide access to documents giving details of operations, including some aspects of tradecraft, and the transcripts of meetings between agents and case officers (CIA 2012).

We know some things about spies through what spies tell us themselves, though if we ask, 'Why do people spy?' we should certainly ask, 'Why do they write about spying?' Whether we believe them depends on our judgements. Many memoirs are exercises in self-justification and often in self-aggrandisement. The accounts of people whose lives have been lived through deception clearly need to be read with care. And if that goes for what they write in retirement (or exile) it goes for what they say when serving, to journalists and others. Disclosure can reflect active agendas and/or internal disputes. The published history of espionage is nevertheless important for the justification of espionage for the reason that success, and the means by which it is achieved, generally needs to remain secret.

Whether we believe accounts of former adversaries is a further question. While Kim Philby's *My Secret War* attracted scorn in the West, the accounts of Yuri Modin (KGB desk officer and handler for the Cambridge moles) and Victor Cherkashin have been taken more seriously (Philby 1968; Modin 1994; Cherkashin 2005). So, too, have collaborations between the KGB's Oleg Tsarev and Western writers, based on Tsarev's access to KGB archives (Costello and Tsarev 1993; West and Tsarev 1999; West and Tsarev 2009). Rather different forms of collaboration and access were enjoyed by Oleg Gordievsky, whose *KGB: The Inside Story* was co-authored with Christopher Andrew and based on Gordievsky's access to KGB files as *Rezident*-designate to London (Andrew and Gordievsky 1990).

Is the Great Game worth the candle?

So what? Why does espionage matter? An obvious distinction is between spying on spies and spying on governments. With the latter one answer is counterfactual – it is possible to identify cases where espionage might have prevented intelligence failure. One lesson Americans learned from Pearl Harbor, for example, was the need for a foreign intelligence-gathering organisation (as well as a central intelligence machinery to evaluate, integrate and disseminate). The events of 9/11, the invasion of Iraq in 2003 and the question of Iran's weaponisation of its nuclear programme have underlined what many see as the need for espionage, while also demonstrating the problems and challenges of acquiring and running agents.

Various examples of espionage have been mentioned above, which illustrate the potential benefits of spying. Systematic evaluation is beyond this chapter, not least because such scrutiny requires careful examination of how the products from each spy were assessed, integrated into the analytical process (if there was one) and then used by decision-makers. Some of the risks of espionage have also been explained. Nazi Germany would have been best served if the *Abwehr* had not even attempted espionage against the British during the war. The gathering of secret intelligence can be a double-edged sword. Getting it wrong can be worse than if the attempt had never been made.

A different focus concerns the impact of espionage on public attitudes, political culture and international trust. During the Second World War, Britain and America decided not to spy on the USSR, their wartime ally. They were unaware of Soviet espionage, which only began to become apparent after the defection of a GRU cipher clerk, Igor Gouzenko, in September 1945. In the United States the discovery of Soviet spies in the American government and the Manhattan Project greatly fuelled the rise of McCarthyism and the grip of Cold War paranoia. Cold War espionage became a feature of Cold War culture, and of the distrust at the heart of East–West relations. The portrayal of espionage in cinematic and literary representations also reinforced an influential political discourse: the view that East and West were morally symmetrical and fought each other in the same way for the same ends. Le Carré's *The Spy Who Came in From the Cold* was an early portrayal of this (Le Carré 1963).

Spying has been described as, 'the second oldest profession and just as honorable as the first'.[1] Certainly some would share Immanuel Kant's view of espionage as, 'intrinsically despicable' (Herman 2004: 180). Not all states engage in espionage or have organisations with such specific responsibility. Some states are better at spying than others. Yet the nature of threats and risks in international society – arising from the actions of both states and non-state actors – will for many generate a felt need for espionage (as well as a need to protect against the espionage). The causes for which people spy may change. The reasons why they spy show no signs of disappearing.

Note

1 Michael J. Barrett quoted in (Knightley 1986: 1). Why comparisons should be drawn with chartered accountancy is unclear to this author.

10

ECONOMIC INTELLIGENCE

Peter Davies

I have always been puzzled by economic intelligence.

(Geoffrey Littler 1967)[1]

Walter Laqueur's celebrated characterisation of economic intelligence as 'what economists do in and for intelligence agencies' (Laqueur 1993: 40) encapsulates its *epistemological* (nature, methods and techniques employed, strengths and weaknesses of the knowledge provided), *sociological* (participants and their backgrounds) and *institutional* (machinery, culture and environment) features. What it lacks is the historical perspective so essential to a profound understanding of any government activity. Intelligence history must capture what is unique about intelligence and the features it shares with other government activities and institutions. This chapter investigates the history of economic intelligence in the UK where it first emerged as a distinguishable field, paying especial attention to two of its distinctive characteristics. Economic intelligence (1) serves an unusually wide range of government departments engaged in both international and domestic policy-making; and (2) outside defence intelligence an unusually high proportion of the information is either openly available or acquired by the government during the normal course of its activities.

In the lexicon of intelligence studies economic intelligence is simultaneously a *secret* and a *mystery*. It is a *secret* because (notwithstanding the extensive literature on assessments of the Soviet Union's economic strength and military spending) so little has been written about it. The *mystery* is why this should be so. Economic intelligence has long been a core government capability, while throughout the Cold War efforts to acquire knowledge of the Soviet economy and its ability to support its major social, political and strategic goals was almost certainly the 'largest single project in social science research ever undertaken' (Kennedy 1991: 1). In a world of finite resources where every government objective has financial and resource implications economic intelligence sheds light on almost all political, military, and scientific and technological questions. It holds the key to assessing the industrial and financial strengths and weaknesses that advance or impede the attainment of a foreign state's domestic and international objectives.

Two concepts of economic intelligence

Intelligence is knowledge of a foreign entity as a society and a threat. Economic intelligence contributes to both these objectives. This broad prospectus is evident in the range of economic intelligence targets contained in a 1962 paper by the UK Ministry of Defence's Joint

Intelligence Bureau (JIB) for an Intelligence Research Methods Conference (Crick 1962: 4). Economic intelligence 'subjects' were listed therein as:

(i) Strategy for economic growth, effectiveness in realising economic capacity, acceleration or deceleration of growth, the amount of slack and degree of flexibility.

(ii) Increases or decreases in the economic cohesion and coordination of international groupings.

(iii) Economic factors which may lead to internal disturbances, serious dissatisfaction or political instability.

(iv) Strategic vulnerability of the economy.

(v) Resource allocation trends as bearing both on the evolution of the defence effort as a whole, and on changes within the defence effort in terms of the balance of weapons, their development and production.

(vi) Developments in external economic relations, trade and aid, and the extent to which some countries can serve as economic models for others. Degree of self-sufficiency.

The overarching administrative problem for governments has been how to acquire, analyse, assess and disseminate political, economic, military, and scientific and technological intelligence both holistically and in a timely manner. With almost infinite resources and lacking a long departmentally based intelligence tradition, the US created the CIA. This was not a feasible option for the UK. The British intelligence machinery operated within a culture that abhorred centralisation, where departments retained autonomy in their own fields, with national or coordinated assessments achieved through an interdepartmental committee. This outlook was reinforced by the constitutional accountability of ministers for their departments.

In mid-1943 Colonel Geoffrey Vickers VC, the Deputy Director of the UK's Ministry of Economic Warfare (MEW) – the department responsible for providing assessed economic intelligence to the Services and Whitehall – and its representative on the Joint Intelligence Committee (JIC) – circulated a systematic review of the nature of intelligence, the types of organisation needed to practise it effectively, and the special role of economic intelligence within it (Vickers 1943). Vickers identified six types of intelligence organisation. These included: (1) *joint intelligence organisations* 'typified by the JIC and its joint staff . . . who are specialists in nothing except in integrating their respective departments views into a combined appreciation'; (2) *specialists in departmental subjects* serving one particular master for which 'no case for centralisation arises' (e.g. the separate Service intelligence directorates); and (3) *specialists in subjects used by a range of departments* (where the only example was economic intelligence, all of which was analysed, collated and appreciated centrally in the MEW for the benefit of all potential users). Vickers proposed that centralisation should be adopted only where different departmental interests overlap and special expertise was required. *Ceteris paribus*, 'a department will always be better served by doing its own intelligence work itself', but centralised intelligence was 'entirely appropriate when the different users have much the same point of view' and necessary when the appreciation process 'can only be effectively be carried out by a monopoly'. It was also 'essential to establish an organic connection between the centralised organisation and its users' by 'drawing its staff from user departments and giving user departments a share in its control; and by establishing machinery by which user departments prescribe what is wanted and regularly test and pronounce on the result'. How well did Britain's economic intelligence capability dovetail with the central intelligence machinery?

Economic intelligence before the Cold War

British economic intelligence has a longer pedigree than the JIC and is the precursor of inter-departmental intelligence coordination in Whitehall. It emerged as an identifiable field in the absence of an authoritative intelligence machine. Its origins are found in the realisation by the fighting services and (to a much more limited extent) the FO in the late 1920s of the potential impact of rapid industrial and technological development on Britain's interests and security. While the FO's perspective was the role of economics as the harbinger of conflict of which rearmament was only a symptom, the Services emphasised how technological progress facilitated rapid mobilisation and the economic sustainability of military operations (Milne 1928; Wellesley 1930). These political and military concepts of economic intelligence, reflecting respectively support for foreign policy and for strategic military planning, were complementary: the former sought to explain why states act as they do, the latter how these intentions were translated into military capabilities.

The Services soon recognised that they lacked the professional expertise to address the economic and industrial dimensions of industrial mobilisation. This required 'a high degree of centralisation and the closest coordination' and that only 'a single organisation could deal with the problem with any prospect of success' (War Office 1931). Consequently, in 1931 the Industrial Intelligence Centre (IIC) was created as a specialist organisation targeting enemy industrial strengths and vulnerabilities and war mobilisation capabilities. Over time the IIC developed a more holistic economic approach to assessing capabilities and intentions. As the prototype of a non-departmental organisation working under the auspices of a formal committee the IIC was incontrovertibly an 'important innovation probably unique among the intelligence bureaus of the major powers in the interwar years' (Wark 1985: 159–160).

Where the Services' focus was limited to mobilisation speed and vulnerability, the FO's proposal was much more wide-ranging. Its Deputy Secretary, Sir Victor Wellesley, saw economics (in the guise of tariffs and modern industrial development, the unequal distribution of the world's natural resources and the ability of stronger nations to maintain their living standards at the expense of the weaker states) as one of the three principal causes of war. Yet the FO's organisation was predicated on a 'complete divorce between political and economic work' to the extent that no political 'department could produce a comprehensive survey of the economic position of any given country and deduce from it the probable political implications'. Wellesley's solution was a central politico-economic department working to the Permanent Under-Secretary, to collect and coordinate political and economic information and disseminate assessments to its political departments.

The two concepts developed independently and both encountered opposition from the organisations they were set up to serve. Few FO officials accepted the need for an economics department and Wellesley succeeded only in establishing a small coordination section. The Services resented the IIC's growing authority. In September the IIC and the FO's small capability were incorporated into the Intelligence Branch of the new Ministry of Economic Warfare (MEW) under the IIC's Director, Major Desmond Morton. Intelligence Branch was in two parts. Blockade Intelligence targeted Germany's external trade and efforts to limit economic relations with neutral states, thus reflecting Morton's long-held conception of economic warfare as a fourth fighting service. The smaller Economic Warfare Intelligence element, with the IIC's staff as its nucleus, was to provide the MEW's operational branches, the fighting services and other departments with targeting and strategic intelligence, including estimates of how long the German economy could continue to support war objectives, and assess its impact on shaping Germany's strategic intentions.

Economic intelligence may have been the vanguard of intelligence coordination, but the seeds of Cold War jurisdictional problems were evident throughout the 1930s. The advantages of bringing together both the IIC and the FO's limited capability (and therefore the two concepts of economic intelligence) within a dedicated ministry were considerably offset by the Services insisting on their right to receive and assess economic intelligence for their own purposes. Initially this resulted in a return to duplication of effort and competitive assessments, and a waning of the limited interdepartmental cooperation on economic intelligence achieved during the previous decade. The Services also refused to countenance military officers serving as part of an integrated civilian-military intelligence staff under civilian command even though they relied on the MEW rather than their own intelligence directorates.

In 1941 the MEW's Intelligence Directorate was rechristened Enemy Branch. Soon after his appointment in April 1941 Vickers began its transformation into a purely intelligence organisation. Support for the blockade was significantly reduced in favour of operational intelligence for the Services, especially air and land operations. Enemy Branch became the major Allied source on Russia. It developed 'new methods of economic research and measurement' and a more comprehensive 'understanding of the nature, strength and vulnerability of "war potential"'.[2] By mid-1943 it employed half the Ministry.

The Second World War consolidated economic intelligence as a separate field. Vickers was an enthusiastic advocate of the importance of a centralised economic intelligence capability to support both foreign policy and military strategy. Even so, economic intelligence was 'centralised to a greater extent than any other intelligence field' this was within 'a temporary ministry which has little organic connection with the fighting services and less with the Foreign Office and which is likely to be among the earliest wartime Ministries to disappear. It is performed almost entirely by temporary civil servants having no connections with any of the user departments' (Vickers 1943). The question of where an economic intelligence organisation meeting the different requirements of all departments should reside in peacetime had yet to be resolved. Should it be centralised in a single location or compartmented around Whitehall's economic, political and military departments?

The decision on the post-war location of economic intelligence rested with the Machinery of Government Committee (MGC) tasked with reviewing the future of the wartime departments within its wider study of the lessons of the war for Whitehall's post-war organisation. In January 1944 the MGC agreed to the early transfer of Enemy Branch to the FO to enable it to oversee the economic issues arising from the liberation of occupied Europe, for which it was the coordinating department. This took place in April 1944. However, the MGC had failed to properly grip two fundamental problems. First, the FO had no intention of becoming the repository of economic intelligence for Whitehall. It was determined to house only a small capability limited to collating, appreciating and distributing economic intelligence for its own departmental purposes, and would 'not include "specialists" who remain in it indefinitely on account to alleged expertise' (Ronald 1944). When its Economic Intelligence Department (EID) was eventually established after the end of the war in Europe it found itself at the bottom of the FO's food chain without executive responsibilities. Its life also proved to be a short one. EID ceased to exist on 29 February 1952, with the FO citing 'the overriding national need to make stringent economies'. Second, the Services would reject any dependence for military-related intelligence on the FO. In August 1945 the Chiefs of Staff agreed that the new JIB would provide economic intelligence on industrial war potential and economic vulnerability.

Cold War economic intelligence architecture

Vickers' conception of centralised economic intelligence was not implemented and in July 1945 he left Whitehall to return to his legal practice. With economic intelligence for foreign policy and defence conducted respectively in the FO and the JIB the field had reverted into its threat and societal/political compartments, with national assessments coordinated interdepartmentally though the JIC. Working relationships between the respective staffs were close. Sir Douglas Evill's 1947 report into Whitehall's intelligence organisation emphasised the 'close correlation' between their work and their use of much of the same material and suggested 'there would almost certainly be economy and general benefit from a very close touch between the two Departments' (Evill 1947). But he accepted that EID 'exists and works for a purpose entirely other than the JIB' and did not consider bringing together their respective economic functions into one agency.

The EID's demise in 1952 left the MOD in sole possession of Whitehall's economic intelligence baton. While its primary focus remained the communist bloc and Soviet threat, the range of economic intelligence topics continued to evolve and to embrace non-defence work for other Government Departments (OGDs). The creation in September 1954 of an informal interdepartmental Economic Intelligence Group (EIG) (which the JIB chaired, provided the secretariat and drafted the vast majority of studies) to assess economic developments in the communist world and secure interdepartmental agreement confirmed the JIB's economic intelligence primacy in Whitehall. It was the *de jure* lead department for all aspects of the communist economies and until the mid-1960s the *de facto* lead department for non-Bloc economies. Economic intelligence was effectively centralised in the MOD, but without any organic connection with its non-military customers. In purely organisational terms this makeshift arrangement offered no longer-term stability. Even so, it was generally effective when the all-consuming intelligence interest of the economic departments was on the communist economies and professional economic expertise in departments was almost non-existent. Bur in purely organisational terms this makeshift arrangement offered no longer-term stability.

In 1964 the JIB was assimilated into the MOD's new Defence Intelligence Staff (DIS) and its economic capability became the Directorate of Economic Intelligence (DEI). The DEI's three main customers were: (1) the MOD for defence intelligence appreciations for policy-making, procurement and defence planning; (2) the Joint Intelligence Organisation (JIO) for general intelligence assessments and current intelligence reporting; and (3) single departments and the interdepartmental machinery for economic issues outside the defence field. DEI studies were also made available NATO and allies at appropriate classification levels. It also prepared reports requested by economic departments to support British industries' export drive, some of which were passed to firms, chambers of commerce and industrial federations. In all an estimated that 80 per cent of DEI's work was of interest to OGDs (MOD 1970). Indeed, demand for its product from the civil departments had led to some DEI branches shifting their emphasis from 'largely defence to more non-defence reporting'. It was also a flexible organisation with the capacity to react to changing demands for intelligence.

Economic intelligence and the 1968 reforms

By the early 1960s it was evident that the interdepartmental economic intelligence machinery required revamping. A start was made in 1962 with the creation of the Economic Intelligence Steering Committee (EISC) as the economic counterpart of the JIC within the Cabinet Office committee system. Membership was at Under-Secretary level and its terms of reference specifically addressed the economic and applied science and technology interests of the civil departments relating to the communist block or by their activities elsewhere. It was also required to provide 'specific and concrete information about Soviet Bloc decisions or intentions, to serve as a guide to our own actions, in, for instance, trade negotiations' (EISC 1962). However, the Treasury was determined to ensure that the EISC did not stray to embrace non-bloc interdepartmental studies. When the Committee appeared to be moving in that direction the Treasury, which had hitherto played only a supporting role in interdepartmental economic intelligence, prevented it from doing so. For the Treasury economic expertise took precedence over all other considerations and detailed country-specific knowledge. Irrespective of the weight of evidence and other departments' requirements for wider politico-economic-military assessments, the Treasury could not accept that its authority and expertise should be subjected to an overriding interdepartmental review.

With the creation in the mid-1960s of the Government Economic Service (GES) – which had little professional regard for DEI's economic competence – and Whitehall's economic intelligence priorities now evolving beyond the communist world, retaining a large economic intelligence capability in the MOD as the overriding authority was no longer tenable. Although the Cabinet Secretary, Sir Burke Trend, remained convinced of the value of economic intelligence to formulating economic policy he acknowledged the failure to embed the EISC into the mainstream Cabinet Committee system as a major gap in the intelligence machine. Trend attributed this to the secrecy associated with intelligence and the 'corresponding reluctance' of the economic departments 'to be prepared to make the necessary effort of collaboration which is required of them if they are to derive any benefit from the system' (Trend 1967). He drew the lesson that an effective economic intelligence capability as part of a more professional intelligence organisation could only benefit economic policy if it was under the effective control of the Treasury and the economic departments. Economic intelligence thus formed a crucial component of his planned reorganisation of the central intelligence machinery. Consequently, in April 1968 the new Treasury-chaired JIC(B) with a remit to address economic intelligence subjects without a direct military dimension (which would be retained within the politico-military JIC(A) replaced the EISC.

Placing the JIC(B) under the control of the economic departments was but a necessary and not a sufficient condition for success. Trend also recognised that the new Committee required a permanent staff. In the short term the only source of this expertise was the DEI. A report by the Intelligence Coordinator proposed a Central Overseas Research Department (CORD) in the Cabinet Office to assume 'most of the function of the DEI and the Joint Research Department of the Foreign Office and the Commonwealth Relations Office 'and then extend its scope in the light of experience' (Intelligence Coordinator 1968). The CORD would employ specialists more effectively and also put them at the disposal of the whole government. The Cabinet Office claimed manifest advantages: removal of departmental constraints would increase the effectiveness of DEI outside the military field and of JRD (undervalued by the FCO); create a critical mass of staff 'to allow extended coverage and greater specialisation'; 'shield policy departments' from some JIC work; reduce overlapping and duplication leading to greater rationalisation and staff savings in departments. In the longer term the CORD would progressively take over functions from other departments (Gildea 1968).

This was a bold initiative. Embedding a centralised economic intelligence capability of around 100 research staff represented a major departure from Whitehall's traditional departmental system, while establishing a new committee for economic intelligence – thereby sundering the holistic link between the threat and societal elements of economic intelligence – ran counter to the philosophy of Whitehall's central intelligence machinery predicated on a multi-disciplinary approach to assessments. Both the FCO and MOD were strongly opposed. An enquiry commissioned by the Permanent Secretaries Committee on Intelligence (PSIS) and undertaken by Ronald McIntosh (Deputy Secretary in the Cabinet Office) and Ian Bancroft of the Civil Service Department (a future head of the Civil Service) came down firmly against the project (McIntosh and Bancroft 1969).

Their report identified 'two very different schools of thought in Whitehall' on the relationship between the collection and analysis of information and its integration with policy. It was 'a firm principle' that intelligence 'should be entirely separated from policy and operations; situations must be assessed objectively by people who have no Departmental or other axe to grind'. This principle had been compromised in the UK to the extent that it was 'customary to make an interdepartmentally agreed assessment of political and military intelligence as a separate exercise – even if some of those involved . . . are concerned with the subsequent action'. On the other hand, the economic departments had no 'tradition of separating the collection and analysis of information from the formulation and execution of policy'. The intelligence model was incompatible with the overarching 'emphasis on the need for individual Departments to do much more research-based policy planning'. McIntosh and Bancroft were categorical that the 'most effective deployment of highly qualified staff . . . is likely to occur if the Departments which are responsible for policy are also made accountable for the related research work'. Consequently, 'the principle of associating the research effort closely with policy . . . should be generally followed outside the strictly military field'.

The report also proposed the abolition of the DEI with its communist bloc expertise transferring to the FO to work alongside its political departments. It argued that the specialist techniques required for handling information on communist countries were not easily availably nor quickly acquired, relied to a much greater extent on covert information, and demands 'experience of Communist ways of thinking, since their economic concepts are very different from those of the West; and in this field, perhaps even more than elsewhere, economic and political developments are closely related and neither can be understood without the other'. The communist countries were therefore a special case allowing for political and economic intelligence to be brought closer together. When this proposal also proved unacceptable to the MOD the PSIS accepted that it could neither proceed with the CORD nor implement the McIntosh–Bancroft proposals.

DEI and JIC(B) survived, but both had been seriously wounded. DEI was subjected to a series of internal MOD reviews, which significantly reduced its capability to report on non-bloc issues. The JIC(B) also limped on without the promised support from the economic departments. Before passing the Cabinet Secretary's baton to his successor in 1973 Trend reported that:

> I have been concerned for some time about the JIC(B). We created this second JIC Committee on a rather experimental basis in order to ascertain whether there really was a case for JIC machinery to deal with economic intelligence separately from the politico-military intelligence which is the concern of JIC(A). But it has also been a weakly child liable to suffer from neglect and indifference on the part of the Departments which ought to be its foster parents; and I have been tempted from time to time to wind the whole thing up.
>
> (Trend 1973)

But he could not bring himself to do so. Instead he commissioned a review by the JIC(B)'s new Treasury chairman, which severely circumscribed the Committee's role. Whereas Trend had conceived the interdepartmental machinery as having a high profile role as a basis for action, the Committee was now to be a mere facilitator, responding to the requirements of the economic departments, focusing only on policy requirements. The JIC(B) was rebranded as the Overseas Economic Intelligence Committee (OEIC) so as to avoid any implication that assessments were grounded on covert information. While this was hard to reconcile with all intelligence problems having an economic dimension (and DEI's all-source practice), the existence of a separate high-level economic committee in the intelligence machine conflicted with the British philosophy of a committee coordinating intelligence as a whole. The paradox was resolved only when the OEIC was dissolved in 1980 and replaced by a JIC subcommittee chaired by the Treasury working primarily on the communist bloc and with the authority to issue reports without seeking prior JIC approval.

Recurring themes

Throughout the 50 years surveyed in this chapter, economic intelligence was a core British government intelligence objective and a major capability. It was also exceptional as, for almost all of the Cold War period, the UK's locus of economic intelligence was the MOD, from which the JIB provided Whitehall departments with assessments on the widest range of economic, financial and industrial issues. It is difficult to offer a satisfactory narrative of British intelligence without according substantial roles to Whitehall's largest assessment organisations, whose detailed studies proved to be the cornerstone of so many JIC assessments.

The conviction that economic intelligence for all departments could be delivered more effectively through a central Cabinet Office resource was alien to Whitehall's prevailing departmental culture. That economic intelligence survived at all in a separate Cabinet Office committee for as long as it did was a testament to the vital role of the DEI with its acceptance of remits when other departments went into hiding. DEI remained the intelligence machine's organisation of last resort. Whitehall departments were never confronted with the consequences of the decision to rule out a central resource and rely on the traditional committee approach. Meanwhile, in stripping DEI of much of its non-bloc resources MOD adopted an insular and not a Whitehall view of national economic intelligence requirements.

This failure of the economic departments to support JIC(B)/OEIC exhibited the hubris and false consciousness of the new swathe of GES economists, their belief in the universality of neoclassical economic theory trumping special knowledge of a foreign country, and confidence that published or otherwise accessible data through international economic organisations rendered classified intelligence redundant. Whereas intelligence analysis offered the 'faculty for imaginative insight into the decision processes of other societies and cultures, and a facility for surveying the totality of international affairs' (Strong 1968: 224), the economic departments conceived studies of the industrialised and developing worlds as purely economic questions. They therefore failed to build on the advantages of a holistic approach setting economic assessments in the context of the overall national capabilities and ambitions of foreign countries.

Laqueur's definition of economic intelligence was US-centric. The historical evidence confirms that its overtly technical approach has only limited application to the UK where economic intelligence problems were viewed rather more in *intelligence* than in *economic* terms and where the application of intelligence skills was as important as professional economic qualifications. With few classically trained economists and overriding security concerns limiting access to academic expertise, British practice is characterised as that of staff in intelligence agencies tackling intelligence problems with an economic dimension, i.e. how intelligence analysts treated economic issues.

Economic intelligence was a casualty of Whitehall's departmental system, its abhorrence of centralisation, and its generalist culture which undervalued specialist research. In contrast to the

US, where the CIA gradually acquired jurisdiction over economic intelligence and extended its field of responsibility, the UK held fast against a centralised holistic capability. The result was a net loss of capability at the very moment it was required to assess emerging global issues. Britain was less well informed about its competitors' economic conditions and, at worst, ill-equipped to judge their capabilities. Historical analysis of the institutions and practice of economic intelligence offers evidence to support the conviction that the 'collective interest is too often dominated and distorted by sectional interests' (Blackstone and Plowden 1988: 12–13).

Notes

1   TNA, BA 25/41 (Littler 1967).
2   TNA, T 223/53, *Report on the Demobilization of the Ministry of Economic Warfare*, 19 May 1943.

11

MEASUREMENT AND SIGNATURE INTELLIGENCE

Matthew M. Aid

MASINT in the real world

You may not know what it is or what it does, but measurement and signature intelligence (MASINT) has been around for decades; you just probably never recognised it as such. Here are a few examples demonstrating the importance of MASINT during the Cold War era:

- Through much of the Cold War, a pair of AN/FPS-17 long-range surveillance radars at Pirinclik, Turkey, and Shemya Island, Alaska, were among the most important sources available to the US intelligence community for reliable information on the performance characteristics of new Soviet ballistic missiles being tested from the Kapustin Yar and Tyuratam missile test centres, such as the missile's speed, thrust, trajectory, acceleration, course and altitude. These radars also proved to be an important means of also detecting and tracking Soviet manned and unmanned space launches from Tyuratam (Zabetakis and Peterson 1964).
- During the 1962 Cuban Missile Crisis, the US Navy put modified Geiger counters on helicopters and flew them over the Soviet merchant ships coming in and out of Cuba in an attempt to determine if any of these ships were carrying nuclear weapons (GMAIC/JAEIC/NPIC 1962).
- In the 1960s the US Air Force secretly installed long-range surveillance radar inside a radome at Tempelhof airfield in West Berlin, which gave the US intelligence community complete coverage of all Soviet and Warsaw Pact military and civil flight activity over East Germany, as well as western Poland and parts of northern Czechoslovakia. The data from the Tempelhof radar was of enormous importance in the months leading up to the Soviet invasion of Czechoslovakia on 20 August 1968, picking up a dramatic increase in Soviet Air Force flight activity in East Germany and western Poland as early as 20 June 1968 (COM 1968).
- At the height of the 1973 Middle East War crisis, a US Navy clandestine intelligence unit in Istanbul, Turkey set off alarm bells across Washington, DC, when it reported that its nuclear intelligence (NUCINT) sensors had detected what were believed to be nuclear weapons in the hold of a Soviet merchant ship that was steaming through the Dardanelles bound for Alexandria, Egypt (CIA 1973).

- The first, and perhaps the only, time that MASINT was utilised to its fullest potential and with any degree of coherency was during Operations Desert Shield/Desert Storm in 1990–91, when a wide-range of MASINT sensors provided timely and critically important intelligence information about Iraq's nuclear, chemical, and biological warfare activities, as well as Scud ballistic missile launch activities. For example, during Operation Desert Storm, DSP satellites successfully detected all 88 Iraqi Scud launches and were able to provide approximate locations for the launchers (Chapman 1997: 19).

What is MASINT?

For the past 40 years, American intelligence officials have struggled with the nagging question of just what MASINT is. There are plenty of unclassified definitions around, both official and unofficial, but no one can seem to agree on just one. For example, the Defense Intelligence Agency (DIA), which has always been responsible for managing the US intelligence community's MASINT collection and analytic programs, has defined MASINT as intelligence 'derived from specific sensors for the purpose of identifying any distinctive features associated with the source, emitter, or sender, and to facilitate subsequent identification of the same' (DIA 2 1979: 26).

But, as the reader will readily agree, this highly ambiguous definition does not answer the question of what MASINT actually does because it could apply just as aptly to the heat sensors in a toaster oven as a technical intelligence sensor. So the definition of what MASINT is has changed repeatedly as its partisans have tried time and again to get the US intelligence community to accept it as an intelligence discipline deserving of the same level of resources and respect as the larger and better established human intelligence (HUMINT), signals intelligence (SIGINT), and imagery intelligence (IMINT) programs.

A big part of the problem is that MASINT began as a budgetary compartment into which were placed all non-SIGINT or IMINT technical intelligence collection systems. In the mid-1970s the US DIA coined the idiom 'MASINT' so that it could lump together into a single budgetary line-item all of the non-SIGINT or IMINT technical collection sensors that it was responsible for getting Congress to approve money for. The term stuck simply because it was a simple and effective way for harried congressional staffers and officials at the Office of Management and Budget (OMB) to categorise these systems for budgeting purposes. It is from these humble beginnings that MASINT traces its origins (DIA 1 1994: 8–9).

As has been the case since the term was first coined almost forty years ago, MASINT remains a hodgepodge of dozens of unrelated technical intelligence collection programs and one-off purpose-made sensors which monitor what American intelligence professionals obliquely refer to as geophysical phenomena, such as seismic, acoustic, hydroacoustic, hydromagnetic, electro-optical, radio frequency and infrared emissions, as well as a host of other radiating or emitting sources. In other words, MASINT is involved in monitoring any foreign weapons systems, vehicles, devices and/or industrial processes that emit what is euphemistically referred to as a 'signature', which as one can imagine covers a lot of ground. See Figure 6.1 for a listing of the six intelligence sub-disciplines, which comprise MASINT today.

Among the kinds of intelligence products that MASINT sensors produce are detailed reports on the unique heat signatures of ICBM launches or plants engaged in the manufacture of fissile materials for nuclear weapons, electronic emissions from unshielded computer systems, radar/infrared signatures of ballistic missiles in flight, or the unique acoustic signatures of submarine propulsion plants. MASINT is also concerned with the collection and analysis of seismic and hydroacoustic data, as well as nuclear particulate and gaseous effluents that are the detritus of nuclear weapons tests (Morris 1996: 24; Fulghum 1999: 50).

Take for example the different kinds of information that MASINT sensors can provide about an ordinary helicopter in flight. A MASINT acoustic sensor can identify the exact make and model of the helicopter by comparing the acoustic signature generated by its rotor blades with those of other helicopters. A MASINT radar sensor can provide fine-grained signature data on the craft's exact size, shape, weight, and flight performance, such as its speed and altitude. And MASINT infrared scanners can track the helicopter's movements at night by focusing on the heat signature generated by the aircraft's engine, and can usually tell you roughly how many passengers are inside the helicopter by counting the heat sources in the cabin.

To the layperson, this would seem to be an inordinate amount of time and precious resources being spent collecting highly esoteric information about a lowly helicopter, which, it could be argued, would be of marginal interest to the average intelligence analyst or high-level consumer of intelligence reporting. This is indeed true. But anyone with a passing familiarity with the way intelligence organisations work will recognise that in every country's intelligence service there will always be a small constituency of engineers, analysts and consumers, the so-called 'techno nerds', who want exactly this kind of arcane technical information. MASINT is their intelligence discipline.

The result is that many (but not all) senior American intelligence officials I have spoken to over the past 25 years believe that MASINT is not a coherent and clearly definable intelligence discipline per se, but rather a catch-all, *omnibus gatherum* collection of technical intelligence sensor systems that have been lumped together as a matter of convenience because they cannot be neatly fit for categorisation purposes anywhere else. These critics may be correct from a strictly business management point of view, where coherency, rationalisation and synergies determine who gets the budget resources and who does not.

MASINT may be the misunderstood and underappreciated stepchild of the US intelligence community, but there is no denying that it has always been a source of critically important intelligences.

MASINT sensors

In order to give the reader a clearer sense of what MASINT is all about, what follows is a selective, but by no means comprehensive, listing of different kinds of MASINT collection programmes and sensor systems that have been used in the past or are still in use today by the US intelligence community:

- Since 1947, the US Air Force has operated on behalf of the US government what is generically referred to as the Atomic Energy Detection System (AEDS), whose mission it is to detect nuclear weapons explosions around the world using a wide array of manned and unmanned MASINT sensor systems. Compared with the CIA and NSA, the AEDS was a relatively small endeavour. As of 1984, 1,300 military and civilian personnel were operating 19 detachments, four operating locations and more than 50 unmanned equipment locations in the US and 35 countries around the world engaged in monitoring foreign nuclear weapons testing activities (US Air Force 1984). The AEDS system is still functioning today under the aegis of the Air Force Technical Applications Center (AFTAC), whose headquarters is located at Patrick Air Force Base, Florida. Among the $300 million worth of MASINT collection systems currently utilised by AFTAC are ground-based seismic, hydroacoustic and electromagnetic pulse (EMP) detection stations, reconnaissance aircraft engaged in airborne nuclear particulate collection, and VELA satellites designed to detect the unique signatures of atmospheric nuclear weapons explosions (AFTAC 1997).

- The Sound Surveillance System (SOSUS) was the US Navy's principal source for operational intelligence on movements and deployment patterns of Soviet submarines during the Cold War. At its height in 1983, there were 50 SOSUS hydrophone arrays installed in four major ocean basins in the North Atlantic and Pacific Oceans that were connected to 17 shore-based processing facilities called Naval Facilities (NAVFACs) – nine in the Pacific and eight in the Atlantic littoral – manned by about 150 US Navy officers and 1,800 enlisted men. The SOSUS hydrophone arrays provided the US Navy with a 24/7, all-weather capability for detecting and tracking the movements of Soviet and other foreign submarines over large portions of the North Atlantic and Pacific Oceans, including the Norwegian and Bering Seas. Depending on its mode of operation and sea conditions, SOSUS could detect Soviet submarines out to a range of 5,000 nautical miles with an extraordinary degree of accuracy (Weir 2006).
- The first Defense Support Program (DSP) early warning satellite was launched in November 1970 into geosynchronous orbit 22,000 miles above the Earth. These satellites were equipped with extremely sensitive 12-foot-long infrared telescopes, which were capable of spotting the heat plumes generated by foreign missile and space vehicles immediately after they were launched. In the 1980s the infrared sensors on the DSP satellites were so accurate that they could detect the location of a missile launch down to less than three miles, and could determine in less than ten seconds if the missile's azimuth track indicated an attack on the United States (Richelson 1999). For example, on 12 June 1981, DSP satellites detected the near-simultaneous launch of three Soviet SS-20 intermediate-range ballistic missiles (IRBMs) from the Drovyanaya missile complex to the Kamchatka Peninsula (DEFSMAC 1981). DSP is being replaced by a new early warning satellite system called the Space-Based Infrared System (SBIRS) (Richelson 2012: 243).
- The US Air Force flew three RC-135S COBRA BALL reconnaissance aircraft, which were used to monitor the terminal phase of Soviet ballistic missile tests beginning in October 1969 (Strategic Air Command 1973: 89). These aircraft not only carried a very sophisticated automated telemetry intercept suite, but also a number of fine-grained optical intelligence sensors that are capable of measuring with extraordinary accuracy the size, weight and other physical parameters of the missile warheads. These COBRA BALL aircraft are still flying intelligence collection missions around the world monitoring foreign missile tests and space launches (US House of Representatives 1996: 153).
- COBRA DANE was a one-of-a-kind phased-array radar system located on Shemya Island, Alaska. Between July 1977 and the mid-1990s, Cobra Dane took detailed radar measurements of the terminal phase of all Soviet ICBM and SLBM re-entry vehicles before they impacted at the Klyuchi impact area on the Kamchatka Peninsula, as well as monitored the flight paths of Soviet manned spacecraft and unmanned satellite systems in orbit over the Earth (Air Force Space Command 1990).
- COBRA JUDY was a one-of-a-kind shipborne phased-array radar system mounted on the deck of a converted freighter called the USNS *Observation Island*, which was used to monitor the terminal phase of Soviet ballistic missile tests to Kamchatka and the mid-

Pacific. During the Cold War, the *Observation Island* cruised just off the coast of Kamchatka or in the mid-Pacific for 200 days a year taking detailed radar measurements of every Soviet ballistic missile test, which allowed American intelligence analysts to accurately gauge the missiles' size, performance and the accuracy of their re-entry vehicles. COBRA JUDY is still operational, but now used for monitoring the occasional Chinese or North Korean ballistic missile test (*Cryptologic Quarterly* 1983: 79). *Observation Island* and its COBRA JUDY radar are still operational, sailing periodically from its home base at Pearl Harbor, Hawaii, to monitor foreign missile tests. But it does not operate alone. In the 1990s the US Air Force fielded a new shipborne missile monitoring system called COBRA GEMINI, which consisted of two X- and S-band radars placed on a Military Sealift Command ship called the USNS *Invincible*. With a range of 1,200 kilometres, these radars can track with incredible precision the flights of ballistic missiles being tested by less-developed nations around the world, while *Observation Island* focuses on strategic targets like Russia and China.

- The E-8C Joint Surveillance Target Attack Radar System (JSTARS) aircraft is an example of a currently operational airborne radar intelligence (RADINT) collection system. Fielded in the 1980s, each JSTARS aircraft carries an electronically steerable 25-foot radar antenna, which is so accurate that it can provide with incredible precision information about enemy troop movements and the locations of troop concentrations and weapons systems on the battlefield (Chapman 1997: 19).

- In the 1970s the US Navy fielded an airborne acoustic intelligence (ACOUSTINT) system called BEARTRAP on five P-3 Orion anti-submarine warfare patrol aircraft, which was used to track the movements of Soviet submarines and monitor their sonar emissions and underwater communications. Some of the sensors on these planes were so sophisticated that they could measure the strength of the submarine hulls they were monitoring.

- The Navy also fielded in the 1970s a sophisticated intelligence collection suite on four P-3 ORION ASW aircraft called Clipper Troop, which consisted of SIGINT as well as photo, nuclear, acoustic and infrared MASINT sensors, which were used to covertly collect intelligence on the activities of Soviet warships and submarines around the world. The gamma-neutron detector sensors on the aircraft could even determine if there were nuclear weapons on board the Soviet ships.

- Since the launch of the first SSN-637 Sturgeon-class nuclear attack submarines in March 1967, every US Navy attack submarine has been equipped with a broad range of SIGINT as well as MASINT intelligence collection systems. For example, each Sturgeon-class submarine carried a series of very sensitive acoustic intelligence (ACOUSTINT) systems, which recorded and analysed the sonar emissions of enemy warships, submarines and anti-submarine warfare aircraft, as well as homing torpedo signals. Each Sturgeon-class boat also deployed a wide array of sophisticated optical intelligence (OPTINT) sensors attached to the sub's periscope, which allowed the boat's commander to take incredibly fine-grained photographs of enemy ships, submarines and shore installations while surfaced or even submerged (US Navy 1985).

- Some MASINT sensors are extremely specialised and esoteric in nature. For example, in the early 1980s the US Army wanted more information about the laser rangefinders being used on the new generation of Soviet T-62 and T-72 tanks. In response, the US Army Intelligence and Security Command (INSCOM) developed and built a series of new 'laser intelligence', or LASINT, sensors specifically for this purpose. In 1982, these sensor system, codenamed CEILING SEARCH, CAIRN TRIUMPH and CAIRN EMPEROR, were placed on top of a tower on the West German border near the town of Wobeck, from where they could monitor the annual field manoeuvres conducted by the Soviet Third Shock Army across the border at the Letzlinger Heide Training Area in East Germany (Odom 1982).

- MASINT even has battlefield applications, but on a very limited scale. In the 1980s the US Army fielded a system called REMBASS (Remotely Monitored Battlefield Sensor System), which consisted of small seismic, acoustic, magnetic and infrared sensors that could be easily hidden on the battlefield and used to monitor in real-time enemy vehicular traffic and troop movements out to a distance of 100 kilometres from the sensor monitoring team. The US Army tried to use REMBASS in Afghanistan after the October 2001 invasion of that country, but without much success. For instance, an unattended seismic sensor array emplaced along a strategic mountain pass north of the city Kandahar had to be abandoned after US Army troops tired of repeatedly responding to alert signals every time local villagers and their horses or donkeys were detected travelling the pass on their way to sell their goods or wares in Kandahar (Dominguez 2003).

- America's clandestine intelligence operators also are practitioners of MASINT. The CIA's Office of Technical Collection (OTC) and its antecedents have been heavily involved in clandestine MASINT collection for decades. For example, during the Cold War, the CIA and the US military experienced considerable success intercepting electronic emissions from unshielded typewriters, printers, computer systems and cipher machines inside foreign government offices, embassies and consulates. In February 1986, the KGB seized a railroad freight container that was travelling across the USSR on the Trans-Siberian Railway from Japan to West Germany. When the container was opened, the Soviets found that it contained an array of CIA technical intelligence-gathering equipment. The CIA project, designated CK-ABSORB, was a $60 million project designed to monitor the shipment of Soviet nuclear warheads along the Trans-Siberian Railway. This operation was compromised by a KGB spy inside the CIA, Aldrich H. Ames. The Soviets put the CK-ABSORB equipment on show in Moscow in August 1987 (JDW 1987).

A square peg in a round hole: MASINT management woes

As important as the intelligence derived from the individual MASINT sensors has been over the past 50-plus years, managing these collection assets has proven to be nothing short of a nightmare for the US intelligence community.

In the early 1980s, the US intelligence community stepped into the morass in an attempt to better manage the various disparate MASINT programmes. In March 1983, the Director of Central Intelligence organised a MASINT Subcommittee of the National SIGINT Committee as the first step towards formally recognising that MASINT was fast reaching national-level importance as a source of intelligence (SIGINT Committee 1983). But it was not until 1986 that a separate MASINT Committee was established to determine national policy for this intelligence discipline, as well as validate collection and processing requirements submitted by intelligence consumers. In 1992, a Central MASINT Office (CMO) was established by the DIA to perform oversight and centralised management over all MASINT collection and processing activities (DIA 1 1994: 8–9).

But the CMO proved to be a failure as a programme-management tool. It was unable to build consensus or recognition within the US intelligence community for the importance of

MASINT. And, as a management tool, the CMO failed to effectively meld all six MASINT sub-disciplines into a single integrated programme. In the aftermath of 9/11, the US intelligence community finally recognised that the MASINT system was failing and was in urgent need of a drastic makeover. On 15 December 2004, Director of Central Intelligence Porter J. Goss told the intelligence community in no uncertain terms that 'Past efforts to manage MASINT have been hampered by an unrealistic view of MASINT as a single enterprise. MASINT in the National Foreign Intelligence Program is too diverse to be managed, functionally or otherwise, by a single authority' (Goss 2004).

Which brings us back to where this chapter began, which is that the fundamental problem with MASINT is that it is not really an intelligence discipline at all. Rather, it is a loose conglomeration of, for the most part, unrelated and very technical intelligence collection sensors and vehicles that have little, if anything, in common with one another other than the fact that they have all been lumped together because they do not neatly belong anywhere else. According to long-time intelligence scholar Dr Jeffrey T. Richelson, 'In many ways, MASINT is more a description of the product, stemming from a particular type of analysis of the data produced by a variety of collection activities, than a coherent collection activity itself' (Richelson 2012: 241).

Lacking any discernible coherency, with few synergistic ties that bind its various components together, and without any meaningful high-level patronage within the US intelligence community, MASINT has always been generally looked upon by senior US intelligence officials as the bastard stepchild of the intelligence community.

As a result, MASINT has never been truly understood or appreciated within the US intelligence community, and as such, has never been used to its fullest potential. A 1996 congressional study found 'MASINT, as a specific and unique discipline, is not well understood by both the IC [intelligence community] and user communities. Therefore, the potential of its future contributions may be limited' (US House of Representatives 1996: 144).

Almost ten years later, not much had improved. In the aftermath of the 2002 Iraqi Weapons of Mass Destruction intelligence failure, a 2005 review panel still found a 'general lack of understanding of, and respect for, MASINT' (WMD Report 2005: 242, fn 754).

Even the DIA, historically MASINT's strongest advocate within the US intelligence community, admitted that ignorance of its capabilities within the US intelligence community is the core problem with MASINT. The DIA has spent decades trying, sometimes half-heartedly, to proselytise within the military services for greater recognition and respect for MASINT, but with only marginal results to show for its efforts. A 1994 secret report stated that:

> the full war fighting potential of this diversified technical intelligence collection discipline has not been fully realised. Despite the lessons learned from DESERT SHIELD and DESERT STORM, a general lack of understanding and awareness of how existing (or future) MASINT capabilities could be applied in support of military operations prevails.
>
> *(DIA 1 1994: 1–2)*

The six MASINT sub-disciplines

Electro-optical intelligence

Electro-optical intelligence (EOINT) is concerned with the collection of emitted or reflected radiations across the optical portion of the electromagnetic spectrum, i.e. visible, ultraviolet and infrared, using sensors like radiometers, spectrometers, non-literal imaging systems, lasers or laser radars. Electro-optical intelligence is broken down into three general sub-disciplines: infrared intelligence (IRINT), optical intelligence (OPTINT) and laser intelligence (LASINT):

1. Infrared intelligence (IRINT) includes sensors that collect data across the infrared portion of the electromagnetic spectrum.
2. Optical intelligence (OPTINT) involves collection across the visible, ultraviolet and near-infrared portions of the electromagnetic spectrum.
3. Laser intelligence (LASINT) gathers data on foreign laser communications systems, target illuminators, laser rangefinders, or directed-energy weapons, such as space- or ground-based laser systems.

Radar intelligence

Radar intelligence (RADINT) is intelligence information obtained by tracking foreign military activities, manned and unmanned space flights, and weapons systems testing by use of a variety of radar sensors. A number of different radars have been, or are currently being, used by the US for intelligence-gathering purposes, such as line-of-sight, monostatic or bistatic, phased array, synthetic aperture radar (SAR), and over-the-horizon (OTH) radar systems.

Radio-frequency (RF) intelligence

RF Intelligence comprised two sub-disciplines: radio-frequency/electro-magnetic pulse intelligence (RF/EMP), and unintentional radio intelligence (RINT):

1. RF/EMP intelligence involves the collection of electro-magnetic pulse (EMP) signals associated with nuclear weapons or high-energy weapons testing activities.
2. Unintentional radiation intelligence (RINT) is intelligence derived from the collection and analysis of non-information-bearing elements extracted from the electromagnetic energy unintentionally emanated by foreign electronic devices, equipment, and systems (excluding those generated by the detonation of atomic weapons).

Geophysical intelligence

Geophysical intelligence (GEOINT) is concerned with characterising and measuring the geo-physical phenomena normally associated with nuclear weapons detonations, such as acoustic, seismic, and magnetic waves. Acoustic intelligence refers to the collection of intelligence information derived from monitoring sounds, pressure waves or vibrations radiated through air (ACOUSTINT), water (ACINT) or the earth's surface (Seismic). Examples of ACINT sensors include sonar sensors, which detect the presence and location of ships and other weap-ons systems in the water; SOSUS underwater acoustic sensors, which are used to monitor the movements and locate submarines; or ground-based acoustic sensors, which can detect pressure waves from atmospheric nuclear weapons blasts.

Materials intelligence

Materials intelligence is the collection of atmospheric trace elements; gaseous, liquid or solid particulates; effluents or debris. This discipline is focused primarily on foreign nuclear, chemical or biological weapons research, development, and testing activities, although it does have other non-military applications as well.

Nuclear intelligence

Nuclear intelligence (NUCINT) refers to the collection of intelligence information about the nuclear radiation or other physical phenomena associated with nuclear weapons detonations, such as the identification and characterisation of the fissile materials used in the weapons (plutonium, uranium or both), and the monitoring of radio frequency emissions resulting from nuclear weapons detonations, such as electromagnetic pulse (EMP), X-ray, gamma-ray, and neutron emissions from nuclear weapons detonations.

(Source: Defense Intelligence Agency (DIA) 1 (1994) 2–5, DIA FOIA)

12

OPEN SOURCE INTELLIGENCE

Stevyn D. Gibson

The problem of definition: get over it

The exploitation of open sources of information is not new. Its contemporary prevalence is a reflection of the increasing volume, immediacy and accessibility of today's mobile digital information and communication technologies (ICT). Like the concept of intelligence, the definition of open source intelligence (OSINT) is debatable. OSINT is defined here as 'the exploitation of information legally available in the public domain'. The definition works, but it is problematic. What is the public domain? How do we determine 'legally available'? Who does the exploitation? When WikiLeaks dumped thousands of secret documents into the public domain via the internet during 2010–11, the US Library of Congress, bizarrely, was forbidden from using them in its own assessments because they remained classified. Yet, they were available to anyone with an internet connection, including, presumably, Library of Congress researchers on PCs at home.

OSINT's contribution is usually 'measured' in efficiency terms – inputs related to outputs. It is more useful to explore its effectiveness – what it can do for the intelligence function. In terms of efficiency OSINT claims 80 per cent of intelligence output; yet, despite this, remains 'second-class' to closed 'ints'. In terms of effectiveness, it can replicate 'secret' sources, form the matrix to bind all other intelligence sources together, and has its own distinct attributes to offer; but, is no more a 'silver bullet' for policy than those same closed 'ints'.

Hidden in plain sight

In March 2002, John Darwin canoed out into the North Sea from the English seaside town of Seaton Carew and faked his suicide. By February 2003 he had moved back into the family home to live secretly with his wife Anne. In March 2003 a death certificate was granted and his wife began the fraudulent process of recovering the insurance on her husband's supposed death. Between 2003 and 2007 the couple travelled abroad and constructed a new life away from the UK authorities as well as a few suspicious people at home. They set up a home and business in Panama. Then, in December 2007, John Darwin walked into a London police station claiming amnesia; he was 'reviving' his identity in order to satisfy new Panamanian investment laws. The police had already begun investigations into possible fraudulent activity three months earlier. Yet, they failed to connect Anne Darwin's frequent trips abroad with her husband's adventures in Panama. Five days after his return the *Daily Mirror* published a photograph of the Darwins with their Panamanian estate agent. The photograph had been taken in 2006 and published on the internet as part of the estate agent's marketing campaign. This photograph had been discovered by a 'suspicious' member of the public, who had simply typed 'John', 'Anne' and

'Panama' into Google. She informed Cleveland police of the result. They expressed 'surprise' at the simplicity of this public-spirited piece of detective work, but it took the *Daily Mirror* to convince them. The information had been openly available in plain sight for 18 months.

Hindsight is a wonderful thing – the scourge of intelligence practitioners. This is but one of myriad examples of information in support of law enforcement being hidden in plain sight. Today, such is the proliferation of social networking that law enforcement, security, and intelligence agencies exploit these mobile, digital, internet-based resources for evidence of law-breaking, self-incrimination and acts preparatory to law-breaking. Whether they do this routinely, efficiently and effectively, let alone ethically, and without subverting privacy or justice, remain important arguments.

There is nothing new under the sun

In 1808, Wellington assembled his generals before departing for the Peninsular War and admonished them for their ignorance of Napoleon's new French infantry formations being openly reported in *The Times*. In 1826, Henry Brougham, the radical Whig politician, established the Society for the Diffusion of Useful Knowledge. Its aim was: 'to impart useful information to all classes of the community'. This utopian dream of knowledge transforming society sounds strikingly similar to that of Google today: 'To organize the world's information and make it universally accessible and useful'. The society closed in 1848. Its product was considered erratic and miscellaneous. One might add idealist, naïve and absent of political purpose. It thought that the provision of information was the end game, and in doing so elevated means to ends. Contemporary open source evangelists – WikiLeaks – pioneer similar utopian visions for 'open' information. Finally, for the nineteenth century, Jane's commercial open source publication *Fighting* Ships was established in 1898.

The formation of institutional 'state-sponsored' organisations by which open sources of information are exploited for 'modern' or 'industrial' intelligence purposes can be pegged to the creation of the UK's BBC Monitoring Service in 1938 (now BBC Monitoring). Its US equivalent – Foreign Broadcast Monitoring Service, later Foreign Broadcast Information Service (FBIS), and today's Open Source Center (OSC) – emerged in 1941. Both were formed in response to the invention of radio; in particular, its use in the 1930s as a tool by the Axis Powers for the dissemination of propaganda. Not only did they monitor broadcast media as a collection activity in its own right, but they also gauged the response to our own propaganda broadcast as part of wider and more nuanced information operations – much as they do now.

That 'monitoring' became categorised as 'open' and 'interception' as 'closed' was partly a reflection of the intended nature of the data transmitted – public versus secret – and partly to conceal from the target that it was being collected against. As the two world wars merged into the Cold War, TECHINT and SIGINT penetrated the secretive nature of 'Eastern Bloc' society, and the satellite platform became to collection what the internet is to collection today. 'At home' secrecy dominated the capabilities-orientated intelligence requirements of the Cold War in order to protect sources, methods and product from 'the enemy'. Although OSINT played the junior partner to closed collection, organisations such as the Soviet Studies Research Centre in the UK evolved alongside the BBC Monitoring Service to reveal secrets – capabilities – and chip away at mysteries – intentions – through examination of open source media.

Today, contemporary ICT, built on digitisation and miniaturisation, and enhanced by the cellphone, provides new platforms for intelligence, as well as a 'new', more 'open' globalised society. OSINT is re-blooming in both this technological evolution and the 'opening up' of formerly closed societies.

The '80 per cent rule': the elephant in the room

> A proper analysis of the intelligence obtainable by these overt, normal and aboveboard means would supply us with over 80 percent, I should estimate, of the information required for the guidance of our national policy.
>
> *(Allen Dulles, in Grose 1994: 525–528)*

Allen Dulles's testimony to the Senate Committee on Armed Services (25 April 1947) was only nine pages long and hastily written; but, in it, he began the process of the demystification of the art of intelligence, adding:

> Because of its glamour and mystery, overemphasis is generally placed on what is called secret intelligence, namely the intelligence that is obtained by secret means and by secret agents . . . In time of peace the bulk of intelligence can be obtained through overt channels, through our diplomatic and consular missions, and our military, naval and air attachés in the normal and proper course of their work. It can also be obtained through the world press, the radio, and through the many thousands of Americans, business and professional men and American residents of foreign countries, who are naturally and normally brought in touch with what is going on in those countries.

This 80 per cent claim originated the now revered quantification of open source contribution to intelligence. This contribution is widely repeated by many practitioners, commentators and customers. NATO considers that OSINT provides 80 per cent of final product for arms control and arms proliferation issues (NATO 2002). Hulnick suggests that 80 per cent of US Cold War analysis could have been taken from open sources (Hulnick 2004: 6). Steele's view is that, across the board, OSINT can provide 80 per cent of what any government needs to know and 90 per cent for private-sector organisations.[1] For some collection agencies, 90 per cent is the norm: NATO; EUROPOL; UK MOD; Swedish MOD; Dutch MOD; US DIA; CIA; and UK HMRC-LE to list a few in public/government sectors. The CIA's Bin Laden unit, noted that '90 percent of what you need to know comes from open source intelligence' (Glasser 2005). EUROPOL suggests that the contribution might be as high as 95 per cent for counterterrorism issues (Gibson 2007: Appendices, Interview EUROPOL 4). Similarly, the 1996 Aspin–Brown Commission remarked that: 'In some areas . . . it is estimated that as much as 95 per cent of the information utilised now comes from open sources' (Brown–Aspin 1996). Responding to the report of the 1997 US Commission on Secrecy, the grand-master of US foreign policy, George F. Kennan, wrote to Commission Chairman Senator Daniel P. Moynihan:

> It is my conviction, based on some 70 years of experience, first as a Government official and then in the past 45 years as a historian, that the need by our government for secret intelligence about affairs elsewhere in the world has been vastly overrated. I would say that something upward of 95 percent of what we need to know could be very well obtained by the careful and competent study of perfectly legitimate sources of information open and available to us in the rich library and archival holdings of this country. Much of the remainder, if it could not be found here (and there is very little of it that could not), could easily be nonsecretively elicited from similar sources abroad.
>
> *(Kennan 1997)*

Finally, but not exhaustively, in 2005, a former Deputy Assistant Director of Central Intelligence for Analysis and Production stated that 95–98 per cent of all information handled by the US intelligence community derives from open sources. It would seem, then, that OSINT constitutes a significant majority of the intelligence effort as recorded by those who best know.

The elephant: the '80 per cent rule': is not a gorilla but a fish

However, this oft-quoted estimate that 80 per cent or more of final intelligence product is generated from open source exploitation is also a mischievous 'red herring'. How is the figure calculated? What is the yardstick of measurement? Where are the repeatable corroborable data by which it is determined? The evidence is anecdotal; subjectively assessed rather than methodically derived. Moreover, while 80 per cent represents a substantial elephant in the intelligence room, and may inform how input is related to output, it should not be misconstrued as an evaluation of effectiveness.

Furthermore, this broad 80 per cent estimate does not equate to all intelligence subjects equally, or simultaneously.[2] In the mid-1990s the US government's Community Open Source Program (COSP) estimated OSINT contribution to be in the range of 40 per cent overall, while specific contributions, depending upon target difficulty, ranged from 10 per cent in denied-area, secret-issue matters, to 90 per cent on international economics. This COSP estimate may be the only methodically derived data-point for the evaluation of OSINT's contribution. As Markowitz suggests, much of the chatter surrounding the 80 per cent claim might be no more than circular reporting of Dulles's original estimate.[3] Once stated by respected members of the intelligence community it passes into lore.

Even if these estimates are correct, at best they are only expressions of efficiency – an important argument for the allocation of scarce intelligence resources – but they do not reveal any understanding of OSINT's contribution to decision or policy-making effectiveness. Certainly, this 80 per cent label is not matched by the weight of an 800lb gorilla in terms of those scarce resources devoted to it (Johnson 2003b).

Regardless of the general attribution and subjective estimate of OSINT's contribution, the obvious question ought to be 'What is it 80 per cent or 95 per cent of? Is it output measured by paragraphs in a final intelligence report, actions enumerated by arrests and threat interdictions, or clearly observable policy achievements?'

Any obsession should be with the meaning rather than the number. As RAND and Gill and Phythian have all noted, intelligence effectiveness is a slippery concept to pin down, let alone measure (Gill and Phythian 2006: 18; RAND 2006: 26–29). Odom, similarly, bemoans the fact that nowhere within the intelligence community are inputs related to outputs:

> Because the DCI has never made the effort to impose a similar system (to the Defense Department) on resource management in the Intelligence Community, its consolidated Intelligence Community budget does not effectively relate inputs to outputs.
>
> *(Odom 2003: 32)*

Instead of traditional benchmarks of quantity and quality of data gathered, Odom argues that effectiveness should be measured according to how much output is used by, and meets the needs of, its customers. Interestingly, the US Army begins to construct such an argument: 'determining whether PIRs [priority intelligence requirements] have been answered' (US Army 2004: 1–8). The US Joint Chiefs expand it by recognising that intelligence evaluation is undertaken by the customer, based upon: 'the attributes of good intelligence: anticipatory, timely, accurate, usable, complete, relevant, objective, available' (US DoD 2004: III, 56–57).

The UK intelligence community similarly confuses efficiency with effectiveness. Its Intelligence and Security Committee relates inputs to outputs through 'top-level management tools' ensuring 'business' objectives are met within the Intelligence Agencies; the resulting Public Service Agreements and Service Delivery Agreements reflecting a transfer to resource-based accounting processes. Worse, they equate process for purpose and confuse means with ends.

Thus, today's 'best' determination of effectiveness seems to reside with the customer or the accountant. Yet, customer satisfaction, business targets and balancing scorecards generate little meaningful illumination upon the effectiveness of intelligence in relation to policy objectives. In order to evaluate OSINT's contribution, it seems crucial to understand how it is effective both absolutely within the intelligence function and relatively to closed intelligence.

Open source exploitation: intelligence's 'silver bullets'

> Compared with the more traditional or esoteric intelligence techniques, it is often faster, more economical, more prolific, or more authoritative.
>
> *(Herman L. Croom, in Croom 1969)*

In 1969, Croom – a CIA officer – summarised much of the contemporary debate surrounding OSINT in just seven pages. He recognised the key benefit of OSINT's contribution – a more equitable policy towards intelligence resource allocation. He argued a case for its efficacy using nuclear weapons proliferation and the developing international situations of Africa, Latin America and South-East Asia as case studies. He recommended the establishment of an open source agency – *outside* the CIA – specifically instructed to treat this intelligence species.

More recently, Sands articulated five contributing factors that OSINT offers relative to closed: an assessment frame of reference; the protection of closed material; credibility; ready access; and enhanced assessment methodology (Sands 2005: 63–78). This author's research across contemporary intelligence, security, law enforcement and corporate organisations establishes seven high-order factors describing the contribution of OSINT – its effectiveness – to the wider intelligence function (Gibson 2007).

1. *Context:* without exception all intelligence agencies recognise that open sources of information represent a 'matrix' in which to conduct their work. Described variously as 'a first port of call', 'stocking filler', 'background' or simply 'contextual material', it represents the most widely acclaimed attribute of OSINT. Rolington's description of President Clinton's intelligence needs succinctly demonstrates the significance of context (Rolington 2006).
2. *Utility:* utility is a synonym for speed, volume and cost. Intelligence practitioners – public and private – recognise that it is quicker, more productive and cheaper to collect open sources of information before closed. It is simply more immediately useful to analysts.
3. *Benchmark:* closed single-source intelligence collection agencies use OSINT as a benchmark against which their sources are gauged. They recognise that it is uneconomic and unprofessional to disseminate intelligence product derived from closed sources when it resides publicly. Moreover, benchmarking is used both ways – closed information can also be used to challenge open source information. Confusingly, some single-source agencies now claim difficulty in distinguishing open from closed sources.
4. *Surge:* clandestine intelligence, particularly HUMINT, is not an activity that can be turned on and off like a tap. Conversely, open sources, already 'out there' are more easily 'surged'

than traditional sources. They provide an holistic all-source capability: satellite imagery is available commercially off the shelf; 'news' can be aggregated, searched and sorted on the internet; 'citizen journalists' or 'bloggers' help unravel the mysteries of 'uncertainty'; while the sharing of intelligence via an 'Intelipedia' moves analysis towards a real-time product. When 'surprise' happens – kidnap to revolution – analysts and policy-makers turn to OSINT for a 'first cut'.

5. *Focus:* open sources can be used to both direct further collection efforts as well as provide the illusive here and now of 'point' information. Thus, focus implies both direction – targeting onto new 'leads' – as well as acuity – high granularity.

6. *Communicability:* practitioners claim that information derived from open sources is easier to share and disseminate. Security concerns shrink to who collects it rather than who from. Yet, the dominant culture of secrecy confounds this theoretical patency.

7. *Analysis:* analysis is designed to achieve three things: situational awareness; an understanding of situations; and some tentative forecasting effort. Broadly, this comprises at least five varieties of product: current intelligence; database or knowledge creation; forecasts; warnings and indicators; and 'red teaming'. Each of these is achievable and undertaken by OSINT. However, the degree to which open source collectors undertake analysis varies considerably. In private information brokerages, analysis is undertaken by individuals or groups comfortably interchanging between all functions of the intelligence cycle in order to create product. In public-sector agencies, analysts and collectors are broadly separated. Interestingly, today, BBC Monitoring acknowledges that it formally conducts analysis of its own collection. Similarly, open source procedures vary between 'push' and 'pull' systems. In some agencies a 'push' system operates whereby open source expertise sits (literally) alongside an analyst or team of analysts. In others a 'pull' system operates where analysts have to go to centralised open source cells with their requirements and wait for a response.

Notwithstanding these high-order factors, they still only represent what OSINT can do for the intelligence function. They are no evaluation of effectiveness advancing the ideological or political objectives of decision-makers that intelligence supports.

All animals are equal, but some are more equal than others

In George Orwell's *Animal Farm*, the seven laws of animalism eventually become a single law: all animals are equal, but some animals are more equal than others. By the same token, regardless of the '80 per cent rule', the proportion of resource devoted to OSINT is nowhere near comparable to closed. OSINT may be formally and deliberately exploited within the intelligence community, but it is regarded as less equal than others.

Many myths and misconceptions serve to confound OSINT's contribution to intelligence: that it is in competition with secret intelligence, rather than complementary to, if not thoroughly enmeshed with, closed; that it resides solely on the internet rather than magnetic, film, paper and other non-digital sources; that it is exclusively text-based and in English, rather than also oral, image-based and in many languages; that it is conducted overtly, when collectors may hide their interest at a conference, mask their intentions in the academic papers they read or 'anonymise' their IP address when interrogating websites; that OSINT is exclusive to the public sector, when, by definition, it is available to many with a cause, including the private, academic and other non-governmental sectors; that it is free to collect or assess, rather than requiring specialised effort and increasingly expensive effort as greater value is added; that the greatest added value may come from traditional intelligence providers – private-sector product is not 'inferior' to public-sector product, nor OSINT necessarily 'inferior' to closed 'ints'; that OSINT is excused the usual 'rules' of information-working commonly applied to construct assessment in support of decision-making, rather than be validated for accuracy, relevance and timeliness in the same way that journalism and research should be; and, not least, that OSINT cannot provide a 'smoking gun', when many historical examinations of 'intelligence surprise' show those surprises being pre-trailed in the press, and countless examples of contemporary social networking media 'confessions', demonstrate that much evidence is already in plain sight in these media.

Thus, the concern with effectiveness is important in one key regard: it should prioritise, or at least influence, the treatment of OSINT within agencies and across national intelligence machineries. All of these cultural, organisational and technical misconceptions underline the necessity for a distinct OSINT tradecraft, appropriate tools and techniques, specialised software and equipment, a 'familiarity' with contemporary ICT (more likely to be found in those aged under 55 in 2013), and a befitting budget. The establishment of the OSC in the US goes part way to realising Croom's vision; but, as Bean observes, remains inside a closed environment and subject to high-level office politics (Bean 2011).

Not everything that 'twitters' is gold

History has witnessed several significant transformations in ICT: the invention of the alphabet to enable writing; the cipher to aid mathematics; the printing press to democratise communication; electricity, the telegraph and transistors to deliver instant communication; the steam and internal combustion engines to deliver the messenger; and chips with everything. Notably, the printing press contributed to two revolutionary periods – the Renaissance and the Reformation. Contemporary ICT – particularly the combination of mobile phone and internet – has similarly contributed in recent decades to 'revolution', change and the democratisation of decision-making. Certainly, the democratisation of information is increasing if one 'counts' the number of people being 'connected' to the internet and the amount of information available on the internet.

There are some cautionary notes. First, the availability of more information in the public sphere may confer a quantitative rise, but does not infer any similar qualitative improvement. One of the 'complaints' of contemporary information-working is the cliché of 'drinking at a fire hydrant'. Yet, if information is your business, where else would you want to drink? If you cannot apply the necessary filters, funnels, adapters and pumps to control the flow then you may be consigned to sup with a straw from obscure puddles. Second, the increased immediacy of information does not excuse the necessary activity of analysis. The '90 per cent of everything is crap' rule also pertains. Nowhere does this seem more apparent than in the 140-character confines of the aptly named 'twittersphere'! Third, regardless of the medium of communication, communicators still need to have something meaningful to say. In the political sphere, while Twitter, Facebook, SMS messaging or the Gutenberg printing press can contribute significantly to political processes, the primacy of any political movement remains the strength of its motivating idea. Moreover, the rules of information-working apply as much to these new sources as they do to traditional sources. Thus, *sapienta* is as likely (or not) to come from open source exploitation as it is from the exploitation of secret sources (Gibson 2009).

While the achievement of strategic or operational objectives more meaningfully reflects the effectiveness of both open and closed exploitation, the contribution of a wider democratisation of information to optimal decision-making remains to be seen.

Move on please: there are no more silver bullets here

The problem with spies is they only know secrets.

(Robert Steele, in Steele 2002: 43)

The purpose of intelligence – support to decision-making, truth to power, who knows what in sufficient time to make use of it – remains extant. By contrast, the conduct of intelligence – how it is done – is continually evolving commensurate with changing ICT. The increasing availability, immediacy and volume of open sources generated by the latest transformation in ICT is reflected in the formal and deliberate acceptance of OSINT as a new information class alongside HUMINT or TECHINT. Certainly, today, open sources remain recognised and exploited across the intelligence, security and law enforcement communities.

Open source exploitation is but one information-working discipline; subject to the rules of all information-working disciplines. OSINT's specific contribution to intelligence can be evaluated by high-order factors: context; utility; benchmark; focus; surge; communicability; and analysis. These factors could further direct the intelligence function in three important ways: the allocation of resource; the focus for training, policy and doctrine; and the efficient tasking of the intelligence community. Yet, the paradoxical location of OSINT inside the established closed environment, its weak resource allocation, and the stubborn culture of intelligence practitioners and customers – 'classification-obsession', bureaucratic resistance to change, 'office politics' – hamper OSINT's full integration, appropriate weighting and status.

OSINT's effectiveness in relation to outcomes beyond the confines of the intelligence function remains illusive. Like intelligence more broadly, measures of effectiveness reside in perceived added value to the customer, accounting procedures and pseudo-scientific scorecards. These subjective self-affirming yardsticks hinder any linking of the intelligence function to political, ideological or economic goals. OSINT is not the be-all-and-end-all of intelligence. It may be a lifeline for the intelligence function in today's globalised open world, but it is no 'silver bullet' for decision-makers. Effective open source exploitation confirms to the grown-up sceptic that ideological purpose remains a mystery to those naïve enough to predict it.

However, globalisation, mobile digital communications and the democratisation of information render a deeper contextual understanding; visible to others beyond just intelligence, security and law enforcement communities. The 'predictors' seem unable to detect readily apparent concerns: a post-Cold War ideological vacuum; a risk management decision-making framework substituting for proper political leadership; and the contemporary ascendancy of the pursuit of security over the pursuit of liberty (Gibson 2012: 204–221). Steele implies not that spies should know something more than secrets – secrets are precisely the currency of spies – rather that decision-makers should know something more of the world beyond spies. Whether intelligence communities can deliver this or decision-makers recognise the deficit remain debatable issues.

Thus, the challenges for the total information business, of which intelligence and OSINT are parts, are not simply how to deal with the increasing volume of information, the sharing of classified sources, or honestly balancing open and closed capabilities. These can be dealt with procedurally by technological means and culturally by attitudinal shifts. The greater challenges for the intelligence community reside in presenting a genuine picture of reality to their masters; regaining confidence in judging rather than measuring intelligence effectiveness; and reconnecting power and society with purpose in the sense of what we are for, rather than deferring to process and what we are against.

Notes

1   Correspondence, Robert David Steele–Gibson, October 2003.
2   Conversations with Michael Herman (former secretary to the UK JIC), Dr Joe Markowitz (former Director of COSP) and the UK's Open Source Joint Working Group.
3   Conversation with Dr Joe Markowitz, October 2003.

PART IV

Systems of intelligence

13

THE UNITED KINGDOM

Michael S. Goodman[1]

Intelligence in the United Kingdom has a long and distinguished history. Its roots can be traced back to the sixteenth century, and attempts by Lord Burghley and Sir Francis Walsingham to safeguard the throne of Queen Elizabeth I. Military historian Sir Basil Liddell Hart has spoken of the 'British Way in Warfare'. Surveying historical trends, he argued, revealed a distinctive British approach to warfare, based on 'mobility and surprise' and the strengths of a maritime strategic policy (Liddell Hart 1932). In the same way it is possible to talk about a 'British Way in Intelligence' – a distinct way in which intelligence is approached in the United Kingdom. To understand this we need to look not only at how intelligence is organised, but at the underlying rationales behind its structure and how it fits within the wider governmental machinery. This chapter will also focus on current threats and pose some thoughts on how British intelligence might develop in the future.

Despite its modern origins in 1909, British intelligence was once labelled as the 'missing dimension' of political history (Andrew and Dilks 1984). This view, now several decades old, would be difficult to justify today: not only are there myriad declassified intelligence files in the archives, but the official histories of the Second World War, Falklands War and Desmond Morton, not to mention the authorised histories of MI5 and SIS, mean that we are at an unprecedented level of openness. Understandably, the level of coverage gets thinner as we approach the present. In addition, there have been a number of reviews of intelligence but these have tended to deal with the constituent elements of the intelligence process. An exception is to be found in the first chapter of Lord Butler's report into pre-war intelligence on Iraqi WMD (Butler 2004). In an interesting chapter entitled 'The Nature and Use of Intelligence' written by Peter Freeman, then historian for GCHQ assigned to assist the Butler inquiry, we find the first serious exposition of how the British intelligence community actually works. This chapter, designed to 'describe the nature of intelligence', does so in a distinctly British way.

In the common usage of the English language 'intelligence' refers to not just the nature of the product itself, but also the means of procurement and analysis, and the organisations that deal with it. Yet this conceals differences in how English-speaking countries approach intelligence. The post-war US system saw intelligence as geared towards avoiding surprise; in Britain and the Commonwealth it has been seen far more as a function of statecraft, to help improve the quality of decision-making.

The most common, albeit problematic, approach to discussing intelligence is to perceive it as a cyclical process, traditionally encompassing everything from direction, collection, analysis and dissemination – in essence every aspect that an intelligence organisation deals with.[2] Butler took a similar approach, describing the iterative processes of collection, validation, analysis, assessment and dissemination (Butler 2004: 7–14). While this is a useful way to explain the nature of intelligence itself, it does not go far enough.

If we are really to comprehend how intelligence works in the UK then we need to deconstruct it into its component parts; furthermore this split should not just be by organisation, but by characteristics too. Doing so is instructive, for we can begin to see how 'intelligence' is identified in the British context. Based on an overarching belief that intelligence adds value to decision-making across civil and military, domestic and overseas, domains, there are several defining and interrelated characteristics of British intelligence that influence at its heart. This is achieved through an inherently joined-up intelligence community; the committee-style approach; the drive for consensus; the necessity of having single source information validated and analysed in the collection agencies themselves, but not assessed; and the capability for intelligence to go from the agencies directly to their customers as well as to central all-source assessments.

Britain's intelligence community has a large and very central role to play in the affairs of state (ISC 2010–11).[3] At its heart has traditionally been the Joint Intelligence Committee (JIC), which not only plays a role in the process through which information leaves the intelligence machinery and enters the policy-making realm, but also organises what goes on in the rest of the community. So, how is British intelligence organised? The only organisational chart to be found for British intelligence depicts it through lines of ministerial responsibility (Cabinet Office 2010). In fact, it was only with the publication of the first booklet on the 'Central Intelligence Machinery' in 1993 that an official diagram was produced (Cabinet Office 1993). While this is useful, it does not explain the interrelated nature of the intelligence community, or how it functions with officials and ministers. To explore this, it is necessary to consider how British intelligence has evolved.

Origins

Britain can be seen as one of the earliest pioneers of intelligence and espionage; indeed, the word 'intelligence' itself traces its roots to sixteenth-century 'Intelligencers', people charged with acquiring information on behalf of Her Majesty's Government. Of these people, Sir Francis Walsingham is often seen as the first 'spy master' (Alford 1998).[4] Walsingham ran a successful network of informers, agents and decrypters, both in England and abroad, and dealt with various conspiracies and plots against the reign of Elizabeth I. It is fascinating to consider Walsingham's intelligence network. Operating in the latter half of the sixteenth century, it was short of money and resources yet ran a number of agents and counterespionage operations. Interestingly Walsingham, whose official title was 'Principal Secretary of State', was also primarily responsible for foreign policy. This linkage between intelligence, foreign affairs and officialdom continued. In 1782, for instance, the Foreign Secretary assumed responsibility for administering the Secret Vote – the intelligence budget.

The modern British intelligence system can trace its roots back to 1909, with the founding of the Secret Service Bureau. This was created amid fears of a growing German threat to British interests. As such a domestic department, MI5, and an overseas department, MI1c (which would become SIS), were formed. From their earliest days both departments had specific, different tasks. MI5 was responsible for internal security and spent much of its time monitoring Germans living in the UK, while also assuming responsibility for countering Irish terrorism. MI1c, operating out of a flat in central London, concentrated on foreign threats and recruiting agents abroad to watch for signs of German mobilisation (Andrew 2009; Jeffery 2010).

Until the outbreak of the Second World War, British intelligence was a predominantly military discipline. Not only were both Secret Service departments staffed largely by ex-military figures but their outlook was far more concerned with enemy capabilities than political intentions. This process gradually began to change from the mid-1920s onwards. At this time the Foreign Office (FO) saw itself as the only government body capable of offering advice on political and diplomatic matters. Furthermore, British intelligence was a very disjointed matter. MI5 and SIS (including the SIGINT organisation GC&CS) were the only two 'civilian' agencies, for although they had a military designation and comprised former military officers, they were all retired. In addition the three services – Army, Navy and Air Force – all had their own intelligence staffs, as did the FO, in an unofficial capacity (Goodman 2007).

In 1936 it was proposed by Sir Maurice Hankey, the secretary to the Cabinet and to the Committee of Imperial Defence, and founder of the cabinet system of British governance, that some kind of committee was needed to overcome the problems of duplication of effort, and to ensure that the Chiefs of Staff (COS) and government had the best possible information at its disposal. The result was the creation of the JIC and, though it would take some time to become properly established, it was to become the centrepiece of British intelligence.

The intelligence cycle

Requirements and priorities

Before any activity can take place, requirements are placed upon the collection agencies. In the British system, responsibility for allotting intelligence priorities has historically resided with the JIC. This Committee will be discussed in more detail below, but it is worth highlighting that membership includes the heads of the intelligence agencies and senior figures within policy-making departments. Since 2010, however, the process of combining intelligence and policy concerns into the requirements process has been assisted by the creation of the National Security Council (NSC). This was set up to 'coordinate responses to the dangers the UK faces, integrating at the highest level the work of the foreign, defence, home, energy and international development departments, and all other arms of government contributing to national security'. In other words, it exists to fuse elements of intelligence and policy, and this is reflected in its composition, which is more senior than that of the JIC. The Prime Minister chairs the NSC and, besides senior ministers, its attendees also include the National Security Adviser, the JIC Chair, the heads of the three intelligence agencies and the Chief of the Defence Staff. It is based on the principles of a committee approach and the importance of consensus.

In 2010 the NSC published the UK's first 'National Security Strategy', which, among other things, provided an assessment of the risks to British security. The Strategy (NSC 2010) identified the most pressing priorities as:

- acts of terrorism affecting the UK or its interests;
- hostile attacks upon UK cyberspace;
- a major accident or natural hazard (e.g. influenza pandemic);
- an international military crisis between states, drawing in the UK and allies.

These areas form the broad contours of the requirements facing the intelligence and security community. Within them the JIC then sets more detailed prioritisation in the form of 'Strategic Priorities', which is an annual process. To add further flexibility to the system, the NSC, in its weekly meetings, can then enforce an immediate realignment of resources if a particularly urgent situation requires it (ISC 2011–12). These priorities are especially relevant to the work of GCHQ and SIS; the anomaly is MI5, the Security Service, which is guided by the overall national priorities but retains a statutory duty: 'the protection of national security and, in particular, its protection against threats from espionage, terrorism and sabotage, from the activities of agents of foreign powers and from actions intended to overthrow or undermine parliamentary democracy by political, industrial or violent means' (MI5 1989). Here, then, at the very start of the intelligence process, we can identify the crucial role played by committees, consensus and the need for the intelligence community to function with the instruments of state. This requirement setting process is, in itself, cyclical in that the JIC and NSC also assess the agencies' successes in meeting their targets.

Collection

There are three primary agencies responsible for the collection of intelligence, and their roles can easily be divided. Perhaps the most well-known agency is the Secret Intelligence Service (SIS) or, as it often referred to, MI6. Despite being founded in 1909, it was not until 1992 that the British government officially announced the existence of SIS. Its role was placed on a statutory basis that year through the Intelligence Services Act, which defined the functions of the Service and the responsibilities of the Chief.

SIS has, perhaps, the most mystique about what it actually does; there are scant official details about its activities. The principal functions of SIS are to 'obtain and provide information relating to the acts and intentions of persons overseas in the fields of national security . . . the economic well-being of the UK . . . in support of the prevention or detection of serious crime' (SIS 2012a). To meet these requirements SIS 'conduct[s] covert operations and . . . act[s] clandestinely overseas in support of British Government objectives'. This is done through the running of human agents and, as its website states, 'SIS collects secret intelligence and mounts covert operations overseas' (SIS 2012b). SIS therefore is primarily a collection agency, it has a small in-house operational analytical function, but above all its role is to collect information on behalf of the government (Butler 2004: 9). SIS is largely tasked directly by customers, and its priorities reflect annual community requirements.

While SIS may be the most secret of the agencies, GCHQ has, historically, been the one about which least is known (Aldrich 2010).[5] Communications intelligence has a long history in the United Kingdom, stretching back to at least the seventeenth century when John Wallis became the chief cryptographer for Parliament (Smith 1917). The modern SIGINT agency is the Government Communications Headquarters (GCHQ), located in Cheltenham, Gloucestershire. In 1994 GCHQ acquired a legal framework and statutory basis. GCHQ takes its priorities and requirements from the JIC and 'provides intelligence in support of Government decision-making in the fields of national security, military operations and law enforcement . . . the battle against terrorism and also contributes to the prevention of serious crime' (Cabinet Office 2010: 8).

GCHQ is and always has been the largest of the agencies. It is also the most expensive to operate because of the importance of keeping abreast of the latest technology. In addition to its SIGINT role, GCHQ also takes the lead in 'information assurance' – in other words, keeping 'Government communications and information systems safe' (Cabinet Office 2010: 8). Its most recent role has been to accommodate the Cyber Security Operations Centre (CSOC): a small organisation comprising secondees from across government, located in GCHQ but administered by the Office of Cyber Security in the Cabinet Office (Cabinet Office 2009). In this way GCHQ has both an offensive and a defensive function. Despite having a significant analytical component, GCHQ is predominantly a collection agency. Both SIS and GCHQ are government agencies accountable to the Foreign Secretary.

The third of the major intelligence agencies is the Security Service, better known as MI5. MI5's origins stretch back to 1909 but it was not given a statutory basis until 1989; it is accountable to the Home Secretary. The legislation of the 1989 and 1996 Security Service Acts set forth the functions and parameters of MI5. These are, according to its website, to 'frustrate terrorism; prevent damage to the UK from foreign espionage and other covert foreign state activity; frustrate procurement by proliferating countries of material, technology or expertise relating to weapons of mass destruction; watch out for new or re-emerging types of threat; protect Government's sensitive information and assets, and the Critical National Infrastructure (CNI 2011); and reduce serious crime through assistance to law enforcement agencies' (MI5 2012a). MI5 collects its own intelligence, through human agents, surveillance and interception of communications (MI5 2012c). Unlike the FBI, to which it is often compared, MI5 has no police powers of arrest and so needs to work very closely with law enforcement in collecting evidence and arresting suspects.

In addition to the three main intelligence agencies, there are a number of other organisations that collect intelligence. Within the Ministry of Defence, Defence Intelligence (DI) is funded through the Defence Vote. DI was founded (as the Defence Intelligence Staff) in 1964, by the bringing together of the single Service intelligence staffs, and incorporated the Joint Intelligence Bureau. It was initially designed as the first tri-service military intelligence establishment. DI is traditionally headed by a serving three-star officer, with a civilian deputy, and throughout the organisation there is a fusing of military and civilian personnel. The Chief of Defence Intelligence (CDI), as its head is known, is also 'responsible for the overall coordination of defence intelligence throughout the Armed Forces and single-Service Commands'. DI serves a variety of functions, far more than the other agencies with an important analytic capability. Serving under the CDI is a two-star deputy civilian, who is responsible for analysis and production of intelligence, and a two-star military officer, responsible for collection, including signals, satellite and human intelligence (MOD 2012a). While it contributes to JIC requirements, it is not solely tasked by it as DI ultimately serves the Chief of the Defence Staff and the Secretary of State for Defence. Since 2010 this has made for a slightly convoluted yet simpler process in as much as CDS's priorities are now those of the NSC, which are also those of the JIC. DI's objectives are largely orientated towards supporting military operations, but they also support the JIC priorities (MOD 2012b).

Analysis

An important caveat needs to be made here about terminology – many commentators describe 'analysis' as a single stage between collection and dissemination, but the practicalities are not so straightforward. Lord Butler differentiated between 'validation', 'analysis' and 'assessment'. These are very useful distinctions, especially their applicability to British intelligence. The first of these processes – validation – occurs within the collection agency itself. Simply put, this is a procedural stage, designed to test the authenticity and legitimacy of the information – that is, it is not considering the information itself, but the means by which it was procured (Butler 2004: 9).

The 'analysis' stage may occur in the collection agency itself, but more likely will take place in one of the analytical components of the intelligence machinery. To a great extent this still depends on the subject but, from 1964, the largest concentration of effort has been within DI. As well as having a large collection effort, DI is the largest analyser of intelligence in the United

Kingdom, particularly on military and counter-proliferation subjects. At this stage experts will consider the information provided and try to establish its significance (Butler 2004: 10). DI receives collected information on an array of matters, not just military. Its work on economic, logistic, and scientific and technical intelligence is unique within Whitehall. In addition, other agencies will receive intelligence depending on its nature: intelligence on criminal matters would be analysed by the National Crime Agency, and intelligence on terrorism would be the responsibility of the Security Service.

The final step of this process is 'assessment'. At this stage the newly analysed information is compared, contrasted and possibly incorporated with existing information. This stage can take place within the all-source assessment procedures employed by DI, though it need not necessarily always be all-source (Butler 2004: 11). More generally this takes place within the central intelligence machinery in the Cabinet Office. Created in the depths of the Second World War, though not formally known as the Assessments Staff until 1968, this is the highest level of assessment of the whole British intelligence machinery. The Assessments Staff, a group of approximately 30 figures from diverse backgrounds across the agencies, diplomatic service, defence and civil departments, are seconded for a period of two to three years. Each member is assigned a topic or desk, be it topic-specific like proliferation, or country-specific like Afghanistan.

Generally speaking, the Assessments Staff are not always experts in their particular field. Rather their role is to collate all incoming intelligence (be it secret material passed to them from the collection agencies or open source reporting) and assess it, in consultation with experts in the departments. Their reports – the topic is pre-chosen or sponsored by a government department – are then discussed in Current Intelligence Groups (Butler 2004: 13). In the CIGs, papers are discussed with all the relevant experts, once more drawn from across the breadth and depth of the government. Once a paper is agreed it is passed to the JIC for comment, approval and distribution. In the event that a paper is too time-sensitive to go through the JIC itself, the Chief of the Assessments Staff can issue it in his/her name (Cabinet Office 2010: 24).

This practice follows the broad characteristic of British intelligence, where customers are organised by topic, collectors by type. This is especially evident in the case of terrorism. The Joint Terrorism Analysis Centre (JTAC), created in 2003, is located within MI5 and is answerable to its Director-General. However, it is a separate entity in that it is staffed by members of the wider intelligence, security and policy community who are seconded to it for a period of time. At present this includes 16 different home departments (MI5 2012d). JTAC analyses and assesses all intelligence on Islamist terrorism, both domestic and international. What is crucial is that JTAC provides a subject-specific forum in which relevant members can meet to assess intelligence on terrorism and provide threat levels.

Dissemination

Dissemination of intelligence in the United Kingdom can take place at various levels. For instance, if the information is actionable it might be that it is passed straight to those with law enforcement powers – in other words, the police or customs. If something is extremely time-sensitive, then it might be that it bypasses the more strategic level of approval of the JIC. Generally, however, assessments are passed to officials or ministers through the JIC. It is at this stage that the central characteristics of British intelligence – the committee approach and the drive for consensus – are most evident.

The JIC has had various functions over the course of its history (Goodman 2013). Generally speaking, its official remit is to 'give direction to, and keep under review, the organisation and working of British intelligence activity as a whole at home and overseas in order to ensure efficiency, economy, and prompt adaptation to changing requirements'. To achieve this, the Committee has several specific responsibilities:

- to assess events and situations relating to external affairs, defence, terrorism, major international criminal activity, scientific, technical and international economic matters and other transnational issues, drawing on secret intelligence, diplomatic reporting and open source material;
- to monitor and give early warning of the development of direct and indirect threats and opportunities in those fields to British interests or policies, and to the international community as a whole;
- to keep under review threats to security at home and overseas and to deal with such security problems as may be referred to it;
- to contribute to the formulation of statements of the requirements and priorities for intelligence gathering and other tasks to be conducted by the intelligence agencies;
- to maintain oversight of the intelligence community's analytical capability through the Professional Head of Intelligence Analysis;
- to maintain liaison with Commonwealth and foreign intelligence organisations as appropriate, and to consider the extent to which its product can be made available to them.

(Cabinet Office 2010: 26)

Looking at the JIC over its evolution we can see that it sits in a unique position within the intelligence machinery and wider governmental system: it is at the apex of a multibillion-pound intelligence community, setting requirements and monitoring performance; yet at the same time it reports upwards, producing high-level assessments for use by policy-makers. The NSC is the continuation of this trend.

The committee approach

The committee-based approach at the centre of British intelligence owes its origins to the growth of the centralised cabinet system of government, first introduced in 1916 by Maurice Hankey. At its heart is the principle of collective decision-making. It was in this tradition that the JIC was created in 1936, designed to remedy the lack of coordination within British intelligence. How does the system work in practice? Here the joined-up approach that is representative of British intelligence becomes visible. The JIC comprises a Chairman; the heads of the three main intelligence agencies; the Chief of Defence Intelligence; and senior officials involved with policy from the Ministry of Defence; the Foreign and Commonwealth Office; the Home Office; the Department for International Development; the Treasury and the Cabinet Office (and others as required); and finally the Chief of the Assessments Staff.

The mixture of senior people is deliberate. The mix of intelligence professionals (or producers of intelligence) and those from the policy arena (consumers) means that assessments produced are 'washed in the blood' of the policy community[6] – that is, assessments are written and disseminated in such a way as to be useful, relevant and timely for those to act upon them. As mentioned above, the JIC does not draft the assessments; instead it approves them and issues them in its name. The real engine of the machinery operates one level down, with the Cabinet Office Assessments Staff. It is worth noting here that the assessments produced and issued by these bodies include both long-term and short-term assessments. What is central to all is that they represent the common viewpoint.

It is at this level that issues of oversight and accountability are exercised. This happens in various ways: the JIC constantly reviews the performance of the intelligence agencies in their collection requirements and, in addition, two other, external, mechanisms exist to review the work of the intelligence community. The highest level is the 'Intelligence and Security Committee' (ISC). This was created in 1994 with the role of providing oversight of the intelligence community. It is a cross-party committee and members of both Houses of Parliament sit on it. The ISC is responsible for examining the expenditure, administration and policy of the intelligence agencies but, unlike its American counterparts, it has no authority to investigate or oversee operations. In addition there are two external Commissioners, both of whom are law Lords, and who oversee the work of the Agencies. All three of these bodies produce annual reports.

Striving for consensus

The British intelligence community is based on a committee-style approach. The joined-up nature of this is reflected not only in the diverse backgrounds of those involved, but also in the nature of the produced assessments themselves. As mentioned earlier, the origins can be traced back to the cabinet system of government, and this is important in that all such discussions proceed on the basis of commonality: in other words, the belief in the British system that policy-makers should only be provided with one, universally agreed, assessment. The British approach contrasts significantly with the competitive American system of alternative assessments in the 'National Intelligence Estimates', where dissenting views are provided in footnotes, including who the dissident is and why they disagree. In the UK, on the rare occasions when the intelligence is ambiguous or lacking, and when the JIC is unclear, the Committee is allowed to report 'alternative interpretations of the facts'. However, 'in such cases all the members have to agree that the interpretations they are proposing are viable alternatives' (Butler 2004: 13).

One recent innovation following the Iraqi WMD affair has been the creation in the UK of an option to include dissenting views: in theory the JIC Chairman can identify any items with particularly difficult or troublesome conclusions; yet it is a characteristic of the joined-up approach that, if there is disagreement, the preferred course of action is to iron it out before producing the final assessment (ISC 2005–06: 23). The criticism often levelled at the British system is that consensus invariably leads to the lowest common denominator. By contrast, the American alternative competitive model allows policy-makers to choose what intelligence fits best with preconceived policy options. The basis of this search for consensus lies in more general questions about the role of intelligence, and how the intelligence and policy-making communities should interact with one another.

Looking to the future

There does not exist an official definition of 'intelligence' in the United Kingdom; rather we have to infer it from how it is approached (MOD 2011: 1–9).[7] Through an examination of the interrelated stages of the intelligence cycle it is possible to begin to understand how intelligence in the UK is defined. The organisation of British intelligence is a microcosm of the political system it operates within. Perhaps this is why the myriad replications of the JIC created during and after the war never really worked in those countries with a very different system of governance to the UK (Valero 2000; Murphy 2002). This is particularly the case given the apolitical role that senior policy-makers play within the British system, as opposed to political appointees in other countries (Omand 2012a).

Through a centrally coordinated requirements and priorities process, the British intelligence community is tasked by those who make policy to collect information on targets of importance. Not only does intelligence have to be timely and reliable in order to be useful, it crucially also has to be relevant. Through its committee-based approach and drive for consensus, British intelligence is predicated on the need to address policy-makers' concerns. At every stage before intelligence estimates reach decision-makers there is a policy-input – from the choice of target to the approval of assessments – and this ensures that the process has a relevance that is difficult to achieve in any other way.

The most recent 'innovation' in the UK was the creation in May 2010 of the NSC, yet it has historical roots. In 1903, amid a fear that the Cabinet should not be left to deal with crises on its own, a Committee of Imperial Defence (CID) was created. Chaired by the Prime Minister, just as the NSC is, the CID had an advisory and warning role, and was designed to fill a strategic void at the centre of government (MacKintosh 1962; Prins 2011). In a similar way, the JIC originally supported COS planning and requirements, and today this role has been superseded by the NSC and its priorities.

The British intelligence machine, including the NSC, has evolved over the decades to counter the present threat; if it were to be created afresh, in the twenty-first century, it is very unlikely it would look as it currently does. How might these threats change in the future and what might happen to the intelligence machinery? In the early 1990s the JIC discussed whether it was legitimate for an intelligence organisation to produce an assessment that contained no classified intelligence. Increasingly, as the intelligence community moves from the dearth of intelligence it faced in the Cold War to the overload of information it confronts today, there will be an increasing necessity to focus on analysis of open source intelligence. This is particularly the case as threats and concerns become more global. Furthermore, as the world continues to change and previously marginal subjects come to the fore – such as energy security, the importance of natural resources and the rise of civil conflicts – 'intelligence', as it is currently understood, may need to be redefined. This shift is something already under way in the military, with post-conflict reconstruction efforts increasing as war-fighting potential decreases. This does not mean, though, that there will no longer be a need for more traditional methods of intelligence gathering. The human spy on the ground will always be as important as the most sophisticated means of technical espionage, but it does suggest that the machinery will need to adapt. This is not the first time that the community has had to do so: after the end of the Cold War the Soviet threat disappeared, to be replaced by the triple challenges of new priorities, technological adaptation and changing social attitudes. The current division of HUMINT, SIGINT and security will need to continue, but increasingly the analytical efforts devoted to understanding the world will need to expand. For Britain, its historical legacy in intelligence excellence will stand it in good stead.

Notes

1 Disclaimer: This chapter is drawn only from released official records and published sources, and the views expressed are the author's alone and do not represent the views or carry the endorsement of the government.
   An earlier version of this chapter, more historical in focus, was published as 'The British Way in Intelligence' (in Grant 2011: 127–140). I am immensely grateful to various people having read earlier drafts of this, including Jane Knight and Sir David Omand.
2 For more on the intelligence cycle, see David Omand's chapter in this volume (Chapter 6).
3 The current budget is somewhere in the region of £2 billion (ISC 2010–11).

4   In fact this is slightly erroneous in that Walsingham adopted an intelligence network from his pred-
    ecessor, Sir William Cecil. Walsingham was responsible for enlarging the network and making it more
    professional in nature (Alford 1998).
5   GCHQ does release archival files but these are quite limited for the post-war period.
6   I have borrowed this great phrase from Sir David Omand.
7   There is a slight exception to this: a military training manual has a definition of intelligence but this has
    not been adopted elsewhere: 'the directed and co-ordinated acquisition and analysis of information to
    assess capabilities, intent and opportunities for exploitation by leaders at all levels' (MOD 2011).

14

THE UNITED STATES

Stephen Marrin

Intelligence as a function of government plays an important role in the creation and implementation of United States (US) foreign and domestic policy. Most treatments of US intelligence take its role and function as given, and focus on describing and evaluating the existing structures and processes. These scholarly contributions effectively address different aspects of American intelligence, but a by-product of this focus on the particular is that there is much less focus on the general. So how do intelligence organisations work together, within a broader conceptual framework that puts each in context of the other's role and function? How does American intelligence and all of its organisational components work together as a system? This chapter first emphasises the reasons why intelligence exists and how it fits into the broader framework of US government and governance before focusing on the actual ways in which intelligence supports policy-making.

American government and governance

The purpose of government is to channel society's aggregated power in the same way that a riverbed channels a river flowing through the countryside. An individual's power can be derived from a number of sources, including wealth and potential use of force. Individuals join together into various groups, and these groups join with others to create the incredibly complex interlocking systems that make up societies. Their power aggregates similarly, as water does in the way that streams join together to form tributaries and tributaries lead to rivers. In order to operate efficiently, societies must have some way of organising power, and governments have become the structures, the channels, which direct the country's river of power. In the US, each of the 50 states is a tributary for the river, which consists of the national government.

Government wields society's power. How this is done and towards what ends seems to be the defining characteristic of different political systems. When many share the sources of power and desire to wield it, rules of competition become necessary to prevent it from becoming a brutal struggle for the reins of power. The development of democracy grounds the basis of governmental legitimacy in the aggregated will of the people. This creates a situation where the sources of power are held in many hands, and where rulebooks become necessary for the conversion of general will into political choice. These rulebooks – constitutions – form the basis for the political structure of the society. As a result, in constitutional democracies or republics, power flows through the governmental structures defined and created through the constitution.

The US government was created under unique political, economic and social conditions, and it was these conditions that influenced the writers of the US Constitution. As power was held in a variety of diverse regional hands, the application of power needed a coordinating mechanism, and so the US government was born. The Constitution created the forms through which various groups compete for power, and the structures that apply power once it is won according to the rules. The rationale behind the structure was the doctrine of separation of powers and checks and balances in order to prevent inordinate acquisition or arbitrary application of power.

Each of these governmental structures serves a different purpose. There must be a body that defines the uses towards which power is used: the law-making function. In the US this function is met through the complicated arrangement of two legislative houses, the Senate and the House of Representatives. Then there is the body that applies power and enforces the laws: the executive function. This consists of the Presidency and the rest of the executive branch. Finally, there is the arbiter of disputes: the judicial function. At the national level, this is the Supreme Court as well as the rest of the federal judiciary. These, then, are the governmental structures that channel the river of power in the US.

Once power is aggregated and structured, it must be used. This is the role of the elected leadership, sailing the ship of state along the river of power. However, there are a variety of normative goals towards which power can be used, such as the defence of the regime or the people, maximising economic welfare or individual freedom, or providing internal security, economic egalitarianism, and advancement of a particular religious or ideological agenda. Political leaders are elected to provide the vision and manage the process of using this aggregated power to achieve specified ends. The elected leaders cannot necessarily change the will of the people, but they can decide how far or how fast the government responds to that will through application of power. The act of governing and governance involves the making of choices, and the management of the people's power.

Within this framework of government and governance, the purpose of intelligence is to act as a lookout for the officers on the ship of state as it sails along the river of power. The lookout has the spyglass, evaluating the ship's environment for dangers and opportunities. If the branches of government provide the structures that channel the river of power, then the elected leadership and those they appoint to positions of authority are those who control the ship of state. These elected leaders are the ones who decide when, where, and how state power will be employed. The purpose of intelligence is to support the making of policy. It involves the acquisition of information and creation of knowledge or understanding to improve decision-making.

Much of the information, knowledge and understanding required by those in government can be acquired through normal channels: policy departments, the media and other sources. What distinguishes intelligence from these other sources of information is that, due to the requirements of competition, the acquisition of the information or its assessment must be done in secret in order to ensure that there is a benefit to the decision-maker (Marrin 2007; Sims 2009; Warner 2009b). As such, the only aspect of intelligence that is different from any other decision support activity within government is that it is secret. This means that intelligence matters in only a limited subset of cases where decisions are required, but in that limited subset of cases the advantage provided by intelligence can be significant.

The intelligence function provides the elected leadership with the ability to look ahead and prepare for both dangers (hidden rocks or shoals, potential for floods), as well as opportunities (new harbours, speedier lanes). This can involve the offensive use of power, to gain an advantage over a competitor; or it can involve the defensive use of power, to prevent negative outcomes from occurring. In the end, intelligence as a governmental function is to ensure that the decisions made lead to the most effective and efficient use of power.

Foreign intelligence

When most people think about intelligence, they are thinking about foreign intelligence. This is the collection and evaluation of intelligence geared to support foreign or national security policy. The purpose of institutionalised foreign intelligence is to provide information to decision-makers so that they can use the economic, political or military power at their disposal more effectively. To accomplish this purpose, foreign intelligence agencies covertly acquire, analyse and disseminate information regarding threats to national security. A covert information acquisition capability supplements overt information collection because much of international relations is conducted in secret. The only way to apply power effectively in an area where so much is kept secret is by uncovering the capabilities and intentions of enemies and potential competitors.

The primary benefit of intelligence is that it enables power to be applied with greater precision and with less collateral damage, or with greater efficiency and effectiveness. Properly understood, the role of intelligence is the collection and analysis of information. In terms of foreign intelligence, the benefit of intelligence is easiest to illustrate in the application of military power. For example, imagery from aerial platforms can provide the information necessary to more effectively put bombs on targets. If intelligence does not provide correct information, then military power cannot be applied as effectively. Similarly, foreign intelligence also assists in the effective and efficient application of economic and political power.

Historically, American intelligence capabilities had been organised ad hoc for military purposes because the negative impact of losing wars was so significant. However, once the war was won, the intelligence capability was disbanded. Perhaps this was due to American conceptions of safety due to the protective effects of two oceans (Ford 1995), or perhaps it was due to American exceptionalism: as Secretary of State Henry Stimson said in 1930, 'Gentlemen do not read each other's mail' (Titus 2002).

Such ethical objections to foreign intelligence were quickly overridden in the face of military threats and transition to world power status. During the Second World War and the Cold War the US did not eschew any intelligence capabilities. The attack on Pearl Harbor and subsequent American involvement in the Second World War changed the need for and use of intelligence precisely because the use of power had increased. During the Second World War, the US increased its overseas presence, and this necessitated the creation of a global intelligence capability commensurate with the US's expanded global role. After the Second World War ended, American political leaders decided that the US needed an intelligence agency capable of integrating disparate pieces of information distributed throughout the military and other government agencies to prevent another Pearl Harbor. As a result, in 1947 the Central Intelligence Agency (CIA) was created to prevent future surprise attacks by focusing on threats to national security.

Over time a more expansive role for foreign intelligence agencies developed, providing intelligence to support foreign policy-making more generally rather than limiting the focus to national security threats. The term national security is notorious for its ambiguity and flexibility. As Joseph Romm (1993: 3) observed, the phrase national security 'had become so widely used by 1947 that the National Security Act, which established . . . the National Security Council (and the Central Intelligence Agency), did not bother to define the term but left it open to broad (i.e. not purely military) interpretations'. He went on to say that the ambiguity inherent in the term national security comes 'from the inherent subjectivity in determining the threats to any nation's security'. Narrow definitions of national security focus tightly on military issues, but broader definitions can incorporate political, economic, social and environmental considerations. As definitions of security expand, so do perceptions of threats to national security.

During the Cold War, 'national security' could reasonably incorporate all aspects of foreign and domestic policy. Distinct from pure security considerations, a foreign policy is a government's attempt to advance its interests internationally. In the case of the US, the primary interests are mentioned in the Constitution: 'Provide for the common defense, promote the general welfare, and secure the blessings of liberty.' To achieve the goals of greater defence, welfare or liberty requires the application of military, economic or political power internationally through a foreign policy. During the Cold War, economic and political matters were interpreted through a security prism, and national security considerations seemed to incorporate all aspects of foreign policy because of the huge level of effort required to be prepared to fight World War III. In this heightened security environment, threats to national security were perceived to arise from all corners, including economic, military and political competitors. The foreign intelligence community fulfilled its task by monitoring the world as best it could.

When the Cold War ended and the primary threat to national security disappeared, it became obvious that intelligence agencies had expanded their role to provide intelligence relevant to foreign policy support more generally rather than exclusively for national security concerns. In the early 1990s, debates over the direction of post–Cold War intelligence roles and missions highlighted the importance of changing perceptions of national security threats. Those who emphasised the primacy of economic matters in the future wanted the Intelligence Community to focus on economic intelligence. Those who believed that interdependence would make the power of states less relevant focused their attention on other transnational issues, such as narcotics trafficking, terrorism and the environment. And those who believed that the US should focus its power only on narrowly defined national security threats argued for a smaller, more targeted intelligence capability.

This demonstrates the degree to which intelligence policy is really part and parcel of foreign policy-making. Once intelligence collection capabilities are built for purposes of threat perception and warning, they can and most likely will be used for broader foreign policy-making as well. For example, information acquired on a foreign country's transportation infrastructure for a defence capabilities study can be adapted to provide assessments of port or rail carrying capacities prior to humanitarian interventions. Information collected to assess how a foreign leader responds in different national security situations can be provided in the form of foreign leader profiles to trade negotiators to provide an edge in negotiations. Absent a clear security threat and outside the context of the Cold War, these activities are more accurately conceived as foreign policy support rather than national security threat perception and warning.

To achieve these ends at the national level, the US government is organised along a hub-and-spoke model where the spokes consist of policy departments wielding different kinds of power. The Defense Department wields military power, and is supported by a constellation of many variegated intelligence collection and analysis entities so as to ensure that power application is as efficient and effective as can be. These Defense Department organisations include the agencies that meet the intelligence collection needs of the US government, such as imagery and signals intelligence. It also includes the intelligence branches of each of the military services with the Defense Intelligence Agency as centralising focal point.

The same basic kind of structure exists for diplomatic and economic power and federal law enforcement, with intelligence components supporting their policy-making and implementation through the acquisition and evaluation of information. The coordinating function of the different forms of power is at the level of the National Security Council, the National Security Advisor and the President. The CIA's analytic function is located at this hub, supporting the decision-making that employs all elements of national power as well as the distributed informational needs of the intelligence and policy communities. Directly supporting this power coordination function is the intelligence community coordinating function in the form of the Director of National Intelligence and associated staff. This is the same role previously performed by the Director of Central Intelligence and the Community Management Staff, with new powers and authorities conferred through passage of the 2004 Intelligence Reform and Terrorism Prevention Act (IRTPA).

In sum, foreign intelligence exists to provide information to decision-makers at all levels of government so that they can apply the power they have at their disposal more precisely.

Domestic intelligence

Just as foreign intelligence enables the effective and efficient application of power internationally, domestic intelligence enables the effective and efficient application of power domestically. For example, informants can provide information leading to the arrest of people suspected of committing crimes, and wiretaps can provide law enforcement agencies with sufficient information to arrest suspects before they can carry out criminal or terrorist activities. In addition, domestic intelligence can provide correct information to law enforcement personnel so that misapplication of power such as false arrests or intruding on the wrong address or house does not occur.

In theory, this domestic intelligence could be combined with foreign intelligence through centralisation of all internal and external functions in a single agency. But due to concerns about an excessively powerful government, in the US foreign and domestic intelligence collection are separated from each other to protect domestic civil liberties. As Stewart Baker (2001), a former senior high ranking national security official, observed, 'Combining domestic and foreign intelligence functions creates the possibility that domestic law enforcement will be infected by the secrecy, deception, and ruthlessness that international espionage requires. Dividing the responsibilities among different agencies reduces that risk.'

In the US, domestic intelligence has been a perennial component of governance that historically has been institutionalised ad hoc to address specific threats to domestic security. Unlike other countries that established permanent domestic intelligence agencies to monitor citizen behaviour in the face of long-term insurgencies or violent political factions, the US historically had few reasons to institutionalise a national domestic intelligence capability. As Richard Morgan (1980: 16) observed, 'The first century and a half of American democracy was marked by intermittent episodes of internal intelligence gathering. Monitoring dissent, by the federal government at least, was undertaken only in response to a crisis of the moment; with the passing of the crisis the monitoring ceased, and the federal machinery that supported it was dismantled or retooled for other tasks.'

As with the foreign policy arena, however, domestic policy involves a mix of economic, political, and security (law enforcement) power. The difference is that these powers are structured by the US government through policy-making organisations such as the Departments of Agriculture, Education and Energy. Each department acquires the information it needs, but in the domestic context most of this information is not considered intelligence because it does not have to be acquired covertly. On the other hand, other domestic policy departments, such as Justice, Treasury and Homeland Security, contain components that collect and evaluate intelligence, consisting of the subset of information that needs to be acquired or assessed in secret in order for it to have value for decision-makers.

Historically there was a reluctance to create a permanent domestic intelligence capability at the federal level because, for the most part, the function could be met by existing capabilities at the state and local levels. But that changed during the twentieth century. The creation of the Federal Bureau of Investigation (FBI) in the early 1900s led to the institutionalisation of an intelligence function at the federal level. Over time the FBI became the federal government's primary law enforcement agency investigating violations of federal criminal law. During the Cold War its domestic intelligence capabilities expanded to counter increased perception of threat, and then shrunk in the 1970s because of public opposition to practices and a backlash against abuses. Following the 2001 terrorist attacks, the FBI has devoted much additional attention to the counterterrorism mission.

Since 2001 the federal government has made many changes to its security and intelligence agencies to improve their operations. The September 2001 terrorist attacks provided a security rationale analogous to Pearl Harbor for expanding existing national domestic intelligence capabilities into permanent bureaucracies dedicated to domestic intelligence collection and analysis. These changes include the creation of the Department of Homeland Security, the incorporation of the Secret Service into the Department of Homeland Security, the shift of the Bureau of Alcohol, Tobacco and Firearms from the Treasury Department to Justice, and the growth in FBI intelligence collection and analysis capabilities.

Supplementing these efforts at the national level are growing intelligence capabilities at the state and local levels. Unlike foreign intelligence, domestic intelligence in the US involves governing authorities at different, and sometimes overlapping, jurisdictions. Power in society is divided in many different ways. State governments, local governments, and tribal authorities each have power also, and use that power in different ways. Together they make up the US governmental system. But sometimes jurisdictions overlap. For example, preventing terrorist attacks in New York City could be seen as the responsibility of the federal government, the New York State government and its Office of Counter Terrorism, or the New York City government and its New York City Police Department's Counter Terrorism Division. Adjudicating roles and responsibilities when jurisdictions overlap can be difficult.

As different kinds of domestic intelligence capabilities are developed for counterterrorism purposes, new mechanisms have been created to coordinate the flow of information between the various levels or seams in governmental responsibilities. The bulk of domestic intelligence is collected by state and local law enforcement agencies in the course of their daily street patrols and other activities. Most of this information is not stored or aggregated into broader assessments of criminal activity, and once the information in case files is used to arrest or prosecute individuals, it is archived or disposed of according to local guidelines. Yet the sharing of information collected between the various levels of government could prove quite useful in the various missions of domestic security: counterintelligence, counterterrorism, crime prevention, and so on. But sharing this kind of information means creating new mechanisms called fusion centres to coordinate the horizontal flow of information between agencies at the national level. The other purpose of fusion centres is to coordinate the vertical flow of information between national, state and local levels of government. Due to the number of agencies, organisations and jurisdictional authorities involved, this is a very complex process.

Fusion centres that address vertical information sharing between levels of government are more complicated to manage than those which coordinate power horizontally at a single level of government. In the state and local context, power tends to be divided along geographic jurisdictional lines rather than the functional lines that the federal government uses. This difference in division of power also explains why it has been very difficult to establish lines of communication vertically between the federal, state and local governments. Theoretically, it could be possible to establish functional differentiations at the state and local levels similar to those that exist at the federal level, specifically by breaking down how power is applied in those domains that correspond with the organisations that exist at the federal level. But, for most small jurisdictions, this kind of breakdown based on functional specialisation would not be effective given relatively limited resource base. As a result, what happens is an awkward melding of different kinds of organisational structures at the federal, state, and local levels.

Despite the difficulties in bridging the gaps in domestic jurisdictions, domestic intelligence exists for the same reason that foreign intelligence does: to provide information to decision-makers so that they can apply the power they have at their disposal more effectively and efficiently.

Checks and balances

The US government was built in such a way as to ensure that power was divided both within the national government as well as between the national and state governments. The nature of the balance between national and state governments in the American political system has been the subject of debate and argument for more than two centuries. More diffuse power leads to a lesser ability to apply it. The early experiences with the Articles of Confederation demonstrated that diffuse power does not necessarily lead to the effective application of power.

Centralised power does allow for greater leverage in its application, and so over time power has become more and more centralised. History shows that power initially flowed from the streams to the river, with each of the states acting as tributaries to the national government's river. But now the flow appears to have reversed, with just as many distributaries as tributaries. General consensus exists that the national government has over time become predominant, and while some may dispute the rightness of it, it seems to parallel the requirements for organisation and efficiency driven by the need to protect from external threat and to advance economic interests.

As the country expanded, it began to form a unified nation-state with greater identification to the whole over the specific parts. In particular, the external threat of war during the twentieth century and the provisions made to meet it drew the country together. In addition, the gains in economic efficiency that resulted from more uniform rules and regulations led the locus of power to shift from the regional state centres to the national government. As the country has developed from multiple regional perspectives and identities into a nation-state the initial plan of government that called for a sharing of power between the forms of government has had to adapt to meet the changing conditions.

As the intelligence capabilities of the executive power of government grow, there is also a need to check or balance that growth of power through other branches of government. At the federal level, that means through Congressional authorisation and appropriations process, as well as continued oversight. The competition over the ends of aggregated power is what produces the partisan and interest group struggles within the legislative arena where the trade-offs in national goals are debated and decided. The attempt to govern is an exercise in competition, negotiation, and compromise. Despite popular dissatisfaction with partisanship, it will continue in perpetuity because that is what democracy is for.

There are, of course, passengers on this ship of state, who also just so happen to own the ship of state as well. Every few years they choose a new captain. The passengers themselves could become crew if they want to, or even try to become captain themselves. Or they could remain both passengers and owners. Regardless of the role they play, they tend to take a proprietary interest in the success or failure of the ship of state, both because they are on the ship, but also because they actually own the ship. The legislative arena is where the owners of the ship discuss where the ship should go, and periodically get into significant debates with the captain when he wants to go in a different direction. They also look over his shoulder and demand accountability when things go badly, thus ensuring a healthy tension in the relationship between owner and operator.

The degree to which the government employs domestic intelligence to monitor for threats internally is an ongoing debate. The passengers do not necessarily like the captain and the crew to have too much power over them. And yet at times it may be necessary for the captain and crew to protect the majority of the passengers from a violent minority. Having the crew member with the spyglass turned on the passengers could be very useful for that. But that does not mean the passengers like it either. So there is an ongoing debate over the extent to which the captain and the crew will obtain – or retain – domestic intelligence capabilities, and it changes according to the perception of threat.

Questions of the constitutionality of domestic intelligence collection and analysis programmes are embedded within a broader debate of the relative importance of national security vis-à-vis civil liberties. Two sets of partisans engage in this debate: those who advocate increased application of governmental power to protect national security (Baker 2001; Posner 2001), and those who emphasise the inviolability of civil liberties, such as the American Civil Liberties Union. The differences between partisans are not as wide as is conventionally assumed. All participants in the skirmishes agree that national security and law enforcement goals should be pursued within constraints established to protect civil rights and liberties. The US Constitution, after all, indicates that the government should both 'provide for the common defense' and 'secure the blessings of liberty'. However, while the Constitution's goals are ideal in theory, in practice the programmes to achieve one goal can conflict with another, and in the end trade-offs are necessary in order to realise some acceptable outcome. Conflicts arise because people define 'acceptable' differently, some prioritising national security or law enforcement over liberty, and others vice versa. Even though the skirmishes are fought on the margins of agreement does not mitigate the ferocity of the resulting battles.

While skirmishes have been fought over a wide front, the battleground with greatest implications for civil liberties is that of the government's acquisition and analysis of domestic intelligence because through this mechanism the potential exists for monitoring the behaviour and activities of every American citizen, and not just those suspected of crimes. Since the 2001 terrorist attacks state power partisans have had an advantage due to the public's increased perception of threat and greater willingness to compromise civil liberties to address it. As a result, civil libertarians have engaged in a strategic retreat and the battle lines have apparently shifted as a result of this retreat. Whether these new lines are temporary or permanent has yet to be determined.

Looking ahead

The purpose of intelligence is to guide the ship of state along the river of power. What started out as a small river in the late 1700s has now become a raging torrent; the world's superpower. More and better intelligence is required to ensure that the decisions are as good as they can be because the consequences of getting it wrong now are much more significant than they used to be. Looking to the future, it appears likely that demand for intelligence will only continue to grow.

In terms of foreign policy, the amount and kind of foreign intelligence needed varies according to the level of international engagement (e.g. power applied) and the type of foreign policy pursued. Isolationist policies require less information; interventionist policies require more. A militaristic policy will require primarily military information, a mercantilist policy will need primarily economic information, and a revolutionary or status quo policy will need primarily political information. In other words, the mission and targets of the American intelligence community will depend upon the foreign policy of the US, and it will be possible to explain and predict intelligence analysis coverage given US foreign policy priorities and the mix of power applied. Given that the US is the most powerful country in the world and is likely to remain so for the foreseeable future, it is highly likely that levels of foreign intelligence required to support both foreign policy and national security will remain quite high.

In terms of domestic policy, the amount of domestic intelligence needed also varies according to the amount and kind of power applied. Much of the effective management of social policy can be done openly through government agencies where intelligence is not required. But as threats increase, or are perceived to increase, ensuring security may require that more and more domestic intelligence be acquired in order to defend against those threats.

Since 2001, the increased perception of the threat from terrorism has led to an increased desire for domestic intelligence, but in the future the threat may be even greater than it is today. The threat to security is growing because technological knowledge inevitably diffuses. As knowledge increases, greater power is available at less cost and requires the efforts of fewer and fewer people. Technology provides people with tools, which are intrinsically neither good nor bad, but acquire normative value based on the uses to which they are put. Technological advances have provided huge benefits in many fields, including communications, education, medicine and food production, but the same technology that can be used to create can also be used to destroy. As technological capabilities get more advanced, the need to monitor smaller and smaller groups to prevent the development and deployment of new kinds of weapons, or ways of disrupting society, becomes increasingly important. This will lead to an increasing need for domestic intelligence capabilities in the future.

In addition, once intelligence capabilities are developed for one purpose eventually they can also be used for other purposes. For example, the government will most likely employ counterterrorism surveillance capabilities for general law enforcement purposes. Over time, technological advancements will only increase domestic surveillance capabilities and the ability of those in power to ensure domestic security. In addition, domestic intelligence information could be used for purposes other than ensuring security, such as the targeted distribution of goods and services. Once information is collected, it can be used for purposes other than those initially intended, and it likely will, because of increased efficiency and effectiveness of policy-making. This will also lead to an increasing need for domestic intelligence capabilities in the future.

Ultimately it is up to the elected leadership, reflecting the will of the people, to decide the degree to which power is applied either domestically or internationally. In the analogy to the government as channelling the flows of power as it might a river, initially the US government was a small river. As it has gotten older, though, the river has become much larger, and has reversed the flows from the streams from which it originally came. The three branches of the river have each gotten larger, and their respective ratio of water flow has changed. As a result, the banks have changed over time, and in places the river flows over different ground than it used to. The channel has grown deeper to accommodate the greater flow of water. The ship of state has grown larger and now moves faster along this river power, which increases the need for a lookout function like intelligence to help decision-makers choose the most effective path. That the US government has been able to accommodate to the changes that it has, and even thrive in the midst of a raging torrent, is quite an accomplishment and no small achievement. This is, in the end, a testament to the skill of the captains who have been chosen to sail the ship of state along this river of power, as well as to the able assistance of their lookouts.

15

CANADA

Andrew Brunatti

The genesis of Canadian intelligence as a national endeavour can be traced back to the Second World War, which prompted Canada's involvement in the collection and analysis of new forms of intelligence (Jensen 2008). Canada's close cooperation with Britain, the United States, Australia and New Zealand during the war years set the stage for its inclusion in the post-war alliance structures that encouraged burden-sharing and cooperation between these five states; a network that would become known as the 'Five Eyes'. Most important for Canada was its inclusion in the UK–USA Communications Intelligence Agreement (the 'UKUSA Agreement') of 1951 as a 'second party' (UKUSA Agreement 1951).[1]

The UKUSA alliance framework set the tone for Canada's Cold War intelligence community (IC), in much the same way NATO and NORAD[2] set the tone for its larger foreign and defence policy. Given Canada's population and economic size, burden-sharing through alliance structures appealed to Ottawa's fiscal and policy conservativeness. Additionally, Canada's preference for stability and negotiation in foreign policy was reinforced by the Cold War balance of power, which left little room for aggressive middle-power foreign policies (Bromke and Nossal 1983: 336–337). This preference for stability in foreign policy was matched in domestic policy, where concerns over national unity and economic stability were consistent trends.

The end of the Cold War removed the direct threat of East–West nuclear conflict but introduced a widened, more fluid threat environment alongside conflicting national and international policy demands. This multifaceted context has been exacerbated by the 9/11 attacks on the United States, the resulting Canadian involvement in Afghanistan and the post-2008 global financial crisis. To these largely external factors one must add the noted lack of an 'intelligence culture' in Canada, which derives from a risk-averse approach to defence and security issues in general (Horn 2006: 386; Lefebvre 2009: 85–86). Far from being detached from its national political environment, the Canadian IC is greatly impacted by these larger enabling and constraining dynamics. Canada's IC and intelligence policy-makers have often had to tread a fine line, balancing a need for intelligence to support government operations with a national political culture that has traditionally viewed intelligence at best with apathy, and at worst with suspicion. As a result, Canada's overall approach to intelligence has been defined by minimalism. Yet the Canadian IC has adapted and evolved in order to balance complex environmental demands, resulting in a maturing IC that is very much the product of Canadian interests and policies.

The chapter will explore this thesis by doing two things. First, it will provide an overview of the contemporary Canadian IC, with particular focus on collection, analysis and assessment, and coordination. Second, it will identify key trends in Canadian intelligence in order to provide a wider perspective.

Intelligence collection

Similar to its other Westminster allies, Canada has defined the mandates of its collection agencies largely by collection discipline rather than geography. The Canadian Security Intelligence Service (CSIS) is Canada's national agency for deriving intelligence from human sources and technical surveillance. Section 12 of the CSIS Act of 1984 gives CSIS primary responsibility for the collection and analysis of security intelligence, while Section 16 enables the Service to collect foreign intelligence at the request of the Minister of Foreign Affairs or the Minister of National Defence (CSIS Act).

In a distinction that can be outwardly confusing, there is no legislated territorial limit on CSIS's collection of security intelligence, however the Service's collection of foreign intelligence is limited to within Canadian borders.[3] Canada has defined security and foreign intelligence by target type rather than by geography, however there is an inherent overlap that is managed on the basis of whether the intended target is a Canadian citizen or not. In a recent review of the CSIS Section 16 Program, the Security Intelligence Review Committee (SIRC) identified that the lines between security intelligence and foreign intelligence were increasingly blurred. This has resulted in a rise in what has been termed 'blended collection', where the Service's Section 12 and Section 16 priorities are addressed simultaneously (SIRC 2010b). Additionally, CSIS now has a stronger international presence that extends beyond traditional liaison and further into operational activities in order to meet rising Government of Canada intelligence requirements (SIRC 2012: 21–22). While increases in overseas operations and foreign intelligence collection continue to raise questions about a 'foreign intelligence service in increments' (Forcese 2011), the statutory foundation for CSIS thus far remains unchanged.

While CSIS has principal responsibility for the collection of HUMINT and has traditionally been focused on security intelligence, the Communications Security Establishment Canada (CSEC) has principal responsibility for SIGINT and has focused primarily on foreign intelligence. Unlike CSIS, CSEC remained without a statutory mandate until 2001 when the Anti-Terrorism Act amended the National Defence Act (Lefebvre 2010: 260). CSEC's mandate, now laid out in statute, consists of the provision of foreign intelligence to the Government of Canada, provision of information security services and advice to government departments, and 'technical and operational assistance to federal law enforcement and security agencies' (ND Act 1985).[4]

The widened threat environment has significantly impacted CSEC's activities. Canada's proficient but limited SIGINT capability had always faced more targets than it had resources, but the post-Cold War environment exacerbated this considerably. Keith Coulter, Chief of CSEC from 2001–05, stated that SIGINT requirements from numerous government departments are constantly worked down to the essentials (Coulter 2005). Additionally, the growth in counterterrorism through the 1990s and certainly after 9/11 forced the Government of Canada to re-evaluate the balance that existed between CSEC's capabilities and the protection of Canadians' privacy. The 2001 amendments to the National Defence Act introduced a regime of ministerial authorisations that allows CSEC to target foreign communications where there is the possibility of a Canadian citizen or resident being involved (ND Act 1985; Lefebvre 2010: 260–261). Shelly Bruce, Deputy Chief for SIGINT at CSE in 2010, stated, 'we needed these new tools, because the combination of the internet revolution and the security agenda together comprised the biggest challenge ever faced by the SIGINT world' (Bruce 2010).

A recent administrative change illustrates CSEC's evolving place within the Government of Canada. In November 2011, CSEC was made a stand-alone agency within the National Defence portfolio (SI/2011–96). Previously CSEC had been a semi-autonomous agency within the Department of National Defence, with the Chief of CSEC answering to the Deputy Minister of National Defence and to the National Security Advisor (PCO 2001: 9). With the new arrangement, the Chief of CSEC holds the full responsibilities of a deputy head, including that of accounting officer for CSEC's new stand-alone budget, and is directly responsible to the Minister of National Defence for the administration and operations of the agency. This change signals a vote of confidence by the government in CSEC's maturity as an organisation, and indicates a desire to move the national SIGINT mission out from the control of a single department.

In contrast to the civilian agencies, defence intelligence has often been overlooked as part of the Canadian intelligence enterprise. However, the structures under the Chief of Defence Intelligence (CDI) represent Canada's third national intelligence collection organisation. The Defence Intelligence Review of 2004, which created CDI, began to move defence intelligence towards a more integrated model that would support operational joint headquarters and strategic national requirements (Cox 2011). The current CDI organisation encompasses six directorates, four of which unify intelligence production, capabilities development, information management and policy (DND 2009). The Director General for Military SIGINT (DGMS) integrates the activities of the Canadian Forces Information Operations Group (CFIOG) with national SIGINT capabilities housed in CSEC. Lastly, the Director for Geospatial Intelligence (D Geo Int) acts as Canada's national geospatial and imagery intelligence centre, overseeing the Mapping and Charting Establishment, the Canadian Forces Joint Imagery Centre and the Joint Meteorological Centre (Thompson 2009).

While SIGINT has traditionally been dominant for strategic and operational consumers, the role of geospatial intelligence (GEOINT) is steadily increasing. Concerns over arctic sovereignty and maritime security have placed a focus on what the Canada First Defence Strategy termed a 'system of systems' comprising aircraft, sensors, drones and satellites that will monitor Canada's vast northern territories and equally vast coastlines (DND 2008: 17). In perhaps the most significant step forward for Canada's GEOINT capability, DND's Polar Epsilon project, which exploits imagery from the RADARSAT-2 satellite in a public–private partnership, will eventually be complemented by the RADARSAT Constellation Mission, which will be wholly owned and operated by the Government of Canada in support of arctic and maritime surveillance missions (Mahmood 2009; Shanko 2012).

A more recent addition to the IC is Canada's financial intelligence unit, the Financial Transactions Reports Analysis Centre (FINTRAC). The investigation of terrorism financing has been identified as a key, but inherently challenging, aspect of modern counterterrorism (Major 2010b). FINTRAC receives and analyses financial reporting from numerous types of financial organisation, and disseminates relevant material to other intelligence and law enforcement actors (Capra 2010).

One of FINTRAC's principal customers is Canada's federal police force, the RCMP. When the security service function was separated from the RCMP in 1984, the force lost its national security intelligence role. However, the RCMP still retains the national lead for criminal intelligence. It exercises this role principally through the leadership of the multi-agency Criminal Intelligence Service of Canada and through its own Criminal Intelligence Program (RCMP 2009; CISC 2012).

Finally, there is need for a brief discussion of the long-running debate regarding whether Canada should have a 'foreign intelligence service' (Cooper, B. 2007; Livermore 2009). This terminology confuses the situation by implicitly defining 'foreign intelligence' geographically (i.e. intelligence collected externally), contrary to Canadian's tradition of defining it by target type (i.e. intelligence collected about *foreign actors*). Canada does collect intelligence about foreign actors through numerous means, the most apparent being CSEC's SIGINT collection and the CSIS Section 16 Program. The Department of Foreign Affairs and International Trade (DFAIT) collects foreign intelligence of the grey[5] variety through the longstanding Interview Program and the more recent Global Security Reporting Program (Jensen 2004; Swords 2007). Of course a significant amount of foreign intelligence is also derived from the diplomatic reporting of DFAIT's Foreign Service officers. Additionally, imagery and geospatial intelligence obtained by CDI will often fall under the definition of foreign intelligence. The debate regarding whether there is a gap in Canada's intelligence collection really focuses on whether there should be a particular functional capability (clandestine HUMINT) operating in a particular geographic environment (outside Canada). Given this, the key question actually becomes: 'Should Canada have a separate clandestine HUMINT organisation to collect foreign and security intelligence extraterritorially?' It has been pointed out that this question must ultimately be answered through a realistic cost–benefit analysis of Canada's intelligence needs (Livermore 2009). To date the question appears to have been answered in the negative. The expansion of niche capabilities such as DFAIT's Global Security Reporting Program and the CSIS Foreign Collection Program indicate that the Government of Canada is satisfied to adapt and evolve existing structures to meet increased needs.

Intelligence analysis and assessment

Given Canada's strong adherence to the Westminster tradition of ministerial responsibility and the close involvement of the UK during the IC's formative years, it is perhaps unsurprising that Canada, like Britain, ended up with centralised intelligence collection but decentralised analysis and assessment (Davies 2002). Intelligence is fed into departmental analytic organisations, such as DFAIT's International Security Branch, CDI's Director General of Intelligence Production, CSIS's Intelligence Assessments Branch, or Transport Canada's Intelligence Branch, where it is then used to support departmental operations including the formulation of advice to decision-makers. The division between validation, analysis and assessment within the Canadian system is, correspondingly, very similar to that of the British system (Butler 2004: 9).

While validation and analysis of intelligence takes place within the collection agencies or in departments, four organisations have responsibility for different types of assessment. The first is the International Assessments Staff (IAS) within the Privy Council Office. As its name implies, IAS focuses on assessing international dynamics in support of senior customers such as cabinet ministers and their deputies (PCO 2010: 10–11). IAS frequently draws on departmental expertise where possible, particularly CDI when military matters are concerned. CDI itself produces assessments on defence matters for senior readers when decisions are being taken about military deployments or force posture (DND 2009). CSIS's Intelligence Assessment Branch has primary responsibility for national assessments on threats to security, and operational threat assessments relating to terrorism are the responsibility of the Integrated Terrorism Assessment Centre (ITAC).

Until relatively recently, the national assessment function within the Canadian IC was impeded by the lack of an interested audience. As Greg Fyffe, a former Executive Director of IAS, has pointed out, 'Before 9/11, the input of intelligence material into decision-making, particularly international decision-making, was modest' (Fyffe 2011: 11). In the post-9/11 environment, ministers and their deputies have taken a greater interest in intelligence assessments, resulting in the strengthening of the assessments process, particularly at the centre of government (Fyffe 2007).

Coordination and management

As in other Westminster systems, there is a fine balance in Canada between devolved departmental management and central coordination. This is as true for the IC as it is for any other sector. The creation of Public Safety Canada (PSC) in 2003 unified the core public safety agencies under a single ministerial portfolio. PSC has since taken a lead coordinating role in counterterrorism, cybersecurity, critical infrastructure protection and federal law enforcement policy (PSC 2012).

However, not all intelligence relates directly to public safety, and important actors including CSEC, CDI, DFAIT's International Security Branch and FINTRAC necessarily fall within different ministerial portfolios. This ensures that the Prime Minister and Cabinet, and hence the Privy Council Office, remain the focal point for strategic coordination. As in Britain, a web of interlocking committees coordinates the national intelligence effort (Last and Milne 2005: 150). At the centre of this web are the Cabinet Committee on National Security (CCNS) and the Cabinet Committee on Foreign Affairs and Defence (CCFAD) (PMO undated). The Deputy Ministers' Committee on National Security (DMNS) supports these ministerial bodies by acting as the management board for the IC. Subcommittees operating under DMNS focus on particular themes, including intelligence programmes and border security (PCO 2012). The Intelligence Assessment Coordinating Committee (IACC), chaired by the Executive Director of IAS, maintains a watching brief over the national assessment and analytic effort (Fyffe 2007). Lower-level committees and working groups are also formed on an ad hoc basis in order to address particular interdepartmental assessments, policy issues or joint projects.

The process for defining national requirements and priorities for intelligence has been identified by review bodies as a consistent weakness in the Canadian community, but one that is being improved with experience (OAG 1996, 2009). Generally, the principal intelligence agencies forward draft priorities, including coverage requested by major customers, to PCO annually where they are reviewed and rationalised through the DMNS machinery. Agreed draft priorities are submitted to CCNS for review and approval. Once approved, National Intelligence Priorities for Security Intelligence are provided to CSIS, Foreign Intelligence Priorities are provided to CSEC[6] and Defence Intelligence Priorities are provided to CDI (OCSEC 2007; SIRC 2010a; DND 2011: 19). The agencies then construct collection plans that will guide collection activities in order to address the annual priorities. While these documents provide consistent guidance, much day-to-day interaction occurs bilaterally through requests for information, or RFIs, which are compared against the standing priorities to ensure consistency before being actioned.

Key trends in Canadian intelligence

The preceding sections have provided a necessarily brief overview of the contemporary Canadian IC. By casting a wider gaze, however, one can also identify several key trends that have played a dominant role in shaping Canada's intelligence community.

The first key trend is the development and management of *increasing interdependence* between actors. While each organisation can satisfy its own narrow mandate, the success of the *national* intelligence effort depends on the agencies trading resources between themselves. For instance, CSIS operations can benefit CSEC by providing information that allows for more efficient deployment of SIGINT capability. Conversely, CSIS relies on CSEC's foreign intelligence SIGINT in order to more effectively identify and prioritise security threats. The Service also relies on CSEC to provide specialist assistance under 'mandate C' to its Section 12 investigations (Mosley 2009). Interdependence is also reinforced through comparative advantage in analysis. PCO and DFAIT cannot hope to replicate the specialist knowledge sitting in CDI, and vice versa. Similarly, CSIS assessments on terrorism greatly benefit from the specialist financial knowledge housed in FINTRAC, while FINTRAC relies on wider CSIS analysis to help target its limited analytic capacity.

As the importance of these interdependencies has grown, the need to structure and manage resource exchanges increases in order to minimise risks to civil liberties and build trust between agencies. In response, the Canadian IC has crafted legislative mandates for its collection agencies that are nuanced and interoperable, as witnessed by the Mosley ruling of 2009 (Mosley 2009). The community has also made wide use of memoranda of understanding (MOUs) in order to regularise interagency business. For instance, there is a tri-ministerial MOU between CSIS, DFAIT and DND that governs the Section 16 Program, as well as one between the RCMP and CSIS that has evolved considerably since 1984 (SIRC 2000: 28–29, 80). Additionally, review bodies have been developed that focus on high-risk areas, namely the Security Intelligence Review Committee that reviews CSIS investigations and relationships, and the Office of the Communications Security Establishment Commissioner, which does the same for CSEC. These measures formalise, guide and review organisational interaction, allowing the agencies to safely exploit interdependencies in the face of increased environmental complexity.

The second key trend has been *tight fiscal control* of the intelligence community, sometimes bordering on strangulation. As early as the 1950s, the RCMP Special Branch was 'hopelessly understaffed and underequipped' (Sawatsky 1980: 105). Likewise, by the late 1970s, Canada's SIGINT effort in general was 'understaffed and ill-equipped', with its cryptanalysis effort 'literally on the point of extinction' (Robinson 1992: 24). A 1987 review of foreign intelligence assessment indicated that both defence and foreign intelligence assessment units were stretched dangerously thin (Marchand 1987: 39–41). The post-Cold War 'peace dividend' cuts prompted DFAIT to shed the foreign intelligence assessment function altogether in an effort to save other programmes (Farson 1999: 12).

Canada's IC has adapted in several ways to a consistently tight fiscal environment. First, it has focused on building capabilities around niche requirements. Prime examples of this are the CSIS Section 16 Program, DFAIT's Global Security Reporting Program, and the development of the RADARSAT satellite. While these initiatives are limited in scope, they each target a valuable niche requirement for the IC as a whole. Second, the community has tried to exploit technology for cost-effectiveness. For instance, CSIS's employment of lawful interception and electronic surveillance capabilities under Section 21 of the CSIS Act represent cost-effective methods of investigation when compared with alternatives. In another example, through the 1990s, as the defence budget was being subjected to continuous cutbacks, DND and CSEC converted the SIGINT intercept stations at Alert, Gander and Masset to remote operations controlled centrally from Ottawa (Rudner 2001: 108). Lastly, the IC has exploited its access to Five Eyes allies as a force multiplier, on which more will be said shortly.

While tight fiscal control of the intelligence community can avoid empire building and drive efficiency, going too far can leave agencies spread too thin and risk costly mistakes. The O'Connor Commission, which investigated events surrounding the Maher Arar affair, strongly indicates that a lack of surge capacity in both CSIS and the RCMP due to fiscal constraint contributed to the foundations of the affair (O'Connor 2006: 14–47). There is no doubt that massive investment over the last decade has left the Canadian IC in much better shape. However, the death of Osama bin Laden, the withdrawal of Canadian forces from Afghanistan, and the precarious global economic situation have already prompted some significant attempts towards a 'peace dividend', most recently targeting the follow-on RADARSAT project (Ivison 2012).

The third key trend is Canada's deliberate strategy of remaining a *net intelligence importer*. This phrase has been used to illustrate that the amount of intelligence Canada produces through its own national capability is far smaller than the amount of intelligence it imports from its Five Eyes partners. Margaret Bloodworth, a former Canadian National Security Advisor, has stated that Canada 'must contribute in order to receive, and this is all the more important given that we are a net importer of intelligence. If we were to try and replicate the benefits of these relationships within our own resources, it would cost tens, if not hundreds of millions of dollars' (Bloodworth 2007). For Canada, participation in the Five Eyes network is a force multiplier: relatively little investment in intelligence results in a disproportionate return (on the Five Eyes, see Cox 2012). Because Canada has lacked an 'intelligence culture', any significant expansion of Canada's intelligence capability risks political as well as economic costs. Given this larger context, the strategy of remaining a net intelligence importer strikes a shrewd balance.

Canada's IC: minimalist, but adaptive

The mounting complexity of the global environment has increased government's need for intelligence to assist decision-making. However, Canada's national political culture has oscillated between apathy and suspicion towards its intelligence community. Because of complex, often contradictory, environmental pressures, Canada's intelligence community has been defined by minimalism. However, within these constraints the IC has proven adaptive. The community has progressively recognised and managed interdependencies between actors in order to increase overall value. It has managed in many cases to balance tight fiscal control with the maintenance of operational capabilities, although long-term degradation has proven difficult to overcome. And lastly, the IC has managed its international partnerships in ways that ultimately benefit Canadian national security.

There have, of course, been problems, some of which seem intractable, like the tension between the RCMP and CSIS stemming from the 'intelligence versus evidence debate' (Major 2010a). However, the Canadian intelligence community is ultimately a maturing and learning organisation like any other. Given this, and because of the complexities involved, problems are inevitable and solutions inevitably difficult to determine. Perhaps the truly revealing feature is in how problems are addressed once they arise. In this sense, as in many others, the Canadian intelligence community ultimately reflects the country it serves: collegial yet cautious, purposeful yet modest.

Notes

1 Although Canada had been included in earlier iterations of the UKUSA Agreement, it was not until inclusion of Appendix J in the 1951 agreement that the Canadian position was explicitly stated.
2 North Atlantic Treaty Organization and North American Aerospace Defense Treaty, respectively.
3 Definitions relevant to 'security intelligence' and 'foreign intelligence' are included in the CSIS Act and the National Defence Act of 1985, respectively.
4 Referred to as mandate A, mandate B and mandate C, respectively.
5 Grey referring to the fact that these activities are not clandestine in nature, but not overt either.
6 These priorities also probably provide guidance to DFAIT's GSRP and Interview Program.

16

AUSTRALIA

Frank Cain

The Australian intelligence community is composed of six independent agencies, most of which were established during the Cold War. The oldest is the Australian Security and Intelligence Organisation (ASIO), followed by the Australian Secret Intelligence Service (ASIS), the Defence Signals Directorate (DSD), the Defence Intelligence Organisation (DIO) and the Office of National Assessments (ONA), and the latest is the Defence Imagery and Geospatial Organisation (DIGO).

Origins of surveillance in Australia

The surveillance of citizens considered to be a threat to the state was instituted in Australia during the First World War. The Intelligence Branch of the Australian Army led the surveillance and prosecution of opponents of the war for fear of them dissuading men from enlisting in what was the all-volunteer national army. Letters were opened, speeches recorded and pamphlets censored by the army, assisted by seconded police officers. An outpost of MI5 was established in Australia during the war, but there were few duties for it and it aided in the suppression of the anti-militarist and Marxist-styled Industrial Workers of the World (IWW), which had arrived from America before the war. Despite this, opposition to the war expanded and enlistments to the army continued to decline.

The government's concerns over left radicalism, stirred by the effects of the Bolshevik revolution, led to it establishing the Investigation Branch located in the Attorney-General's Department. It took over the large collection of files from the Intelligence Branch and some of its military staff, focusing on the Left and the nascent Communist Party of Australia (CPA). It maintained connection with MI5 through the wartime cipher it retained. The Investigation Branch was reluctant to keep watch on the right-wing proto-Fascist private armies established during the Great Depression nor on the local sections of the German Nazi Party sponsored by the German consulates after 1933.

The Cold War and establishment of ASIO

The Investigation Branch went into abeyance during the Second World War, to be replaced by the wartime Security Service, which continued to monitor the CPA and conduct security clearances for workers in the munitions industries. The Branch re-emerged after the war renamed the Commonwealth Investigation Service (CIS), but it was to be displaced by the establishment of Australian Security Intelligence Organization (ASIO) in 1949. ASIO was established as a result of the operations of the US Signal Security Agency in Arlington Hall, outside Washington, DC. The Agency had long experience in breaking the Soviet diplomatic, intelligence and trading codes used in the traffic between Moscow and the dozens of Soviet embassies and consular offices in the world. The operation was named 'Venona' or sometimes 'Bride', and gave the Agency access to traffic between Moscow and the Soviet embassy in Canberra (Benson and Warner 1996: vii–xxxiii). The embassy communicated with Moscow via telegrams, using a code book converted into five-figure blocks with add-on random numbers. Assuming this technique to be impenetrable, the telegrams were sent through the local post office in Canberra. From there they were plucked out of the transmission cycle by the Australian Army signals section and given to the Americans without the knowledge of the Australian government.

These American-decoded messages revealed the names of officers in the Australian Foreign Ministry and the sending of documents to Moscow. A combined committee of US State and Defense officials examined the issue and inappropriately decided that Australia was untrustworthy, and it banned the transmission of all US classified information to Australia. The UK was also affected through its alliance with Australia in conducting guided missile research that built on the developments in German rocket research, most of which had been captured by the Americans after the war. The British and Australians were building a missile testing range in the barren centre of Australia in which the British sought to use range instrumentation from the US. Hoping to persuade the US to lift the ban, the British Labour Prime Minister, Clement Attlee, wrote to President Truman about the issue saying that he would offer the services of MI5 to assist the Australians in establishing a new counterespionage system, which was a proposal acceptable to the Labor Prime Minister Chifley in Australia (Cain 2008: Ch. 4). The Australian government was aware of how intelligence bodies tend to become anti-left institutions, and Chifley's ministry had the new ASIO placed under the directorship of a Supreme Court judge to stop that bias evolving. The Americans lifted their ban on information, but only slightly to the level of 'confidential' for which the new government under Robert Menzies expressed gratitude. Meanwhile Menzies geared up ASIO to aid him in banning the CPA. He replaced the judge with the former Director of Military Intelligence, and expanded ASIO's staff to 141 officers. ASIO thereby converted to a secretive surveillance agency that worked directly and indirectly with Menzies' conservative government for much of the Cold War.

The Australian Secret Intelligence Service (ASIS)

The Australian Secret Intelligence Service (ASIS) emerged from the planning by R.G. Casey, a senior minister in Menzies' conservative government and who had connections with British intelligence work and the Central Intelligence Agency (CIA) through friendship with the Dulles brothers, especially Andrew Dulles, head of the CIA. He prodded the government to establish a local version of the British Secret Intelligence Service, also known as MI6. Three young men were selected in May 1950 to train with MI6, and on 13 May 1952 Cabinet approved the establishment of an Australian Secret Service that was to function by being hidden in Australian embassies. The Australian Secret Intelligence Service, as it was later named, functioned under a veil of secrecy with its costs concealed and recruitment conducted through the proverbial tap on the shoulder. Its existence was publicly revealed by another conservative Prime Minister in October 1977.

Casey intended that ASIS would collect foreign intelligence and have an operations arm. These combined functions in one officer placed some agents in stressful situations abroad. In 1993, ASIS agents in India and Egypt suffered breakdowns through their taxing duties and, after

162

receiving no assistance from their department, they aired their complaints on national television. Information emerged of how Australia had paid funds to political parties in Malaysia, and the Foreign Minister quickly established a Royal Commission to silence discussion on it. The Commission, conducted by Justice Samuels and Michael Codd, produced a 900-page report in April 1995 recommending, among other things, that ASIS be brought under its own parliamentary act. This change was made on 25 October 2001 with the passing of the Intelligence Services Act 2001 (Royal Commission Report 1995).

ASIS maintained a clandestine training centre outside Melbourne for its agents to learn skills in firearms and explosives. In November 1983 the centre staged a training exercise involving a 'hostage rescue' conducted in a leading Melbourne hotel, which went badly wrong. Automatic weapons and handguns were produced and a door bashed down with a sledgehammer, police were called and the participants arrested, although much of its impact was hushed up (Toohey and Pinwell 1989: Ch. 11). Thereafter weapons training ceased, although it has recently been reintroduced and permits ASIS agents to carry weapons for which they do not require to hold a gun licence. However, the discharge of the weapons has to be reported to the Inspector-General of intelligence. At the end of the Cold War, ASIS began to retrench staff numbers, but the events surrounding 9/11 led the Howard government to expand its staff numbers and finances. The present role of ASIS is one of providing human intelligence capability and secret intelligence not readily obtained by other means that may affect the interests of Australia and the well-being of its citizens. It conducts counterintelligence activities and liaises with its counterparts in other countries. It also provides support to the Australian Defence Force in its military operations (Cornall and Black 2011: 11).

The Defence Intelligence Organisation (DIO)

The Defence Intelligence Organisation also evolved out of the Second World War, in imitation of Britain's Joint Intelligence Bureau (JIB), by bringing together senior representatives of the three Australian defence services to analyse future enemy threats then confined to the region of the Soviet Union and communist China (Hall 1978: Ch. 15). In February 1970 JIB expanded its research analysis beyond the purely military issues to include foreign policy matters. This led to it being renamed the Joint Intelligence Organisation and headed by a Foreign Ministry appointee (Richelson and Ball 1985: 52–56). In 1977, the body was divided in two, with JIO continuing as a mainly military assessing organisation. The second body, to be known as the Office of National Assessment (ONA), was formed to include the other specialisations that are discussed below. In 1989 the defence intelligence bodies were reviewed resulting in it adopting the new title of Defence Intelligence Organisation (DIO). Its focus then became the provision of strategic intelligence drawn from all sources in the Australian intelligence community with the intention of supporting the current and potential operations of the Australian Defence Force. Its focus on anti-terrorism requires it to continually assess the military capabilities of countries and foreign non-state actors while also making technical assessments of weapons system, cyberthreats and defence-related technologies (Cornall and Black 2011: 13–14).

The Defence Signals Directorate (DSD)

The Defence Signals Directorate is mainly involved in collecting information from communication satellites in Australia's region and deciphering those parts of the traffic that have a bearing on Australia's security interests. It has its origins in the years of the Pacific War when the Australian and American military joined in decoding Japanese radio transmissions from sites around the Pacific. This joint operation contributed to the defeat of the Japanese forces. Eavesdropping on the wireless communications of neighbouring countries can be a valuable asset and, at the end of the war, the UK, US, Australia, Canada and New Zealand joined together to coordinate the collection of wireless traffic for alliance and security use. This was known as the UKUSA Agreement and this alliance continues today. DSD maintains stations to receive traffic from the International Telecommunication Satellites, or 'Intelsat', hovering above numerous countries in the Pacific region; it draws out the messages from fax, phone, emails or wireless telephones. These messages are put through high-speed Cray computers and, by using an Echelon program, the computers can select messages containing key words inserted in the program's 'dictionary' (Poole 1998: 4, 5, 7, 13). These selected messages are then computer-translated or copied within DSD for distribution to Australian intelligence agencies. DSD maintains a number of receiving stations with one at Shoal Bay near Darwin, one in the North West Cape and in Geraldton in WA, and one at Carbalah near Toowoomba in Queensland. These are linked through the army's radio network based in Watsonia in Melbourne and then transmitted to DSD in Canberra for sending on to the National Security Agency (NSA), which maintains a huge signals intelligence centre in Fort Meade outside Washington, DC.

The CIA also maintains a tracking station in Pine Gap near Alice Springs, which receives messages from its observation satellites passing in orbit over Russia and China. DSD's existence remained secret until revealed by the conservative Prime Minister in 1977 after which DSD, ASIS and DIO were individually covered by the Intelligence Services Act in 2001. In addition to collecting COMINT and SIGINT from people or organisations in the local geographic region, DSD provides assistance to the state governments and the Commonwealth on matters relating the security and integrity of information that is processed, stored or communicated by electronic or other means. It also provides support to the Defence Force in its military operations, and provides assistance in cryptography, communication, computer and other specialised technologies as well as helping in local search and rescue operations (Cornall and Black 2011: 11–12).

The Office of National Assessment (ONA)

The Office of National Assessment (ONA) was established by Prime Minister Fraser of the Liberal Party-led government in 1977 by splitting off the clearly non-military aspects from long-term national security planning. The Royal Commissioner appointed by the Whitlam government suggested such changes that would embrace the scientific, economic and geographic issues no longer appropriate to what became the DIO. ONA was established under its own act titled the Office of National Assessments Act 1977 and its Director-General is an independent statutory officer who is not subject to external direction on the contents of ONA assessments. He is Australia's senior intelligence figure. The Office has responsibility for Australia's Open Source Centre. ONA employs a permanent staff to which are added visiting academics on a contract basis, and analysts and military officers from other departments. ONA monitors all important issues in the world that would affect Australia, and prepares an intelligence assessment for presentation to the National Security Committee of Cabinet. These reports are confirmed through 'four eyes' inspections, meaning that the UK–US alliance of English-speaking countries also reads and comments on those studies. DSD serves the national interest by increasing government understanding of international developments by providing assessments to the government on international matters that are of political, strategic or economic significance to Australia (Cornall and Black 2011: 14).

In March 2003, Prime Minister Howard joined Australia to the US and the UK in the invasion of Iraq. The Americans had determined to attack Iraq as far back as 21 November 2001 and the following years were spent finding reasons to invade, ranging from it having WMDs to it importing yellow cake from Niger (Woodward 2004: 1–2). Andrew Wilkie was a senior officer in the ONA who resigned in 2003 in protest at Howard joining the war. In 2004 he published a book titled *Axis of Deceit*, showing how the allies went to war ignoring the advice of their intelligence agencies. These reports provided details of WMDs, but added qualifications about their limitations, and that their production had stopped. The leaders ignored the qualifications and the cessation of production. The ONA and other sources warned about the falsity of the yellow cake incident, but the British and Australian leaders ignored that advice and pretended the yellow cake matter was correct intelligence. After the war these national leaders deflected accusations for having made selective reading of those reports. A parliamentary inquiry in Australia led to a leading opposition member saying that 'The exaggeration and the sense of immediacy was the work of politicians, outside the intelligence advice they were being presented with – at least from the Australian agencies and, I would suggest, their American and British counter-parts' (Wilkie 2004: 119–120). Wilkie explained that his resignation was the only valid path he could see for attracting the publicity that might divert Howard from what Wilkie labelled 'this unnecessary war'. He wrote that 'The country [Iraq] did not pose a serious enough security threat to justify a war, too many things could go wrong, and it was plainly stupid to use force while other options remained' (Wilkie 2004: 186).

The Defence Imagery and Geospatial Organisation (DIGO)

The Defence Imagery and Geospatial Organisation (DIGO) was established on 8 November 2000 within the Department of Defence under a Cabinet Directive. It was an amalgamation of the Australian Imagery Organisation, the Directorate of Strategic Military Geographic Information and the Defence Topographic Agency. DIGO was incorporated into the terms of the Intelligence Services Act in 2005. Its role is to collect geospatial intelligence from a variety of sources including satellites, reconnaissance aircraft and unnamed aerial vehicles and takes the form of electro-optical, infrared and radar images or video. It was formed in response to the greater use of satellites to produce photo imagery in real time of any target in the world. The imagery can be obtained from commercial suppliers or from American security sources, and it is not known if DIGO part-owns a satellite source. It aids in collecting foreign intelligence and supports the defence force in its operations, which includes targeting and training. DIGO supports the states in national security functions and in emergency response functions by providing digital and hard-copy maps and tailored imagery (Cornell and Black 2011: 12).

ASIO and the Cold War

ASIO functioned under the Prime Minister's charter from 1949 until 1956 when Menzies agreed to the Director-General's request to pass an ASIO Act in order to give its officers continuity of employment. ASIO had achieved a political win over the Petrov Affair in 1954 that damaged the political prospects of the Labor Party. Petrov arrived in Australia in 1951 as a coding clerk for the Soviet embassy, and ASIO contacted him in the hope that he would defect and provide access to more Venona material. He defected in 1954 bringing non-Venona papers and Menzies immediately ordered a Royal Commission hoping to repeat the coup initiated in Canada by the defection of Gouzenko, another Soviet coding clerk, who exposed communists in the higher levels of the Canadian government (Cain 2003: Ch. 7) However, nothing eventuated because the Americans wanted to keep Venona a secret and refused to release this valuable material simply to prosecute a few communists in distant Australia. The ASIO Act was amended in October 1979 by the Fraser government, but more significantly in 1986 when the Hawke government made sweeping changes included the establishment of the Inspector-General's office to oversee ASIO.

In 1965 Menzies joined with the US in supporting South Vietnam in the Vietnamese civil war by sending troops to aid the South. This required select conscription for young males to fill out the army's ranks. Both actions received the popular endorsement at the time against the 'falling dominoes theory' that China might invade Australia. However, by 1969 popular opin-ion turned against the war, as it had in the US. The Menzies government was slow to recognise this political change, particularly among its middle-class voters who now feared losing their sons to this guerrilla war. ASIO maintained its surveillance on the growing numbers of dissenters, and photographed people that led voters to imagine a government secret service operating on behalf of the Menzies government.

When the Labor Prime Minister, Gough Whitlam, took office in 1972, he planned to make ASIO (then with a staff of 400) more accountable, and appointed Justice Bob Hope to conduct a Royal Commission into the AIC. Hope's report was sent to the next Fraser government, which in 1979 actually expanded ASIO's powers and made it less accountable. The election of the Hawke Labor government saw the long-awaited changes made in 1986. An Inspector-General of Intelligence and Security (IGIS), to act under the terms of the Human Rights Act, was appointed to oversee the intelligence agencies. A Joint Parliamentary Committee on ASIO, and other intelligence agencies, later to be known as the Parliamentary Joint Committee on Intelligence and Security (PJCIS), was appointed to review the functioning of the agencies. A confidential annual report was to be presented to parliament by ASIO and an extract made available to the public. A small legal section was established within the Attorney-General's Department to monitor and advise ASIO on legal questions. By then ASIO had a staff of 734. Some of the critics who had condemned ASIO for being a secret state within the state were placated by these changes.

The end of the Cold War, marked by the implosion of the Soviet Union and the vast economic growth of communist China, led to reductions in the intelligence community and shedding of staff. ASIO had to reduce its staff numbers by 50 officers to reach 684. But this winding-down was suddenly reversed following the events of 9/11 in the US. The conserva-tive Prime Minister, John Howard, was a friend of President George W. Bush and was actually in Washington when the Pentagon was attacked. He returned home intent on aiding President Bush's war on terrorism and punishing any Australian with terrorist links to the Middle East.

Terrorism and the expansion of ASIO's powers

Prime Minister Howard moved immediately to have 40 pieces of legislation passed by which the powers of the Federal Police and ASIO would be expanded to conduct the 'war on terrorism' with staff numbers expanded to 1,769 by 2011 (ASIO Report to Parliament 2011: 161). ASIO was given new powers to seize suspected persons on 28-day warrants, hold them in a secure place and have them interrogated by ASIO agents. The suspects were to be denied access to lawyers or friends and, after being strip searched, they could be held incommuni-cado for an indefinite period under a series of rolling 48-hour warrants. Detainees revealing the events occurring during this process of interrogation would be jailed, as would journalists reporting those events. It would have converted ASIO from being an undercover surveillance body into a form of secret police with holding cells and unlimited questioning powers. The

Joint Parliamentary Committee on ASIO and other political agencies divided over the bill on political party lines. After firm opposition from human rights groups, university law schools and particularly the newspaper corporations, who feared for their reporters' freedoms, Howard's conservative government withdrew the bill on 12 December 2001 and presented it again in March 2003 greatly modified and with a three-year sunset clause attached.

ASIO and the war in Iraq

In March 2003 Howard's government dispatched Australian troops to assist the British and Americans imposing regime change in Iraq on the basis of intelligence later found to be fabricated. The Office of National Assessments handled this bogus information and one of its officers, Andrew Wilkie, resigned in protest at the government going to war based on this unreliable information, as discussed above. There were few Australians found to have links to Middle East terrorism: one assessment identified approximately ten Australians who were arrested and charged under anti-terrorist legislation, but in most cases the charges were not sustained while others led to long legal challenges. Outside of this number was the case of two Australians caught in the tentacles of the Guantanamo Bay prison camp. More importantly, however, a large number of terrorist convictions were obtained against two groups of mainly Muslim working-class men. One group was charged with conspiracy over a possible bombing activity in Melbourne that never eventuated and another group of men was convicted of conspiracy involved in a possible raid on the Holdsworthy army barracks to capture military weapons contained therein. Space does not allow an analysis of these lengthy legal cases that went far beyond ASIO's resources and involved hundreds of state and federal police officers. The cost of these multiple trials was estimated to amount to hundreds of millions of dollars.

ASIO and the renditioning of Mamdouh Habib

The renditioning of Mamdouh Habib, a duel Australian-Egyptian citizen, who was held in America's hands while being tortured in Cairo, reflected badly on the Howard government. Public opinion was initially critical of him, but a wider publication of his case while imprisoned after being sent by the US to Guantanamo Bay led to support flowing to him. Habib was held for two and one half years without charge. He was eventually released and wrote a book about his experiences, titled *My Story: The Tale of a Terrorist Who Wasn't* (Scribe Publications, Melbourne, 2008). In December 2010, the Labor Prime Minister, Julia Gillard, asked the Inspector-General of Intelligence and Security, Dr Vivienne Thom, to 'conduct an inquiry into the actions of Australian intelligence agencies in relation to the arrest and detention overseas of Mr Habib from 2001 to 2005'. Dr Thom called for thousands of pages of documents and summoned 24 current or former Commonwealth officers and Mr Habib to appear before her on oath. The public part of her report was issued in December 2011 and while Dr Thom's investigation covers the same time period as that described in Habib's book, there is nothing in common between the two publications because they were drawn from differing sources. Dr Thom was concerned only with the involvement of Australian officials and Habib's assertions about his contacts with these officials were discounted by the Inspector-General through lack of documentation.

Habib (2008: 32) was born in Egypt in 1956 and naturalised in Australia in 1980, after which he raised a family in Sydney and became involved in local Muslim politics, which led to ASIO trying to recruit him as an informer. Hoping to establish an agency business with Pakistan, he travelled to Islamabad and then to Kabul in Afghanistan, but on witnessing the 9/11 events on television there he immediately returned to Australia starting with a bus trip to Karachi, only to be taken off the bus by Pakistan police near Quetta on 5 October 2001 (Habib 2008: Ch. 3). ASIO learned of the arrest soon after, as well as a report saying that 'he might have had prior knowledge' of the 9/11 events (IGIS Report 2012: 26). That statement seems to have been accepted by ASIO without questioning its origins. It led ASIO to assume that Habib was a terrorist and it sent an agent, Mr L, to Islamabad to interview Habib in jail and also to offer him consular help. It was improper for the Australian High Commissioner's office in Islamabad to allow Mr L to assume that role of consular adviser. Then suddenly Habib was flown to Cairo on 10 November 2001 for renditioning.

ASIO and other departments discussed the matter of sending Habib to Cairo from as early as 24 October 2001 and Dr Thom found little resistance from them to him being handed over even with no charge against him. She was surprised to find no documentation of how this agreement was reached. She was also surprised to find that on 24 October ASIO handed over to Egyptian intelligence the papers and laptop taken from Habib on the bus saying that it would 'have severe consequences' for Habib facing Egyptian officials known to practise torture. She criticised Dennis Richardson, Director-General of ASIO for the lack of official documentation about this important handing over of Habib. Habib (2008: 103–108) described in his book his interrogation and torture in Cairo, about which Dr Thom was not interested because her inquiry was confined to actions of Australian officials. In March 2002, Dennis Richardson decided that Habib had been cleared of terrorist activities against him (IGIS Report 2002: 58–59). But instead of having him return to Australia, he was taken over by US officials, who flew him in mid-April 2002 to Guantanamo Bay. Australian officialdom apparently did not learn of this transfer until 3 May 2002. The Consul-General in Washington, Derek Tucker, visited him there and the Australian Foreign Office asked the US officials to charge him or release him, but the Guantanamo affair had become highly politicised in Washington by then. His real rescuer was the American human rights lawyer, Joseph Margulies, who had Habib's amazing story published in the *Washington Post* on 6 January 2005, from where it was picked up by Senator Durbin then questioning the Attorney-General designate, Alberto Gonzales, who was testifying at his Senate confirmation (Margulies 2006: 194). Three weeks later Habib was released and flown to Sydney in a specially hired Gulfstream business jet. Margulies assured Habib (2008: 228) that the CIA had arranged for his quick release through not wishing to see the details of Habib's Cairo torturing episode brought out in court hearings.

The Inspector-General found ASIO, the AFP, the Foreign Ministry, the Prime Minister's Department and the Attorney-General's Department all to be wanting in their protection of Habib's human rights. Dr Thom condemned them for leaving Habib in American hands just because he could not be prosecuted if brought home. She remarked that 'insufficient regard was had to the fact that Mr Habib was being held without charge and without access to any legal process for over two years, and no Australian government agency positively satisfied itself that the detention had a proper basis in law. Mr Habib's best interests should have been the subject of more attention and action by Australian government agencies,' her report noted (IGIS 2012: 102). The importance of Dr Thom's investigation was that the intelligence agencies, the Federal Police and the Foreign Affairs Department were called on to account for their actions and that ASIO's secret files and document had to be produced and shortcomings in their compilation was criticised by the Inspector-General. One can be assured that the large ASIO staff, now approaching 1,800 officers, will be more meticulous in the immediate future with their record-keeping procedures should a similar case arise.

Future directions for the Australian intelligence community

Those parts of the intelligence community that had not been given their own legislative authority such as ASIS, which had functioned as part of the Foreign Affairs Department, DSD, which was part of the Defence Department, and DIGO, which established new defence technology within the Defence Department, gained legal status in 2001 with the adoption of the Intelligence Services Act of that year. The official thinking seemed to be that with the end of the Cold War these individual bodies should be given greater permanency and continuity rather than looking to merge them into a new post-Cold War collective of intelligence bodies. The Parliamentary Committee on Intelligence and Security was also given the status of permanency even though it was a committee of parliament rather than part of the AIC. The possible leakage of secrets through parliamentary members and staff seemed to be the motivation for this legislation.

The legislation did not lead to greater cooperation between community members established during the years of the Cold War, and the so-called 'stove piping' tendencies continued. The first decade of this century witnessed the assertion by the Prime Minister's Department that sought greater cooperation within the intelligence community. On 23 December 2010, Prime Minister Gillard acted by establishing an 'Independent Review of the Intelligence Community'. Its two members, Robert Cornall and Rufus Black, took a year to interview a large number of senior public servants who were associated with intelligence leadership both in Australia and overseas. The reviewers remarked the 'The intelligence community has grown substantially over the last ten years in response to increasing demand, mainly in relation to terrorism, fighting wars and countering espionage (including cyberattacks), proliferation of weapons of mass destruction and people smuggling.' The part of the review released to the public was disappointing. It did not recommend mergers in the community and it opposed any move to separate domestic security intelligence from foreign intelligence when the threats of that period were emanating from external influences (Independent Review of IC 2011: 22).

However, the Parliamentary Joint Committee on Intelligence and Security took action during the Cornall/Black inquiry to ensure that the legislation controlling the 'intelligence community members was appropriate and effective for dealing with the local counter-terrorism and security issues . . . and contain[ed] appropriate safeguards for protecting the rights of individuals'. To this end the Joint Committee legislated for the appointment of a 'National Security Monitor' under a new act known as the 'Independent National Security Legislation Monitor Act 2010'. A Sydney barrister, Bret Walker SC, was appointed as the inaugural Independent Monitor in April 2011 and, by 16 December 2011, he had presented his first Annual Report. With appendices, this report extended to 116 pages that cannot be summarised here other than to note that Mr Walker examined some of the legislation introduced in haste by the Howard government in 2001, including the amended ASIO Act that he intended to examine in his succeeding reports (Walker 2011).

In other changes affecting the AIC in 2012 was the establishment in the Office of Prime Minister and Cabinet (PM&C 2012) of the National Security and International Policy Group Executive. Included in this Executive was the position of National Security Adviser who is to develop partnership within the national security community and oversee the implementation of all national security policy arrangements. The Adviser will report to the Secretary of PM&C, who is the most senior official next to the Prime Minister. One of the aims of the PM&C is to establish by 2020 the pooling of all information in the national security community that will produce 'the smooth flow of people, ideas and activities across boundaries' (Dept PM&C, NSIPGE: 2012: 1–3). Each desk associated with the pooled office will have a screen and keyboard, and 'the users will be able to switch between classification domains with ease. Individuals will have secure desktop video and teleconferencing and will have secure mobile voice and data communications for when they are away from the office' (Chief Information Officer 2009). The concept of the AIC, as it stands today, will be converted with these changes by 2020 into data collection agencies gathered under the aegis of the PM&C Department. Record collection and the tight security around this has been an essential factor with Australian intelligence agencies. How much they will permit sharing that secret information through secure videoconferencing links within a large national body will be an indication of how far the AIC has moved on from its distant origins embraced in secrecy in the years of the Cold War and afterwards in present times.

17

FRANCE[1]

Pierre Lethier

'Our borders may know no threats, but threats now know no borders' – the adage was blatantly simple but patently relevant. This formula set the tone of public discourse in France just over four years ago on the whole question of *le renseignement*, and it soon became all-pervasive. It was in simplistic terms of this nature that the French government launched an initiative in June 2008, the aim of which was to convince the public that it had had little option but to make the decisions and take the measures it had in defence and security policy and in intelligence, three areas which from then on would be linked in government literature. In making this point, the centre-right government elected in 2007 was also trying to avoid upsetting the near-complete consensus on defence that had been in place in France for more than 30 years.

Surely it would do no harm just this once. It was a significant decision, a surprise even, for a French government to unveil its policy on secret intelligence and hope for immediate public support. The precedents were few and far between, and had generally coincided with times of international crisis. They had also been quickly forgotten. The one possible exception was the remarkable moment when, during the Stresa Conference of April 1935, France's short-lived and ill-fated prime minister Pierre-Etienne Flandin decided to show his hand. National secrecy had been laid on the negotiating table, and the incident remains etched on public memory.

The timing of Flandin's unprecedented act – France was the first country to take such a risk – was striking. At this point successive French governments, which seemed to take over from one another at a frenetic pace, had sought to address the gaps and failures in the country's legal, statutory and legislative system, and to devise a more precise definition of secrecy in matters of state and of defence. Violations of these categories of secrecy would be punished with increasing severity. Flandin and his delegation lifted the lid on all of France's secret intelligence not only to Great Britain and Italy – whom they were trying (in vain) to bring round to their viewpoint – but to the whole world. This information concerned not only the general threat posed by Nazi Germany and its specific plans, which went far further than mere revenge, but also the capacity and scale of its espionage, involving diplomacy, the military and the police – a closely guarded secret until this point.

The rhetoric of border and threat employed in 2008 was radically opposed to that of 1935, and it drew attention to the ends and means of secret intelligence in a more unequivocal fashion. The one, momentary, dissenting voice came from a group of army officers worried about the country's future military capabilities, which were to remain under the cover of the pseudonym *Surcouf*. On the whole the general public – less well informed than these anonymous experts but anxious to feel secure in the immediate – responded enthusiastically: the government's general plan of defence, security and intelligence was felt to be coherent, and its redefinition of the aims and organisation of what it now referred to as the national intelligence community was considered timely. The dissenters made an unsuccessful attempt to denounce the simplistic and inconsistent nature of the White Paper on Defence and National Security of June 2008 in the media; shortly afterwards, opinion polls showed that the general outline of the government's plan had been well received, and that in its new dispensation the intelligence services enjoyed a positive image, especially in the specific area of foreign intelligence. The picture presented in 2008 was a reassuring one.

This new-look intelligence community, conceived in a time of budget cuts and reductions in military personnel and civil service staff, was an amalgamation of six specialised departments and special services, four of which were of long-standing – created in the mid-1930s, and frequently reformed and renamed under the Fourth and Fifth Republics – the other two of more recent foundation. All were statutorily placed under the authority of three key government ministries: the ministry of defence looked after the DGSE (foreign intelligence), DRM (defence intelligence) and DPSD (the ministry's security service), the ministry of the interior was in charge of the new DCRI (homeland intelligence), which essentially consisted of the former DST (counterespionage) and of a few elements of the RG (political and general information), and the ministry of finance was responsible for the DNRED (customs intelligence) and TRAC-FIN (financial intelligence).

These six departments had previously been both strictly separate from one another and individually compartmentalised. Now, though, while the relevant ministries would continue to control their operations, the very highest level of the state would coordinate them, bringing them closer together, harmonising their activities and facilitating exchange and mutual support between them. This collection of specialised organisations would employ a total of nearly 15,000 career agents drawn from various civil servant corps, notably from the police and – accounting for half of this burgeoning community – from the military. Henceforth all would be obliged to cooperate, and together they would share an effective monopoly on all activities and resources, human and technical, in secret fact-finding, clandestine action, armed forces intelligence and security, and detection and prevention of attacks on state security; their remit would also include counterespionage, counterterrorism and counterinsurgency, as well as customs investigations and inquiries into suspicious or fraudulent money trafficking.

The White Book on Defence and National Security of 2008 was a short initial statement, just a few pages and a single graph, but it nonetheless represented something entirely new – previous White Books had given very little, if any, space to the state's secret activities. Clandestine operations have never been mentioned in this programmatic literature, only activities of 'analysis and synthesis', generally in succinct and uncomplimentary language. For example, the White Paper of 1972 confined itself to a single but incisive phrase deploring the paltry nature of assessment activities, while the 1994 paper included one paragraph exhorting the services to maximise their efforts to present government authorities with quality synthesis.

The 2008 document – which, unlike many previous White Papers, was made public – was not concerned with this end of the intelligence chain, in which substantial investment in human resources had already been made, slowly at first, but had now reached completion. Instead, it focused on establishing formally the role of the special services within the context of the country's general defence and security programme, the way in which they were to be organised and the overall system of command and control of the services. Around the time this general outline of the administration and financing of intelligence appeared, a number of complementary announcements were made, for example the creation of a National Intelligence Council, a National Intelligence Coordinator, an Intelligence Academy and a Parliamentary Mission on Intelligence.

When France's new socialist president, François Hollande, was elected to office on 6 May 2012, the intelligence question was left hanging. The manifesto he had presented in the course of his long electoral campaign gave no indication of whether he would retain or modify the intelligence legacy bequeathed to him by his conservative predecessor Nicolas Sarkozy. When he was formally invested as head of the state on 15 May, President Hollande pledged that his prime minister – Jean-Marc Ayrault, whom he had appointed the same day – would have full powers restored to him according to articles 20 and 21 of the French Constitution. This means that Prime Minister Ayrault, far more than his predecessor François Fillon, will have complete responsibility for the direction of government policy and the running of the entire administration. In these conditions, one might ask if the new president will retain absolute control over government intelligence – President Sarkozy having been effectively in the driving seat on intelligence matters – or whether he will go back to the system that had lasted from the time of General Charles de Gaulle until the accession of Nicolas Sarkozy and François Fillon, in which the overall command and, above all, the instruments of control belonged to the prime minister.

In 2008 the CNR (National Intelligence Council) replaced the CIR (Interdepartmental Intelligence Commission), the new coordinating body enjoying a higher status than its predecessor. From the beginning of the Fifth Republic, the CIR had been under the prime minister's supervision, along with all other interdepartmental organisations implementing national defence policy. Today, though, the all-powerful CNR brings together the prime minister and five senior ministers – interior, defence, foreign affairs, finance and industry – plus the heads of the intelligence and security services, all under the authority of the president, to whom they report. This presidential council decides the overall direction of intelligence, defines its priorities, establishes the state's intelligence needs and hence its main research objectives, and in doing this decides on the distribution of resources and investment, delineates areas of activity and manages any possible sources of friction – between the services themselves or with other ministerial departments, such as foreign affairs or treasury. The office of permanent secretary of the CNR is filled by the national coordinator of intelligence, a senior civil servant whose secret remit is supervised by the president's general secretary, the true right arm of the head of state. While the coordinator is effectively the intelligence services' means of access to the president, he does not possess the authority of a full-blown intelligence community manager.

From the year 1959 the intelligence coordinator, after the fashion of the old CIR, had operated under the control of the prime minister, and hence was not a director of national intelligence either. His role was strictly confined to synchronising police intelligence and foreign intelligence activities aimed at countering the various threats France faced in the days of the Algerian war; it was not to last. After the constitutional reform of 1962, which introduced further presidential control over the new regime, it was replaced by a twin leadership, the job of receiving and assessing intelligence briefs and (when absolutely necessary) of coordinating these operations now falling to both the presidential palace and the prime minister's office. This division of labour between the Elysée (strategic direction) and Matignon (notably in matters of secret funding) placed control in the hands of a hybrid civil-military superior hierarchy, and proved perfectly stable and indeed virtually undisputed until the end of Valéry Giscard d'Estaing's presidency and Raymond Barre's government. After that, things began to drift, and the system was criticised by a number of intelligence chiefs and aides who served during the period dating from the political transition of 1981 to that of 2007. Many of those who had fallen out of favour most rapidly published their memoirs or gave testimonies, in which they typically claimed that, far from being an efficient line of communication between themselves and the two heads of the national executive, the chain of command was akin to a double screen, which often served to cut them off from the heart of elected power. This structure was in fact the antithesis of a global management system, and in the past had effectively separated the interior and exterior services, and even set them against one another. A very provisional solution to the problem was tested under Prime Minister Michel Rocard in 1990–91, at a point when intelligence reforms were being prepared that would involve the military – more specifically the SIGINT and ELINT, the areas in need of most urgent attention in the wake of the First Gulf War. This conclusion recognised what was considered an intolerable unevenness in technical intelligence resources between the allies of the coalition. However, under Rocard's government a permanent intelligence committee would convene once a month, attended by all the heads of the different intelligence services – in the presence not of the prime minister and his ministers, but of their respective chiefs of staff or principal private secretaries.

While it may not be an essential priority in these first days of the new presidency of 2012, the question of where and how national intelligence is directed could rapidly become more important in the months ahead. The president is head of all the armed forces and sole master of the nation's nuclear arsenal (article 15), guarantor of national territory and of all treaties (articles 5 and 52) – in other words, the supreme head of Diplomacy. He could decide to follow the example created by his predecessor Nicolas Sarkozy and choose to maintain the apparent coherence created by the new presidential *imperium* over national intelligence: after all, the aim of the 2008 reform had been to simplify the system, to provide some clarity where an increasingly unhelpful ambiguity had reigned since the mid-1980s. This had been painfully evident during the three periods of political *cohabitation* – 1986–88, 1993–95 and 1997–2002 – between a president and prime minister from opposing parties, who were often rivals for the presidency in the following elections.

To an extent, the ambiguity of the system had been revealed to the public during the famous *Rainbow Warrior* affair in 1985. Attempts were made in France to discover not only who, legally and in actuality, had been in command of the clandestine operation, but who was responsible for it politically. A deafening silence from the executive prompted theories of a dirty trick played by a service that had gone rogue or factional, or both. This time however, the principle of plausible deniability was not an option for the government, especially since from the outset the opposition had been whipped up into a frenzy by two former intelligence and security hierarchs – experts in clandestine operations who had been rudely dismissed during the political transition of 1981 – and were fanning the flames of controversy as hard as they could. The sabotage of Greenpeace's flagship in Auckland had gone disastrously wrong when an innocent bystander was killed by the second underwater bomb used in the action, after which two French agents were captured. It was a bold and risky operation, which would inevitably have been traced back to France, but in truth it was death of the young Portuguese journalist and the arrest of the two Service Action officers which really turned public opinion. Without the tragedy and disgrace which resulted some would have been amused by the affair; experts might even have praised the skill and bravery of the sailors and divers, risking their lives in exceptionally turbulent ocean waters during the southern winter.

The order to carry out the sabotage was issued to the head of the DGSE, Admiral Pierre Lacoste, by the minister of defence, Charles Hernu, and then confirmed by the president's personal military chief of staff, General Jean Saulnier, while the allocation of special funds for this expedition to the antipodes was authorised by the prime minister's principal private secretary, Louis Schweitzer. The normal procedure of authorisation for clandestine operations – unknown to the general public at this point – had been followed faithfully. However, there was no indication that the prime minister himself, Laurent Fabius, had ever been informed of the real purpose of the southern expedition. This raised the question of whether the prime minister, traditionally considered as occupying 'the worst of all jobs' under the Fifth Republic, should always be held responsible for everything the state did. In this particular case it was decided that he should not, and that his role in the minister of defence's clandestine operations was not to be probed. To complete the story, it is worth recalling the unswerving loyalty the head of the government showed both to the country's secret services and to the president who appointed him. In order to give the handful of agents who were still in or near New Zealand in July 1985 a chance to escape their pursuers, Laurent Fabius went along with the famous and wicked government inquiry which spent the summer bungling and delaying its investigations for as long as possible.

The ambiguity of the pre-2008 system stemmed as much from a lack of higher legislation as it did from the way the services were run. Since France has chosen not to possess an Intelligence Services Act per se, the president has no explicit – let alone absolute – prerogative. Hence secret intelligence does not strictly, or even naturally, belong to the 'private domain' of the president, except in cases when it is directly concerned with the head of state's exclusive right in matters of diplomacy – for example, the decision to expel a great number of Soviet diplomat-spies in the early 1980s, and later a high-ranking American intelligence officer and his four agents in the mid-1990s, was taken or at least authorised by the president himself. In times of political *cohabitation*, even more than in the more customary situation of the president and the parliamentary majority (and by extension the government) being of the same party, strategic intelligence is part of the 'shared territory' belonging jointly to the president and the prime minister. In actuality, the president's role is sometimes further reduced.

A compelling example occurred in the spring of 1988. Prime Minister Jacques Chirac decided to dispatch Service Action to the frontline in New Caledonia to suppress a rebel Kanak group – the insurrectionists had taken up armed resistance against local legal representatives when a law was passed aimed at destroying their hopes of legally gaining independence in the future. Although the socialist president François Mitterrand was in favour of a completely different policy, he decided not to risk a clash with the conservative prime minister. In short, he gave in, and Service Action's intervention – violent, by definition – was out of his control.

A third example of a different type from the same decade – one which the passage of time has allowed historians to give some consideration – demonstrates the ways in which the president, on occasions when the prime minister chooses to step out of the affair, can exploit the secret services for his own personal diplomatic ends, secret or otherwise. This would include instances where the minister of foreign affairs and senior diplomats are not completely in agreement with the president's foreign policy, and the president decides to forestall, circumvent or even counteract their initiatives. Such as it exists, secret diplomacy is the exclusive preserve of the president, and his instrument for the purpose is the foreign intelligence service. It was in this manner that President Mitterrand dismissed the arguments of his minister Claude Cheysson – who belonged to the left wing of the party – and effectively shut him out by offering aid to the British in their recapture of the Falkland Islands in the spring of 1982. This military aspect of this affair has been widely misunderstood. The type of action Mitterrand implemented required a smokescreen, but ignorant commentators have confused this with the vague appearance of a double game. A pertinent example occurred as the conflict was drawing to a close, at a point when neither London nor, of course, Paris was aware of the exact date when the Argentines would formally surrender. French sources in contact with Argentina's naval air force had gathered vital intelligence concerning the placement of the five French-made jets and their anti-warship missiles on Tierra del Fuego (outside the official war zone) – missiles which had had a devastating effect on several previous occasions – but this information was not immediately made available to British forces. The intelligence reached the frontline belatedly, it must be said, but a false impression soon spread of inefficiency or, worse still, insincerity on the part of Mitterrand and the secret action he had authorised. The final special operation, codenamed after an exotic operetta by Gilbert and Sullivan, was launched with assistance from Chile – at that point the regime France abhorred more than any other – and it was a failure.

However, secret diplomacy entrusted to the intelligence services has more often been adopted as a course of action by the head of state in order to resolve a crisis, defuse a conflict or as a secret intermediary in disputes between warring neighbours. For several decades this was something of a speciality of the SDECE and then the DGSE in French-speaking Africa, from the Sahel to the Great Lakes.

Because of its fluidity and its ability to change course swiftly, secret action also allows the president in certain instances to keep his political options open. This was the case for two decades in Lebanon, where a bewildering array of players was involved – many of them acting in Syria's interests – who constantly shifted their demands and allegiances, or who only came to participate during the afterlife of the crisis in the region. In instances of the latter, secret action became a feature of the long conflict between communities, deploying every possible component of intelligence, counterinterference and armed intervention. The cost of this activity was considerable, and special government funding was required in great quantity and with great frequency – this, then, presupposed a minimal level of governmental consensus, despite the hardships and the frequent failures of counterterrorism. When secret action was applied to very precise geographical areas – for example, in the border area between Lebanon and Israel for discreet mediation between Amal Shiites and the Israel Defense Forces, or, later, in the Sahel belt during the Touareg rebellions for talks between governments and separatists – established experts were required, seasoned campaigners of the 'old school', as it were. This type of intermediation is run directly, or very closely, by the director general and his project leaders, and is always sanctioned by the president; it is deployed in advance of regular diplomatic activity, but acts in harmony with it, not antagonistically. Its use also gives the political authorities reliable opportunities to evaluate the intellectual calibre and technical dependability of their special services.

Certain operations of this type have been described by intelligence chiefs and agents who have subsequently published their memoirs – invariably these operations were fairly delicate in terms of day-to-day activities, but in the long run proved not to be terribly dangerous or politically toxic, and were probably unveiled for this very reason. Nobody ever seemed to take offence at their being made public. On the other hand, secret actions with a potentially explosive political or diplomatic dimension – for example, active support for guerrilla organisations, pressure groups or revolutionary movements or retaliation against foreign secret services and terrorist groups, generally in the Middle East – are obviously commented on retrospectively far less by this particular type of author. Exceptions to this usually occur when the author is no longer in sympathy with the organisation he once served, or was an unwilling and truculent victim of one of the purges that invariably occur during a change of government: in this case he will tend to be implacably opposed to the prevailing ideology at the point of his removal from the service. These disgruntled individuals are often keen to feed stories to the public that combine their professional experience and their personal understanding (or lack thereof) of the naturally impenetrable, complex system that had employed them. This was conspicuously the case during the decade following de Gaulle's second elevation to office, which saw the publication of a swathe of corrosive memoirs. However, it was far from being the only time. This literary sub-genre, following epic accounts by Philippe Thyraud de Vosjoli, Marcel Leroy-Finville and Roger Wybot, has become well established in France.

Over the years, several French politicians have expressed their surprise, and often their dismay, at the existence of what at first sight seems to be an enigma and a paradox at the very heart of national intelligence.

On the one hand, it is effectively tolerated that, in the publications that they produce every now and then, secret service chiefs and agents will chip away slightly at secrecy. However, this spirit of tolerance, which has been exploited extensively since 1981, could evaporate if any of these writers overstep the mark – for example, if they were to compromise the security of their sources, give a breakdown of the budget allocated to recruiting and maintaining informers both within the country and internationally, or give a little too much away regarding the workings of secret inquiries and interventions, the techniques of HUMINT or the technology employed in SIGINT or ELINT. In any case, the success of these publications does not rely exclusively on the revelation of a scandalous irregularity in these affairs, but also on the author's respect for the narrative rules of the genre: a generous dose of collective eulogising and professional vanity, a few notes of bitterness or even pique, and often, for good measure, a bit of penance. Indeed, a few extremely informative texts have been denied real success in bookshops because they failed to observe these rules of composition or provided inadequate context.

On the other hand, it is remarkable how rarely, if ever, French secret agents defect or commit acts of treason in order to further the aims of rival powers. It is true that several agents have come under suspicion and been broken by a ruthless system of internal security – a system that is sometimes disgracefully unfair, since more often than not it acts on accusations made by allied foreign services that are poorly substantiated or, worse still, pure fabrication. Yet, for all these tenacious investigations, there is no example in the recent history of the French services of a traitor *extraordinaire* of the calibre of Kim Philby or Gabriele Gast, still less of Aldrich Ames or Robert Hanssen. In France at least this remains a surprise, but the observation is made typically in order to decry a completely different kind of damage inflicted by a few agents who have turned rebellious. These are generally not serious attacks on national defence and security, but pot-shots taken at the political authorities by subversive or vengeful commentators, and the battleground for these writers tends to be national rather than international. France has certainly had its fair share of traitors, but as they have generally come from other sectors of the administration and from wider society, a typology of the French renegade has emerged, exemplified by the internationalist agent Jean Cremet, the born conspirator André Labarthe, and the accidental spies George Pâques and Jean de la Granville.

It is also for this reason – in order to reinforce the tranquillity and, ultimately, the stability of the state – that the reform undertaken in 2008, like the great statutory and legislative overhaul of the mid-1930s, essentially comprised a revision of procedures surrounding the protection of state secrecy. This tightening of secrecy was introduced in a context of increased and more highly developed surveillance methods and technology. Probably the most sensible innovation in this two-fold project – the appeasement of the secret state and the strengthening of the surveillance state – was the implementation, alongside these new procedures, of a process that would eventually lead to genuine parliamentary control over intelligence. Henceforth the most trusting among the French could harbour genuine hopes that a newly created parliamentary commission on intelligence would offer a serious, independent guarantee not only of the efficiency of the secret services, but also of their impartiality. And henceforth the services themselves could hope, as an indirect result, that they would no longer find themselves in the public eye only when their failings or inevitable misfortunes made the headlines. Thus, in a few rare instances when circumstances dictated, the head of this bi-partisan commission considered it advisable to explain, as succinctly as possible, the conclusions reached by the group – eight specialists drawn from the National Assembly and the Senate. Two recent examples were the outbreak in Tunisia and Egypt of the long and widespread movement known as the Arab Spring, which seemed to have taken the government completely by surprise in December 2010, and the killings in Toulouse and Montauban in March 2012 – the single act of terror inspired by

Islamic radicalism to be committed on French soil for many years, in this case by a home-grown terrorist. In both cases the eight eminent members of the parliamentary commission emphasised that, here as before, they saw no failings or inadequacies in the government's intelligence plan as implemented, let alone any act of disloyalty on the part of the new intelligence community.

This assertion is significant in the context of secret service history, which abounds with cases of misuse of secret knowledge perpetrated by agents who were duty-bound to observe scrupulous political neutrality. The loyalty of agents to institutions has frequently been called into question – to such an extent, in fact, that on more than one occasion, typically when a major election is on the horizon, the question of the politicisation of the intelligence and security services has been raised. There have been several instances of outcry against the infiltration of the services by political militants and activists, and it must be said that a bad example has often been set at the highest level. The (almost) untouchable chief of police Jean Chiappe in 1934 and the head of counterespionage Roger Wybot in 1958, for example, were quite prepared to undermine the governments they served by taking a clandestine role in forcing constitutional change.

Furthermore, under France's Fifth Republic no head of state, in office or in waiting, and regardless of his reputation for virtue or corruption, seems to have escaped attempts at political destabilisation by individuals working either for factions on the fringes of the secret police or for the foreign branch – or, more often than not, for both. Every single Fifth Republic president – De Gaulle in 1965, Pompidou in 1968, Giscard d'Estaing in 1976 and 1979, Mitterrand in September 1985, Chirac in 1996 and Sarkozy in 2004 – has been a victim of partially or totally forged intelligence produced by agents or, more often, correspondents, and in one particular case even heads of interior and foreign intelligence. Conspiracies of this kind have never managed to achieve all of their aims, even though a considerable number of them have been supported or taken over by political leaders, by magistrates or by journalists (who have tended to be obliging before turning militant).

However, the point at issue here is not the ethos of the intelligence services in itself – in any case, it would be extremely difficult to consider this array of widely differing remits and activities as a homogeneous ontological unit without committing gross inaccuracies and distortions. Rather, it is the failings – the vices even – of successive recruitment policies that hired senior staff as more or less sympathetic sources and helpers. This has been the heart of the problem since the creation, or re-creation, of the services in the aftermath of the Second World War. Like many of their counterparts in other countries, the French services were far too ready to turn to politically active circles for their management, their secret infrastructure and their information. Several talented writers of memoirs – Alexandre de Marenches, Pierre Lacoste, Claude Silberzahn and Rémy Pautrat, for example – have made an important contribution to discussions of the morality and loyalty of the special services, and the specific levels of discretion that must be observed by agents who have uncovered sensitive material or find themselves in possession of privileged and toxic information. They have also commented on the harm done by more or less clandestine political networks. However, like those who came before and after them, these men had neither the time nor the freedom to transform the services they ran – whether the DGSE or the DST – into completely neutral bodies and to eradicate the pernicious influence of pressure groups.

The immediate future – which now belongs to the centre left in France – will tell whether in this respect the reforms begun in 2008 by the centre right were more efficient, and indeed whether they were sincere. For the time being, though, there is doubt in the air.

In any case, the new government did not even wait for the results of the June 2012 parliamentary elections before advising the head of the DCRI to resign from his post. The director of intelligence at Paris police headquarters (who had no direct link with the structure which runs the national intelligence community), the head of the DGSE and the coordinator of intelligence may similarly not have to wait for long before they are served their notice. A spoils system prevails, an almost perfectly accepted norm in French political practice. However, the new government's attention, unlike that of the incoming socialists in 1981, is not focused primarily on the foreign branch as it seeks to scrutinise and evaluate the intelligence services – on this occasion its sights are trained on the DCRI and its chief, Bernard Squarcini, in particular. Squarcini has become a prominent figure in the mediasphere since he has played a central role in the government's configuration of the special services between 2007 and 2012. As such he has also been subjected far more intensely to the problems posed by the demands of the head of state and his entourage than his opposite number in the foreign branch. A former detective who made his way up the ranks of the police hierarchy over the course of three decades, and a recognised authority on violent sub-state actors and on security policing, in his latest role he aroused the ire of the CNCIS (National Commission for the Control of Security Interceptions) and the criminal courts which – in a very rare move – charged him with breach of privacy by illegal means. Squarcini – too enthusiastic and unconditional a supporter of the previous head of state in the eyes of his critics – was faced with another very rare phenomenon, a revolt by his staff in the police force. In part this was an open rebellion by a number of low-ranking counterespionage personnel, organised by their professional union, in protest at Squarcini's senior recruitment policy. They voiced their disquiet when a few young graduates were appointed to senior posts that, in their quite reasonable opinion, should have gone to people with far more experience in the job, acquired over a long period of time in the field. There was another, far more serious side to the revolt, however – an act of covert rebellion by some of his close associates who went to the media and questioned, rightly or wrongly, his political activism. By doing this they helped to strengthen the legal case against him. What these signs of unrest reveal more than anything is the extremely difficult situation even a senior officer such as Squarcini faced if he was to implement the reform of 2008: he was tasked with grafting onto the new homeland intelligence service the rigid rules and very peculiar procedures of an authentic secret service, rules that, by definition, imposed a far greater level of discipline, restriction and abnegation on practising agents than they had ever experienced before, with no scope for argument on their part. Yet in all his successful career as a policeman, Bernard Squarcini had never worked in counterespionage or as an intelligence agent. Similarly, the last two national coordinators at the Elysée Palace and even the head of the foreign branch have never themselves worked in secret intelligence in their previous careers. By contrast, Squarcini's successor Patrick Calvar, appointed on 30 May 2012, hails from a completely different background, having spent most of his career in interior and foreign intelligence.

The nature and extent of the threats facing the nation will undoubtedly be re-evaluated in the summer of 2012. In the course of his general address to the Assemblée Nationale, Prime Minister Jean-Marc Ayrault was already announcing the submission of a White Book on Defence and National Security for the beginning of 2013. If and when the discussion turns to this central compartment within national intelligence, it will probably focus on three questions – organisation, status and scope of activities. First, whether the emphasis should still be placed on constructing a truly secret interior service, which should be modernised further in a wholesale upgrade of its scope and capability, or whether it would be preferable to concentrate efforts on what is called proximity intelligence within French society – the latter would mean reviving or resurrecting, though with major changes from top to toe, the tarnished old RG (Renseignements Généraux), which in 2008 was reduced to the SDIG and placed under the direction of the criminal investigation department, the Sûreté Publique. Next, whether the administrative status of the DCRI should be raised to a par with its foreign equivalents – whether this mere central coordinating body should become a general directing body (like Britain's MI5 or America's FBI), and hence enjoy budgetary autonomy and independence from the police force. Finally, whether the scope of activities and the means of the homeland security service should be increased, especially in the most sensitive and pressing scientific areas such as protection of state communications and cybersecurity.

The French have long been hostile to the idea, and no doubt to the possible risks, of gathering into a single national body all the most costly and high-grade technology used in intelligence acquired by scientific sources and in offensive countermeasures. For this reason, until now successive governments have never seriously considered the possibility of constructing an agency along the lines of America's NSA, and have preferred to scatter intrusion and interception activities and technology, as well as counterintrusion, across a range of bodies – both the different services that comprise the national intelligence community and a number of external organisations that are closely linked to it, such as the GIC (Interministerial Control Group) and the ANSSI (National Security Agency for Information Systems). On several occasions French scientific authorities have proposed arguments for technical and financial rationalising of the intelligence services, but political or, occasionally, military arguments have always carried more weight. For the same reason, there would seem to be little chance of success for the idea, frequently proposed in the past, of relieving the DGSE of its sizeable SIGINT component and constructing an intergovernmental agency along the lines of the GCHQ – a plan that was briefly studied by a select committee before the political transition of 1981.

In this context of re-evaluating threats and examining priorities, which has been planned for the period from July to December 2012, a few subsidiary questions remain concerning the coordination and monitoring of the state's special activities. There are two obvious areas that the previous administration left to lie fallow. The first of these is the question of encouraging and controlling relations and exchanges between the services that comprise the French intelligence community and equivalent organisations in other countries. The first intelligence coordinator of the Sarkozy administration made an unsuccessful attempt to reach a 'No Spy' agreement with the United States. Although it was vigorously supported by America's Director of National Intelligence himself, this proposal aimed at stabilising Franco-American relations was not approved by the White House. In the final analysis, Washington was not interested in a formal treaty with France on intelligence matters. Both the French coordinator and the American director lost their job. It is highly unlikely that Paris will undertake such an uncertain venture in the near future – France's intelligence community might well wonder whether and, if so, how it could ever embark on efforts at cooperation with an ally so immeasurably more powerful in terms of manpower and finance, but particularly difficult and demanding to deal with. The French intelligence community has never agreed to participate in any special American initiatives that could be construed as legally contentious – rendition being a notable example – just as it never subscribed to the theories evoked in order to justify the war in Iraq in 2003. The rendition programme was debated in Paris in the winter of 1985 by American emissaries shortly after the *Achille Lauro* affair, but the French authorities issued an immediate point-blank refusal to cooperate. However, the same intelligence authorities have found themselves in concrete situations where they lack the means of intervention, and where America has then deployed its forces. In the Sahel – for example in Mali and Somalia – France's intelligence and special action have more often than not been held in check. Lack of security is on the increase in the region and France's room for manoeuvre is very limited. As was the case in Chad in the 1980s, where no large-scale operation or decisive action was possible without extensive financial and technical support from America's clandestine services, here again France – if it wants to act – finds itself obliged to share the task. The Sahel is an especially turbulent zone, where Westerners, French nationals in particular, have regularly been taken hostage by radical Islamist groups such as AQIM, by separatists or by pirates – American intelligence has concluded that it is of paramount importance to have a genuine clandestine military force in the region, a form of Service Action multiplied several times over and coordinated tactically by Special Forces command. The operational reinforcement of the different special military forces it possesses will probably force Paris to give some thought to the matter of harmonisation. For a long time, especially during the period stretching from the days of the Balkan crisis to the recent operations against pirates in the seas around Somalia, French special forces have wanted the fighters of Service Action to move back over to them from the DGSE. The tactical adroitness of these elite fighters – operating discreetly rather than secretly – during the long Libyan campaign in 2011 was duly recognised, but it was concluded, correctly and not for the first time, that they performed far more effectively when deployed in conjunction with military forces supported by advanced technology, rather than in small clandestine units that, though extraordinarily courageous, often had to operate with resources that were far too primitive.

If, by chance, the government elected in 2012 went against national tradition and decided to break the traditional mould – to which the 2008 reform has merely added a few stopgap measures – by gathering all its special services into two or three large interoperative bodies – scientific, security and military – it could perform a corresponding rhetorical shift. In 2012 public opinion would have little difficulty moving away from its old adage and embracing a new formulation: 'Insidious and persistent the threats to our front, ingenious and consistent our front to those threats.'

Note

1   This essay was written in the summer of 2012.

18

INDIA

Rudra Chaudhuri[1]

On 19 January 2010, Hamid Ansari (2010), the Indian Vice-President, forcefully argued that there was 'no reason why a democratic system like ours [India's] should not have a Standing Committee of Parliament on intelligence'. A former diplomat, and re-elected to his post as Vice-President in 2012, Ansari (2010) intimated that 'compulsive secrecy' has every potential to undermine effectiveness.

The speech, as one former intelligence chief wrote, generated the kind of 'sustained interest' few others had in the past (Tharakan 2010). It was no mistake that it was scripted for a lecture to remember Rameshwar Nath Kao, the founding Chief of the Research and Analysis Wing (R&AW), India's external intelligence agency. It was also no mistake that the Vice-President underlined the need for greater transparency to an audience largely of spooks working for an organisation that has no legal mandate whatsoever. In fact, constitutionally, R&AW does not exist (Raghavan and Chaudhuri 2010). This of course is a matter of some debate, especially since the so-called intelligence failure in 2008, when a ten-man squad launched well-calculated and devastating attacks across 11 pre-arranged sites in Mumbai, India's financial capital.

Post-Mumbai, or post-26/11 – as the three-day siege that began on 26 November is popularly remembered – introspection around the utility, coordination capabilities and efficacy of India's intelligence agencies strengthen. As one editorial stressed, the bottom line was that there was a dire need for 'system-wide reform' (*The Hindu*, Anon 2011). Importantly, as a former R&AW officer turned commentator argued, greater transparency was deemed imperative to surge public confidence (Raman 2010). What was needed was a degree of learning as to whom and what spooks were. After all, as has been widely established in Britain, and as the Director General of the Security Services (MI5) astutely noted in the Foreword to the Service's first official history, 'public understanding and support' is considered 'vital' to 'success' (Andrew 2009: xv).

These remarks did not fall on deaf ears. As the Vice-President too stressed, the process of transparency first requires 'greater openness with regard to the history of intelligence institutions' (Ansari 2010). This is especially important for a country with no tradition of official histories in intelligence – something of a paradox given that Kao himself favoured establishing a historical division (Raman 2007: 27), where public domain debates around intelligence are a fairly new phenomenon, and in which the few books on intelligence tend to be authored by former officers rather than historians or dispassionate observers, doing much for intrigue but little for rigour.

This chapter is an attempt to introduce Indian intelligence since 1947. It is divided into two parts. The first looks at the history and structure of Indian intelligence agencies during the Cold War. The second examines their evolution since the fall of the Soviet Union, focusing on key crises leading to what are commonly called – but not always substantiated – 'intelligence failures'. Notably, it deals with the inability to spot Pakistani-backed incursions into Indian Territory in 1999, which led to the outbreak of war, and the terrorist attacks in Mumbai in 2008, highlighting the attempts at reform and the state of Indian intelligence in the current milieu.

The end of empire and the rise of 'independent' intelligence: an Indian intelligence bureau

In early 1947, Sir David Monteath, the Permanent Undersecretary at the India Office in London, noted that 'in theory', the 'Secret Service cannot operate in British Commonwealth territory'. From now on, he wrote, India was to be treated as a 'foreign country' (Jeffery 2010: 638–639). Such directives were in keeping with what came to be called the 'Attlee doctrine' – that is, a general principle mooted by Prime Minister Clement Attlee that the Secret Intelligence Service (SIS), or MI6, was barred from gathering intelligence in Commonwealth countries without Whitehall's 'full' knowledge (Jeffery 2010: 638–639). To maintain security linkages in erstwhile colonies, MI5's 'E' branch – dedicated to overseas operations – relied primarily on a Security Liaison Officer (SLO) (Murphy 2001: 107–108). Indeed, in the case of India, this was authorised by Prime Minister Jawaharlal Nehru's government (Andrew 2009: 442). The position of the SLO – first held by one Lt Colonel Kenneth Bourne – was deemed especially important. An independent India, MI6 argued, would either be 'unwilling to cooperate' with Britain or 'unreliable' even if it did so (Jeffery 2010: 638).

Yet, and within a decade of Indian independence, such premonitions proved faulty. The relationship between MI5 and the Indian Intelligence Bureau (IB) survived the larger chill in Indo-British relations informed by events such as Nehru's condemnation of the Suez invasion and India's refusal to censure Russian suppression in Hungary in 1956. According to Roger Hollis, MI5 Director General, the IB's second director, B.N. Mullick, shared MI5's 'views on Communist penetration' in India much more so than the Indian government (cited by Hollis in Andrew 2009: 445–446). Indeed, Mullick confessed that the Indian Ministry of External Affairs (MEA) was suspicious of IB's linkages with British intelligence. 'There are too many people,' he told Bourne's successor, 'who would be happy to break up the liaison' (cited by Hollis in Andrew 2009: 445–446).

In many ways, Mullick's predisposition towards Britain was all but natural. After all, the IB was the successor organisation to the Central Special Branch (CSB) created in 1887. Parts of this morphed into the Department of Criminal Intelligence (DCI) instituted in 1904 at the behest of Lord Curzon, who himself left India a year later (Popplewell 1995: 57–91). In 1920, following the First World War, the CSB was renamed the Intelligence Bureau – or what was then called the Delhi Intelligence Bureau (DIB) – and reported directly to the Governor General of India. Bureaucratically, it was placed under the Home Department (Subramanian 2005).

In 1947, the IB came under the full control of the Indian government and was led by its first Indian Director, Sanjeevi Pillai. Mullick took over in 1950. In the Indian constitution, introduced on 26 January 1950, the IB's status – mentioned only in what is known as the Union List (Seventh Schedule, Article 246) – fell under the jurisdiction and responsibility of the Central Government in New Delhi and remained ambiguous at best (Mazumdar and Kataria 1997: 118, 245–246). It had no formal charter, and, much like in previous decades, answered directly to the Home Ministry (Subramanian 2005: 2147–2150).

IB and the intelligence cycle

As is widely accepted, and inked in Sherman Kent's 1946 classic on 'strategic intelligence', the term 'intelligence cycle' refers to a four-stage process: requirement, collection, analysis and production, and finally dissemination to a variety of 'customers', including political elites, the military and law enforcement agencies. There are of course deep-seated issues with the 'cycle' as it stands but, by and large, spooks and analysts alike are seduced by the simplicity inherent in a process that makes for a clear diagram (Johnson 1986: 1; Hulnick 2006). Mullick (1971: 502–505), too, was much taken by this.

As the main civilian intelligence organisation, at least in the initial two decades following Indian independence, IB assumed responsibility to collect both domestic and strategic intelligence. Within India, the rise and activities of the Communist Party – the main opposition party following the first three general elections in 1952, 1957 and 1963 – and its more extreme affiliates served as the primary targets for espionage. Indeed, communist infiltration and growth was closely watched by both MI6 and the Central Intelligence Agency (CIA). MI5 was even given access to IB's records of the Communist Party of India's (CPI) finances (Andrew 2009: 445). CIA reporting on India for much of the 1950s too was inundated by speculations around levels of communist influence in the armed forces and the upper echelons of government. Some of these assessments were nothing short of ludicrous.

To take one example, a report in 1959 suspected Major General B.M. Kaul of being 'sympathetic towards Communism'. The reason: he was found to prefer 'social contact' with communist officers during his time in Korea, where he served as the number two to General Thimayya, the Chairman of the Neutral Nations Repatriation Commission (National Intelligence Survey (Anon 1959), cited in Dhar 2009). Little did these reporters realise that Kaul would be the one charged – and zealously accepted – to take on the Chinese in 1962. That he failed in his task is another matter altogether.

Strategic intelligence dealt with the potential material and moral strength of identifiable foes – such as the People's Republic of China and Pakistan, and fell within the IB's domain. 'Operational intelligence', or intelligence gathered by way of interrogation of prisoners and details from the 'front', was entrusted to the Military Intelligence Directorate (MI). IB, according to Kaul, collected and evaluated intelligence, passing the same to the MI Directorate, its biggest customer during the late 1950s and the early 1960s – that is, before, during and right after India's war with China in October–November 1962. The task of assessment and dissemination, again according to Kaul, lay with the military (Mullick 1971: 505).

To be sure, and as Srinath Raghavan (2009) clearly documents, basic principles of intelligence – separating collection from assessment – were in fact decidedly sullied during the China crisis. For one, despite Kaul's defence of IB's operational modus operandi, the fact remained that the IB was collecting *and* assessing intelligence. This, as Raghavan (2009) points out, 'violated the fundamental principle that the reporting agency should not be asked to assess its own reports'. Further, IB's own analysis was somewhat obscure and even contradictory. In one briefing it confidently argued that Indian occupation of posts along the border would deter Chinese offensives, while previous assessments suggested that the Chinese were set to unpick Indian posts (Raghavan 2009). Hence, which was it?

Compounding these obvious lapses in both methodology and conflicting conclusions, there was little or no coordination between the IB and the MI Directorate (Vaughn 1993: 2–4). Predictably, the latter was tasked to the Ministry of Defence (MOD). Further, the Joint Intelligence Committee (JIC) was responsible to the Chiefs of Military Staff. Much like Britain until

1957, following which the JIC was moved to the Cabinet Office, the JIC in India largely represented the views of the MI Directorate and, more specifically, the Director of Military Intelligence (DMI) (Goodman 2008: 51–53). That it was led by an MEA official mattered little. In short, the JIC was all but 'defunct' (Raghavan 2009), leaving no opportunity to independently assess IB's reporting. The organisational collapse of Indian intelligence, whether it was IB's dual tasking or an ineffective JIC, was all but evident. Brigadier M.N. Batra, the DMI during the China War, himself supported the idea of reconfiguring an intelligence apparatus essentially handed down by the Raj (Singh 2007: 29–30). This, coupled with a surprise attack backed by Pakistan in Kashmir in 1965, led to far-reaching changes in the construction and very shape of Indian intelligence.

Shock of defeat and the birth of R&AW

'R&AW,' said one senior former Taliban official, incites nothing less than 'paranoia' in the 'minds and hearts' of Pakistani intelligence and military personnel. It is the reason, he continued, 'Pakistan will *never* accept India in Afghanistan' (author's interview with a former Taliban official, 2011). Indeed, ever since the R&AW came into being on 21 September 1968, it has been widely perceived as an omen to Pakistani security and autonomy. Whether it is India's role in Afghanistan since the US-led intervention in 2001 (Khan 2011: 130–131), its links with Baloch Nationalists – Balochistan is the largest province in the settled areas of Pakistan with a history of bloody rebellion – or, in fact, just about anything considered detrimental to Pakistani interests, 'R&AW' is the first call on the lips of Pakistani security elites. In some ways, and much like communism in America in the 1960s and 1970s, it's something of a convenient contraction to mask shortcomings that don't always have anything to do with Indian intelligence.

Established by way of an Executive Order from the Prime Minister's Office (PMO), the R&AW of the Cabinet Secretariat, as is the inclusive designation, was created at the behest of Indira Gandhi, India's third Prime Minister. It was carved out of the IB's External Wing, which was hitherto led by Kao, the 'shy' 'founding father' of the new unit responsible only to the PMO (Raman 2007). Almost immediately, the annual budget for external intelligence quadrupled from $5 million to $20 million (Gupte 2009: 372). There was no doubt that R&AW enjoyed the support of the sitting incumbent (Malhotra 1989: 125). To be sure, Kao, who joined the Indian Police Service in 1940, held his post in R&AW until he retired in January 1977. He later served as a Senior Advisor to both Mrs Gandhi and her son Rajiv Gandhi, India's sixth Prime Minister (*Times of India*, Anon 2002). He died in January 2002, leaving only taped recordings of what presumably are his biographical accounts. They remain undisclosed (Raman 2007).

With an initial strength of 250, R&AW was primarily staffed by IB officers, themselves mainly from the military or the police. Direct recruiting started only in 1985 (IDSA Task Force Report 2012). By the early 1970s, its personnel – according to a former officer – 'numbered several thousand' (Singh 2007). There is of course no way of establishing the veracity of such accounts. As the same officer argues, 'there is no official document that gives out the history of RAW. Neither is it possible to get an accurate picture of its evolution, organisation and present status' (Singh 2007). Not even Indian Parliamentarians have access to its precise organisational structure. In short, what 'we', the general public and observers, know requires patching bits of information mainly from operations and campaigns where R&AW's input has been documented elsewhere.

'Kaoboys' in action

On 3 December 1971, Pakistan launched a pre-emptive attack against India. The response was swift and firm. On 4 December, the Indian army began ground operations against Pakistan on both the Western border – with present-day Pakistan – and the Eastern sector, bordering what is now Bangladesh. Thirteen days later, the Commander of the East Pakistani Army surrendered, and hence was born the new and independent state of Bangladesh. The history of the war, which effectively bifurcated Pakistan, can be found elsewhere (e.g. Sisson and Rose 1990). What is imperative, from the point of view of this chapter, is the role played by R&AW, then barely three years old.

The R&AW's objectives were three-fold. First, to provide intelligence to elites and mainly the army – then led by General (later Field Marshall) S.H.F.J. Manekshaw, who, ironically, had been investigated by Mullick a decade or so before for links with communism; second, to train Bengali – the majority population in the East – freedom fighters in dedicated training camps supported by R&AW; and, third, to make sure that reports of West Pakistani massacres in the East were widely known (Raman 2007: 10). A Monitoring Division within R&AW provided signals intelligence, often recording phone conversations including that of General Yahya Khan, the third President and second military dictator of Pakistan.

The war also allowed R&AW to exercise what were then slowly developing covert capabilities. Officers raided the hill tracts known to house insurgent leaders in north-eastern India, on the border with Bangladesh. In short, and as suggested in the available and open source literature, to a large extent, 1971 validated both Kao's leadership abilities and R&AW's operational capabilities. Those taking part in operations were allegedly popularly called 'Kaoboys of the R&AW'.

Yet, on the other hand, R&AW was found handicapped by its limited ability to collect human and technical intelligence (HUMINT and TECHINT, respectively), especially when it came to intelligence about India's non-neighbours like the US. This was imperative. President Nixon ordered the US Navy's Seventh Fleet into the Bay of Bengal during the crisis, to deter India from expanding the War to the West. R&AW did not detect this (Raman 2007: 39–40). Further, neither IB nor R&AW was able to track an alleged informant – suspected of being a Cabinet Minister – on the CIA's payroll.

On balance, these were early days. Such misdemeanours were hardly matters of consequence, especially as the war's objectives had been achieved. Indeed, and somewhat bizarrely, R&AW was assisted by the CIA in developing technical capabilities. The latter would not help when it came to Pakistan, but was more than willing in the case of China. For instance, in 1971, while Richard Nixon and Henry Kissinger 'tilted' towards Yahya Khan, the CIA helped India create an Aviation Research Centre (ARC) for aerial reconnaissance.

IB and a 'constitutional coup'

With the R&AW's exclusive focus on external intelligence, the IB's attention was squarely trained on domestic threats. To a large extent, the growing Maoist insurgency served as a primary target for sleuths. However, and at the same time, the organisation began to be seen as a political instrument used to spy and collect data on opponents rather than defend the realm. Indeed, as one notable practitioner turned scholar argued, soon, and for much of the period covering the Cold War, the IB 'tended to function on the whims and fancies of whoever happened to be its director' (Subramanian 2005: 2147–2150). In turn, more often than not, the director was found to be loyal to the Prime Minister of the day. This seemingly expedient rapport was most palpable for the period in which India was placed under 'Emergency' between 26 June 1975 and 21 March 1977.

Shaken by a High Court order – in Allahabad, a city in the northern Indian state of Uttar Pradesh – which held Prime Minister Indira Gandhi responsible for manipulating election results in the 1971 General Assembly elections, Mrs Gandhi declared a state of emergency. In a radio broadcast she claimed that 'communal passions' and 'forces of disintegration' threatened Indian sovereignty (Guha 2007: 493). Rather, the declaration itself was nothing less than what one insider called a 'constitutional coup' (Verghese 2010: 212).

Blaming the CIA for destabilising the nation and supporting opponents, the Prime Minister unsuccessfully tried to rally the nation. In this time, political opponents were arrested under what was called the Maintenance of Internal Security Act (MISA). Press freedom was censored, and the IB was said to keep tabs not only on opponents but also those within the Congress, the Prime Minister's own party (Malhotra 1989: 166–167). The IB and R&AW also bypassed the JIC and reported directly to the PMO. Indeed, officers from these services were 'lent' to the Ministry of Information and Broadcasting, which led many to believe that the spooks on loan were to 'make the media behave' (Raman 2007: 50).

Following the emergency and the installation of the *Janata* government, made up of erstwhile opponents, the IB's role was placed under the scanner. A Commission led by a senior judge lambasted the service for impropriety and made a strong case for defining its charter. The idea was to prevent it from being 'lent' as an 'instrument of politicians or an agency for controlling the opponents of the ruling party or elements within the party in power with which the high command of the party does [did] not see eye to eye' (Subramanian 2005: 2150).

For the first time, the Commission highlighted the need for democratic control over intelligence. Yet, and until the turn of the twentieth century, there was little evidence of intelligence reform. Unlike Britain, where Peter Wright's *Spy Catcher* and Chapman Pincher's classic *Their Trade is Treachery* provoked Margaret Thatcher to address the need for legislation, India's stimulus for change would come not from allegations of moles in the Security Services but the much more blatant episode of a military attack sponsored by neighbouring Pakistan.

'The most dangerous place in the world'

On 11 and 13 May 1998, India tested five nuclear devices. On 28 May, Pakistan tested five of its own. South Asia had gone nuclear, and Kashmir, according to Bill Clinton, became the 'most dangerous place on earth' (Misra 2008). Conflict in and *for* the region could well spark a nuclear emergency as potent as the Cuban Missile Crisis. Indeed, the Clinton White House faced exactly this presentiment in the summer of 1999.

On 8 May 1999, the Indian Military Operations Directorate reported clashes with a Pakistani patrol. Subsequently, an Indian soldier was found missing. Four days later, General V.P. Malik, the Chief of Army Staff, received reports from Headquarters Northern Command – in charge of guarding the border with Pakistan – that between 100 and 150 'jihadi militants' had infiltrated an Indian district called Kargil, along the 740-kilometre Line of Control (LoC) between India and Pakistan (Malik 2006: 106). For almost 11 weeks, the Indian army fought what turned out to be mostly Pakistani regulars – which quickly multiplied in numbers – initially disguised as mujahedeen fighters. The war ended on 26 July 1999, with India taking back all positions temporarily occupied by Pakistan. As far as Clinton and indeed most of the world was concerned, Kargil was nothing less than Pakistan's 'wrongful incursion' (Clinton 2005: 865).

Following the war, a non-statuary four-member Committee found that the Pakistani armed intrusion 'came as a complete and total surprise to the Indian Government, Army, and intelligence agencies' (Kargil Committee Report, Anon 2000). Further, the Committee made plain that it did not 'come across any agency or individual' who was able to predict large-scale Pakistani military intrusion (Kargil Committee Report, Anon 2000). Clearly, and at some level, India experienced a colossal failure of intelligence. Who exactly was to blame, and what impact did both the war and the Committee report have on India's intelligence apparatus?

Kargil: an intelligence failure?

In the aftermath of the Kargil War, senior army officers and former and serving intelligence officials locked horns. General Malik (2006: 80–81) blamed almost all aspects of the existing intelligence infrastructure for the 'failure to anticipate or identify military action'. Specifically, he argued that failure could be 'attributed' to the JIC, which had been given little or no attention by the government of the day. To an extent, this was of course surprising. In April 1999, the JIC was morphed into the newly created National Security Council Secretariat (NSCS), working directly under the National Security Advisor (NSA). Clearly, slighter attempts to reform India's national security apparatus did little for intelligence coordination (Malik 2006: 80–81).

Responsible mainly for tactical intelligence collection, the MI's role, as underlined in the Kargil Committee Report, was inherently limited (Kargil Committee Report, Anon 2000). Apart from issues of remit, the MI is barred from collecting external intelligence; the committee found that the military were unwilling to share intelligence with other agencies. Malik, too, made the point that, at the tactical level, army intelligence was 'inadequate'. For instance, unit commanders simply did not maintain contact with local civilian populations, undermining a key resource for intelligence collection (Malik 2006: 86).

For its part, the R&AW reported directly to the Prime Minister, completely bypassing the JIC. Much like the IB during the China War, the agency provided conflicting conclusions with little evidence and almost no follow-up. For instance, in April 1998, an R&AW report argued that, for Pakistan, 'waging war against India in the immediate future will not be a rational decision'. Yet, a few months later, another report stated that Pakistan could engage in a 'limited swift offensive threat'. When asked for details by their military consumer, neither the JIC nor R&AW provided a response, let alone evidence backing its claim (Malik 2006: 80–81).

According to one observer of intelligence and counterterrorism, some 40-odd intelligence reports had been produced between May 1998 and July 1999, signalling the need to focus on cross-border activity. However, only two were presented to the Prime Minister (Mahadevan 2011: 7–9). In the end, the inability to predict or detect the infiltration appears to have been not only because of the failure at the level of collection, assessment and analysis, but also because of what might be considered elite cognition and bias.

First, despite reports of cross-border activity, no one in the Indian intelligence establishment suspected large-scale infiltration. Indeed, the 45 intelligence inputs mentioned above were among some 8,000 others (Mahadevan 2011: 7–9). Information overload is of course a common problem among the world's leading intelligence agencies. Nonetheless, and as Richard Betts (2007: 4–15) puts it, the 'producers' presentation must make it speak to consumers'. In the case of Kargil, the producers themselves seemed unclear about what they were producing. This was evident as neither the JIC nor IB and R&AW was able to provide detailed analysis or support its inputs. Indeed, according to the Kargil Committee, the R&AW's approach to 'collection, coordination and follow-up' was 'weak' (Kargil Committee Report, Anon 2000).

With regards to India's intelligence apparatus as a whole, the committee found that there was simply 'no institutionalised process' whereby different intelligent arms 'interact periodically at levels below the JIC'. In the concluding section on intelligence, committee members bluntly stated that there were 'no checks and balances' to ensure that the 'consumer gets all the intelligence that is available and is his due'. Importantly, agencies were found to be 'preserving' their 'own turf and departmental prerogatives' rather than working towards an interagency process to serve the interests of a state forced to war (Kargil Committee Report, Anon 2000).

Second, Indian and Pakistani rapprochement and diplomatic dialogue in the early part of 1999 made it arguably difficult, if not almost impossible, to conceive of Pakistan's planned deception. As Raghavan (2009) points out, Indian leaders 'believed that relations with Pakistan were on the mend'. Consequently, cognitive selection could well be considered a reason for not addressing the few reports that were produced on infiltration. As Robert Jervis (2010: 163–165) points out, there is an inherent tendency for policy-makers to resist information contrary to the policy being pursued. Given the upward trend in Indian and Pakistani relations in the first quarter of 1999, cognitive bias, according to Jervis's logic, might well have led to deflecting or even ignoring independent and contrarian judgements of a foe the government was trying hard to befriend.

Similarly, institutionalised beliefs among elites also add to 'cognitive predispositions' undermining the value of the intelligences collected and assessed. For instance, both military and intelligence elites believed that a Kargil-like operation was unlikely because it was simply irrational. As Jervis (2010: 169) stresses, in cognitive psychology, it is a 'confirmed proposition' that 'once a belief or image is established', in this case the miasma of irrationality, 'discrepant and ambiguous information' tends to be 'ignored'. Arguably, this is exactly what happened. Hypnotised by the scepticism underlying even the possibility of a major clandestine intervention, security elites were conditioned into ignorance. To be sure, the Committee picked up on this. While underlining that Pakistan's behaviour 'was not rational', the report made a case to more closely study 'behaviour patterns' and bring in those from the outside – such as academics and specialists – to develop 'White Wings' (Kargil Committee Report, Anon 2000).

Some further suggestions were also included in the 340 recommendations made by what came to be called the Group of Ministers' (GoM) report on 'Reforming the National Security System'. This was accepted by the Cabinet Committee on Security (CCS), India's apex policy-making body on security, chaired by the Prime Minister (IDSA Task Force Report 2012). Indeed, in 2001, the government created the Intelligence Coordination Group (ICG), chaired by the NSA and meant to 'provide systematic intelligence oversight'. In 2003, the Technical Coordination Group (TCG) was set up to oversee technical requirements and resources (IDSA Task Force Report 2012: 91). Yet, the inability to implement systematic reform – opposed to simply create new structures for intelligence governance – was once again palpable in November 2008, when Mumbai was placed under siege. This is of course not to suggest that the attacks completely undermined attempts at intelligence development, rather that Mumbai shed light on how much more attention needs to be given to the very question of reform.

The Mumbai attacks and intelligence reform

The central intelligence-related questions with regards to the attacks – details of which can be found elsewhere (Tankel 2011: 207–235) – have to do with how the attackers arrived in Mumbai unnoticed and why various aspects of their surveillance prior to the attacks escaped detection within India. As Stephen Tankel investigates and explains in his stunning book on the Lashkar-e-Taiba, the Pakistani state supported militant organisation that executed the attacks, ten armed men were able to make their way to Indian waters on a ship they boarded in Karachi on 23 November. They took control of an Indian fishing trawler, bringing them as close as four nautical miles from the Indian coast before they hopped onto an inflatable dinghy that docked in Mumbai on the night of 26 November (Tankel 2011: 209–210).

Barely a week following the attacks, the new Indian Home Minister stated that there were clear lapses (the minister in charge during the attacks was suitably removed from office). He was doing his 'utmost' to 'improve the effectiveness of the security systems in the country' (Weaver 2008). The minister's remarks were tellingly warranted. Allegedly, both R&AW and IB received intelligence to suggest that an attack was conceivable. The latest warning was provided only few days before the gunmen set foot in Mumbai, yet agencies failed to either share intelligence among themselves and the local police, or provide details and specifics to substantiate the same (Rabasa *et al.* 2009: 9).

Further, what soon became clear was that intelligence coordination capabilities and structures were poorer than expected. For instance, IB did not have direct access to foreign internal intelligence. There was no common database on terrorism. R&AW's covert capabilities were literally non-existent. Those serving in the NSCS were found to be less qualified. And there was no streamlined process by which diplomats and officials in the External Affairs Ministry could be in regular contact with intelligence agencies (Raman 2010: 195–201). In the following few years, the government spent millions of dollars on technological upgrading and police modernisation but, as one editorial put it, this 'much vaunted' and visible change 'has just not delivered' (*The Hindu*, Anon 2011).

The key, it would seem, has less to do with new toys and gadgetry, and much more to do with better coordination, and exposing analysts and agents to the less tangible but imperative task of finding innovative conceptual tools to examine intelligence inputs. This would require getting over, or at least finding a way around, the rigid cognitive biases explained above. For this to happen, and as highlighted in the introduction to this chapter, it is crucial to revisit past examples of both failures and successes, while looking at ways to make R&AW and other agencies accountable to elected elites. Indeed, it is worth studying why other agencies, such as MI5, took to reform and legislation. Interestingly, rather than shun change, MI5 Chief Anthony Duff enthusiastically supported reform, presumably to transform the image of an otherwise shadowy organisation popularly associated with shadowy figures in trench coats lurking in dark and wet corners. Such far-reaching attempts at change are perhaps a stretch for those chiefs dotting the bureaucratic landscape in India, but a considered debate around the same would be a starting point. To be sure, both B.N. Mullick and R.N. Kao would probably approve.

Note

1 The author would like to thank Sunil Khilnani, Stephen Tankel and Pranay Sharma for their deep insights, comments and critiques, and Josh Webb for editorial assistance.

19

CHINA

Nicholas Eftimiades[1]

China's use of intelligence

Chinese intelligence operations and methods are relatively new to the Western world. They are not, however, new in themselves. The practice of espionage in China dates back to at least the fifth century BC, when the proper employment of spies was detailed in a military manual, Sun Tzu's *The Art of War*. In what has become a classic work on the fundamentals of military tactics and strategy, Sun Tzu put a high value on accurate and timely intelligence in daily affairs of state and in support of military campaigns. He attributed a commander's foreknowledge to the proper employment of espionage agents, saying that 'no one in the armed forces is treated as familiarly as spies and no one is given rewards as rich as those given to spies'.

Sun Tzu was not alone in his appreciation of accurate and timely intelligence in support of diplomatic and military campaigns. China's military history is replete with examples of using espionage to attain policy and military objectives. In the book *Chinese Ways in Warfare*, Frank A. Kierman, Jr, describes ancient Chinese battle narratives such as the *Tso-Chuan* (Tradition of Tso) of the Eastern Chou period (*c.*770–403 BC) (Kierman and Fairbank 1974). These narratives are divided into a sequence of preparatory and operational phases, and among the preparatory phases are the collection and analysis of military and relevant diplomatic intelligence information.

Even in ancient times China had developed and documented an understanding of intelligence needs and practices for military and diplomatic activities. At that time, information requirements were relatively simple: enemy unit size, weaponry, location and morale; biographical information on enemy commanders; terrain features; and the intentions of neutral and allied forces. In addition, the *Tso-Chuan* describes intelligence operations employed not only to collect information but also to deceive the opposition and deny them militarily significant information.

Today, the People's Republic of China's (PRC) intelligence needs are far more numerous and complicated than those of ancient times. Yet today's policy-makers show the same appreciation for the value of foreknowledge and the proper application of espionage activities in support of the affairs of state. The PRC's intelligence apparatus is more than just a support department for policy-makers. It is inextricably linked to the foreign policy decision-making process, and internal methods of economic development and political control.

For centuries intelligence services have served their constituents by collecting information about friends and adversaries alike. Espionage has been described by insiders as 'the world's second oldest profession'. To comprehend the structure, roles and nature of China's intelligence system it is first necessary to understand that such intelligence activities are tied to governments' decision-making processes. Just like diplomatic or military campaigns, intelligence operations in the modern world require careful planning, command and control, communication, and tremendous financial resources. These elements must be organised in some way to accomplish their respective tasks.

Intelligence agencies worldwide share the same overall goal: to provide accurate and timely intelligence to their consumers. To do so they collect raw information from a variety of human and technical sources, and collate and analyse that data. The completed analytical product, intelligence, is then disseminated to the consumer, whose information requirement started the process. That person or group is then in a position to ask for additional analysis or to implement policy based on the intelligence received. The entire process is known as the intelligence cycle.

Like other regional or global powers, the leadership of the PRC bases its policies and actions on its military, political and economic self-interests. Many of those interests involve reaping financial and technological benefits from close commercial ties with advanced industrialised nations. In recent years, China's human rights and economic policies have alienated some policy-makers among the Western democracies and, in the case of the United States, restricted its access to some categories of advanced technology. China's intelligence services have therefore played a large role in supporting national policy objectives by targeting and information on the technological, economic, political and military infrastructures of the developed nations.

Espionage and other intelligence activities rarely require the proverbial cloak and dagger, but they are far more complicated than mere theft of a foreign government's classified materials. Espionage is an orchestrated, all-encompassing attempt to extract information from multiple levels of society. At the national level, desirable intelligence falls into several categories. Each of these should be considered separately to piece together the true role of intelligence collection and analysis as practised by the PRC:

- *foreign political situations:* all the affairs of state that determine a nation's future actions domestically and internationally;
- *leadership figures:* the histories and personalities of those individuals who influence the affairs of state, now or in the future;
- *military force structures and capabilities:* information such as the table of organisation and equipment for military forces; the locations, strengths and missions of those units;
- *technology:* commercial and defence-related technology to aid Chinese economic and military development;
- *science and related technological issues:* the overall level of sophistication in civilian and military sectors as well as a society's ability to develop and use technology;
- *economic conditions:* strengths and weaknesses of a nation's economy, and how economic factors might influence domestic and foreign policies;
- *sociological factors:* religious, cultural and customary practices of a society and how those factors might affect its actions and decisions.

In democratic societies much of this information is available in the open press. In addition, a great deal of usable information can be gathered simply by watching a society function on a daily basis. General attitudes of the populace, political personalities and trends, and economic conditions are all topics addressed daily in any major Western newspaper. Intelligence agencies therefore spend considerable time and effort identifying, collecting, translating and analysing information from published *open sources*.

Framework for analysis

For the purposes of analysis, China's human-source intelligence operations can be divided into four broad categories: overt collection; clandestine directed at classified data or defence restricted technology; commercial or economic espionage; overt action.[2]

Overt intelligence activities are those collection and analysis functions that can be identified and attributed to a specific country. For example, when military attachés attend another country's military exercises they are engaged in overt intelligence collection. The host government expects that the attachés will report the event and any relevant information from it to their own governments. This information might include unit strengths, proficiency, procedures, equipment, tactics, and biographical data on commanders. In turn, the host government will attempt to gather information from the attending attachés – and they will do the same among themselves in the course of normal conversation. This type of activity, and other forms of direct observation and contact (e.g. a diplomat holding discussions with local inhabitants or government officials), is generally considered overt collection.

Clandestine activities are intelligence collection operations that, even if detected, cannot be attributed to a specific nation. These operations usually involve the recruitment of spies and are designed to hide the involvement of the nation that is behind them. For example, one might suspect clandestine collection activities if classified or restricted equipment was discovered in the hands of a third world nation that did not have the technical capability to produce it. One can assume that the equipment was stolen, although the thief and the exact method remain unknown.

Commercial or economic espionage collection activities are targeted against foreign high technology and commercial trade secrets. In the case of China these operations are often characterised by limited or poorly executed espionage tradecraft. It is difficult to determine the extent to which the Chinese government is using such practices. The decision is largely dependent on one's definition of the Chinese government. The complete political, personnel and managerial control extended by the Chinese Communist Party over leadership governing state, quasi-state and private high-technology defence-related industries gives credence to the notion that, at a minimum, the Chinese government is ignoring economic espionage being conducted by these firms. More evidence indicates that the PRC state mechanisms are actively engaged in the act (McGregor 2011: 72ff). In 2011, the United States publicly identified China as the world's most active and persistent perpetrator of economic espionage. China was further described as an aggressive and capable collector of sensitive US economic information and technologies, particularly in cyberspace (Office of the National Counterintelligence Executive 2011).

Covert action operations are not intelligence collection activities per se. Instead, they are efforts such as economic and military assistance programmes that are designed to manipulate a foreign government or other entity. Covert action operations can be divided into four general categories: political, economic, paramilitary and those that feature disinformation.

China's intelligence information objectives

In general, intelligence activities, whether open or clandestine, are directed at either satisfying information requirements or covertly advancing national objectives. The former are known in intelligence circles as information objectives (IOs): specific requests for certain kinds of data, assigned to human or technical intelligence collectors by a nation's policy-making apparatus. The IOs of the PRC's leadership are unique to its strategic political and military concerns. In military terms the PRC is still strictly a regional power, not a global power. General military policy in China has been under intense review since the early 1980s and has been evolving since the early 1990s. Military officials have shown considerable interest in the strategy and tactics used by the US and the multinational coalition in the Iraq wars. However, despite the military's intense modernisation efforts, the political leadership is still reliant primarily on the country's size and large population as a defence against perceived military threats from the outside world.

The PRC's perception of internal and external threats dictates the information require-ments levied on its intelligence services. It has little to gain from intense espionage and analysis activities directed at global political–military alliances outside its region of influence. For mili-tary intelligence purposes, the PRC focuses its intelligence collection activities on issues that more directly affect its internal stability, regional security, and technological and economic development:

- Russian Republic (historic animosity and territorial disputes still exist between China and Russia);
- India (the long-standing distrust between India and the PRC is based on political differ-ences, the 1962 border war and the Chinese subjugation of Tibet);
- Muslim states north of Xinjiang (the resurgence of fundamentalist Islam in the central Asian states of the former Soviet Union threatens to weaken Beijing's internal control over the Muslim population of Xinjiang province, and Beijing still highlights terrorism in the area as a high national security concern);
- South China Sea (China has intensified its interest in this region to enforce territorial claims to support economic development).

Also of considerable interest to Beijing are American, Japanese, South Korean and Taiwan-ese military activities along China's eastern seaboard and in the Sea of Japan. Overall, the information objectives revealed in an analysis of nearly 200 Chinese espionage cases from 1994 to 2012 reveals the following information objectives of interest to China's intelligence apparatus:

- high technology for military, civil, and commercial uses – the United States, Europe and Russia are key target areas for China's military technology collection programme, but technologies for commercial and civil applications are collected from a wide variety of nations;
- trade secrets, economic and commercially related information are collected on a global scale by the Ministry of State Security (MSS);
- national security policies and related information;
- foreign policies and trends (from bilateral policy and trade issues to identifying and influ-encing governments and events); and
- dissident groups (e.g. democracy advocates, Fan Lungang, Taiwanese nationals).

Ministry of State Security

China's preeminent civilian intelligence collection agency is the MSS (*Guojia Anquan Bu*). It was formed in June 1983 by combining the espionage, counterintelligence and security func-tions of the Ministry of Public Security (MPS) and the Investigations Department of the Chi-nese Communist Party central committee (Richelson 1988: 277). Prior to the reorganisation China's leading intelligence service was the MPS, which still has a role in counterintelligence investigations and operations due to bureaucratic infighting and its pervasive presence at the lower levels of local government (Du Xichuan and Zhang Lingyuan 1990: 135).

The MSS, assisted by several deputy ministers, oversees all the bureaus within the ministry. Since 2007, Geng has been a member of the 10th CPPCC National Committee and the 17th CPC Central Committee, and is widely seen as an expert on America.

Each government ministry responsible for overseas operations has a foreign affairs bureau, and most such ministries also contain a separate Taiwan affairs department as well as a Hong Kong and Macao affairs office. China's premier foreign policy body, the Ministry of Foreign Affairs (MFA), is further subdivided into eight geographic departments, including African Affairs, European Affairs and Latin American Affairs (PRC Ministry of Foreign Affairs 2012). Research institutes affiliated with the foreign affairs apparatus and intelligence agencies (including the MSS) use similar geographic divisions. It would make sense, then, for the MSS to follow this pattern and have a foreign affairs bureau consisting of the standard geographic divisions, plus separate departments for Taiwan and Hong Kong/Macao.

Geographic divisions allow work units to specialise in a particular area of expertise but do not permit work to be accomplished by functional expertise. The structure of the MSS must therefore be divided not only by geographic considerations but by functional expertise as well. The next question, then, becomes what sorts of functional assets does the MSS need to conduct espionage and counterespionage in China and abroad?

First and foremost, it needs qualified personnel. Each employee must be recruited, screened, trained, paid, supplied, transported, fed and occasionally housed. Support services are needed, such as logistics, records or database management, planning and accounting; these essential services can be found in all Chinese ministries (Barnett 1967: 250). The universal practice within intelligence agencies of compartmentalising information indicates that each of these services probably exists as a separate department in the MSS as well.

Because the MSS is active domestically as well as abroad, operational sections and many support functions should be similarly divided. The result is that the MSS has separate departments at the bureau level for internal and external espionage investigations and operations. The fact that Yu Zhensan, identified as the former chief of the MSS's foreign affairs bureau, defected in 1986 confirmed the existence of such a structure (Hong Kong AFP 1986: K1).

Public exposure of Chinese intelligence activities in Taiwan, Japan and the United States – carried out by intelligence operatives posing as businessmen and diplomats – confirms that the MSS conducts clandestine collection operations overseas. It also indicates that the MSS is capable of fielding case officers under both official government (legal) covers and non-government (illegal) covers. In the case of the Chinese intelligence services, official cover has a wide range of applications. The PRC is represented overseas by accredited diplomats, trade and industry figures, commercial officers, military attachés, journalists, scientists and students. Many of the aforementioned positions are used as legal cover for overseas espionage activities.

The use of legal covers by Chinese intelligence officers is a well-established practice in the global espionage trade. In a number of publicised spy scandals, PRC intelligence officers were exposed while operating under cover from the New China News Agency (NCNA), the Chinese People's Friendship Association, the Ministry of Foreign Affairs, the Ministry of National Defense, the United Front Works Department, the International Liaison Department and official trade offices. The consistent use of legal covers over a long period (1960 to the present) is evidence of the depth of China's intelligence experience and its commitment to espionage as a tool of foreign policy.

China also makes extensive use of illegal covers. This is a more sophisticated and difficult method of operation because the case officer is not affiliated with his or her government. As a result, a separate system of control and clandestine communication must be established to direct the illegal operative and receive information in return.

This process is dangerous for the illegal case officer because he or she has no diplomatic immunity. If this individual is caught by a foreign government, he or she usually faces imprisonment, or worse. Recent espionage cases in the United States and Taiwan provide first-hand examples of how China uses illegal networks.

The PRC's detailed knowledge of these types of espionage techniques comes out in its public announcements of counterespionage successes. In press reports MSS representatives have claimed that spies from Taiwan and other foreign powers have been caught in possession of the aforementioned equipment by various provincial MSS offices (*Zhongguo Xinwen She, K8* 1988). Such reports lead to five conclusions:

1. The MSS has the operational knowledge to provide technical support for espionage operations.
2. The MSS has a public or external affairs unit.
3. The national MSS supervises the provincial offices.
4. In domestic counterespionage, the MSS has an investigative role.
5. MSS officers are trained to identify the operational tactics and technical equipment used to conduct espionage.

The MSS's current structure can be seen in greater clarity when juxtaposed with the known activities of the Ministry of Public Security (MPS). The MPS's political security section used to conduct counterespionage operations against foreign intelligence services. It was also responsible for counterintelligence investigations of citizens who had travelled overseas or maintained foreign contacts (Barnett 1967: 222–223).

The organisational structure of the MSS indicated that the agency runs a wide range of administrative and functional operations both domestically and overseas. One can only speculate about the existence of other mission-orientated bureaus within the MSS. It is particularly difficult to identify the exact titles – as opposed to the functions – of bureaus and departments because their designations are changed periodically to enhance security. (Butterfield 1990: 334) Analysis of the structure, however, produces an assessment of the organisation's roles and capabilities.

Military Intelligence Department

The Military Intelligence Department (MID) of the People's Liberation Army's (PLA's) General Staff Department (GSD) is the second largest organisation in the PRC involved in HUMINT collection. Known as the Second Department (*Er Bu*), it is similar to many such organisations all over the world in that it is charged with providing timely intelligence support to the military command structure (Sources 1 and 5; Tan Po Cheng Ming 1996: 28–31; Global News Wire 2006).

The function of the GSD is to implement and monitor the policies of the central committee's Military Commission (MC) and to run daily affairs of the PLA (Global News Wire 2006). So one would expect that the GSD and MC are the primary recipients of finished intelligence produced by the Second Department. Other consumers would be the Ministry of National Defense (MND), the headquarters of the different services, the military-industrial complex and unit commanders.

The Second Department's HUMINT collection activities support three types of military intelligence requirements: tactical, strategic and technological. At present the bulk of the MID's effort is dedicated to the tactical intelligence task of identifying and assessing potential military threats on China's borders. This focus is slowly changing. As the PRC attempts to secure a greater position in regional affairs, collection and analysis of politico–military and military–economic information will have to increase to support Beijing's regional aspirations. The responsibilities of the Second Department can be divided into the following categories (Kent 1949: 32–38): order of battle (i.e. the size, location, equipment and capabilities of armed forces (military and insurgent) that exist in immediate proximity to the PRC); military geography; military doctrine; plans and intentions (i.e. the military plans and intentions of current and potential enemies, allies and neutral nations); military economics; biographical intelligence (about foreign military officials); nuclear targeting; and military intelligence watch centres, providing intelligence for immediate use and mid-term planning. It defeats the purpose of military intelligence collection not to have a system in place for bringing the most recent information to the attention of policy-makers and military commanders. The function of such a system is to provide indications and warnings of potential or impending military threats. It can be assumed that the Second Department maintains a network of regional and national 'watch centres' to support various levels of command.

The Second Department is also active in the field of collecting foreign high technology, especially if there are military applications (Chen 1987). In fact, according to some accounts, the MID is China's preeminent intelligence agency in this regard (Sources 1 and 5). Based on the limited number of PRC military attachés, the Second Department does not appear to have the overseas presence necessary to be the nation's primary collector of foreign high technology; but since many Second Department personnel serve under cover as consular officers, the number of collectors may actually be quite high (Source 1).

Due to its close relationship with the consumer – China's military-industrial complex and armed forces – the Second Department probably has some measure of authority in the planning and conduct of intelligence operations designed to acquire foreign military technology (Richelson 1986: 41).

The MID must have a structure that supports HUMINT collection operations domestically and abroad to fulfil information requirements from tactical commanders, the military-industrial complex, and military and civilian policy-makers. Logically, there must be some way of compiling and prioritising these collection requirements to accomplish tasks and to prevent duplication of effort. The locus for the collection and dissemination of intelligence supporting tactical-level requirements takes the form of a regional intelligence centre. Intelligence seems to be passed to other MACs at the headquarters level. This process appears to parallel that of the PLA's civilian counterparts, where information exchanges occur at the regional level. For example, 'to strengthen the cooperative relationship among Chinese military personnel stationed in Hong Kong and Macao, the director of the Political Department and the chief of staff of the General Staff of Guangzhou Military Area Command (MAC) cooperate in exchanging intelligence' (Defense Intelligence Agency 1984: 33, 34).

Tactical information is collected by the PLA, PLA Navy and PLA Air Force reconnaissance units. PLA and PLA Navy special operations units conduct visual reconnaissance and electronic intercepts for combat unit commanders (JPRS-CAR-90–075, 10 October 1990). PLA reconnaissance elements exist at the company level in group armies (GAs) and MAC border units. Border units are one part of the MAC structure; the others are garrison and internal defence forces. The composition of these forces can vary among MACs due to area-specific tactical requirements. However, regardless of the composition of forces, the combat unit commander dictates the conduct of his reconnaissance unit's collection activities (Defense Intelligence Agency 1984: 33–34). Each service arm collects, compiles, analyses and disseminates through its own intelligence analysis centre, which exists under the intelligence division headquarters in times of peace. In wartime the collection and analysis functions would be placed under the direct control of the front command.

As MAC combat forces are ultimately subordinate to a national command structure, so too are MAC intelligence collection units subordinate to the Second Department at the national level. It is not known, however, exactly to what degree the Second Department may allocate collection duties to tactical forces. PLA doctrine encourages commanders even in the lower echelons to be aggressive and to conduct independent reconnaissance activities to meet their intelligence needs.

The contention that MAC intelligence forces are coordinated at the national level is supported by the fact that the Second Department maintains a tactical reconnaissance bureau (*Jun Jiancha Zhu*, or Second Bureau) to foster communication among intelligence division commands in each MAC (Defense Intelligence Agency 1984: 33). Also at work in the MACs is the Second Department's First Bureau, which divides its collection responsibilities among five geographic divisions: the Beijing area, Shenyang, Shanghai, Guangzhou and Nanjing. The First Bureau is one of seven functional entities within the Second Department that allows HUMINT collection and analysis work to be conducted along functional lines. These comprise two collection bureaus, four analysis bureaus, and one newly formed research bureau dedicated to science and technology (Source 5).

At the national level the Second Department's HUMINT programme includes PRC military attachés who collect in support of strategic military intelligence requirements. These individuals belong to the department's attaché bureau, which contains more than 400 people. The attaché bureau, also called the Third Bureau, is subdivided into several groups (*Xiao zu*), with one of the most important and active ones being based in Turkey.

PRC military attachés collect data on foreign weapons technology, order of battle, and military doctrine, economics and policy. While much of this information is available from open sources, sensitive technology generally must still be approached in a clandestine manner. These attachés fulfil their responsibilities by conducting both overt and clandestine HUMINT operations. In their circles this sort of work is called 'half open, half closed'.

Because PRC military attachés have clandestine collection responsibilities, an internal training programme is needed to develop these skills. The requirement to compartmentalise information and the secretive nature of intelligence organisations dictate that this course of study should be offered by a separate entity under the Second Department, rather than by the training academies of other military departments or civilian agencies. The Nanjing Foreign Affairs institute – recently renamed the PLA Institute for International Relations – is the Second Department's school for espionage tradecraft and foreign languages.

The Second Department has its own analysis bureau to process and disseminate military intelligence. Personnel from this bureau conduct preliminary all-source intelligence analysis. The term *all-source* refers to the use of information from all intelligence disciplines – HUMINT, signals intelligence (SIGINT) and imagery intelligence (IMINT) – in reaching analytical conclusions. Each day at 7 a.m. the analysis bureau produces a report of the significant military intelligence events that occurred over the previous 24 hours. The report is circulated to members of the central committee's Central Military Commission (CMC), the politburo and chiefs of the general departments. The bureau is located in building no. 11 of the GSD's Beijing headquarters.

The analysis bureau is largely integrated with the China Institute for International Strategic Studies (CIISS), established in October 1979 under the name Beijing Institute for International Strategic Studies. CIISS states its mission as conducting the analysis of international strategic situations, China's national security, international politics and the economic environment. The institute consults and offers policy advice to China's military and related institutions. Its 100 research members include military officers, diplomats and university professors. The current chairman of the organisation is Xiong Guangkai, former Major General and Chief of the Second Department. Xiong ultimately rose to be PLA's deputy chief of staff (Barnett 1985: 124; Lin 2011).

The Second Department has three intelligence analysis bureaus in addition to its analysis unit (which conducts preliminary analyses only) and its associated military research institutes. The first two of these three bureaus produce and disseminate in-depth intelligence analyses about specific geographic targets: the Fourth Bureau covers the political and military policies of the Russian Federation and Eastern Europe; and the Sixth Bureau focuses its efforts on the Asian nations that border China (Sources 4 and 5; *Hong Kong Economic Journal* 2006). The other component of this trio is called the America/Western Nations Analysis Bureau, or the Fifth Bureau. It uses primarily open source publications in its political and economic analyses.

Institutions (academic or otherwise) that conduct research on foreign military doctrine strategy or capabilities are adequate only for basic or estimative analysis. The most important part of military intelligence analysis is the production of current intelligence. Just as intelligence centres in each MAC support the headquarters elements of tactical commands, the CMC and general departments need to have a focal point for indications-and-warnings intelligence in the event of a national military emergency. This military intelligence would be required to synthesise all-source intelligence from the MACs and overseas diplomatic posts to provide timely support to national-level commands. It is likely that this centre exists as a part of the analysis bureau due to that entity's access to all-source data, which would be used to confirm and detail impending military threats.

The last of the Second Department's so-called functional bureaus is the Bureau of Science and Technology, also called the Seventh Bureau. Established in the late 1980s, this unit's role is to research, design and develop technology, including the development of espionage equipment and the provision of the bureau's own computer centre (Sources 4 and 5). The very existence of the Seventh Bureau indicates that the Second Department is thinking about and planning for espionage directed against foreign science and technology well into the future. This is also made apparent by the presence of two electronic factories under the bureau's control. A well-established relationship between military technology collectors and scientific research centres is strong evidence of a clearly defined role for technical intelligence support in the development of weapon systems. Long-term planning such as this provides some insight into the quality and foresight of the management structure. Also, the Second Department clearly does not depend on its civilian counterpart, the MSS, for technical support.

In addition to the functional bureaus involved in collection and analysis, the Second Department has a number of administrative and support bureaus and divisions. These entities are collectively referred to as non-functional bureaus. Two of the most striking units are the Records/Archives bureau, which receives, translates and stores open source publications from overseas (Source 3), and the Confidential bureau (*Jiyao ju*), also known as the Secret Documents Bureau, which is responsible for handling, transmitting, and storing classified documents (Source 5). Based on the number of bureaus, the PLA Second Department appears to rival the MSS in size.

Conclusion

Major powers conduct espionage to support their interests. In this setting, China is no different from other nations with global interests. Also, gathering information on friends and adversaries should not necessarily be viewed as an evil act. Often, lack of knowledge about another country's intentions serves to destabilise relations between states. Particularly in the military arena, in many situations foreknowledge of a nation's intentions can lead to diplomatic or other policy initiatives that can avert a costly arms race or even military conflict.

Simply put, espionage is a normal activity between nations. It is extremely rare for the conduct of espionage to affect bilateral relations between states. However, one cannot accept the premise that the PRC is simply executing a government function by engaging in espionage. Since China's economic expansion, Beijing's strategic intelligence objectives include suppressing political opposition, support to foreign and economic policy, and developing its military-industrial base and force projection capabilities.

Notes

1 The views expressed in this study are those of the author and should not be construed as representing positions of the Department of Defense or the US government.
2 Cyber espionage is not considered in this article as it is primarily the responsibility of the Peoples Liberation Army's Third Department, Seventh Bureau and, as such, is considered a signals intelligence (SIGINT) function.

20

JAPAN

Ken Kotani

Japan possesses a number of self-contained intelligence institutions: the Cabinet Intelligence Research Office (CIRO), the Public Security Intelligence Agency (PSIA) and the various ministry-embedded apparatus: Defense Intelligence Headquarters of the Ministry of Defense (DIH/MOD), the Public Security Department of the National Police Agency (NPA), and the Intelligence and Analysis Service of the Ministry of Foreign Affairs (MOFA). These institutions form a Japanese intelligence community in appearance. However the community is very small compared to that of other nations and it lacks a unifying force for coordinating the various intelligence services. There are approximately 5,000 members of staff within the Japanese intelligence community and it is estimated that the budget is less than 150 billion yen (US$1.8 billion) per year.

Intelligence organisations of Japan

The Cabinet Intelligence and Research Office (CIRO)

The CIRO is Japan's central intelligence agency based in the Cabinet Office. CIRO has a staff of around 170 people, 100 of whom are on loan from other ministries and agencies, and most of the chief positions are occupied by police officers. It is tasked with collecting open source information and coordinating with other intelligence agencies, but the staff shortages makes carrying out these duties particularly difficult. The head of the CIRO is required to advise the Prime Minister weekly, but according to Andrew Oros (2002: 6), '[m]any experts give the CIRO poor marks on its primary mission of dealing with intelligence on national strategy, particularly in the post Cold War period'. The CIRO expanded with the creation of a subordinate organisation, the Cabinet Satellite Intelligence Centre, which was established in 2001. The centre employs 320 staff, 100 of whom are IMINT analysts, and it has four optical satellites and one radar satellite. Additional optical and radar satellites are scheduled to launch in 2012. The latest version of the satellite (IGS-6A) was launched in September 2011 and is said to have a 60 cm resolution (Lele 2013: 195).

Ministry of Foreign Affairs (MOFA)

In comparison to other agencies the MOFA has a relatively long tradition of collecting intelligence overseas. The Investigation Department, initially established in 1934, was later absorbed by and incorporated within the International Intelligence Department in 1991; this has subsequently become the Intelligence and Analysis Service. In the absence of a foreign intelligence collection agency, MOFA's service is regarded as a kind of overseas intelligence. However, as all MOFA personnel are trained and employed as diplomats, they are not able to function as true intelligence operatives, often facing difficulties engaging in covert intelligence activities in foreign countries. It is believed that around 80 members of staff are assigned to the intelligence section of the MOFA. While the section can collect diplomatic information through hundreds of embassies and consulates all over the world, overseas embassies are in fact able to bypass the intelligence department and send information to MOFA's policy-making departments directly (*Taigai Joho Kinou Kyouka ni Kansuru Kondankai* n.d.).

Defense Intelligence Headquarters/Ministry of Defense (DIH/MOD)

The Defense Intelligence Headquarters (DIH), established in 1997, is the largest intelligence apparatus in the Japanese intelligence community, with more than 2,400 members of staff, most of whom come from the various arms of the military service. The DIH falls under the control of the Defense Minister and the director of DIH advises him directly on a weekly basis. Until the founding of the DIH, Japanese military intelligence was handled separately by the respective intelligence sections of the Japan Ground Self-Defense Force (JGSDF), the Japan Maritime Self-Defense Force (JMSDF) and the Japan Air Self-Defense Force (JASDF), and for a long time it was difficult to break down the walls between them.

The main duty of the DIH is to collect and analyse signals intelligence through six interception bases in Japan. The former body of the DIH, the 2nd Investigation Bureau of the JGSDF, had intercepted Soviet signals throughout the Cold War. The most famous case occurred in 1983, when a Su-15 jet fighter shot down a *Korean Air* Boeing 747 on 1 September; the bureau intercepted signals between the Su-15 and a Soviet air base in the Far East. The Prime Minister, Yasuhiro Nakasone, decided to pass the secret information to the US government against protests by the MOD, prioritising the maintenance of good diplomatic relations between the US and Japan over this security matter (Nakasone 2012: 343–344). The Soviet Union did not officially admit its involvement in the incident, but the interception record was released by the US government.

Additionally the DIH possesses an imagery intelligence section, an analysis section and a joint intelligence section, all of which work together with the JGSDF, the JMSDF and the JASDF.

Public Security Intelligence Agency (PSIA)

The PSIA is an internal investigation agency, similar to the British Security Service (MI5). Its staff is estimated at 1,500. The PSIA was established as a division of the Ministry of Justice in 1952 with the purpose of monitoring nationalist and communist activities in Japan. Unlike the police, the agency cannot force someone to cooperate with its investigation. In fact, the PSIA is thought to be little more than an enforcement organisation of the Subversive Activities Prevention Law, aiming to prevent radical groups from carrying out terrorist acts and violent activities on Japanese soil. The law is widely regarded as ineffectual and it has been invoked only in a limited number of cases; indeed, it was not even applied to the case of the Aum Shinrikyo sarin gas attack in March 1995, in which the cult released the poisonous gas in Tokyo underground stations. The Public Security Examination Commission did not agree that the Subversive Activities Prevention Law applied, and the weak response led to public discussions on the future existence of the agency. After the sarin gas incident, the PSIA struggled for its survival, and it has increasingly come to focus upon new dangers, such as drug dealing and terrorist threats. Since its reorganisation in 1996, there has been a clear shift it its mission, from internal investigations to foreign intelligence collection.

National Police Agency (NPA)

The NPA assumes a role similar to that of the FBI in the United States, and is responsible for policing the entire nation, and protecting against foreign espionage and terrorism. In fact the NPA is the most influential apparatus in the Japanese intelligence community. Its ability to carry out its responsibilities is dependent upon its 300,000-strong police force (a force far greater than that of the military services) and its links with the chief intelligence officers of other agencies. The NPA regularly sends senior police officers to the Director of Cabinet Intelligence, CIRO, the deputy director of the Cabinet Satellite Intelligence Center, the head of SIGINT section of DIH, and the Director of the first intelligence department of the PSIA. The highly centralised NPA can collect information through the intelligence sections of these other agencies. The Public Security department is the central body of the NPA's intelligence and is responsible for counterintelligence in the country. The department is made up of the Foreign Affairs section, the International Terrorism section and the Public Security section.

After the Second World War, Japanese intelligence was rebuilt for monitoring communist activities in Japan, and the police was suitable for carrying out these duties. Moreover, the role of the Japanese military forces was limited in the Cold War period, and the police took over the role of military service. For example, in 1976, when Lieutenant Ivanovich Belenko of the Soviet Air Force, flew to Hakodate airport with his MIG-25 fighter jet seeking political asylum, the Japanese police force tried to keep military officers out of the airport. It was a typical case of bureaucratic factionalism and a humiliating incident for the military, which was not allowed to scrutinise the MIG during the initial phase of the incident (Okoda 2001: 138; Sato 2012: 27).

The NPA has also shown interest in international cooperation, and has been increasingly involved in exchanges with foreign agencies to fight common threats. After Japan signed the Mutual Assistance Treaty together with members of the US, Korea, China and Russia, the NPA was able to share information directly with the police forces of these countries over the head of the MOFA. However, despite this growing influence, the NPA remains essentially an organisation of law enforcement; it collects information for its investigations, but it does not seek to shape foreign and security policy.

A brief history: the Cold War to the present

In the early 1950s, under the auspices of Prime Minister Shigeru Yoshida, the Chief Cabinet Secretary Taketora Ogata and Jun Murai, chief of the security section of the National Police Agency, tried to set up an entirely new body of intelligence, with the intention to establish a central intelligence machinery similar to the US Central Intelligence Agency (CIA) (Kitaoka 2007: 166–178). However, the press bitterly opposed the plan, and Yoshida was obliged to compromise, establishing a Research Center (which later became the CIRO) in the cabinet office headed by Murai in April 1952 (Haruna 2000: 521–530). The centre was allocated only 30 members of staff and had a poor legal grounding. It was expected to collect and analyse open source information and to aggregate the information of other ministries and agencies. However, the shortage of staff and the legal restraints placed upon it resulted in a body that barely functioned as an intelligence apparatus throughout the Cold War period.

The end of the Cold War had a significant impact on the Far Eastern security environment, and the Japanese government – in the face of international and internal difficulties – started to discuss organisational reforms of the country's security and intelligence apparatus. The Japanese intelligence community was shocked by the North Korean launch test of a Tepodong-1 ballistic missile in August 1998, which was fired over Japan. This failure to anticipate the firing of the missile led to the Prime Minister's decision to launch reconnaissance satellites.

Domestically, the Aum Shinrikyo attack on the Tokyo underground in March affected more than 5,000 people. The NPA and PSIA failed to prevent the attack, and this prompted discussions over internal security reforms. The September 11 attacks by Al Qaeda further pushed the need for reform on to the agenda. In recent years, the Cabinet Office, MOFA, the Liberal Democratic Party (LDP) and the PHP Research Institute (a Japanese private institution) have all published different plans for intelligence reform (e.g. PHP 2006).

The Cabinet Office published a new report, *The Improvement of Intelligence Functions of the Prime Minister's Office*, based upon these plans in February 2008 (*Kantei ni okeru joho kihou no kyouka no houshin*). The report made the following recommendations: (1) to establish equal relations between policy-making and intelligence elements in the Cabinet Office; (2) to enhance intelligence-gathering activities; (3) to promote intelligence-sharing among ministries and establish the Office of the Prime Minister's control over information flows in the Japanese government; (4) to develop intelligence infrastructure; (5) to overhaul the security system. Indeed, this report proposed the creation of a committee system as the central intelligence machinery, based on the British model. The Cabinet Office also issued a proposal, *The Improvement of Counter-intelligence Functions*, in August 2007, and based upon this the CIRO established the Counter-intelligence Center in the Cabinet Office in April 2008 (*Kaunta interijyensu kinou no kyouka ni okeru kihon houshin*). Finally, the CIRO summarised the points of these reports for the discussion of the 4th council on security and defence held in the Prime Minister's Office (*Kantei*) in February 2009 (*Anzenhosyou to boueiryoku ni kansuru kondankai (Dai 4 kai)*).

Issues

Lack of overseas human intelligence collection capabilities

Japan has not had an apparatus for overseas human intelligence since the end of the Second World War. While not permitted to engage in covert activities, Japanese diplomats have played a central role in overseas information gathering, collecting information through their diplomatic networks and open sources in the host country. The NPA, PSIA and MOD also send members of staff to Japanese embassies abroad to serve as secretaries or military attachés; one of their duties is to collect political and military information.

Usually, HUMINT gathers information that is not accessible through diplomatic means; since the Japanese government is not able to operate outside of these diplomatic channels in foreign countries, it cannot collect overseas information. Moreover, it is almost impossible to gather information in countries that have no diplomatic relations with Japan. The Japanese government has acknowledged that there are 17 abducted Japanese citizens in North Korea, for example, but it is has been unable to learn anything about their status given the lack of diplomatic relations with the country. According to the WikiLeaks documents, the Director of CIRO, Hideshi Mitani, confessed that Japan's best insights into North Korea came not from a secret source but rather from the published memoirs of Kim Jong Il's former sushi chef (Dorling 2011). In February 2011, the WikiLeaks documents suggested that the Japanese government had established a new HUMINT agency for collecting information on North Korea and China, but the report was based upon false information.

Lack of central machinery and poor information sharing

Under the present Cabinet Office, CIRO is modelled upon the American CIA style, while the Cabinet Intelligence Committee (CIC)/Joint Intelligence Committee (JIC), as explained below, is based on the British JIC. The Japanese bureaucratic culture is similar to that of the US, exhibiting a strong sectionalism, and significant rivalry and friction between the various ministries. However, the Japanese political system is similar to that of the UK, with consensus decision-making under a parliamentary cabinet system. Thus, it can be said that this mixture results in the contemporary hybrid intelligence system, with the effect that neither system works effectively.

The Japanese system of government is built around individual ministries and agencies, which tend not to communicate or share information either with one another or with the cabinet office. The former Director of Cabinet Intelligence, Yoshio Omori, wrote that he was not given any intelligence from the MOFA and MOD, even though he was the head of central intelligence (Omori 2005: 37–38). He was unable to overcome the divisions and barriers between the CIRO and other ministries. In recent Japanese history, the government has never succeeded in managing the central intelligence system effectively.

In 1952 the Japanese government established the CIRO, modelling it upon the CIA. However, despite a promising start, the Japanese government had not sufficiently understood the nature and operation of the CIA. The CIRO's responsibilities were significantly restricted, and it did not have the authority to force other institutions, departments and agencies to share information with it. According to the Order for Organization of Cabinet Office, the CIRO's 'duty is to collect and analyze information relating to the policy-making of the cabinet and to liaise and coordinate with other ministries' (Order for the Organization of the Cabinet Office 1952).

However the CIRO does not possess any means of information gathering except for IMINT, and the MOFA, MOD and NPA are not obliged to pass any information on to the agency. These ministries continue to send their staff to the Prime Minister's Office as aides and personal secretaries, and are consequently able to bypass the CIRO and to deliver information personally and directly to the Prime Minister himself (PHP Research Institute 2006: 22). Moreover, the CIRO is influenced by the NPA, with many chief positions being held by former members of the police force. Consequently there is a police-style culture, rather than an intelligence-gathering and assessment culture (Oros 2002: 6–8). Unless the underlying tension is addressed, it is hard to see the information-gathering problem ever being resolved, however much the CIRO is strengthened as an institution. In the half century that has passed since the office was established, the CIRO has been Japan's central intelligence organisation, yet its function has not adapted to the contemporary context; serious changes are required.

By the 1980s, the Japanese government had begun to realise that the highly centralised structure of the CIRO was ineffective. Initially, senior officials simply thought that the American system was not suitable for the Japanese context. There was a subsequent attempt to introduce the British system in 1986, without dismantling the CIRO; the CIC was born. The CIC is made up from deputy secretaries and chief secretary class, with only two meetings a year, each meeting lasting around one hour, which is lacking in responsive capability (PHP Research Institute 2006: 23). In addition, the JIC holds bi-monthly meetings of the Bureau Chiefs who are much more involved in actual operations. The British committee system is fundamentally based upon the idea of collegiality, and Japanese bureaucrats, favouring a compartmentalised system, did not welcome the committee system. As a result, the reality of the committee has been more akin to table-talk than to a serious discussion on national intelligence. This is, in part, the result of the fact that the committee does not possess a bureau office, nor does it have a staff that is responsible for writing assessment papers for the committee.

In April 2008, the CIRO appointed five analysts: they were tasked with drawing up the National Intelligence Estimate draft, in the hope that it would improve the management of national intelligence. For writing the estimate, the CIRO is given an authority to coordinate other ministries and how the Japanese intelligence agencies come to share intelligence at the JIC. An intelligence officer said, '[i]ntelligence sharing among ministries and agencies has been drastically improved by the JIC and National Intelligence Estimate' (Kaneko 2010: 62).

Malfunction of the intelligence cycle

In order for intelligence collection and reporting to be useful to the state, the intelligence community commonly needs some political guidance (Lowenthal 2003: 144). However, the Japanese intelligence agencies are not briefed about intelligence requirements by policy-makers, and as such they face significant difficulties. In determining foreign policy, political leaders are usually far more concerned with establishing a consensus among the various political groups than with carefully examining intelligence. In other words, Japanese politicians or policy-makers tend to put political goals ahead of intelligence or information on the ground.

Too much time is expended in Japanese policy-making as a result of this need to build a consensus. Moreover, new information that emerges after a consensus has been reached is actually undesirable; this can lead to information being suppressed, even when it appears to be accurate. Thus, politicians do not require information from the intelligence services to assist in developing policy; rather they need internal information on their political opponents. There is a malfunction in the intelligence cycle.

Prior to the Second World War, there was no centre of power in the Japanese political arena. The Prime Minister was essentially a 'first among equals', and he faced significant difficulties in building a consensus on Japanese foreign policy. After the war, the position of the Prime Minister was strengthened, but consensus-building remained important. Article 65 of the Japanese Constitution states that, 'administrative power is vested in the Cabinet'. In other words, the Japanese Prime Minister cannot decide anything without obtaining the consent of other cabinet members, and the cabinet usually works on a basis of unanimity. The Prime Minister must often go to great lengths to persuade the Minister of Education or the Minister of Health of the importance of overseas and security matters. In this decision-making process, the Prime Minister does not need secret intelligence for deciding overseas policy. Richard Betts (2007: 192) suggested that 'the importance of successful intelligence ultimately varies with the policies it has to support', but Japanese intelligence has largely been overlooked by political leaders.

In 1986, the Prime Minister was granted the authority to convene the Security Council of Japan in case of emergency. The council comprises nine ministers, who engage in overseas and security matters. However, the role of the council is only to consider and discuss the situation; it is not a decision-making body. During the Cold War period, the Japanese government did not confront delicate international matters. As a result of US dominance in the region, the Far Eastern international context was relatively stable. Nevertheless, Japanese politicians' need for secret information remains very low in the post-Cold War context. Indeed, it was not until 2006 that the Prime Minister, Shinzo Abe, proposed the institution of the National Security Council (NSC) to replace the existing Security Council. The new council would be designed for swift decision-making in foreign and security policy (Hitoshi 2006: 8–9). Moreover, the NSC was expected to act as a counterpart to the intelligence community, giving requirements and receiving intelligence. Thus the Japanese NSC was designed to activate the intelligence cycle between the Prime Minister's Office and the intelligence community. However, the sudden resignation of Abe in September 2007 frustrated the plan.

A somewhat secure system

In May 2012, it was widely reported that the Japanese police suspected Li Chunguang, first secretary of the Chinese Embassy in Tokyo, of engaging in espionage activities in Japan. Four secret documents from the Ministry of Agriculture, Forestry and Fisheries of Japan were leaked to a private association in China; Li was not only involved in this association, but he also had substantial connections with the senior figures of the Ministry in question. However the police were not able to make an arrest because the Japanese government does not have an anti-spy law or a security act. As a result, the police were able to charge him only with a very minor offence that was in violation of his residency. However, Li managed to escape and return to China before any charges could be brought against him. The scandal was headline news in Japan and the two ministers were dismissed from their posts.

In contrast with other systems of intelligence, there is also a lack of counterintelligence structures that could prevent enemy spy activities. Before the Second World War, under the Military Secret Law and the National Defense Security Law, 'foreigners involved in spy activities or their Japanese agents could be punished with the death penalty or unlimited penal servitude with a minimum of three years' (Hidaka 1937: 24). Even in the famous Sorge Incident in 1940 this was considered sufficient.

However, at the end of the war, when these laws were abolished, there was no legislation put in place to cover a counterintelligence structure. In August 1954, Yuri Rastropov, a KGB defector to the US, confessed that hundreds of Japanese agents, including several diplomats of the MOFA, collaborated with him; this incident highlighted the inadequacies of the existing legislation. After Rastropov's confession, three Japanese diplomats – Nobunori Hikarashi, Shigeru Takamore and Hiroshi Shoji – were accused of collaboration. Hikarashi committed suicide during his interrogation, Takamore was sentenced to eight months' imprisonment for the breach of the obligation to maintain secrecy as a civil servant under the National Public Service Law (NPSL) and Shoji got the benefit of the doubt (Tanaka 1980: 364–376).

Indeed, Japan was 'spy heaven' for Soviet spies during the Cold War period. The leniency of the legal system was further demonstrated in the Kononov Incident (1971), the Miyanaga Incident (1980), the Levchenko Incident (1982) and other cases involving Soviet spying activities (Levchenko 1988; Gaiji Jiken Kenkyu Kai 2007: 186–189). After Levchenko, former KGB major, was granted asylum in the US, he testified that there were a number of Soviet spies active in Japan; this testimony caused spy fever within the Japanese government. The Prime Minister, Yasuhiro Nakasone, attempted to pass a State Secrets Bill (anti-spy law) in June 1985, but was forced to yield to furious public opposition (Kaneko 2007: 123). Japanese public opinion has been greatly influenced by the liberal tone of the press and the general resistance towards matters of intelligence, and Japanese politicians, who are acutely aware of this climate, are hesitant to discuss the topic openly.

Weaknesses such as these continue to act as a barrier for the exchange of intelligence with other countries. The US Deputy Secretary of State, Richard Armitage, published a famous report in 2000, *The United States and Japan: Advancing Towards a Mature Partnership*, setting the tone for the strengthening of US–Japan security cooperation. In addition to promoting the idea of cooperation in the intelligence arena, this document also called for a greater degree of intelligence sharing within the Japanese government, an increased participation by the Japanese parliament in intelligence operations, and increased public and political support for legislation concerning an Official Secrets Act (INSS 2000).

Legislation concerning intelligence security predominantly relates to the duty of civil servants to maintain state secrecy under the NPSL. Breaking the law carries a maximum of one year's imprisonment. The November 2001 amendments to the Self-Defense Force Law (SDFL) in connection with military secrets, which covers government institutions as well as private corporations, set the maximum prison sentence at no more than five years. Similarly, in connection with intelligence that was received from the US within the framework of the Mutual Support Agreement (MSA) concerning 'Special Military Intelligence', the maximum sentence was set at no more than ten years (Secrets Protection Law). Japan signed the General Security of Military Information Agreement (GSOMIA) with the US in August 2007, and the hope is that this will not remain limited to military secrets alone, but rather that will lead to the development of a comprehensive intelligence security system, has been expressed. According to expert indications, there are currently at least 1,000 people engaging in activities on behalf of China within Japan (PHP Research Institute 2006: 25). The NPA warned the Japanese government that, 'the means of Chinese information gathering are quite slick: hiring Japanese agents on the ground, whilst simultaneously fostering friendly Sino-Japanese relations on the surface' (*Shouten* 2004: 43).

On 4 November 2010, a Japanese Coast Guard officer, Masaharu Isshiki, also known as 'sengoku38', uploaded a video file to YouTube. The Japanese public was surprised that the video had been leaked, given the fact that the Japanese government considered it to be secret. The film shows a collision between a Japanese coast guard ship and a Chinese poacher's fishing boat near Senkaku islands in Japanese waters; the coast guard held the fisherman in custody. The Japanese government concealed the film out of diplomatic consideration for China, but it was leaked by a coast guard officer, who was frustrated by the government's temporising policy.

The leak shocked the government, and the Democratic Party of Japan started to discuss an official security law. The Council of Advisers for Legislation on Security Law submitted a proposal to the Prime Minister, Naoto Kan, on 8 August 2011. According to the proposal, the Japanese government would introduce the notion of 'Special Secret' as the highest level of secrecy in Japan, and any violations of the act would be subject to five or ten years of imprisonment (Report of the Council of Advisers for Legislation on Security Law n.d.). However the Democratic Party abandoned efforts to pass this piece of legislation. The reason for this concession is unclear, but it is said that the government wanted to assign the highest priority to the consumption tax increase in the Diet session of 2012. In a twist of irony, just a few months later the Chinese spy incident was broadcast extensively.

Conclusion

Japan's main intelligence targets are China and North Korea, but in the absence of an efficient HUMINT agency, the Japanese government relies solely upon IMINT and SIGINT, which is insufficient for sound policy-making. The government has sometimes relied on intelligence offered from the US intelligence community, however.

As far as counterintelligence is concerned, the NPA and PSIA face significant problems in monitoring Chinese espionage activities. While the number of Chinese spies in Japan has increased rapidly, the NPA and PSIA lack effective measures to monitor them. For example, the Japanese police are not allow to eavesdrop on phone conversations and emails for information-gathering purposes, and have no choice but to watch and tail suspects directly. The limited manpower of the NPA cannot effectively counter Chinese espionage activities and the lack of anti-spy law makes the situation much more difficult. Reforms of the small and somewhat secure intelligence system must be initiated immediately.

21

ISRAEL

Uri Bar-Joseph

Intelligence collection, processing, distribution and consumption had been an important part of Jewish history since Biblical times. The most notable spying mission in this history was that of the 12 spies who were sent by Moses to the land of Canaan that was promised to the Jews by God. Until today this mission is a fine example of the intricate web between high-quality intelligence collection about the nature of the country, which was defined by the spies as 'a land of milk and honey'; popular political pressure by the Israelites, who feared confronting the strong enemy that inhabited the land; motivated biases in the estimation process, which led ten of the spies to yield to the pressure and reassess the land as 'a land that eateth up the inhabitants thereof'; and a mistaken leadership decision by Moses, which ultimately left him and his people deep in the desert for another 40 years (Numbers 13). Some Biblical lessons have been adapted by Israel's more modern spies. For years the motto of the Mossad was 'For by wise counsel thou shalt make thy war' (Proverbs 24:6). This was later replaced by 'Where no counsel is, the people fall, but in the multitude of counselors there is safety' (Proverbs 11:14).

Close to 2,000 years of life in the Diaspora, mostly as second-class citizens, furnished the Jews with the tools needed to build an effective intelligence community: the need not to excel among the gentiles and to live life in the shadow, the knowledge of foreign languages and cultures, and links with other Jewish communities all over the world. Recognition of the importance of intelligence was well evident since Jews started returning to the Promised Land in the late nineteenth century. During the First World War, a Jewish spy network that was known by its acronym as NILI provided the British with detailed information about Turkish military activities in Palestine. This intelligence was used effectively by General Allenby in his Palestine campaign in 1917–18. During the British Mandate years (1917–48) the *Yishuv*, the Jewish community in Palestine, built an impressive set of intelligence organisations. The Political Department of the Jewish Agency (the de facto government of the *Yishuv*) had since the early 1920s a foreign policy intelligence section. In 1940 the *Haganah* ('Defence'), the *Yishuv*'s paramilitary organisation, established its own intelligence and counterintelligence unit, known as the Information Service (*Sherut Yediot*, or 'Shai'). Shortly afterwards the *Haganah*'s Striking Force (*Palmach*) established its 'German platoon', made of Jews of German origin who were to operate, in coordination with the British SOE, behind the German lines, and the 'Arab platoon', composed of Jews from Arab countries disguised as Arabs, who operated in the Arab sectors of Palestine, and in Syria and Lebanon (Dekel 1959; Black and Morris 1991: 1–54; Katz 1992: 9–24).

Israel's intelligence community was born in June 1948, in the midst of the War of Independence. The *Haganah* was turned into the Israeli Defense Force (IDF) and its Information Service became Military Intelligence known by its Hebrew acronym Aman. A few weeks later the counterintelligence section of the Information Service was turned into the Security Service (later known as the General Security Service, or Shabak). Until August 1950 it belonged to the IDF and then it was transferred to the Prime Minister's Office. June 1948 also saw the establishment of the Political Department in charge of collection in non-Arab countries in the Foreign Office, replacing the intelligence unit of the Jewish Agency. Due to operational failures, ineffective management and insufficient coordination with Aman, this unit was dismantled. On 1 April 1951 responsibility for collection and operations abroad was transferred to a new agency in the Prime Minister's Office: the Institute for Intelligence and Special Operations, aka the Mossad. This was the last major shift in the structure of the intelligence community (Melman and Raviv 1989: 41–74; Black and Morris 1991: 54–97; Avivi 2012; Erlich 2012; Glaser 2012).

Although the Mossad is Israel's most famous intelligence agency, the community's senior organisation is Aman. Until 1974 Aman was solely responsible for Israel's national intelligence estimates. Following its failure to warn against the Arab sudden attack of the 1973 Yom Kippur War, a research branch was established in the Mossad and the Research Department of the Foreign Office was enhanced. Nevertheless, Aman maintained its seniority in strategic intelligence. Moreover, its budget is far larger than that of the Mossad and the Shabak, primarily since it is Israel's main collector of signals intelligence (SIGINT) and visual intelligence (VISINT). It is also the biggest agency in terms of manpower.

Aman's status as *primus inter pares* is derived from the fact that conventional military threats, primarily a combined Arab surprise attack, had always been considered as the main threat to Israel's national security. In late 1948 its prime task was defined as 'the provision of a warning to the state of Israel of a coming attack by the Arab armies . . . in order to allow the General Staff to mobilize forces and deploy the army in time to meet the threat'. Despite considerable changes in Israel's strategic environment during the past 35 years – changes that yielded a decline in conventional military threats, and a rise in terrorism and non-conventional threats – Aman still maintains its status as Israel's leading intelligence organisation (Bar-Joseph 2009).

Coordination between the Mossad, Aman and Shabak is conducted by a special organ known as the Committee of the Heads of the Services, or Varash. Its chair is the chief of the Mossad and according to a law that was passed in 2008, the Prime Minister's Military Secretary (an officer at the rank of Major General) and the head of the National Security Council also participate in the committee's meetings. Varash is not a decision-making forum and does not convene on a regular basis; it meets ad hoc to update and coordinate intelligence and operational activities.

Being the world's most 'fightoholic' nation in the post-1945 era gave Israel's intelligence community a special status, unlike in any other Western-type democracy. Perceiving themselves as a small community challenged constantly by a large unstable environment, the Israelis consider intelligence the nation's first line of defence. Service in the community is regarded not only as an important service but also as a patriotic mission. It is also prestigious and can be rewarding. Retired officers from Aman's SIGINT unit (Unit 8200) are highly sought after in the high-tech market and 8200 itself is considered as the main engine behind Israel's status as a high-tech state and start-up nation. Heading one of the services secures a good chance for a high-ranking position in the economic or political sector after retirement, as evidenced by the fact that a number of former chiefs of Aman, Mossad and Shabak serve as members of the parliament or as cabinet ministers. Notably, Zipi Livni, who ran for premiership and headed Kadima, which became the largest party in the 2009 elections, was considered to have sufficient experience in national security affairs because of her four years' junior service in the Mossad.

Israel's intelligence community gains considerable respect from foreign communities as well. In 1956 the Shabak succeeded in getting hold of Khrushchev's secret speech, which started the de-Stalinisation process in the communist bloc. A copy of the secret document was given to the CIA, and this act laid the foundation for a close cooperation between the Israeli and the American intelligence communities. Similar cooperation was reached with other Western organisations, primarily British, German and French. Since 11 September 2001, this cooperation deepened and now comprises many other intelligence agencies, including Muslim and Arab. By many foreign reports Israel plays a major role in the global war against terrorism as well as against Iranian efforts to become nuclear. Even if there is some degree of exaggeration in defining the Israeli services as the world's best, there is no doubt that their record is quite impressive, and by any standard they show a high level of professionalism, creativity and daring.

The intensive and colourful history of Israel's intelligence community has attracted over the years considerable public interest, as reflected in the growing number of fiction and non-fiction books about its real and imaginary operations, primarily those of the Mossad. Some of these accounts are more popular than accurate, but others present a rather solid, though mostly anecdotal, history of operations (e.g. Black and Morris 1991; Katz 1992; Bar-Zohar and Mishal 2012; Melman and Raviv 2012). Less attention has been devoted so far to collection of information as well as its analysis, which constitutes the main bulk of the community's work and responsibility. Consequently, the rest of this chapter will focus on Israel's SIGINT, human intelligence (HUMINT) and estimation records, primarily with regard to preventing strategic surprises.

SIGINT[1]

The roots of Israel's SIGINT can be traced back to the Mandate years. Since the early 1940s the Shai routinely monitored and deciphered the Morse communications of the British Criminal Investigations Department, police, army and naval units. Towards the end of the British rule it systematically tapped telephone talks of senior British officers and commanders of local Arab paramilitary forces. In the summer of 1947, when the UN Special Committee on Palestine conducted its hearings concerning the future of the country, the Shai bugged its meeting room in the Palace Hotel in Jerusalem and provided the Jewish leaders with a daily account of the discussions. A few months later, when war began, it started systematically wiring the telephone lines between Jaffa, Jerusalem, and Haifa and Arab countries, thus gaining significant information about Arab planned operations.

When Aman was established in June 1948, Shai's SIGINT unit was organised as Intelligence Service 2. During the war it broke the ciphers of the Egyptian and Jordanian armies and provided useful information, which, among other things, helped the IDF win the battle for Lydia in July 1948, take over the city of Beer Sheba and sink the Egyptian flagship, the frigate *Amir Farouq*, in October 1948, as well as listen to the instructions to the Egyptian delegation in the armistice talks of early 1949.

In the early 1950s, and now known as Unit 181, Aman's SIGINT organ was made up of approximately 150 soldiers and civilian experts, and in 1952 its headquarters moved to its current location, Camp Glilot, north-east of Tel Aviv. Its main means of collection continued to be COMINT and its main target was the routine military activity in the neighbouring Arab countries. Although the larger share of its activity was wireless traffic, some collection was done by tapping military telephone lines. In December 1954, five Israeli soldiers were caught while replacing batteries in an eavesdropping device to the central telephone line of the Syrian army in the Golan Heights. It can be assumed that similar activities took place along the other borders as well. Unit 181 also developed embryonic electronic intelligence (ELINT) capabilities that were used for the first time in combat to block Egyptian wireless traffic during a border incident in November 1955.

On 28 October 1956, a day before the start of the Sinai/Suez war, Unit 181 tracked the flight course of two Ilyushin 14s that carried the Egyptian high command to talks in Syria. One of the planes was shot down by an Israeli fighter upon return. Although the unit missed the flight of the second, which carried Egypt's Chief of Staff, Field Marshal Abed Hakim Amer, the loss of 14 senior commanders on the eve of the war hampered Egyptian efforts during the fighting.

The beginning of the decade between the 1956 and the 1967 wars was relatively calm but, following a major failure to detect a large-scale deployment of the Egyptian army near the Israeli border in February 1960 (see below), Aman started increasing its collection efforts, especially in the realm of strategic warning. Accordingly, Unit 515, as it was now called, purchased new listening equipment, increased its coverage deeper into the neighbouring Arab states and improved its ELINT capabilities. The top requirement of this build-up was to allow a fast reaction to the threat of an Egyptian air assault of the nuclear reactor at Dimona. This threat (codenamed 'Senator') ranked highest in Aman's priority intelligence requirements until the war of 1967.

The ongoing improvement of Unit 515's capabilities led to a number of major achievements, the most important of which was detailed coverage of the Egyptian Air Force in its bases west of the Suez Canal and ground forces activity in the Sinai. The performance of the Egyptian radar system was mapped by ELINT means, enabling the Israeli Air Force (IAF) to locate the low-altitude flight paths that were used on 5 June 1967 to attack the Egyptian Air Force (EAF). ELINT was also used in the first hours of the war to blind the Jordanian radar in Ajloun that could provide Egypt with a warning of the take-off of the whole IAF.

Aman's communications intelligence (COMINT) capabilities during this period were quite impressive. In February 1960, Unit 515 intercepted and deciphered a cable from Gen. Amer, who was in Damascus, ordering his army to deploy along the Israeli border in the Negev to deter the IDF from attacking Syria. Egypt and Syria were then politically united in the framework of the United Arab Republic. From the early 1960s Arab states started using radio-telephone systems, and covering them had been another major priority of the unit. In December 1966 it intercepted a telegram sent from Amer's plane en route to Pakistan to President Nasser in Cairo, concerning a possible deployment of the army in the Sinai in response to a large-scale IDF reprisal in Jordan. During the second day of the 1967 war, Israel released a recording of a talk between President Nasser and King Hussein of Jordan, who agreed to blame the US and Britain for their alleged participation in the air strike that had destroyed the EAF a day earlier. These few examples constitute a good indication of the quality of Aman's SIGINT coverage throughout this period.

The occupation of the Sinai, the West Bank and the Golan Heights in the 1967 war opened a new era for Unit 515 (now renamed Unit 848). Its main new bases were located far closer than before to the Arab centres of military activity, in Mt Hermon (2,814 m above sea level) in the Golan and in Um Hashiba (723 m above sea level) in the Sinai. Aman invested extensively in building up considerable SIGINT and ELINT capabilities, including electromagnetic, electro-optical, acoustic and seismic sensors (especially in Um Hashiba), as well as VISINT capabilities (especially in the Hermon). Consequently, Unit 848 grew rapidly and became one of the largest units in the IDF.

The military conflict that intensified after the 1967 war, primarily the Egyptian–Israeli War of Attrition (1969–70), led to an organisational build-up, too. The escalating Soviet role led to the creation in late 1967 of a unit specialising in Russian COMINT ('Masrega', or 'knitting needle'). Even more important, in 1969 three separate elements – Aman's technological unit, which specialised in building up listening devices, the General Staff Reconnaissance Unit

('Sayeret Matkal'), which specialised in intelligence operations in enemy territory, and a small unit that specialised in the preparation of intelligence for operations – were combined into a new organ known as Special Operations (Mivtzaim Meyuhadim, aka Mem Mem). From this stage on, Aman operated two SIGINT units.

During the War of Attrition, Aman's SIGINT units provided highly useful intelligence support, especially to special operations such as commando raids deep in Egyptian territory in 1968 or the capturing of a Soviet P-12 radar system in December 1969. During the three years between the end of this war and the War of Yom Kippur it focused on improving its capabilities to provide a war warning. A critical element here were listening devices planted by Sayeret Matkal in February 1973 on key Egyptian military communications lines. These 'special means of collection', as they were referred to among the few in the know, were considered by the Prime Minister, the Minister of Defence and the Chief of Staff as the main guarantee against the possible surprise of an Egyptian attack.

Strange as it might sound, on the eve of the war Aman's director, Maj. Gen. Eli Zeira, who was certain that war was unlikely, refused to operate the means. He also avoided distributing critical COMINT information that indicated that the war might be near. At the same time he told his superiors that his low probability estimate rested also on information from the special means of collection. This was a major factor that convinced them, until the very last moment, that no emergency moves, primarily the mobilisation of the reserve army, were required. Ultimately, despite the fact that Aman's SIGINT units had excellent potential to provide a strategic warning, Israel was caught unprepared by the Arab attack and was saved, by a complete surprise, by HUMINT.

Although the fiasco of the Yom Kippur War was mainly the outcome of erroneous intelligence estimation and not of collection, it served as a catalyst for a major build-up of Aman's collection apparatus. The returning of the Sinai in the framework of the peace agreement with Egypt compelled Unit 8200 – as it has been named since the war – to rely far more on airborne platforms and more advanced sensors. At the same time the peace with Egypt, the eight years of the Iran–Iraq war, the destruction of much of Iraq's army in Operation Desert Storm and the collapse of the USSR, decreased significantly the threat of an all-out Arab surprise attack. Accordingly, since the early 1990s strategic warning ceased to be the prime task of Unit 8200. It was replaced by the requirement to provide the IDF with operational intelligence, primarily in its low-intensity conflicts with the Palestinians in the occupied territories and Hezbollah in Lebanon.

8200 became the largest unit in the IDF and, with the exception of the IAF, also enjoys the biggest budgets. Since 1973 Aman's other SIGINT unit, Special Operations, had undergone a similar process in terms of importance, size and budget allocation. An indication of this is the fact that, when it was established in 1969, the rank of its commander was Lieutenant Colonel while now it is Brigadier General. Both units contributed significantly to the success of the attack on the Iraqi nuclear reactor (operation 'Opera') in June 1981, the destruction of the Syrian anti-aircraft systems in the Bakaa valley (operation 'Artzav 19') in the Lebanon war in June 1982, the destruction of Hezbollah heavy rockets arsenal (operation 'Specific Gravity') in the 2006 Lebanon war, and the destruction of the heavy rockets arsenal of the Hamas at the beginning of operation Pillar of Defense in November 2012. In addition, Aman's SIGINT units have provided much of the intelligence information needed to carry out small-scale operations, primarily in the West Bank and Gaza since the beginning of the second Intifada in late 2000.

The intensified cooperation with field units and the growing demand for combat intelligence added another dimension to Unit 8200's classic SIGINT activity. In 2011 it established its first field regiment whose soldiers are divided into teams that are staffed to other IDF units in their combat missions. By the end of 2012 the regiment was already active and with considerable operational experience. At the same time the cyber revolution added a third dimension to its activity. Officially the IDF invests in cyberdefence and Unit 8200 plays a leading role in this domain. Unofficially and according to various sources, the virus Stuxnet, which attacked Iran's nuclear infrastructure, was developed, at least partially, by 8200. If this, indeed, is the case it constitutes further proof of the excellent technological capabilities of Aman's SIGINT units. Finally, the Arab Spring, which started in late 2010 and is technically geared by Facebook and Twitter, became a fourth dimension of Aman's SIGINT activity.

HUMINT[2]

HUMINT is considered as a major source of the strength of Israel's intelligence community, especially when compared to similar communities in the West. But, when it comes to providing a strategic warning, the record of Israeli HUMINT is somewhat less impressive. For example, no HUMINT warning preceded the Arab invasion of Palestine on the day the British Mandate ended, although some sources of the Arab Department of the Palmach provided partial reports on Syrian preparations for invasion. During the war, HUMINT provided some operational information but mainly of tactical importance.

Bureaucratic competition between Aman and the Mossad, combined with a low level of professionalism, led to a rough start. In July 1954 a network of Egyptian Jews who were recruited and trained by Unit 131 of Aman to serve as saboteurs, were caught following an order of activation. As a result the Egyptian *Mukabarat* caught also Maj. Max Bineth, who started a separate spying mission in Cairo in 1952. The fiasco, known as 'the unfortunate business', triggered the worst political scandal in Israeli history, known as the 'the affair', which lasted until the mid–1960s.

Aman's HUMINT section, now Unit 188, froze its activities in the Arab world and underwent a rebuilding process. Towards the late 1950s it renewed its activities, focusing on Egypt and Syria, where Israel was left for years without any significant human sources. To fill this gap Unit 188 recruited and trained two Israelis – Zeev Gur Arie (cover name Wolfgang Lutz, code name 'Samson') to be the main human asset in Egypt, and Eli Cohen (cover name Kamil Amin Ta'abet, code name 'Menashe' or 'warrior 88') to do the same in Damascus. Their main task was to provide strategic warning of an incoming Arab attack. Both integrated very well in the local political and military elites, both acquired highly useful information of strategic value, and both were exposed and arrested in early 1965, thus leaving Israel with no major HUMINT sources in the years that preceded the 1967 war. This gap in HUMINT was bridged effectively by SIGINT and VISINT means of collection.

In 1963, following the resignation of the Mossad chief and the nomination of Aman's director to head the Mossad as well, Unit 188 was transferred to the Mossad. Aman was left with Unit 154 (later 504) that operated local Arab agents, mostly near the border and on tactical missions. The Mossad, which acquired a monopoly on HUMINT in foreign countries, had two departments: Caesarea, which was based on Unit 188 and used 'warriors', i.e. trained Mossad men and women like Eli Cohen in spying missions; and 'Tzomet' ('intersection'), whose collection officers handle foreign agents, primarily Arab ones. No change had taken place with regard to the Shabak that maintained its HUMINT functions in counterespionage and, later, counterterrorism.

Israel's golden age of strategic HUMINT took place between the wars of 1967 and 1973, a period in which Egypt initiated the War of Attrition (March 1969–August 1970) and then, with Syria, launched the War of Yom Kippur (October 1973). Learning from the tragic way by which Lutz and Cohen ended their long-term missions, the Mossad now relied less on its own 'warriors' and more on local agents, primarily in Egypt, which was the key to Arab war initiation. This entailed 'Tzomet' a critical role in providing Israel with a war warning.

In the years before the outbreak of the Yom Kippur War, Tzomet had a number of sources in Egypt, usually with good access and high reliability record. With the exception of one, their identities have not yet been exposed. These HUMINT assets proved their value especially in the year before the war. A few of them warned, by the end of 1972, that President Sadat decided to renew hostilities without waiting for certain Soviet arms, which were considered until then as a necessary precondition for a successful war. In April 1973 they provided concrete warnings concerning an Egyptian decision to start a war in mid-May. Two of them informed shortly afterwards that the decision was postponed, as indeed was the case. One source warned a week before the war that the large-scale military exercise for the crossing of the canal that was scheduled to start a day later was a disguise for the intention to launch a war. Finally, the warning that convinced the Israeli leadership to accept that war would break out within hours came from a Tzomet source as well.

This source, Ashraf Marwan (code name 'the angel'), was the jewel in the crown of Israel's HUMINT history. Being the son-in-law of President Nasser and a close assistant of President Sadat, he had almost free access to all of Egypt's secrets. Since the late 1970s, when he offered his services to the Mossad, he gave his handlers, among others, the Egyptian army's complete order of battle, its detailed war plans, including the most secret one that was concealed from the Syrians and was used in the war, the protocols of Sadat's talks with his generals, the protocols of Soviet–Egyptian discussions at the levels of state leadership, ministers of war and Chiefs of Staff, and the minutes of Egyptian high command meetings. Zvi Zamir, the Chief of the Mossad during this period, defined Marwan as 'the best source we have ever had'. Others who were aware of his contribution concluded that, because of him, Egypt was 'an open book for Israel'. The warning he gave Zamir in their secret meeting in London about 15 hours before the outbreak of the war was the most important piece of secret information in Israel's history. It prevented a far more devastating situation at the first stage of the war, including the occupation of the entire Golan Heights. Given that Marwan provided this information all alone and for so many years (his Mossad service ended in 1998) he can be considered as the best HUMINT source any nation had in the post-1945 era.

Although it was HUMINT rather than SIGINT which contributed the information that prevented a complete surprise, the declining threat of an all-out Arab surprise attack and improved VISINT and SIGINT capabilities in the era after the war eroded the need for HUMINT to provide a war warning. Nevertheless, the rise of new threats, primarily the nuclearisation of Iran and global terrorism, combined with Israel's unique advantages in this type of collection, justified the continued allocation of considerable resources to HUMINT, primarily in the Mossad. This is likely to remain the situation also in the foreseeable future.

Research and analysis[3]

Israel's fine record of SIGINT and HUMINT in meeting the fundamental challenge of Arab war preparations and intentions to go to war was not met by a similar record of strategic analysis. With only one exception, Aman's Research Department (Israel's sole national intelligence estimator until 1974) failed during its first 20 years of existence in this task.

In September 1955 Aman's analysts completely missed Egypt's arms deal with the Soviet bloc, believing that Nasser would not challenge the Western monopoly of arms sales in the region. After the deal was announced, it took Aman more than six months to provide a good estimate of its magnitude. In February 1960 Israel was surprised when it was found that most of the Egyptian army, including 500 tanks, was deployed near the border, ready to invade the Negev. The IDF had fewer than 30 tanks in the area and had to take emergency measures (operation 'Rotem') in order to deploy the entire regular army to meet the threat. Despite being aware of the fact that Gen. Amer had ordered the deployment, Aman's analysts avoided warning their bosses since they regarded Egypt's intentions as defensive.

Following the 1962 Egyptian military intervention in the civil war in Yemen, Aman developed a conception according to which Nasser would avoid any significant move against Israel as long as his army was stuck in the Yemenite swamp. With this conception in mind, the agency estimated in February 1967 that war was unlikely before 1970. After 15 May, when the Egyptian army started deploying in the Sinai, thus igniting the crisis that preceded the war, Aman's analysts continued to estimate that Nasser had no desire for escalation. Accordingly, they maintained, 'closing the Straits for Israeli shipping is not likely in the immediate future'. A few hours after this assessment was issued, Nasser gave the order to close the Straits of Tiran to Israeli shipping – a move that made war inevitable.

The outbreak of the War of Attrition constitutes an exceptional case of estimate success. In autumn 1968, Aman assessed that in the coming spring Egypt was likely to launch a war aimed at regaining the territory lost in June 1967. This assessment was the foundation for the order to complete all war preparations by 1 March 1969. The War of Attrition broke out a week later. In the war itself, however, Aman's experts missed the threat of a Soviet active intervention in the conflict. Despite SIGINT warnings, they continued to adhere to the conception that the Kremlin would avoid such a move for fear of a confrontation with the US. When their mistake became evident in March 1970, an entire Soviet anti-aircraft division was already deployed in Egypt.

The surprise of Yom Kippur constitutes a rare case even in its own category of events. On the eve of Barbarossa, the Soviets had all the information needed to conclude that the German attack was inevitable, but Stalin rejected his experts' estimates and continued to believe otherwise. In December 1941, the US had no clear indication that Pearl Harbor might be the target of the Japanese attack. In contrast, in October 1973 Aman had all the information needed to conclude that an Arab attack was highly likely, and there was no political disagreement with such an estimate. The causes for this failure are beyond the scope of this chapter. Suffice to say here that it reflected, more than everything else, mirror imaging, i.e. the belief that Sadat would not attack since he knew that Egypt would be defeated, and self-confidence regarding the outcome of such a conflict in light of Israel's military superiority.

If, prior to the 1973 war, Aman's mistaken estimates reflected a tendency towards a Pollyanna syndrome, after the fiasco they naturally turned to Cassandra's direction. Between 1974 and 1975 Aman issued, without sufficient evidence, a number of war warnings. None of these materialised. Moreover, throughout this period, Aman completely ignored the fundamental change in Egypt's attitude towards Israel, a change that culminated in Sadat's dramatic visit to Jerusalem in November 1977 and the Egyptian–Israeli peace accord. On the eve of the visit Aman's director estimated that Sadat's initiative might be a cover for offensive intentions.

Aman's estimation record during the last 30 years is a more mixed bag. In June 1982 its analysts were right when warning that Israel should not rely on the Lebanese Phalangists. Israeli politicians preferred, however, a different estimation given by the Mossad, and the outcome was the fiasco of Israel's grand plan in Lebanon. The Shabak and Aman failed to see the coming of the first Intifada in late 1987 – a case of surprise that so far has attracted insufficient attention. Similarly, both Aman and the Mossad were surprised by Iraq's invasion of Kuwait in August 1990. However, both estimated correctly the US response and the final outcome of the military conflict. Aman's experts were also right in estimating that Iraq would launch Scuds armed with conventional warheads on Israel in order to disintegrate the American-led coalition but would avoid the use of chemical warheads as long as there was no threat to the regime.

In the aftermath of the 1991 war, an internal debate concerning a possible strategic shift in Syria took place within Aman. While its director estimated that Assad was ready to sign a peace treaty with Israel in exchange for the Golan, his analysts were more sceptical. As is clear today, the analysts were wrong. During the late 1990s Aman also estimated that an IDF withdrawal from Israel's self-proclaimed security zone in southern Lebanon would lead to an escalated conflict and a possible confrontation with the Syrians. They were wrong again. Israeli difficulties in assessing social events in the Arab world were reflected in the failure of both Aman and Shabak to predict the Hamas victory in the Palestinian elections in January 2006, and the failure to grasp the magnitude of the Arab Spring since 2010. Aman's director estimated in early 2011 that '[c]urrently, there is no threat to the stability of the regime in Egypt'. Three weeks later Mubarak's regime collapsed.

The main threat that has haunted Israel during the past decade is that of an Iranian bomb. Aman warned in the mid-1990s that Iran will have the bomb by 2000 and then moved the dates to 2003, 2005, 2009 . . . and so on. It is not clear if the Mossad, which leads the Israeli campaign against nuclear Iran, erred similarly.

All in all, none of these mistaken estimates comes close to the 1973 fiasco, but they nevertheless present a rather poor record of strategic analysis. In some cases (e.g. the 2006 Palestinian elections and the 2011 revolution in Egypt) the failure was not unique to the Israeli services. In others, such as the expected date for an Iranian bomb, self-negating prophecy may count for the variance between the estimate and the outcome. In most other cases, it was a combination of a number of factors: mirror imaging (the Arabs will not make such clear mistakes, as in 1967); underestimation – which may be the result of Aman being a military body and its analysts are career military officers – of complicated political considerations and overestimation of military factors; and a personal tendency, which is more typical to military organisations than to civilian ones, towards a high for cognitive closure – a well-known psychological mechanism that hampers the processing of new information, especially when it contradicts one's conception of the situation. And, in any event, intelligence strategic estimation is a well-known minefield. In this sense the poor performance of Aman's analysts is not an exception in their profession.

Notes

1   This section is based on the following sources: Tirosh (2012), Geffen (2012), Lapid (2012), Argaman (2007), Bar-Joseph (1995), Shalev (2006) and various articles in the Israeli press.
2   This section is based on the following sources: Goren (2012), Segev (2012), Bar-Joseph (2011), Black and Morris (1991), Katz (1992), Melman and Raviv (2012), Bar-Zohar and Mishal (2012), and Zamir (2011).
3   This section is based on the following sources: Laslau (2012), Adamsky and Bar-Joseph (2006), Bar-Joseph (2005), Shalev (2006), Sobelman (2003), and Melman and Raviv (2012).

22

GERMANY

Anna Daun

Introduction

This chapter gives an overview of the institutional structure and some major trends in German intelligence. It begins with a glimpse at Germany's strategic conditions, before giving a brief description of the German intelligence community. Finally, I will assess the impact of both systemic change and transnationalisation processes on the organisation of German intelligence in the past two decades.

Strategic conditions and the role of intelligence

The changes in the international system after 1989 resulted in a profound shift of Germany's strategic position. First, through its reunification and recovery of full sovereignty, Germany turned into a 'normal state' again. Since then, it has resumed its particular position in the heart of the continent, sharing borders with nine states, and thus exhibiting a high interdependency with the co-players of the European international system (Schwarz 1994). Germany, as an important ally at the Cold War front, had previously been guided and protected by the United States – particularly in terms of intelligence. However, the United States' shift in focus since the end of the Cold War has brought with it the challenge for Germany to develop a foreign security policy of its own.

These necessities emerging out of the international context have been considered by the successive German governments to a certain extent. Generally, there is a broad consensus that Germany should continue its keen involvement in bi- and multilateral cooperation structures. However, with the Balkan war German foreign policy and security actors began to perceive a gradual deterioration of the transatlantic relationship. There was an obvious shortage of intelligence sharing, in addition to some significant operational deficiencies in German (and European) intelligence (and general military) capabilities. In the end, the involvement in the Balkan war directly motivated the institution of major German operational intelligence capabilities, including satellite imagery intelligence and a reform of the BND, which I will discuss at more length in the following section. On the strategic level, Germany has indeed extended its geographical intelligence outreach (confidential interviews), but in general intelligence does not seem to provide any significant contribution to national decision-making. On the part of the government there is no request for institutionalised, long-term, strategic intelligence analyses (confidential interview) and German intelligence agencies have not developed any strategic intelligence capabilities of the speculative-evaluative kind (Kent 1949; Schwarz 1994). Correspondingly, high-ranking BND officials have often deplored the fact that only the coalition government of Chancellor Gerhard Schröder (Social Democrats) and foreign minister Joschka Fischer (the Greens) have attached any particular value to intelligence, while former governments have expressed their disdain of the services more or less publicly. The current Merkel/Westerwelle government (Christian Democrats/Liberals) is said to have barely any relationship with the services. For instance, even though the BND claims to have cautioned against the war in Afghanistan, and against problems arising from economic and demographic developments in the Arab world, its assessment was requested only *after* decisions had been made within NATO or the UN Security Council. More generally, the lack of national strategic intelligence estimates symbolises Germany's general difficulties in discussing and shaping a prioritised strategy that would serve as a compass for its foreign policy decision-making.

The institutional framework of German intelligence

Germany has three official intelligence services: The *Bundesnachrichtendienst* (BND: Federal Intelligence Service), the *Verfassungsschutz* (BfV/LfV: Federal Office for the Protection of the Constitution) and the *Militärischer Abschirmdienst* (MAD: Military Counterintelligence Service). The BND is the foreign intelligence service, the Verfassungsschutz is the internal intelligence service and the MAD is primarily responsible for counterintelligence in the German military. According to the division of responsibilities they each answer to another principal: the BND is controlled directly by the office of the Chancellor (subsequently referred to as the Chancellery); the *Verfassungsschutz* forms part of the Ministry of the Interior; and the MAD belongs to the Department of Defence. In addition to these three services, there is a further military intelligence agency (although it is not officially defined as such), which is concerned with technical intelligence (including SATINT) abroad as well as electronic warfare: the *Kommando Strategische Aufklärung* (KSA: Strategic Intelligence Command). In the following paragraphs, I will briefly introduce these four main German intelligence organisations.

Foreign intelligence: the Bundesnachrichtendienst *(BND)*

The BND is the successor of the *Organisation Gehlen*, which was established in 1946 by Reinhard Gehlen, a former Nazi intelligence director, on behalf of the US government. Under the wings of the CIA, the *Organisation Gehlen*'s purpose was to access intelligence that had been collected by German officials during Hitler's campaigns so that it could be used against Russia (Critchfield 2003). After ten years of being under CIA direction, the *Organisation Gehlen* was officially transferred to the German government under the name of the *Bundesnachrichtendienst*. In 1990, the BND was given a legal basis, defining its mission abroad and restricting its activities on German territory. The budget of the BND is not public. Just over 10 per cent of its 6,500 employees are military personnel, including four Generals who occupy leading positions. The BND produces political, economic, military and scientific technological intelligence and it uses both human and technical (SIGINT) means to collect information.

The BND's intelligence production process – the intelligence cycle – is administrated by the Chancellery, the head of which is the German intelligence manager (*Beauftragter für die Nachrichtendienste*). The Chancellery has a unit of approximately 20 officials at its disposal who are responsible for the political and legal supervision of the BND. One of its tasks is to prepare the basic secret direction plan, which is updated once a year (confidential interviews). The plan defines the mid- and long-term intelligence requirements, and those German ministries with a stake in foreign policy and security are involved in the prioritisation process – most significantly the ministries of foreign affairs, defence, economics and the interior (ibid.). The intelligence catalogue includes regions and countries like the Middle East, Central Asia (including Afghanistan and Pakistan), Russia, West Asia, North and East Africa, the Balkans, Turkey and East Asia, including China and India (ibid.). These countries are assigned to three levels of priority, each of which determines the extent and depth of intelligence collection; all means of intelligence collection are utilised for countries at the highest priority level. By contrast, intelligence collection relating to countries at the second level of importance does *not* involve HUMINT efforts, and countries in the third category are covered only to the extent that open information is available (confidential interview). In addition to these regional foci, the list defines certain functional, cross-regional intelligence targets, particularly Islamic terrorism, the proliferation of weapons of mass destruction (especially in Iran and North Korea) and organised crime. It is remarkable that the German intelligence direction plan is, in some ways, an operationalisation of concrete German interests abroad, which are practically unconsidered in the sphere of public policy.

In addition to these longer-term intelligence targets, the Chancellery is updating and adapting to immediate intelligence requirements, collaborating with high-ranking officials of the respective ministries as well as with experts of the BND (confidential interviews). Finally, the BND is deals with daily requests for information by its usual 'customers', such as the ministries and the chancellery. The biggest share of these requests comes from the military's command authorities (confidential interview).

Due to a major BND reform which was completed in 2009 (Uhrlau 2009), the BND's organisational structure has changed in that HUMINT collection and analysis are now pooled in four major 'production divisions'. On the one hand, there are two regionally orientated divisions ('region A' and 'region B'); on the other hand, there are two issue-orientated divisions ('terrorism and organised crime'; 'proliferation') (BND 2011). The production of regional intelligence operates along an organisational divide of collection and analysis. Here, the respective departments for collection and analysis are organisationally (and geographically, until the BND's move to Berlin) separate from one another (confidential interview). By contrast, in the area of terrorism and proliferation, collection and analysis are pooled within the same departments (ibid.). The idea behind this newly introduced 'desk principle' is to reduce bureaucratic and cultural barriers as well as hostilities between collectors and analysts, which have long characterised their mutual relationships (ibid.).

The BND draws on a large network of stations abroad (*Residenturen*), which are usually attached to German embassies (confidential interviews). If possible, they are recognised and authorised by the host country, but if diplomatic relations are strained the BND may establish unofficial stations (Schmidt-Eenboom 1995). The 'residents' (chiefs of station) coordinate with partner organisations within the host countries, and these partners are becoming increasingly important intelligence sources for the BND (confidential interviews). However, German HUMINT capabilities are supposed to be rather weak (confidential interviews). SIGINT is the most important, and by far the most expensive, element of German intelligence. The BND operates fixed COMINT facilities both at home and abroad (Schmidt-Eenboom 2011). In the case of the latter, the host country usually agrees to BND presence and activities, and often participates in one way or another (confidential interview). SIGINT technologies are developed by the private sector in cooperation with the BND (confidential interviews).

Finally, at the turning point of the cycle the finalised intelligence product is disseminated to intelligence customers via various standardised channels. The most important 'clients' are the Chancellery, the relevant ministries (foreign, defence, economics, interior), and the other security and intelligence services (including the Federal Criminal Police Office (BKA), the

BfV/LfV, Customs Service (ZKA) and MAD). Among the standard operating procedures for disseminating intelligence, the weekly oral briefing in the Chancellery stands out. It is actually a two-fold meeting under the direction of the intelligence manager or his or her deputy (confidential interviews). The first part of the meeting is composed of the heads of the three intelligence services, the intelligence management of the Chancellery and the state secretaries of the Foreign Ministry (AA), the Ministry of the Interior (BMI), the Ministry of Justice (BMJ), the Ministry of Defence (BMVg) and the Ministry of Economics (BMWi). Since 9/11, the head of the Federal Criminal Police Office (BKA) and the Attorney General have also participated (ibid.). In the meetings, the heads of the intelligence and security services provide an assessment of the current security situation (ibid.). The second part of the meeting is even more restricted, involving only the heads of the three services and the federal police, the secretaries of the relevant departments and the intelligence manager with his or her deputy. The Chancellor is not present but is to be briefed by the head of the Chancellery (ibid.).

Military intelligence: the Kommando Strategische Aufklärung *(KSA)* and the Militärischer Abschirmdienst *(MAD)*

There are two intelligence organisations under the authority of the Ministry of Defence: the MAD – which is especially concerned with counterintelligence in the military – and the *Kommando Strategische Aufklärung* (KSA) – which is the military TECHINT organisation. Leaving aside the topic of the MAD as a security intelligence organisation, the focus here is on the KSA, the military intelligence institution concerned with 'positive' intelligence (Kent 1949).

The KSA was founded in 2002, and today it has about the same number of employees as the BND. In contrast to the intelligence structures of the US, where these TECHINT collection and electronic warfare are assigned to different agencies, the KSA is in charge of both. However, responsibility for SIGINT collection is divided between the BND and the KSA, with the head of the BND being the official 'SIGINT coordinator'. The KSA is also in charge of the German imagery intelligence (IMINT) project, SAR–Lupe. It produces strategic, operational, and tactical intelligence using both home bases and mobile units in the operational areas of the *Bundeswehr*.

As a result of its recent involvement in multilateral military operations, Germany's military intelligence needs have increased. These requirements are met by both the BND and the KSA, and in the operational and tactical arenas, each agency complements the work of the other. The BND specialises in the covert collection of intelligence, in interrogation and in certain parts of technical intelligence, especially COMINT. Meanwhile, the KSA's SIGINT collection covers the whole electromagnetic spectrum, i.e. the collection of short-wave signals from German territory, mobile forces participating in military operations, the conduct of SIGINT vessels and aircraft, and, finally, the operation of the German SAR–Lupe SATINT capability. Since 2007, Germany has launched five radar satellites that are capable of producing IMINT, even in cloudy or dark conditions. It takes a minimum of two hours (and a maximum of 12 hours) for the information to be received (confidential interview). As in the case of the other intelligence services, the budget of the KSA is not public.

Domestic intelligence: the Verfassungsschutz *(BfV/LfV)*

The *Verfassungsschutz* is responsible for domestic intelligence and counterintelligence activities (BVerfSchG § 1 (1)). It is organised according to the German federal principle, meaning that its authority is divided among 16 different agencies (*Landesämter für Verfassungsschutz (LfV)*), each being the primary operating agency of the respective German *Land*. At the same time, the authority of the *federal* agency (*Bundesverfassungsschutz (BfV)*) is limited. The BfV is in charge of coordinating the agencies of the *Länder* without having discretionary power itself. For example, it is only allowed to recruit a source after consulting the appropriate agency at the *Länder* level (LfV) (confidential interview). Moreover, the BfV assumes command in cases where several *Länder* agencies are involved or when the nation as a whole is affected. Nevertheless, the *Länder* agencies (LfV) are expected to inform the BfV of all operations which involve more than one *Land*. The share of the federal budget allocated to the BfV amounted to 190 million euros in 2012, not including the budgets of the respective *Länder* agencies (BMI 2012). The federal agency alone (BfV) employed approximately 2,600 members of staff in 2011.

Since the *Verfassungschutz* is acting within German territory, it is strictly bound to German law. In principle, the management and direction of the *Verfassungschutz* are not devised by the government, but are rather derived from the agency's mission to protect political order and the security of the homeland. Nevertheless, the heads of the services are political officials and, thus, are controlled by the government. In order to fulfil its duties, the *Verfassungsschutz* is allowed to use diverse intelligence collection and camouflage methods and may obtain information from financial, post, aviation and telecommunication services (BVerfSchG § 8). It also has access to a number of federal databases such as the central migration register and the register for licensed vehicles, as well as to other government sources of information, such as asylum date. In spite of being responsible for domestic intelligence the *Verfassungsschutz* is increasingly involved in countering transnational threats, as I will outline below.

Effects of systemic change

Since nearly all West German intelligence had been focusing on Warsaw Pact states during the Cold War, the breakdown of the USSR caused an existential crisis among the German services. This was particularly true for the BND, which had been established in direct response to the Soviet threat and had developed and directed all its capabilities towards this end.

However, with the proliferation of military operations since the 1990s, Germany's transition into a fully sovereign state, as well as the emergence of other major powers that challenged Western dominance, there were strong incentives for new intelligence capabilities and the reorganisation of existing structures. A significant effect of systemic change on German intelligence was the institution of operational military intelligence capabilities. It was during the Kosovo war that Germany realised that it was not able to 'see' without American support because it lacked IMINT capabilities. Consequently, the German government decided to develop its own 'eyes' with the SAR–Lupe radar satellite project, which was finally assigned to the newly established *Kommando Strategische Aufklärung* (see above). The BND, which had long been the country's only military intelligence organisation, also expanded its capabilities in operational military intelligence. A reorganisation of its basic structure began in the 1990s and was completed in 2009 (Uhrlau 2009). According to the agency's former head, Ernst Uhrlau, the most important characteristics of the reform are the emphasis on 'actionable intelligence' and the close cooperation with the German military (ibid.). The increased emphasis on military intelligence is reflected in both the new division 'operational areas external relations' (ibid.) and in the sharp increase in military personnel within the BND. In 2007, for example, there were 280 soldiers in the BND; by 2011, that number had almost tripled, with 750 members of staff claiming a military background. The protection of German military personnel abroad has become one of the BND's main duties.

Another effect of systemic change at the beginning of the 1990s was the expansion of intelligence targets. During the Cold War, the USSR and East Germany were by far the most important targets of the BND, with other regions, such as the Middle and Far East, being of subordinate importance. However, following the collapse of the bipolar system, Germany expanded its intelligence capabilities all over the world. This was especially true in those regions where the German military was operating, such as in the Balkans and Afghanistan. But German intelligence has also extended to other geographical areas, including those that are important for a stable political order in the country's eastern neighbourhood, those that might contribute to its international standing (e.g. regarding counterproliferation) or those that are crucial for its economic well-being. Germany's wealth depends heavily upon an undisturbed export of goods and an import of natural resources from all over the world.

Transnationalisation effects

Soon after organised crime came to the fore of German intelligence as the first transnational phenomenon (Singer 2002), it became clear that there were also *political* transnational threats including the proliferation of weapons of mass destruction and transnational terrorism. German intelligence services had already reacted to these kinds of threats as early as the 1990s, with the creation of new departments specifically concerned with transnational terrorism, for example. However, the attacks on the US in 2001, on Madrid in 2004, and on London in 2005 had an even bigger impact on German threat perception and the organisation of its security organisations. First, it led to an increasing fusion of law enforcement and intelligence activities; and, second, it blurred the divisions between internal and external security, provoking an internationalisation of both law enforcement and intelligence.

Convergence of law enforcement and intelligence

While organised crime had previously been the exclusive domain of law enforcement agencies, at the beginning of the 1990s the German intelligence services also integrated it into their respective responsibilities. In doing so, they engendered further competition between intelligence and police authorities. The police, for their part, called for 'police intelligence' and 'criminal intelligence', demanding more *preventive* rather than *reactive* competences (Stock 2009).

The rivalry between police and intelligence services was further reinforced by the perception of Islamic terrorism a decade later. After 9/11, both the *Verfassungsschutz* and the Federal Police Office profited from an extraordinary initial budget of three billion euros in 2002, which was used to establish new departments for counterterrorism. The BfV created a new division of 'International Terrorism', but in terms of competences, budget and employees, the BKA, which had been assigned the 'primary responsibility' in national counterterrorism, gained even more from the new threats. In the aftermath of 9/11 the BKA had hosted a broad interagency investigation (which included a large number of FBI agents) directed at uncovering any German connections to the 9/11 attackers. This effort led to the creation of a new division, 'International Coordination', as well as a new subdivision, 'Islamic Terrorism', within the 'State Security' branch. A significant new measure introduced by the BKA is the so-called 'preventive competence' measure. This doctrine allows the agency to pursue any individuals who it believes might engage in terrorist activity in the future, even if he or she has not yet done so.

In order to overcome the divisions between intelligence and police functions – at least to some extent – the German Ministry of the Interior built up a ' *joint* counterterrorism structure' (emphasis added). In 2004, a new counterterrorism department was created with the specific aim of overseeing international and interagency cooperation. Second, the overlap of law enforcement and intelligence has been compensated for by the establishment of 'joint centres' where the different security agencies (police, intelligence, customs, immigration and others) share information and produce joint analyses in specific issue-areas. This trend began in 2004 with the foundation of the *Gemeinsames Terrorismusabwehrzentrum* (Joint Counter-terrorism Center: GTAZ) as a platform for operational intelligence sharing and for coordinating activities between 38 German authorities involved in counterterrorism. The GTAZ was modelled on the Joint Terrorism Analysis Centre in London (JTAC), which had been established by the British partners one year earlier (confidential interview). In the following years, the same model was adopted in a number of other issue-areas apparently requiring an interagency approach. Thus, in addition to the GTAZ, a joint centre for cybersecurity, a joint centre concerned with illegal immigration, and a joint centre for countering right-wing terrorism have been established (see Figure 22.1, below).

In addition to these issue-orientated 'joint centres', in 2006 a 'joint counterterrorism database' was created, which is fed into, and which receives requests from, all 38 security agencies at the federal and *Länder* levels. The database has two levels of access. One contains basic personal data and is directly accessible to all 38 agencies. The other level contains more detailed personal data, including information relating to an individual's education and profession, religion, civil status and travel movements, as well as their telecommunications and internet use, and whether they possess any firearms, or have had any contact with terrorist associations (Bundesrat 2006). The database is said to be a one-way street with intelligence flowing from the intelligence to the police authorities but not the other way around (confidential interview).

The creation of this joint counterterrorism database had been discussed for years without reaching a consensus. The critics feared that the merging of bureaucratic knowledge would be at the expense of civil liberties. Although this is a common concern of many liberal democracies in the wake of 9/11, the German case is unique in one significant respect. After the Second World War, and following Germany's experiences under the Nazi regime, a legal barrier was constructed to prohibit the fusion of intelligence and police. This organising principle is referred to as *Trennungsgebot* (dividing imperative): both authorities – intelligence and police – are to be organisationally separate from one another in order to prevent the emergence of an uncontrollable power. Thus, the question of whether the institutional changes described above (e.g. joint centres and joint databases) are actually undermining the *Trennungsgebot* principle, and if so to what extent, is a matter of some debate in Germany. Moreover, the very characteristics of these 'new threats' have raised serious questions over the continuing validity of the principle.

Overlap of internal and external security, and the internationalisation of intelligence

It is now widely accepted that the transnationalisation of threats is rendering any clearcut distinction between external and internal security obsolete. Starting from this assumption, both the internal as well as the external services have incorporated transnational threats into their respective portfolios, and each has established new functional divisions in order to deal with the new threats. Organised crime had already been defined as an area of responsibility for German intelligence services at the beginning of the 1990s, and this was followed by WMD proliferation in the middle of the decade. Finally, in the summer of 2001, just before the attacks on New York and Washington, the BND created a new division specifically concerned with addressing terrorism, narcotics, money laundering and immigration issues (BND 2005). The *Verfassungsschutz* even considers counterterrorism to be a primary focus. The observation of Islamic terrorism was outsourced from its former division of foreign extremism and established as a division (*Abteilung 6*) in its own right.

Meanwhile, both services have expanded their international cooperation. The BND, who had already begun to spin a web of intelligence partnerships across the developing world since the 1960s (Schmidt-Eenboom 1995), expanded this network to the east after the dissolution of the Warsaw Pact. Since then, numerous partnerships have been established with intelligence services in various Eastern European and Asian countries, including Russia with whose services the BND maintains a formal intelligence sharing agreement (confidential interview). By the end of the 1990s, the BND had reached the threshold of one hundred bilateral intelligence partnerships, some of which have become more active as a result of the global 'war on terrorism' (confidential interviews).

In principle, one has to distinguish between intelligence partnerships that are established to produce joint intelligence, and those that are restricted to the exchange of intelligence information (Westerfield 1996). The former involve the sharing of operational details, and for this reason they are feasible only within stable and well-regulated partnerships where the protection of sources and methods is guaranteed. The latter, in contrast, can be realised either within an institutionalised cooperation agreement or on an ad hoc basis. The origins of shared information – that is, the sources through which and the methods by which information is obtained – are usually concealed from partners. Consequently this sort of cooperation can be achieved without a particular level of trust being generated by a long-standing reciprocal partnership. Therefore, it is especially this kind of cooperation – most commonly in the form of an ad hoc exchange of personal data – that has most notably increased in the defence against transnational threats. In the context of the 'war on terror', the German services have benefited particularly from their Middle East partnerships, in addition to their close and permanent relationships with the US, France, the UK and Israel (Johnson and Freyberg 1997; Daun 2011). Correspondingly, there is significant variation in the levels of cooperation and the degree of intelligence sharing among the different issue areas: cooperation is closest in the areas of proliferation and terrorism. An additional tool for the direct and rapid exchange of operational information is the GTAZ; it is not only useful for German interagency cooperation, but also for the strengthening of international ties, especially those with the US and the main European counterterrorism partners, that is the UK, France, Italy, and Spain. In contrast to transnational terrorism and proliferation, however, intelligence cooperation is less common in the areas of organised crime and economic intelligence.

Although it was legally determined in 1996 that all international intelligence contacts must be established through the BND, after 9/11 the BfV also dispatched liaison officers to Washington and Paris. However, the secondment of BfV personnel abroad remains an exception and most of its international relations take place inside Germany. Information is usually exchanged between the BfV and the respective intelligence representatives who are delegated to the embassy of their countries. These representatives are also invited to expert conferences, and sometimes, if interests converge, the *Verfassungsschutz* may even cooperate with a foreign intelligence service in a joint operation. A successful operation against a group of Islamists preparing for a terror attack against US targets in Germany in 2007 provides a recent example of such a joint operation, as US and German agencies worked together. Such events are rare, however. Finally, there is even a degree of internationalisation at the *Länder* level, despite the fact that it is only the federal agency (BfV) that has the formal authority to establish international partnerships. While, in some cases, *Länder* maintain well-established, cross-border ties with their direct neighbours in issues relating to regional affairs, in others, international partners actually approach the *Länder* agencies directly, albeit with varying degrees of success. In sum, international intelligence cooperation of the *Verfassungsschutz* has increased significantly since 9/11.

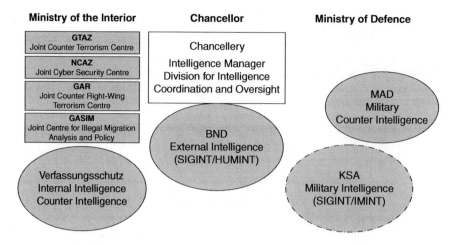

Figure 22.1 The German intelligence community

The internationalisation of intelligence also affects other security agencies such as the police and customs, both of which are increasingly concerned with intelligence. The internationalisation of the BKA began in the wake of the 'war on drugs' in the 1980s. Since then, the BKA has been extending its international network and maintains about 60 liaison officers working abroad today. Similarly, the German Customs Service (ZKA) has built up external relations. In contrast to the BKA and the BfV, whose investigational authority is relatively limited due to the federal structure of German security agencies, the ZKA is a national institution and as such is always authorised to investigate independently. Since 1992 it has been allowed to open letters and to conduct SIGINT operations. Like the BKA, the ZKA has dispatched liaison officials who are familiar with the bureaucratic structure of the host country, in order to maintain contacts with the local authorities. This applies to both formal administrative assistants and informal contacts, the latter being especially important for sharing urgent operational information. So far, the ZKA has dispatched liaison officers to the capitals of 14 countries, including the US, France, the UK, Italy, Spain, the Netherlands, Poland, the Czech Republic, Bulgaria, Croatia, Turkey, Russia, Lithuania, Afghanistan and China. Most of its partner countries have also dispatched a liaison officer to Germany.

All in all, especially the *internal* services are affected by transnationalisation effects: their budget and competences have increased, and shall compensate for the increased border permeability inside the country. The German intelligence community is illustrated in Figure 22.1.

Conclusion

The processes shaping the international system in the last two decades have had significant effects upon German intelligence. The internal agencies, *Verfassungsschutz* and the BKA, have been upgraded in terms of budget and competences, and international cooperation has been enhanced by all agencies. Meanwhile, the increase in operational intelligence capabilities is, in part, due to the fact that Germany has been involved in several multilateral military operations since the 1990s. On the other hand, there is *no* clear trend in terms of strategy. In a sense, the lack of strategic intelligence at the national level is just another indicator of a more general problem: the tabooing of security issues in Germany.

23

RUSSIA

Reginald Brope

After a short hiatus during the 1990s, Russian intelligence and security services are once again prominent in the international political, security and media spotlight. Sources of their recent fame include the arrest of senior Estonian Defence Ministry figure Herman Simm in 2008 and his conviction on charges of treason through spying for the Russian intelligence services, the accusations against and investigation of Katia Zatuliveter of being a spy at the heart of the British parliament, as well as the 'spy rock' scandal when the Russian security services exposed a British operation in Russia. Indeed, Russian intelligence and security services are considered to be very active in NATO and its member states – illustrated by the uncovering of the spy network in the US in 2010. According to some, this network was evidence of Russian intelligence activity in the US that was equal to, or greater than, even that of the Cold War. Similarly, the head of MI5 stated in 2007 that the Russian intelligence effort in the UK was equal in scope to Soviet activities during the Cold War.

At the same time, Soviet and Russian intelligence services feature prominently in the media and in film, most recently in the movie *Tinker Tailor Soldier Spy*, as well as in both fictional and documentary television series such as *Spooks* and *Modern Spies*. As a result, the Russian intelligence services offer one of the most emotive and contentious subjects of research in international and security studies, demonstrating a heady mix of sex and glamour, historical and ideological conflict, and political and commercial intrigue.

The link with the Cold War is important both in perception and in reality. In terms of perception, Russian intelligence and security services are often confused and conflated with the Soviet services. Sweeping accusations are frequently made both in public policy and media circles referring to today's intelligence services as simply the actions of the Komitet Gosudarstvennoi Bezopasnosti (KGB), or to reforms of the Russian intelligence services as an attempt to recreate the KGB. This echoes the accusation that today's Russian leadership is comparable to that of the Stalin-era USSR and is trying to reinvent the USSR. Of course, in reality, the Russian intelligence and security agencies did emerge directly from the Soviet services and, despite numerous reforms, the new, separated services initially retained many of the same functions, personnel and techniques.

Analyses of the Russian intelligence and security services must simultaneously consider a multiplicity of immediate questions and difficulties. Some of these are similar to those faced in addressing the intelligence services of other states – not least of which are the more general shrouds of secrecy in which the Russian intelligence services naturally operate, as well as the myths and legends surrounding them; conspiracy theories about Russian intelligence services are just as prominent, if not more so, than those about Western intelligence services. Other questions, however, are more specific to the Soviet and Russian environment. What was the nature of the transition from the intelligence and security services of the USSR to those of the Russian Federation? What are the key Russian structures? What is their role in political life in Russia? It is these latter, more specifically 'Russian' questions that this chapter seeks to address.

In providing an overview of the Russian intelligence and security services, this chapter first discusses some of the most prominent myths associated with them. It then considers the transition and evolution of the services after the collapse of the USSR in two ways: First by tracing the transition from the KGB to Russian services, then by exploring their relationship with Russian politics and society. Although the chapter will seek to frame the main overall structures and the relevant controversies, given the limitations of this context the main focus will be upon the successors to the KGB: the Federalnaya Sluzhba Bezopasnosti (FSB) – which deals with counterintelligence and security matters, and has become the most powerful and prominent of the intelligence and security services – and the Sluzhba Vneshnei Razvedki (SVR) – the foreign intelligence service. The chapter will not deal with Russian military intelligence, the GRU.

The 'Litvinenko effect'

Russian intelligence and security services are shrouded in a fog of myth and conspiracy. As one Russian expert has noted, the KGB was the subject of many myths (see Sever 2009). A recent controversy is the accusation that the FSB was involved in mass murder to enhance Vladimir Putin's political prospects. In September 1999, four bomb explosions destroyed apartment blocks in the cities of Moscow, Buynaksk and Volgodonsk, killing 293 people. The question of responsibility for the bombings flared into a conspiratorial debate, as some suggested that the Russian authorities, specifically the FSB, had planned the attack to generate support for Vladimir Putin and to justify a new war against Chechnya. According to Russian journalists (Soldatov and Borogan 2010: 110), this ballooned into a 'crisis of confidence in the FSB', which was only further accentuated by reports of a foiled fifth attack in the city of Ryazan, but which the authorities subsequently announced to have been an FSB exercise. Official explanations failed to resolve the confusion, however, and subsequently the flames of conspiracy were fanned by a series of apparently suspicious coincidences, including the deaths of two people who were investigating the explosions, the arrest of a third on dubious charges, and a closed trial of two suspects, which raised further questions about why it was held amid such secrecy.

Specialists on the subject both recognise the clumsiness with which the Russian officials handled the unfolding events, and yet refute the idea that the FSB were responsible for the bombings. They note that the accusers were unable to offer substantial evidence (Soldatov and Borogan 2010: 110), and suggest that, on the contrary, either Chechen or Chechen-aligned Wahhabi militants were responsible for the attacks. Nevertheless, the conspiracy theory has survived, largely on a life support machine powered by the public relations activities of a number of prominent anti-Putin Russian exiles, though it was reinvigorated by a second major controversy – the murder of former FSB officer Alexander Litvinenko in London. Following the granting of his asylum in the UK, Litvinenko became an increasingly controversial figure, propagating numerous conspiracy theories and scandals about the Russian authorities. Indeed, in cooperation with Yuri Felshtinsky, he published a book asserting that the FSB had used the apartment bombings to foment war in Chechnya (Litvinenko and Felshtinsky 2007) – though a publisher could not be found until after his death. The book subsequently gained prominent media coverage, thereby further reviving the conspiracy theory.

The murder has been extensively discussed in the media – with many attributing it to the FSB, either directly, or through ex-KGB proxies or 'rogue agents'. The UK's Crown Prosecution Service has sought the extradition of prime suspect Andrei Lugovoi, a former FSB officer like Litvinenko, in order to bring him to trial. The Russian authorities have refused to extradite Lugovoi. Since the trial is pending, UK authorities have not yet released the evidence for public scrutiny and we must wait to see its strength. Nevertheless, there is a wider point to be made. Individual conspiracy theories thrive in contextual 'normalisation' – when conspiracy theorists assert that conspiracy is everywhere. Litvinenko's death came at an important time in Russian politics, with widespread concern growing about Putin's appointments of former and current intelligence and security services personnel to key official positions. Moreover, not long before Litvinenko died, the journalist Anna Politkovskaya was murdered in Moscow, another crime many immediately blamed on the FSB.[1] The wider context of Litvinenko's death was more important, therefore, than the actual guilt of Lugovoi – or the FSB. For many, convinced by the easy access to active political opponents of Vladimir Putin (such as Boris Berezovsky), it served to illustrate the wider conspiracy that former KGB Lieutenant Colonel Vladimir Putin had led the FSB – or rather the KGB – back into power in Russia and was using the methods of the Soviet secret police to enforce their rule and punish dissent.[2] The entwined murders and bombings have blurred into one larger climate of conspiracy.

The KGB

The KGB was officially established in 1954, the result of a process that began with the merger of the Ministry of State Security (MGB, Ministerstvo Gosudasrtvennoi Bezopasnosti) and the Ministry of the Interior (Ministerstvo Vnutrennikh Del, MVD) in 1953 and the subsequent detachment of the KGB from the MVD a year later. It was the organ of state security and the 'sword and shield' of the Communist Party of the Soviet Union (CPSU); the shield for protecting the party leadership, the sword the means by which the leadership attempted to impose its will both within and outside the USSR.

In essence, though, the KGB was the successor organ to what was initially established in 1917 – the Vse-Rossiiskaya Cherezvechainaya Kommissiya or VChKa, often shortened to ChK (Cherezvechaninaya Kommissiya). Its agents were known as 'Chekists'. Former KGB General Oleg Kalugin quotes Joseph Stalin in describing the nature of the ChK: it was the 'punitive organ of Soviet power . . . something like a court martial, set up to save the revolution from the assaults of counter-revolutionary bourgeoisie and their agents' (Kalugin 2009: 13). As the security arm of the Bolshevik Party, the ChK's focus was the suppression of political opposition and desertion. After 1922, Soviet state security organs evolved, experiencing a number of name changes, including, most notably, the Obedinyonnoe Gossudarstvennoe Politicheskoe Upravleniye (OGPU), 1926–34, and later the Narodniy Kommissariat Vnutrennykh Del, 1934–43 (NKVD), as well as undergoing a number of evolutions in their role.[3]

These background points are important because of the continued significance of this history today: Russian intelligence and security agents, particularly those in the FSB, are often referred to as 'Chekists', and the term carries with it a great deal of cultural and political baggage. Of further importance is the fact that, at the time of its founding, the KGB sought to distance itself and its activities from its predecessors in the interests of political legitimacy, emphasising that it was neither the legal heir nor the political successor to these organs, nor did it employ the same brutal methods (Albats 1995: 8). During the following years, the KGB sought to promote a new, younger generation of officers, 'untainted by the crimes of the Stalin era' (Kalugin 2009: 22), and freed from any association with former head of the secret police Lavrenti Beria. If it distanced itself from these 'ancestors', however, the KGB nevertheless continued with similar functions, monitoring the Soviet public for dissent and subversion throughout the USSR and Warsaw Pact states, and it was central to the suppression of both the Hungarian revolution in 1956 and the Prague Spring in 1968.

Thus, while many in the West considered the KGB to be the broad equivalent, or the Soviet version, of an amalgamation of the US's CIA and FBI, or the UK's MI5 and MI6, because it represented both foreign intelligence and counterintelligence services, this was misleading. The KGB was more than just the internal and external intelligence services of the country; it was also a secret police monitoring its own society. Michael Waller has framed the philosophical distinction thus: if the CIA and FBI have a national security mind-set of secrecy distinct from the population, this is the nature of the profession – the keeping of secrets in the interests of a democratic society. The KGB differed from this because its approach linked secrecy with the conspiracy to repress democratic values, and its focus was the constant search for enemies among its own people on a national scale. It abused intelligence and counterintelligence to create, sustain and preserve a totalitarian political power that saw all opposition as enemies (Waller 1994: 9–11).

There were a number of practical and structural differences. While the CIA and FBI are agencies, the KGB was a vast apparatus, bringing together into a single unit the separate organs of foreign intelligence, counterintelligence, military and police counterintelligence, information collection and analysis, special investigations, covert operations, assassinations, ideological enforcement as well as internal troops and a large army of border guards, all supported by a vast structure and network of administrative, logistical and informal employees (for a full list, see Waller 1994: 3).

Throughout its existence, the KGB underwent a number of reforms and structural changes intended to enhance its effectiveness, to respond to reversals or to correct deficiencies. Latterly, the KGB's structure was based on five Chief Directorates: The 1st Chief Directorate for operations conducted abroad; the 2nd Chief Directorate, responsible for counterintelligence and control of the civilian population within the Soviet Union and based throughout the USSR; the unnamed Border Guards Directorate; the 5th Chief Directorate for the suppression of ideological dissidence; and the 8th Chief Directorate which monitored and attempted to decipher foreign communications. Subordinate to these were a number of Directorates, Departments and Services.

Overall, therefore, the role and scale of the KGB meant that it played a 'transcendent' role in Soviet policy and society (Barron 1983: 12). Indeed, in the words of Gordon Bennett, the KGB was the 'most powerful security organisation ever created' – it was omnipresent in the USSR, had an extensive international network, and enjoyed 'almost unlimited funds, facilities', and the ability to place its personnel into any soviet organisation (Bennett 2000a: 2). It also pursued counterintelligence activities in other intelligence organs, such as the military intelligence service, the GRU. The structure of the KGB evolved further during the 1980s: In 1982, the 3rd Directorate, which oversaw military discipline, intelligence and counterintelligence, again became a Chief Directorate, and in 1989, the 5th Chief Directorate became Directorate Z for the protection of constitutional order, but overall the KGB remained largely untouched by the reforms instigated by Mikhail Gorbachev's perestroika. However, the KGB's role in the coup in 1991 resulted in Gorbachev abolishing the KGB of the USSR in late 1991, with the organisation being fragmented into four structures.

Two further points merit mention. First, given the observation of its power, is the question of oversight. The KGB was a pillar of Soviet rule, and as such wielded considerable power, answerable only to the Politburo. However, while this was not a question of public scrutiny, at least not until 1989, it was also not without check. In terms of civil control, the CPSU Central Committee retained oversight; all KGB officers were of course party members and thus subject to party discipline. Also, the leadership occasionally sought to bring the KGB to heel: Khrushchev for instance cut pay, perks and pensions in the mid-1950s (Kalugin 2009: 19, 22). Finally, Bennett notes that the CPSU's patronage exerted ideological control: the CPSU expected the KGB to confirm or to support its ideological theories, especially about the West (Bennett 2000a: 3).

But CPSU control depended on the party itself being unified – when the party began to lose direction, the security services increased their influence. This was further accentuated by the repeal of Article 6 of the Soviet constitution, which weakened the CPSU's main mechanism of control. Equally, oversight structures created during perestroika were rendered ineffective because they were filled with those friendly to the services (Waller 1994: 152). Related to this, there was significant competition between the GRU – the military intelligence – and the KGB, both in terms of intelligence operations and in internal politicking.

Overall, the break-up of the KGB altered the configuration of Russian intelligence in important ways, breaking the organisation into separate services and changing the structure of authority. Despite some continuity of serving personnel, one of the results of the break-up was the dispersion of officers, whether serving, retired or resigned, into wider society. The line separating the secret services from society was erased as personnel permeated every level of civil society and business (Waller 1994: 289).

From the Soviet KGB to the Russian FSB

The transformation from the KGB to the FSB was long and arduous, taking place in the period between autumn 1991 and autumn 2004. Following the break-up of the KGB, Boris Yeltsin sought to establish separate Russian services, and by early January 1992 there were five new Russian structures, all of which Yeltsin himself controlled alone.[4] The KGB 1st Chief Directorate became the SVR, the 8th Chief Directorate became the Federal Agency for Government Communications and Information (FAPSI), the KGB Border Guards initially became the Committee for Protection of Russian Borders,[5] and the 9th Directorate became the Main Guard Directorate. The largest was the fifth main structure, initially the Ministry of Security, which encapsulated the 2nd Chief Directorate, the 3rd Chief Directorate, and four other KGB Directorates, including those tasked with surveillance and those focusing on economic crime and corruption. In 1993, the Ministry of Security became the Federal Counterintelligence Service until 1995, when it became the FSB.

This process of break-up in the early 1990s was accompanied by much rhetoric about reforming, even reconstructing, the services, as well as by considerable infighting – not least of all because Yeltsin wanted to weaken cooperation between the separate organisations. For instance, as Bennett notes, the head of the SVR, Yevgeni Primakov, had to battle 'on all fronts to save the SVR' (Bennett 2000a: 6). However, with all organs reporting to him directly, Yeltsin had accrued considerable power over the services themselves, which in turn generated significant political power. Indeed, some suggest that Yeltsin also became increasingly dependent upon the services, and as a result their powers were not constricted, but rather began to grow (Knight 1996: 37). While there is a common understanding that it is Putin who has led the return to power of the ex KGB and now FSB, it was, in fact, Yeltsin who began this process of continuing, maintaining, and strengthening the intelligence and security services – not least through the appointment of Putin – even though he had presided over their initial fractures.

During the 1990s, the two main Russian intelligence and security services, the SVR and the FSB, experienced considerable constriction. The Russian economy was in free-fall both in the aftermath of the collapse of the USSR and in the wake of the economic crisis of 1998, and many officers left the services to enter the private sector. This was largely the result of sackings, reorganisations and the extremely low salaries within the services. Moreover, the services suffered numerous professional setbacks. For the SVR, dealing with foreign special services continued to be an important concern, as was obtaining political and technical information, and in this respect, the US remained the top priority. Other tasks included disinformation and the manipulation of the media. The SVR endured some high-profile scandals, including the arrests of several agents, and furthermore was faced with accusations of failing to curtail its activities in Europe, despite the ongoing attempts at establishing international partnerships.

The FSB's tasks include counterintelligence, economic security, which involves cooperation with the business community (new legislation had also given them influence on private companies), and counterterrorism, which includes a coordinating role alongside other law enforcement bodies in the Interdepartmental Anti-Terrorist Commission. Additionally, it now deals with border security, information security and monitoring domestic dissent (for a detailed discussion, see Ushakov 2006: 63–90). Moreover, its structure, which had evolved as 14 directorates, was reconfigured and reduced to five departments and six directorates in 1997, and it was further re-organised in 1998. Directors of the FSB publicly announced their successes: in 1995–96, the FSB reported uncovering the activities of some 400 foreign intelligence agency staff members, and in 1997 the Director equated the level of foreign intelligence activity in Russia with that last seen during the Second World War.

But the depredations of the wider economic and social context in Russia, which led to many officers leaving the services were accentuated by poor coordination and leadership, despite, or perhaps because of, the constant reforms. Simultaneously, therefore, the FSB was degrading while facing increased problems: it had to manage a swell in internal chaos in Russia, including a surge in organised crime, as well as the war in Chechnya, which 'was a FSB nightmare' (Bennett 2000b: 13–19). According to Bennett, the changing roles did not sit well with the new FSB. They saw their function as pursuing foreign spies, the numbers of which were perceived to be increasing significantly, particularly from the US, and they expected to be rewarded for their efforts in this task. Instead they had to chase and investigate petty crooks, domestic mafia and various extremists, for which they received inadequate reward (Bennett 2000b: 33).

Putin's arrival in office led to increased support for the intelligence and security services, though, as noted above, it also coincided with growing concern in Russia and abroad about the recreation of the KGB. He ordered increased funding and support for the services and, in 2003, announced the largest reforms of the Russian security services since 1992. With regards to funding, the share of budget spending (in terms of share of GDP) devoted to the power agencies increased rapidly from 1999; it began to stabilise in 2005 before increasing again from 2006 onwards (for detailed discussion about funding, see Cooper, J. 2007). The reforms were to the considerable advantage of the FSB, since the large Border Guard Service was incorporated within it as a substructure. The personnel, infrastructure and functions of FAPSI were transferred both to the FSB and the Ministry of Defence, which may have benefited the GRU. The reforms also created the state Committee of the Russian Federation to Control the Trade in Narcotics and Psychotropic Substances (Gosnarkokontrol), which in turn benefited from the disbanding of the Federal Tax Police.

Overall, the intelligence services remain under the purview of the president, though formally the Procurator General's office retains legal oversight for the FSB (Ushakov 2006: 150–159). In foreign matters, the FSB coordinates with the SVR, and, in internal matters, with the other law enforcement bodies, including the Ministry of the Interior (MVD), the General Procurator's Office (GP) and the Investigative Committee (SK).

The FSB (and other law enforcement bodies) continued to suffer reversals, most notably illustrated by the terrorist attacks in Moscow in 2002, Beslan in 2004, and Moscow again in 2010 and 2011. However, these have served to emphasise the focus on strengthening structures, and the FSB has been granted wider powers, particularly in the fight against terrorism, including the legal authority to hunt and kill suspected terrorists abroad and to give warnings to Russian citizens. The FSB has succeeded in locating and liquidating most of the Chechen terrorist leadership and has announced ever larger successes against the activities of foreign intelligence agencies.

The influence of the intelligence and security services in Russian politics

As noted above, the belief that Putin's victory in the 2000 presidential elections hailed a rise to power of ex-KGB figures after a period of Yeltsin-led democracy during the 1990s, is misleading. Intelligence officers had spread throughout society, permeating business and politics in 1991, and many senior figures within these arenas, particularly in the latter, have a background in intelligence. Igor Sechin, a prominent figure in both the Russian energy sector and in political circles, is one such example of a senior business figure alleged to have a security services background. Similarly, in the political arena, one of the competitors in the 1999 elections was Yevgeniy Primakov, and a number of other leading parliamentary opposition figures also have KGB backgrounds: Gennadiy Zyuganov, leader of the Russian Communist Party, which has been the major opposition party since the collapse of the USSR, was a colonel in the Soviet KGB, as was Gennadiy Gudkov, a senior figure in the Just Russia party. It is also alleged that the Liberal Democratic Party of Russia (LDPR), another important parliamentary party, was created by the CPSU and KGB.

There are a number of former KGB and FSB officers at the centre of political power in the Kremlin and government, and former KGB officers lead the main law enforcement ministries. Permanent members of the Security Council (SC), the main organ for coordinating authority and policy formulation, are long-serving intelligence and security officers, and since 2008, Nikolai Patrushev, former KGB officer and Yeltsin-appointed Director of the FSB from 1999–2008, has been the Secretary of the SC, a body over which Putin himself retains overall control. This group of intelligence and security officers is often referred to as the 'siloviki'; its members are representatives of the Russian power ministries and they are considered to be statist and conservative in outlook.

It is important to note, however, that despite the presence of senior intelligence and security services officials at the core of Russian formal policy-making, and who thus wield considerable influence, they only form part of a wider group that includes lawyers, economists and financiers. Furthermore, the 'siloviki' do not represent a single unified whole, and despite reforms some friction between the main services remains, not least of all resulting from unclear boundaries of responsibilities. One of the major trends in recent analysis about the intelligence and security services is that there has been a 'war of the siloviki', that the major clans have been engaged in internal conflicts. This is often illustrated with reference to the Tri Kita (Three Whales) furniture smuggling case, as a result of which a number of senior law enforcement officials from the FSB, MVD and GP were dismissed. Another example of this competition is the apparent conflict between the FSB and the Gosnarkokontrol, an ongoing case in which the FSB appears to have uncovered drug trafficking within Gosnarkokontrol being the latest incident.

Conclusions

The Russian intelligence and security services are increasingly active. They have undergone significant change since the collapse of the USSR. Most obviously, they have lost the ideological element that was a centrepiece of the KGB's work. At the same time, they have undergone numerous reforms and restructuring since the early 1990s to improve their functions and to enhance coordination between structures. Although the reforms have left some gaps or overlaps in responsibilities, the overall results of the reconfigurations are that the FSB is the major Russian intelligence and security agency, tasked with neutralising both internal and external threats and responsible for overall law enforcement coordination and counterterrorism. Reforms may continue. There has long been rumour of a merger of investigative bodies to create an equivalent to the FBI, for instance, though the creation of such a body is likely to face internal obstacles: while a 'war of the siloviki' is overstating the case, the responsibilities of services partly overlap and there appears to be some competition between the bodies.

The Russian intelligence and security services continue to face significant internal and external challenges: most recently, they were in the headlines for working with the Ukrainian security service to foil a plot to assassinate Vladimir Putin after the presidential elections. Their role stretches beyond intelligence and security, however, and former KGB officers hold key positions in Russian politics and business. Yet the fear of a return to the secret police-style security services of the Soviet period is exaggerated and sensationalist: if they are increasingly active, today's FSB and other services perform very different functions to the KGB and ChK.

Notes

1   The investigation into this murder is also still under way. As with Litvinenko's murder, the accusations vary – that the FSB was directly involved, or that it was former FSB agents working with a criminal gang, or that the FSB was protecting the real culprit.
2   It is noteworthy that Boris Berezovsky himself was one of those who had played a prominent role in Putin's rise and electoral victory in 2000.
3   The FSB website details the history of the service (see www.fsb.ru).
4   The precise details of the break-up of the KGB, Yeltsin's take over of the Russian KGB in early 1991 before the collapse of the USSR, and the impact of the struggle between Gorbachev and Yeltsin on senior service personnel, are complex and cannot be covered here (see Waller 1994; Knight 1996).
5   This organ became the Border Troops under the Ministry of Security in June 1992, and then the Federal Border Service in 1993.

24

SPAIN

Rubén Arcos

As with most national intelligence systems in Western democracies, the past decade has seen substantial changes in the structure of the Spanish system of intelligence. These reforms have resulted in a system formed by an array of national and departmental bodies and structures of intelligence, operating at the various different levels of the system, in order to ensure coordination between organisations. Since the attacks of 11 March 2004 (henceforth referred to as 11-M), the creation of intelligence coordination centres has become the general focus of many governments, and is largely a response to the flaws and deficiencies that have become apparent within their intelligence systems. However, in Spain this institutional development is not accompanied by a complementary system of directives and standards for the intelligence community. The construction of the Spanish intelligence community still seems to be a work in progress, if community is to be understood as a coordinated set of national intelligence and departmental services sharing information and working as a unit to achieve common planned objectives according to a security strategy.[1] In fact, such a strategy did not exist until June 2011, when the government published the *Spanish Security Strategy: Everyone's Responsibility* (Gobierno de España 2011).[2]

At the same time, with regards to the public's knowledge and understanding of the function of intelligence services, the last decade has seen the introduction of intelligence as an object of study in Spanish universities. The National Intelligence Centre (CNI) has developed a policy of openness and seeks to educate stakeholders through the progressive signing of agreements with public universities. However, this policy of developing a culture of intelligence conflicts with the pre-Constitutional Official Secrets Act (1968) still in force, creating a significant barrier to the study of intelligence in Spain.

A one-service system at the national level: the National Intelligence Centre

In spite of the creation of new intelligence structures and coordination centres in the aftermath of 11-M, the main intelligence reforms to date were developed prior to the Madrid train bombings. In May 2002, for example, two key changes were made within the intelligence community: the CNI and the Government Delegate Commission for Intelligence Affairs (CDGAI) were established by Act 11/2002, Regulatory of the National Intelligence Centre, and the Organic Law 2/2002, which regulates the preliminary judicial control of CNI activities, was also enacted.

The CNI replaced the Higher Centre for Defense Information (CESID), which was created on 4 July 1977 by a Royal Decree. Initially, the CESID came under the direct control of the

Minister of Defense, as a departmental body responsible for providing information of interest to the National Defense (see Royal Decree 1558/1977 and Royal Decree 2723/1977). The CESID came to replace the Central Documentation Service (SECED) of the Presidency and the intelligence section of the High General Staff. However, since 1982 the CESID mission was also tasked with providing intelligence to the Prime Minister (see Ruíz Miguel 2005). Royal Decree 2632/1985 of 27 December established an internal structure that integrated the divisions for foreign intelligence, domestic intelligence, counterintelligence, and economy and technology,

In contrast to the systems of intelligence in most other countries, Spain models a single intelligence service at the national level, which has functions of foreign and domestic intelligence and counterintelligence. CNI is charged by Act 11/2002 with the main mission of 'providing the Government with the necessary information and intelligence to prevent and avoid any risk or threat to the independence or integrity of Spain, the national interests, and the stability of the rule of law and its institutions'. More specifically, the CNI is the national intelligence agency responsible for the analysis and dissemination of information as well as for the development of studies and proposals to be presented to the Prime Minister and the Government in order to enabling the anticipation and prevention of security threats (cf. Section 1 of Act 11/2002). According to Section 4 of the Act, the CNI has seven functions:

1. Collecting, evaluating, and interpreting information and disseminating the necessary intelligence to protect and promote the political, economic, industrial, commercial and strategic interests of Spain, being able to act both inside and outside of the national territory.
2. Preventing, detecting, and enabling the neutralisation of any actions by foreign intelligence services, groups or individuals that may jeopardise the constitutional order and citizen rights and freedoms, and/or threaten the sovereignty, integrity and security of the State, the stability of its institutions, the national economic interests and the well-being of the population.
3. Promoting cooperation and collaborative relationships with the intelligence services of other countries and international organisations, for a better fulfillment of its objectives.
4. Obtaining, evaluating and interpreting the traffic of signals of a strategic nature for the fulfilment of the assigned intelligence objectives.
5. Coordinating the action of the different bodies of the Administration that use cipher, ensuring the security of information technologies in this area, reporting on the coordinated acquisition of cryptologic equipment, and training both their own staff and that of other departments in this field to ensure the proper fulfillment of the Center's mission.
6. Ensuring compliance with regulations on the protection of classified information.
7. Ensuring the security and protection of its own facilities, information and material, and human resources. (Cf. Section 4 of Act 11/2002.)

According to Act 11/2002 the CNI came under the control of the Prime Minister and the government, and was attached to the Ministry of Defense. However, the ministerial restructuring undertaken by the Spanish government after the general election of November 2011 has entailed a change in the administrative location of the CNI and it is now attached to the Ministry of the Presidency, under the responsibility of the First Deputy Prime Minister and the Minister of Presidency.

As previously stated, Spain has a single intelligence agency at the national level and there is no security intelligence service charged with a mission complementary to that of the CNI. Rather, the Spanish intelligence model integrates the State Security Forces, the Corps' information services, and other military and civil bodies of the administration. According to Act 11/2002, the responsibility for coordinating all these elements of the system is charged to the CDGAI, which is chaired by the Vice-President of the government and the Minister of Presidency; its members include the Minister of Foreign Affairs and Cooperation, the Minister of Defense, the Minister of Home Affairs, the Minister of Economy and Competitiveness, the Secretary of State-Director of the Cabinet of the Presidency, the Secretary of State for Security, and the Secretary of State-Director of the CNI, the latter acting as Secretary of the Commission. The Act also states that the Undersecretary of Presidency will be included in the Commission's meetings, as will other high bodies and directors of the administration where appropriate.

In addition to this task of coordinating the intelligence community, the CDGAI is also responsible for providing guidance on intelligence priorities through the annual Directive of Intelligence, and for monitoring and evaluating the accomplishment of the objectives of the CNI. This positions the CDGAI as an institution of executive control and oversight complementary to the internal control exerted by the Secretary of State-Director of the CNI and the Secretary General. The Directive is prepared on the basis of a preliminary draft of intelligence requirements prepared by the CNI; it is then presented to the Commission for review and subsequently proposed to the Prime Minister (Bregante 2007: 119).

With regards to the Spanish IC, Act 11/2002 could not be more ambiguous since it neither defines the concept of Spanish intelligence community, nor clarifies its structure. This ambiguity, together with the lack of a transparent system of complementary directives for ensuring the operational coordination of the community, are significant problems that must be resolved.

By virtue of Act 11/2002, the Director of CNI is also the National Intelligence and Counterintelligence Authority and Director of the National Cryptologic Centre (CCN). The CCN, established by Royal Decree 421/2004 on 12 March 2004, is attached to the CNI and, under the authority of the Secretary of State-Director, is tasked with ensuring the security of information technologies and with protecting classified information transmitted through these means). The Director of the CNI is also the National Delegated Authority for the Protection of Classified Information (ANS-D). The National Security Office (ONS) is the working body of the ANS-D for the protection of NATO Classified Information, in addition to that of the European Union, Western European Union, and European Space Agency. The function of the ONS is to ensure compliance with the regulations relating to the protection of national Classified Information, including any data given by foreign nations or international organisations under treaties and agreements.

In addition to these bodies, the basic structure of the CNI comprises three technical directorates, namely Intelligence, Support to Intelligence, and Resources. Each falls under the direct authority of the Secretary General, who is appointed to the position on the basis of acknowledged professional experience and expertise in intelligence. This basic structure also includes the Legal Affairs Office and the Office of the Director, as well as offices abroad.

According to Section 5.1 of Act 11/2002, 'the activities of the CNI, as well as its organisation and internal structure, resources and procedures, personnel, facilities, databases, sources of information, and the information or data that could lead to the knowledge of the matters above, are top secret classified information'. However, details relating to its personnel and budget, for example, have been made accessible. In the case of the former, statements from official sources have reported that the number of CNI employees stands at 3,500 and that foreign deployments covers a range of 64 countries. Similarly, it is stipulated in the General State Budgets

Bill 2012 that R 221.2 million has been allocated for the 'Assessment for Protection of the National Interest', which is reserved for CNI. Of these funds, EUR 166.28 million are allocated for public servants of the CNI, and EUR 17.8 million are assigned for confidential activities (Arcos 2012).

The parliamentary oversight of these confidential funds, which are classified as top secret, is exercised by the Commission for Control of the Appropriations for Confidential Funds. This commission is the parliamentary oversight body of the CNI. It is chaired by the President of the Congress and includes those members of Congress who have access to classified information, namely the leaders of the parliamentary groups. The content of the Commission's meetings is also classified as top secret. While the Commission has access to reports and other materials related to the CNI and the Directive of Intelligence, However, the Commission is not author-ised to view any classified information as regards the sources and methods of the Centre, nor is it privy to the information provided by foreign intelligence services and international organi-sations. According to Act 11/1995 a report on the confidential funds should be submitted to the Commission on a semi-annual basis. The overall control of the CNI budget falls under the auspices of the Spanish Court of Auditors and the General Comptroller's Office of the State Administration.

According to the Organic Law 2/2002 of 6 May, certain activities of the CNI that might affect rights enshrined in the Spanish Constitution – namely the right to privacy of communica-tions and the right to the inviolability of the home – are also subject to preliminary judicial con-trol. In such cases, the Secretary of State-Director of the CNI has to seek authorisation for the use of such measures from the judge of the Supreme Court who is in charge of this control. The Director is obliged to submit a written request explaining the following points: (1) the specific measures requested; (2) the facts supporting the request, the aims that prompted the request and the reasons for it; (3) which individual or individuals will be affected by the measures adopted; (4) the period of time in which the measures will be carried out. The duration of these measures cannot exceed 24 hours if the inviolability of the home is affected, or three months in the case of intervention or interception of communications. However, if necessary, it can be extended for a further period of equal time (cf. Section 1.2). In terms of authorisation, the judge must reach an informed decision within a maximum period of 72 hours, or 24 hours in the case of urgent situations. The law also states that any obtained information that is not directly related to the aims of these measures or for the specifically authorised purposes must be destroyed.

Military intelligence

The Armed Forces Intelligence Centre (CIFAS) was created by a Ministerial Order on 19 April 2005 (Order DEF/1076/2005). The CIFAS is responsible for disseminating military intelli-gence to the Minister of Defense, through the Spanish Chief of Defense Staff, and to other mili-tary authorities. The overall aim is to provide the necessary support for military operations, and to warn of potential crisis situations of military interest coming from abroad. The tactical intel-ligence organisations of the Army, Navy and Air Force are functionally dependent on CIFAS, which leads the gathering and analysis of strategic and operational military information and intelligence. The mission of the CIFAS is complementary to that of the CNI, which oversees the Joint Military Intelligence Plan and provides directives for coordination and cooperation. Indeed, the Director of the CNI must report to the CDGAI on the activities of the CIFAS. As part of its functions, the CIFAS collaborates and maintains relations with the intelligence structures of international defence organisations of which Spain is a member, and with those of allied countries.

Law enforcement intelligence

As noted above, the Information Services of the State Security Forces and the Corps of the Ministry of Home Affairs are fundamental elements of the intelligence system. These services are primarily concerned with law enforcement intelligence duties against terrorism, organised crime and criminal activities. Since the officials of the CNI are not law enforcement agents, with the exception of those tasked with security and protection, the smooth working of the system depends upon smooth communication and coordination between the CNI and those bodies of the Ministry of Home Affairs with intelligence competencies. This points to the need for trust-based, bidirectional reporting between the CNI and the law enforcement agencies, in order both to support the decision-making process and to undertake specific measures against threats. Since the 11-M attacks, policy-makers have tended to focus on creating intelligence coordination structures in the fight against terrorism and organised crime, and far less attention has been paid to building and ensuring the working of the system as a community.

In an effort to address this problem, the Executive Committee for the Unified Command of State Security Forces and Corps (CEMU) was established on 7 May 2004 by a Ministerial Order initiated by the Spanish Socialist Party. This committee was replaced with the Executive Commission for Coordination of the State Secretary for Security on 17 February 2012, following a ministerial restructuring undertaken by the Popular Party Government. The CEMU was tasked with strengthening the operational coordination between the intelligence and judicial police in the National Police Corps and the Guardia Civil, among other responsibilities.

Since the dismantling of the Unified Command, the National Police Corps and Guardia Civil have separate General Directorates under the State Secretary of Security of the Ministry of Home Affairs. The National Police Corps integrates the General Commissariat of Information and the General Commissariat of Judicial Police under the Attached Operational Directorate. The General Commissariat of Information is in charge of the 'collection, reception, treatment and development of information of interest to the public order and security in the area of competencies of its General Directorate, and the operation or operational use of that intelligence, especially in the field of terrorism, nationally and internationally' (Section 3.3. of the Royal Decree 400/2012). The structure, organisation and means of the General Commissariat of Information are classified as top secret. However, in 2004 the testimony of the General Commissioner of Information at the 11-M trial reported that, since 2001, the Commissariat has consisted of a general secretariat and four operational units: the Intelligence Central Unit, in charge of analysis; the Domestic Information Central Unit, responsible for dealing with the ETA terrorist threat and that of other radicalist movements; the External Information Central Unit; and the Operational Support Central Unit. In addition to these four key units, the commissariat has a unit for surveillance as well as provincial information squads. The External Information Central Unit (UCIE) was formed by integrating three services: Arab and Islamist Affairs, Technology and External Coordination. This amalgamation of departments was unveiled in July 2004 by the Parliamentary Commission of Inquiry on 11-M.

The functions of the General Commissariat of Judicial Police, on the other hand, include investigations of and efforts at supra-territorial offences, especially drug-related crimes, organised crime, economic, financial and technological crimes, and the control of games of chance. Moreover, Royal Decree 400/2012 states that the Commissariat is also in charge of the 'direction of the investigative services on monetary crimes and currency-related crimes' and is required 'to collaborate in these matters with the corresponding services of the Bank of Spain'. Its structure and units were defined by the Ministerial Order of 1 July 2005 (Order INT/2103/2005), integrating a General Secretariat, the Drug and Organized Crime Unit (UDYCO), the Violent and Specialized Crime Unit (UDEV), the Economic and Fiscal Crime Central Unit (UDEF), the Criminal Intelligence Central Unit (UCIC) and the Central Unit for International Police Cooperation (UCPI).

In the fight against illegal immigration, the General Commissariat of Borders and Aliens is responsible both for controlling entry to and exit from the Spanish territory, and for the prevention and investigation of illegal immigration networks. It has a specialised unit, the UCRIF, with a service of intelligence and risk assessment, for addressing this mission.

With regards to the Guardia Civil, the responsibilities of the General Director include the 'collection, centralization, analysis, assessment and dissemination of any information which is necessary to carry out operational missions and, in addition, liaising and coordinating with other national and international information bodies' (Section 4 of the Royal Decree 400/2012). Under the command of the attached Operational Directorate are the Department of Information and the Department of Judicial Police of the Civil Guard. The mission of the Department of Information is to plan, organise, direct and manage the collection, processing, analysis and dissemination of information of interest to public order and security, and its duties include the operational use of information, particularly that which relates to national and international terrorism. Its structure includes the Central Unit for Logistical Support (UCAL), the Group of Operational Support (GAO) and several other departments (UCEs), which have specific areas of concentration. While the Department of Information's specific structure, organisation and means are classified as top secret, it became known that, by July 2004, there were four such specialised units: the Central Special Unit One (UCE-1), focused on ETA; Central Special Unit Two (UCE-2), concerned with international terrorism; the Central Special Unit Three (UCE-3), focused on social conflicts (e.g. related to racist movements or sects); and a fourth unit providing specialised support to the ones in areas such as surveillance.

The Department of Judicial Police of the Guardia Civil is in charge of organising and managing investigations of, and operations against, crime. It is also tasked with developing forensic, identification, analysis and technical research services, as well as collaborating with national and international police forces in these areas. Guardia Civil is also responsible for the surveillance of coasts, borders, ports, airports and territorial waters, as well as the control of illegal immigration. This latter function is charged to the Fiscal and Borders Department, which also has responsibilities in combating smuggling and illicit drug trafficking (Section 4 of the Royal Decree 400/2012).

Under the authority of the General Director of the Guardia Civil is the Technical Office, which incorporated the Centre of Analysis and Foresight (CAP). The CAP is in charge of the research and foreknowledge of security-related matters and also of collaborating with universities and other institutions that develop research and studies on security.

Coordinating centres and protection of critical infrastructures

In mid-May 2004 at the CEMU's organisational meeting, it was agreed that a National Counterterrorism Centre would be established, and on May 28 the Council of Ministers approved the creation of the National Counterterrorism Coordination Centre (CNCA). Organisationally, the CNCA falls under the authority of the State Secretary for Security and, until February 2012, it was functionally dependent on CEMU as a non-political and non-operative missions structure, integrating members from the National Police Corps, Guardia Civil and CNI. It also includes members of Penitentiary Institutions. The CNCA's key responsibilities are the integration, analysis and assessment of all available information on terrorism, and its main objectives are the provision of regularly updated terrorist threat assessments, maintaining the leading role in counterterrorism and the identification of possible scenarios of intervention in order to plan responses to terrorist attacks.

As part of the ministerial restructuring outlined by Royal Decree 991/2006 of 8 September 2006, the Centre of Intelligence against Organized Crime (CICO) was established. The CICO has a coordination function and, like the CNCA, operates under the authority of the Secretary of State for Security. Subsequent legislation has not modified its original responsibilities. The CICO does not *gather* intelligence, but rather is tasked with analysing information and producing strategic intelligence in order to combat organised crime. It is responsible for developing operational coordination criteria for the joint action of the relevant bodies in cases where their remits coincide (Section 2.3.c). Furthermore, the CICO periodically prepares assessments on organised crime, among other issues, particularly in relation to Spain.

Similarly, the National Centre for Critical Infrastructure Protection (CNPIC) is organically dependent on the Secretary of State for Security. The CNPIC was established by Act 8/2011, of 28 April, following the Council of Ministers Agreement of 2 November 2007. Its mission is to 'drive, coordinate and supervise all the activities on critical infrastructure protection assigned to the State Secretary for Security'. According to Royal Decree 704/2011on Regulations for Critical Infrastructures Protection, the CNPIC is responsible for collecting and analysing all available information on strategic infrastructures coming from institutions, police services, private operators and international partners, and for the distribution of its assessments to CNCA and other structures (see Section 7).

Economic and commercial intelligence

In order to promote and protect Spain's economic, commercial and industrial interests, the CNI's intelligence and counterintelligence functions in these areas are supported by a network of economic and commercial offices that are part of Spain's diplomatic missions abroad. The offices provide information and support by means such as the monitoring and analysis of economic and commercial developments in foreign countries, as well as compliance with trade agreements.

The Spanish Institute for Foreign Trade (ICEX) of the Ministry of Economy and Competitiveness, operating through these economic and commercial offices, is responsible for promoting the internationalisation of Spanish businesses and improving their competitiveness. The Institute assists small and medium-sized enterprises in particular.

In June 2011, the Council of Ministers approved the Spanish Security Strategy. This document assumes that economic security is a fundamental dimension of security and calls for the creation of a System of Economic Intelligence (SIE).

Consumers, other structures and crisis management

The main consumer of the intelligence produced by the CNI is the Prime Minister's Cabinet (Díaz Fernández 2010), although the Ministry of Foreign Affairs and Cooperation, the Ministry of Defense and the Ministry of Home Affairs also usually receive CNI intelligence reports, according to the service's website.

According to Royal Decree 83/2012, of 13 January, the Prime Minister's Cabinet is a body for political and technical assistance with the duty of providing information and advice to the Prime Minister (Section 1), among its other responsibilities. It is headed by the Secretary of State, who is also the Secretary of the Government Delegate Commission for Crisis Situations (CDGSC). The Director of the CNI is a member of the CDGSC.

In July 2012, the Spanish government created the Department of Homeland Security under the authority of the Deputy Director of the Cabinet, as the permanent advisory and technical supporting body of Presidency for homeland security affairs. The Department of Homeland Security replaced the former Department of Infrastructure and Monitoring of Crisis Situations (DISSC), assuming the responsibilities of the latter in providing support to the structures of the National System for Crisis Management (SNCSC), keeping and ensuring the proper functioning of the National Center for Crisis Management (CNCSC) and of the special communications of the Presidency, monitoring crisis and emergency situations at both national and international levels, in direct coordination with other relevant bodies and authorities, and proposing the procedures of the SNCSC (cf. Section 4 of the Royal Decree 1119/2012 of 20 July 2012).

A key deficiency in the area of security is the lack of a council. Spain has a National Defense Council and a Foreign Policy Council, but no security council.[3] The National Defense Council was established in November 2005 by the Organic Law 5/2005 of the National Defense, as the collegiate body to coordinate, advise and inform the Prime Minister in the area of defence policy. The Director of the CNI is a member of the Defense Council. The Foreign Policy Council was created by a Royal Decree on July 2000, as a collegiate supportive body with similar functions in the area of foreign policy. In accordance with the holistic approach to security that has been adopted within the country, the creation of a National Security Council is a central aspect of the Spanish Security Strategy.

Preparing for the future: intelligence culture and non-governmental stakeholders

Prior to the mid-2000s, the presence of intelligence in university courses was anecdotal at best. The causes of this notable absence are diverse but are probably linked to Spain's pre-democratic history, given the fact that intelligence is inextricably linked with the political system it serves. In any case, the consequence of intelligence not being taught in universities was a general mistrust and lack of knowledge concerning matters of intelligence the services' stakeholders. This has changed considerably as a result of the implementation of a policy of openness more recently adopted by the CNI. This policy has been enacted through the CNI's Intelligence Culture Initiative and through the signing of agreements with universities, which has, in turn, led to the development of intelligence studies in Spain. While it aims to stimulate and generate knowledge in the field of intelligence, the initiative also has a strategic dimension, seeking the expertise of academic scholars and other non-IC stakeholders. Since intelligence and information services have traditionally resisted openness, the effectiveness of analytic outreach depends upon the capacity to build and manage bidirectional trust between the IC and outsiders, with academia being key. Intelligence-related events, workshops and university courses have emerged as spaces of interaction. This environment brings intelligence officials and outsiders closer together (Arcos and Antón 2010), helping to overcome the culture of secrecy and mistrust, and replacing it with one based upon transparency and trust.

Notes

1   Some views in this chapter have been previously stated in Arcos, 2012.
2   In May 2013 the document was revised an updated as *National Security Strategy*.
3   The functions of the future National Security Council are determined in Chapter 5 of the National Security Strategy 2013.

PART V

Contemporary challenges

25

COUNTERTERRORISM AND INTELLIGENCE

Neal A. Pollard and Lt John P. Sullivan

> In recent years we appear increasingly to have imported from the American media the assumption that terrorism is 100% preventable and any incident that is not prevented is seen as a culpable government failure. This is a nonsensical way to consider terrorist risk and only plays into the hands of the terrorists themselves. Risk can be managed and reduced but it cannot realistically be abolished, and if we delude ourselves that it can, we are setting ourselves up for a nasty disappointment.
>
> *(Jonathan Evans, Director General, British Security Service)*

With this statement, the head of Britain's internal intelligence service thus characterised the reality of intelligence in counterterrorism. Counterterrorism is an intelligence war, without wartime objectives. The intelligence community (IC) plays a central role in counterterrorism, in at least four key ways. Counterterrorism relies on intelligence to understand the threat, to give warning of adversaries' intentions and capabilities, to find and disrupt the adversary, and to measure the effectiveness – or lack thereof – of counterterrorism policy, strategy and operations.

Director-General Evans' quote above indicates that intelligence 'failures' against the terrorist threat should not be measured in terms of successful terrorist attacks, or even failed terrorist attacks such as that nearly perpetrated on Christmas Day 2009 by Umar Farouk Abdulmutallab, in his self-inflicted failure to blow up Northwest Airlines Flight 253 from Amsterdam to Detroit. Rather, the role of intelligence, and its successful planning, execution, and use against terrorism and asymmetric threats, is to manage effectively and reduce the risk of those threats. Success here is measured in whether the policies, tools, resources and processes of intelligence are best calibrated and applied against the threat, and whether some effect against the threat can be attributed to effective intelligence.

This chapter describes the role of intelligence and its evolution in counterterrorism. It also offers observations on challenges that still remain in the practice and use of intelligence against terrorism and other transnational threats, after a decade of significant combat against Al Qaeda and affiliated groups, the rise of transnational criminal organisations, and massive shifts in the organisation and missions of some Western intelligence agencies.

Transnational terrorism

This chapter will focus on the role of intelligence in countering specific non-state terrorist groups that pose a 'transnational' national security threat. The priority for national security and intelligence agencies should be those transnational groups that have sufficient regional or global aspirations, resources and reach to enable them to cross international borders and hold vital national interests at risk.

Transnational terrorist groups exploit the engines, trends and technologies of globalisation: cheap intercontinental travel, transnational commerce, and global information and communications technology. Like legitimate transnational actors, terrorists exploit globalisation to increase their productivity. They also exploit the geopolitical environment and the erosion of sovereign boundaries resulting from globalisation (Pollard 2009: 119). As former DNI, Mike McConnell, stated:

> The end of the Cold War and the advance of globalization enabled the acceleration of threats stemming from international terrorism, weapons of mass destruction (WMD) proliferation, failed states, and illegal drug trafficking. These threats, among others, move at increasing speeds due to technology and across geographic and organizational boundaries, blurring the distinction between foreign and domestic, and between strategic and tactical events.
>
> *(McConnell and Redd 2007)*[1]

The primary terrorist threat against the United States and its allies continues to be Al Qaeda and its affiliates, including groups in the Near East, South Asia and Africa. These affiliate groups, such as Al Qaeda in the Arabian Peninsula (AQAP), Al Qaeda in Iraq, Tehrik-e-Taliban Pakistan (TTP), and potentially even Lashkar-e-Tayyiba (LT), pose more of a current and active threat to the US homeland than the core Al Qaeda cadre that struck on 9/11 (Olsen and Olsen 2011). Additionally, the Iran-backed Hizb'allah still remains a hostile and global terrorist organisation (Gistaro and Leiter 2007; Olsen 2012: 3). Moreover, Al Qaeda and regional affiliates are reaching a broader audience through 'the spread of radical – especially Salafi – Internet sites', as well as globalisation trends and recent technological advances (in communications as well as mobility) that enable 'small numbers of alienated people to find and connect with one another, justify and intensify their anger, and mobilize resources to attack' (Gistaro and Leiter 2007). Because of their online presence, their interest in weapons of mass destruction (Clapper 2012: 2) and their demonstrated intent to attack the US homeland, AQAP is the best example of the expanding terrorist threat (Clapper 2012: 2).

Policy and action against transnational terrorist groups

The Obama administration articulates eight goals in its National Strategy for Counterterrorism, as follows.

1. Protect the American people, homeland, and American interests;
2. Disrupt, degrade, dismantle, and defeat al Qa'ida and its affiliates and adherents;
3. Prevent terrorist development, acquisition, and use of weapons of mass destruction;
4. Eliminate safehavens;
5. Build enduring counterterrorism partnerships and capabilities;

6. Degrade links between al Qa'ida and its affiliates and adherents;
7. Counter al Qa'ida ideology and its resonance and diminish the specific drivers of violence that al Qai'da exploits;
8. Deprive terrorists of their enabling means.

(White House 2011: 8–9)

Counterterrorism strategy and operations seek to achieve these goals by disrupting the key underlying capabilities and processes in the 'terrorist lifecycle': ideological and operational leadership and organisation; safe havens; recruitment, training and indoctrination; financial sources and infrastructure; planning, targeting, preparation and resourcing; adoption and use of critical technology; mobility for personnel and materiel; operational planning and execution; and exploitation of attack (Pollard 2009: 120–122). These elements make the difference between a localised 'homegrown' marginal threat, and a sustained terrorist threat with global reach, resources and ambitions, able to disrupt and degrade strategic national interests.

A group's ability to grow, adapt and wage an effective global (or even sustained regional) terrorist campaign depends on its ability to build and use these elements. The same holds true for regional or global transnational criminal organisations. Consequently, attacking these capabilities and processes can produce measurable strategic effects against a transnational threat (Pollard 2009: 122). Thus, the job of intelligence collection and analysis should be targeting and reporting on terrorist and criminal groups' capabilities and processes supporting these elements.

Requirements for intelligence against transnational terrorist groups

Intelligence requirements for counterterrorism span a matrix of strategic, operational and tactical analytical levels, and offensive and defensive measures and actions. Strategic defence requires intelligence for identifying long-term strategic vulnerabilities, how vulnerabilities might arise over time, or methods by which policy-makers might receive strategic warning and reduce vulnerabilities to terrorist attack and future terrorist capabilities.[2] Operational defence requires intelligence to gain insight into how terrorists build and use capabilities, build networks of support, secure safe havens, establish training regimes, or seek, adapt and employ technology and related technological skills and specialists. Tactical defence requires intelligence that can warn of planned attacks, or movement of terrorist personnel, matériel or finance (McConnell and Redd 2007; Pollard 2009: 122–123).

Strategic offence requires intelligence to support national policy for long-term efforts, such as countering violent extremist ideology, anticipating and preventing the rise of specific terrorist groups and movements, and anticipating strategic surprise, such as a quantum leap in terrorist employment of critical technologies such as cyber or biological (McConnell and Redd 2007). Operational offence requires intelligence for targeting and disrupting key terrorist capabilities, processes, and infrastructure that support the viability of terrorist groups, such as safe havens, financial infrastructure and networks, mobility capabilities, leadership and command channels, and avenues of sponsorship (Pollard 2009: 122–123). Tactical offence implicates intelligence requirements to support direct, tactical action to disrupt terrorist individuals and cells, such as apprehension or direct action against a terrorist, disruption of an attack, or seizure of finances or materiel from a specific network (McConnell and Redd 2007). These various levels of intelligence requirements, and the insight they yield in support of specific actions, are portrayed in Table 25.1.

Table 25.1 Intelligence requirements[3]

	Strategic	*Operational*	*Tactical*
Defence	Reduce long-term vulnerabilities to emerging terrorist capabilities	Identify terrorist exploitation of infrastructure	Warn of attacks or terrorist movements
Offence	Counter violent extremist ideology	Disrupt transnational financing network	Capture or kill terrorist leaders

To accomplish these intelligence goals, intelligence operations target transnational groups and their leaders, suppliers, sponsors and facilitators. This is a shift from the origins of the modern US intelligence community, which was built to focus on states, namely the Soviet Union and Warsaw Pact states during the Cold War. Forcing that shift has been the focus of intelligence reform in the US and other countries after 9/11.

The requirements for intelligence during the Cold War were different than those for a war against extremist groups. During the Cold War, enemy forces were easy to find and observe but hard to neutralise, and operated mainly overseas. Intelligence during the Cold War focused on orders of battle, numbers, strength and movement of warfighting materiel, intentions of leaders, and punctuated activity of force movements or even regional conflicts during otherwise vacuums of hostile activity. During the Cold War, intelligence placed a priority on strategic indications and warning (I&W) of hostile intent or action, changes in warfighting or intelligence capabilities and long-term plans. Tactical activity would be obvious, or at least easier to obtain than strategic intent. The 'steady state' of normalcy was, simply, nothing happening.

Intelligence for counterterrorism is the opposite. Enemy forces are easy to neutralise, once found. Finding them is the challenge: terrorists are less organised than a nation-state, their 'forces' smaller and more diffuse in number, and they hide among civilians and legitimate commerce. Terrorist groups generally do not mask their intentions, capabilities, or long-term plans, but do project their intentions to multiple audiences, making it difficult to parse their tactical intentions, and frustrating efforts to drive strategic intelligence to tactical opportunities for action. Terrorist activities do not occur in vacuums of hostile activity, but rather are constant but faint signals of activity hidden within the persistent stream of the noise of global commerce and movement. The 'steady state' of normalcy is constant 'chatter'.

These differences in the terrorist threat present an overall intelligence challenge arguably more difficult to manage now than during the Cold War, because of a number of reasons. Terrorists blend in with civilian populations and commerce even inside the homeland (Hoffman 1998), and rely on surprise, small organisational cells, and intense secrecy of operations and communications to achieve their tactical ends (Wardlaw 1989: 131–136). The terrorist threat is less 'bounded' or discrete than the Soviet Union or other states (by fewer geographic, political or operational constraints). Terrorist groups are more reactive to the policies and counterterrorism efforts of their target states, not necessarily subject to deliberative, independent strategic considerations, thus making their actions less determinate and predictable. Events that create, drive or result from terrorist groups (and thus change the threat environment) unfold and affect threat dynamics more rapidly than events that affected the Soviet Union and the Cold War balance of power.

Evolution of intelligence: terrorism to transnational crime

The attacks on the United States on 9/11 brought a new awareness of the risk of terrorism. As a result, the intelligence community and all levels of government sought to build new capabilities to combat transnational threats. Both terrorism and global crime pose significant challenges to both intelligence and law enforcement agencies. These networked adversaries blend political and economic motivations with fanaticism (i.e. jihadism or *narcocultura*) into criminal enterprises that challenge the rule of law and exploit the seams between crime and political conflict.

In the United States, two major approaches were developed to address the new threat environment, based on the experience of local law enforcement both in the United States and Europe. The first was the New York Police Department (NYPD) approach, based on strengthened criminal intelligence and a network of international liaison officers to extend 'sensing' capabilities. NYPD's liaison programme is based on the premise that 'The war on terrorism has no national boundaries and now the NYPD doesn't either.' It is referred to by New York's Police Foundation (which partially funds the programme) as 'Global Policing in the 21st Century'. The NYPD deployed detectives to at least ten cities worldwide: Toronto, Montreal, Santo Domingo, London, Paris, Lyon, Madrid, Tel Aviv, Amman and Singapore. These NYPD detectives are unarmed and are not directly involved in investigations and enforcement actions. Their role is solely liaison and information exchange.[4]

The second approach was the networked Los Angeles Terrorism Early Warning (TEW) group that sought to leverage the 'co-production of intelligence' from a multilateral, multidisciplinary network (Wirtz and Sullivan 2009). Again, this model built on lessons learned in the experience of European nations dealing with internal terrorism and insurgent campaigns, focused on law enforcement and internal intelligence collection and analysis. These models emphasised local and regional agencies, as opposed to national-only agencies, as producers as well as users of intelligence.

This approach recognised that both transnational terrorism and organised crime, although they span borders and even continents, nevertheless have local dimensions and presence. Thus, local police are best positioned to understand their communities and local threat environment. Yet transnational terrorist and criminal enterprises link in interactive networks. In response, these models enable local police agencies to cooperate with their counterparts at national and foreign liaison agencies to understand and counter the threat both globally and locally. Global metropolitan policing is the term used to describe this emerging trend in police cooperation in sharing intelligence and best practices, focusing on three elements: (1) cross-border, (2) transnational and (3) global. It includes both national and metropolitan police, as well as linkages with intelligence organisations, non-governmental organisations (NGOs) and private/corporate security entities (Wirtz and Sullivan 2009). NYPD's International Liaison Program and the TEW model are two distinct expressions of the trend to integrate law enforcement and intelligence to address global, transnational threats.

Since 9/11, intelligence and law enforcement agencies have focused on overcoming not only organisational and political hurdles, but technical hurdles as well. A significant technical hurdle persists in dealing with the sheer amount of data available that might or might not contain indications of a terrorist threat. Information and data about terrorist groups, activities and processes are scattered, difficult to isolate, and must be plucked from countless sources in broader information bases with lower quality and less context (Fishbein and Treverton 2004: 8). All of this presents a difficult intelligence target in itself; social, political, economic and technological trends exacerbate these challenges for intelligence agencies, and will do so into the future.

Continuing issues

Transnational threats are not static: they can evolve, adapt and morph as quickly as any other effective multinational entity or global social network. Over at least the past ten years, the world's intelligence and counterterrorism agencies have tried to reorientate their requirements, operations and analysis accordingly. That said, intelligence agencies will face continuing challenges in adapting their own business processes, innovative sources and methods, and technological tools, to keep up with transnational threats to their nations as well as operational threats to their own tradecraft.

New technology tools and trends will present challenges to intelligence agencies in countering terrorism – not just because of the advanced threat they might bring, but also because of the difficulty in bridging the necessary operational, analytical and technical expertise within the intelligence community to confront the threat as it evolves. Globalisation will not abate, and the future will continue to see highly beneficial technology that is cheap, widely available, easier to use and potentially very dangerous if used in the wrong way. Cyber- and biotechnology are two examples. Terrorists will also continue to exploit technology to increase their own productivity. Moreover, intelligence agencies should watch closely for terrorist intent to adapt cybertools or weapons, as well as weapons of mass destruction: nuclear, biological, chemical or radiological weapons. Any such intent would portend a very serious threat.

Keeping up with globalisation: the consequences of being modern

As transnational threats hide in a sea of information noise, intelligence agencies will need to exploit innovative tools and techniques to make sense of the deluge of data and find the signal in the noise. At the same time, intelligence agencies will have to cope with a world where public databases, big data analytics and social network media erode the ability to keep secrets, common commercial transactions use embedded biometrics, and online video surveillance pervades every street corner and dark alley. These trends make life difficult for criminals, but they also present challenges for spies.

Intelligence agencies do not have the configuration, manpower, funds or even authorities to observe directly the multitude of urban settings and globalised infrastructures, hiding millions of shady or illegal channels, through which terrorists move money, people, weapons and plans. For this, they must take advantage of data mining, analytics and non-obvious link awareness to strengthen open source collection, and augment and focus clandestine foreign intelligence collection. The pace of technology will make this difficult enough, not to mention the precarious challenge of managing the ever-shifting ground of unreconciled privacy standards among allies, privacy restrictions on democratic governments, and privacy obligations for corporations and citizens.

Cyberterrorism: the consequences of being right

Headlines shriek regularly with fears of cyberterrorism. Media warn of spectacular electronic attacks on computer-supported infrastructures such as the air traffic control system, nuclear power plants and electric power grids. So far, that threat has not emerged: those with capability have not demonstrated intent, and vice versa. Nonetheless, intelligence agencies should remain vigilant for indications of emerging cyberterrorism threats – a threat that is amorphous and poorly understood, but one that could rapidly and unexpectedly emerge given the pace of technology, the adaptability of terrorist groups and the emergence of new vulnerabilities.

Currently, terrorist use of the internet is a greater danger to the US when computers are used as tools, rather than as weapons or targets. Nations and terrorist groups have shown some interest and investment in capabilities to wage electronic attack against the US. As far back as 1996, a US Defense Science Board report documented such interest by states and terrorist groups. However, these scenarios of computers as weapons or targets currently pose less of a terrorist threat to the US than does terrorist use of computers as tools: the threat here lies in groups' abilities to enhance the effectiveness of their operations, while hampering efforts and denying opportunities to thwart them. Furthermore, although the threat of destructive cyber-terrorist attacks is currently relatively low, terrorists' continuing pursuit of information technology (IT) as a tool could precipitate terrorist use of IT as a weapon. Intelligence services should continue to watch for signs of convergence between those with intent, and those with capabilities, to launch destructive cyberattacks.

Many groups have shown interest in cyberweapons, or have defaced or disrupted websites. But these have been low-level threats, notable more for conceptual advancement than technological sophistication. Terrorists innovate more conceptually than technologically, driven by opportunity and strategic imperatives, with 'high-concept/low-tech' advances such as the 9/11 attacks and simultaneous truck bombs. Terrorists seek spectacular attack, not easily yielded by cyberattack, which carries greater risk of failure than a truck bomb. Furthermore, most terrorist groups are operationally conservative, will not innovate for the sake of innovation, and tend to keep with weapons that are proven.

That said, terrorist groups are constantly evolving and exploring ways to increase their effectiveness, and any trend or technology that increases the effectiveness of the current terrorist threat is a danger. Terrorist groups continue to exploit IT to increase effectiveness in recruitment, propaganda, training, logistics, secure communication, surveillance and targeting. Websites and chat rooms are known to be effective fora for propaganda and training material, joining disparate groups of discontents and facilitating radicalisation. Encrypted wireless and email communications allow terrorist operatives to plan and coordinate securely. Open information on the web, and services such as Google Maps, allow terrorists to identify, assess and surveil targets. Emerging online activities such as Second Life and similar massively multiplayer online games (MMOGs) facilitate group cohesion, and provide a forum to plan and conduct 'virtual' training and attack test runs.

Terrorist use of IT also might reduce opportunities to interdict attacks, if IT can provide a cybersubstitute for terrorist activities previously occurring in 'real world', where terrorists are more vulnerable. Physical surveillance and training are two examples of critical 'real-world' functions that might be replicated in cyberspace. If terrorist planners and operators can use online resources and maps to surveil a target, or MMOGs and security social networking to build esprit de corps and a network of collaborators and facilitators, then they are accomplishing in cyberspace tasks and activities that before would have potentially exposed them to security forces. Thus, moving these activities to cyberspace can deny intelligence and security agencies opportunities to interdict.

As terrorist groups pursue IT as a tool, to enhance effectiveness and frustrate counterterrorism efforts, such groups will necessarily acquire technical resources, skills, abilities and experience in the offensive use of IT. This could enable terrorist groups to overcome the technical or operational barriers preventing effective use of IT as a true cyberweapon, and thus precipitate or accelerate convergence between intent and capability for cyberattack. A handful of terrorist leaders who are also proficient in IT, and can demonstrate the potential of cyberattacks, could lead fellow terrorist planners to see the potential of IT as a weapon, and overcome their own reticence to innovate.

Intelligence services should track trends of intent *and* capability in the transition of IT from tool to weapon or target. This means watching carefully for the emergence of terrorist operatives who have influence over their leadership and sponsors, while extolling the virtues of cyberwarfare. Similarly, intelligence services should watch for indications and trends of skilled computer scientists, engineers and hackers increasingly gravitating towards existing violent extremist groups, and terrorist recruiters and infrastructure.[5]

Weapons of mass destruction terrorism: the consequences of being wrong

The priority challenge for intelligence and counterterrorism focuses on terrorist use of WMD. When one crosses this much uncertainty with this much consequence of getting it wrong, it is hard to make good policy decisions. This increases policy-makers' reliance on intelligence, and raises the stakes for the intelligence community.

Few groups have shown an interest in acquiring and using weapons of mass destruction,[6] even fewer have attempted such an attack, and no extremist group has wrought 'mass destruction' using chemical, biological, radiological or nuclear weapons. However, intelligence agencies should remain vigilant against this threat, given geopolitical trends in the Near East and South Asia, the decreasing costs and increasing availability of underlying technologies, the difficulty of detecting groups' intents and capabilities for using these weapons, and the consequences if such groups are successful.

Intelligence for preventing weapons of mass destruction (WMD) terrorism requires insight into the intent and capabilities of state and non-state suppliers of materials, expertise, logistics and financial support; facilitators such as financiers, smugglers and traffickers; and non-state terrorist groups and facilitation networks that seek to acquire materials and skills, and deliver a weapon clandestinely. All of these actors operate in a highly clandestine environment. In particular, terrorist groups – already a difficult target for intelligence – that seek WMD compartmentalise those programmes and strictly limit access by their own personnel, making their WMD efforts the most secretive part of an already secretive enterprise, and among the hardest information to collect against any terrorist group. Additionally, there simply are not that many terrorist groups, if any, currently trying to acquire WMD. Thus, intelligence efforts are confronted with a difficult challenge, locating a 'signal', fortunately small in existence but unfortunately designed to be clandestine, within the sea of 'noise' that characterises globalisation. As one senior intelligence analyst put it to this author, never have so many analysts chased so few data points.

Terrorists have clearly indicated interest in chemical, biological, radiological and nuclear weapons.[7] In 1984, the Rajneeshees religious cult in Oregon employed salmonella as a biological agent to sicken 751 people in hopes of influencing an election (Tucker 2000: 115–137). In 1995, Japanese cult Aum Shinrikyo killed 12 people and injured thousands with sarin nerve gas, after attempting 20 other biological and chemical terrorist attacks in Japan in 1990–95 (Tucker 2000: 207–226). Al Qaeda has directed several operational leaders to acquire or develop nuclear, chemical or biological weapons (Graham *et al.* 2008: 4–5, 10–12, 20). In 2012 testimony to the Senate Armed Services Committee, DNI James Clapper stated that AQAP continues to express interest in chemical, biological or radiological weapons (Clapper 2012: 2). However, relatively few people have been killed by terrorist biological or chemical attacks, and there have been no successful nuclear or radiological terrorist attacks. In terms of terrorists delivering true 'mass destruction' with WMD, it appears that, as with cyber, those with intent lack capability and those with capability lack intent.

The reasons for this are probably a combination of factors. First, most terrorist or criminal groups would have relatively little use for a nuclear or biological weapon: the expense, the risk of operational failure, the risk of increased scrutiny and attacks from security forces, and the potential backlash that might decrease recruits and financial or logistical support from sympathisers, all reduce the value of WMD when compared to proven conventional weapons that more readily and securely support groups' political and operational goals.

Second, one should not underestimate the technical requirements for a non-state group to develop WMD. For transnational groups desiring to develop and deliver a weapon of mass destruction, they have to overcome three scientific and operational hurdles: acquisition of the required basic skills and materials, weaponisation of those materials into a functional device, and delivery of that device to a target. These hurdles require different skills, tools and processes: weaponising highly enriched uranium to produce an improvised nuclear device requires relatively rare skills and tools that might not be as helpful in smuggling that device past security forces to its intended target.

The examples of the Rajneeshees, Aum Shinrikyo and Al Qaeda illustrate these technical hurdles. Aum had access to extraordinary financial resources and scientific expertise, Al Qaeda enjoyed safe haven in Afghanistan, and both sought WMD. Yet neither succeeded in causing casualties with either biological or nuclear weapons, and Aum killed only 13 people using a chemical weapon that, while potent, failed because its delivery system was ineffective. That said, in 2006 congressional testimony, Charles E. Allen, Under Secretary for Intelligence and Analysis at the Department of Homeland Security, noted that the threat of bioterrorism could rise if a terrorist group were able to recruit technical experts who had experience in a national biological warfare programme, with knowledge comparable to that of the perpetrator of the 2001 anthrax letter attacks (Graham *et al.* 2008: 11). Similarly, US government officials have testified that Al Qaeda probably does not currently have the skills or material to produce a nuclear weapon; however, officials also have stated that the threat can change significantly if a group can recruit a few people with access to weapons-usable nuclear material or nuclear weapons engineering expertise (Graham *et al.* 2008: 20). Pakistan and Syria are two countries that have a worrisome mix of political instability, proximity to hostile terrorist groups and networks, and weapons of mass destruction (Graham 2008: 65–75). Thus, the threat of WMD terrorism shares another aspect with the threat of cyberterrorism: intelligence services should be concerned more with scientists and engineers becoming terrorists, than terrorists trying to become scientists and engineers (Graham *et al.* 2008: 11).

These characteristics of WMD terrorism provide sets of indicators on which intelligence analysts should focus. The technical hurdles described above can help to identify terrorist groups' attempts to bridge intent and capability. Similarly, extremist groups' efforts to recruit scientists and engineers, as well as trends of scientists and engineers gravitating towards groups' recruitment leaders or processes, should provide indications of both intent and capability.

WMD terrorism lies at the nexus of proliferation and terrorism, bridging supply and demand. Efforts to counter WMD terrorism also ought to bridge supply and demand, and focus on that nexus. However, in government security and intelligence services, the counterterrorism world often is a different discipline, if not a different world, than counterproliferation. Counterproliferation traditionally focuses on state programmes and institutions, which are composed of bureaucracies, with individuals cycling in and out (albeit with some continuity among scientists and leadership), and such institutions do not tend to evolve as quickly as transnational groups' strategies, plans, and personnel. By comparison, counterterrorism focuses more on individuals than institutions. Scientists might engage in clandestine and illicit proliferation activity, their capabilities as scientists are often widely known, often through their scientific publications, whereas terrorist leaders and operatives work to keep secret details on both personnel and capabilities.

As mentioned above, the 9/11 Commission focused on intelligence failures in the counterterrorism mission: intelligence failed to interdict a plot that existed. By contrast, the WMD Commission focused on intelligence failures in the counterproliferation mission: intelligence indicated the existence of a plot that did not exist. Although these two commissions combined to effect the changes in the US intelligence community over the past eight years, the CT lessons from these commissions are different from the CP lessons. As the Graham-Talent Commission noted:

Among the conclusions drawn by the CT analysts after 9/11 was that they must be far more forward-leaning in their threat assessments and must be willing to think creatively and take analytic risks. In contrast, the lessons the CP analysts drew from the 2002 Iraq WMD National Intelligence Estimate were to check and recheck every source, fully vet all information, clearly distinguish what is known from what is judged, and be extraordinarily cautious, even reticent, when preparing intelligence and presenting it to policymakers.

(Graham et al. *2008: 96)*

The remaining challenge for the intelligence community is to bridge those differences. In particular, intelligence analysis should focus on how different nodes of the demand – scientists, poorly guarded supplies of materials, terrorist group leadership, smuggling operations and routes, financiers and funding streams, and other nodes – interact with one another. This challenge is a function both of information processing and analytic tradecraft.

Conclusion

There are few solutions to transnational threats; there are instead tools and techniques to manage risks. This provides the basis of a reasonable measure of effectiveness for intelligence and counterterrorism agencies: are they optimised, and using the best tools, techniques and procedures, in the most effective ways, to identify and manage all risk elements that are under their control, and are they making progress at gaining more control over more risk variables? Echoing Jonathan Evans' words earlier, these are the most reasonable of expectations a nation can lay upon its intelligence community, to reduce the risks of terrorism.

Those tools, techniques and procedures include aforementioned technologies and processes for data mining, big data analytics and non-obvious link awareness. But they include broader, less exotic organisational practices. This includes creating operational units that bring closer together, as their core organisational principle, collectors (including open source specialists), analysts and technologists, to work specific functional and regional issues, such as cyberterrorism or foreign fighter movement across regions. Technologists in this sense include specialists on threat technologies, but also, for example, technologies and tools, as well as business and social trends, on social networking media.

Here, the US intelligence and counterterrorism community offers some examples of effective organisation, especially among units focused on WMD terrorism. It will be important for governments and legislatures to continue to identify, emphasise and support similar examples of collaboration and innovation seen over the past ten years, as transnational threats adapt to and exploit emerging technologies, commercial trends and business processes, cut across the regional and functional boundaries governments set for themselves and the world, merge with other transnational actors with witting or unwitting common objectives, and move seamlessly through the fabric of globalisation. For modern intelligence services, managing risk is a function of managing globalisation.

Counterterrorism and intelligence efforts must adapt to the decentralised and transnational nature not only of the threats themselves, but the engines of globalisation (e.g. social networking media) and areas of industry (e.g. biological sciences) the threats exploit. Most of these areas of industry have transnational communities themselves, and strong interest in seeing that their products and services are not used in illicit means. This offers not only a source of potential information, but a strong incentive to strengthen public–private cooperation and information sharing.

Notes

1 The authors wish to express their appreciation to Miss Emelie Rodriguez of Sewanee: The University of the South, for her assistance in researching and editing this chapter. Miss Rodriguez contributed as an intern and research assistant for summer 2012 in support of writing this work, and other efforts on counterterrorism and cyber security (Rodriguez 2012).

2 This strategic/tactical breakdown of intelligence support to counterterrorism missions is a part of the US Intelligence Community's 'Analytic Framework for Counterterrorism', described by VADM J. Scott Redd in his testimony, cited above (McConnell and Redd 2007). The author has added the additional element of operational intelligence support (Pollard 2009: 122–123).

3 This table was first published in Pollard (2009: 123).

4 See New York City Police Foundation, International Liaison Program at http://www. nycpolicefoundation.org/global.asp.

5 See Chapter 26 on a discussion of cyberthreats and hacktivism, as distinguished from terrorism and violent extremism.

6 For the purposes of this chapter, the author uses WMD as shorthand denoting chemical, biological, radiological or nuclear weapons.

7 See, generally, Tucker (2000) for numerous examples and case studies.

26

CYBERSECURITY

Dave Clemente

Eventually everything connects – people, ideas, objects . . .
the quality of the connections is the key to quality per se.

(Charles Eames)

Cyberspace – and the physical, logical and social layers that comprise it – presents significant challenges and opportunities for intelligence organisations. Thanks to rapid advances in technology, capabilities that were once the sole domain of nation-states are now widely available to individual actors. In addition, the relative anonymity offered by cyberspace means that these capabilities can be employed with few restraints. This has resulted in an environment in which the classic intelligence descriptive 'wilderness of mirrors' is particularly apt.[1] Cyberspace also presents opportunities for many stages of the intelligence cycle.[2] Collection in cyberspace is particularly desirable given the low risks and potentially high rewards. There is no physical danger because collectors sit behind computers in secure government buildings, probing target networks on the other side of the globe. This reduces the political risk associated with intelligence and increases the attractiveness of cyberspace for intelligence customers.

The part of cyberspace most people are familiar with – the web (just one of the many kinds of traffic that runs on the internet) – has its origins in the US defence community of the 1960s (Leiner, Cerf *et al.* 2012). In addition, as the birthplace of the transistor and information theory – the twin pillars of modern ICT – the US started with a natural advantage in this arena (Gertner 2012). The UK has also made significant contributions to computing and to the development of the web (Dyson 2012):

> . . . the information revolution took off in the 1940s with the realization that any task could be subjected to mathematical processes (with their accompanying speed, volume, and precision) if it could be expressed in the form of an algorithm. The result has been an accelerating shift of work and communications tasks to computerized (i.e. digital) processes, swiftly followed by an equally momentous connecting of these processes to one another over networked channels. If the analogue revolution was a discontinuous shift in the technology of acquiring and sharing information, then its digital counterpart represents yet another discontinuous shift in the technology of acquiring, sharing, and storing information.
>
> *(Warner 2012c: 143–144)*

Both countries retain significant institutional memory regarding the foundational elements of the digital environment. However, this 'first-mover' advantage is eroding as cyberspace becomes truly globalised. Dependence on the US – to provide connectivity and expertise – is waning and being replaced with talent drawn from countries around the world. This trend will continue as the next generation of 'digital natives' emerges, who are fully immersed in, and conversant with, the information age.

The impact of cyberspace on the intelligence community is a story of evolution, not revolution. This is a community intimately familiar with technology and change, however there are qualitative differences between the current environment and that of previous generations. One defining characteristic of the information age is that it revolves around the management of abundance – not scarcity (Naughton 2012; 112). The business of intelligence is no exception. As more data become available (and is gathered) greater effort is required to interpret them and to uncover meaning and relevance. Managing the signal to noise ratio is a task of supreme difficulty, with irrelevant, extraneous data crowding out the important or critical. Finding ways to detect the signal has always been a challenge – even more so in the current environment.

The rapid expansion of cyberspace (i.e. infrastructure and connected users and devices) and the relative ambiguity that it provides for individuals means that many threats are difficult to measure and mitigate. The challenges of cybersecurity look less like puzzles – where pieces are known to exist and can be collected and fit together, and more like mysteries – where ambiguity and uncertainty abound (Treverton 2007), and where dense feedback loops between myriad actors create immense complexity (Geer 2008).[3]

This chapter aims to provide a nuanced perspective on cybersecurity and the contemporary challenges and opportunities it presents to the intelligence community. These are both internal and external – that is, cyberspace challenges intelligence organisations to move ever faster in the cycle of offence and defence – collecting externally while protecting internally. Security and insecurity are two sides of the same coin. Those who can master the former (internally) while inducing the latter (externally) will reap disproportionate rewards. This chapter will examine a number of key issues through three lenses: first, the political challenges of intelligence and cybersecurity; second, the human and social dimension; and, third, the technological nature of intelligence in the information age. Individually and combined, these lenses colour all elements of the intelligence cycle.

Political challenges

The political dimension of cybersecurity and intelligence is evolving, and in many ways is driven by technical advances (e.g. faster processors, larger storage capacity, finely calibrated sensors, advanced data mining algorithms, powerful encryption), which open new avenues for collection and analysis. These advances have been embraced by some governments and treated with wariness by others, in part depending on the extent to which entrenched interests are challenged.[4] Cyberspace lowers the political and physical risks of intelligence collection, making it attractive as a low-risk and high-payoff activity. Yet there are significant political challenges. The biggest of them is misunderstanding the nature of cyberspace, in particular underestimating the power it provides for decentralised action at the individual and small-group level.

It is natural for contemporary threats to guide the focus of the intelligence cycle. Over the past decade, as technology advanced relentlessly, the dominant threat narrative in the US and Western Europe has focused on Islamist-inspired terrorism. The terrorism narrative has embedded itself firmly in the public consciousness, and when combined with cyberspace it tends to produce dramatic headlines. Tens of thousands of scholarly articles can be found on the web that address the phenomenon of 'cyberterrorism', yet they struggle to identify a single instance where terror was created. More recently, interstate tensions in cyberspace (e.g. regarding economic espionage and cyberconflict) have started to move to the fore, rivalling counterterrorism as the lens through which intelligence-gathering and analysis are viewed.

Diffusion of power

Cyberspace offers significant opportunities for diffusion of power, including autonomous or collective action. The possibilities and implications of this diffusion are vast, for 'permissionless innovation' and the development and deployment of new technologies that disrupt established systems and entrenched interests (Schewick 2010). Intelligence organisations are forced to adapt to this environment and to the creative public uses of technology.

Powerful capabilities such as high-resolution satellite imagery and geo-location are now widely available to anyone with an internet or data-enabled device. Advances in miniaturisation permit powerful devices to be transported and concealed with ease. Many of these advances have emerged from the private sector in response to commercial demand. This level of sophistication had traditionally been the preserve of nations, not individuals, and the diffusion of this power is perceived by many governments as a significant challenge.

In order to address these challenges, intelligence organisations have been forced to adapt by hiring specialised talent, including contractors. Over the past decade, the private sector has made significant inroads into the intelligence business, in a move partially driven by the growth of government counterterror funding (Priest and Arkin 2012). These companies develop sophisticated surveillance and reconnaissance platforms, data mining software, and a host of other technical tools, which are often marketed to intelligence and law enforcement agencies around the world. Other companies provide a full range of collection and analysis – combining assets on the ground with open source intelligence (OSINT) including satellite imagery and expert analysis. The sum of these activities means that, for governments, as sources of information have proliferated, data collection has become easier. But analysing and understanding global dynamics, and communicating meaningfully to policy-makers, remain significant challenges, in large part due to the flood of data that analysts must work with.

In addition, instantaneous communication and ease of information transfer make it difficult to prevent leaks and impossible to retract information that has been made available online. For intelligence organisations, there is a constant tension between the 'need to share' (encouraged in Washington after 11 September 2001) and the more secretive 'need to know'. The 2010 disclosure by WikiLeaks of 250,000 US State Department cables serves as a prime example of the delicate balancing act between sharing enough information to connect the dots, and sharing only with only those people that need to know.

Uncertainty

One role of an intelligence organisation can be viewed as 'bounding uncertainty'. As part of this, it is necessary to understand 'the forces at work in any situation – the key variables and drivers and our adversary's perspective. It is the difference between strategic understanding and tactical command of an issue' (Petersen 2011). Intelligence-gathering from a position of asymmetric information brings significant advantages. In other words, anything that permits a wider field of view than the adversary (e.g. espionage, information sharing alliances, nuanced data mining) can help to obtain or maintain a qualitative edge.

Network and data security is an enduring cybersecurity and counterespionage concern. When defending against advanced intrusions it can be extremely difficult to discern whether the intruder is conducting espionage or hostile reconnaissance (Lewis, J. 2011). Both are a concern, but the latter is arguably more severe, given that it could be preparing the battlefield for an attack. This ambiguity is greater when, as in many cases, intrusions are discovered long after information has been stolen and computer logs have been erased. In these circumstances, forensic analysis may be impossible and damage estimates vague and speculative.

On the defensive side, although diffusion of technology can strengthen societal resilience by reducing single points of failure, there is an asymmetric component for countries with significant cyber capabilities. They tend to also be countries that are heavily networked. Their citizens and critical infrastructure are dependent on cyberspace, and as a result the country is more vulnerable to electronic attack and disruption (Brenner 2011).

A significant majority of critical infrastructure is owned and operated by the private sector. They are also a rich source of intellectual property, which makes them prime intelligence targets. Few of these critical companies can independently and successfully resist the intelligence efforts of a determined and well-resourced nation-state adversary. Yet information-sharing barriers (e.g. divergent incentives) prevent coordinated public–private-sector defensive action, which increases general uncertainty regarding the quantity and quality of cyberthreats. From a public perspective there is a shortage of specific threat information, which hinders calculation of even a basic risk equation (risk = threat $\times$ vulnerability $\times$ impact) (Bejtlich 2005).

Opening up

For better or worse, modern ICT offer intelligence customers the chance to engage in near real-time analysis of raw data. It also gives them access to numerous sources, many of which are unaffiliated with government (e.g. media outlets, blogs, social media). Open source intelligence collection has a decades long history, and has traditionally included 'television and radio broadcasts, newspapers, trade publications, internet websites, and nearly any other form of public dissemination' (Leetaru 2010: 18). This is rapidly expanding, however: 'Now vast quantities of information about target cultures and countries, their economies, culture, physical geography, climate and so on are available . . . A whole branch of intelligence work is having to be created to access (not a straightforward matter), monitor and exploit such internet-based material' (Omand 2010b: 31).

Intelligence organisations are responding by developing departments that focus exclusively on OSINT (e.g. CIA Open Source Centre) (Dozier 2011). They sift through a torrent of data, sometimes to find the needle in a haystack, but increasingly to discern patterns across different data categories (e.g. email, SMS, geo-location, health/tax/legal/criminal records).[5] This is axiomatically considered a desirable state of affairs, yet quantitative growth does not equal qualitative improvement. There are many sources of intelligence competing for the attention of both intelligence analysts and customers, but time remains finite.

Human and social challenges

Cyberspace poses challenges for the human and social aspects of intelligence. Although data collected in cyberspace can augment and complement HUMINT, it cannot supplant it. Humans are indispensable in the processing and analysis phases. Computers excel at processing vast quantities of data. But they are limited in their ability to provide contextual analysis, an area where humans are indispensable. On the spectrum of Data > Information > Knowledge > Wisdom, computers dominate the handling of the first two categories while humans are essential for the latter two.

The human element comprises both the weakest link and the greatest point of strength in cybersecurity. The potential for social engineering (i.e. manipulating or tricking people into creating a security vulnerability) is one of the most consistently exploitable weaknesses in any organisation. Yet only a human can turn data into knowledge, or identify false positives in computer-generated results. The challenge is knowing when the human 'in the loop' is the failsafe, and when they are the liability (Geer 2012).

Collection in cyberspace brings an interesting twist when compared to other domains. Validation of some kinds of data is less problematic when extracted from inside a target's network. This is a significant advantage over collection from a human source, where information may be suspect and require multiple sources of validation. This, of course, depends of the type of data that are collected. Design blueprints taken from inside a target network would have a high degree of validity, whereas emails and memos represent a record of what was said, and may not be the truth or the most accurate version of the truth.

Cyberspace can serve to exaggerate biases, and reliance on familiar tools can also produce a distorted picture. For example, the contribution of social media to the spread of protests and uprisings (e.g. in Iran or Egypt) is regularly overestimated. The increase in connectivity assists, but will never replace, the value of field reporting. This bias – in the perception of cause and effect (Heuer 1999: 127–129) can occur in any field of intelligence, and cyberspace is no exception. The digital domain also makes 'othering' very easy, by facilitating the projection of familiar culture norms and values onto strangers. This is a familiar challenge for intelligence organisations, and is not unique to cyberspace. However the digital environment strips away the social and cultural nuances that are gained from personal interaction.[6] Human responses to digital stimuli are far less evolved than in the physical world. Trust mechanisms that have developed over millennia, and in many cases are contextually and societally specific, have few parallels in the digital domain (Schneier 2012).

The intelligence community is grappling with these challenges. In addition to cultural nuance, there is also the task of manipulating immense data sets, also known as 'big data' (Manyika, Chui *et al.* 2011). The analysis phase – reducing ambiguity and making sense of data by examining it in the light of multiple variables – is increasingly considered to be equally as valuable as the collection phase (Quan 2012).

> In the messy environment of the twenty-first century, the analyst's value took a quantum leap. Regardless of the resources committed to collection, and regardless of the instruments and assets available, the volume of data that must be collected in an era of globalization guarantees gaps in that collection. Only analysts' judgements can bridge those gaps. In order to arrive at sound judgements as expeditiously as possible, moreover, analysts require technologies that can facilitate the search for and organization of data, identify commonalities and conflicts, and produce parallel benefits that conserve for analysts the time to think.
>
> *(Immerman 2011: 166)*

This places emphasis on talent acquisition and retention, both of which are growing problems for intelligence organisations, who must compete on the open market for this scarce resource (Jowitt 2011).

Technological challenges

Technological advances present new challenges as well as opportunities for intelligence organisations. However, there is arguably less ambiguity here, as the problem space is historically familiar and relatively well understood. Relative to other government departments, intelligence organisations tend to be early adopters of new technologies. On the supply/demand curve of collection, the supply side is continually opening up thanks to new sources of data and methods of collection. These opportunities themselves present new challenges, given the torrent of data that can now be aggregated. The possibilities are beyond the wildest dreams of pre-cyberspace intelligence organisations, and the current and potential future gains are lucrative enough to justify significant investment in people, processes and technology.

Counterintelligence and network defence are constant challenges for intelligence organisations, while at the same time they attempt to infiltrate the networks of other governments. Designing and configuring secure networks is highly labour-intensive, with a change in one area often requiring a series of associated changes across the network (Metz 2012). To defend against vulnerabilities introduced by the human element, robust access and identity management is widespread in both the public and private sectors (e.g. secure government facilities, or biological or chemical research labs). Although these systems are costly and require calibration and regular oversight, the WikiLeaks disclosures demonstrate the costs of improper access management.

Identity

Analysts are not the only ones dealing with the implications of cyberspace. Technology diffusion and increased networking has opened new possibilities for many aspects of intelligence, yet at the same time it has raised barriers in other areas. One notable challenge is the spread of sophisticated, often biometric, controls at border crossings. It has become much harder to create multiple identities for intelligence personnel who travel regularly to the same country. This difficulty will only increase as biometric controls, including iris scans, become more widely used around the world (Stein 2012). This will be compounded by advances in facial recognition technology, which will impact intelligence officers and undercover police (Barwick 2011), as well as political dissidents or anyone who wishes to remain anonymous.

Diffusion of advanced technology has made aspects of 'traditional' HUMINT tradecraft more difficult, and the issue of identity has clear implications in many areas. It is harder to create believable 'digital debris' in cyberspace, to assist in the creation of a cover or other aspects of a false or augmented identity. While it is true that the digital world is rife with misinformation, an identity with a shallow or non-existent online footprint is doomed to failure. Although search engines can be seeded with false information, the daily activities of an average internet user leave a trail that is difficult to forge. On the other hand, however, cyberspace makes it easier to communicate back home or exfiltrate electronic data. And many tried and true methods of tradecraft retain their utility. Physical secret writing is less likely to be discovered, as young analysts focus on the digital domain and consign microdots to the history books.

While governments retain the edge in physical and virtual surveillance, it is becoming more difficult to conduct operations undetected. This was brazenly demonstrated in 2010 when Israeli agents assassinated a Hamas military leader in Dubai. Although the Israeli team exited the country without being captured, both they and their overseas handlers left extensive and inevitable digital footprints, which Dubai authorities meticulously reconstructed using closed-circuit TV and technically advanced law enforcement capabilities (Baer 2010). The result was swift and embarrassing exposure of Israeli involvement, and a lesson in the power of modern surveillance and digital forensics.

The future: golden age or going dark?

It has been noted that 'in terms of stealing other people's secrets, technology is making this the golden age of signals intelligence' (Ulizio 2012). This seems consistent with the historical changes of the past 20 years, where possibilities for collection are unprecedented as online data and communications grow exponentially. Another perspective, often voiced in the US, is that their intelligence organisations are 'going dark' and losing access as their technological advantage deteriorates relative to other states or non-state actors. They argue that new capabilities and surveillance powers are needed to counteract this degradation (Swire and Ahmad 2011).

One example is encryption, which, under the Clinton administration, was permitted to be exported more freely (Gross 2012). Implemented properly, encryption provides increased security for online communication and financial transactions. Yet code-breaking and surveillance, for national security and law enforcement purposes, have become more difficult in environments where encryption is prevalent. The current government trend of mandating telecoms companies to provide back-door network access for interception purposes looks set to continue, even though these intentional vulnerabilities are open to abuse by anyone with sufficient knowledge of the system (Prevelakis and Spinellis 2007; McCullagh 2012).

The direction one leans in this debate depends largely on perspective. Early adopters of distributed networking have reaped the rewards, but other countries are catching up as the internet becomes truly global. US influence over the internet's physical, logical and political components is fading as a result (Markoff 2008). This is natural, and indeed it would be historically inconsistent if technological advances did not spread beyond borders, particularly in today's highly interconnected world. The amount of available data far surpasses the pre-internet era, making this the golden age of signals intelligence.

An important component of this debate revolves around society and surveillance. It is essential to engage in open debate on the balance between privacy and security, given the increasing ways individuals can be monitored as they go about their lives. Threats cannot always be avoided, no matter how good the intelligence, and an informed public is the foundation of a resilient nation.

Conclusion

Thanks to the information age, intelligence has gone from a retail to a wholesale business. Many facets of intelligence are now about handling abundance. Plummeting storage costs make it more feasible to collect every possible data point and store it for analysis. At the same time, the popular interpretation of Moore's Law (really an observation) continues to hold true, with semiconductor speeds doubling approximately every 18 months (Mack 2011: 203). This tidal wave of data and speed is forcing intelligence organisations to develop new methods of deriving signal from the noise. And this is just the beginning. Every year hundreds of millions of users and billions of devices get online for the first time. Both threats and opportunities are multiplying as the surface of cyberspace grows exponentially.

Consistent investment and R&D are mandatory for countries that wish to gain, maintain or improve their cyberintelligence capabilities. As emerging countries grow and their connectivity and technical expertise increases, the balance of power between national intelligence organisations will reflect fewer outliers (i.e. very strong or very weak intelligence capabilities). Collective cybersecurity and defence mechanisms are at an early stage, and there is scope for significant global growth. A strategic perspective is also necessary. Intelligence is best viewed as a means to an end; as an essential component of national political, social and economic objectives.

Notes

1 The author is grateful to all those who kindly provided their personal and professional insight to this chapter.
2 Defined as: (1) planning and direction, (2) collection, (3) processing, (4) analysis and production, (5) dissemination, and (6) feedback. It is cyclical in theory but rarely in practice. It is increasingly common for stages of the cycle to run in parallel, occasionally with experts co-located to facilitate information-sharing and analysis (Hulnick 2006).
3 'Puzzles can be solved; they have answers. But a mystery offers no such comfort. It poses a question that has no definitive answer because the answer is contingent; it depends on a future interaction of many factors, known and unknown. A mystery cannot be answered; it can only be framed, by identifying the critical factors and applying some sense of how they have interacted in the past and might interact in the future. A mystery is an attempt to define ambiguities . . . During the cold war, much of the job of US intelligence was puzzle-solving – seeking answers to questions that had answers, even if we didn't know them' (Treverton 2007).
4 One notable and early example of this came in 1997, when former French President Jacques Chirac openly dismissed the internet as an 'Anglo-Saxon network' (Cohen 1997).
5 'The power of OSINT to peer into closed societies, to predict major events and to offer real-time updates cannot be overstated . . . former Deputy Director of Central Intelligence William Studeman estimated in a 1992 speech . . . that more than 80 per-cent of many intelligence needs could be met through open sources' (Leetaru 2010: 20).
6 'An understanding of history and culture is key to coming to grips with the assumptions that underpin much of our analysis. And I am not talking about our history and culture, but the history and culture of the countries we work on *as the people and leaders of those countries understand them*. Every analyst – regardless of discipline or role – needs a deep appreciation of how a people see themselves, their historical ambitions, and their grievances. For analysts focused on foreign leaders, or politics, or economics, it is essential that they understand how power is acquired, the preferred way of exercising power, and the acceptable and unacceptable uses of power, as well as the defining life experiences of the key actors in the countries they specialize in' (Petersen 2011).

27

GLOBALISATION AND BORDERS

Zakia Shiraz and Richard J. Aldrich

The globalisation debate

Intelligence has grown exponentially over the last decade. America and its closest allies now spend over a $100 billion a year on intelligence. In this chapter, we suggest that the dominant explanation of this dramatic expansion – the spectre of 'new terrorism' – reflects a misapprehension. Instead it is globalisation that has driven the acceleration of intelligence and which, by equal turns, also presents stark challenges to the future of intelligence agencies. Globalisation has accelerated a wide range of sub-military transnational threats, of which the 'new terrorism' is but one example. Most importantly, the blurring of international borders has impacted intelligence agencies across the world. Economic reforms designed to stimulate international trade and investment have rendered national borders increasingly porous. Meanwhile the long-promised engines of global governance intended to manage the attendant problems remain weak. In their absence, the dark underside of a globalising world is increasingly policed by 'vigilant states' that resort to a mixture of military power and intelligence power in an attempt to address these slippery problems. Yet the intelligence services cannot meet the improbable demands for omniscience made by governments, nor can they square their new enforcer role with vocal demands by global civil society for improved ethical practice.

We are conscious that globalisation itself is a contested concept and its definition is worthy of a chapter in itself. We use 'globalisation' here to denote a process that has resulted in profound social change: not merely internationalisation or universalisation but a profound deterritorialisation in which time and space are altered making many things more proximate. We have seen an acceleration of transborder exchanges of every kind driven by the fact that communication, production and trade have decreasing geographic and temporal constraints. The Westphalian idea of things that lie definitively inside or outside a border is under constant assault. These trends are not difficult to substantiate – but perhaps hardest to measure is the underlying sense that more people have become aware of the world as a single whole. Often associated with the end of the Cold War, we would instead assert that the rise of globality has figured centrally in the lives of a large proportion of humanity since the late 1950s (Scholte 2000: 49, 87).

While globalisation constitutes a central component of current debates about the nature of security, its impact on intelligence has been neglected. At the end of the Cold War the largely peaceful wave of democratisation and the end of a number of longstanding conflicts that were driven by superpower rivalry prompted an optimistic consensus that a reduction in armed conflict would occur. The concept of humanitarian intervention became widely accepted by the international community as a means to prevent and resolve conflicts. However, the end of the Cold War also triggered a spate of civil conflicts in the Balkans, the Caucasus and Africa marking a shift in scholarly attention from superpower rivalry to new intrastate problems. Conflict moved into a lower key – civil wars, terrorism, insurgencies, ethnic conflicts, separatist movements, guerrillas and other forms of intrastate strife were accompanied by waves of illegal trafficking in people, drugs, weapons, counterfeits, timber, human organs and diamonds. Governments everywhere are now fighting a secret war against the terrorists, insurgents, proliferators and international traffickers that move in the seams between our jurisdictions.

A significant body of literature has emerged that addresses these developments. For Mary Kaldor, globalisation is conceived of as the 'intensification of global interconnectedness – political, economic, military and cultural' (Kaldor 1999: 71). This process is presented as contradictory, even paradoxical; involving integration and fragmentation, homogenisation and diversification, globalisation and localisation, and is framed as the primary cause of contemporary conflicts. The ideology of Cold War politics provided a common vocabulary on which to build transnational civil society. During this period, military cooperation increased; state armies were tied into inseparable cooperative international frameworks through military alliances, international arms production and trade, forms of military cooperation, and arms control agreements (Kaldor 1999: 5). Cold War rivals provided economic and diplomatic assistance to Third World states in the competition for control and assistance, deepening their reliance on global frameworks and ultimately leading to the erosion of the monopoly of legitimate organised violence. Now, according to Kaldor, the decline of state legitimacy is promoting rivalry among non-state actors, meanwhile the distinction between public and private authority is blurred as the state's monopoly over violence declines, spreading criminality and corruption. In short, globalisation presents an alarming duality; first, it brings about the erosion of state authority; second, it generates increased opportunities for illicit economic gain in the context of civil war.

Mark Duffield has also highlighted the dangers of a radically interconnected world. He argues that the underdevelopment of the Global South is presented as a dangerous threat to international security that foments armed conflicts, criminal activities, massive displacements and terrorism. Therefore, the permanent emergency posed by these threats demands that states play a central role in the protection and security of the Global South and has defined the moral grounds for Western interventions through the responsibly of the West to 'protect'. This in turn has prompted two decades of liberal adventurism (Duffield 2001, 2007). Paul Rogers goes further, insisting that the post-Cold War security paradigm that seeks to address contemporary security threats – crime, disease, poverty, violence and terrorism – through military force is fundamentally misguided and unsustainable (Rogers 2002: 8). The writings of both these authors offer contextual explanations as to why globalisation presents a multitude of risks, threats and uncertainties which have increasingly required a more interventionist style and which has also brought intelligence to the fore.

Collectively, this literature highlights the challenges of a 'borderless world'. However, since 9/11, the very conception of borders and the distinction between the internal and external has emerged as an important security debate in itself. States increasingly rely on the concept of the border in order to frame their reading of security (Vaughan-Williams 2009: 3). Geopolitically, borders constitute and 'render visible that otherwise hidden link between earth and law'. In a globalised world, the sources of threat and risks are increasingly intermingled with a complex conception of borders including 'forward borders' (Vaughan-Williams 2011: 284). Moreover, the growing interconnection offered by the 'crime–terrorism nexus' and the dependence on security forces by states to counter such problems has had important implications on the use of the secret services by states. The long-term transformation of the secret services is therefore best viewed through the prism of globalisation.

Globalisation and the rise of secret services

The end of the Cold War called into question the very existence of some secret services. The perceived lack of major security threats led to significant budget cuts for the intelligence services and some US Senators even spoke of the abolition the CIA. Twenty years later the CIA basked in resources beyond its wildest expectations. In 2012, the US intelligence budget was approximately three times its Cold War level, at a dizzy \$75.4 billion per annum. Similar narratives abound in other Western countries. The Dutch foreign intelligence service was actually abolished in the early 1990s and then hurriedly re-established with improved funding. The UK Security Service, known colloquially as MI5, has doubled in size since 2001. Similar trends can be observed in the Global South where intelligence agencies have grown exponentially to address domestic and international security threats. However, despite the unprecedented growth of these agencies, few intelligence service chiefs are optimistic about the future. Notwithstanding healthy budgets, the accelerated pace of globalisation since the end of the Cold War has had a deleterious impact on the realm of the work-a-day intelligence officer.

Meanwhile, the recent academic literature on intelligence remains myopic. There is an ever expanding range of literature exploring Western intelligence and security agencies through the prism of the 'War on Terror'. Much ink has been expended exploring the intelligence background to the events of 9/11, on the invasion of Afghanistan, on drones, Guantanamo and the hunt for bin Laden. Innumerable essays have been produced that seek to analyse the Iraqi WMD fiasco. The attacks in Europe, including the Madrid bombings in 2004, 7/7 bombings in London as well as the numerous plots foiled by the police and security services, have led to another wave of literature (Posner 2005; Wright 2007; Zegart 2007). However, despite the ever growing scholarly attention to the area of intelligence, little effort has been put into connecting intelligence with mainstream debates within international security or international relations. Our discussion of globalisation and intelligence represents an effort to begin that process of connection.

Life has come to resemble art. In a fascinating essay on Ian Fleming's iconic creation 'James Bond', Peter Earnest and James N. Rosenau comment on this curious phenomenon. Fleming's first spy novels were set against the background of the Cold War. But he soon lost interest in this glacial struggle, and the more infamous Bond villains – Dr No, Goldfinger and Blofeld – were essentially post-Cold War figures. They are not far from the real enemies of the last two decades – part master criminal, part arms smuggler, part terrorist, part warlord. These characters endanger the security of the whole world. Although no real-life equivalent yet boasts a private monorail, remarkably, drug cartels in Colombia have begun to use their own submarines to move cocaine to the United States. Like our modern enemies, Bond villains prefer a borderless world and thrive on secrecy. In the 2008 film *Quantum of Solace*, counterterrorism was already yesterday's business and, instead, Bond looked forward to the next decade where the enemies exploit climate change and environmental hazard (Earnest and Rosenau 2000).

It is not easy to capture the spirit of an epoch. Yet despite the anxious rhetoric of political leaders across the globe, the idea that we inhabit an era defined by 'New Terrorism' is somewhat questionable. Since the end of the Cold War it is the complex debate over the nature of the changes associated with globalisation, their texture and meaning, that has formed the dominant theme in international relations. This is reflected not only in academic discourse but also wider public understanding. The more influential popular books on international affairs over the past ten years have focused not on terrorism, but on the impact of globalisation, global economic crisis and related issues of global justice (Stiglitz 2002; Wolf 2004; Friedman 2005; Lewis, M. 2011). Moreover, the most problematic issues confronting us over the next decade are mostly associated with broader problems of 'global uncertainty', including third world debt, financial instability, climate change and pandemics, coupled with a range of networked threats involving diverse illegitimate actors (Cronin 2002; Barkawi 2006; Guelke 2006). The current economic downturn has also led to a greater emphasis on intelligence to defend economic security. However, we have seen few attempts to consider the connections between the intelligence services and the broader currents of globalisation (Gibson 2005; Aldrich 2006).

Intelligence is exposed to the impact of globalisation in at least four ways

New targets

First, and most obviously, this manifests itself in terms of difficult new targets that are mobile, diverse and elusive. Globalisation has created a borderless world in which states are bound by international regulation whereas their well-resourced illicit opponents are able to move people, funds and weapons faster than government agencies. Globalisation delivered improved levels of trade and, until recent years, fabulous new wealth. However, as Moisés Naím has argued, it is unevenly distributed and also offers a breeding ground for new criminal activity and political violence that spans continents. Naím suggests that illicit activity goes well beyond organised crime and highlights the parallel effects of money laundering, corruption, weapons proliferation and the rise of kleptocractic regimes – which he denotes as the 'Five Wars of Globalisation that we are losing'. While international crime is nothing new, he suggests that we are now seeing novel adaptive and undifferentiated structures that are highly decentralised, horizontal and fluid. They specialise in cross-border movement and are also very proficient in the use of modern technologies. In short, they are the miscreants of globalisation (Naím 2005).

New partners

A second impact is a growing dependence on intelligence partners in the Global South – perceived as the home of the new enemy. The shift towards transnational targets in far-flung corners of the world has meant that services are increasingly sharing intelligence. Whereas traditionally agencies have cooperated reluctantly with preferred partners on a bilateral basis, intelligence services have now been forced to share more widely. This also takes the form of forging precarious friendships with 'enemy' states and private agencies in an effort to keep up with their elusive opponents, as well as multilateral intelligence liaison arrangements. The increasing important of human intelligence (HUMINT), the lack of expertise in gathering this type of intelligence by American services and the growth of the importance of domestic security services in the Global South has led to an extraordinary set of relationships in which Western intelligence services have recently collaborated with the intelligence services of countries that the State Department list as sponsors of terrorism.

Covert action

A third impact of globalisation is the shift towards disruption, covert action and pre-emption. Economic globalisation is well advanced, but the engines of global governance that were supposed to help to police it have not arisen naturally and, in so far as they exist, they have proved to be notably weak. By the late 1990s, national governments had to place their intelligence and security services in the front line against a range of elusive but troublesome opponents. The new targets that secret services are confronting are more ruthless and violent than those we encountered during the Cold War. Taken together with the kinetic business of counterterrorism, the result has been that the secret services are doing less analysis and estimating, and more 'fixing', enforcing and disrupting. Western governments have moved their intelligence services away from pure intelligence towards the kind of intervention that looks more like covert action. Some of this is being franchised out to the new private military companies and freelance secret services.

The end of secrecy

Fourth, globalisation has led to a corrosion of state secrecy. In recent decades a vast network of global civil society and human rights campaigners has emerged. In their wake they have brought high expectations for ethical foreign policy, regulation, transparency and accountability. One result has been that the European intelligence and security services – including those in the UK – went through a regulatory revolution in the 1990s in which the European Convention on Human Rights was incorporated into their governance. The US practice of extraordinary rendition is an example of how 'secrets' soon became public knowledge and prompted formal enquiries in Europe and North America. Intelligence services used to operate in the shadows, but they now work under the spotlight of a globalised media that is no longer much troubled by rules of state secrecy. Increasingly, accountability now seems to flow from a globalised network of lawyers, activists and journalists, not from parliamentary oversight committees (Dover and Goodman 2009).

These developments amount to a paradox – a more active secret service and yet less secrecy – and are suggestive of an emerging crisis. Governments today make more use of spies and special forces than ever before. However, in spite of their unprecedented expansion these services do not have the capacity to deal with all the ills of globalisation that governments are asking them to address. Indeed, over the past decade, while they are surged against the 'new terrorism' there has been little capacity left for them to address other important issues. In short, it is a great time to be a drug dealer or a cybercriminal. Traditional counterintelligence has also fallen by the wayside. Western secret services are faced with a plethora of threats, however they cannot be, at one and same time, tough enough to deal effectively with their ruthless new opponents, or soft enough to satisfy human rights activists. Meanwhile governments and ministers urge extraordinary new powers, and the intelligence and security services are taking much of the blame for the erosion of civil liberties at home and human rights overseas.

The challenges of a borderless world

The internet is the leitmotif of an increasingly borderless world. The symptoms include the growing complexity and volume of deregulated financial and commercial transactions that in many cases defy government regulation or taxation. Other hallmarks of state sovereignty are suffering erosion, including the privilege of secure communications. After a complex technical and legal battle in the 1990s, states are no longer the sole custodians of high-grade encryption, which is now available to private organisations and even individuals. Open source intelligence providers now rival the state agencies, since vast amounts of detailed information is now freely available about countries, commercial entities and individuals by mining the 'deep web'. Where this is not available from open sources it is offered for sale, often from companies run by former police and intelligence officers. Open source intelligence is used by a range of private-sector and non-state actors who build business intelligence enterprises and offer expertise in global risk analysis. In short, sophisticated technical activities in the field of information, communications and intelligence are no longer the preserve of states.

The decline of communications infrastructures dominated by the sovereign state presents major challenges for intelligence services. For several centuries, intelligence and security services have made use of the channels and choke points created by the Westphalian order to pursue their business. A key example is signals intelligence, or SIGINT, which has produced information on an industrial scale since the Second World War. The telecommunications revolution of the past 20 years has undermined SIGINT agencies such as NSA and GCHQ, which were once the aristocrats of the intelligence world. Public key cryptography has been extended to private individuals, who enjoy the privilege of secret writing that for centuries was mostly the preserve of princely 'black chambers'. Although in practice only a minority of malevolent groups resort to sophisticated packages like 'Pretty Good Privacy', a degree of immunity to interception is offered to all by the sheer exponential growth in global communications. Over 300 billion emails are sent every day – that's close to three million a second. Even if the agencies could collect all this material, they would not know what to do with it. The main challenge since the 1990s has been the problem of processing new streams of data that are growing at exponential rates. Practitioners often liken this to trying to pour a glass of water with a fire hose.[1]

Meanwhile intelligence agencies are embroiled in a race against publicly available technology. The signals intelligence agencies like GCHQ and NSA have long been involved in a cryptographic arms race with their competitors in the realm of diplomatic communications. Today, technology in the hands of the public is also a problem. Scientific advances provide us with novel forms of personal intercommunication such as Skype, a voice over internet protocol system, every two or three years. During the 1970s, the ease with which the agencies could intercept telephone traffic carried by microwave and satellite, then analogue mobile phones, resulted in an intelligence bonanza. However, today telephone calls are migrating to the internet and falling out of reach. Each telecom provider will have its own protocol, effectively providing a layer of encryption that will have to be stripped away, rendering SIGINT much more labour intensive and, together with the growing volume of traffic, this poses an almost insuperable problem. Agencies can, of course, search for evidence retrospectively, or target the communications of individuals who they know are of interest, but in a world of anonymous threats, agencies wish to screen the ever larger volumes of international communications traffic. Perhaps we will see the task of technical collection devolved to the internet service providers (ISPs) in some countries.

Signals intelligence also highlights one of the most intractable problems posed by globalisation – the increased need for intelligence cooperation. Despite the public commitment of policy-makers to achieve wider intelligence cooperation, the vast majority of intelligence cooperation remains clumsily bilateral. Early examples of this problem were visible in the 1990s during the larger peacekeeping operations in the former Yugoslavia. Here a United Nations compound often contained numerous National Intelligence Cells (NICs) all living in their secure containerised accommodation, reflecting absurd local compartmentalisation driven by the fear of sharing SIGINT (Wiebes 2003). This same phenomenon has been visible in Afghanistan, a theatre of war that has been described as a veritable 'Special Forces Olympics' with elite elements from many states. However, intelligence support to these special force elements over the past five years has been lumpy due to national restrictions on the release of SIGINT and satellite imagery, which remain heavily compartmentalised.[2]

Intelligence sharing is viewed favourably among politicians and the press. It is seen as a logical way of countering transnational threats. However, the problem of sharing will not be overcome easily, even if some magical answer is found to issues of national ownership and source protection. The hard truth is that many services are simply not configured to handle the increasing amounts of data that might be pooled. As Stephen Lander, former Director General of MI5, has observed, the uncritical sharing of large volumes of material can do more harm than good: 'Some states collect haystacks and keep haystacks, some services collect haystack and keep needles, some services only collect needles.' If America's NSA shared its data with all of its domestic and overseas partners the result would simply be overload (Lander 2004).

Increasing levels of intelligence cooperation with the domestic security services in the Global South are also ethically problematic as intelligence here often takes the form of abrasive secret policing. The collaboration of the CIA with Middle Eastern state security services is a notable example of this. Indeed, the onset of the Arab Spring and the regime collapse in Egypt, a key Western ally, is of particular worry to intelligence practitioners. However, in other regions of the world, the US and UK have sought to implement security sector reform by providing considerable intelligence training and military aid. This type of convergence can be observed in the case of Colombia where, in 1990, the US sent a 14-member team to restructure the country's intelligence network. The wide range of representatives included members of the CIA, the US Southern Command, US Embassy's Military Group and the Defence Intelligence Agency. Despite the persistent condemnation of US and Colombian intelligence ties from human rights organisations and the Colombian agency's notoriety as an incompetent and corrupt institution, recent successes are undeniable and there have also been reputational improvements (Boraz 2006).

South–South intelligence cooperation is the next wave. The recent increase in intelligence sharing between Colombia and Mexico is an important expression of the regionalisation of intelligence in which the domestic services in the Global South are a new regional force. Intelligence cooperation between the two states to combat drug trafficking includes information on drug smuggling routes and targets, as well as transnational police operations. These initiatives aim to constrain the vast range of transnational activity related to drug trafficking and organised crime, such as terrorism, kidnapping, money laundering, and the trafficking of weapons and humans. Increased South–South cooperation could lay the foundation of an international standardisation of intelligence practice that would support not only sharing but also the greater deployment of intelligence as evidence in criminal trials.

Disrupting, fixing and enforcing

The role of the intelligence and security services has shifted from ideas to action. Superficially this reflects the simple fact that their opponents are now more ruthless and violent than those we encountered during the Cold War. More fundamentally it may be symptomatic of societies that find it increasingly difficult to tolerate risk, especially among the G20 countries. In retrospect, the Cold War landscape now looks rather passive – a period when intelligence was seemingly about missile-counting or else persuading ballerinas to defect. Admittedly, the distinctions can be overdrawn. Certainly some of the human agents that the West employed in the Soviet Union, Eastern Europe, China and especially North Korea came to a violent end. Covert action was also an important part of Cold War secret service. Notwithstanding this, there was distinct shift in the nature of secret service by the late 1990s towards more kinetic activity (Maddrell 2006: 142–147; Shiraz 2011).

Secret services are now confronting violent non-state actors. Describing the post-Cold War transition of SIS, the Lord Chancellor, Lord Mackey of Clashfern, observed that this was 'not purely an information-gathering service' adding, rather delicately, that it was now also 'tasked by Government to carry out other valuable services' (House of Lords 1993: 1029). Even as he spoke this, the trend towards more disruption and enforcement was being exemplified by an accelerating anti-narcotics operations in Colombia where SIS superintended a combined operation involving customs officers and special forces. In recent years large British companies have hired former UK special forces to protect their economic activities, which illustrates a wider trend in which security consultants are used extensively to assist in improving the performance of security forces in foreign countries (Pallister *et al.* 2003). Over the past decade, the United States has led a new culture of enforcement. Pugnacious slogans such as 'find, fix and finish' were adopted by senior US intelligence officials like General Michael Hayden (Hayden 2007). Intelligence is therefore no longer a support activity that focuses on estimating intentions and capabilities. It is now inherently more operational. The kind of problems presented by globalisation demand intelligence agencies to 'action' the information themselves – often quite quickly – rather than pass it to policy-makers (Johnston and Sanger 2002).

The Global War on Terror has witnessed a significant increase in action operations. Since 2004, the CIA has used broad, secret authority to join with special forces to mount attacks against militants in Syria, Pakistan and elsewhere. Reportedly, the Presidential Order relates to 20 countries with different levels of approval applying to each state – for example, operations into Pakistan require presidential approval. In 2006, a US Navy Seal team reportedly raided a compound of suspected militants in the Bajaur region of Pakistan. This was watched in real time at the CIA headquarters in Langley, since the mission was captured by the video camera of a Predator drone aircraft. The raid on Syria on 26 October 2008, by no means the first, was directed by the CIA with commandos operating in support (Schmitt and Mazzetti 2008).

Private security agencies are less troubled by the legal constraints that state intelligence services face. Increased pressures on intelligence services to fulfil a wider set of demands and operate on a timely basis have overstretched government agencies. Some clandestine work is therefore franchised out to private security agencies that are less troubled by issues of jurisdiction. State agencies that were run down in the early 1990s do not have the capacity to address counterterrorism, the wars in Iraq and Afghanistan, together with the 'old new threats' of the 1990s such as organised crime, and now the revived issues of counterespionage presented by Russia and China. The growth of private military companies (PMCs) has been widely commented on and need not be rehearsed in detail here (Merle 2006; Scahill 2007). However, the extent to which some PMCs are also to some degree private intelligence services is often overlooked. One PMC operating in Iraq – CACI, Inc. – came to public notice because it provided some of the interrogators and interpreters for the Abu Ghraib prison. Another company – called Diligence, Inc. – was founded by William Webster, who previously headed both the CIA and the FBI. Its senior executive, Mike Baker, was CIA field officer for some 14 years (Shorrock 2008).

Regulation, accountability and global civil society

Growing expectations of ethical practice present a key challenge for intelligence in an era of globalisation. Intelligence agencies grapple with a wide range of contradictory demands – more active operations, increased global cooperation, and a wider set of security threats – all set against the expectations of ethical behaviour and good governance from global civil society. The rhetoric of global humanitarianism, used freely by politicians and officials since the end of the Cold War is replete with references to improved accountability, transparency and above all a culture of regulation, which reflects an increased sensitivity to risk. This manifested itself most clearly in the rush to put European intelligence and security services onto a statutory basis in the 1990s. Despite initial misgivings on the part of intelligence officers, the result has been greater clarity and confidence regarding routine operations. Whereas in the past, intelligence and security services might act only if they felt they could do so discreetly, they now carry out operations because they feel they are working on a sound legal basis. This, in turn, has also resulted in a higher volume of operations.

However, the blurring of borders complicates the oversight of intelligence. Traditionally, all intelligence and security services have benefited from the distinction between domestic and foreign, or 'internal and external'. States were able to employ this divide to resolve some of the abiding tensions between security and liberty. This was achieved by permitting greater licence to foreign intelligence services, compared to domestic security services. For example, technical agencies have often enjoyed unfettered communication interception activities abroad, while requiring warrants for some kind for interception at home. Current technological developments mean the distinctions between domestic and international communications are eroding. Now a 'hotmail' message sent between two addresses in London may travel via the United States or China on its journey. Is this a domestic communication or an international one? Domestic agencies also play an ever increasing role in an international context and have as many representatives overseas as the CIA.

The blurring of domestic and foreign intelligence collection is well illustrated in the NSA 'warrantless intercept' controversy. NSA, the Americans signals intelligence agency, is permitted to intercept foreign communications freely but is forbidden to eavesdrop on Americans without a warrant. However, this law was designed for the era of the telegraph and the telephone rather than the internet. Moreover, the increased mobility of US citizens means that the NSA sometimes finds itself intercepting Americans abroad unwittingly when both callers are geographically outside the United States and perhaps speaking in Spanish. All these problems are underlined by a case that was before the federal judge in northern California in 2008. In a class action suit, it was alleged that AT&T Corporation was working with the NSA to implement a vast warrantless surveillance programme that collects both domestic and foreign communications, and illegally monitors the communication records of millions of Americans (Mohammed 2006). The obvious question is why the NSA has been doing this illegally when warrants are easily obtainable from the Foreign Intelligence Surveillance Court? The answer is probably a desire for 'wholesale' surveillance and data mining in a forlorn attempt to catch up with a wired world in which the distinction between domestic and foreign means little (Schneier 2005).

National assemblies and parliaments are not always in a position to provide accountability mechanisms for the intelligence services when they work globally. Growing international intelligence cooperation, the formation of precarious friendships with state security services and the growing use of private intelligence render parliamentary oversight bodies powerless since they can only inquire into activities by their own national agencies. Typically, rendition has involved partnerships between the United States and countries such as Egypt, Jordan and Syria, together with private companies. These limitations apply to routine standing committees and also special commissions. In Canada, the inquiry by Justice Dennis O'Connor into the Mahar Arar rendition case was able to call Canadian security personnel as witnesses, but failed to persuade any Americans – even the American ambassador in Ottawa – to appear before it. The obvious limitations of old-style political oversight bodies have prompted courts and judges to take a stronger interest in multinational intelligence cooperation.

Multinational intelligence cooperation has also promoted international enquiries. In 1998, when this idea was first suggested by David Bickford CB, previously a legal adviser to both MI5 and SIS, few took the idea seriously (Schneier 2005). However, since 2005 we have seen real examples of such inquiries. At the regional level there have been twin investigations into renditions and secret prisons by the Council of Europe and the European Parliament. Unusually, General Michael Hayden, then Director of CIA, responded by briefing a number of European ambassadors at a lunch hosted as the German Embassy in Washington. His remarks, which were widely reported, were effectively a CIA response to the European inquiries – perhaps a modest 'first' in the realm of transnational intelligence oversight. More unusual still is the investigation into the assassination of the Lebanese Prime Minister, allegedly by persons close to Syrian and Lebanese intelligence services, which has been undertaken by a United Nations International Independent Investigation Commission (Harris 2007).

In reality, commissions and inquiries at all levels are now démodé. In a world where information is super-abundant and secret services less secret, the main driving force for intelligence accountability comes from a global network of human rights campaigners, activists and journalists. Global governance may be weak, but global civil society has proved to be a surprisingly effective sentinel (Florini 1998). In June 2007, mundane open source material, accessed by journalists and researchers, led to courts in Munich identifying the names of CIA officers and issuing arrest warrants (Goetz, Rosenbach and Stark 2007). CIA officers involved in rendition in Italy have also been named and their home addresses publicised. Although national governments have been keen to assert public interest immunity in these matters, in a globalising world it is increasingly hard to keep a secret. The very same processes of globalisation that have degraded individual privacy are also eroding the state secrecy that hitherto protected intelligence officers from exposure.

Like privacy, secrecy is shrinking. This trend will be exacerbated by the contracting-out of intelligence activities. Traditionally, CIA officers who retire have, with very few exceptions, dutifully submitted their memoirs to Langley and go through an official clearing process for sanitisation (Moran and Willmetts 2011). However, it is unlikely that those working for Blackwater and Aegis will observe the same niceties. Admittedly, it is hard to think of these world-weary warriors as active promoters of transparency. However, the reality is that we already know far more about intelligence during the past decade than we ever thought possible. Little of this information has come to us through the formal channels of oversight, enquiry or declassification. Ironically, while Western governments now display an increasing appetite for secret work, globalisation ensures that few of these matters will remain hidden for very long. Meanwhile global intelligence cooperation on a myriad of growing areas – counterterrorism, counternarcotics, WMDs – has led to a spread of knowledge across a growing range of agencies and countries. Therefore, in the twenty-first century, one of the most likely impacts of globalisation upon intelligence will be a growing climate of 'regulation by revelation'. Whatever the future direction of the vigilant state, the intelligence services look increasingly likely to become unsecret services, and their activities are unlikely to be very far from the public gaze (Aldrich 2009b).

Notes

1 In 2005, the United States was thought to undertaking somewhere short of a billion 'intercept events' a day across the spectrum of all communications. Private information.
2 Private information.

28

WEAPONS OF MASS DESTRUCTION

James J. Wirtz

Although intelligence analysts have long identified weapons of mass destruction as an important issue for collection and analysis, the field of intelligence studies has not singled them out as a specific topic that requires a unique set of methodologies or concepts. The absence of a separate sub-field of study can probably be best explained by the fact that weapons of mass destruction forms a far-ranging issue when it comes to the practice and study of intelligence. 'Weapons of mass destruction' is a term that embodies nuclear, biological and chemical weapons and radiation dispersal devices (so-called dirty bombs) that have the potential of causing catastrophic levels of death and destruction. Intelligence analysts are most interested in discovering the size and capability of a competitor's weapons of mass destruction arsenal, the characteristics of associated delivery systems, and the nature of employment, deployment, declaratory and procurement doctrines that are linked to various weapons systems. Intelligence agencies often make the collection and analysis of intelligence related to weapons of mass destruction their highest priority, and develop sophisticated capabilities to understand the physics, biology and chemistry as well as the associated scientific, engineering, strategic and policy disciplines that contribute to the creation and employment of these weapons.

Efforts to build or acquire weapons of mass destruction clandestinely, to sidestep legal prohibitions or international norms against proliferation is another topic that is high on the agendas of intelligence managers around the world. Monitoring suspected instances of chemical and biological weapons proliferation is complicated by the fact that many dangerous substances or organisms can be created from materials, cultures and processes that have legitimate scientific, commercial or medical applications. The effort to enrich uranium or create plutonium for use in nuclear weapons has virtually no significant 'dual use' application for peaceful purposes, but commercial nuclear power generation in many instances has served as the scientific, technological and material basis for nuclear weapons programmes. Identifying and understanding the proliferation of nuclear, chemical and biological weapons and associated technologies is a complex issue involving a variety of collection efforts, analytical methodologies and an ability to overcome the best efforts of dedicated opponents who seek to hide their efforts from the prying eyes of intelligence agencies. Detecting and understanding the nature of various chemical, biological and nuclear arsenals is at the heart of today's intelligence enterprise.

Despite the wide-ranging nature of the intelligence issues related to weapons of mass destruction, it is possible to identify a key question related to 'actionable intelligence' when it comes to informing contemporary counterproliferation decisions that preoccupy students and practitioners of intelligence. Specifically, when should intelligence analysts warn policy-makers that a nation or non-state actor is about to acquire or use a weapon of mass destruction and that the time has arrived to launch a preventive war or pre-emptive strike to destroy an opponent's nascent capability or existing arsenal? This is the question that animates debate about how the United States should respond to Iran's apparent effort to acquire clandestinely a nuclear weapons capability or arsenal, and the ongoing debate about the role of intelligence in the American and British decision to launch the Second Gulf War to prevent Saddam Hussein from restarting his nuclear weapons programme (Pfiffner and Phythian 2008).

Although the terms are often used interchangeably, 'preventive war' and 'pre-emption' are different concepts. Preventive war is based on the notion that conflict is inevitable, and that it is better to fight immediately while the costs are low rather than in the future because the costs of war will increase. It is a deliberate decision to begin a war that occurs when 'preventive motivations for war' overcome policy-makers' general inclination to seek peaceful ways to avoid conflict. From an intelligence perspective, the decision to launch a preventive war is an analytical issue because it requires analysts to identify a 'window of opportunity' – the time when it is still possible to destroy an emerging capability before it becomes an operational threat. Pre-emption is nothing more than a quick draw. Upon detecting evidence that an opponent is about to attack, one beats the opponent to the punch and attacks first to blunt the impending strike. Pre-emption involves 'indications and warning intelligence' – an ability to predict an opponent's attack by understanding and detecting movement towards an attack posture. Both intelligence problems are highly demanding, although analytical judgements related to issues of preventive war are likely to be politically significant and often give at least the appearance of being highly politicised. The decision to launch a preventive war, or the decision to take bold actions that run a significant risk of hostilities in response to a suspected instance of clandestine proliferation, is the critical issue behind intelligence related to weapons of mass destruction.

The remainder of this chapter explores the intelligence challenges faced by both parties in a strategic setting that creates the possibility of preventive war. It does so by identifying the incentives that shape the way actors attempt to acquire clandestinely weapons of mass destruction, which in turn influences the incentives and opportunities of states or coalitions that are determined to prevent proliferation. It then identifies the intelligence and strategic challenges faced by both parties, which constitutes the strategic context for the issue of actionable intelligence to prevent the proliferation of weapons of mass destruction. The chapter explores these issues by first describing the incentives faced by states bent on acquiring weapons of mass destruction and the strategic and intelligence demands created by their policy, which can be characterised as a need to pass through a 'window of vulnerability'. It then describes the incentives and intelligence challenges faced by parties intent on stopping clandestine proliferation programmes, which culminate in the need to identify a 'window of opportunity' to stop clandestine weapons programmes. The chapter will then describe how the involvement of non-state actors or the effort to develop certain types of weapons create variations in the strategic incentives and patterns of behaviour that create the setting for weapons of mass destruction intelligence. The chapter concludes by describing how the strategic setting created by the effort to identify and monitor a clandestine weapons of mass destruction programme creates enduring challenges for those tasked with developing actionable intelligence related to weapons of mass destruction.

The strategic and intelligence challenges of a clandestine programme

States that seek to initiate or complete a clandestine programme to acquire weapons of mass destruction generally face militarily superior opponents that are sometimes even armed with weapons of mass destruction. Additionally, states or non-state actors contemplating clandestine weapons programmes often seek to surprise their opponents with new capabilities – announcing their intentions could lead competitors to initiate their own programmes to develop weapons of mass destruction. Opponents or the broader international community also can be expected to impose significant political and economic sanctions or material and technical embargoes in the face of suspected proliferation efforts, increasing the cost and slowing the potential progress of covert weapons programmes. All things being equal, armament programmes involving chemical, biological or nuclear weapons are best carried out quietly, especially when they are undertaken in the face of highly capable opponents who can be expected to take political or even military action to prevent acquisition of a significant arsenal. The 'window of vulnerability', created by the possibility of damaging sanctions or even more damaging military action, looms large in the minds of those considering a clandestine weapons development programme (Lebow 1984). The key issue for actors contemplating the risks and benefits of a covert weapons programme is to find a way to pass through this 'window of vulnerability' – to acquire a significant weapon of mass destruction capability before opponents can take actions to derail or destroy a nascent programme.

Initially, actors seeking to develop clandestine programmes emphasise secrecy, denial and deception to hide their activities from the prying eyes of opposing intelligence agencies. This strategy is compelling because it is often easy to hide tell-tale signatures of secret activity while weapons programmes are in their infancy. Early efforts also might be difficult to distinguish from legitimate scientific, technical or medical research. Research and development activities generally create few noticeable material or logistical demands, potential signatures that are easier to detect as programmes move towards large-scale manufacturing activities. Of course all activities create some sort of distinct signature. Soviet intelligence, for instance, estimated that the United States was developing a nuclear programme when a whole generation of nuclear experts simply ceased to publish in the usual academic journals (Holloway 1983: 18). It thus behoves actors contemplating a clandestine weapons programme to do everything in their power not to raise suspicions about their activities, which could prompt their opponents to redirect their collection and analytical efforts to detect the first hints of their nascent activity. Secrecy, based on operational security and the presence of cover stories that can provide legitimate explanations to account for suspect activity, are a sine qua non of early efforts to acquire weapons of mass destruction.

Sometimes secrecy, denial and deception are sufficient to hide the existence of clandestine programmes from outsiders. It is still unclear, for instance, if the outside world has a complete picture of the scope and nature of the massive Soviet biological weapons programme – a vast undertaking that was largely unknown to intelligence agencies during the Cold War (Alibek and Handelman 1999). Similarly, the US intelligence community also failed to detect Albania's chemical weapons programme during the Cold War (Mahnken 2005). US intelligence agencies also required the help of a high-ranking defector before they were able to recalibrate their collection and analysis efforts to identify tell-tale signs of Saddam Hussein's secret biological weapons programme (Jervis 2010). Neither is it far-fetched to suggest that, somewhere in the world today, some state or non-state actor is hard at work on a programme to acquire or create a chemical, biological, nuclear or radiological weapon, and that only a small circle of trusted agents are aware of these activities. Nevertheless, those working on a clandestine programme cannot simply assume that they can indefinitely keep their actions secret from outsiders. As activities progress from research and development to prototype testing to serial production, suspicions are likely to emerge about clandestine programmes. Signatures are likely to be created by the testing and manufacturing process, which more limited types of research or development activity do not generate. Even for non-state actors, the very effort to transform a 'device' into a 'weapon' implies the creation of associated delivery systems, doctrine, training, and command and control networks – activities that are likely to draw the attention of analysts charged with monitoring existing military units or terrorist cells (Lavoy, Sagan and Wirtz 2000). All things being equal, as a programme to develop a weapon of mass destruction moves from a conceptual stage to a full-blown militarily significant capability, it becomes increasingly difficult to hide. Those bent on the covert development of a weapon of mass destruction have to come to terms with the problem of what to do when their opponents and the broader international community finally recognise that they are working on fielding a nuclear, radiological, chemical or biological weapon.

Detection by outsiders, especially if the detection of nefarious activity becomes politically salient, is the moment of crisis faced by clandestine proliferators that is at the heart of the 'window of vulnerability'. By definition, it occurs before an emerging capability has been fully developed and deployed to operational units. Because of their effort to develop a weapon of mass destruction, leaders find themselves facing the wrath of neighbours or the international community for undertaking a clandestine programme without the fielded capability needed to deter attack or even to undertake a preventive or pre-emptive strike of their own. The urgent need to avoid preventive attack thus motivates a shift in strategy that is often adopted by those caught with a clandestine programme before weapons development is complete. In other words, if attempts to hide or 'explain away' suspicious activities are no longer successful, actors will begin to exaggerate their progress to create the impression that they already possess a politically or militarily significant weapon. They will do everything possible to create the impression in the minds of their opponents that their programme has progressed to the point in which they have already fielded and can employ a weapon of mass destruction.

Creating the impression that a programme is advanced when it is in fact still in its more preliminary phases generally involves highlighting the elements of the programme that involve the weaponisation of test devices or prototypes. In other words, it is not necessary to test, demonstrate or provide an actual weapon for inspection – it is not necessary to provide incontrovertible proof to the opponent that a weapon is not only available, but can be used by operational forces. Instead, it is only necessary to reveal that associated delivery systems, military infrastructure, doctrine, and command and control networks are already in place to give the impression that a weapon of mass destruction has been fielded with operational forces. Denial and deception does not have to confirm the basic proposition that a clandestine programme is under way. Instead, it has to suggest that a newly discovered covert programme is further advanced than available information suggests.

Denial and deception programmes that are intended to exaggerate a nascent capability generally succeed because they exploit a 'rationality' bias that often affects analysts and policy-makers when they are forced to use inconclusive or incomplete information to estimate the degree of progress enjoyed by suspect activity (Jervis 1976: 321). In the absence of definitive information, people tend to judge the actions of others by identifying how they expend resources (Jervis 1970). Thus, resources devoted to infrastructure, training, designation of special units, or unique command and control procedures are generally considered to be evidence of the existence of actual capability and not part of an elaborate deception campaign intended to exaggerate a nascent programme. Even if the exact purpose behind a denial and deception campaign remains unclear, analysts will tend to assume that the expenditure of resources to undertake such a campaign is prima facie evidence that the opponent in fact has something of importance to hide. If no definitive information is available in the presence of a concerted denial and deception campaign, observers sometimes are willing to take this lack of information as evidence of the success of denial and deception, not the fundamental absence of suspect activity. This is in fact the assumption the US intelligence community made about Iraqi weapons of mass destruction programmes in the months leading up to the Second Gulf War (Jervis 2006: 28). To conclude otherwise – to estimate that denial and deception is actually an effort to hide the absence of progress or capability – would fly in the face of what is perceived to be 'rational' behaviour on the part of the opponent.

German re-armament during the interwar period provides the quintessential example of the way a clandestine armament programme implements this pattern of denial and deception. The Germans went to great lengths to preserve as much of their war industries as possible from the prying eyes of the Inter-Allied Control Commission, which was established in September 1919 to police the disarmament provisions contained in the Treaty of Versailles. Initially, equipment for aircraft production and existing inventory was either hidden or moved out of the country, and traditional arms manufacturers (e.g. Krupp) shifted production into civilian pursuits while preserving their skilled engineering and manufacturing workforces. By the mid-1920s, German governments had exploited an easing of restrictions on military activities by creating a large paramilitary police force and undertaking various research and development efforts in the fields of armoured vehicles and advanced military aircraft. Several aviation training facilities that were publicly described as 'glider clubs' were established and Germany arranged with foreign suppliers to provide submarines and various types of aircraft for training purposes. Most famously, following a secret agreement with Moscow, Germany began to test armoured vehicles on Soviet territory in 1927 (Whaley 2002).

German rearmament increased in scope and pace throughout the early 1930s and reached a feverous pitch after Adolf Hitler became Chancellor in 1933. By 1935, German policy switched from 'shy concealment to intimidating bluff'. According to Barton Whaley:

> The essence of the new propaganda was bluff, to portray a force far stronger than it was. Accordingly, it was shown off at its best: in photo magazines that caught the world's attention; at the vast Nazi rallies at Nuremberg; by entering souped-up, prototype aircraft in international air shows (1936–39); and by giving carefully conducted tours to visiting British, French and American experts (1936–38). Military attaches and selected foreign dignitaries were invited to the first, full-scale manoeuvres (1937) that, along with tours, were specifically designed to imply more than was shown. The Condor Legion fighting in Spain (1936–39) was publicized to prove the excellence of German 'volunteers' and equipment.
>
> *(Whaley 2002: 69)*

The policy of bluff was given such a high priority, that it actually detracted from a more rational re-armament policy that focused on building a force that could be sustained if it ever was engaged in combat. 'By opting for show over substance,' according to Whaley, 'Hitler deliberately made the better choice for a strategy of bluff but the poorer one in the event of war' (Whaley 2002: 78). The German policy of concealment and bluff, however, allowed German re-armament to pass through its 'window of vulnerability', providing the Nazis with the opportunity to initiate hostilities at the moment of their choosing.

Assessing the 'window of opportunity'

States bent on detecting, derailing or destroying a clandestine weapons of mass destruction programme face a number of political and strategic issues that are tied closely to the fundamental intelligence challenge of penetrating the shifting denial and deception strategies that are used to hide clandestine chemical, biological and nuclear weapons programmes. At the heart of the challenge is the fact that the decision to launch a preventive war is an extraordinarily difficult political issue. Policy-makers will always hope that diplomacy, international safeguards, sanctions or international pressure on the part of individual states and collective actors will eventually sidetrack or halt a clandestine weapons programme. There will always be pressure to resist the judgement that war is in fact 'inevitable' and that it is better to fight a war now to prevent another actor from acquiring weapons of mass destruction, rather than later when an actor fields an actual weapon. Political judgements thus rest on estimates of trends (Gartner 1997), and whether or not time is on the side of the angels or if delay to allow peaceful initiatives to take hold will only provide an opportunity to cross the threshold of weaponisation.

Another political and strategic issue that looms large in the minds of policy-makers is perceptions of the 'regret factor'.[1] In other words, are there alternate ways to deal with the emergence of a new chemical, biological or nuclear arsenal on the strategic landscape? Policy-makers will have to estimate if deterrence can contain a newly armed state, or if newfound capabilities will embolden actors to bank on the stability–instability paradox to pave the way for local aggression or to exert unwanted influence vis-à-vis their neighbours. Concerns will also emerge about how a specific instance of weapons of mass destruction proliferation will impact the overall effectiveness of various non-proliferation regimes and how neighbouring states will respond to the presence of dangerous new capabilities on their borders or in their region. Scholars and policy-makers alike argue about whether specific challenges will weaken or strengthen non-proliferation regimes, but in reality, idiosyncratic factors make it difficult to anticipate the long-term consequences of how a breakdown in the non-proliferation regime will affect international norms against acquiring chemical, biological or nuclear weapons.

Policy-makers' confidence in the accuracy of the intelligence they receive about alleged covert programmes is another critical factor when it comes to selecting a policy to deal with a suspected proliferation threat. Because of the nature of the intelligence problem posed by a clandestine weapons of mass destruction programme, however, it might be difficult for intelligence analysts and managers to instil that confidence. When programmes remain in the research and development stage, it will be difficult if not impossible to develop definitive estimates that would break through political and strategic barriers that impede decisive political or military action. Many benign explanations will suggest themselves for suspicious activity – dual-use applications exist for many processes, materials or organisms that are associated with chemical, biological or nuclear weapons programmes. Secrecy and the provision of plausible cover stories will be enough to sow doubt about the ultimate purpose behind programmes, making it likely that policy-makers will opt for delay to see how suspect activities actually pan out.

As clandestine programmes mature and move towards weaponisation of devices and serial production of prototypes, more information about the scope and nature of covert activities is likely to become available to intelligence analysts. Analysts and policy-makers will begin to move into the so-called 'window of opportunity' – a period when an opponent's operational capability is still in the future but current trends point to activities that are directed towards fielding an operational weapon. At this juncture, analysts will be forced to make a series of important judgements based on limited or contradictory information. On the one hand, intelligence reports might still be based on incomplete or questionable information, or indicate that progress towards actual weaponisation is limited. On the other hand, the opponent's denial and deception efforts might shift towards highlighting progress in a clandestine programme. Models or prototypes of delivery systems might be displayed as production weapons. Doctrinal or propaganda pronouncements might be issued to describe policies or operational concepts related to capabilities that are still years away from reality. Real or fake infrastructure might be revealed to create the impression that a programme is far too extensive to be eliminated in a single preventive military strike. Although analysts might be able to penetrate this clutter of conflicting information and indicators, and develop an accurate estimate of the actual state of a clandestine weapons of mass destruction programme, their estimates will always incorporate qualifications based on the presence of legitimate doubts about the quality of the information used in their analysis and the presence of alternative explanations for events on the ground. In other words, it will be hard to offer a definitive judgement about whether they are entering or are about to exit their 'window of opportunity' to take military action to curtail a clandestine weapons programme. And if policy-makers wait for definitive proof of the fact that a clandestine programme has culminated in a weapon, they will miss their window of opportunity to prevent an opponent from acquiring a weapon of mass destruction – definitive proof will come in the form of a test, use in war or other compelling evidence that a weapon actually exists.

The ultimate paradox analysts face is that if they are successful ex ante in estimating that the time is ripe for acting on their estimates, they will be criticised ex post for their judgements. This is because the best time to launch preventive attacks to stop a clandestine weapons programme is before that programme reaches fruition, before an arsenal is actually fielded by an opponent. By definition, a preventive strike to stop a weapons programme before it reaches fruition must occur before an opponent deploys an operational force. Thus, even if they are successful, evidence uncovered after the attack will suggest that the preventive attack was unnecessary because the opponent lacked a complete arsenal or weapons infrastructure. Analysts also might be accused of being duped by an opponent's denial and deception schemes – the effort to give the appearance that a secret programme has produced an operational capability – that were intended to deter preventive attack. For the side seeking to stop a clandestine programme, the most critical intelligence challenges are centred on the need to identify the opponent's real intentions, and the need to estimate when time is no longer on the side of the angels and that the moment has arrived to either move decisively to end an effort to acquire a weapon of mass destruction, or learn to live with another actor that is armed with chemical, biological or nuclear weapons.

Caveats

In light of this description of the incentives, constraints and behaviours of those seeking to develop weapons of mass destruction and those seeking to block those activities, there are two caveats that could potentially alter the logic and dynamics surrounding the issue of actionable intelligence related to weapons of mass destruction. First, the likelihood of detecting clandestine programmes to develop weapons of mass destruction is related to the scope of the activity needed to produce a weapon, and the difficulty of discriminating between weapons programmes and legitimate scientific, medical or industrial endeavours. In this regard, biological weapons constitute a significant issue because it is extremely difficult to distinguish legitimate from nefarious activity because both can be conducted in virtually the same facility or laboratory. The pace of scientific discovery in the fields of chemistry and biology also is so rapid, that it is difficult to fathom the possibilities created by new techniques, organisms and compounds (Moodie 2012). Sometimes tell-tale signs of malicious activity can be detected. Use of a virulent strain of anthrax when a non-virulent strain would be appropriate, for instance, can and should raise alarm bells within regulatory regimes or the scientific community. Nevertheless, compared to programmes to develop nuclear weapons, secrecy and efforts to hide dangerous initiatives as legitimate scientific or medical research are relatively easy when it comes to the production of biological weapons. States that are developing biological weapons might never reach the point where they face an incentive to exaggerate the success of their clandestine activities.

The same logic would also apply to a secret programme to develop chemical weapons, especially if the programme was intended to develop a limited amount of dangerous material. The act of diverting small quantities of precursor chemicals to weapons production or the temporary diversion of a legitimate chemical production facility to covert activity might be difficult to detect. But as production increased to yield the large stockpiles of chemicals necessary for battlefield use, or the serial production of delivery systems or actual munitions began to unfold, the probability of detection would increase. Still, efforts to produce a small quantity of dangerous material for use in a terrorist attack might be easily hidden by good operational security.

Second, non-state actors bent on acquiring weapons of mass destruction face operational and resource constraints that will tend to limit both their interest and ability to use denial and deception to give an inflated impression of their capabilities. Because they often operate within civil societies that object to their activities and goals, non-state actors generally prefer to 'hide in plain sight' by blending into society as they work to achieve their objectives (Wirtz 2008). They frequently use denial and deception to maintain secrecy and the appearance of normalcy – secrecy thus constitutes the sine qua non for many non-state actors that are bent on malevolent activity because detection of their initiatives and intentions would lead to prompt action on the part of national authorities or the international community (Bell 2002). Moreover, because they often suffer from severe resource constraints, they may lack the capability to undertake denial and deception campaigns to create an exaggerated impression of their activities (Bell 2002). In effect, unless a non-state actor is intent on creating the perception that they possess a capability when none actually exists for purposes of intimidation, it is unlikely that they will be willing or able to exaggerate the threat they pose in an effort to deter counteraction by national authorities or the international community.

When faced with certain types of weapons proliferation or by threats posed by non-state actors, the problem confronting intelligence analysts could be limited to penetrating denial and deception intended to maintain secrecy and the appearance of normalcy. This is a difficult task because it relies on the detection of anomalies in normal patterns of behaviour that are unlikely to constitute prima facie evidence of a clandestine effort to develop weapons of mass destruction – the type of evidence that would provide a compelling political justification for an immediate and forceful response. Nevertheless, an understanding of what might indicate the possibility of nefarious activity by non-state actors or in chemical and biological research and manufacturing activities would greatly facilitate an accurate assessment of potential threats.

Conclusion

Intelligence analysts face two fundamental problems when it comes to providing actionable intelligence related to clandestine programmes to develop weapons of mass destruction. First, the incentives of those intent on undertaking a clandestine weapons development programme drive the overall nature of the intelligence problem. Initially, they will try to minimise the intensity and nature of the signals created by their nefarious activity, while attempting to ensure that any information that does become available will resemble legitimate or otherwise 'dual use' activities. Secrecy, denial, good operational security and cover stories intended to portray normalcy will be adopted to protect clandestine programmes in their early stages of research and development. As suspicions are raised that 'normal' activities are not what they appear to be, they will shift their efforts to give the appearance that operational capabilities are available to allow them to pass through the 'window of vulnerability'. In a sense, they want to prevent their adversaries from obtaining confirmation of their plans before they come to fruition by preventing them from obtaining accurate data in the first place and then convincing them that their 'window of opportunity' to act has already passed.

The denial and deception strategy adopted by clandestine proliferation programmes is effective because it interacts with the strategic and political problems faced by those intent on halting proliferation. Even if signals are obtained that point to a nascent weapons of mass destruction programme, it will be difficult for policy-makers to justify prompt military action or draconian sanctions to stop a programme that is possibly years away from producing a usable weapon. And if signals are obtained that point to a more advanced weapons programme, analysts and officials will be faced with a denial and deception campaign intent on suggesting that it is no longer militarily feasible to strike a quick blow to eliminate a weapons capability. Those bent on proliferation hope that, when it becomes increasingly possible politically to take strong action against proliferation, analysts and policy-makers might just conclude that it is no longer militarily feasible, in terms of the costs and risks involved, to take action to eliminate a weapons of mass destruction programme.

Because the decision to launch a preventive war is probably the most difficult challenge faced by policy-makers, the effort to tip that decision towards inaction is clearly an inviting target for a denial and deception campaign. Penetrating that denial and deception by providing an accurate and timely estimate of the true state and trajectory of a clandestine weapons of mass destruction programme is also one of the most important, and difficult, problems faced by intelligence analysts. Knowing the incentives of both parties in this situation, and how those incentives shape the strategic interaction among those parties, is the first step in understanding the dynamics and issues involved in developing actionable intelligence to stop a clandestine weapons programme before it becomes a fait accompli.

Note

1   I would like to thank Eric Edelman for laying out the elements that constitute the 'regret factor'.

29

ENERGY AND FOOD SECURITY

Petra Dolata

Energy and food security have become prominent concepts in the last couple of years. They highlight potential vulnerabilities in an interconnected world and point towards the intricate relationship between traditional and human security concerns. These vulnerabilities have existed before but their systematic inclusion into academic studies occurred only recently, thereby contributing to the widening of the concept of security (Buzan 1997). Because energy or food disruptions potentially constitute threats to the well-being of citizens, but also the functioning of national economies, both concepts need to be addressed from an intelligence studies perspective in order to provide useful data on the probabilities of these threats and to offer responses that go beyond ad hoc measures and contribute to improved resilience.

Traditionally, the availability of food and energy was a key factor in waging war and was included in military considerations. However, the current debate goes well beyond this immediate link. Food and energy are crucial for human survival and according to the 'freedom from want' dictum (United Nations 1948) should thus be considered a basic need that has to be secured by governments and the international community. From an economic perspective, energy is considered to be a basic resource (Strange 1988). While food may be equally essential as a staple product it does not hold the same salience in terms of macroeconomics. Partly this has to do with the fact that in Western countries food is in ample supply. This is not the case with energy. One of the reasons why energy security has become such a significant issue in international politics is its uneven distribution in the world, and the fact that important international players such as China and the United States, as well as many developed countries, lack sufficient indigenous supplies and compete for these resources. Energy is also deemed more important because it is a finite resource, which may run out soon, while food is considered an infinite resource. Another reason why more attention has been accrued to energy is its function as a fuel for a country's economy, making it 'the precondition of all commodities' (Schumacher 1977: 1–2). It is needed to generate electricity, for transport, for heating or cooling and many other activities and products in modern life. Despite efforts to use energy more efficiently, world demand will still be increasing over the next couple of years particularly because of India's and China's expanding economies (IEA 2007). In addition to, and as a consequence of, its central economic role, energy is also deemed a critical infrastructure (Yergin 2006: 70).

Climate change

To understand the increasing political currency of both terms, one needs to turn to climate change. It is through this debate that the security aspects of food and energy have been emphasised. And it is also through climate change that the two concepts are interlinked. As fossil fuels such as oil and coal were deemed to constitute less acceptable energy resources because of their high carbon intensity, the search for alternatives has become extremely important, particularly in transport, which is still heavily fuelled by petroleum products. One of the major alternatives to gasoline is biofuels. As a consequence, bioethanol from corn and sugar cane has been propagated as a viable substitute, and is produced and exported on a large scale by Brazil and the United States. However, corn and sugar cane are also foodstuffs. Putting aside a large part of annual crops for fermentation into bioethanol removes it from the food market and may thus contribute to food insecurity. In an extreme scenario this contributes to conflict. One example would be the 2007 'tortilla crisis' in Mexico. Food prices doubled within a year because there was a shortage of corn as the world's largest exporter, the United States, was using an increasing share of its crops for biofuels. Massive protests followed, potentially destabilising the Mexican government (Nash 2007: 473). This sparked an intense discussion revolving around the issue of 'food versus fuel' (Zhang *et al.* 2010).

Despite this link between energy and food the two are rarely discussed together in security studies investigations. More prominent is the linkage made between climate change on the one hand, and energy security or food security on the other. These linkages underscore an important analytical point. Because the effects of climate change are more indirect and not intentionally brought about by a clearly defined actor (Briggs 2012: 658), they are to be distinguished from intentional acts by governments, groups or individuals who target the secure supply of energy and food. Without the latter both food and energy security could simply be subsumed under the concept of environmental security (Allenby 2000). However, it is this two-fold nature that makes it difficult to conceptualise them as such. Briggs proposes to differentiate between risks and threats to denote these different challenges posed by intentional action on the one hand and non-intentional developments on the other. He argues that intelligence activity should focus on possible action by enemies disrupting food and energy supplies. At the same time the impact climate change may have on energy and food systems should also be studied (Briggs 2012).

Governments have recognised the impact of climate change on security, and various military and intelligence studies have examined its role as a facilitator of conflict (German Advisory Council on Global Change 2008; National Intelligence Council 2008; US Department of Defense 2010; Defense Science Board 2011). In April 2007, energy, security and climate change were discussed at the highest level at the United Nations Security Council (UNSC 2007). However, in the academic debate this nexus remains contested (Luft, Korin and Gupta 2011). Not only has it been criticised as a very European perspective, outlining how that linkage was not prominent in United States political discourse, but it is also seen as adversely affecting analytical clarity since it prioritises environmental risks and downplays intentional threats by enemies. Thus, the question is how does one conceptualise energy security?

Energy security studies

Before addressing the concept of energy security it is important to note that the difficulties we encounter in defining the term relate to its wide use by both academics and practitioners. It is employed to describe specific circumstances in international and domestic politics; it is used to justify certain policy responses such as large-scale energy projects, a phenomenon that has been described as the securitisation of energy; and it is applied as an analytical category to understand all the aforementioned events, decisions and processes.

There are several possible ways of studying energy security more systematically. One such way is to address the multiple approaches that different academic disciplines take. This would link the social and natural sciences, and highlight energy systems. Cherp and Jewell suggest a comprehensive, multidisciplinary approach to energy security studies that brings together the different disciplinary methods, theories and perspectives. They argue that the social sciences, particularly political scientists, have introduced a 'sovereignty' perspective concentrating on the question of 'who controls energy resources and through which mechanisms', thus focusing on external threats (Cherp and Jewell 2011: 204, 206). They admit that this energy security literature has been the most vocal and sophisticated. In contrast natural scientists and engineers use the image of robustness while economists prefer talking about resilience when discussing energy security. A holistic approach would integrate all these and would not only foster a better understanding of the complexity of energy systems but also facilitate better responses to energy security challenges (Cherp and Jewell 2011).

Another way of conceptualising energy security is to focus on its historical development. This approach allows the researcher to revisit past debates as well as previous government responses in order to understand how political actors have made sense of the concept of energy security over time and how that understanding has changed. In addition, it allows for national differentiation demonstrating different experiences and policy responses, thus helping to reconcile divergent views on the same energy challenges. Discussions around energy security do not really start before the twentieth century when the war efforts of European powers were increasingly based on petroleum, which, unlike coal, was not readily available to all. Most scholars refer to the example of the British navy switching from coal to oil on the eve of the First World War (Yergin 2006). However, it was not until after the Second World War that secure access to oil became a geopolitical issue beyond the war effort. An international oil market emerged and one of the most powerful actors in the international system, the United States, became increasingly reliant on oil imports, leading the government to institute import quotas in the late 1950s (Mead and Sorensen 1971; Zeiler 1990).

The early focus on petroleum has shaped discussions on energy security ever since and explains why much of today's debate continues to revolve around fossil fuels, particularly oil and more recently gas. Energy security has really been about oil security. Partly this is because oil is needed for transport and electricity, the two most important aspects of economic production and distribution. More generally, it is a consequence of the emergence of an international petroleum market, which gradually shifted power away from traditional consumer countries such as the United States to emerging centres of oil reserves and production elsewhere in the world, mainly in the Middle East. With the increasing nationalisation of oil companies in these regions after the founding of OPEC in 1960, the power centre with regards to international pricing of oil gradually moved to the Middle East. This did not constitute a strategic problem while there was an abundance of oil supply but, as soon as the market changed into a seller's market, consumer countries became more vulnerable. This was best symbolised by the events of 1973/74 when the Organization of Arab Petroleum Exporting Countries (OAPEC) decided to discontinue its petroleum shipments to a number of Western states that supported Israel during the Arab–Israeli War, foremost among them the United States. The resultant oil (price) crisis revealed the petroleum dependence of the United States and the strategic significance of secure supplies (Willrich 1976; Licklider 1988).

The United States reacted by incorporating energy security into its foreign policy agenda, making it an integral part of its national security narrative (Stern 2006; Yergin 2006; Taylor and van Doren 2008). This strategic understanding of oil diplomacy was reinforced by the 1980 Carter Doctrine, which saw the Soviet invasion of Afghanistan as an attempt to take control of Middle Eastern oil and expressly stated that 'an attempt by any outside force to gain control of the Persian Gulf region will be regarded as an assault on the vital interests of the United States of America, and such an assault will be repelled by any means necessary, including military force' (Carter 1980). Thus, an energy security paradigm (Yergin 2006: 69) emerged that would be valid over the next three decades. It was characterised by the realisation that the United States was dependent on petroleum supplies from unstable and insecure regions, which made the country vulnerable. To overcome these vulnerabilities the United States resorted to diversification strategies targeting both the energy mix and the regional origin, as well as strategies to improve resilience (Yergin 2006: 76). However, it is important to note that, strictly speaking, United States vulnerabilities were not as much a result of physical supplies from the Middle East as of price hikes that resulted from events in those unstable regions (Stokes 2007).

During the 1980s and early 1990s, oil prices dropped because of the discovery of new reserves and the positive effects of globalisation. After the end of the Cold War there was also hope that oil would just be another commodity (Bielecki 2002; Helm 2005). However, the energy security paradigm remained in place. The early years of the twenty-first century witnessed a revival of the debate and added another dimension to the concept of energy security. In the wake of the 9/11 attacks, the US government realised its energy infrastructure vulnerabilities, and how important it was to secure refineries, pipelines and sea lanes for tankers against terrorist attacks. Critical energy infrastructure protection (CEIP) became an important aspect of United States intelligence activities (Rudner 2008).

The energy security paradigm persisted but not all allies agreed with it. Most Western European countries – while acknowledging their dependence on the same insecure sources in the Middle East – continued to rely on commercial solutions to their vulnerabilities. Instead of aiming for less dependence they championed the management of their energy dependency. The tools for that management were economic and not political. Until recently this constituted a crucial difference between the United States and many Western European countries. This indicates a fundamental philosophical discrepancy in conceptualising energy and is an expression of distinct national approaches to the regulation of energy. It pitches strategic strategies against market-orientated approaches. This changed slightly with events in Eastern Europe between 2005 and 2009, when disputes over gas supplied through pipelines broke out between Russia and its neighbours, jeopardising deliveries to Western Europe (Baran 2007; Umbach 2010).

These events, together with the challenges of a continuously globalising energy market and high prices, put energy security back on the international agenda. In 2006 the G8 summit placed energy security centre stage, and so did President Bush in his State of the Union address when he warned that 'America is addicted to oil' (Bush 2006). NATO began to consider whether it should include energy security in its new strategic concept. In April 2007, at the request of the UK government, energy, security and climate change were discussed at the United Nations Security Council (UNSC 2007). This attests to the prominence these issues had attained.

The divergent perspectives on energy security among transatlantic partners guide us to a third way of conceptualising energy security. Differentiating between economic, political, social and strategic meanings, it is useful to engage in a more philosophical debate about the concept of energy security. While a number of European countries define energy as a commercial good, the United States classifies it as a strategic good. This has implications for the chosen strategies to deal with energy security, and the relationship between markets and politics. If energy is a market commodity then states rely on commercial measures and essentially depoliticise energy security. It is through market mechanisms and trade relations that energy supplies are secured. If energy security is seen as a strategic good then this has implications for national security, foreign policy and the intelligence community. The strategic significance of energy security is mainly propagated through a geopolitical understanding of energy addressing conflict and the specific spatial dynamics of international energy diplomacy (Le Billon 2004). It defines threats to energy security as politically motivated disruptions of energy.

The above differentiation between strategic and commercial good also affects the prioritisation of agency. It changes the group of actors researchers will focus on: national governments are central to the understanding of the strategic aspects, while energy companies are more important when looking at the commercial relationships. This market versus politics division is also reflected in the different disciplinary approaches of international relations and international political economy. The former focuses on state actors, foreign policies and energy diplomacy; the latter looks at non-state actors and dependencies. However, the conceptual differentiation between state and non-state actors is not particularly useful as it has become increasingly difficult to classify international oil companies (IOCs) and national oil companies (NOCs) along such a dichotomy. While NOCs may be closely wedded to national governments, they are also expected to make profit like IOCs. Equally complex is the classification of interests along functions in the energy system. It is true that consumer countries are worried about securing affordable and uninterrupted supplies. Opposed to that, a producer is more interested in continuity of demand and high prices, and transit countries in infrastructure and investment security. Yet, most countries are increasingly both – producer and consumer, or transit and consumer state.

In addition to its nature as a commercial or strategic good, energy can also be regarded as a public or common good. This would entail an increasing role of government and regulatory activity. More recently, the idea of energy as a common good has been introduced to the debate by energy-poor countries such as India, whose approach to energy security is based on the assumption that everyone should have equal access to energy (Srivastava and Rehman 2006). In addition, this characterisation comes into play when energy security is linked to climate change issues, and points towards the fact that energy security and climate change are both global challenges that cannot be successfully dealt with on a national level. Instead it is interpreted as a common challenge to the international community. Thus, while strategic and economic interpretations of energy security underscore national strategies, the understanding of energy as a common good both localises (energy poverty of individuals and small communities) and globalises (global governance) the issue.

What is energy security?

Despite Cherp's and Jewell's (2011) contention that the social sciences have been most vocal in discussing energy security, the concept itself remains rather under-theorised. While it has been examined within the disciplines of international political economy, international relations and security studies there is no consensus on its analytical features (Klare 2008; Sovacool 2011; Orttung and Perovic 2012). Instead there are many competing definitions. What can be said is that, until the late 1990s, much of the debate was dominated by producers.

Discussions in the West have so far focused on supply security. This is reflected by academic definitions such as the one provided by Barton *et al.* (2004), who state that energy security is 'a condition in which a nation and all, or most, of its citizens and businesses have access to sufficient energy resources at reasonable prices for the foreseeable future free from serious risk of major disruption of service' (Barton *et al.* 2004: 6). Many share this definition (CIEP 2004; Klare 2008). The International Energy Agency (IEA) also defines energy security from a supply perspective, calling for 'adequate, affordable, and reliable supplies of energy' (IEA 2007: 160). Sovacool and Brown, in their review of the academic debate, contend that energy security includes aspects of 'availability, affordability, efficiency, and environmental stewardship'

(Sovacool and Brown 2010: 77). This is also the language used by the European Union in its statements on energy security (European Commission 2001).

All these definitions aim to arrive at a systematic approach to energy security through classifications. However, there are also some who propose quantification through the development of measurable indicators. Sovacool and Brown created an index system that allowed them to compare the level of energy security among selected states (Sovacool and Brown 2010).

What is food security?

Food security is a much more easily definable term, even though it is a fairly new topic in security studies. It was traditionally examined by development studies scholars, who regarded food disruptions as endemic to the developing world. However, since around 2007 a number of studies have emerged in developed countries that specifically address food security (DEFRA 2006; European Parliament 2011; Foresight 2011). Historically, the United Nations Food and Agriculture Organization defined food security to denote access to safe and nutritious food (FAO 1996). The inclusion of nutritional security adds a qualitative dimension to the otherwise quantitative concept. Food security focuses on individuals and households, and acknowledges that failure to obtain food or increase in food prices may develop into a security risk because of potential civil unrest and mass migration (McDonald 2010). Food sovereignty denotes the ability of nation-states to provide sufficient food for their citizens. Generally food security is closely related to human security as it propagates 'access by all people to enough food to live a healthy and productive life' (Pinstrup-Andersen 2009: 5). As with energy security, it is useful to differentiate between the absence of food supplies and high prices for food. Both are a consequence of 'declining investments in agriculture, water scarcity, biofuel production, slowing rates of crop yield growth, crop failures, lower levels of grain reserves, and rising oil and fertilizer costs' (Madramootoo and Fyles 2012: 307). Paradoxically, per capita global food production is currently sufficient to nourish the world's population, however approximately 925 million people were not food secure in 2010 (Ingram 2011: 417–418). As Boutros Boutros-Ghali explained at a conference in Washington in 1993, the problem is a political one and needs a political solution (Shaw 2007). Most studies agree that such a solution would need to focus on food production since an increase in production is seen as the best response to food insecurity. In contrast, the FAO definition focuses on the human security aspect.

Conflict, energy and food security

In determining the power of states in the international system, natural resources – energy and food – have played an important role. Realists deem them as constitutive of a country's material capabilities. On the other hand, energy is important for the smooth running of the global economy, which is conducive to a stable international system. Hence, supply disruptions become a major challenge to international stability. It potentially changes the distribution of power in the international system and affects questions of security, development and conflict.

Some of this debate intersects with the question of whether energy sources are finite and whether we have reached and passed the peak point of supplies (Heinberg 2006). This peak oil debate has been extremely powerful in drawing media and public attention to the issue of energy dependence. However, some of this debate is flawed. It is based on the assumption that we know scientifically what the total deposits are. But, as new finds and unconventional resources highlight, numbers can change quickly. While there is agreement that these finite resources will diminish over time, there is no agreement as to how quickly this will happen.

A number of authors have examined the link between energy and conflict (Klare 2001; Le Billon 2004; Le Billon and El Khatib 2004; Peters 2004; Pascual and Zambetakis 2008). Linkages exist in three major ways. First, in a world that relies on fossil fuels that are unevenly distributed, energy can be used as a foreign policy weapon. States may threaten to disrupt supplies in order to facilitate a political outcome favourable to them. The AOPEC tried to do so in 1973 while, more recently, Russia has been criticised for resorting to pipeline shutdowns. The potential closing down of vital shipping lanes may also count as an energy-related weapon. A good illustration would be Iran's threat to close down the Strait of Hormuz, through which most of the Gulf oil and liquefied natural gas (LNG) from Qatar is shipped to customers in Asia, Europe and America. In addition, attacks on vital transport infrastructure – pipelines or shipping lanes – may also be employed as tactics by non-state actors such as terrorist and pirate groups.

Second, having power over world energy supplies may become so important that countries aspiring to be great powers may do anything possible to attain control of energy, including going to war (Le Billon 2004; Klare 2008). Klare even sees a new international energy order emerging, in which power is defined through ownership of oil and gas (Klare 2008). Predicting a scramble for remaining resources is predicated on the peak oil theory, which warns of depleting reserves and highlights the rivalry between old (United States, Europe) and new (China, India) consumers. Some authors argue that US policy in the Middle East is driven mainly by such a 'blood for oil' agenda, particularly with reference to the 1991 Gulf War and 2003 invasion of Iraq (Klare 2001; Pelletière 2004; Noël 2006–07; Stokes 2007). Others mention Russia's energy relations with Central Asia and Chinese energy diplomacy in Africa as good examples (Hall and Grant 2009). China is pursuing relationships with African oil-producing countries without respecting human rights issues, and even supplying these countries with weapons and other military equipment (Tessman and Wolfe 2011). Yet, the academic verdict on China's role is still pending. Some argue that China as a latecomer to the oil game has no other choice than to deal with countries that have been shunned so far, for example Angola (Dorraj and Currier 2011).

These conflicts born out of energy resource competition have been described as old wars (Kaldor 1999). Since the end of the Cold War the world has seen a number of internal or transnational conflicts that were either fought over oil and gas or with the help of energy revenue. Thus, internal destabilisation provides a third dimension to the energy and conflict nexus. This includes more theoretical debates on the link between resources and governance, but also colonial legacies. Friedman coined the term 'petro states' to denote an inverse causal relationship between fossil fuel wealth and internal political freedom (Friedman 2006). Countries like Russia, Iran, Venezuela, Nigeria and Sudan are often referred to as good examples. Others see a clear connection between resource wealth, corruption and civil war, discussing such phenomena as the 'resource curse' and 'rentier states' (Berdal and Malone 2000; Watts 2004; Collier and Hoeffler 2005).

Conclusion

Energy and food security may not be central issues in intelligence studies, but they pose complex challenges to both national and human security in the twenty-first century. The biggest global energy challenge will be the decarbonisation of the global energy system (Nuttal and Manz 2008), as well as universal access to both energy and food. Either as risk or threat they need to be fully understood in order to provide responses and solutions. These responses need to find a working balance between free market agendas and national security strategies (Barton *et al.* 2004: 472).

30

INTELLIGENCE SHARING

James Igoe Walsh

Introduction

This chapter explores intelligence sharing.[1] Intelligence sharing occurs when a state (commonly termed the sender) communicates intelligence it has developed with another state (the recipient). It devotes little attention to related phenomena, including operational cooperation among intelligence agencies of different countries. After defining intelligence sharing and discussing the range of forms that this practice can take, the chapter lays out the benefits that sharing states hope to secure, and the costs and risks they run when they engage in this form of cooperation. I then describe theoretical attempts to understand the conditions under which states share intelligence, focusing on explanations that emphasise mutual trust, institutions and monitoring, and hierarchy. The chapter next discusses how researchers have in practice analysed the conditions facilitating intelligence sharing, focusing particular attention on the work of historians, policy analysts and political scientists specialising in international relations. The chapter closes with a brief suggestion: while ethical issues characterise discussions of most other areas of intelligence, they have played too small a role in developing our understanding of intelligence sharing, and future work could focus fruitfully on this area.

Benefits of intelligence sharing

Intelligence sharing is a long-standing practice among states (a very valuable review is Crawford 2010). Most dyads of countries share no intelligence with one another. When states do share intelligence, sometimes one participant sends intelligence in exchange for something else, such as foreign aid, security assurances or diplomatic support. Other arrangements see the participating states all sharing intelligence with one another. Agreements also vary in how much intelligence each state shares. Some, such as the sharing between the United States and Great Britain during the Second World War under the terms of their BRUSA agreement, see states regularly sharing intelligence on a wide range of issues. Most, though, limit intelligence sharing to only some topics. Many contemporary intelligence-sharing arrangements between the United States and countries in the Middle East and South Asia, which focus on intelligence concerning terrorist groups, take this form. Another dimension of variation among intelligence sharing arrangements is the degree to which one party has control over the intelligence activities of another. The intelligence sharing between the United States and Britain during the Cold War saw little of this; instead, the two states collaborated closely but ultimately retained the authority to determine their intelligence activities. But, in other cases, powerful states such as the US take a direct and active role in the priorities and activities of intelligence services in other countries.

States value shared intelligence for the same reason that they value intelligence produced by their own services – decision-makers often face a great deal of uncertainty about international politics, and more and more accurate intelligence can reduce this uncertainty. The most important benefit from sharing intelligence is that it can provide decision-makers with new perspectives on the problems they face and the likely effects of the policies that they select.

The benefits from sharing increase when participating states specialise. Specialisation allows each to develop greater expertise in the targets, or better collection and analysis techniques than would be possible if carried out by a single country. Concrete examples would include countries that exchanged intelligence from their signals intercept stations, reconnaissance aircraft or satellites that cover different areas of the world, which employ different means of intelligence collection on the same target and then share the results with one another, or coordinate their networks of agents that provide human intelligence so that they do not overlap. Cooperating states that agree to specialise in their intelligence efforts can collectively generate more and better intelligence than would be possible if they each tried to provide adequate coverage for the same targets.

Costs and risks of intelligence sharing

Given these benefits, why might two states *not* share intelligence with each other? Theories of international negotiation identify two general barriers to cooperation in situations where mutual benefit is possible: the bargaining problem and the enforcement problem.[2]

States interested in sharing intelligence need to identify potential partners, agree on what intelligence each would collect, and what intelligence will and will not be shared, any side-payments such as military assistance or diplomatic assistance that one provides to the other, and a range of related issues. Each of these issues imposes costs on one participant and provides a benefit to another. The countries must negotiate an agreement that splits these costs and benefits in a way that is acceptable to all participants. This may not be possible for a number of reasons. First, the states must decide if the shared intelligence on offer is worthwhile. Each country would want the sharing agreement to focus more effort on its priorities for intelligence collection and analysis. Countries might also have different preferences regarding the quality control, human rights, and security standards that should be met by participants. Participants must expend effort to devise a sharing arrangement that would survive unforeseen developments, such as if the targets of the intelligence collection efforts unexpectedly changed their behaviour. Disagreements over who pays what costs to set up and maintain the sharing agreement would also probably emerge. The intelligence-sharing agreement might seek to reap the gains available from specialisation by calling for each country to shift towards concentrating on some activities while relying on their partner to supply other types of intelligence. Shifting in this direction would mean that both countries would need to pay some costs to hire or retrain personnel, and to invest in new equipment and technology, and they might differ over the extent to which such changes should be paid for by the other partner.

While the bargaining problem is an important barrier to intelligence sharing, the enforcement problem is even more important in this domain. This occurs when states promise to share intelligence, and then renege on or 'defect' from this promise. Defection may be either deliberate or involuntary, in the sense that lower-level state officials defect without such approval. A sender can defect by altering intelligence content, withholding it or exaggerating the accuracy of its sources. Senders that defect deliberately manipulate shared intelligence with the intent of influencing the recipient's subsequent actions. Alternatively, individuals within a sending government might be operating under the control of another power or group that controls the intelligence they pass to other states. Corruption or other administrative weaknesses might limit the state's ability to collect intelligence effectively in the first place. And sending states might also not share fully or honestly if some of their personnel who control relevant intelligence disagree on political or policy grounds with the decision to share it.

Recipients can also defect in ways that harm the interests of a sender. A recipient might forward shared intelligence to a third country. This constitutes reneging since intelligence-sharing agreements usually prohibit sharing with other states or actors. Such a recipient concludes that its interests are served by passing along intelligence even if this might conflict with the interests of the sender. A recipient also might inadvertently forward shared intelligence to third parties. Individuals that have access to its intelligence may be agents of a third state or other outside group, and violate their government's policy by sharing intelligence with their controllers. Sending states must carefully assess the loyalty of individuals and politically influential groups in the receiving state before sharing intelligence.

The costs of defection can be large for both senders and receivers, which is one reason why the enforcement problem looms particularly large when states consider sharing intelligence. Recipients may be deceived into providing benefits to senders that provide them with low-quality intelligence. More important, though, are the potential indirect costs of cooperating with a sender that defects. A recipient may base very important foreign policy decisions involving the use of force on flawed or misleading intelligence shared by other states. Costs for sending states can also be substantial, including sharing secrets or sources and methods with third parties. These costs increase when the participating states have developed specialised and complementary intelligence efforts. Specialisation increases the costs of defection. The most valuable sharing partners have much valuable intelligence but can do the most damage when they defect from promises to share. Defection can remove access to the partner's specialised assets and seriously weaken the ability to gather useful intelligence on a target.

Another reason the enforcement problem is a particularly powerful barrier to intelligence sharing is because it is difficult to determine if a partner has reneged or not, for at least three reasons. First, decision-makers face uncertainty when crafting foreign policy, and this is one reason they seek intelligence from other states. But this uncertainty increases their vulnerability to defection. Second, intelligence almost always includes an analytical element. The analytical component of intelligence may be more easily manipulated by a state that the raw information upon which it is based. Third, and perhaps most important, intelligence by definition includes secret information. Most intelligence producers do use both open sources of information as well as secret or clandestinely obtained information. States go to great lengths to secure secret intelligence, and to prevent their targets from discovering their sources and methods of intelligence collection and analysis. For this reason, intelligence agencies are reluctant to share all intelligence even within their own governments. This concern for security makes it very difficult for one state to determine if another has defected on a promise to share intelligence. Keeping details of intelligence collection and analysis secret is, on the one hand, recognised as a legitimate security practice but, on the other, it makes it easier for a sending state to alter or fabricate information it passes to others. The barriers to sharing created by security also pose difficulties for sending states. Sending states want to ensure that recipients secure the shared intelligence and do not pass it along to enemies, either deliberately or inadvertently. But recipients do not want to divulge their security arrangements to prevent others from illicitly gaining access to intelligence they possess. This makes it difficult for the sending government to ensure that the security procedures are effective in protecting the secrets that is shares. As I argue elsewhere (Walsh 2010):

There is thus an important difference between the exchange of intelligence and the exchange of a tangible good. Tangible goods can be inspected after purchase to ensure that they conform to the buyer's expectations. But 'buyers' of intelligence cannot easily monitor the 'seller' to determine if the intelligence it provides has been collected diligently and analyzed properly. Sellers of intelligence have difficulty ensuring that buyers treat the intelligence as securely as they would prefer.

Explaining intelligence sharing

If bargaining and enforcement problems make sharing intelligence difficult, when can these barriers be overcome? The most common explanation in the literature on intelligence sharing is mutual trust. Stéphane Lefebvre (2003: 528) writes that 'trust in, and respect for, other [countries' intelligence] agencies is foremost when the time comes to decide on the extent of intelligence sharing arrangements', and that 'confidence and trust are essential ingredients' for intelligence sharing. Chris Clough (2004: 603) concludes that 'mutual trust is the most important factor' driving sharing, and Derek Reveron (2006: 456) holds that 'engaging foreign intelligence services . . . requires high levels of trust on the part of all countries involved'.

Trust is a complex and multifaceted concept. In this context, researchers typically understand trust as the expectation on the part of one state than another state will not exploit its cooperation to secure immediate gains. Where does such trust in other states originate? This question has been investigated by multiple research traditions in political sociology (Coleman 1990; Hardin 2002), social psychology (Hovland, Janis and Kelley 1953), international relations and rational choice theory (Crawford and Sobel 1982). All identify similar interests as a key condition for the emergence of trust and the sharing of information. All of these theoretical understandings of trust conclude that parties discount the value of shared information that they cannot verify themselves when they fear that their partner's interests diverge from their own. This divergence of interests may create an incentive to deliberately communicate incorrect intelligence to convince the receiver to select the action that produces the outcome most favourable to the sender.

There is much evidence that mutual trust facilitates the reliable exchange of information. But we know, too, that high levels of trust are not a necessary condition for intelligence sharing – that is, that countries would not be able to share if they did not trust one another at a high level. Lefebvre's conclusion that trust is an 'essential ingredient' for intelligence sharing, and Clough's that it is the 'most important factor' driving sharing, suggest that trust *must* be present for sharing to occur. But as many of the actual investigations of intelligence sharing make clear, countries can share intelligence even when they do not place a great deal of trust in one another. This problem is not limited to intelligence sharing, though. As the large literature on the enforcement problem should make clear, this barrier to cooperation exists in many other domains of international politics as well. It is possible, then, to apply theoretical explanations of cooperation in the face of defection to the area of intelligence sharing.

One promising approach is liberal institutionalism. This seeks to understand the conditions under which states that do not have a great deal of trust in one another can nonetheless cooperate by deploying carefully crafted bargaining strategies aimed at reassuring partners, and by creating institutions designed to monitor for defection (key works here are Keohane 1984; Fearon 1998). Liberal institutionalism has a sophisticated and nuanced understanding of the conditions facilitating cooperation in addition to high levels of mutual trust, and has been widely applied in multiple domains of international politics. Liberal institutionalism may not apply well to intelligence sharing, though. The inherent secrecy that is common in this domain makes it difficult to implement liberal institutionalism's prescriptions. States interested in cooperating, but worried about defection by other participants, can charge an independent third party, such as an international organisation, with independently monitoring compliance. This can provide independent evaluation of compliance. But this option of independent monitoring conflicts with states' desire to secure and keep secret their intelligence activities, since it requires that intelligence agencies divulge detailed information about their actions. This is one reason that attempts at multilateral intelligence sharing through formal international organisations or ad hoc arrangements are so rare. It is much easier for states desiring to share intelligence to organise the process on a bilateral basis with only one other participant to monitor.

Another way that states can address concerns about enforcement is by ensuring that that defection harms the defecting state's reputation. Having a reputation for keeping commitments is valuable. States with a reputation for defecting from agreements may find it more difficult to persuade other countries to take a chance on cooperating with them in the future. The desire to maintain a reputation for honest dealing sometimes leads states to forgo the short-term benefits they would accrue from defection (Downs and Jones 2002), but this only influences the choice to comply or to defect if it knows that its decision will be communicated to other states. Concerns about security complicate efforts to reassure partners by undertaking publicly observable intelligence-sharing commitments that, if violated, would undermine a government's reputation. The details of most intelligence-sharing arrangements are kept secret from third parties. This makes it problematic for one partner to harm another's reputation through an accusation of defection, since doing so necessitates revealing details about the intelligence that has or was supposed to have been shared.

Elsewhere (Walsh 2010) I have suggested another way that intelligence sharing can occur under conditions distinct from those identified by a focus on trust and on institutions. Intelligence-sharing agreements between states can be constructed as a hierarchy. Hierarchy differs from anarchy in that a subordinate state voluntarily gives up some autonomy to a dominant state. The dominant state can monitor the subordinate state for defection and to punish such defection when it occurs.

This sort of hierarchical relationship can maximise the benefits from sharing intelligence when the participants specialise in one aspect of intelligence collection and analysis. As discussed above, specialisation leaves each more vulnerable to the actions or inactions of the other. Hierarchy reduces the considerable costs of defection. A hierarchical relationship has a more powerful dominant state and one or more subordinate states. The dominant state takes the role of making important decisions about the form of the intelligence-sharing partnership. Subordinates give some of their decision-making autonomy, substituting the leadership of the dominant state. In return for its effort and circumscribed autonomy, the dominant state provides the subordinate with some combination of its own shared intelligence, diplomatic support, economic assistance, and other valuable goods and services. Hierarchy provides one possible solution to the enforcement problem by allowing the dominant state to take direct and intrusive steps to ensure that the subordinate is not defecting from its promise to share intelligence securely. Hierarchy does not characterise all or even most intelligence-sharing arrangements. This is because maintenance of a hierarchy involves costs for the participants. The dominant state must provide valuable goods and services to the subordinate, which must in turn sacrifice some of its autonomy. States should agree to pay these costs only when they are outweighed by the benefits of more and more reliable intelligence sharing.

These three approaches to intelligence sharing – trust, neoliberal institutionalism and hierarchy – can each explain cooperation in intelligence sharing under the proper conditions. For example, hierarchy can allow states that do not trust one another very much to still share intelligence. Hierarchy also adds to the institutional repertoire that states can design to overcome concerns about cheating and defection. Neoliberal institutionalism explores only international institutions that are consistent with the assumption that states exist in truly anarchic relations with one another. Conversely, drawing attention to hierarchy or neoliberal institutionalism is not really necessary in cases where the states involved trust one another implicitly; here, trust alone can drive extensive sharing.

Studying intelligence sharing

Broadly speaking, there are three main approaches to studying international intelligence sharing. The first is historical. The majority of studies of intelligence matters are written by historians, who are most interested in developing a full narrative of particular cases (important histories are Richelson and Ball 1985; Alexander 1998; Cockburn and Cockburn 1991; Andrew 1994; Smith 1996; Tamnes 1991; Jakub 1998; Aldrich 2002). Historical work is very important for our understanding of the practices of intelligence sharing. Good historical work relies on primary sources of evidence, especially declassified documents. However, this emphasis can also lead to a focus on cases of intelligence sharing that may not be representative of the practice. The focus on narrative and primary sources leads historians to place much of their effort on analysing episodes of intelligence sharing for which many sources can be obtained. This is often impossible, though, because governments are typically reluctant to release much information about their intelligence-sharing practices. A second approach focuses primarily on policy concerns. This valuable stream of work often explores recent intelligence developments and provides guidance as to how to avoid the problems of the recent past. But, as with historical investigation, this can lead to analysis of a restricted range of types of cases of intelligence sharing.

Elsewhere I have suggested that the study of intelligence sharing, and of intelligence more generally, can also be fruitfully analysed using the common tools of the social sciences, including the systematic description of patterns of behaviour, the development of hypothesised causes of this behaviour, and a clearly articulated and methodical research design that allows for the rigorous collection of evidence. To the extent that this approach has merit, it has implications for the study of intelligence, and for the relevance of this work for decision-makers and for the evaluation of intelligence policies.

These approaches to studying intelligence sharing are not directly competitive, and our understanding of the practice can be enhanced by combining insights from all three. Work produced by historians or policy analysts, for example, might benefit from a more sustained interaction with the theories and empirical research practices that are commonly employed in the social sciences. The brief review above suggests at least two ways that the study of intelligence sharing could be strengthened through such an interaction. First, theories drawn from other areas of social life may illuminate questions and answers that otherwise might not arise. For example, hypotheses drawn from liberal institutionalism and from theories of contracting highlight how states can structure their relationships to better realise joint gains from cooperation. A second reason for integrating the study of intelligence sharing with the study of international relations more generally is that it is difficult to make any sort of generalisation without theory. The analysis and conclusions of those that reject serious theorising are in fact influenced by an implicit theory or theories of action. But the fact that these theories are not clearly articulated makes it more difficult to challenge their precepts.

Theory provides value, though, only if it is married with rigorous factual and empirical research. Carefully thought-out research designs allow the careful evaluation of theoretical propositions, but can have important practical consequences and improve the policy relevance of studies of intelligence. To take an example from my work on hierarchy and intelligence sharing (Walsh 2010), practitioners of intelligence regularly explain intelligence sharing as a product of mutual trust between states. Mutual trust certainly facilitates intelligence sharing. It is not, though, a necessary condition for sharing. States that do not place a high degree of trust in one another can, under the right conditions, still share intelligence. The commonly accepted idea that trust drives cooperation in this area turns out to be an important part of the story, but not the whole story. This means that the options open to decision-makers seeking to share intelligence differ from those prescribed by the conventional wisdom on the topic.

Another example is the work of Aydinli and Tuzuner (2011). They seek to develop a systematic dataset that describes interactions between the intelligence agencies of the United States and those of other countries. They do so by using advanced information retrieval and automated textual analysis tools. This approach has the great advantage of providing a systematic set of data on intelligence sharing that is not limited by the selection of cases or the time and effort a researcher can spend investigating archival documents. They use this dataset to demonstrate that intelligence sharing between democracies is no more common than it is between non-democracies. This theory draws on the large literature in international politics, which concludes that cooperation is more likely when the participating states are democracies. Their effort moves the field forward by combining innovative data collection with a theoretical grounding in mainstream international relations literature.

Evaluating intelligence sharing

One important area that has received too little attention is the normative and ethical implications of intelligence sharing. States share intelligence to make themselves more secure. But should such sharing come before all other goals? Should, for example, democratic states share intelligence with counterparts that engage in torture or other forms of human rights abuses in order to generate intelligence? This question has direct and immediate relevance for the intelligence-sharing practices of major democratic states, especially the United States. But questions such as these have received little systematic attention from students of intelligence sharing. Future efforts in this area could devote resources to better understanding not only the political and security trade-offs involved in sharing intelligence, which have been the focus of this chapter, but also the ethical trade-offs that such exchange involves.

Notes

1   There is a large literature on intelligence sharing. Important works include Richelson (1990), Aldrich (2002), Clough (2004), Ellis and Kiefer (2007), Lander (2004), Lefebvre (2003), Warner (2004), Sims (2006) and Wirtz (1993).
2   This distinction is developed in Fearon (1998) and Mattli (1999). Gruber (2000), Krasner (1991), and Oatley and Nabors (1998) are representative analyses of bargaining. There is a large literature on enforcement; three of the most important works are Keohane (1984), Oye (1985) and Stein (1990).

31

COMMUNICATION, PRIVACY AND IDENTITY

Robert Dover

> The expansion in the use of surveillance represents one of the most significant changes in the life of the nation since the end of the Second World War. Mass surveillance has the potential to erode privacy. As privacy is an essential pre-requisite to the exercise of individual freedom, its erosion weakens the constitutional foundations on which democracy and good governance have traditionally been based in this country.
>
> *(House of Lords 2009)*

It is an inalienable truth of the modern era that there has been a revolution in communications technology. Indeed, in the past 20 years the accessible forms of communication have progressed from the written letter and the landline telephone, where access to someone's personal photographs would only have been possible had they invited you round to their house, to a culture whereby nearly every member of society over the age of 14 has a mobile phone with a camera installed on it, and membership of a social networking website that allows them to share their (sometimes intimate) pictures with their friends and acquaintances and, depending on their privacy settings, the whole world.[1] Prior to the great gains made by social networking sites, it required some level of personal connection to get to know another person's most intimate details; now it just requires several clicks of a button. This particular change in society has been presented as a moment of personal empowerment, but within these new freedoms have come extreme dangers. The amount of information that can be discovered about an individual, routinely and without the cause that they are a person of concern, the profiling that can be done on that information and the exploitation of it not only by friendly intelligence agencies, but by competitor agencies too, has brought the ordinary citizen much closer to the intelligence agencies than ever before. Privacy campaigners often invoke the East German 'Stasi' as a cultural reference point for the modern era of electronic surveillance, but the unpleasant truth is of course that the Stasi could only dream of the opportunities that modern intelligence agencies (and private investigators) have with the wealth of technology and information available to them.

Social media and communications technology is only one aspect of the technological revolution in privacy, however. Since 2000, and across all Western democratic states, the affordability and technical ability to create population-wide databases has also facilitated the collection of large pools of information about individuals that also fundamentally change the relationship between the individual and the state. The international NGO, Privacy International described eight states in 2007 as being 'endemic surveillance societies': China, Malaysia, Russia, Taiwan,

Thailand, Singapore, the United Kingdom and the United States. This research was updated in 2011 with a European focus and, again, the UK did poorly, but with Sweden and Belgium being flagged for concern, too (Privacy International 2011). Of the 2007 report countries, only the UK and the US can be described as fully functioning democracies, so their inclusion in such a list should be concerning. Endemic surveillance is normally what one would expect of authoritarian states in recognition that, to sustain their rule, compulsion is required.

This chapter explores the evolving relationship between technology, identity, privacy and intelligence. It focuses on the technological changes that have driven this area, and then considers the impact this has had on the ordinary individual in society, their interactions with their peers and the impact these changes have had on the security picture. In particular, this chapter focuses in particular on how Western intelligence agencies have sought to keep up with and counter threats produced by the rapid developments to communications technology.

This is a constantly evolving area, and it is one in which the pace of technological development is moving more quickly than legislation and political developments can keep up with. Within Western democracies, the pace of change has transformed our social and political relations, and unparalleled freedoms of expression and virtual association have quickly produced a governmental backlash that is almost universally described as authoritarian in character. Within the autocracies of the Middle East and North Africa this technology has been used to fuel uprisings and revolutions: the sheer numbers of those taking part in these uprisings have swamped the highly sophisticated (and Western) technology used to try to track and counter dissident messages (Timm and York 2012). Because this area of study is so large, this chapter focuses only on the most prominent technological and political trends to emerge from it, and as such it examines instantaneous communications, the Arab Spring, the implications for identity and the implications for privacy.

Instantaneous communications

The ability to instantaneously communicate is not new. The wire telegram system, radio communications, the telephone and the fax machine were the original means by which ordinary citizens (to varying degrees) were able to communicate with one another. For the ordinary citizen, many of these tools were out of reach, and for much of the twentieth century the telephone and, latterly, the fax machine were the preserve of business and government. The importance of being able to encrypt radio messages (and of course break them) came to prominence in both world wars for the delivery of operational and tactical-level communications, but especially during the Second World War, where the British efforts to break the German 'Enigma' codes resulted in the development of the earliest forms of computer (Copeland 2012). This cryptographic arms race continued on throughout the Cold War, as both NATO and the Warsaw bloc countries sought to communicate securely while simultaneously unpicking what their adversaries were communicating to one another – all part and parcel of an adversarial relationship typified by hyper-competition (Aldrich 2010). The means of instantaneous communication grew, both in terms of their sophistication and, more importantly, in terms of their sheer numbers (studies suggest that, in 2012, across the whole globe, 79 per cent of the world's population owned a mobile telephone, with a large number of countries where mobile phones outnumber people: Brazil, for example, has an ownership rate of 135 per cent, the United Kingdom 122 per cent, the United States 104 per cent, where multiple phone ownership reflects business use in the main). In the early 2000s the exponential growth in the numbers of devices available posed the problem of how to store the amount of data that could be collected by agencies, but as storage has become wider and cheaper, the problem now is how to analyse the sheer quantity of information pouring in to government servers. This particular conundrum has given rise to many research-led initiatives: the ability to detect stress in voice calls, keyword identification, word pattern identification and voice identification are just a few examples. The aim of all of these new technologies is to sift the important pieces of data from that which can be discarded; some have typified the problems faced by agencies as aiming a fire hose at a pint glass. Jihadist terrorists, in particular, responded to the new surveillance techniques in three ways: in the first instance by using satellite phones (which were harder to monitor), by using voice over internet protocol telephony – known by the name of one of the key players in the field, Skype (which was also hard to monitor because of the particular way that the calls were dispersed across the entire network of users, i.e. there was not a single line to be intercepted), and then third by avoiding electronic communications technology altogether and relying on military cultural understandings between combatants, and word-of-mouth communications within a cell (meaning that intelligence agencies would need to have identified and penetrated the cell to successfully roll it back). The next section explores an emblematic technology that popularised instant communications: the BlackBerry phone.

BlackBerry Messenger (BBM)

BlackBerry telephones, with their micro-scale 'qwerty' keyboards and an emphasis on emailing over telephony, became ubiquitous in business circles during the first decade of the 2000s. Their popularity spread more widely and made the BlackBerry phone as much of a fashion accessory for the youth population as the iPhone had become for affluent twentysomethings. One aspect of the BlackBerry that was particularly notable was the BlackBerry Messenger (BBM) system. This was a more advanced and encrypted version of the SMS system that most non-BlackBerry users used: BBM messages could be sent only to other BlackBerry devices, and only via a PIN system. The messages are free to send and receive, are not restricted in length like SMSs, and are routed through dedicated servers. While this had obvious benefits to the business community, particularly in keeping discreet messages private, it took on a more sinister edge in the August 2011 London riots. At this time the BBM system was used by rioters to inform others about where to meet to be involved in violent action, where opportunities to loot were arising, about police movements and other tactical intelligence (Lammy 2012: 25). The policing services involved in trying to curtail the riots complained publicly about their inability to intercept BBM, while some legislators called for the BBM service to be switched off. Because of the high probability of a repeat of the riots in 2012 there had not at the time of writing been a public explanation of how the various policing and intelligence agencies tackled the problem of collective action and mobilisation via social networks and BBM. There are several possibilities, however: GCHQ was briefly touted as having been tasked to be involved in the problem of decrypting BBM and, with the BlackBerry servers being located in Slough (UK), there was ample legislation available to the enforcement agencies to compel Research in Motion (the parent company) to provide de-encryption and access to these messages in real-time (Dodd and Halliday 2011).

This is not the first time that BlackBerry devices and their encryption software have caused issues with national jurisdictions: both India and Indonesia have threatened to ban the use of BlackBerry devices if the encryption is not lifted off them so that those people of interest to their respective intelligence agencies can be appropriately monitored (Apostolou 2011). The same has been the case in Saudi Arabia and the United Arab Emirates, where difficulties of monitoring what users are doing with their BlackBerrys had resulted in some of the functionality being blocked by the authorities. This also gives us an indication of the level of interception that is considered normal by intelligence authorities over mobile communication devices.

The Arab Spring: the first social media revolution

The Arab Spring, which saw an end to the entrenched dictatorships in Egypt, Libya and Tunisia, as well significant public uprisings in Bahrain and Syria, was facilitated – to a great extent – by users of the Twitter and Facebook platforms. It was these platforms on which virtual groups formed prior to taking to the streets, that tactical and operational intelligence was shared, and video and photographic footage of security force brutality was aired to mobilise yet more of the population against the authorities. In the countries of the Arab Spring it was these democratising electronic platforms that gave relatively unimpeded access to freedom of speech for politically active youths, which provided momentum for protests against entrenched governments. In Tunisia, it was the progressive measures of 31 per cent of young adults having been to university, and 33 per cent regularly being connected to the internet (with 24 per cent being members of Facebook) that contrived to provide a catalyst for the political violence that was seen in early 2011. Of those surveyed at the height of the Arab Spring in Egypt and Tunisia, some 90 per cent said that they were using Facebook and Twitter to organise the protests and to disseminate the key messages from them. What is more is that more than 80 per cent of the protests called on Facebook ended up finding their way on to the streets, making this kind of online coordination potentially very potent indeed.

It is very difficult to make an accurate judgement about the true role of Facebook and Twitter in the Arab Spring, and in mobilising political violence in the Middle East and North Africa. What can be said, however, is that in the London riots of August 2011 there were highly audible concerns about the role that the Twitter platform was said to be playing. High-profile research by the London School of Economics and the *Guardian* newspaper into the role that social media played in the London riots suggested that the riots played more of a function in providing a news service about what had happened, rather than as a tool of mobilisation (Richards and Lewis, 7 December 2011). It is also important to note that there were a number of high-profile prosecutions as a result of messages written on social media sites. The LSE research strongly suggested, however, that mobile phones and the instant messaging option to be found there had assisted the rioters to gain a foothold in August 2011 (Ball and Brown 2011). Twitter and Facebook had received the adverse publicity in London because the messages could be read by the media and by the public. The BBM messages were obscured from public view and thus did not receive the same attention, while providing the real effect on the ground.

The difference between the Arab Spring and the London riots is also that the mobile phone signal was regularly jammed in the countries affected by the Arab Spring, which may have also contributed to the emphasis on internet-based platforms, while in London – for those on the streets and wanting to participate in anarchy – the mobile platform made more sense. Since the initial round of the Arab Spring in early 2011, the growth in Facebook membership, in particular, in these countries, has remained strong: all the Arab Spring countries have experienced growth levels in users in excess of 30 per cent in the year, part of which is likely to be because of the perceived role of Facebook in supplying political change to the region and as a continued part of the political dialogue in these countries (in Egypt, 88 per cent of those surveyed said they got the majority of their news information from social media, which was 20 per cent higher than those who consulted the independent local media, and a further 6 per cent higher (57 per cent) than those who consulted international media sources like the BBC World Service). Even within Western democracies, those under 25 are more likely to acquire their knowledge of current affairs via social media than they are through the mainstream established media. Furthermore, and of interest to Western policy-makers, the Arab Spring demonstrated the futility of trying to block access to social media sites, with more than half of those polled in Egypt and Tunisia saying that the block had inspired them to go further with their protests, to find new ways of organising and to encourage others to participate, too. So, in times of unrest the authorities are likely to be better served by leaving social media channels open, but to monitor and understand what is going on within them, and what this will mean for the political violence they are facing.

Identity

The development of an individual's identity has become more readily discoverable in the past ten years. For those in their teenage years today, unaware of how valuable close personal information and the development of identity and ideas are, the move towards almost total transparency presents as many risks as it does opportunities. One of the clearest dissections between opportunity and risk is in the ability for anyone possessing basic computing skills to become part of transnational interest groups (be these focused around the benign adoration of popular musicians at one end, or the malign support of radical anti-capitalist groups at the other). It is the absence of effort required to engage with these groups, coupled with the perception of anonymity that comes with the internet, that has made for notable cases of problematic engagement on the internet. The Norwegian mass-murderer Anders Breivik is one of the best examples there is of self-radicalisation and connection with extremist groups via the internet. In this instance it led to the murder of 77 law-abiding mainstream political activists at a summer camp. So the internet has allowed people to explore their interests and their fanaticism for all sorts of legitimate and peaceful pursuits, but it has also allowed a window into people's minds. This window provides data that can be stored and analysed, and in producing a new form of engagement between people – one that magnified the ability to remain in instantaneous contact with and exchange ideas with people from any part of the globe – the internet simultaneously created a new plain on which the social world operates, but also undermined the existing physical plains on which the social world had previously operated.

For those caught up socialising only via electronic means, research suggests they experience greater levels of isolation and a higher incidence of mental illness. For intelligence agencies this transformation resulted in a greater number of lone-wolf people of concern, of narratives (like radical Islamism) that they have struggled to control, and the development of problems that are simultaneously from abroad but nested at home. Counterbalancing this is the greater ability to see the narratives and the actors involved. The internet has presented new problems and new challenges to intelligence agencies, but it has not democratised information away from government control: organisations like WikiLeaks are the exceptions that prove the rule, and the ongoing tussle being played out in the media and in the British and Swedish courts over Julian Assange is an indication of how this remains unresolved.

For individual identity, part of the risk picture comes, for instance, in the hormonally charged development of political identity and political thoughts during adolescence. In the UK, the previous Labour government had within its senior ranks ministers who had – in their formative days – been members of the Communist Party of Great Britain or of the Campaign for Nuclear Disarmament (CND), a left-wing unilateralist group that was strongly monitored by a unit of the British Ministry of Defence and the intelligence services during the 1980s (Byrne 1988). In the 1970s and 1980s there was some monitoring done by telephone intercept, but mostly it was done on the basis of human intelligence collection. While there continued to be some suspicion about those individuals who had been members of these groups, they had been able to rise up through mainstream political movements because it was merely their membership that was publicly known, not the minutiae of their thoughts or actions during this time. That is simply not the case now; in all likelihood it would be the minutiae of the detail of these thoughts that would be available to any enforcement agency interested in it, via internet forums, social networking sites, and if serious enough then via their email and mobile phone messages, too. Much of this information would also be available to the ordinary public, able to search through public internet records. So, one danger of these developments is that, collectively, we will know too much: our previous and stable elites had some colourful past lives, but a colourful life is becoming problematic and so the further 'blanding' of our politics is likely to result.

For intelligence agencies and policing units that rely upon being able to insert individuals into groups of concern, the transparency that comes from the internet, the wide sharing of images, and the development of commercial and government-owned facial recognition software presents a threat to their ability to conduct their business. As a random, but illustrative example, of the 200 or so students to whom I have taught intelligence and security in the past two years, more than 95 per cent of them possessed a social networking account, and the vast majority of them had a publicly available picture of themselves on the internet. So, one can crudely extrapolate that only a tiny percentage of those coming through British universities will be technically able to be used as undercover operatives, and some of them will have rendered themselves completely unusable due to the sheer quantity of electronic detritus they have left online for all to see. A recent example of this risk can be seen in a news story from Belgium where intelligence officers had posted their job titles on the professional networking site LinkedIn and had, therefore, effectively outed themselves and the confidential roles they play within government (Vanhecke 2012). If we were trying to spot a future trend, it might be that the use of human intelligence will be on the wane, while open source and technical collection will necessarily improve.

Large-scale databases, be they commercially held 'loyalty card' schemes at supermarkets (which go far beyond just the food in your basket) or government information-sharing schemes (such as national health records), or pan-European and international data-sharing enterprises such as the EU's Visa Information System (VIS), the Schengen Information System (I and II) and the EU–US Passenger Name Record (PNR) system, contain sufficient information (often individually, but certainly collectively) to allow for the widespread profiling of individuals using the data stored within them. And even this realisation comes with nuance: the European Parliament rejected the PNR agreement with the United States twice on the grounds of what was likely to happen to the information held on EU citizens in the US; campaign groups continue to worry about the use to which governments put sensitive data on population-wide databases. However, the rising spectre of cybersecurity and attacks by third countries (usually thought of as being China and Russia) provide a greater level of concern: this sensitive profiling data could be used by our adversaries to gain strategic advantage over us. The Director-General of MI5, Jonathan Evans, suggested in June 2012 that cybercrime (mostly the theft of intellectual property from private companies) had caused one particular firm to lose £800 million, while the Cabinet Office estimated that losses from cybercrime amounted to £27 billion, or 1.8 per cent of British GDP (Evans, J. 2012). There is, therefore, sufficient scale and sophistication in these efforts to pose a very real threat to government databases (which have many physical entry points, or terminals) and which could give substantial advantages to competitor nations. Similarly, the analysis done to open source social media data provides home intelligence services with the ability to track and profile people and organisations of concern: but it provides competitors with the same opportunity.

The formation of individual identity is being moulded by new technologies and new ways of interacting with others. Key markers of identity are increasingly stored on mass population databases and are subject to profiling techniques and being shared transnationally. The threat from adversaries tapping in to these data sources remains very high.

Privacy

Staff and students alike are often told not to email anything they would not shout across an open room. Following the great inquiries into why the government chose to go to war in Iraq (Butler 2004; Chilcot 2012 and ongoing), into the relationship between politicians and the media (Leveson 2012), and into the behaviour of bankers based in London in allegedly fixing the inter-bank lending rate (LIBOR) (July 2012) means that we might amend this dictum to never write anything on email that you would not want published on the front of a national newspaper. Enshrined within English law is freedom of information that can give access to work-based correspondence and documents, and work-based email accounts, for example, belong to the employer rather than the employee. So, contrary to popular perception, there is no right to privacy on work-based email or telephone communication.

More significantly, however, is the shift from a political and social culture that used to privilege the right of the individual to privacy over the right of governments to breach that privacy, unless there was a significant and pressing reason to do so, to a prevailing culture where breaching privacy is the norm and a right to privacy is the exception. Part of this shift is generational. Those under 25 have had their formative years immersed in internet culture and therefore think nothing of sharing intimate details online, whereas older folk are far more conscious of their privacy and try to guard it more closely. But there is an observable shift away from the right to privacy, and this can be best observed through the ubiquity of closed-circuit television on the streets (in the UK this is particularly true in London where the local authorities run more than 8,000 cameras alone, without considering the number of privately run cameras) and facing outwards from private residences. Calculating the number of CCTV cameras in the UK is made more difficult because there is no need to register them. Studies suggest, however, that numbers run to 1.85 million – that's one camera for every 32 people, although in London it is estimated that a person moving around the city quite normally would be recorded by at least 70 cameras a day (CCTVUserGroup 2008). The development of face-recognition software has meant that individuals can be tracked automatically moving from one zone to another and, coupled with video content analysis (VCA) and voice recognition devices, both the conversation and the tenor of the conversation can be monitored and alerts signalled automatically to relevant authorities. In America, the 1967 case of Katz vs the United States (389 US 347) held that there was a right to privacy in public spaces – in this particular case, that a citizen was entitled to hold a private conversation in a public place and that it remain private, so there is a legal precedent which would suggest that some elements of CCTV activity infringes core human rights.

The right to private communications is also being subverted as part of the Western world's response to jihadist terrorism. US authorities already have the power to intercept any electronic communication that emanates outside of the US, and that crosses through US servers. In the UK the 2008 Interception Modernisation Plan, or to paraphrase Richard Aldrich (2010), the plan to collect everything and anything, was derided and shelved as the Labour government came fitfully to a close in 2010. However, this plan was reactivated by the Conservative-Liberal Democrat government in the 2010 Strategic Defence and Security Review (SDSR) and appeared in the legislative programme for 2012–13 as the Communications Capabilities Development Programme (CCDP), which aimed to capture (via private providers) every email, telephone call and instant message sent and received in the UK (Home Office 2012b). As with the Katz judgement above, the expectation in the wider population is that private communications remain just that, unless there is a compelling reason to subvert this general rule. The CCDP reverses this basic assumption.

The development of population-wide databases, such as the proposed DNA database in the UK, in addition to biometric databases, puts a large amount of sensitive and identifiable information at the click of a mouse for those working in these sectors. While a case can be made that such databases make public service delivery more efficient, they also change the relationship between state and citizen (a need has been established that details should be known by the state), and as described in the case of Passenger Name Records, above, this has further complications at the pan-European and transatlantic level.

Conclusion

The advances in communications technology in the early part of the twenty-first century have fundamentally altered the way that ordinary citizens communicate with one another and with their governments. This has demonstrably changed the character of social relations in Western societies, patterns of commerce, and the relationship between the citizen and the state. As technical collection and storage has become more accessible to a greater range of government departments, so the number of mass population databases and the like have emerged that lay bare a wealth of sensitive information to government agencies and those they engage with, in the name of service delivery or security. These agencies are not limited to intelligence and policing agencies, but also extend to include local government and tax collection authorities, for example. This is a large extension of the powers granted to agencies not engaged in security and policing work. The use to which data are put by domestic authorities has caused considerable concern to privacy campaigners (being as they include information on biometrics, images, voice records, medical records and private communications, among many classes of information) but it is the leakage of these data into the private sector (and the use they might be put to), and the number of access points where data could be illegally accessed by adversaries, that is a separate and large cause for concern. The pace of technological change and innovation has outstripped regulation, law and oversight in the past ten years. Without radical reappraisals of the law and oversight covering these technologies and practices, and without some form of public debate over the extent of surveillance by public and private sources, the disjuncture between the common perception of private communications remaining private and the reality will grow ever wider.

Note

1   For example, and according to Internet World Statistics, 49.9 per cent of North Americans are members of Facebook, compared to 28.7 per cent of all Europeans.

32

INTELLIGENCE OVERSIGHT AND ACCOUNTABILITY

Claudia Hillebrand

Introduction

In a relatively short period of time, many liberal democracies made considerable efforts to balance effective (secret) intelligence activities with democratic values and scrutiny demands. In 1975, William Sullivan, former head of the FBI's Domestic Intelligence Division, stated before the Senate Select Committee to Study Governmental Operations with Respect to Intelligence Activities (1976), the 'Church Committee', which investigated misconduct by the US Intelligence Community:

> During the ten years that I was on the US Intelligence Board . . . never once did I hear anybody, including myself, raise the question: 'Is this course of action which we have agreed upon lawful, is it legal, is it ethical or moral?' We never gave any thought to this line of reasoning, because we were just naturally pragmatists. The one thing we were concerned about was this: will this course of action work, will it get us what we want, will we reach the objective that we desire to reach?

Such ignorance of legal and moral restrictions concerning the intelligence realm has been replaced in many democratic states by an understanding that intelligence, despite its particularities, is an inherent part of the decision-making process within the executive branch of government and, as such, requires clear mandates, guidelines and regulations like other executive bodies. Moreover, intelligence, and its purpose and limitations, are now more openly discussed than ever before. A striking example is the public speech delivered in November 2011 by British Foreign Secretary William Hague on the role of secret intelligence in the realm of foreign policy. He admitted that '[t]his is an unusual topic for a Foreign Secretary to discuss in public' (Hague 2011). Yet the controversies surrounding allegations of torture by, and collaboration of the British intelligence services with their US counterparts in the context of extraordinary renditions and the wider war on terror led him to speak out in public. Hague (2011) acknowledged that '[i]ntelligence throws up some of the most difficult ethical and legal questions'.

A crucial mechanism for exploring ethical and legal questions concerning intelligence and ensuring clear guidelines and regulations is a functioning intelligence oversight system. This chapter will briefly outline the purpose and forms of intelligence oversight and accountability; it will go on to discuss some of the contemporary challenges for existing oversight bodies and it will finally consider and address some recent and ongoing reforms of oversight bodies.

The purpose of intelligence oversight

A defining feature of intelligence, according to most scholars and practitioners in the field, is the element of secrecy (Shulsky and Schmitt 2002: 171; Gill and Phythian 2006: 7). On the one hand, secret intelligence is – as the Director of SIS put it – 'important information that others wish you not to know' (Sawers 2010). On the other hand, secrecy is perceived as a necessary condition for the success of many intelligence operations and methods: 'If our operations and methods become public, they won't work' (Sawers 2010). The emphasis on secrecy and, consequently, the lack of transparency creates significant challenges from the perspective of democratic governance. The opaque nature of intelligence is in sharp contrast to basic democratic values, such as openness and participation. Moreover, the work of intelligence services often clashes with the right of individuals, for example with respect to privacy rights concerning communication surveillance or the right to life concerning lethal drone attacks conducted by the Central Intelligence Agency (CIA). Liberal democratic societies are based on the principle of the rule of law and the protection of human rights and, again, intelligence interferes with those features on a daily basis. Marvin Ott (2003) has outlined some of the major clashes between democratic ideals and intelligence practice, which are summarised in Table 32.1.

Despite these obvious contradictions, there are rarely calls to curtail the basic activities of intelligence services. Rather, the work of intelligence actors is perceived as being useful and necessary to protecting national security. This is in particular the case in times fraught with insecurities. For example, the events of 11 September 2001 and subsequent terrorist attacks in Europe have led to an upsurge of intelligence-related activities in many countries, fostered by increased intelligence budgets and numbers of personnel as well as extended mandates and powers. The fact that intelligence now plays such a crucial part in many areas of national and international politics also means that its impact is far-reaching concerning day-to-day social interactions within democratic societies (Scott and Jackson 2004: 1; Dover and Goodman 2009: 1).

Yet intelligence services and their work pose a dilemma in democratic, liberties-based societies in which executive intrusions on individual rights are legitimised only under certain, justifiable circumstances. While such societies are strongly committed to legal as well as moral limitations on state action, intelligence efforts often conflict with such values. Though this dilemma becomes particularly visible to the wider public in the context of intelligence 'scandals' and controversial operations, the work of agencies requires constant, difficult decision-making

Table 32.1 Democratic values and intelligence practice

Value	Democratic ideal	Intelligence realm
Openness and participation	Free flow of information; free media; high degree of governmental transparency	Secrecy; need-to-know; compartmentalisation of classified information
Power	Disaggregated	Centralised; concentration of authority and access to secrets
Rule of law	Root of democracy; law based on societal values	Often requires special exemptions under domestic law; regularly violates the law of other countries
Privacy	Fundamental right	Intelligence activities frequently infringe privacy; employers are polygraphed; publications need to be 'cleared'
Mutual trust	Trust among citizens; trust between citizens and government	Distrust; price of security is vigilance – engrained suspicion concerning the co-workers

Source: adapted from Ott (2003)

regarding its legal and moral limitations. To juggle the democratic demands of the public and the effectiveness of the intelligence sector's activities, oversight institutions and mechanisms were set up in order to scrutinise and 'check' intelligence services and their work. The term oversight is to be distinguished from the managerial, internal control within intelligence agencies. Rather, it 'refers to a process of superintendence of the agencies that is concerned not with day-to-day management but with ensuring that the overall policies of the agency are consistent with its legal mandate' (Gill and Phythian 2006: 151). This includes, in particular, the investigation of proper conduct, efficacy and effectiveness. Within the existing national landscapes of intelligence oversight, a range of bodies and channels can be identified through which the intelligence sector can be scrutinised, such as executive institutions, parliamentary committees, and judicial bodies. Roughly speaking, intelligence oversight comprises four main elements: executive, legal, judicial and public oversight. Non-executive forums are of particular importance from a perspective of democratic security governance to ensure that an 'outside' check of executive actions takes place (cf. Krieger 2009: 210).

Accountability is a wider concept than oversight and can be described as 'being liable to be required to give an account or explanation of actions and where appropriate, to suffer the consequences, take the blame or undertake to put matters right, if it should appear that errors have been made' (Oliver 1991: 22). Hence, an accountability forum is an institution to which actors explain and justify their actions; which ensures their responsibility; and by which the actors possibly face sanctions. Mechanisms of accountability were set up to ensure that the agencies are limited in their activities and responsible for them at the same time. Depending on the accountability holder in question, the main aim might be to ensure the intelligence work's legality, budgeting, effectiveness and efficiency, or to examine its wider policy and administration. The work of such accountability holders, exercised through a range of institutions and statutory mechanisms, contributes to the more formalised oversight system. Scrutiny by the news media or human rights organisations, for example, can lead to public accountability, for example through elections, or 'the public-at-large can hold intelligence accountable' in the sense that intelligence officials ought to question themselves whether their actions would be justifiable to the wider public (Hastedt 2010: 27; see also Hillebrand 2012). The significance of public accountability has been emphasised by Admiral Stansfield Turner, former CIA Director, who emphasised that '[t]here is one overall test of the ethics of human intelligence activities. That is whether those approving them feel they could defend their actions before the public if the actions became public' (quoted in Quinlan 2007: 124).

Intelligence oversight in practice

Intelligence oversight manifests itself in a variety of forms, depending on the geographical, political and social context. While most parliamentary oversight bodies were created as of the mid-1970s, West Germany, for example, had already set up a – rather informal – parliamentary body in 1956, although it was initially only to oversee one of the intelligence services, the *Bundesnachrichtendienst*, and lacked a legal basis. A forerunner of today's main parliamentary committee responsible for overseeing the three national intelligence services (*Parlamentarisches Kontrollgremium*) was put on a legal footing in 1978. In the US, the findings and recommendations of the Church Committee and related inquiries led to the creation of the Senate Select Committee on Intelligence (SSCI) in 1976, and the House Permanent Select Committee on Intelligence (HPSCI) was subsequently established in 1977. In the UK, even the existence of the individual intelligence services was not officially acknowledged for a long time. One important factor towards the public recognition and legal regulation of the Security Service (MI5) was the jurisdiction by the European Court of Human Rights (ECtHR). When allegations against MI5 concerning the abuse of surveillance powers to fight domestic subversion were to be taken to the ECtHR by two later Cabinet ministers, Patricia Hewitt and Harriet Harman, who were subject to heavy surveillance for their political activism, the British government decided to introduce the 1989 Security Service Act (Phythian 2007: 77). The Secret Intelligence Service (MI6) and Government Communications Headquarters (GCHQ) received a legal mandate with the 1994 Intelligence Services Act. The Act also set up the Intelligence and Security Committee (ISC), comprising parliamentarians of both the House of Commons and House of Lords, appointed by the Prime Minister.

Existing comparative academic work on intelligence oversight helps us to understand the scope and purpose of various oversight mechanisms (Born, Johnson and Leigh 2005; Born and Caparini 2007; Bruneau and Boraz 2007; Johnson 2007). As suggested earlier in this chapter, four broad categories of oversight mechanisms can be distinguished: executive, legislative, judicial and public oversight.

Executive oversight in the intelligence realm primarily refers to ministerial directions and responsibility. For example, although the British Prime Minister has overall responsibility for matters of intelligence and national security, the British MI6 is primarily responsible to the Foreign Secretary. The French General Directorate for External Security, as well as the US National Security Agency, are directed by the Ministry of Defence, respectively. One recent example of the implications of ministerial responsibility for the work of the intelligence services is the case of Britain's former Foreign Secretary Jack Straw. Together with former senior MI6 official Sir Mark Allen, Straw is currently facing legal action in the context of the alleged extraordinary rendition case concerning the Lybian Abdel Hakim Belhadj. Straw allegedly authorised Belhadj's rendition to Libya and, if this proves to be correct, would therefore be complicit in the detainee's torture abroad (Cobain 2012).[1]

Legislative oversight refers to the role of parliaments in providing mandates for the intelligence realm as well as legislation on intelligence and matters of national security. In practice, it appears that the effectiveness of legislative oversight bodies depends strongly on the investigative powers (including the right to access information and adequate resources), which the bodies hold, their political will to inquire complex and controversial issues, their independence and their ability to maintain secrets. As will be discussed below, several existing legislative oversight bodies have been criticised in recent years for their unsatisfactory performance. This is also partly due to reasons related to the wider political environment in which legislators have to carry out their work. In a recent study into the oversight performance of the Congressional intelligence oversight committees Amy Zegart (2011: 115–116) suggested, for example, that, compared to other policy areas,

> [i]ntelligence is in many respects the worst of all oversight worlds: It concerns complicated policy issues that require considerable attention to master, deals with highly charged and controversial policies that are fraught with political risk, requires toiling away in secret without the promise of public prestige, and provides almost no benefit where it counts the most, at the polls. Intelligence oversight may be a vital national security issue, but it is a political loser.

Judicial oversight is primarily exercised by national as well as, to a lesser extent and only where appropriate, the European courts, but it can also be exercised by more specialised bodies, such as tribunals, commissioners and ombudsmen. There is a general tendency for courts to hesitate to decide on matters of national security and refer to the primacy of the executive in this area, also due to the necessary handling of secret material. Yet there has been an increase in the role of the judiciary in overseeing intelligence, in particular concerning anti-terrorist legislation and activities since the 9/11 attacks (Manget 1996; Leigh 2011: 232f).

Public oversight, finally, is less formal in nature than the three categories described above. Yet, particularly in times of crisis, as in the post-9/11 era, intelligence services need to ensure the trust of the wider public and allow for meaningful public debate (Chesterman 2011: 80–81). A rather formal mechanism of public oversight refers to public inquiries and investigations, such as the work of the National Commission on Terrorist Attacks Upon the United States (2004; '9/11 Commission'), which investigated the circumstances leading to the terrorist attacks of 11 September 2011.

Challenges for intelligence oversight

Some of the more recent developments in the field of intelligence outlined in this volume pose serious challenges to existing oversight bodies. The following section will focus on two developments only, which became particularly significant in the post-9/11 era: the demands for increased cooperation at all policy levels, in particular the international one; and the increased involvement of corporate security actors.

International cooperation

Political demands in the context of the fight against terrorism at the beginning of the twenty-first century have led to intensified cooperation between security authorities across the globe. Intelligence liaison has, of course, always posed a particular challenge to existing oversight systems. Their work is based within a particular national, political framework and focuses on the performance and wrongdoing of the respective domestic intelligence actors (see also Krieger 2009: 233). As a consequence, matters of liaison have always been subject to scrutiny through oversight bodies in a haphazard manner, if at all. Yet in the post-9/11 era, 'the "black hole" presented by liaison is . . . too big to ignore' (Aldrich 2009a: 54). This has become strikingly obvious with respect to cases of so-called extraordinary rendition. Exposures and allegations concerning these controversial CIA-led practices have led to a situation in which, in countries such as the UK, 'the intelligence community is under scrutiny as never before' (Omand 2009: 238). Yet the inquiries that have so far taken place into the rendition campaign have also demonstrated serious shortcomings concerning existing oversight mechanisms (Hillebrand 2009; Wright 2011; for a discussion of related reform suggestions, see below). For scholars studying the democratic accountability of intelligence efforts, this raises an important question: do the number and nature of the inquiry bodies actually give any indication of the degree of democratic quality of the intelligence sector in question? A crucial achievement of the various inquiries so far has certainly been the 'visualisation' of some aspects of this form of intelligence cooperation, allowing for crucial insights into liaison practices and the work of intelligence services more generally (e.g. Council of Europe 2006).

Yet, the ongoing demand for further inquiries into intelligence-related matters ought to be understood as an indicator of the eroding trust of the public in the intelligence communities. So far, it seems that most European governments (allegedly) involved in one or more of the rendition cases have not found a convincing strategy to (fully) restore public trust in the intelligence sector. More notable has been the ongoing hesitation, or reluctance, by American intelligence oversight bodies to investigate the CIA's activities in these matters, however. For example, the SSCI decided to investigate the CIA's interrogation and detention practices only in 2008/09.

The Chairman of the SSCI, Sen. Dianne Feinstein, maintained on 29 November 2011, before the Senate plenum, that the preliminary findings suggest that 'coercive and abusive treatment of detainees in US custody was far more systematic and widespread' than the SSCI had thought, and that 'the abuse stemmed not from the isolated acts of a few bad apples but from fact [*sic*] that the line was blurred between what is permissible and impermissible conduct' (Congressional Record 2011). Yet the investigation strongly divided the SSCI and has been slow – and the final report remains classified.

Judicial oversight has been severely hampered by governmental efforts to provoke the state secrets privilege and therefore to shut down litigation on the grounds of national security. This continued under the Obama administration, which, for example, used the privilege in February 2009 in a case involving five former detainees who were allegedly tortured.[2] Finally, the idea of a truth commission to investigate the Bush administration's responsibility concerning renditions and torture allegations, suggested by Patrick Leahy, chairman of the Senate Judiciary Committee, was never seriously discussed and no senior US official has been hold to account in a meaningful way so far.

Overall, the reluctance of American oversight bodies to investigate the CIA's activities and the wider political context has created an accountability gap. The case of extraordinary renditions and secret detentions suggests that the existing patchwork of national oversight bodies is insufficiently willing or capable of overseeing at least some forms of intelligence cooperation. While we have also seen the increased involvement of oversight forums at the European level, most notably in the form of the Council of Europe's Parliamentary Assembly, it remains crucial that the respective national oversight bodies work properly. Intelligence cooperation is likely to remain an important part of intelligence work and therefore accountability forums have to adapt to the situation.

Privatisation

The privatisation of security has attracted much attention in recent years, but scholars have so far paid little attention to private intelligence provision both in a military as well as a civilian context (but see Dover 2007; Chesterman and Fisher 2009). Thanks to few individual studies of the intelligence aspects of the phenomenon, it is obvious that the number of contractors in the field of intelligence has been growing to a considerable extent in the post-9/11 era (Chesterman 2011: Ch. 4). Illuminating work in this context has been conducted in the framework of the *Washington Post*'s Top Secret America project, but no detailed account of contractual intelligence spending is publicly available.[3] For the US, a report of the HPSCI stated in May 2007 that even 'Intelligence Community leaders do not have an adequate understanding of the state and composition of the contractor work force, a consistent and well-articulated method of assessing contractor performance, or strategies for managing a combined staff-contractor workforce' (HPSCI 2007).

While private companies have provided goods and services for state intelligence customers for a long time – for example, concerning information technology support, it appears that they are increasingly involved in what in the American context is referred to as 'inherently governmental' activities. It is this aspect of the privatisation of intelligence that, in particular, challenges the existing mechanisms of oversight. This has become obvious with respect to revelations in the post-9/11 era. For example, contractors were involved in interrogations at the CIA's secret detention facilities, the abuse of prisoners at Abu Ghraib prison, and acts of waterboarding; and a private company provided the flights used in the context of the CIA's extraordinary rendition programme (Jones and Fay 2004; Mayer 2005, 2006; SSCI 2008). Such examples suggest that intelligence services might 'outsource' particularly controversial, illegal or unethical work in order to avoid being held to account for misconduct. As Chesterman (2009: 195ff) suggested, the use of contractors in the intelligence realm challenges appropriate oversight of the sector for at least three main reasons. First, the degree of secrecy surrounding intelligence contractors, including the above-outlined lack of basic information concerning the extent of contractors' involvement, makes the work of oversight bodies extremely difficult. Second, engaging private actors in state security matters introduces a profit motive to the sector. The intelligence 'market' is opaque, however, and difficult to scrutinise for outsiders, such as parliamentarians. Related to this, the abuse of secret information is more likely in areas where contractors are involved. Moreover, in post-9/11 America the chances of earning a higher salary led to a 'brain drain' from the state intelligence sector to the private security sector. Third, Chesterman suggests that there is a lack of political guidance concerning the determination of inherently governmental activities by intelligence services. Those functions would be allowed to be conducted only by government personnel.

The struggle for reforms

The controversies surrounding intelligence in the post-9/11 era have led to calls for improved and strengthened oversight of the intelligence services in several countries, such as the UK, Germany and the US. In the UK, there are currently two major reform suggestions under discussion concerning legislative and judicial scrutiny mechanisms, respectively. With respect to the ISC, the proposals are aimed at strengthening its independence; turning it from a committee of parliamentarians to a parliamentary committee; widening its mandate, remit and investigatory powers; and increasing its resources (HMG 2011: 40ff; ISC 2011: 81ff).

Yet while the parliamentary powers are to be fostered, the British government wants to restrict the open use of secret intelligence in courts in the future. This proposal is the result of a court case concerning British resident and former Guantánamo detainee Binyam Mohamed. The British government had eventually to disclose some secret intelligence, most notably a CIA account that British officials received from their American counterparts prior to his interrogation by an MI5 official in Pakistan in 2002. The government had argued that the disclosure of the account would harm the intelligence relationship between the UK and the US, but the judges emphasised the overwhelming public interest in this matter. As a consequence, the government considered changes concerning the capability of courts to investigate matters of intelligence. In particular, it suggested the introduction of legislation that would facilitate the use of closed material procedures (CMPs) in civil proceedings when sensitive material would be considered (HMG 2011: Ch. 2). If the Justice and Security Bill were passed, special security-vetted lawyers would consider sensitive material in private. While the government hopes that this measure would ensure that too much knowledge about its services and their work would be revealed to the public and could therefore be exploited by terrorist groups or other opponents, CMPs would also exclude the defendants from consulting the evidence used against them. Original legislative plans also concerned the introduction of secret court hearings, but they met fierce criticism on the grounds of open justice and were subsequently not taken forward.

In the US, the 9/11 Commission's report of 2004 described congressional oversight as 'dysfunctional' and proposed a number of potential changes, such as creating a joint committee on intelligence (National Commission on Terrorist Attacks Upon the United States 2004: 420). Yet, despite some structural and institutional changes, Congressional oversight has not been improved in a meaningful way since (Zegart 2011).

Moreover, the Obama administration has been surprisingly determined to pursue (alleged) whistleblowers regarding matters of intelligence, and national security more broadly. It has prosecuted an unusually high number of leak-related cases (six) so far, although with limited success, and it is to introduce new rules to facilitate the detection of in-house whistleblowers by the intelligence services.

Conclusion

This chapter has outlined the purposes as well as the main bodies and channels of intelligence oversight. It discussed some major challenges for intelligence oversight and briefly outlined a few ongoing debates about reforming oversight.

Squaring democratic demands with maintaining effective intelligence work will continue to be a societal and political challenge in the foreseeable future. Recently, the UK government has, for example, proposed a bill that would update the existing Regulation of Investigatory Powers Act (RIPA) and require internet service providers to keep a wide rage of data, such as emails, the use of social network sites and voice calls over the internet. These would then be available to the security authorities under certain circumstances. Security authorities consider this to be crucial. As MI5 Director Jonathan Evans (2012) put it: 'It would be extraordinary and self-defeating if terrorists and criminals were able to adopt new technologies in order to facilitate their activities while the law enforcement and security agencies were not permitted to keep pace with those same technological changes.' Yet only transparent and continuous political debates can deliver a meaningful societal consensus on which measures are necessary, adequate and least intrusive for ensuring national and global security without excessive interference with individuals' rights. Through their work, intelligence oversight bodies can stimulate such discussions, and contribute to them. Yet, crucially, once the legal and ethical off-limits of intelligence work are agreed, a major purpose of oversight bodies is to ensure that those limits are respected by the intelligence agencies and their political masters.

Notes

1   In a similar case, the Libyan Sami al Saadi accepted a settlement of £2.2 million from the UK government in December 2012. Al Saadi and his family were rendered from Hong Kong to Libya in 2004, where al Saadi had to face imprisonment and torture. Evidence for the UK's involvement in this rendition case was maintained in CIA correspondence found in the office of Libya's former Foreign Minister Moussa Koussa after the fall of Tripoli (Leigh 2012).

2   The Appeals Court's decision is available at http://www.ca9.uscourts.gov/datastore/opinions/2010/09/07/08–15693.pdf.

3   The Top Secret America project is available at http://projects.washingtonpost.com/top-secret-america/. One of the rare accounts of contractual intelligence spending is the revelation by Terri Everett, a staff member of the US Office of the Director of National Intelligence, in May 2007 that 70 per cent of the US intelligence budget was dedicated to contractors. The DNI later refuted the figures as anecdotal evidence. For a similar estimation see Shorrock (2008).

33

ORGANISED CRIME

Peter Gill

The National Crime Agency will be a UK wide crime-fighting agency, which will have a highly visible, national profile committed to protecting the public. It will lead the UK's fight against serious, organised and complex crime, provide a new focus on economic crime and strengthen policing at the border.

Law enforcement agencies have told us that they do not have the tools they need to tackle increasingly complex economic crimes. Investigations can take several years and cost millions of pounds, with no guarantee of success, which means victims wait far too long for reparation. Or indeed receive no payback at all.[1]

Introduction: studying intelligence and organised crime

There has always been a very large gulf between governments' rhetoric about 'wars on' or 'fighting' organised crime and the reality of what they are actually able to do about it. UK government statements on launching the legislation to bring about the National Crime Agency, like the first one above, show that the rhetoric remains intact but, in order to consider what role is or might be played by intelligence in the 'fight' or, indeed, whether such language is simply misleading, it is necessary first to examine key conceptual issues including how 'organised crime' is defined. For example, the second quote above, made within days of the first by a member of the same government, also refers to the challenge of complex economic crimes but strikes a very different tone; this is not a 'fight' but an attempt to avoid long investigations with uncertain outcomes in return for some combination of plea bargaining, compliance and reform.

Hitherto, intelligence studies have concentrated their attention on foreign and military intelligence, especially in respect of matters of war and peace and, more recently, on terrorism. One reason for this is that the majority of those studying intelligence would describe their academic interests in terms of international relations and/or history, and the increasing availability of documentary evidence in official archives provides enough material to keep generations of scholars happy. By comparison, intelligence matters regarding crime and internal security have been studied by few, with far less archival material available and less mileage to be gained with publishers who have become just as entranced with terrorism as many governments have become obsessed in the last decade. The main link between these fields – intelligence, crime and internal security – has been made by those officials and academics representing organised crime as a threat to 'national security', usually, but not always, *via* terrorism.

This representation became significant in the 1990s after the end of the Cold War during which time security debates shifted significantly. Western agencies, having lost their primary target, and facing budget reductions, needed to find new foes and, with globalisation processes accelerating, transnational criminal organisations fitted the bill perfectly. A related but less opportunistic development of the 1990s was the academic and official broadening of the notion of security away from its roots in *national* or *state* security and to a broader notion of *human* security (e.g. OECD/DAC 2004). The former was not downgraded because security institutions remained powerfully represented in governments and, anyway, there is an entirely coherent argument that reductions in poverty and improvements in health and education are dependent on some minimum level of physical security, but the shift was reflected in the important idea of security sector reform as the basis for much work in democratisation among former authoritarian states. After 9/11, official and academic security interests shifted back to more traditional concerns, albeit to a more complex mix of non-state (especially Al Qaeda) and state (Iraq, Iran, . . .) threats.

This lack of interest in organised crime from 'intelligence studies' reflects the interaction between the politics and government of crime and researchers' view thereof. In the United States – home to most students of intelligence – the imbalance between, say, studies of foreign intelligence and criminal intelligence is that the former is viewed as an entirely legitimate exercise of state power, while the latter smacks of tyranny and invasion of human rights, and is tolerated, if at all, very reluctantly. For one thing, while 'political policing' has been as endemic in US history as in, say, Europe, you would not know this from reviewing the mainstream 'intelligence studies' literature (Donner 1990). Nor does this literature provide much examination of 'organised crime' even though the concept was essentially invented in the US. However, the domain of organised crime is studied primarily by criminologists and, with some notable exceptions (e.g. Sheptycki 2009; Brodeur 2010), they have shown such little interest in intelligence that we might conclude it is as much a 'missing dimension' of crime studies as it was of international relations. Given the academic imperatives for research grants and publications, the traditional inaccessibility of intelligence practitioners to scholars' inquiries and inapplicability of the quantitative research methods normally required by research grant donors, have combined to keep law enforcement intelligence a largely research-free zone. Given the suspicion of 'outsiders' that is endemic within police cultures, this suits cops just fine: the lack of scholarly curiosity and police secrecy are mutually reinforcing.

What is 'organised crime'?

If some criminal activities are 'organised' then it is implied that others are not; that they are essentially 'opportunistic'. Indeed, a good proportion of 'volume' crime, including thefts, burglaries and assaults, occur, if not exactly 'on the spur of the moment', then certainly with a minimum of organisation and planning. As it happens, the immediacy of becoming a victim of such a crime means that these essentially 'predatory' crimes make up a high proportion of reports to police, to which they will feel more or less obliged to respond. In some cases perpetrators may 'graduate' to more sophisticated criminality, but there is an important distinction between this predatory criminality, which essentially just 'redistributes' money from victims to criminals, and 'enterprise' crimes which involve the production and distribution of new goods and services (Naylor 1997: 3).

Deploying this concept of 'enterprise' crime helps to cut through some of the more arcane debates on how to define 'organised crime' (cf. Edwards and Gill 2002; Dean *et al.* 2010). Organised crime can be characterised as the provision of goods and services either deemed illegal by states or, where the provision is subject to regulation, providing them more cheaply. But, if we are interested in the idea of crimes committed within organisational contexts, would we want to include also categories such as corporate crime and white-collar crime?[2] The former is certainly 'organised crime' in that the perpetrators are engaged in enterprise aimed at the generation of profits, while the latter may have more similarity with predatory 'street' crime, the difference being in the perpetrator's class position and the site of the criminal opportunity. So, for the purposes of understanding the role of intelligence, it is most useful to think, first, in economic terms of people as criminal entrepreneurs operating in markets, sometimes as part of 'firms' (legal or otherwise). The United Nations Office on Drugs and Crime (UNODC) now focuses on criminal markets as the most effective target for analysis (IPI 2011: 3).

But organised crime raises issues of government as well as markets. A distinctive aspect of 'organised' crime is that it thrives most where it is able to corrupt police, border, court and other officials, and so threatens the integrity of the rule of law. The connections between 'under' and 'over' worlds may be quite extensive in that certain services that are required, for example, to launder the proceeds of crime, require the assistance of professionals in law and financial services (cf. Van Duyne 1997). In some places criminal organisations may achieve such significance within particular areas that they become what Michael Warner (2009b: 19–20) calls 'non-state sovereignties' – groups prepared to use force in order to control people, territory and resources – but such groups do not just use force but also provide other state-like services such as security and jobs. Indeed, taking a longer historical perspective, Charles Tilly (1985) demonstrated the links between war-making, organised crime and the development of states in Europe.

Thus the question of relationship between states and organised crime is central; while it might seem obvious that the object of the former is to suppress the latter, in fact the relationship is far more complex. On the one hand, organised crime is represented as a threat to states (e.g. HMG 2011a: 9) and fragile or 'failed' states may be seen as both perpetrator and victim of international crime (Gros 2003: 64–67).[3] Williams and Godson (2002: 315–322) summarise a number of key propositions as to these relationships: weak states provide a congenial base for criminal organisations; the weakening of authoritarian states facilitates the expansion of criminal activities, even more so where there is also transition to a free market; and states suffering civil conflict will also see an increase in organised crime as entrepreneurs, criminal or otherwise, take advantage of the great opportunities to supply goods and services otherwise unobtainable. The authors suggest that, by comparison, legitimate democratic states will keep organised crime on the defensive, but we should note that 'corporate' crime emanating from stronger, wealthier states can cause at least as much, if not more, harm (Slapper and Tombs 1999: 54–84). The financial crash of 2008 and successive banking scandals, originating in the wealthiest and most democratic states, included their fair share of organised criminality (as well as greed and stupidity) but were followed by few criminal investigations outside of the US.

How is crime 'organised'?

This is an important question if one is thinking about targeting intelligence. There has been debate in the organised crime literature going back nearly 50 years as to whether hierarchy or networks best describe the organisation of crime. Early work in the US argued that crime – specifically Italian-American – was organised on a bureaucratic model complete with bosses, lieutenants and soldiers, and this image retains a hold in some law enforcement circles but, in part, this can be seen to result from mirror-imaging (Gill 2000: 61–64). Certainly the model has fewer advocates in Europe; in the UK, for example, networks have always been seen as the more useful metaphor. Thus networks tend to be the dominant view now but analysis varies from the essentially descriptive mapping to more analytical and explanatory use of social network analysis (e.g. Klerks 2003). The form taken by networks will vary between the different criminal activities in which they are involved (Bruinsma and Bernaso 2004). However, it is not a very fruitful debate since the two are not empirically independent (cf. Von Lampe 2009: 96): a market can be described as a more or less formal network of actors, some of them individuals, some hierarchical organisations.

It is obvious, but worth noting, that the central problem in organising illegal activities is that a number of the routines available to organising legal activities are not available. It is the flip side of the 'brass plate' problem: criminal organisations, no more than terrorist groups, are not in the *Yellow Pages* (or yell.com), their agreements with other groups are not enforceable through the courts, and their employees cannot be sacked for incompetence. Instead, a full range of informal understandings and sanctions exist, including codes of loyalty based on family or clan membership, oaths of secrecy only broken at risk of exclusion and violence, and constant fear of 'attack' from competitors or authorities. Criminal networks therefore rely heavily on trust. Other things being equal, trust is higher within familial, tribal or ethnic relationships, and all of these do play a significant role in the organisation of crime, including transnationally where diasporas provide ready-made networks.[4] But if and when trust fails, then authorities have the opportunity to penetrate the network.

Intelligence and the governance of organised crime

Organised crime is conducted covertly and there are major problems of measurement (examples of the issues are provided by Burnham 2003; Gregory 2003; Levi and Maguire 2004); if intelligence is about the production of useful knowledge for policy-makers, then a major potential contribution would be to assess the extent and costs of crime. Threat assessments are a useful device in order to get some sense of the problem, especially within fragile or transition states, but they are fraught with problems (cf. IPI 2011: 2–3). For example, there may just be a lack of data or there is overreliance on law enforcement data that is collected for purposes other than social research. Even in the UK – a country with many years of experience of developing intelligence and collating crime statistics – extremely vague and contradictory estimates might be provided by government: 'Total cost of economic and social harm caused to the UK by organised crime is estimated at between £20 billion and £40 billion each year' (Home Office 2012a).[5] There is similar vagueness over the numbers of published targets: in July 2011 this was *c*.38,000 individuals involving around 6,000 criminal groups; in May 2012 it was *c*.30,000 individuals and 7,000 groups. The fact that there is always far more than enough 'organised crime' to keep police occupied at the tactical level in developing specific operations against markets, firms and so on, means that little time may be devoted to strategic initiatives of trying to anticipate future developments, including the unintended outcomes of changes in laws and regulation. Williams and Godson (2002: 347–351) identify a number of techniques that might tackle the 'formidable' problem of anticipating developments in organised crime, including 'red team' approaches, more extensive information gathering both from open and covert sources, analysing travel patterns, assessing vulnerabilities in business and government, and 'knowledge fusion'. However, the reactive drives out the proactive in law enforcement and the consequences of organised crime, never as spectacular as 'terrorism', may not engage policy-makers' attention or resources enough for the development and implementation of a broad strategic effort across the whole of government.

What are the objectives of intelligence operations? The way in which crime is viewed is crucial to developing strategies – for example, if the threat is defined in terms of specific 'firms' and entrepreneurs, such as 'Mr' and/or 'Ms Bigs', then the idea of 'taking down' via arrests and similar means is the logical way forward, and this remains a dominant law enforcement approach to the extent that the aim is the prosecution of offenders. On the other hand, if the problem is viewed in terms of the operations of illegal markets then it might lead to more multi-agency approaches, including disruption. These may be part of broader containment or 'regulation' strategies based more on notions of risk assessment than law enforcement per se (Gill 2002). Prosecution and, possibly, incarceration may be part of a disruption strategy, but may be viewed as just another 'business risk', and it does not necessarily remove people from positions of influence within criminal organisations; equally, the fact that crime is embedded within particular local or national economies, such that it provides the livelihoods for many, means that others will quickly come forward to fill any gaps. Prosecution, of course, requires the development of evidence rather than just intelligence, and is relatively expensive as well as uncertain in terms of outcome; hence the attraction of disruption. But this also has uncertain outcomes – criminals may just be diverted into other and possibly more damaging enterprises and, in terms of legality, the whole process takes place beyond any judicial oversight (Gill 2000: 234–236; Sheptycki and Ratcliffe 2004: 206–207).

The use of some intelligence methods, such as informers, is as old as detective policing, and information collection has been transformed for police as for other agencies by the information and communications revolution and developments in monitoring technologies such as the miniaturisation of cameras. The development of analytical methodologies in relation to organised crime advanced considerably from the 1960s onwards (e.g. Andrew and Petersen 1990) and now constitutes an extensive list of both strategic and analytical methods (e.g. Ratcliffe 2008: 91–114; Gottschalk 2010: 118–121). Martin Innes and colleagues (2005) provide an interesting account of how such analytical methods are actually deployed within policing and are adapted to traditional modes of policing rather than necessarily increasing its rationality. This reflects the continuing marginal status of analysis within policing (cf. Evans, M. 2012: 135–136) and demonstrates the imperfect embedding of intelligence as 'knowledge' work within the more action-orientated policing culture.

The contemporary history of policing organised crime in the UK provides an interesting case study of trying to increase the intelligence contribution to policing organised crime, and parallels broader discussions of the use of 'hard' and 'soft' power (cf. Gill and Phythian 2012: 121–126). The establishment of the Serious Organised Crime Agency (SOCA) was announced in 2004 and it became operational in April 2006. SOCA was to bring about the merger of the National Criminal Intelligence Service (NCIS) and the National Crime Squad (NCS) (which had themselves reflected the 1990s centralisation of regional squads originally established in the 1960s), and those from customs and immigration departments involved in the investigation of trafficking (Gill 2000: 81–89). This attempted a more coherent strategy after a history of poor working relations between the separate agencies and was an explicit attempt to create more of an 'intelligence' than a 'police' body. Despite the adoption of 'intelligence-led' policing in the UK in the early 1990s, and the promulgation of the National Intelligence Model in 2001, the unpublished Spedding report about the intelligence community had been critical of the ability of police and NCIS to produce intelligence on organised crime (Harfield 2006: 744–747). This shift was further symbolised by the appointment of Stephen Lander, former MI5 Director General, as the first SOCA Chair. SOCA's first 'generic priority' was to 'build knowledge and understanding of serious organised crime, the harm it causes, and of the effectiveness of different responses'. Assessment of its performance was to be made with reference to 'trends in underlying harms caused by organised crime' and 'evidence of dislocation of criminal markets, including evidence that criminal groups are finding the UK a less attractive market' (SOCA 2006: 7–9).

However, this talk of harm reduction and intelligence analysis regarding market disruption was all rather different from traditional police concerns with 'feeling collars' and 'locking up the bad guys', and the 'paradigm shift' (Harfield 2006) of creating SOCA did indeed generate some problems at SOCA with the conflicting organisational cultures of its constituent elements. It seems that the opposition quickly became convinced that SOCA was not delivering adequately since, in July 2010, the new Coalition government announced the establishment of a 'powerful new National Crime Agency (NCA) to lead the fight against organised crime and strengthen our border security' (Home Office 2010). The change in tone from just five years earlier was very clear – the Factsheet published with the Bill establishing the NCA included 'fight' or 'fighting' crime four times in the first three paragraphs, and the NCA would provide 'hard-edged enforcement' through prosecution where practicable (HMG 2011b: 6).

Conclusion: some continuing 'challenges' in policing organised crime

Once crime becomes a 'business' depending on continuous operations and embedded to a greater or lesser extent in communities (defined either spatially or by consumption), maintaining profitability demands greater resilience in order to protect people's livelihoods. Viewed from the perspective of the criminal organisation, this is all part of risk management vis-á-vis both rivals and law enforcement (Williams and Godson 2002: 335–339). One key element of this is the ability of criminal groups to adapt to authorities (e.g. Dorn 2003). Another is that some of the significant profits generated are available for the purposes of counterintelligence, including corrupting officials. For example, the US Department of Homeland Security Inspector General, giving evidence to a congressional committee in March 2010, said: 'We have found the tactics used by the drug trafficking organisations in their corruption activities are similar to the processes or tactics used by foreign intelligence services as they attempt to recruit or otherwise compromise our officers and agents' (Frost 2010: 180).

The problem of sharing between fragmented intelligence units is one familiar to any student of intelligence; problems of information sharing are aggravated to the extent that there are multiple police forces that see themselves in competition (e.g. Sheptycki and Ratcliffe 2004: 199–202). For example, the development of intelligence within locally based police forces in the UK from the 1960s onwards resulted in 200 separate crime and intelligence databases by 2010, but it was only in 2011 that the first stage of a Police National Database became operational, enabling officers to access national intelligence with respect to child protection and counterterrorism (NPIA 2011). The US, with around 18,000 separate police departments, is an extreme case of fragmentation and developed some of the earliest examples of organised crime 'task forces' as a means of bringing together police from different agencies, and to overcome bureaucratic and legal obstacles to information sharing (e.g. Gill 2000: 46–48). The counterterrorist 'fusion centres' that have proliferated in the US and Europe since 9/11 are similarly inspired. As between nations, there are further obstacles in the form of languages and incompatible legal structures; however, there have also been extensive efforts to overcome these, often driven by the internationalisation of US law enforcement and, within Europe through the standardisation of procedures such as the European Arrest Warrant and the European Police Office (Europol), an essentially police intelligence organisation furthering cross-national collaboration (Andreas and Nadelmann 2006).

Perhaps the greatest obstacle in the way of managing 'organised crime', however, is its volume and permeation through all societies, rich and poor. As we have seen, 'guesstimates' of its extent vary widely and there is a consequent danger of a moral panic that can be made use of by the growing security-industrial complex to further its influence and profits. Having said that, however, if one takes a broader notion of organised crime to include corporate crime as well as family, clan or tribally based groups, then the extent of human misery and environmental degradation resulting from trafficking, fraud, illegal logging and extraction of minerals which, in turn, may fuel intercommunal violence is clearly such as to require *some* effort at control.

Analytically, this requires attention to the economic and the governmental; thus the best way of approaching it is through some notion of political economy. Equally, in examining transnational organised crime, some notion of illicit international political economy as sister of international political economy (IPE) is a productive approach (Andreas 2004). The extent to which informal economies, enterprise crime, corruption, illegal markets and so on are embedded in contemporary societies, and the interdependence of 'over' and 'under' worlds, means that it is absurd to talk about 'fights' and 'wars' on crime. The only feasible policy is one of multi-agency governance (including containment, suppression, negotiations, etc.) in attempts to increase human security in respect of safety and health that requires more 'joined-up thinking' than is indicated in the opening quotes (see also Edwards and Gill 2003).

Intelligence has a crucial role to play both in the estimation of organised crime and development of policy. The first requires not just the use of covert sources such as are crucial at the tactical level but also careful use of open sources including social research. Intelligence works on a preventive logic, and developing policy requires careful analysis of the likely outcomes – both intended and unintended – of new regulation. Given the extent to which it dominates discussion about transnational organised crime, drugs trafficking and the transparent failure of prohibitionist policies would be a good place to start. Concentrating on the supply side of the market (mainly poorer, developing countries) means that the negative impact of policies in terms of poverty and human rights is greater there than in the richer, consuming countries (Andreas and Nadelmann 2006: 250–253; Mena and Hobbs 2010).

'Wars' against organised crime are not only unwinnable, their consequence may be even more dangerous than the crime itself; in a climate of uncertainty due to the lack of specific data about the extent and cost of crime, governments are dependent on vague estimates to persuade people to accept the ever more intrusive measures they say are required. In the worst case, states, and their intelligence agencies, may be more a part of the problem than the solution. This may range from a simple refusal to acknowledge the existence or impact of organised crime through failures to provide adequate legal frameworks, or to investigate properly active collusion or involvement in rent-seeking behaviour. Careful control of policy and oversight of activities are required in order to guard against this and the ever-present dangers of corruption given the large sums of money generated and the significance of covert information gathering as well as strategies of disruption.

Notes

1 The first quotation is from Home Office, *Crime and Courts Bill Fact Sheet* (Home Office 2012a). The second is UK Justice Minister Crispin Blunt introducing the idea of Deferred Prosecution Agreements on 17 May 2012, available at http://www.justice.gov.uk/news/features/new-tool-to-tackle-economic-crime.

2 See, for example, Wright (2006: 21–24) and Madsen (2009: 7–11) on taxonomy. These debates are not trivial for policy-makers and practitioners but are not crucial for the purposes of this chapter.

3 To the extent that organised crime is linked with terrorism it may represent a serious threat to the state. Links between the two certainly exist but may be exaggerated; while terrorists want to undermine governments, organised criminals want them in place to retain a degree of market stability and to repress unwelcome competition.

4 Unfortunately, too much of the literature and official discourse on organised crime speaks of it in ethnic terms – Sicilian Mafia, Japanese Yakuza, Chinese triads, Jamaican posses and so on – which has

enabled the problem to be presented as one of ethnic 'others', whereas in all countries most 'organised criminals' are native citizens. Ethnicity is one of a number of variables that are useful in explaining *how* crime may be organised but rarely *why* it happens. However, Ianni (1974) proposed 'ethnic succession' as an explanation for waves of immigrants in the US responding to deprivation and discrimination by a combination of political and criminal means to obtain money and influence. For a comprehensive historical examination of how the original Italian Mafia myth developed in the US, see Woodiwiss (2001: 97–104, 243–265).

5 Confusing things further, in 2009 the Cabinet Office had published estimated costs for different types of organised crime totalling £68.4 billion (Cm 7665, Annex 2). It is instructive to compare these estimates with those for the costs of tax avoidance (legal) and tax evasion (illegal) in the UK: tax avoidance costs the UK £25 billion a year; tax evasion £70 billion a year; and uncollected tax amounts to £27 billion to £28 billion; cf. http://www.taxresearch.org.uk/Blog/2010/03/30/time-to-face-tax-realities/ (accessed 31 May 2012).

REFERENCES

Ackoff, R. (2004) 'Transforming the Systems Movement', PLA Conference Paper, 26 May. Online. Available: http://tinyurl.com/Ackoff-Prime (accessed August 2012).

Adamsky, D. and Bar-Joseph, U. (2006) '"The Russians are not Coming": Israel's Intelligence Failure and the Soviet Military Intervention in the "War of Attrition" in 1970', *Intelligence and National Security*, 21(1), 1–25.

Agrell, W. (2002) *When Everything Is Intelligence – Nothing Is Intelligence*, Sherman Kent Center for Intelligence Analysis, Occasional Papers, 1. Online. Available https://www.cia.gov/library/kent-center-occasional-papers/vol1no4.htm (accessed 15 August 2012).

Agrell, W. (2009) 'Intelligence Analysis after the Cold War – New Paradigm or Old Anomalies', in G.F. Treverton. and W. Agrell (eds) *National Intelligence Systems*, Cambridge: Cambridge University Press.

Aid, M. (2003) 'All Glory Is Fleeting: SIGINT and the Fight Against International Terrorism', *Intelligence and National Security*, 18(4), 72–120.

Aid, M. (2009) 'All Glory Is Fleeting: SIGINT and the Fight Against International Terrorism', in C. Andrew, R. Aldrich and W. Wark (eds) *Secret Intelligence: A Reader*, London: Routledge, 40–77.

Aid, M. and Wiebes, C. (2001) 'Introduction on the Importance of Signals Intelligence in the Cold War', *Intelligence and National Security*, 16(1), 1–26.

Air Force Space Command (1990) *Space Detection and Tracking: A Chronology: 1957–1983*, US Air Force Freedom of Information Act: History Office, Secret.

Air Force Technical Application Center (AFTAC) (1997) *Organization and Functions Chart Book*, Center Instruction 38–101, US Department of State Freedom of Information Act, Secret, 21 April (AFTAC), Center Instruction 38–101, *Organization and Functions Chart Book*, 21 April, US Air Force Freedom of Information Act: Secret. USAF FOIA.

Albats, Y. (1995) *KGB: State Within a State: The Secret Police and Its Hold on Russia's Past, Present and Future*, London: I.B. Tauris.

Aldrich, R.J. (2001) *The Hidden Hand: Britain, America and Cold War Secret Intelligence, 1945–1964*, London: John Murray.

Aldrich, R.J. (2002) 'Dangerous Liaisons: Post-September 11 Intelligence Alliances', *Harvard International Review*, Fall, 50–54.

Aldrich, R.J. (2006) 'Setting Priorities in a World of Changing Threats', in S. Tsang (ed.) *Intelligence and Human Rights in the Era of Global Terrorism*, New York: Praeger, 158–171.

Aldrich, R.J. (2009) 'Global Intelligence Co-operation versus Accountability: New Facets to an Old Problem', *Intelligence and National Security*, 24(1), 26–56.

Aldrich, R.J. (2009) 'Regulation by Revelation? Intelligence, Transparency and the Media', in R. Dover and M. Goodman (eds) *Known Knowns: British and American Intelligence and the Media*, New York: Columbia University Press.

Aldrich, R.J. (2010) *GCHQ: The Uncensored Story of Britain's Most Secret Intelligence Agency*, London: HarperPress.

Alexander, M. S. (1991) 'In Lieu of Alliance: The French General Staff's Secret Co-Operation with Neutral Belgium, 1936–40', *Journal of Strategic Studies*, 14(4), 413–27.

Alexander, M.S. (ed.) (1998) *Knowing Your Friends: Intelligence Inside Alliances from 1914 to the Cold War*, London: Frank Cass.

Alford, S. (1998) *The Early Elizabethan Polity: William Cecil and the British Succession Crisis, 1558–1569*, Cambridge: Cambridge University Press.

Allenby, B.R. (2000) 'Environmental Security: Concept and Implementation', *International Political Science Review*, 21(1), 5–21.

Alibek, K. and Handelman, S. (1999) *Biohazard*, New York: Delta.

Almond, G.A. and Verba, S. (1963) *The Civic Culture: Political Attitudes and Democracy in Five Nations*, Princeton, NJ: Princeton University Press.

Andreas, P. (2004) 'Illicit International Political Economy', *Review of International Political Economy*, 11(3), 641–652.

Andreas, P. and Nadelmann, E. (2006) *Policing the Globe*, New York: Oxford University Press.

Andrew, C. (1985) *Her Majesty's Secret Service: The Making of the British Intelligence Community*, London: Heinemann.

Andrew, C. (1994) 'The Making of the Anglo-American SIGINT Alliance', in H.B. Peake and S. Halpern (eds) *In the Name of Intelligence: Essays in Honor of Walter Pforzheimer*, Washington, DC: NIBC Press, 95–109.

Andrew, C., (1995) *For the President's Eyes Only: Secret Intelligence and the American Presidency from Washington to Bush* : New York, HarperCollins.

Andrew, C. (2004) 'Intelligence, International Relations and "Under-Theorisation"', *Intelligence and National Security*, 19, Summer, 170–184.

Andrew, C. (2009) *The Defence of the Realm: The Authorized History of MI5*, London: Penguin.

Andrew, C. and Gordievsky, O. (1991) *KGB: The Inside Story*, New York: HarperPerennial.

Andrew, C. and Mitrokhin, V. (1999) *The Mitrokhin Archive: The KGB in Europe and the West*, London: Allen Lane.

Andrew, C. and Neilson, K. (1986) 'Tsarist Codebreakers and British Codes', *Intelligence and National Security*, 1(1).

Andrew, C., Aldrich, R. and Wark, W. (2009) 'Introduction: What Is Intelligence?', in C. Andrew, R. Aldrich and W. Wark (eds) *Secret Intelligence: A Reader*, London: Routledge, 1–2.

Andrew, C. and Dilks, D. (eds) (1984) *The Missing Dimension: Governments and Intelligence Communities in the Twentieth Century*, London: Macmillan.

Andrew, P. and Peterson, M. (eds) (1990) *Criminal Intelligence Analysis*, Loomis, CA: Palmer Enterprises.

Anon (1959) National Intelligence Survey: India, Supplement VI – Communism, CIA released Documents in period 29/7/1958–19/3/1959, Online. Available: http://www.faqs.org/cia/docs/99/0000777829/NATIONAL-INTELLIGENCE-SURVEY-INDIA.html

Anon (2000) *Kargil Committee Report: Executive Summary*. Online. Available: http://nuclearweaponarchive.org/India/KargilRCA.html.

Anon (2002) 'RAW Founder Chief R.N. Kao Dies', *Times of India*, 20 January.

Anon (2011) 'Little Learned from 26/11', *The Hindu*, 15 July.

Ansari, H. (2010) 'Address of the Vice President at the Fourth R.N. Kao Memorial Lecture: Intelligence for the World of Tomorrow', *Outlook India*.

Anzenhosyou to boueiryoku ni kansuru kondankai (Dai 4 kai) Online. Available: http://www.kantei.go.jp/jp/singi/ampobouei2/dai4/gijisidai.html (accessed 5 July 2013).

Apostolou, N. (2011) 'India cracks down on the BlackBerry', *The Register*, London. Online. Available: http://www.theregister.co.uk/2011/08/08/indian_BlackBerry_crackdown/ (accessed 21 September 2012).

AR 15–6 Investigation of the Abu Ghraib Prison and 205th Military Intelligence Brigade LTG Anthony R. Jones and AR 15–6 Investigation of the Abu Ghraib Detention Facility and 205th Military Intelligence Brigade MG George R. Fay (2004) Online. Available: http://news.bbc.co.uk/nol/shared/bsp/hi/pdfs/26_08_04_fayreport.pdf (accessed 20 September 2012).

Arcos, R. (2012) 'Intelligent Design: Restructuring the Spanish Security Apparatus', *Jane's Intelligence Review*, 24, 36–39.

Arcos, R. and Antón, J. (2010) 'Reservas de inteligencia: hacia una comunidad ampliada de inteligencia', *Inteligencia y seguridad: Revista de análisis y prospectiva*, 8, 11–38.

Arendt, H. (1968) *Between Past and Future: Eight Exercises in Political Thought*, New York: Viking Press.

Argaman, J. (2007) *The Shadow War*, Tel Aviv: Ministry of Defense Publishing House.

Asahi Newspaper (2011) 23 September.

ASIO Report to Parliament (2011) Canberra, Commonwealth of Australia.

Atlee, T. (2002) *The Tao of Democracy: Using Co-intelligence to Create a World That Works for All*, Seattle, WA: BookSurge.

Atlee, T. (2009) *Reflections on Evolutionary Activism*, Seattle, WA: CreateSpace.

Atlee, T. (2012) *Empowering Public Wisdom: A Practical Vision of Citizen-Led Politics*, San Francisco, CA: Evolver Editions.

Avivi, S. (2012) 'Founding the Mossad', in A. Gilboa and E. Lapid (eds) *Israel's Silent Defender: An Inside Look at Sixty Years of Israeli Intelligence*, Jerusalem: Gefen, 30–36.

Aydinli, E. and Tuzuner, M. (2011) 'Quantifying Intelligence Cooperation', *Journal of Peace Research*, 48, 673–682.

Baer, R. (2010) 'A Perfectly Framed Assassination', *Wall Street Journal*, 27 February. Online. Available: http://online.wsj.com/article/SB10001424052748704479404575087621440351704.html (accessed 18 May 2012).

Baker, S. (1994/1995) 'Should Spies Be Cops?', *Foreign Policy*, 97, 36–52.

Baker, S. (2001) 'Dangerous Secrets: Don't Give Up Security For a False Sense of Liberty', *Wall Street Journal*, 5 October.

Baldino, D. (2010) *Democratic Oversight of Intelligence Services*, Sydney: The Federation Press.

Ball, D. (1989) *Soviet Signals Intelligence (SIGINT)*, Canberra: Strategic and Defence Studies Centre, Australian National University.

Ball, J. and Brown, S. (2011) 'Why BlackBerry Messenger Was Rioters' Communication Method of Choice', *Guardian*, 7 December.

Bamford, J. (2001) *Body of Secrets: Anatomy of the Ultra-Secret National Security Agency*, New York: Doubleday.

Bamford, J. (2008) *The Shadow Factory: The Ultra-Secret NSA from 9/11 to the Eavesdropping on America*, New York: Doubleday

Bar-Joseph, U. (1995) 'Israel Caught Unaware: Egypt's Sinai Surprise of 1960', *International Journal of Intelligence and Counter Intelligence*, 8(2), 203–219.

Bar-Joseph, U. (2005) *The Watchman Fell Asleep: The Surprise of Yom Kippur and its Sources*, New York: SUNY Press.

Bar-Joseph, U. (2009) 'Military Intelligence as the National Intelligence Estimator: The Case of Israel', *Armed Forces and Society*, Online. Available: http://afs.sagepub.com/content/36/3/505

Bar-Joseph, U. (2011) *The Angel: Ashraf Marwan, the Mossad and the Yom Kippur War*, Or Yehuda: Zmora-Bitan.

Bar-Zohar, M. and Mishal, N. (2012) *Mossad: The Greatest Missions of the Israeli Secret Service*, New York: Ecco.

Baran, Z. (2007) 'EU Energy Security: Time to End Russian Leverage', *Washington Quarterly*, 30(4), 131–141.

Barkawi, T. (2006) *Globalisation and War*, Lanham, MD: Rowman and Littlefield.

Barnett, A.D. (1967) *Cadres, Bureaucracy and Political Power in China*, New York: Columbia University Press.

Barnett, A.D. (1985) *The Making of Foreign Policy in China*, Boulder, CO: Westview Press.

Barrett, D.M. (2005) *The CIA and Congress: The Untold Story from Truman to Kennedy*, Lawrence: University of Kansas Press.

Barrett, D.M. (2012) E-mail correspondence with the author, 29 May.

Barron, J. (1983) *KGB Today: The Hidden Hand*, New York: Reader's Digest Press.

Barry, J. (1993) 'Covert Action Can Be Just', *Orbis*, 37, Summer, 375.

Barton, B., Redgewell, C., Rønne, A. and Zillman, D.N. (eds) (2004) *Energy Security: Managing Risk in a Dynamic Legal and Regulatory Environment*, Oxford: Oxford University Press.

Barwick, H. (2011) 'Social Media Could Render Covert Policing "Impossible"', *Computerworld*, 25 August. Online. Available: http://www.computerworld.com.au/article/398599/social_media_could_render_covert_policing_impossible_/ (accessed 8 May 2012).

Bean, H. (2009) 'Organizational Culture and US Intelligence Affairs', *Intelligence and National Security*, 24, 479–498.

Bean, H. (2011) *No More Secrets: Open Source Information and the Reshaping of US Intelligence*, Westport, CT: Praeger Security International.

Bejtlich, R. (2005) 'Risk, Threat and Vulnerability 101', *TaoSecurity*, 5 May. Online. Available: http://taosecurity.blogspot.co.uk/2005/05/risk-threat-and-vulnerability-101-in.html (accessed 19 February 2012).

Bell, J.B. (2002) 'Conditions Making for Success and Failure of Denial and Deception: Nonstate and Illicit Actors', in R. Godson and J.J. Wirtz (eds) *Strategic Denial and Deception: The Twenty-First Century Challenge*, New Brunswick, NJ: Transaction Publishers.

Bellaby, R. (2012) 'What's the Harm? The Ethics of Intelligence Collection', *Intelligence and National Security*, 27(1), February.

Bennett, A. (1983) 'An Englishman Abroad', in A. Bennett (1991) *Single Spies: A Double Bill by Alan Bennett*, London: Samuel French Limited.

Bennett, A. (1991) 'A Question of Attribution', in A. Bennett (1991) *Single Spies: A Double Bill by Alan Bennett*, London: Samuel French Limited

Bennett, G. (2000a) *The SVR: Russia's Intelligence Service*, Camberley, UK: Conflict Studies Research Centre.

Bennett, G. (2000b) *The Federal Security Service of the Russian Federation*, Camberley, UK: Conflict Studies Research Centre.

Bennett, G. (2003) *FPS & FAPSI – RIP*, Camberley, UK: Conflict Studies Research Centre.

Benson, R.L. and Warner, M. (1996) *VENONA Soviet Espionage and the American Response 1939–1957*, Washington, DC: National Security Agency Central Intelligence Agency.

Berdal, M.R. and Malone, D. M. (2000) *Greed and Grievance: Economic Agendas in Civil Wars*, New York: Lynne Rienner.

Berkowitz, B. (2002) 'Intelligence and the War on Terrorism', *Orbis*, Spring, 289–300.

Berkowitz, B.D. and Goodman, A.E. (1989) *Strategic Intelligence for American National Security*, Princeton, NJ: Princeton University Press.

Betts, R.K. (1978) 'Analysis, War and Decision: Why Intelligence Failures Are Inevitable', *World Politics*, 31(2), 61–68.

Betts, R.K. (1980–81) 'Surprise Despite Warning: Why Sudden Attacks Succeed', *Political Science Quarterly*, 95(4), 551–572.

Betts, R.K. (1988) 'Policy-Makers and Intelligence Analysts: Love, Hate or Indifference?', *Intelligence and National Security*, 3(1).

Betts, R.K. (1998) 'Intelligence Warning: Old Problems, New Agendas', *Parameters*, 28(1), 26–35.

Betts, R.K. (2012) E-mail correspondence with the author (June 23).

Betts, R.K. (2007) *Enemies of Intelligence: Knowledge and Power in American National Security*, New York: Columbia University Press.

Bickford, D. (1999) 'Memorandum: The Accountability of the Security and intelligence Services with Particular Regard to the Security Service', Appendix 2, UK Select Committee on Home Affairs, 3rd Report, *Accountability of the Security Service*, 21 June.

Bielecki, J. (2002) 'Energy Security: Is the Wolf at the Door?' *Quarterly Review of Economics and Finance*, 42, 235–250.

Bimfort, M.T. (1958) 'A Definition of Intelligence', *Studies in Intelligence*, Fall. Online. Available: https://www.cia.gov/library/center-for-the-study-of-intelligence/kent-csi/vol46no3/html/v46i3a02p.htm (accessed 29 December 2011).

Black, I. and Morris, B. (1991) *Israel's Secret Wars: A History of Israel's Intelligence Services*, New York: Grove Weidenfeld.

Blackstone, T. and Plowden, W. (1988) *Inside the Think Tank: Advising the Cabinet 1971–1983*, London: Heinemann.

Bloodworth, M. (2007) *Evidence to the Standing Senate Committee on National Security and Defence*, Senate of Canada, 1st Session 39th Parliament, 26 March.

Boraz, S.A. (2008) 'Colombia', in S. Farson *et al.* (eds) *PSI Handbook of Global Security and Intelligence*, Vol. 1, Westport, CT: Praeger Security International.

Boraz, S.C. (2006) 'Establishing Democratic Control of Intelligence in Colombia', *International Journal of Intelligence and CounterIntelligence*, 19(1), 84–109.

Born, H. and Caparini, M. (eds) (2007) *Democratic Control of Intelligence Services: Containing Rogue Elephants*, Farnham: Ashgate.

Born, H., Johnson, L.K. and Leigh, I. (2005) *Who's Watching the Spies? Establishing Intelligence Service Accountability*, Washington, DC: Potomac Press.

Born, H., Leigh, I. and Wills, A. (eds) (2011) *International Intelligence Cooperation and Accountability*, London: Routledge.

Boyd, E. (2009) 'Large Map of US Counties with Levees', New Orleans: Levves.org. Online. Available: http://levees.org/large-map-of-u-s-counties-with-levees/ (accessed 19 June 2013).

Bozeman, A.B. (1988) 'Political Intelligence in Non-Western Societies: Suggestions for Comparative Research', in R. Godson (ed.) *Comparing Foreign Intelligence: The US, the USSR, the UK and the Third World*, Washington, DC: Pergamon-Brassey's.

Bozeman, A.B. (1998) *Strategic Intelligence and Statecraft: Selected Essays*, Dulles, VA: Brassey's Inc.

Braden, R.A. (2000) 'Environmental Security: Concept and Implementation', *International Political Science Review*, 21(1), 5–21.

Breakspear, A. (2011) 'A New Definition of Intelligence'. Paper presented at the ECPR General Conference in Reykjavik, Iceland, 25–27 August. Online. Available: http://www.ecprnet.eu/conferences/general_conference/reykjavik/paper_details.asp?paperid=1237 (accessed 24 June 2012).

Bregante Otero, N. (2007) 'Los servicios de inteligencia españoles tras los atentados del 11-M', in N. Bonilla and M.A. Esteban Navarro (eds) *Terrorismo global, gestión de información y servicios de inteligencia*, Madrid: Plaza y Valdés, 113–125.

Brenner, J. (2011) *America the Vulnerable: Inside the New Threat Matrix of Digital Espionage, Crime and Warfare*, New York: Penguin.

Briggs, C.M. (2012) 'Developing Strategic and Operational Environmental Intelligence Capabilities', *Intelligence and National Security*, 27(5), 653–668.

Brin, D. (1999) *The Transparent Society: Will Technology Force Us To Choose Between Privacy and Freedom?* New York: Basic Books.

Brodeur, J.P. (2010) *The Policing Web*, Oxford: Oxford University Press.

Bromke, A. and Nossal, K.R. (1983) 'Tensions in Canada's Foreign Policy', *Foreign Affairs*, 62(2), 335–353.

Brown, A.C. (1975) *Bodyguard of Lies*, New York: Harper & Row.

Bruce, S. (2010) Notes for speech delivered at the 6th Annual Conference of the International Association for Intelligence Education (IAFIE', Ottawa, 25–27 May (released to the author under the Access to Information Act).

Bruinsma, G. and Bernaso, W. (2004) 'Criminal Groups and Transnational Illegal Markets', *Crime, Law and Social Change*, 41, 79–94.

Bruneau, T. and Boraz, S. (eds) (2007) *Reforming Intelligence: Obstacles to Democratic Control and Effectiveness*, Austin, TX: University of Texas Press.

Bryden, J. (1993) *Best Kept Secret*, Toronto: Lester Publishing.

Bulloch, J. and Morris, J. (1989) *The Gulf War: Its Origins, History and Consequences*, London: Methuen.

Bundesministerium der Verteidigung (2006) 'Weißbuch 2006 zur Sicherheitspolitik Deutschlands und zur Zukunft der Bundeswehr' (White Paper). Online. Available: http://www.bmvg.de/portal/PA_1_0_LT/PortalFiles/C1256EF40036B05B/W26UYEPT431INFODE/WB2006_mB_sig.pdf?yw_repository=youatweb.

Bundesministerium des Innern. (BMI) (2012) 'Bundesamt für Verfassungsschutz'. Online. Available: http://www.bmi.bund.de/SharedDocs/Behoerden/DE/bfv_einzel.html?nn=109678 (accessed 5 July 2013).

Bundesnachrichtendienst. (BND) (2005) 'Bundesnachrichtendienst Berlin-Pullach: Der Auslandsnachrichtendienst Deutschlands', Pullach.

Bundesnachrichtendienst. (BND) (2011) 'Der Auslandsnachrichtendienst'. BND-Info-Broschüre. Online. Available: http://www.bnd.bund.de/cln_101/nn_1365548/DE/downloads/pdf/BND__Info__Broschuere,templateId=raw,property=publicationFile.pdf/BND_Info_Broschuere.pdf (accessed 5 July 2013).

Bundesrat. (2006) '21. Beschlussniederschrift über die 181. Sitzung der Ständigen Konferenz der Innenminister und – senatoren der Länder am 4. September 2006 in Berlin'. Online. Available: http://www.bundesrat.de/DE/gremienkonf/fachministerkonf/imk/Sitzungen/06–09–04/06–09–04-Beschluss,templateId=raw,property=publicationFile.pdf/06–09–04-Beschluss.pdf.

Burnham, B. (2003) 'Measuring Transnational Organised Crime', in A. Edwards and P. Gill (eds) *Transnational Organised Crime*, London: Routledge, 65–77.

Burns, J.F. (2009) 'Spy Chief in Britain Opens Door a Bit to the Press', *New York Times*, 8 January, A14.

Butler, the Lord of Brockwell (2004) *Review of Intelligence on Weapons of Mass Destruction*, London: The Stationery Office.

Butterfield, F. (1990) *China: Alive in the Bitter Sea*, New York: Random House.

Buzan, B. (1991) *People, States and Fear*, 2nd edn, Hemel Hempstead, UK: Harvester Wheatsheaf.

Buzan, B. (1997) 'Rethinking Security After the Cold War', *Cooperation and Conflict*, 32(1), 5–28.

Byrne, P. (1988) *The Campaign for Nuclear Disarmament*, London: Croom Helm.

Cabinet Office (1993) *Central Intelligence Machinery*, London: HMSO.

Cabinet Office (2009) *Cyber Security Strategy of the United Kingdom*. Online. Available: http://www.official-documents.gov.uk/document/cm76/7642/7642.pdf (accessed 26 June 2012).

Cabinet Office (2010) *National Intelligence Machinery*, November. Online. Available: http://www.cabinet-office.gov.uk/sites/default/files/nim–november2010.pdf (accessed 26 June 2012).

Cabinet Office (2011) 'Supporting the National Security Council (NSC): The Central National Security and Intelligence Machinery'. Online. Available: http://www.cabinetoffice.gov.uk/sites/default/files/resources/Recommendations_Suppporting%20the%20National%20Security%20Council_The%20ce ntral%20national%20security%20and%20intelligence%20machinery.pdf (accessed 26 June 2012).

Cain, F. (2003) 'Governments and Defectors: Responses to the Defections of Gouzenko in Canada and Petrov in Australia', in M. Macmillan and F. McKenzie (eds) *Parties Long Estranged: Canada and Australia in the Twentieth Century*, Vancouver: UBC Press.

Cain, F. (2008) *Terrorism and Intelligence in Australia: The History of ASIO and National Surveillance*, Melbourne: Australian Scholarly Publishing.

Canadian Security Intelligence Service (1985) Canadian Security Intelligence Service Act, R.S.C., c. C-23. Online. Available: http://laws-lois.justice.gc.ca/eng/acts/C-23/ (accessed December 2012).

Canadian Security Intelligence Service (2010) *Public Report 2009–2010*, Ottawa: Public Works and Government Services.

Canadian Security Intelligence Service (2012) *Public Report 2010–2011*, Ottawa: Public Works and Government Services Canada.

Capra International, Inc. (2010) *Final Evaluation Report: 10-Year Evaluation of Canada's Anti-Money Laundering and Anti-Terrorism Financing Regime*, Ottawa: Department of Finance Canada. Online. Available: http://www.fin.gc.ca/treas/evaluations/amlatfr-rclcrpcfat-eng.asp#a8) (accessed January 2013).

Cavendish-Bentinck, A. and Capel-Dunn, D. (1945) *The Intelligence Machine*, Report to the Chiefs of Staff, 10 January.

CCTVUserGroup (2008) 'Counting Cameras in Cheshire', *CCTV User Group Magazine*, 11–15.

Chapman, W.G. (1997) (Major, USAF) *Organizational Concepts for the Sensor-to-Shooter World: The Impact of Real-Time Information on Airpower Targeting*, Maxwell AFB, AL: Air University Press. Unclassified.

Chen, D. (1988) 'PRC in Dilemma over Diplomat's Expulsion', Hong Kong, *South China Morning Post*, 5 December. FBIS daily report – China, FBIS–CHI–88–002, 5 January.

Cherkashin, V. (2005) *Spy Handler: Memoirs of a KGB Officer*, New York: Basic Books.

Cherp, A. and Jewell, J. (2011) 'The Three Perspectives on Energy Security: Intellectual History, Disciplinary Roots and the Potential for Integration', *Current Opinion in Environmental Sustainability*, 3, 202–212.

Chesterman, S. (2011) *One Nation Under Surveillance: A New Social Contract to Defend Freedom Without Sacrificing Liberty*, Oxford: Oxford University Press.

Chesterman, S. and Fisher, A. (2009) (eds) *Private Security, Public Order: The Outsourcing of Public Services and Its Limits*, Oxford: Oxford University Press.

Chief Information Officer (2009) *Australia's National Security Information Environment*, Canberra, Australia: PM&C.

Chilcot, J. (2012) (ongoing) *The Iraq Inquiry*. Online. Available: http://www.iraqinquiry.org.uk/ (accessed 5 July 2013).

Church Committee (1975a) 'Senate Select Committee to Study Governmental Operations with Respect to Intelligence Activities', *Alleged Assassination Plots Involving Foreign Leaders, An Interim Report*, 20 November, Washington, DC: Government Printing Office.

Church Committee (1975b) 'Senate Select Committee to Study Governmental Operations with Respect to Intelligence Activities', *Covert Action in Chile, 1963–1973*, Staff Report, 18 December, Washington, DC: Government Printing Office.

Church Committee (1976) 'Senate Select Committee to Study Governmental Operations with Respect to Intelligence Activities', *Final Reports*, Books I–VI, Washington, DC: Government Printing Office.

CIA (1983) *Fact Book on Intelligence*, Washington, DC: CIA.

CIA, Intelligence Community Staff (1973) 'The Performance of the Intelligence Community Before the Arab-Israeli War of October 1973: A Preliminary Post-Mortem Report', CIA Freedom of Information Act: Top Secret Ruff Zarf Umbra.

CIA, Lt Col. Oleg Penkovsky (2012) 'Western Spy in Soviet GRU'. Online. Available: http://www.foia.cia.gov/penkovsky.asp (accessed 27 June 2012).

CID (1936) *Central Machinery for Coordination of Intelligence*, London: Committee of Imperial Defence.

Clapper, J.R. (2012) 'Unclassified Statement for the Record on the Worldwide Threat Assessment of the US Intelligence Community for the Senate Committee on Armed Services', 16 February.

Clapper, J.R., Jr (2010) 'The Role of Defense in Shaping US Intelligence Reform', in L.K. Johnson (ed.) *The Oxford Handbook of National Security Intelligence*, New York: Oxford University Press.

Clark, K. (2010) 'A New Era of Openness? Disclosing Intelligence to Congress Under Obama', *Constitutional Commentary*, 26, 313–337.

Clark, R.M. (2003) *Intelligence Analysis: A Target-Centric Approach*, Washington, DC: CQ Press.

Clausewitz, C. von (1976 [1832–34]) *On War*, M. Howard and P. Paret (trans. and ed.), Princeton, NJ: Princeton University Press.

Clingendael International Energy Programme (CIEP) (2004) *Study on Energy Supply Security and Geopolitics*, The Hague: CIEP.

Clinton, B. (2005) *My Life*, London: Arrow Books.

Cloake, J. (1985) *Templer: Tiger of Malaya – The Life of Field Marshal Sir Gerald Templer*, London: Harrap.

Clough, C. (2004) 'Quid Pro Quo: The Challenges of International Strategic Intelligence Cooperation', *International Journal of Intelligence and Counterintelligence*, 17, 601–613.

CNI (2011) *How Does the CNI Work?* Online. Available: http://www.cni.es/en/howdoesthecniwork/ (accessed 26 June 2012).

Cobain, I. (2012) 'Libyan Dissidents Launch Action Against UK Government Over Rendition', *Guardian*, 28 June.

Cockburn, A. and Cockburn, L. (1991) *Dangerous Liaison: The Inside Story of the US–Israeli Covert Relationship*, New York: HarperCollins.

Cohen, R. (1997) 'For France, Sagging Self-image and Esprit', *New York Times*, 11 February. Online. Available: http://www.nytimes.com/1997/02/11/world/for-france-sagging-self-image-and-esprit.html (accessed 10 November 2011).

Colby, W. and Forbath, P. (1978) *Honorable Men: My Life in the CIA*, New York: Simon & Schuster.

Coleman, J.S. (1990) *Foundations of Social Theory*, Cambridge, MA: The Belknap Press of Harvard University Press.

Collier, P. and Hoeffler, A. (2005) 'Resource Rents, Governance and Conflict', *Journal of Conflict Resolution*, 49(4), 625–633.

Committee of Privy Counsellors (2004) 'Review of Intelligence on Weapons of Mass Destruction', HC 898, London, 14 July.

Congressional Record (2004) Volume 150, Number 139, US Senate, 8 December.

Congressional Record (2011) Volume 157, Number 181, US Senate, 29 November.

Cooper, B. (2007) *CFIS: A Foreign Intelligence Service for Canada*, Ottawa: Canadian Defence and Foreign Affairs Institute.

Cooper, J. (2007) 'The Funding of the Power Agencies of the Russian State', *Journal of Power Institutions in Post-Soviet Societies*, 6/7.

Copeland, B. (2012) *Turing: Pioneer of the Information Age*, Oxford: Oxford University Press.

Cormac, R. (2010) 'Organizing Intelligence: An Introduction to the 1955 Report on Colonial Security', *Intelligence and National Security*, 25(6).

Cornall, R. and Black, R. (2011) 'Independent Review of the Intelligence Community Report', Australian Government. Online. Available: http://www.dpmc.gov.au/publications/iric/docs/2011-iric-report.pdf p. 318: IGIS Report 2002

Costello, J. and Tsarev, O. (1993) *Deadly Illusions*, London: Century.

Coulter, K. (2005) *Evidence to the Special Senate Committee on the Anti-Terrorism Act,* Senate of Canada, First Session, Thirty-eighth Parliament, 11 April.

Council of Europe, Committee on Legal Affairs and Human Rights (2006) 'Alleged Secret Detentions in Council of Europe Member States', Information Memorandum II, Rapporteur Dick Marty, AS/Jur, 03 rev., 22 January.

Cox, J. (2011) 'The Transformation of Canadian Defence Intelligence in the 21st Century'. Paper presented at the International Studies Association Annual Conference, Montreal, Canada, 16 March.

Cox, J. (2012) *Canada and the Five Eyes Intelligence Community*, Ottawa: Canadian Defence and Foreign Affairs Institute/Canadian International Council.

Cradock, P. (2002) *Know Your Enemy: How the Joint Intelligence Committee Saw the World*, London: John Murray.

Crawford, T. (2010) 'Intelligence Cooperation', in R. Denemark (ed.) *The International Studies Encyclopedia*, New York: Wiley.

Crawford, V. and Sobel, J. (1982) 'Strategic Information Transmission', *Econometrica*, 50(6), 1431–1451.

CREST Collection, 'Soviet Missile Summary', Document No. CIA-RDP81T00618R000101240001–1, National Archives, College Park, Maryland.

Crick, A.J.P. (1962) *Economic Intelligence: Purposes and Prospects*. Released under Freedom of Information Act 16–08–2006095849–001, 4 September 2006, London.

Criminal Intelligence Service of Canada (CISC) (2012) 'Governance, 29 May. Online. Available: http://www.cisc.gc.ca/about_cisc/governance/governance_e.html (accessed January 2013).

Critchfield, J.H. (2003) *Partners at the Creation: The Men Behind Postwar Germany's Defense and Intelligence Establishments*, Annapolis: Naval Institute Press.

Cronin, A. (2002/2003) 'Behind the Curve: Globalisation and International Terrorism', *International Security*, 27(3), 30–58.

Croom, H. (1969) 'The Exploitation of Foreign Open Sources', CIA Historical Review Program, 13(2), 129–136. Online. Available: http://www.gwu.edu/~nsarchiv/NSAEBB/NSAEBB90/index.htm (accessed 5 July 2013) documents 7A & 7B.

Cryptologic Quarterly (1983) 'The Cobra Judy Acquisition', *Cryptologic Quarterly*, 1(4), Winter, Secret, NSA FOIA, p. 79.

Daly, H. (1991) *Steady-State Economics: With New Essays*, 2nd edn, Washington, DC: Island Press.

Daly, H. (1993) *Valuing the Earth: Economics, Ecology, Ethics*, Cambridge, MA: The MIT Press.

Daly, H. (1994) *For the Common Good: Redirecting the Economy toward Community, the Environment and a Sustainable Future*, Boston, MA: Beacon Press.

Daly, H. (2010) *Ecological Economics: Principles and Applications*, 2nd edn, Washington, DC: Island Press.

Dandeker, C. (1991) *Surveillance, Power and Modernity: Bureaucracy and Discipline from 1700 to the Present Day*, New York: St Martin's.

Daun, A. (2011) *Auge um Auge: Intelligence – Kooperation in den deutsch–amerikanischen Beziehungen*, Wiesbaden: VS Verlag für Sozialwissenschaften.

Davis, J. (1986) 'Competing Influences on the Policymaker', Intelligence Policy Seminar, John F. Kennedy School of Government, Harvard University. Recreated by the author from memory of the same information presented by Dr. Gregory Treverton. Online. Available: http://www.phibetaiota.net/2012/03/graphic-competing-influences-on-the-policymaker-treverton/

Davies, D. (1997) 'A Brief History of Cryptography', *Information Security Technical Report*, 2(2), 14–17.

Davies, P.H.J. (2002) 'Ideas of Intelligence: Divergent National Concepts and Institutions', *Harvard International Review*, Fall, 62–67.

Davies, P.H.J. (2004a) 'Intelligence Culture and Intelligence Failure in Britain and the United States', *Cambridge Review of International Affairs*, 17, 495–520.

Davies, P.H.J. (2004b) *MI6 and the Machinery of Spying*, London: Frank Cass.

Davies, P.H.J. (2006) 'Intelligence Analysts and Policymakers: Benefits and Dangers of Tensions in the Relationship', *Intelligence and National Security*, 21(6).

Davies, P.H.J. (2012a) 'The Intelligence Cycle is Dead, Long Live the Intelligence Cycle', Brunel University Interdisciplinary Research Centre. Unpublished paper presented to the International Studies Association Convention, San Diego, April.

Davies, P.H.J. (2012b) *Intelligence and Government in Britain and the United States*, Vols 1 and 2, Santa Barbara, CA: Praeger.

Dawn, O. (1991) *Government in the United Kingdom: The Search for Accountability, Effectiveness and Citizenship*, Milton Keynes: Open University Press.

Day, D.A. (2004) 'Ferrets Above: American Signals Intelligence Satellites During the 1960s', *International Journal of Intelligence and Counterintelligence*, 17, 449–467.

de Graaf, B. (2010) 'How the MfS' Worldview Affected the Intelligence Cycle: A Study Based on Operations Against the Netherlands', in T. Wegener Friis, K. Macrakis and H. Müller-Enbergs (eds) *East German Foreign Intelligence: Myth, Reality and Controversy*, London: Routledge.

De Leeuw, K. (1991) 'The Black Chamber in the Dutch Republic during the War of the Spanish Succession and Its Aftermath, 1707–1715', *Historical Journal*, 42(1), 133–156.

de Lint, W. (2008) 'New Zealand', in S. Farson *et al.* (eds) *PSI Handbook of Global Security and Intelligence*, Vol. 1, Westport, CT: Praeger Security International.

Dean, G., Fahsing, I. and Gottshalk, P. (2010) *Organized Crime: Policing Illegal Business Entrepreneurialism*, Oxford: Oxford University Press.

Dearlove, R. (2010) 'National Security and Public Anxiety: Our Changing Perceptions', in L.K. Johnson (ed.) *The Oxford Handbook of National Security Intelligence*, New York: Oxford University Press.

De Leeuw, K. (1999) 'The Black Chamber in the Dutch Republic During the War of the Spanish Succession and Its Aftermath', *The Historical Journal*, 42(1), 133–156.

Defense Intelligence Agency (1979) *Defense Intelligence Organization, Operations and Management*, Manual No. 56–3, Defense Intelligence Agency Freedom of Information Act, Secret.

Defense Intelligence Agency (1984) *Handbook of the Chinese People's Liberation Army*, DDB-2680-32-84, November. Online. Available: http://www.dia.mil/public-affairs/foia/pdf/PLA_handbook.pdf

Defense Intelligence Agency (DIA) 1 (1994) *MASINT Handbook for the Warfighter*, Defense Intelligence Agency Freedom of Information Act, Secret/Noforn.

Defense Intelligence Agency (DIA) 2 (1979) *Defense Intelligence Organization, Operations and Management, Manual No. 56–3*, Defense Intelligence Agency Freedom of Information Act, Secret.

Defense Science Board (2011) *Trends and Implications of Climate Change for National and International Security*, Washington: Office of the Secretary of Defense. Online. Available: http://www.acq.osd.mil/dsb/reports/ADA552760.pdf (accessed 5 July 2013).

Defense Special Missile and Astronautics Centre (DEFSMAC) (1981) Report Serial No. 5/09/402/81, 12 June, Secret, cited in National Photographic Interpretation Center (NPIC), Imagery Analysis Report, *Soviet Mobile Missile Summary*, July, Top Secret Ruff.

Dekel, E. (1959) *Shai: The Exploits of Hagana Intelligence*, London: Yosellof.

Denécé, E. and Arboit, G. (2010) 'Intelligence Studies in France', *International Journal of Intelligence and Counterintelligence*, 23, 725–747.

Denécé, E. and G. Arboit (2012) 'The Development of Intelligence Studies in France', in Mediterranean Council for Intelligence Studies, *MCIS Yearbook 2012*, 1–64.

Denninger, K. (2011) *Leverage: How Cheap Money Will Destroy the World*, Hoboken, NJ: Wiley.

Dennis, M. (2003) *The Stasi: Myth and Reality*, Harlow, UK: Pearson.

Department for Environment Food and Rural Affairs (DEFRA) (2006) 'Food Security and the UK: An Evidence and Analysis Paper', Food Chain Analysis Group.

Department of Defense (2001) *Department of Defense Dictionary of Military and Associated Terms*, Washington, DC: Department of Defense, 12 April. Online. Available: http://www.dtic.mil/doctrine/jel/new_pubs/jp1_02.pdf (accessed 5 July 2013).

Department of National Defence (DND) (2008) *Canada First Defence Strategy*, Ottawa: Department of National Defence. Online. Available: http://www.forces.gc.ca/site/pri/first-premier/June18_0910_CFDS_english_low-res.pdf (accessed December 2012).

Department of National Defence (DND) (2009) 'Chief of Defence Intelligence', August. Online. Available: http://www.cdi-crd.forces.gc.ca/sites/page-eng.asp?page=1410 (accessed December 2012).

Department of National Defence (DND) (2011) *Report on Plans and Priorities 2011–12*, Ottawa: National Defence.

Der Derian, J. (1994) 'Anti-Diplomacy, Intelligence Theory and Surveillance Practice', in W.K. Wark (ed.) *Espionage: Past, Present, Future?* Ilford, UK: Frank Cass.

Dhar, A. (2009) *CIA's Eye on South Asia*, New Delhi: Manas Publications.

Díaz, F.A.M. (2010) 'The Spanish Intelligence Community: A Diffuse Reality', *Intelligence and National Security*, 25(2), 223–244.

Diaz, M. (2010) 'Forming a Definitional Framework for "Intelligence"', *American Intelligence Journal*, 29(1).

Dodd, N.T. and Halliday, F. (2011) 'MI5 Joins Social Messaging Trawl for Riot Organisers', *Guardian*, 15 August.

Dominguez, J.L. (2003) 'Lessons Learned: A Ground Surveillance Systems Platoon in Afghanistan', *Military Intelligence Professional Bulletin*, October–December. Unclassified.

Donner, Frank J. (1990) *Protectors of Privilege: Red Squads and Police Repression in Urban America*, Berkeley: University of California Press.

Dorling, P. (2011) 'Wikileaks Unveils Japanese Spy Agency', *Sydney Morning Herald*, 21 February. Online. Availible: http://www.smh.com.au/technology/technology-news/wikileaks-unveils-japanese-spy-agency-20110220-1b17a.html

Dorn, A.W. (2012) E-mail correspondence with the author, 18 June.

Dorn, N. (2003) 'Proteiform Criminalities', in A. Edwards and P. Gill (eds) *Transnational Organised Crime*, London: Routledge, 227–240.

Dorraj, M. and Currier, C.L. (2011*)* 'The Strategic Implications of China's Energy Engagement with the Devleoping World,' in *China's Energy Relations with the Developing World*, London: Continuum.

Dover, R. (2007) 'For Queen and Company: The Role of Intelligence in the UK's Arms Trade', *Political Studies*, 55(4), 683–708.

Dover, R. and Goodman, M. (eds) (2009) *Spinning Intelligence: Why Intelligence Needs the Media, Why the Media Needs Intelligence*, New York: Columbia University Press.

Dowell, J.A.E.K. (2011) *Intelligence for the Canadian Army in the 21st Century*, JADEX Papers 5, Ottawa: Department of National Defence.

Downs, G. and Jones, M.A. (2002) 'Reputation, Compliance and International Law', *Journal of Legal Studies*, 31, 95–114.

Dozier, K. (2011) 'CIA Secretly Monitors World on Twitter, Facebook', *MSNBC*, 11 April. Online. Available: http://www.msnbc.msn.com/id/45164661/ns/technology_and_science-tech_and_gadgets/t/cia-secretly-monitors-world-twitter-facebook/ (accessed 10 May 2012).

Du, X. and Zhang, L. (1990) *China's Legal System: A General Survey*, Beijing: New World Press.

Duffield, M. (2001) *Global Governance and the New Wars*, London: Zed Books.

Duffield, M. (2007) *Development, Security and Unending War: Governing the World of Peoples*, London: Polity Press.

Dulles, A. (1977) *The Craft of Intelligence*, Westport, CT: Greenwood.

Dupont, A. (2003) 'Intelligence for the Twenty-First Century', *Intelligence and National Security*, 18(4).

Durant, W. (1916) *Philosophy and the Social Problem*, annotated edn (2008), Frisco, TX: Promethean Press.

Dyson, G. (2012) *Turing's Cathedral: The Origins of the Digital Universe*, London: Penguin.

Dziak, J.J. (1988a) *Chekisty: A History of the KGB*, Lexington, MA: Lexington Books.

Dziak, J.J. (1988b) 'The Study of the Soviet Intelligence and Security System', in R. Godson (ed.) *Comparing Foreign Intelligence: The US, the USSR, the UK and the Third World*, Washington, DC: Pergamon-Brassey's.

Earnest, D.C. and Rosenau, J.N. (2000) 'The Spy Who Loved Globalisation', *Foreign Policy*, 120, 88–91.

Earth Intelligence Network (EIN) (2006) 'Reference: Earth Intelligence Network Analytic Concept'. Online. Available: http://tinyurl.com/EIN-2006 (accessed 19 June 2013).

Economic Intelligence Steering Committee (1962) (EIS(62)) 1st meeting, 12 September. CAB 134/1790, London: National Archives.

Edwards, A. and Gill, P. (2002) 'Crime as Enterprise? The Case of "Transnational Organised Crime"', *Crime, Law and Social Change*, 37(3), 203–223.

Edwards, A. and Gill, P. (2003) 'After Transnational Organised Crime? The Politics of Public Safety', in A. Edwards and P. Gill (eds) *Transnational Organised Crime*, London: Routledge, 264–281.

Ehrman, J. (2009) 'What Are We Talking About When We Talk About Counterintelligence?', *Studies in Intelligence*, 53(2), June.

Ellis, J.D. and Kiefer, G.D. (2007) *Combating Proliferation: Strategic Intelligence and Security Policy*, Baltimore, MD: The Johns Hopkins University Press.

Engler, A., Fischer, D. and Voorst, B.V. (1991) 'The Commander: Stormin' Norman Schwarzkopf on Top', *Time*, 4 February. Online. Available: http://www.time.com/time/magazine/article/0,9171,972270,00.html (accessed 25 June 2012).

Erlich, Y. (2012) 'The Beginning: From an Information Service to a Military Intelligence Service in the War of Independence (1948–1949)', in A. Gilboa and E. Lapid (eds) *Israel's Silent Defender: An Inside Look at Sixty Years of Israeli Intelligence*, Jerusalem: Gefen, 21–29.

Esiemokhai, E.O. (2011) 'National Security, Military Intelligence and You', *Nigerian-Newspaper.com*, 31 July. Online. Available: http://nigerian-newspaper.com/national-security.htm (accessed 12 February 2012).

EUCOM: US European Command (1968) *USEUCOM Joint Intelligence Appraisal*, 20 June 1968, Secret, Washington, DC: National Security Archive.

European Commission (2001) *Towards a European Strategy for the Security of Energy Supply*, Luxembourg: Office for Official Publications of the European Communities.

European Parliament (2011) *Food Security under Threat: Global Response Needed*. Online. Available: http://www.europarl.europa.eu/sides/getDoc.do?type=IM-PRESS&reference=20110216IPR13780&format=XML&language=EN (accessed 5 July 2013).

Evans, G. (2009) 'Rethinking Military Intelligence Failure: Putting the Wheels Back on the Intelligence Cycle', *Defence Studies*, 9(1), 22–46.

Evans, J. (2012) 'The Olympics and Beyond', address at the Lord Mayor's Annual Defence and Security Lecture, London, 25 June.

Evans, M. (2012) 'The Diamond Matrix: A Science-Driven Approach to Policing with Crime Intelligence', *Policing*, 6(2), 133–143.

Evill, D. (1947) *Review of Intelligence Organisations*, 6 November. CAB 163/7, London: National Archives.

Fall, B. (1961) *Street without Joy: Indochina at War 1946–54*, Harrisburg, PA: Stackpole.

Farson, S. (1999) 'Is Canadian Intelligence Being Reinvented?', *Canadian Foreign Policy Journal*, 6(2), 49–86.

Farson, S. and Whitaker, R. (2010) 'Accounting for the Future or the Past? Developing Accountability Oversight Systems to Meet Future Intelligence Needs', in J. Loch (ed.) *The Oxford Handbook of National Security Intelligence*, Oxford: Oxford University Press, 673–699.

Farson, S., Gill, P., Phythian, M. and Shpiro, S. (eds) (2008) *Handbook of Global Security and Intelligence: National Approaches*, Santa Barbara, CA: Praeger.

Farson, S., Gill, P., Phythian, M. and Shpiro, S. (eds) (2008) *PSI Handbook of Global Security and Intelligence: National Approaches: Volume 1 – The Americas and Asia / Volume 2 – Europe and the Middle East*, Westport, CT: Praeger Security International.

FBI (2012) Directorate of Intelligence website. Online. Available: http://www.fbi.gov/about-us/intelligence/intelligence-cycle (accessed 27 February).

Fearon, J. (1998) 'Bargaining, Enforcement and International Cooperation', *International Organization*, 52(2), 269–306.

Ferris, J.R. (2002) 'The Road to Bletchley Park: The British Experience with Signals Intelligence, 1892–1945', *Intelligence and National Security*, 17(1), 53–84.

Ferris, J.R. (2005) 'Intelligence, Uncertainty and the Art of Command in Military Operations', in J.R. Ferris (ed.) *Intelligence and Strategy: Selected Essays*, London: Routledge, 239–287.

Ferris, J. and Handel, M.I. (1995) 'Clausewitz, Intelligence and Uncertainty in the Art of Command and Military Operations', *Intelligence and National Security*, 10(1), 1–58.

Fishbein, W. and Treverton, G. (2004) 'Making Sense of Transnational Threats', *Sherman Kent Center for Intelligence Analysis Occasional Papers*, 3(1), October.

Florini, A. (1998) 'The End of Secrecy', *Foreign Policy*, 111, 50–63.

Food and Agriculture Organization (FAO) (1996) *Rome Declaration and World Food Summit Plan of Action*, Rome: FAO.

Foot, M.R.D. (1966, 2nd edn 1999) *SOE In France: An Account of the Work of the British Special Operations Executive in France 1940–1944*, Government Official History Series, 2nd Edition, Abingdon: Routledge.

Forcese, C. (2011) 'A Foreign Intelligence Service in Increments?', *National Security Law Blog*, 4 January. Online. Available: http://craigforcese.squarespace.com/national-security-law-blog/2011/1/4/a-foreign-intelligence-service-in-increments.html (accessed December 2012).

Ford, H.P. (1995) 'The US Government's Experience with Intelligence Analysis: Pluses and Minuses', *Intelligence and National Security*, 10(4), 34–53.

Foresight (2011) *The Future of Food and Farming: Final Project Report*, London: Government Office for Science.

Frederick the Great (1944 [1747]) *Instructions for His Generals*, trans. Brigadier General T.R. Phillips, Harrisburg, PA: Military Service Publishing Company.

Freedman, L. (1986) 'The First Two Generations of Nuclear Strategists', in P. Paret (ed.) *Makers of Modern Strategy: From Machiavelli to the Nuclear Age*, Oxford: Clarendon Press, 735–778.

Freedman, L. (1986) *US Intelligence and the Soviet Strategic Threat*, 2nd edn, Princeton, NJ: Princeton University Press.

Freedman, L. (2003) *The Evolution of Nuclear Strategy*, 3rd rev. edn, Basingstoke, UK: Palgrave Macmillan.

Freeman, P. (2007) 'MI1(b) and the Origins of British Diplomatic Cryptanalysis', *Intelligence and National Security*, 22(2), 206–228.

Friedman, T.L. (2005) *The World Is Flat: A Brief History of the Twenty-First Century*, New York: Farrar, Straus and Giroux.

Friedman, T.L. (2006) 'The First Law of Petropolitics', *Foreign Policy*, 154, 28–36.

Friedman, W.F. (1991) 'A Brief History of the Signal Intelligence Service', *Cryptologia*, 15(3), 263–272.

Frost, T.M. (2010) 'Statement Before the Ad Hoc Subcommittee on State, Local and Private Sector

Preparedness and Integration, Committee on Homeland Security', US Senate, 11 March, *Trends in Organized Crime*, 13, 179–183.

Fulghum, D.A. (1999) 'Growing Intelligence Operation Focuses on New Types of Signals', *Aviation Week & Space Technology*, 2 August, 50–55.

Fuller, R.B. (1969) *Ideas and Integrities: A Spontaneous Autobiographical Disclosure*, New York: Macmillan.

Furse, G.A. (1895) *Information in War: Its Acquisition and Transmission*, London: William Clowes & Sons.

Fyffe, G. (2007) 'Evidence to the Standing Senate Committee on National Security and Defence', Senate of Canada, 1st Session 39th Parliament, 18 June.

Fyffe, G. (2011) 'The Canadian Intelligence Community After 9/11', *Journal of Military and Strategic Studies*, 13(3), 1–17.

Gaddis, J.L. (2004) *The Landscape of History: How Historians Map the Past*, Oxford: Oxford University Press.

Gaiji Jiken Kenkyu Kai [study group of spy incidents] (2007) *Sengo no Gaiji Jiken [spy incidents after the Second World War]*, Tokyo: Tokyo Hourei Shuppan.

Gallucci, R. (2012) Interview with the author, 19 November.

Gardiner, L.K. (1991) 'Squaring the Circle: Dealing with Intelligence-Policy Breakdowns', *Intelligence and National Security*, 6(1).

Garland, E. (2012) 'Peak Intel: How So-called Strategic Intelligence Actually Makes Us Dumber', *The Atlantic*. Online. Available: http://tinyurl.com/Garland-Intel (accessed 5 April 2012).

Gartner, S. (1997) *Strategic Assessment in War*, New Haven, CN: Yale University Press.

Gates, R.M. (1996) *From the Shadows*, New York: Simon & Schuster.

Geer, D. (2008) 'Complexity is the Enemy', *IEEE Security and Privacy*, Nov/Dec. Online. Available: http://ieeexplore.ieee.org/stamp/stamp.jsp?arnumber=04753682 (accessed 24 April 2012).

Geer, D. (2012) 'People in the Loop: Are They a Failsafe or a Liability?'. Presentation at Suits and Spooks Conference, 8 February. Online. Available: http://geer.tinho.net/geer.suitsandspooks.8ii12.txt (accessed 11 February 2012).

Geffen, H. (2012) 'SIGINT in the Service of Intelligence', in A. Gilboa and E. Lapid (eds) *Israel's Silent Defender: An Inside Look at Sixty Years of Israeli Intelligence*, Jerusalem: Gefen, 197–202.

Gentile, G. (2007) 'American Strategy in Afghanistan Flunks Sun Tzu', *Jerusalem Post*, 2 July.

George, R.Z. (2011) 'Reflections on CIA Analysis: Is It Finished?', *Intelligence and National Security*, 26(1), 72–81.

George, R.Z. and Bruce, J.B. (eds) (2008) *Analyzing Intelligence*, Washington, DC: Georgetown University Press.

Gerecht, R.M. (2001) 'The Counterterrorist Myth', *Atlantic Monthly*, July/August. Online. Available: http://www.theatlantic.com/past/docs/issues/2001/07/gerecht.htm (accessed 11 July 2012).

German Advisory Council on Global Change (2008) *World in Transition: Climate Change as a Security Risk*, London: Earthscan.

Gertner, J. (2012) *The Idea Factory: Bell Labs and the Great Age of American Innovation*, London: Penguin.

Geyer, M. (1986) 'German Strategy in the Age of Machine Warfare, 1914–1945', in P. Paret (ed.) *Makers of Modern Strategy: From Machiavelli to the Nuclear Age*, Oxford: Clarendon Press, 527–597.

Gibbs, T. (2005) 'Studying Intelligence: A British Perspective', in L.K. Johnson (ed.) *Strategic Intelligence*, Vol. 1, Westport, CT: Praeger, 35–64.

Gibson, S.D. (2005) 'In the Eye of the Perfect Storm: Re-imagining, Reforming and Refocusing Intelligence for Risk, Globalisation and Changing Societal Expectation', *Risk Management*, 7(1), 23–41.

Gibson, S.D. (2007) 'Open Source Intelligence (OSINT): A Contemporary Intelligence Lifeline', PhD thesis, Cranfield University. Online. Available: https://dspace.lib.cranfield.ac.uk/handle/1826/6524 (accessed 20 September 2012).

Gibson, S.D. (2009) 'Future Roles of the UK Intelligence System', *Review of International Studies*, 35, 917–928.

Gibson, S.D. (2012) *Live and Let Spy*, Stroud: The History Press.

Gilbert, F. (1986) 'Machiavelli: The Renaissance of the Art of War', in P. Paret (ed.) *Makers of Modern Strategy: From Machiavelli to the Nuclear Age*, Oxford: Clarendon Press, 11–31.

Gildea, D. (1968) Minute to White (Intelligence Coordinator), 25 July. CAB 163/129, London: National Archives.

Gill, P. (1994) *Policing Politics: Security Intelligence and the Liberal Democratic State*, London: Frank Cass.

Gill, P. (2000) *Rounding Up the Usual Suspects?* Aldershot, UK: Ashgate.

Gill, P. (2002) 'Policing and Regulation: What is the Difference?' *Social & Legal Studies*, 11(4), 523–546.

Gill, P. (2008) 'Theories of Intelligence: Where are We, Where Should We Go and How Might We Proceed?', in P. Gill, S. Marrin and M. Phythian (eds) *Intelligence Theory: Key Questions and Debates*, London: Routledge, 208–229.

Gill, P. (2009) 'Theories of Intelligence: Where are We, Where Should We Go and How Might We Proceed?', in P. Gill, S. Marrin and M. Phythian (eds) *Intelligence Theory: Key Questions and Debates*, London: Routledge, 208–229.

Gill, P. (2012) 'Intelligence, Threat, Risk and the Challenge of Oversight', *Intelligence and National Security*, 27(2), 206–222.

Gill, P. and Phythian, M. (2006) *Intelligence in an Insecure World*, Cambridge: Polity Press.

Gill, P. and Phythian, M. (2012) *Intelligence in an Insecure World*, 2nd edn, Cambridge: Polity Press.

Gill, P., Marrin, S. and Phythian, M. (eds) (2008) *Intelligence Theory: Key Questions and Debates*, London: Routledge.

Gilman, N., Goldhammer, J. and Weber, S. (eds) (2011) *Deviant Globalization: Black Market Economy in the 21st Century*, New York: Continuum.

Gistaro, E. and Leiter, M. (2007) 'Implications of the NIE. The Terrorism Threat to the Homeland, Statement for the Record, House Permanent Select Committee on Intelligence and House Armed Services Committee', 25 July.

Glaser, E. (2012) 'Founding the Israeli Security Agency', in A. Gilboa and E. Lapid (eds) *Israel's Silent Defender: An Inside Look at Sixty Years of Israeli Intelligence*, Jerusalem: Gefen, 37–45.

Glass, R.R. and Davidson, P.B. (1948) *Intelligence Is for Commanders*, Harrisburg, PA: Military Service Publishing Company.

Glasser, S.B. (2005) 'Probing Galaxies of Data for Nuggets', *Washington Post*, 25 November. Online. Available: http://www.washingtonpost.com/wp-dyn/content/article/2005/11/24/AR2005112400848.html (accessed 20 September 2012).

Glees, A. (2003) *The Stasi Files: The UK Operations of the East German Intelligence and Security Service*, New York: Simon & Schuster.

Glees, A. (2012) E-mail correspondence with the author, 11 June.

Global News Wire – Asia Africa Intelligence Wire (2006) 'Inside the Chinese Intelligence Agencies', BBC Monitoring International Reports, 8 February. Online. Available: http://www.militaryphotos.net/forums/showthread.php?72090-Inside-the-Chinese-Intelligence-Agencies (accessed 30 September 2012).

GMAIC/JAEIC/NPIC (1962) *Supplement 20 to Joint Evaluation of Soviet Missile Treat in Cuba*, 11 November, Top Secret Multiple Codewords, CREST Collection, Document No.CIA-RDP78T05449A000200230001–6, College Park, Maryland: National Archives.

Gobierno de España (2011) *Spanish Security Strategy: Everyone's Responsibility*, Madrid: Boletín Oficial del Estado.

Goetz, J., Rosenbach, M. and Stark, H. (2007) 'Renditions Scandal: CIA Arrest Warrants Strain US–German Ties', *Der Spiegel International*, 25 June.

Goldman, J. (ed.) (2006) *The Ethics of Spying*, Lanham, MD: Scarecrow Press.

Goodman, M.S. (2007) *Spying on the Nuclear Bear: Anglo-American Intelligence and the Soviet Bomb*, Stanford, CA: Stanford University Press.

Goodman, M. (2008) 'Learning to Walk: The Origins of the Joint Intelligence Committee', *International Journal of Intelligence and Counterintelligence*, 21(1), 40–56.

Goodman, M.S. (2013) *The Anvil of Discussion: The Official History of the Joint Intelligence Committee: Volume I – 1936–56*, London: Routledge (forthcoming).

Goodson, R., May, E. and Schmitt, G. (eds) (1995) *US Intelligence at the Crossroads: Agendas for Reform*, Brassey's Intelligence and National Security Library, Washington DC: Brassey's Inc Publications.

Gordievsky, O. (1995) *Next Stop Execution*, London: Macmillan.

Goren, S. (2012) 'HUMINT in the Service of Intelligence', in A. Gilboa and E. Lapid (eds) *Israel's Silent Defender: An Inside Look at Sixty Years of Israeli Intelligence*, Jerusalem: Gefen, 203–206.

Goss, P. (2004) 'Cooperative Way Forward on MASINT Management, Memorandum Goss to Secretary of Defense et al., December 15', Central Intelligence Agency Freedom of Information Act. Online. Available: http://www.foia.cia.gov (accessed 20 September 2012).

Gottschalk, P. (2010) *Policing Organized Crime*, Boca Raton, FL: CRC Press.

Graham, S.B. *et al.* (2008) *World at Risk*, New York: Random House.

Grant, M. (ed.) (2011) *The British Way in Cold Warfare: Intelligence, Diplomacy and the Bomb, 1945–75*, London: Continuum

Gray, C.S. (1999) *Modern Strategy*, Oxford: Oxford University Press.

Gray, C.S. (2007) *War, Peace and International Relations*, Oxford: Routledge.

Gray, C.S. (2009) 'Out of the Wilderness: Prime Time for Strategic Culture', in J.L. Johnson, K.M. Kartchner and J.A. Larsen (eds) *Strategic Culture and Weapons of Mass Destruction: Culturally Based Insights into Comparative National Security Policymaking*, New York: Palgrave.

Gregory, F. (2003) 'Classify, Report and Measure', in A. Edwards and P. Gill (eds) *Transnational Organised Crime*, London: Routledge, 78–96.

Grey, J. (2012) *Chief of Army's Reading List*, rev. edn, Canberra: Land Warfare Studies Centre.

Griffith, S.B., and Sun Tzu (1963) *The Art of War*, Oxford: Oxford University Press.

Gros, J.-G. (2003) 'Trouble in Paradise', *British Journal of Criminology*, 43, 63–80.

Grose, P. (1994) 'Gentleman Spy: The Life of Allen Dulles, Citing the US Senate Committee on Armed Services, Hearings on the National Defense Establishment', 1st Session, 1947, Boston, MA: Houghton Mifflin.

Gross, M. (2012) 'World War 3.0', *Vanity Fair*, May. Online. Available: http://www.vanityfair.com/culture/2012/05/internet-regulation-war-sopa-pipa-defcon-hacking (accessed 3 June 2012).

Gruber, L. (2000) *Ruling the World*, Princeton, NJ: Princeton University Press.

Guelke, A. (2006) *Terrorism and Global Disorder Political Violence in the Contemporary World*, London: IB Tauris.

Guha, R. (2007) *India after Gandhi*, New Delhi: Picador.

Gupte, P. (2009) *Mother India: A Political Biography of Indira Gandhi*, London: Penguin.

Habib, M. with Collingwood, J. (2008) *My Story: The Tale of a Terrorist Who Wasn't*, Melbourne: Scribe Publications.

Hall, G. and Grant, T. (2009) 'Russia, China and the Energy-Security Politics of the Caspian Sea Region after the Cold War', *Mediterranean Quarterly*, 20(2), 113–137.

Hall, R. (1978) *The Secret State Australia's Spy Industry*, Stanmore: Cassell Australia.

Halliday, F. (1994) *Rethinking International Relations*, Basingstoke, UK: Macmillan.

Halliday, F. (1999) *Revolution and World Politics: The Rise and Fall of the Sixth Great Power*, Basingstoke: Macmillan.

Handel, M. (1993) *Masters of War: Sun Tzu, Clausewitz and Jomini*, rev. edn, London: Frank Cass.

Handel, M. (2001) *Masters of War: Classical Strategic Thought*, 3rd rev. edn, London: Frank Cass.

Handel, M.I. (1983) 'The Study of Intelligence', *Orbis*, 26, Winter, 817–821.

Hannan, L. (1993) 'Access to the Inside: An Assessment of "Canada's Security Service: A History"', *Intelligence & National Security*, 8(3), 149–159.

Hardin, R. (2002) *Trust and Trustworthiness*. New York: Russell Sage Foundation.

Harding, L. (2011) *Mafia State: How One Reporter Became an Enemy of the Brutal New Russia*, London: Guardian Books.

Harfield, C. (2006) 'SOCA: A Paradigm Shift in British Policing', *British Journal of Criminology*, 46, 743–761.

Harris, W.W. (2007) 'Crisis in the Levant: Lebanon at Risk?', *Mediterranean Quarterly*, 18(2), 37–60.

Haruna, M. (2000) *Himitsu no Fairu; CIA no Tainichi Kousaku (Jou) (Secret Files: CIA's Covert Activities in Japan*, Vol. 1), Tokyo: Kyodotsusin.

Hastedt, G. (2010) 'The Politics of Intelligence Accountability', in L. Johnson (ed.) *The Oxford Handbook of National Security Intelligence*, Oxford: Oxford University Press, 719–734.

Hastedt, G.P. (1991) 'Towards the Comparative Study of Intelligence', *Conflict Quarterly*, 11, 55–72.

Hastedt, G.P. (ed.) (1991) *Controlling Intelligence*, London: Cass.

Hauslohner, A. (2012) 'Libya's Central Government Exercises Little Authority Outside Capital', *Washington Post*, 20 September.

Hayden, M. (2002) 'Statement before the Joint Inquiry of the Senate Select Committee on Intelligence and the House Permanent Select Committee on Intelligence', 17 October.

Hayden, M.W. (2007) 'Central Intelligence Agency Director, "Intelligence in the 21st Century"'. Remarks at the Air Force Defense Strategy Seminar, Washington, DC, 19 June. Online. Available: *http://www.af.mil/library/speeches/speech.asp?id=332* (accessed 23 July 2007).

Heidenrich, J.G. (2007) 'The Intelligence Community's Neglect of Strategic Intelligence', *Studies in Intelligence*, 51(2). Online. Available: https://www.cia.gov/library/center-for-the-study-of-intelligence/csi-publications/csi-studies/studies/vol51no2/the-state-of-strategic-intelligence.html (accessed 5 July 2013).

Heinberg, R. (2006) *The Oil Depletion Protocol: A Plan to Avert Oil Wars, Terrorism and Economic Collapse*, Gabriola Island, BC: New Society.

Helm, D. (2005) 'The Assessment: The New Energy Paradigm', *Oxford Review of Economic Policy*, 21(1), 1–18.

Helms, R. with Hood, W. (2003) *A Look Over My Shoulder: A Life in the Central Intelligence Agency*, New York: Random House.

Henderson, D. (1904) *Field Intelligence*, London: HMG Government Printer.

Hennessy, P. (2002) *The Secret State: Whitehall and the Cold War*, London: Penguin.

Herman, M. (1996) *Intelligence Power in Peace and War*, Cambridge: Cambridge University Press.

Herman, M. (2001) *Intelligence Services in the Information Age*, London: Frank Cass.

Herman, M. (2003) 'Intelligence after 9/11', CSIS Commentary 83 (Archived), July (accessed 27 February 2012).

Herman, M. (2004) 'Ethics and Intelligence after September 2001', in L. Scott and P. Jackson (eds) *Understanding Intelligence in the Twenty-First Century: Journeys in Shadows*, London: Routledge.

Herman, M. (2011) 'Academic Intelligence Studies in Britain: The Government's Contribution', IRSEM Laboratoire Strategique, Paris Conference.

Herman, M. (2012) E-mail communication with the author, 10 February.

Herodotus (2004) *The Histories*, trans. C.G. Macauley, ed. and notes by D. Lateiner, New York: Barnes & Noble.

Heuer, R. (1999) *Psychology of Intelligence Analysis*, Washington, DC: Center for the Study of Intelligence, Central Intelligence Agency. Online. Available: https://www.cia.gov/library/center-for-the-study-of-intelligence/csi-publications/books-and-monographs/psychology-of-intelligence-analysis/art14.html (accessed 10 February 2012).

Hicks, D. (2010) *Guantanamo: My Journey*, Sydney: William Heinemann.

Hidaka, M. (1937) *Gunki Hogo-ho* [Military Secret Act], Tokyo: Haneda Shoten.

Hill, C. (2011) *Grand Strategies, Literature, Statecraft and World Order*, New Haven, CT: Yale University Press.

Hillenbrand, C. (2009) 'The CIA's Extraordinary Rendition and Secret Detention Programme, European Reactions and the Challenges for Future International Intelligence Co-Operation', Clingendael Security Paper, No. 9, Netherlands Institute of International Relations. Online. Available HTTP: http://www.clingendael.nl/sites/default/files/20090401_cscp_security_paper_hillebrand.pdf

Hillebrand, C. (2012) 'The Role of News Media in Intelligence Oversight', *Intelligence and National Security*, 27(5), 689–706.

Hilsman, R. (1956) *Strategic Intelligence and National Decisions*, Glencoe, IL: Free Press.

Himitsu Hozen no tameno Housei no Arikata ni Kansuru Yushikisha Kaigi (Council of Advisers for Legislation on Security Law), Himitsu Hozen no tameno Housei no Arikata ni Tsuite (Report of the Council of Advisers for Legislation on Security Law). August 8, 2011 Online. Available: http://www.kantei.go.jp/jp/singi/jouhouhozen/dai3/siryou4.pdf

Hinsley, F.H., Thomas, E.E. and Howard, M. (1979) *British Intelligence in the Second World War*, Vols. 1–5, London: Her Majesty's Stationery Office.

Hinsley, H. (1993) 'The Influence of Ultra in the Second World War'. Speech delivered at the Babbage Theatre, Cambridge, 19 October. Online. Available: http://www.cl.cam.ac.uk/research/security/Historical/hinsley.html (accessed 30 August 2012).

Hinsley, H. (1996), 'The Influence of ULTRA in the Second World War', lecture transcript delivered on Tuesday 19 October 1993 at Cambridge University. Online. Available HTTP: <www.cl.cam.ac.uk/research/security/Historical/hinsley.html>

Hitoshi, Y. (2006) 'Nihon ban NSC no Kadai Issues of Japanese NSC]', National Diet Library: Issue Brief No. 548, September.

Hittle, J.D. (1961) *The Military Staff: Its History and Development*, Harrisburg, PA: Stackpole.

Hitz, F. (2004) *The Great Game: The Myths and Reality of Espionage*, New York: Vintage Books.

Hitz, F. (2008) *Why Spy? Espionage in an Age of Uncertainty*, New York: St Martin's Press.

HMG (2011a) *Justice and Security Green Paper*, October, Cm 8194, London: The Stationery Office.

HMG (2011b) 'The National Crime Agency: A Plan for the Creation of a National Crime-Fighting Capability', Cm 8097, June.

HMG (2011c) 'Local to Global: Reducing the Risk from Organised Crime', 28 July.

Hoffman, B. (1998) *Inside Terrorism*, London: Victor Gollancz.

Hoffman, J. (1995) *Beyond the State: An Introductory Critique*, Cambridge: Polity Press.

Holloway, D. (1983) *The Soviet Union and the Arms Race*, New Haven, CT: Yale University Press.

Holloway, D. (1994) *Stalin and the Bomb: The Soviet Union and Atomic Energy 1939–1956*, London: Yale University Press.

Holloway, D. (1999) 'Physics, the State, and Civil Society in the Soviet Union', *Historical Studies in the Physical and Biological Sciences*, 31(1), 73–193.

Home Office (2010) 'Radical Reforms for Police Announced', Press Centre, 26 July.

Home Office (2012) 'Crime and Courts Bill Fact Sheet', May.

Home Office (2012) *Draft Communications Data Bill*, London: Cm 8359, June.

Home Office (2012) Online. Available: http://www.homeoffice.gov.uk/counter-terrorism/communications-data/ (accessed 12 June 2012).

Hong Kong AFP (1986) 'Intelligence Official's Defection Major Blow', FBIS daily report – China, 2 September.

Hong Kong Economic Journal (2006) Hong Kong (in Chinese), 1 January, BBC Monitoring Asia Pacific – Political, supplied by BBC Worldwide Monitoring, 8 February.

Horn, Col. B. (2006) 'Outside the Wire – Some Leadership Challenges in Afghanistan', *Canadian Military Journal*, 7 (3).

Hotchkiss, J. (1973) 'Make Me a Map of the Valley: The Civil War', in A.P. MacDonald (ed.) *Journal of Stonewall Jackson's Topographer*, Dallas, TX: Southern Methodist University.

House of Lords (1993) Deb 528, 1–12, 9 December, col. 1029.

House of Lords (2009) *Surveillance: Citizens and the State: Report of the Constitution Committee*, London: Stationery Office, 6 February.

Hovland, C., Janis, I. and Kelley, H. (1953) *Persuasion and Communication*, New Haven, CT: Yale University Press.

Howard, M. (1976) *War in European History*, Oxford: Oxford University Press.

Howard, M. (1990) *British Intelligence in the Second World War – Volume Five: Strategic Deception*, London: HMSO.

Hughes, R.G., Jackson, P. and Scott, L. (2008) *Exploring Intelligence Archives: Enquiries into the Secret State*, London: Routledge.

Hughes-Wilson, Col. J. (1999) *Military Intelligence Blunders*, London: Constable Robinson.

Hulnick, A.S. (1986) 'The Intelligence Producer–Policy Consumer Linkage: A Theoretical Approach', *Intelligence and National Security*, 1.

Hulnick, A.S. (1999) *Fixing the Spy Machine*, Westport, CT: Praeger.

Hulnick, A.S. (2004) *Keeping Us Safe: Secret Intelligence and Homeland Security*, Westport, CT: Praeger.

Hulnick, A.S. (2006) 'What's Wrong with the Intelligence Cycle?', *Intelligence and National Security*, 21(6), 959–979.

Hulnick, A.S. (2007) 'Intelligence Reform 2007: Fix or Fizzle?' *International Journal of Intelligence and Counter Intelligence*, 20(4), 567–582.

Hyde, H.M. (1962) *The Quiet Canadian*, London: Hamish Hamilton.

Hyde, H.M. (1982) *The Atom Bomb Spies*, London: Sphere.

Ianni, F. (1974) *Black Mafia: Ethnic Succession in Organized Crime*, New York: Simon & Schuster.

IDSA Task Force Report (2012) *A Case for Intelligence Reforms in India*, New Delhi: IDSA.

Immerman, R. (2008) 'Intelligence and Strategy: Historicizing Psychology, Policy and Politics', *Diplomatic History*, 32(1), 1–23.

Immerman, R. (2011) 'Transforming Analysis: The Intelligence Community's Best Kept Secret', *Intelligence and National Security*, 20 May, 26(2–3), 159–181. Online. Available: http://www.tandfonline.com/doi/pdf/10.1080/02684527.2011.559138 (accessed 8 May 2012).

Ingram, J. (2011) 'A Food Systems Approach to Researching Food Security and Its Interactions with Global Environmental Change', *Food Security*, 3, 417–431.

Innes, M., Fielding, N. and Cope, N. (2005) 'The Appliance of Science', *British Journal of Criminology*, 45(1), 39–57.

Inspector-General of Intelligence and Security (IGIS) (2011) *Annual Report 2010–2011*, Canberra: Commonwealth of Australia.

Inspector-General of Intelligence and Security (IGIS) (2012) *Inquiry into the Actions of Australian Government Agencies in Relation to the Arrest and Detention Overseas of Mr Mamdouh Habib from 2001 to 2005*, Canberra: Australian Commonwealth Government.

INSS Special Report (2000) 'The United States and Japan: Advancing Towards a Mature Partnership', October. Online. Available: http://se2.isn.ch/serviceengine/FileContent?serviceID=10&fileid=DF7 6B344–40F0–95E9–10AB-431693ADE1A7&lng=en (accessed 5 July 2013).

Intelligence and Security Committee (ISC) (2011) *Annual Report 2010–11*, July, Cm 8114, London: The Stationery Office.

Intelligence Coordinator (1968) (JIC(B)) 2nd meeting, 12 July, CAB 181/1, London: National Archives.

International Energy Agency (IEA) (2007) *World Energy Outlook 2007: China and India Insights*, Paris: IEA.

IPI (2011) 'Know Your Enemy: An Overview of Organized Crime Threat Assessments', New York: International Peace Institute, October. Online. Available: http://www.ipinst.org (accessed 5 July 2013).

ISC (1999–2000) *Intelligence and Security Committee Annual Report 1999–2000*. Online. Available: http://isc.independent.gov.uk/files/1999–2000_ISC_AR.pdf (accessed 26 June 2012).

ISC (2005) *Intelligence and Security Committee Report into the London Terrorist Attacks on 7 July 2005*. Cm 6785. Online. Available: http://isc.independent.gov.uk/files/200605_ISC_7July_Report.pdf (accessed 26 June 2012).

ISC (2010–11) *Intelligence and Security Committee Annual Report 2010–11*. Online. Available: http://isc.independent.gov.uk/files/2010–2011_ISC_AR.pdf (accessed 26 June 2012).

ISC (2011–12) *Intelligence and Security Committee Annual Report 201–12*. Online. Available: http://isc.independent.gov.uk/files/2011–2012_ISC_AR.pdf (accessed 20 July 2012).

Ivison, J. (2012) 'Stephen Harper Steps in to Save Radarsat Upgrade after Budget Cutbacks Threatened Satellite Program's Future', *National Post (Online)*, 19 December. Online. Available: http://news.nationalpost.com/2012/12/19/stephen-harper-steps-in-to-save-radarsat-upgrade-after-budget-cutbacks-threatened-satellite-programs-future/ (accessed January 2013).

Jakub, J. (1998) *Spies and Saboteurs: Anglo-American Collaboration and Rivalry in Human Intelligence Collection and Special Operations, 1940–45*, Basingstoke: Palgrave Macmillan.

Jay, J. (1998) *Spies and Saboteurs: Anglo-American Collaboration and Rivalry in Human Intelligence Collection and Special Operations, 1940–45*, London: Macmillan.

JDN-1/10 (2010) *Joint Doctrine Note 1/10: Intelligence and Understanding*, Shrivenham UK: Defence Concepts and Doctrine Centre.

JDW (1987) 'Listening Devices Found', *Jane's Defence Weekly*, 15 August.

Jeffery, K. (2010) *MI6: The History of the Secret Intelligence Service, 1909–1949*, London: Bloomsbury.

Jeffreys-Jones, R. (1989) *The CIA and American Democracy*, New Haven, CT: Yale University Press.

Jensen, K. (2004) 'Canada's Foreign Intelligence Interview Program, 1953–90', *Intelligence & National Security*, 19(1), 95–104.

Jensen, K. (2008) *Cautious Beginnings: Canadian Foreign Intelligence 1939–51*, Vancouver: UBC Press.

Jervis, R. (1968) 'Hypotheses on Misperception', *World Politics*, 20(3), 454–479.

Jervis, R. (1970) *The Logic of Images in International Relations*, Princeton, NJ: Princeton University Press.

Jervis, R. (1976) *Perception and Misperception in International Politics*, Princeton, NJ: Princeton University Press.

Jervis, R. (2006) 'Reports, Politics and Intelligence Failures: the Case of Iraq', *Journal of Strategic Studies*, 29(1), 3–52.

Jervis, R. (2010) *Why Intelligence Fails: Lessons from the Iranian Revolution and the Iraq War*, Ithaca, NY: Cornell University Press.

Jervis, R. (2012) E-mail correspondence with the author, 25 June.

Johnson, L.K. (1980) 'The CIA: Controlling the Quiet Option', *Foreign Policy*, 39, Summer, 143–152.

Johnson, L.K. (1985) *A Season of Inquiry*, Lexington: University Press of Kentucky.

Johnson, L.K. (1986) 'Making the Intelligence Cycle Work', *International Journal of Intelligence and Counter-Intelligence*, 1(4), 1–23.

Johnson, L.K. (1996) 'Analysis for a New Age', *Intelligence and National Security*, 11(4), 657–671.

Johnson, L.K. (2003a) 'Bricks and Mortar for a Theory of Intelligence', *Comparative Strategy*, 22(1), 1–28.

Johnson, L.K. (2003b) 'Preface to a Theory of Strategic Intelligence', *International Journal of Intelligence and Counterintelligence*, 16, 638–663.

Johnson, L.K. (2004) 'Congressional Supervision of America's Secret Agencies: The Experience and Legacy of the Church Committee', *Public Administration Review*, 64, January, 3–14.

Johnson, L.K. (2005a) 'An Introduction to the Intelligence Studies Literature', in L.K. Johnson (ed.) *Strategic Intelligence*, Vol. 1, Westport, CT: Praeger, 1–20.

Johnson, L.K. (ed.) (2005b) *Strategic Intelligence*, Vols I–V, Westport, CT: Praeger.

Johnson, L.K. (2007a) 'Harry Howe Ransom and American Intelligence Studies', *Intelligence and National Security*, 22 April, 403–428.

Johnson, L.K. (2007b) 'A Shock Theory of Congressional Oversight' in L.K. Johnson (ed.) *Handbook of Intelligence Studies*, London: Routledge.

Johnson, L.K. (2008) 'Sketches for a Theory of Strategic Intelligence', in P. Gill, S. Marrin and M. Phythian (eds) *Intelligence Theory: Key Questions and Debates*, London: Routledge.

Johnson, L.K. (ed.) (2010) *The Oxford Handbook of National Security Intelligence*, New York: Oxford University Press.

Johnson, L.K. (ed.) (2011) *Intelligence*, Vols I–IV, New York: Routledge.

Johnson, L.K. (2012) *National Security Intelligence: Secret Operations in Defense of the Democracies*, Cambridge: Polity Press.

Johnson, L.K. and Freyberg, A. (1997) 'Ambivalent Bedfellows: German–American Intelligence Relations, 1969–1991', *International Journal of Intelligence and Counterintelligence*, 10(2), 165–179.

Johnson, L.K. and Wirtz, J.J. (eds) (2011) *Intelligence: The Secret World of Spies*, 3rd edn, New York: Oxford University Press.

Johnson, R. (2005) 'Analytic Culture in the U.S. Intelligence Community: An Ethnographic Study', The Center for the Study of Intelligence. Online. Available: //www.cia.gov/library/center-for-the-study-of-intelligence/csi-publications/books-and-monographs/analytic-culture-in-the-u-s-intelligence-community/analytic_culture_report.pdf

Johnston, D. and Sanger, D.E. (2002) 'Yemen Killing Based on Rules Set Out By Bush', *New York Times*, 6 November.

Johnston, J.M. and Johnston, R. (2005) *Analytic Culture in the CIA*, Langley: CIA Centre for the Study of Intelligence.

Joho Kinou Kyouka Kentou Kaigi (Cabinet Council of Intelligence Enhancement), *Kantei ni okeru joho kihou no kyouka no houshin (Policy Report of Intelligence Enhancement of Prime Minister's Office)*. February 14, 2008, Online. Available: http://www.kantei.go.jp/jp/singi/zyouhou/080214kettei.pdf

Joint Staff (2012) Publication 2–01, *Joint and National Intelligence Support to Military Operations* (revised 5 January 2012).

Jomini, A.-H. (1862) *Summary of the Art of War*, trans. G.H. Mendell and W.P. Craighill, Philadelphia, PA: J.B. Lippincott.

Jomini, A.-H. (1977 [1838]) *The Art of War*, trans. G.H. Mendell and P. Craighill, Westport, CT: Greenwood.

Jones, Lt. Gen. A. and Fay, Gen. G. (2004) 'Investigation of Intelligence Activities at Abu Ghraib', Department of Defence, August. Online. Available: http://www.washingtonpost.com/wp-srv/nationi/documents/fay_report_8-25-04.pdf

Jones, R.V. (1994) 'A Sidelight on Bletchley in 1942', *Intelligence and National Security*, 9(1), 1–11.

Jowitt, T. (2011) 'GCHQ Boss Complains of Cyber Brain Drain', *TechWeek Europe*, 14 July. Online. Available: http://www.techweekeurope.co.uk/news/news-security/gchq-boss-complains-of-cyber-brain-drain-34212 (accessed 10 February 2012).

Kahn, D. (1967) *The Codebreakers: The Story of Secret Writing*, New York: Macmillan.

Kahn, D. (1968) *The Codebreakers: The Story of Secret Writing*, New York: Scribner.

Kahn, D. (1986) 'Clausewitz and Intelligence', in M.I. Handel (ed.) *Clausewitz and Modern Strategy*, London: Frank Cass, 17–26.

Kahn, D. (2001) 'A Historical Theory of Intelligence', *Intelligence and National Security*, 16(3), 79–92.

Kaihla, P. (2000) 'The Technology Secrets of Cocaine Inc' *Business 2.0*, July. Online. Available: http://www.cocaine.org/cokecrime/index.html (accessed 2 August 2007).

Kaiser, K. (1969) 'Transnationale Politik: Zu einer Theorie der multinationalen Politik', *Politische Vierteljahresschrift*, Sonderheft 1(1969), 80–109.

Kaldor, M. (1999) *New and Old Wars: Organised Violence in a Global Era*, Cambridge: Polity.

Kalugin, O. (2009) *Spymaster: My 32 Years in Intelligence and Espionage Against the West*, London: Basic Books.

Kam, E. (1988) *Surprise Attack: The Victim's Perspective*, Cambridge, MA: Harvard University Press.

Kaneko, M. 'Nihon ni Okeru Interijyensu Kaikaku no Doukou [Trend of Japan's Intelligence Reform]', *Intelligence Report*, 20, Tokyo: Intelligence Create, May 2010.

Kaneko, M. (2007) 'Nihon no intelligence community [Japan's intelligence community]', *Sekai no Intelligence [World Intelligence]*, Tokyo: PHP Shuppan.

Kantei ni okeru joho kihou no kyouka no houshin. Online. Available: https://www.kantei.go.jp/jp/singi/zyouhou/080214kettei.pdf.

Kapstein, E.B. and Mastanduno, M. (eds) (1999) *Unipolar Politics: Realism and State Strategies After the Cold War*, New York: Columbia University Press.

Katz, S.M. (1992) *Soldier Spies: Israeli Military Intelligence*, Novato CA: Presidio. Katz v. United States, 389 US 347 (1967).

Kaunta interijyensu kinou no kyouka ni okeru kihon houshin (2007) [Basic Policy on strengthening of counterterrorism], Counter Intelligence Promotion Council, 9th August, Online. Available: http://www.cas.go.jp/jp/seisaku/counterintelligence/pdf/basic_decision_summary.pdf (accessed 5 July 2013).

Kaunta interijyensu Suishin Kaigi [Promotion Council of Counter-intelligence], Kaunta interijyensu kinou no kyouka ni okeru kihon houshin (Policy Report of Counter-intelligence Enhancement in the Japanese Government). August 9, 2007. Online. Available: http://www.cas.go.jp/jp/seisaku/counter-intelligence/pdf/basic_decision_summary.pdf (accessed 5 July 2013).

Kautilya (1992) *Kautilya: The Arthashastra*, ed. L.N. Rangarajan, New Delhi, India: Penguin Classics.

Kavanagh, D. (1972) *Political Culture*, London: Macmillan.

Keegan, J. (1994) *A History of Warfare*, New York: Alfred A. Knopf.

Keegan, J. (2003) *Intelligence in War: Knowledge of the Enemy from Napoleon to Al Qaeda*, New York: Alfred A. Knopf.

Kennan, G.F. (1997) *New York Times*, 20 May, E-17. Need for spy game is overrated. http://tinyurl.com/o7p4ah9 (accessed June 2013).

Kennedy, D.M. (1991) *Sunshine and Shadow: The CIA and the Soviet Economy*, Case Program, No. C16–91–1096.0, Cambridge, MA: Kennedy School of Government, Harvard University.

Kennedy, W.K. (1987) *Intelligence Warfare: Penetrating the Secret World of Today's Advanced Technology Conflict*, New York: Crescent Books.

Kent, S. (1949, 2nd edn 1965) *Strategic Intelligence for American World Policy*, Princeton, NJ: Princeton University Press.

Keohane, R. (1984) *After Hegemony*, Princeton, NJ: Princeton University Press.

Khan, R.M. (2011) *Afghanistan and Pakistan: Conflict, Extremism and Resistance to Modernity*, Baltimore, MD: Johns Hopkins University Press.

Kierman, F. and Fairbank, J. (eds) (1974) *Chinese Ways in Warfare*, Cambridge, MA: Harvard University Press.

Kitaoka, H. (2007) 'Sengo Nihon no Interijensu [Japanese intelligence after the WWII]', in T. Nakanishi and K. Kotani (eds) *Interijensu no 20 Seiki [Intelligence in the 20th Century]*, Tokyo: Chikura Shobo.

Klare, M.T. (2001) *Resource Wars: The Changing Landscape of Global Conflict*, New York: Henry Holt.

Klare, M.T. (2008) 'Energy Security', in P.D. Williams (ed.) *Security Studies: An Introduction*, London: Routledge.

Klepak, H. (2008) 'Cuba', in S. Farson *et al.* (eds) *PSI Handbook of Global Security and Intelligence*, Vol. 1, Westport, CT: Praeger Security International.

Klerks, P. (2003) 'The Network Paradigm Applied to Criminal Organisations', in A. Edwards and P. Gill (eds) *Transnational Organised Crime*, London: Routledge, 97–113.

Knight, A. (1996) *Spies Without Cloaks: The KGB's Successors*, Princeton, NJ: Princeton University Press.

Knightley, P. (1986) *The Second Oldest Profession: The Spy as Patriot, Bureaucrat, Fantasist and Whore*, London: Pan.

Kovacs, A. (1997) 'Using Intelligence', *Intelligence and National Security*, 12(4), 145–164.

Krasner, S. (1991) 'Global Communications and National Power: Life on the Pareto Frontier', *World Politics*, 43(3), 336–366.

Krieger, W. (2004) 'German Intelligence History: A Field in Search of Scholars', *Intelligence and National Security*, 19, Summer, 185–198.

Krieger, W. (2009) 'Oversight of Intelligence: A Comparative Approach', in G. Treverton and W. Agrell (eds) *National Intelligence Systems: Current Research and Future Prospects*, Cambridge: Cambridge University Press, 210–234.

Lammy, D. (2012) *Out of the Ashes: Britain After the Riots*, London: Random House.

Lander, S. (2004) 'International Intelligence Cooperation: An Inside Perspective', *Cambridge Review of International Affairs*, 17(3), 481–493.

Lapid, E. (2012) 'Collecting Information in Preparation for the Six-Day War', in A. Gilboa and E. Lapid (eds) *Israel's Silent Defender: An Inside Look at Sixty Years of Israeli Intelligence*, Jerusalem: Gefen, 65–70.

Laqueur, W. (1985) *A World of Secrets: The Uses and Limits of Intelligence*, New York: Basic Books.

Laqueur, W. (1993) *A World of Secrets: The Uses and Limits of Intelligence*, New Brunswick, NJ: Transaction Publishers.

Lassman, P. and Speirs, R. (eds) (1994) *Weber: Political Writings*, Cambridge: Cambridge University Press.

Last, D. and Milne, G. (2005) 'National Security Decision-Making', in D. Last and B. Horn (eds) *Choice of Force: Special Operations for Canada*, Montreal: McGill-Queens University Press, 135–156.

Lavoy, P.R., Sagan, S.D. and Wirtz, J.J. (eds) (2000) *Planning the Unthinkable: How New Powers Will Use Nuclear, Chemical and Biological Weapons*, New York: Cornell University Press.

Le Billon, P. (2004) 'The Geopolitical Economy of 'Resource Wars', *Geopolitics*, 9(1), 1–28.

Le Billon, P. and El Khatib, F. (2004) 'From Free Oil to "Freedom Oil"': Terrorism, War and US Geopolitics in the Persian Gulf', *Geopolitics*, 9(1), 109–137.

Le Carré, J. (1963) *The Spy Who Came in From the Cold*, London: Victor Gollancz.

Le Carré, J. (1974) *Tinker Tailor Soldier Spy*, London: Hodder & Stoughton.

Le Carré, J. (1989) *The Russia House*, London: Hodder & Stoughton.

Lebow, R.N. (1984) 'Windows of Opportunity: Do States Jump Through Them?', *International Security*, 9, 147–186.

Leetaru, K. (2010) 'The Scope of FBIS and BBC Open-Source Media Coverage, 1979–2008', *Studies in Intelligence*, March, 54(1). Online. Available: https://www.cia.gov/library/center-for-the-study-of-intelligence/csi-publications/csi-studies/studies/volume-54-number-1/the-scope-of-fbis-and-bbc-open-source-media.html (accessed 2 May 2012).

Lefebvre, S. (2003) 'The Difficulties and Dilemmas of International Intelligence Cooperation', *International Journal of Intelligence and Counterintelligence*, 16, 527–541.

Lefebvre, S. (2009) 'Canadian Intelligence Culture – An Evaluation', in R.G. Swenson and S.C. Lemozy (eds) *Democratization of Intelligence: Melding Strategic Intelligence and National Discourse*, Washington, DC: National Defense Intelligence College, 79–98.

Lefebvre, S. (2010) 'Canada's Legal Framework for Intelligence', *International Journal of Intelligence & Counterintelligence*, 23(2), 247–295.

Leibowitz, J. (2006) *Strategic Intelligence: Business Intelligence, Competitive Intelligence and Knowledge Management*, Boca Raton, FL: Auerbach Publications.

Leigh, D. (2012) 'Libyan Family Rendered by UK to Gaddafi Accepts Settlement', press release, 13 December, London.

Leigh, I. (2011) 'National Courts and International Intelligence Cooperation', in H. Born, I. Leigh and A. Will (eds) *International Intelligence Cooperation and Accountability*, London: Routledge, 231–251.

Leiner, B., Cerf, V. *et al.* (2012) 'Brief History of the Internet', *Internet Society*. Online. Available: http://www.internetsociety.org/internet/internet-51/history-internet/brief-history-internet (accessed 12 March 2012).

Lele, A. (2013) *Asian Space Race: Rhetoric or Reality?,* New Delhi: Springer.

Leslau, O. (2012) 'Israeli Intelligence and the Czech–Egyptian Arms Deal', *Intelligence and National Security*, 27(3), 327–348.

Levchenko, S. (1988) *On the Wrong Side: My Life in the KGB*, Dulles: Potomac Books.

Leveson, B.H. (2012) *An Inquiry into the Culture, Practices and Ethics of the Press: Report*, House of Commons Papers, London: The Stationery Office.

Levi, M. and Maguire, M. (2004) 'Reducing and Preventing Organised Crime', *Crime, Law and Social Change*, 41, 397–469.

Lewis, J. (2011) 'The Threat', *Nextgov*, 15 August. Online. Available: http://www.nextgov.com/nextgov/ng_20110815_5884.php (accessed 18 May 2012).

Lewis, M. (2011) *The Big Short: Inside the Doomsday Machine*, London: Allen Lane.

Licklider, R. (1988) 'The Power of Oil: The Arab Oil Weapon and the Netherlands, the United Kingdom, Canada, Japan and the United States', *International Studies Quarterly*, 32(2), 205–226.

Liddell Hart, B. (1967) *Strategy*, London: Faber & Faber.

Liddell Hart, B.H. (1932) *The British Way in Warfare*, London: Faber & Faber.

Lin, J., Hsiao, R. and Stokes, M. (2011) 'The Chinese People's Liberation Army Signals Intelligence and Cyber Reconnaissance Infrastructure', Project 2049 Institute. Online. Available: http://project2049.net/documents/pla_third_department_sigint_cyber_stokes_lin_hsiao.pdf

Lin, L. (2012) 'Top 10 Think Tanks in China'. Online. Available: http://www.china.org.cn/top10/2011–09/26/content_23491278_2.htm (accessed 1 October 2012).

Liszkiewicz, J.Z. (2010) 'True Cost of One White Cotton T-Shirt', *Reconfigure*. Online. Available: http://true-cost.re-configure.org/true_cost_shirt.htm (accessed 5 July 2013).

Littler, G. (1967) Minute to Pitchforth (Treasury), 17 August. BA 25/41, London: National Archives.

Litvinenko, A. and Felshtinsky, Y. (2007) *Blowing Up Russia: The Secret Plot to Bring Back KGB Terror*, London: Gibson Square.

Livermore, D. (2009) 'Does Canada Need a Foreign Intelligence Agency?', Policy Brief No. 3, Centre for International Policy Studies, Ottawa: University of Ottawa. Online. Available: http://cips.uottawa.ca/eng/documents/CIPS_PolicyBrief_Livermore_Feb2009.pdf (accessed January 2013).

Lowenthal, M. (1992) 'Tribal Tongues: Intelligence Consumers, Intelligence Producers', *Washington Quarterly*, 15, Winter, 157–168.

Lowenthal, M. (2003) *Intelligence: From Secrets to Policy*, 2nd edn, Washington, DC: CQ Press.

Lowenthal, M. (2006) *Intelligence: From Secrets to Policy*, 3rd edn, Washington, DC: CQ Press.

Lowenthal, M. (2012) *Intelligence: From Secrets to Policy*, 5th edn, Washington, DC: CQ Press.

Lucas, E. (2012) *Deception: Spies, Lies and How Russia Dupes the West*, London: Bloomsbury Books.

Luft, G., Korin, A. and Gupta, E. (2011) 'Energy Security and Climate Change: A Tenuous Link', in B.K. Sovacool (ed.) *The Routledge Handbook of Energy Security*, New York: Routledge, 43–55.

Lustgarten, L. and Leigh, I. (1994) *In From the Cold: National Security and Parliamentary Democracy*, Gloucestershire, UK: Clarendon.

MacAskill, E. and Norton-Taylor, R. (2012) 'Agent in Underwear Bomb Plot "was British"', *Guardian*, 11 May.

Machiavelli, N. (1998 [1531]) *The Discourses*, ed. and intro. Bernard Crick, trans. Leslie J. Walker, rev. Brian Richardson, London: Penguin.

Machiavelli, N. (2001 [1521]) *The Art of War*, intro. Neal Wood [1965], New York: Da Capo.

Machiavelli, N. (2008 [1532]) *The Prince*, intro. Maurizio Viroli, trans. Peter Bondanella, Oxford: Oxford University Press.

Mack, C. (2011) 'Fifty Years of Moore's Law', *IEEE Transactions on Semiconductor Manufacturing*, May, 24(2), 202–207.

MacKintosh, J.P. (1962) 'The Role of the Committee of Imperial Defence before 1914', *English Historical Review*, 77(304), July, 490–503.

Macridis, R.C. (1961) 'Interest Groups in Comparative Analysis', *Journal of Politics*, 23, 25–45.

Maddrell, P. (2006) *Spying on Science: Western Intelligence in Divided Germany, 1945–1961*, Oxford: Oxford University Press.

Madramootoo, C. and Fyles, H. (2012) 'Synthesis of Findings from the Four McGill Conferences on Global Food Security', *Food Security*, 4, 307–317.

Madsen, F.G. (2009) *Transnational Organized Crime*, London: Routledge.

Mahadevan, P. (2011) 'The Perils of Prediction: Indian Intelligence and the Kargil Crisis', Manekshaw Paper No. 29.

Mahmood, A. (2009) 'RADARSAT-1, RADARSAT-2 and RCM'. Presentation to Ground Segment Coordination Body (GSCB), GSCB Workshop, 18–19 June, Frascati, Italy.

Mahnken, T. (2005) 'Spies and Bureaucrats: Getting Intelligence Right', *Public Interest*, 81, 37.

Major, J. (2010a) *Air India Flight 182, A Canadian Tragedy: Vol. 3*, Commission of Inquiry into the Investigation of the Bombing of Air India Flight 182, Ottawa: Public Works and Government Services.

Major, J. (2010b) *Air India Flight 182, A Canadian Tragedy: Vol. 5*, Commission of Inquiry into the Investigation of the Bombing of Air India Flight 182, Ottawa: Public Works and Government Services.

Malhotra, I. (1989) *Indira Gandhi: A Personal and Political Biography*, London: Coronet Books.

Malik, V.P. (2006) *Kargil: From Surprise to Victory*, New Delhi: HarperCollins.

Manget, F. (1996) 'Intelligence and the Rise of Judicial Intervention: Another System of Oversight', *Studies in Intelligence*, 39(5).

Mangold, T. (1991) *Cold War: James Jesus Angleton: The CIA's Master Spy Hunter*, New York: Simon & Schuster.

Manningham-Buller, E. (2012) *Securing Freedom*, London: Profile Books.

Manocher, D. and Carrie, L.C. (2011) 'The Strategic Implications of China's Energy Engagement with the Developing World', in M. Dorray and C.L. Currier (eds) *China's Energy Relations with the Developing World*, New York: Continuum, 3–16.

Manyika, J., Chui, M. *et al.* (2011) 'Big Data: The Next Frontier for Innovation, Competition and Productivity', *McKinsey Global Institute*, May. Online. Available: http://www.mckinsey.com/insights/mgi/research/technology_and_innovation/big_data_the_next_frontier_for_innovation (accessed 10 June 2012).

Mao Zedong (1972) *Six Essays on Military Affairs*, Peking: Foreign Languages Press.

Marchand, De M. (1987) *Foreign Intelligence Assessment: A Review*, Ottawa: Privy Council Office (released to the author under the Access to Information Act).

Marchetti, V. and Marks, J.D. (1974) *The CIA and the Cult of Intelligence*, New York: Knopf.

Margulies, J. (2006) *Guantanamo and the Abuse of Presidential Power*, New York: Simon & Schuster.

Markoff, J. (2008) 'Internet Traffic Begins to Bypass the US', *New York Times*, 29 August. Online. Available: https://www.nytimes.com/2008/08/30/business/30pipes.html?_r=1&pagewanted=all (accessed 8 March 2012).

Marrin, S. (2007) 'Intelligence Analysis Theory: Explaining and Predicting Analytic Responsibilities', *Intelligence and National Security*, 22(6), 821–846.

Marrin, S. (2009) 'Training and Educating US Intelligence Analysts', *International Journal of Intelligence and Counterintelligence*, 22(1), 131–146.

Marrin, S. (2009) 'Intelligence Analysis and Decision Making: Methodological Challenges', in P. Gill, S. Marrin and M. Pythian (eds) *Intelligence Theory: Key Questions and Debates*, London: Routledge, pp. 131–150.

Marrin, S. (2012) 'Intelligence Studies Centers: Making Scholarship on Intelligence Analysis Useful', *Intelligence and National Security*, 27, June, 398–422.

Marshall, A. (1994) *Intelligence and Espionage in the Reign of Charles II, 1660–1685*, Cambridge: Cambridge University Press.

Martin, D. (1980) *Wilderness of Mirrors*, New York: Harper & Row.

Masterman, J.C. (1972) *The Double-Cross System in the War of 1939 to 1945*, New Haven, CT: Yale University Press.

Mats, B. and Malone, D.M. (2000) *Greed and Grievance: Economic Agendas in Civil Wars*, Boulder, CO: Lynne Rienner.

Mattli, W. (1999) *The Logic of Regional Integration*, Cambridge: Cambridge University Press.

May, E.R. (ed.) (1984) *Knowing One's Enemies: Intelligence Assessment before the Two World Wars*, Princeton, NJ: Princeton University Press.

May, E.R. (1995) 'Studying and Teaching Intelligence', *Studies in Intelligence*, 36, 1–5.

May, E.R. (2000) *Strange Victory: Hitler's Conquest of France*, New York: Hill and Wang.

Mayer, J. (2005) 'Outsourcing Torture', *New Yorker*, 14 February.

Mayer, J. (2006) 'The CIA's Travel Agent', *New Yorker*, 30 October.

Mazumdar, P.K. and Kataria, R.P. (1997) *The Constitution of India*, New Delhi: Orient Publishing.

McConnell, M., and Redd, R. (2007) 'Statement for the Record, Senate Homeland Security and Governmental Affairs Committee Hearing on Confronting the Terrorist Threat to the Homeland: Six Years after 9/11', 10 September.

McCready, D.M. (2003) 'Learning from Sun Tzu', *Military Review*, 83, 85–88.

McCullagh, D. (2012) 'FBI "Looking at" Law Making Web Sites Wiretap-ready, Director Says', *CNET News*, 18 May. Online. Available: http://news.cnet.com/8301–1009_3–57437391–83/fbi-looking-at-law-making-web-sites-wiretap-ready-director-says/ (accessed 12 March 2012).

McDermott, R. (2012) E-mail correspondence with the author, 29 May.

McDonald, B.L. (2010) *Food Security*, Cambridge: Polity Press.

McDowell, D. (2009) *Strategic Intelligence: A Handbook for Practitioners, Managers and Users*, Lanham, MD: Scarecrow Press.

McGregor, R. (2011) *The Party: The Secret World of China's Communist Rulers*, London: Penguin Books.

McIntosh, R. and Bancroft, I. (1969) *Overseas Research Enquiry* (PSIS(69)(5), July. CAB 163/153, London: National Archives.

McNeilly, M.R. (2001) *Sun Tzu and the Art of Modern Warfare*, New York: Oxford University Press.

McNeilly, M.R. (2011) *Sun Tzu and the Art of Business: Six Strategic Principles for Managers*, New York: Oxford University Press.

Mead, W.J. and Sorensen, P.E. (1971) 'A National Defense Petroleum Reserve Alternative to Oil Import Quotas', *Land Economics*, 47(3), 211–224.

Melman, Y. and Raviv, D. (1989) *The Imperfect Spies: The History of Israeli Intelligence*, London: Sidgwick & Jackson.

Melman, Y. and Raviv, D. (2012) *Spies Against Armageddon: Inside Israel's Secret Wars*, Lebanon: Levant Books.

Mena, F. and Hobbs, D. (2010) 'Narcophobia: Drugs Prohibition and the Generation of Human Rights Abuses', *Trends in Organized Crime*, 13, 60–74.

Mercado, S. (2001) 'Open Source Intelligence from the Airwaves: FBIS Against the Axis, 1941–1945', *Studies in Intelligence*, Fall–Winter, 11.

Mercado, S. (2004) 'A Venerable Source in a New Era: Sailing the Sea of OSINT in the Information Age', *Studies in Intelligence: Journal of the American Intelligence Professional*, 48(3), 45–55.

Mercyhurst College, Institute for Intelligence Studies: http://www.iismu.org/ (accessed June 2013).

Merle, R. (2006) 'Census Counts 100,000 Contractors in Iraq', *Washington Post*, December 5. Online. Available: http://www.washingtonpost.com/wp-dyn/content/article/2006/12/04/AR2006120401311.html

Mertsalov, A.N. (2004) 'Jomini versus Clausewitz', in M. Ljubica and L. Erickson (eds) *Russia: War, Peace and Diplomacy: Essays in Honour of John Erickson*, London: Weidenfeld & Nicolson.

Metz, C. (2012) 'Mavericks Invent Future Internet Where Cisco is Meaningless', *Wired Enterprise*, 16 April. Online. Available: http://www.wired.com/wiredenterprise/2012/04/nicira/ (accessed 2 May 2012).

Meyer, A. and Wilson, A. (2003) '*Sunzi Bingfa* as History and Theory', in B.A. Lee and K.F. Walling (eds) *Strategic Logic and Political Rationality: Essays in Honor of Michael I. Handel*, London: Frank Cass, 99–118.

MI5 (1989) 'Security Service Act 1989'. Online. Available: http://www.legislation.gov.uk/ukpga/1989/5/pdfs/ukpga_19890005_en.pdf (accessed 26 June 2012).

MI5 (2012a) 'Objectives and Values'. Online. Available: https://www.mi5.gov.uk/output/objectives-and-values.html (accessed 26 June 2012).

MI5 (2012b) 'Major Areas of Work'. Online. Available: https://www.mi5.gov.uk/output/major-areas-of-work.html (accessed 26 June 2012).

MI5 (2012c) 'How We Operate'. Online. Available: https://www.mi5.gov.uk/output/how-we-operate.html (accessed 26 June 2012).

MI5 (2012d) 'Joint Terrorism Analysis Centre'. Online. Available: https://www.mi5.gov.uk/output/joint-terrorism-analysis-centre.html (accessed 26 June 2012).

Michaelson, G.A. and Michaelson, S. (2010) *Sun Tzu: The Art of War for Managers: 50 Strategic Rules Updated for Today's Business*, Avon, MA: Adams Media.

Milne, G. (1928) *The Need for an Organization to Study Industrial Intelligence (including Industrial Mobilization in Foreign Countries): A Memorandum by the Secretary of State for War*, 9 August. CAB 48/3, London: National Archives.

Ministry of Defence (MOD) (1970) 'Report of Working Group on Overseas Political and Economic Research', 16 April. DEFE 27/1, London: National Archives.

Ministry of Economic Warfare (MEW) (1943) *Report on the Demobilization of the Ministry of Economic Warfare*, 19 May, London: National Archives.

Ministry of National Defense, People's Republic of China (2011) 'The Wisdom of Sun Tzu'. Online. Available: http://www.mod.gov.cn/affair/2011–07/31/content_4286873_4.htm (accessed 5 July 2013).

Misra, P. (2008) 'A Jihad Grows in Kashmir', *New York Times*, 26 August.

Mitelman, L.T. (1974) 'Preface to a Theory of Intelligence', *Studies in Intelligence*, 8(3), Fall, 19–22.

MOD (2011) JDO 2–00: 'Understanding and Intelligence Support to Joint Operations', August, 1–9. Online. Available: http://www.mod.uk/NR/rdonlyres/4169B1A1–179C-459D-B7AD-DABB63EA069E/0/20110830JDP2003rdEDweb.pdf (accessed 26 June 2012).

MOD (2012a) 'Defence Intelligence'. Online. Available: http://www.mod.uk/DefenceInternet/About-Defence/WhatWeDo/SecurityandIntelligence/DIS/ (accessed 26 June 2012).

MOD (2012b) 'How Defence Intelligence Does Its Work'. Online. Available: http://www.mod.uk/DefenceInternet/AboutDefence/WhatWeDo/SecurityandIntelligence/DIS/HowDefenceIntelligenceDoesItsWork.htm (accessed 26 June 2012).

Modin, Y. (1994) *My Five Cambridge Friends*, London: Headline.

MODUK (2010) JDN1/10: *Joint Doctrine Note 1/10: Intelligence and Understanding*, Shrivenham, UK: Defence Concepts and Doctrine Centre.

MODUK (2011) JDP2–00: *Understanding and Intelligence Support to Joint Operations*, Shrivenham, UK: Defence Concepts and Doctrine Centre.

Mohammed, A. (2006) 'Judge Declines to Dismiss Lawsuit Against AT&T', *Washington Post*, 21 July.

Moodie, M. (2012) 'Options and Dynamics: Chemical and Biological Weapons Proliferation in 2020', in J.J. Wirtz and P.R. Lavoy (eds) *Over the Horizon Proliferation Threats*, Stanford, CA: Stanford University Press, 266–290.

Moran, C. and Willmetts, S. (2011) 'Secrecy, Censorship and Beltway Books: The CIA's Publications Review Board', *International Journal of Intelligence and Counterintelligence*, 24(2), 239–252.

Morgan, R.E. (1980) *Domestic Intelligence: Monitoring Dissent in America*, Austin, TX: University of Texas Press.

Morio, S., Sensou, J. and Kyoukun (2012) *The Lessons of the Intelligence War*, Tokyo: Fuyo Shobo.

Morris, J.L. (1996) 'MASINT', *American Intelligence Journal*, 17(1), 24.

Mosley, J.X. (2009) FC 1058 [2010] 1 F.C.R. 460, 5 October.

Mullick, B.N. (1971) *My Years with Nehru: The Chinese Betrayal*, New Delhi: Allied Publishers.

Murphy, P. (2001) 'Intelligence and Decolonisation: The Life and Death of the Federal Intelligence and Security Bureau, 1954–63', *Journal of Imperial and Commonwealth History*, 29(2), 101–130.

Murphy, P. (2002) 'Creating a Commonwealth Intelligence Culture: The View from Central Africa, 1945–65', *Intelligence and National Security*, 17(3), Autumn, 131–162.

Murray, W. (1997a) 'Thinking about Revolutions in Military Affairs', *Joint Force Quarterly*, 16, 69–76.

Murray, W. (1997b) 'War, Theory, Clausewitz and Thucydides: The Game May Change but the Rules Remain', *Marine Corps Gazette*, 81, 62–69.

Myers, K.C. (2010) *Reflexive Practice: Professional Thinking for a Turbulent World*, New York: Palgrave Macmillan.

Naím, M. (2003) 'The Five Wars of Globalisation', *Foreign Policy*, 82(1), 29–37.

Naím, M. (2005) *Illicit: How Smugglers, Traffickers and Copycats are Hijacking the Global Economy*, London: William Heinemann.

Nakasone, Y. (2012) *Nakasone Yasuhiro ga kataru Sengo Nihon Gaikou [Japanese Foreign Policy Since 1945: Yasuhiro Nakasone Oral History]*, Tokyo: Shinchosha.

Nash, S. (2007) 'Decrypting Biofuel Scenarios', *BioScience*, 57(6), 472–477.

National Commission on Terrorist Attacks Upon the United States (2004) *The 9/11 Commission Report: Final Report*, Washington: GPO.

National Defence Act, R.S.C. (1985) c. N-5. Online. Available: http://laws-lois.justice.gc.ca/eng/acts/N-5/ (accessed December 2012).

National Intelligence Council (2008) *Global Trends 2025: A Transformed World*, Washington, DC: GPO. Online. Available: http://www.dni.gov/files/documents/Newsroom/Reports%20and%20Pubs/2025_Global_Trends_Final_Report.pdf (accessed 19 June 2013).

National Policing Improvement Agency (NPIA) (2011) 'Police National Database (PND)'. Online. Available: http://www.npia.police.uk/en/15091.htm (accessed 28 May 2012).

NATO (1975) *AAP-6 (M) Glossary of Terms and Definitions for Military Use* (English and French), Brussels: NATO.

NATO (2002) *Open Source Intelligence Reader*, SACLANT Intelligence Branch.

Naughton, J. (2012) *From Gutenberg to Zuckerberg: What You Really Need to Know About the Internet*, London: Quercus.

Naylor, R.T. (1996) 'From Underworld to Underground', *Crime, Law & Social Change*, 24, 79–150.

Naylor, R.T. (1997) 'Mafias, Myths and Markets', *Transnational Organized Crime*, 3(3), 1–45.

Noël, P. (2006/2007) 'The New US Middle East Policy and Energy Security Challenges', *International Journal*, 62(1), 43–54.

Nolte, W. (2012) E-mail correspondence with the author, 22 June.

North, G. (2012) 'Administrative Law (New World Order) versus Democracy (Live Free or Die)', Phi Beta Iota Public Intelligence Blog, 4 February. Online. Available: http://tinyurl.com/North-Admin-Law.

NSC (2010) *A Strong Britain in an Age of Uncertainty: The National Security Strategy,* Cm. 7953, London. Online. Available: www.direct.gov.uk/nationalsecuritystrategy (accessed 26 June 2012).

Nuttall, W.J. and Manz, D.L. (2008) 'A New Energy Security Paradigm for the Twenty-First Century', *Technological Forecasting & Social Change*, 75, 1247–1259.

O'Connell, A.J. (2006) 'The Architecture of Smart Intelligence: Structuring and Overseeing Agencies in the Post-9/11 World', *California Law Review*, 94, December, 1655–1744.

O'Connell, K.M. (2004) 'Thinking about Intelligence Comparatively', *Brown Journal of World Affairs*, 11, Summer/Fall.

O'Connor, D. (2006) *Report of the Events Relating to Maher Arar: Factual Background*, 1, Commission of Inquiry into the Actions of Canadian Officials in Relation to Maher Arar, Ottawa: Public Works and Government Services.

Oatley, T. and Nabors, R. (1998) 'Redistributive Cooperation: Market Failures and Wealth Transfers in the Creation of the Basle Accord', *International Organization*, 52, 35–54.

Odom, W. (1982) *Odom's Daily Diary: Box 21, Folder 1: Daily Activity Logs: September–December 1982*, Washington, DC: General William E. Odom Papers, Manuscript Division, Library of Congress.

Odom, W. (2003) *Fixing Intelligence for a More Secure America*, New Haven, CT: Yale University Press.

OECD/DAC (2004) 'Security System Reform and Governance'. Online. Available: http://www.oecd.org/dataoecd/8/39/31785288.pdf (accessed 5 July 2013).

Office of the Auditor General (OAG) (1996) 'Chapter 27: The Canadian Intelligence Community – Control and Accountability', *November 1996 Report of the Auditor General of Canada*. Online. Available: http://www.oag-bvg.gc.ca/internet/English/parl_oag_199611_e_1152.html (accessed January 2013).

Office of the Auditor General (OAG) (2009) 'Chapter 1: National Security: Intelligence and Information

Sharing', *Status Report of the Auditor General of Canada to the House of Commons*, Ottawa: Public Works and Government Services.

Office of the Communications Security Establishment Commissioner (OCSEC) (2007) *Review of the Activities of CSE's Office of Counter-Terrorism*, 16 October (released to the author under the Access to Information Act).

Office of the National Counterintelligence Executive (2011) 'Foreign Spies Stealing US Economic Secrets in Cyberspace', October.

Okoda, Y. (2001) *Migu 25 Jiken no Shinsou [The Truth of the Mig-25 Incident]*, Tokyo: Gakushu Kenkyusha.

Olcott, A. (2012) *Open Source Intelligence in a Networked World*, New York: Continuum International Publishing.

Oliver, D. (1991) *Government in the United Kingdom: The Search for Accountability, Effectiveness and Citizenship*, Glasgow: Open University Press.

Olsen, M. (2012) 'Remarks Prepared for Delivery to the American Bar Association Standing Committee on Law and National Security', 16 May. Online. Available: http://www.nctc.gov/press_room/speeches/20120516_Director_Olsen_ABA_Remarks.pdf (accessed 29 July 2012).

Olsen, M. and Olsen, G. (2011) 'Testimony before the Permanent Select Committee on Intelligence, US House of Representatives', 6 October. Online. Available: http://www.nctc.gov/press_room/speeches/dnctc_testimony_before_hpsci_111006.pdf (accessed 23 July 2012).

Omand, D. (2009) 'The Limits of Arowal: Secret Intelligence in an Age of Public Scrutiny', in G. Treverton and W. Agrell (eds) *National Intelligence Systems: Current Research and Future Prospects*, Cambridge: Cambridge University Press, 235–264.

Omand, D. (2010a) *Securing the State*, London: Hurst.

Omand, D. (2010b) 'Evidence to Chilcot Inquiry into the Iraq War'. Online. Available: http://www.iraqinquiry.org.uk/transcripts/oralevidence-bydate/100120.aspx (accessed 5 July 2013).

Omand, D. (2012a) *Securing the State*, London: Hurst.

Omand, D. (2012b) E-mail correspondence with the author, 23 June.

Omand, D., Bartlett, J. and Miller, C. (2012) *Intelligence*, London: DEMOS.

Omori, Y. (2005) *Nihon no Interigensu Kikan [Japanese Intelligence Agency]*, Tokyo: Bunshun Shinsho.

Order for the Organization of the Cabinet Office (1952) No. 219, 31 July. Online. Available: http://www.cas.go.jp/jp/hourei/seirei/naikaku_s.html (accessed 5 July 2013).

Oros, A. (2002) 'Japan's Growing Intelligence Capability', *International Journal of Intelligence and Counterintelligence*, 15(1), 1–25.

Orttung, R.W. and Perovic, J. (2012) 'Energy Security', in V. Mauer, D. Cavelty and M. Dunn (eds) *Handbook of Security Studies*, London: Routledge.

Ott, M. (2003) 'Partisanship and the Decline of Intelligence Oversight', *International Journal of Intelligence and CounterIntelligence*, 16(1), 69–94.

Overseas Economic and Scientific Enquiry (1968) (JIC)(68)(IR), 22 March. CAB 182/73, London: National Archives.

Oye, K. (ed.) (1985) *Cooperation Under Anarchy*, Princeton, NJ: Princeton University Press.

Pallister, D. *et al.* (2003) 'Secret Aid Poured into Colombian Drug War', *Guardian*, 9 July.

Paret, P. (1986) 'Napoleon and the Revolution in War', in P. Paret (ed.) *Makers of Modern Strategy: From Machiavelli to the Nuclear Age*, Oxford: Clarendon Press, 123–142.

Parker, G. (1998) *The Grand Strategy of Philip II*, New Haven, CN: Yale University Press.

Pascual, C. and Zambetakis, E. (2008) 'The Geopolitics of Energy: From Security to Survival', in C. Pascual and J. Elkind (eds) *Energy Security: Economics, Politics, Strategies and Implications*, Vancouver: University of British Columbia Press.

Pedlow, G.W. and Welzenbach, D.E. (1998) *The CIA and the U-2 Program, 1954–1974*, Langley, VA: History Staff, Center for the Study of Intelligence, Central Intelligence Agency.

Pelletière, S.C. (2004) *America's Oil Wars*, Westport, CT: Praeger Publishers.

Perl, R. (2007) 'Combating Terrorism: The Challenge of Measuring Effectiveness', CRS Report for Congress (RL33160) (23 November 2005, updated 12 March 2007).

Permanent Select Committee on Intelligence (HPSCI) (2007) *House of Representatives Report on Intelligence Authorization Act for Fiscal Year 2008*, Report 110–131, 7 May, Washington, DC.

Perrow, C. (2011) *The Next Catastrophe: Reducing Our Vulnerabilities to Natural, Industrial and Terrorist Disasters*, Princeton, NJ: Princeton University Press.

Peters, B.G. (1998) *Comparative Politics: Theory and Methods*, Houndmills, UK: Palgrave.

Peters, D. (2001) 'The Debate about a New German Foreign Policy after Unification', in V. Rittberger (ed.) *German Foreign Policy Since Unification: Theories and Case Studies*, Manchester: Manchester University Press, 11–33.

Peters, S. (2004) 'Coercive Western Energy Security Strategies: "Resource Wars" as a New Threat to Global Security', *Geopolitics*, 9(1), 187–212.

Petersen, M. (2011) 'What I Learned in 40 Years of Doing Intelligence Analysis for US Foreign Policymakers', *Studies in Intelligence*, March, 55(1). Online. Available: https://www.cia.gov/library/center-for-the-study-of-intelligence/csi-publications/csi-studies/studies/vol.-55-no.-1/what-i-learned-in-40-years-of-doing-intelligence-analysis-for-us-foreign-policymakers.html (accessed 10 February 2012).

Pfiffner, J. and Phythian, M. (eds) (2008) *Intelligence and National Security Policymaking on Iraq: British and American Perspectives*, Manchester: University of Manchester Press.

Philby, K. (1968) *My Silent War*, New York: Grove Press.

PHP Research Institute (ed.) (2006) Nihon no Interijensu Taisei; Henkaku heno Rood Mappu [Japanese Intelligence: A Roadmap to Transformation], June. Online. Available: http://research.php.co.jp/research/risk_management/policy/data/seisaku01_teigen33_00.pdf (accessed 5 July 2013).

Phythian, M. (2007) 'The British Experience with Intelligence Accountability', *Intelligence and National Security*, 22(1), 75–99.

Phythian, M. (2012) E-mail correspondence with the author, 24 June.

Phythian, M. (2012) 'Policing Uncertainty: Intelligence, Security and Risk', *Intelligence and National Security*, 38(2): 187–205.

Pike Committee (1976) 'The CIA Report the President Doesn't Want You to Read: The Pike Papers', *Village Voice*, 16 and 23 February.

Pillar, P. (2008) 'The Unending Saga of Intelligence Reform', *Foreign Affairs*, March–April. Online. Available: https://www.foreignaffairs.com/articles/63237/paul-r-pillar/intelligent-design.

Pillar, P. (2011) *Intelligence and US Foreign Policy: Iraq, 9/11 and Misguided Reform*, New York: Columbia University Press.

Pinstrup-Andersen, P. (2009) 'Food Security: Definition and Measurement', *Food Security*, 1, 5–7.

Pollard, N.A. (2009) 'On Counterterrorism and Intelligence', in G. Treverton and W. Agrell (eds) *National Intelligence Systems*, Cambridge: Cambridge University Press.

Polmar, N. and Allen, T.B. (1997) *The Encyclopedia of Espionage*, New York: Gramercy Books.

Poole, P.S. (1998) *ECHELON: America's Secret Global Surveillance Network*, Washington, DC: Free Congress Research and Education Foundation.

Popplewell, R.J. (1995) *Intelligence and Imperial Defence: British Intelligence and the Defence of the Indian Empire*, London: Frank Cass.

Posner, R.A. (2001) 'Security Versus Civil Liberties', *The Atlantic Online*, December.

Posner, R.A. (2005) *Preventing Surprise Attacks: Intelligence Reform in the Wake of 9/11*. New York: Rowman & Littlefield.

Powell, C. with Persico, J.E. (1995) *My American Journey*, New York: Random House.

Powers, T. (1979) *The Man Who Kept the Secrets: Richard Helms and the CIA*, New York: Simon & Schuster.

Prados, J. (2006) *Safe for Democracy: The Secret Wars of the CIA*, Chicago: Ivan R. Dee.

Prahalad, C.K. (2009) *The Fortune at the Bottom of the Pyramid: Eradicating Poverty Through Profits*, Saddle River, NJ: Pearson Prentice Hall.

PRC Ministry of Foreign Affairs (2012) 'Ministry of Foreign Affairs Departments'. Online. Available: http://www.fmprc.gov.cn/eng/wjb/zzjg/ (accessed 30 September 2012).

President Bush (2006) 'State of the Union Address, 2006'. Online. Available: http://georgewbush-whitehouse.archives.gov/stateoftheunion/2006/ (accessed 5 July 2013).

President Carter (1980) 'State of the Union Address, 1980', in J. Carter, *Papers of the Presidents of the United States*, Washington, DC.

Prevelakis, V. and Spinellis, D. (2007) 'The Athens Affair', *IEEE Spectrum*, July. Online. Available: http://spectrum.ieee.org//telecom/security/the-athens-affair (accessed 10 February 2011).

Priest, D. and Arkin, W. (2012) *Top Secret America: The Rise of the New American Security State*, New York: Little, Brown and Co.

Prime Minister and Cabinet Office (PM&C) (2012) *The National Security and International Policy Group Executive*, Canberra: Australian Commonwealth Government.

Prime Minister's Office (n.d.) 'Cabinet Committee Mandates and Membership'. Online. Available: http://www.pm.gc.ca/eng/feature.asp?pageId=53 (accessed January 2013).

Prins, G. (2011) 'The British Way of Strategy-Making: Vital Lessons for Our Times', *RUSI Occasional Paper*, October. Online. Available: http://www.rusi.org/downloads/assets/The_British_Way_of_Strategy_Making.pdf (accessed 26 June 2012).

Privacy International (2011) 'Surveillance Monitor 2011: Assessment of Surveillance across Europe'. Online. Available: https://www.privacyinternational.org/reports/surveillance-monitor-2011-assessment-of-surveillance-across-europe/i-key-findings (accessed 5 July 2013).

Privy Council Office (2001) *The Canadian Security and Intelligence Community: Helping Keep Canada and Canadians Safe and Secure*, Ottawa: Government of Canada.

Privy Council Office (2010) *The Role and Structure of the Privy Council Office*, Ottawa: Government of Canada.

Privy Council Office (2012) 'Deputy Minister Committee Mandates and Memberships', 4 December. Online. Available: http://www.pco-bcp.gc.ca/index.asp?lang=eng&page=secretariats&sub=spsp-psps&doc=comm/mandat-eng.htm (accessed January 2013).

Probst, R.R. (2006) 'Clausewitz on Intelligence', in R.Z. George and Kline, R.D. (eds) *Intelligence and the National Security Strategist: Enduring Issues and Challenges*, Lanham, MD: Rowman & Littlefield, 3–9.

Public Safety Canada (PSC) (2012) 'National Security', 4 December. Online. Available: http://www.publicsafety.gc.ca/prg/ns/index-eng.aspx (accessed January 2012).

Quan, D. (2012) 'Intelligence Analysts Taking Over Leading Role in Spy Game: CSIS Chief', *Canada.com*, 25 June. Online. Available: http://www.canada.com/news/Intelligence+analysts+taking+over+leading+role+game+CSIS+chief/6838216/story.html (accessed 27 June 2012).

Quarmby, N. and Young, L.J. (2010) *The Art of Influence*, Sydney: Federation Press.

Quinlan, M. (2007) *Just Intelligence: Prolegomena to an Ethical Theory*, in P. Hennessy (ed.) *The New Protective State*, London: Continuum, 123–141.

Rabasa, A. *et al.* (2009) *The Lessons of Mumbai*, Santa Monica, CA: Rand Corporation.

Raghavan, S. (2009) 'Intelligence Failures and Reforms', *Seminar Journal*, 699.

Raghavan, S. and Chaudhuri, R. (2010) 'Spooks and States', *Seminar Journal*, 611.

Raman, B. (2007) *The Kaoboys of R&AW: Down Memory Lane*, New Delhi: Lancer.

Raman, B. (2010) *Mumbai 26/11: A Day of Infamy*, New Delhi: Lancer.

RAND (2006) *Towards a Theory of Intelligence*, National Security Research Division & Office of DNI, Washington: RAND.

Random, H.A. (1958) 'Intelligence as a Science', *Studies in Intelligence*, Spring. Online. Available: https://www.cia.gov/library/center-for-the-study-of-intelligence/kent-csi/vol46no3/html/v46i3a02p.htm. (accessed 29 December 2011).

Ranelagh, J. (1986) *The Agency: The Rise and Decline of the CIA*, New York: Simon & Schuster.

Rangarajan, L.N. (ed.) (1992) *Kautilya: The Arthashastra*, New Delhi, India: Penguin Classics.

Ransom, H.H. (1958) *Central Intelligence and National Security*, Cambridge, MA: Harvard University Press.

Ransom, H.H. (1960) 'How Intelligent Is Intelligence?' *New York Times Magazine*, 22 May, 80–83.

Ransom, H.H. (1961) 'Secret Mission in an Open Society', *New York Times Magazine*, 21 May, 77–79.

Ransom, H.H. (1970) *The Intelligence Establishment*, Cambridge, MA: Harvard University Press.

Ransom, H.H. (1975) Remarks to the author, Washington, DC, 20 December.

Ratcliffe, J. (2008) *Intelligence-led Policing*, Cullompton, UK: Willan.

Rathmell, A. (2002) 'Towards Postmodern Intelligence', *Intelligence and National Security*, 17(3), 87–104.

Renier, O. and Rubinstein, V. (1986) *Assigned to Listen: The Evesham Experience 1939–1943*, London: BBC Books.

Report of the Council of Advisers for Legislation on Security Law (2010) Online. Available: http://202.232.146.151/jp/singi/jouhouhozen/housei_kaigi/konkyo.pdf

Reveron, Derek S. (2006) 'Old Allies, New Friends: Intelligence-Sharing in the War on Terror', *Orbis* 50(3), 453–468.

Reveron, D. and Stevenson Murer, J. (2006) *Flashpoints in the War on Terrorism*, London: Routledge.

Rheingold, H. (2012) *NET SMART: How to Thrive Online*, Cambridge, MA: MIT Press.

Richards, J. (2012) 'Intelligence Dilemma? Contemporary Counter-terrorism in a Liberal Democracy', *Intelligence and National Security*, 27(5), 761–780.

Richards, J. and Lewis, P. (2011) 'How Twitter Was Used to Spread – and Knock Down – Rumours During the Riots', *Guardian*, 7 December. Online. Available: http://www.guardian.co.uk/uk/2011/dec/07/how-twitter-spread-rumours-riots.

Richelson, J.T. (1986) *Sword and Shield: Soviet Intelligence and Security Apparatus*, Cambridge, MA: Ballinger Publishing Co.

Richelson, J.T. (1988) *Foreign Intelligence Organizations*, Cambridge, MA: Ballinger Publishing Co.

Richelson, J.T. (1990) 'The Calculus of Intelligence Cooperation', *International Journal of Intelligence and Counterintelligence*, 4(3), 307–323.

Richelson, J.T. (1999) *America's Space Sentinels: DSP Satellites and National Security*, Lawrence: University of Kansas Press.

Richelson, J.T. (2012) *The US Intelligence Community*, 6th edn, Boulder, CO: Westview Press.

Richelson, J.T. and Ball, D. (1985) *The Ties That Bind: Intelligence Cooperation Between the UK/USA Countries – the United Kingdom, the United State of America, Canada, Australia and New Zealand*, Sydney: Allen & Unwin.

Richelson, J.T. and Ball, D. (1990) *The Ties That Bind: Intelligence Cooperation Between the UK/USA – the United Kingdom, the United States of America, Canada, Australia and New Zealand*, 2nd edn, Sydney: Allen and Unwin.

Rischard, J.F. (2003) *HIGH NOON: 20 Global Problems, 20 Years to Solve Them*, New York: Basic Books.

Risen, J. (2006) *State of War: The Secret History of the CIA and the Bush Administration*, New York: Free Press.

Robarge, D. (2007) *Archangel: CIA's Supersonic A-12 Reconnaissance Aircraft*, Washington, DC: Center for the Study of Intelligence, Central Intelligence Agency.

Roberts, P.C. (2012) 'December Net Jobs a 12,000 LOSS – Actual Unemployment 2.6 Times Official Rate or 22.4%', *Phi Beta Iota Public Intelligence Blog*. Online. Available: http://tinyurl.com/Roberts-22-4.

Robertson, K.G. (1982) *Public Secrets: A Study in the Development of Government Secrecy*, London: Macmillan.

Robertson, K.G. (1987) *British and American Approaches to Intelligence*, London: Macmillan.

Robinson, B. (1992) 'The Fall and Rise of Cryptanalysis in Canada', *Cryptologia*, 16(1), 23–38.

Rockefeller Commission (1975) 'Commission on CIA Activities within the United States', *Report to the President*, Washington, DC: Government Printing Office.

Rodriguez, O.R. (2012) 'Mexico Violence: Unidentified Bodies, Missing Cases Mount', *Huffington Post*, 23 July.

Rogers, C.J. (2002) 'Clausewitz, Genius and the Rules', *Journal of Military History*, 66(4), 1167–1176.

Rogers, P. (2002) *Losing Control: Global Insecurity in the Twenty First Century*, London: Pluto.

Rolington, A. (2006) 'Objective Intelligence or Plausible Denial: An Open Source Review of Intelligence Method and Process since 9/11', *Intelligence and National Security*, 21(5), 741–742.

Romm, J.J. (1993) *Defining National Security: The Nonmilitary Aspects*, New York: Council on Foreign Relations Press.

Ronald, N. (1944) Minute to Robbins (War Cabinet Office), 28 November. CAB 21/2562. London: National Archives.

Roxburgh, A. (2012) *The Strongman: Vladimir Putin and the Struggle for Russia*, London: I.B. Tauris.

Royal Canadian Mounted Police (RCMP) (2009) 'Criminal Intelligence Program', 6 January. Online. Available: http://www.rcmp-grc.gc.ca/ci-rc/index-eng.htm (accessed January 2013).

Royal Commission of Inquiry into the Australian Secret Intelligence Service (1995) Canberra, Common-wealth of Australia: Public Edition.

Rudner, M. (2001) 'Canada's Communications Security Establishment from Cold War to Globalization', *Intelligence & National Security*, 16(1), 97–128.

Rudner, M. (2008) 'Protecting Critical Energy Infrastructure Through Intelligence', *International Journal of Intelligence and Counterintelligence*, 21(4), 635–660.

Ruíz, M.C. (2005) 'El CESID: Historia de un intento de modernización de los. Servicios de Inteligencia', *Arbor*, 709, 121–150.

Rumsfeld, D. (2011) *Known and Unknown: A Memoir*, New York: Sentinel.

Russell, B. (1946) *History of Western Philosophy*, London: George Allen & Unwin.

Sakwa, R. (2011) *The Crisis of Russian Democracy: The Dual State, Factionalism and the Medvedev Succession*, Cambridge: Cambridge University Press.

Sands, A. (2005) 'Integrating Open Sources into Transnational Threat Assessments', in J. Sims and B. Gerber (eds) *Transforming US Intelligence*, Washington, DC: Georgetown University Press.

Sato, M. (2012) *Joho Sensou no Kyoukun (Lessons of Intelligence War)*, Tokyo: Fuyo Shobo.

Sawatsky, J. (1980) *Men in the Shadows: The RCMP Security Service*, Toronto: Doubleday.

Sawers, J. (2010) 'The Chief's Speech: Britain's Secret Frontline'. Speech to a meeting of the Society of Editors, 28 October.

Scahill, J. (2007) *Blackwater: The Rise of the World's Most Powerful Mercenary Army*, New York: Nation.

Schecter, J. and Deriabin, P. (1992) *The Spy Who Saved the World: How a Soviet Colonel Changed the Course of the Cold War*, New York: Charles Scribner's Sons.

Schelling, T.C. (1966) *Arms and Influence*, New Haven, CT: Yale University Press.

Scheuer, M. (2005) *Imperial Hubris: Why the West is Losing the War on Terror*, Washington, DC: Potomac Books.

Schewick, B. (2010) *Internet Architecture and Innovation*, Cambridge, MA: MIT Press.

Schiffman, Z.S. (2011) *The Birth of the Past*, foreword by A. Grafton, Baltimore, MD: Johns Hopkins University Press.

Schindler, J.R. (2009) 'Intelligence and Strategy in the War on Islamist Terrorism', in C. Andrew, R. Aldrich and W. Wark (eds) *Secret Intelligence: A Reader*, London: Routledge, 245–258.

Schmidt-Eenboom, E. (ed.) (1995) *Nachrichtendienste in Nordamerika: Europa und Japan: Länderportraits und Analysen*. CD-ROM, Weilheim.

Schmidt-Eenboom, E. (2001) 'The Bundesnachrichtendienst, the Bundeswehr and SIGINT in the Cold War and After', in M.M. Aid and C. Wiebes (eds) *Secrets of Signals Intelligence during the Cold War and Beyond*, London: Frank Cass, 129–176.

Schmidt-Eenboom, E. and Ritzi, M. (2011*) Im Schatten des Dritten Reiches: Der BND und sein Agent Richard Christmann*, Berlin: Links Christoph Verlag.

Schmitt, E. and Mazzetti, M. (2008) 'Secret Order Lets U.S. Raid Al Qaeda in Many Countries', *New York Times*, 10 November.

Schnaubelt, C.M. (2011) 'The Limits of Military Force', *New York Times*, 18 May. Online. Available: http://www.nytimes.com/2011/05/19/opinion/19iht-edschnaubelt19.html.

Schneier, B. (2005) 'NSA and Bush's Illegal Eavesdropping', 20 December. Online. Available: http://www.schneier.com/blog/archives/2005/12/nsa_and_bushs_i.html (accessed 27 July 2007).

Schneier, B. (2012) *Liars and Outliers: Enabling the Trust that Society Needs to Thrive*, Indianapolis, IN: John Wiley & Sons.

Scholte, J.A. (2000) *Globalization: A Critical Introduction*, London: Palgrave.

Schulsky, A.N. and Schmitt, G.J. (2002) *Silent Warfare: Understanding the World of Intelligence*, Washington, DC: Potomac Books.

Schumacher, E.F. (1977) *A Guide for the Perplexed*, London: Jonathan Cape.

Schwarz, F.A.O. Jr and Huq, A.Z. (2007) *Unchecked and Unbalanced: Presidential Power in a Time of Terror*, New York: New Press.

Schwarz, H.-P. (1994) *Die Zentralmacht Europas. Deutschlands Rückkehr auf die Weltbühne*, Berlin: Siedler.

Scott, L. and Jackson, P. (2004) *Understanding Intelligence in the Twenty-First Century: Journeys in Shadows*, London: Routledge.

Scott, L. and Jackson, P. (2004) 'Journeys in Shadows', in L. Scott and P. Jackson (eds) *Understanding Intelligence in the Twenty-First Century: Journeys in Shadows*, London: Routledge, 1–28.

Security Intelligence Review Committee (SIRC) (2000) *SIRC Report 1999–2000: An Operational Audit of the Canadian Security Intelligence Service*, Ottawa: Minister of Supply and Services Canada.

Security Intelligence Review Committee (SIRC) (2010a) *How CSIS Identifies and Addresses Intelligence Priorities*, SIRC 2009–01, 17 February (released to the author under the Access to Information Act).

Security Intelligence Review Committee (SIRC) (2010b) *Review of the Section 16 Program and the Use of Information Collected*, SIRC 2009–02, 12 August (released to the author under the Access to Information Act).

Security Intelligence Review Committee (SIRC) (2012) *Annual Report 2011–2012: Meeting the Challenge – Moving Forward in a Changing Landscape*, Ottawa: Public Works and Government Services Canada.

Segev, S. (2012) *Alone in Damascus*, Tel Aviv: Maariv (Hebrew).

Senate Select Committee on Intelligence (SSCI) (2008) *Annual Worldwide Threat Assessment*, Hearing of 5 February, Washington, DC. Online. Available: http://www.dni.gov/testimonies/20080205_transcript.pdf (accessed 5 July 2013).

Senate Select Committee to Study Governmental Operations with respect to Intelligence Activities (1976) 'Final Report of the Select Committee to Study Governmental Operations with respect to Intelligence Activities', Supplementary Detailed Staff Reports on Intelligence Activities and the Rights of Americans (Book III), 23 April. Online. Available: http://www.icdc.com/~paulwolf/cointelpro/churchfinalreportIIIm.htm (accessed 5 July 2013).

Senior former Taliban official (2011) Interview, 11 February.

Sever, A. (2009) *10 mifov o KGB [10 Myths About the KGB]*, Moscow: Eksmo.

Sever, A. (2010) *FSB*, Moscow: Eksmo.

Shalev, A. (2006) *Success and Failure in Alert: The Israeli Intelligence Assessment Towards the Yom Kippur War*, Tel Aviv: Maarachot.

Shane, S. (2012) 'Inquiry into US Leaks is Casting Chill Over Coverage', *New York Times*, 1 August.

Shanko, B. (2012) 'Arctic Awareness: Canada's Polar Epsilon Program', *Space Quarterly*, March, 40–42. Online. Available: http://technishintoenglish.com/pdfs/Polar%20Epsilon%20SQ.pdf (accessed January 2013).

Sharfman, P. (1995) 'Intelligence Analysis in an Age of Electronic Dissemination', *Intelligence and National Security*, 10(4), 201–211.

Shaw, D.J. (2007) *World Food Security: A History Since 1945*, New York: Palgrave Macmillan.

Sheptycki, J. (2009) 'Policing, Intelligence Theory and the New Human Security Paradigm', in P. Gill, S. Marrin and M. Phythian (eds) *Intelligence Theory: Key Questions and Debates*, London: Routledge, 166–185.

Sheptycki, J. and Ratcliffe, J. (2004) 'Setting the Strategic Agenda', in J. Ratcliffe (ed.) *Strategic Thinking in Criminal Intelligence*, Sydney: Federation Press, 194–210.

Shiraz, Z. (2011) 'CIA Intervention in Chile and the Fall of the Allende Government in 1973', *Journal of American Studies*, 45(3), 603–613.

Shorrock, T. (2008) *Spies for Hire: The Secret World of Intelligence Outsourcing*, New York: Simon & Schuster.

Shouten (Focus) (2004) 'The 50 Years of Security Police', No. 269, September, 43.

Shukman, H. (ed.) (2001) *Agents for Change: Intelligence Services in the 21st Century*, London: St Ermin's.

Shulsky, A. (1995) 'What Is Intelligence? Secrets and Competition Among States', in R. Godson, E.R. May and G. Schmitt (eds) *US Intelligence at the Crossroads: Agendas for Reform*, London: Brassey's, 17–27.

Shulsky, A. and Schmitt, G. (2002) *Silent Warfare: Understanding the World of Intelligence*, 3rd edn, Washington, DC: Potomac.

Shy, J. (1986) 'Jomini', in P. Paret (ed.) *Makers of Modern Strategy: From Machiavelli to the Nuclear Age*, Oxford: Clarendon Press, 143–185.

SI (2011) 'Order Transferring to the Communications Security Establishment the Control and Supervision of Certain Portions of the Federal Public Administration in the Department of National Defence known as the Communications Security Establishment and the Communications Security Establishment Internal Services Unit', P.C. 2011–1305, *Canada Gazette Part II*, 145(25), 26–54.

SIGINT Committee (1983) *Definition of Signals Intelligence*, Memorandum, SIGINT Committee to Acting Director of Central Intelligence, 24 March, Secret, CREST Collection, Document No. CIA-RDP85M00158R000200120035–1, NA, CP.

Sims, J. (2006) 'Foreign Intelligence Liaison: Devils, Deals and Details', *International Journal of Intelligence and Counterintelligence*, 19(2), 195–217.

Sims, J. (2009) 'Adaptive Realism', in G.F. Treverton and W. Agrell (eds) *National Intelligence Systems: Current Research and Future Prospects*, Cambridge: Cambridge University Press.

Sims, J. (2009) 'Defending Adaptive Realism: Intelligence Theory Comes of Age', in P. Gill, S. Marrin and M. Phytian (eds) *Intelligence Theory: Key Questions and Debates*, London: Routledge, 151–165.

Sims, J. and Gerber, B. (2005) *Transforming US Intelligence*, Washington, DC: Georgetown University Press.

Sims, J.E. (2007) 'Smart Realism: A Theory of Intelligence in International Politics', delivered at the International Studies Association Conference in Chicago, 28 February 2007.

Sims, J.E. (2008) *Vaults, Mirrors and Masks: Rediscovering U.S. Counterintelligence*, Washington DC: Georgetown University Press.

Sims, J.E. (2009) 'A Theory of Intelligence and International Politics', in G. Treverton (ed.) *National Intelligence Systems: Current Research and Future Prospects*, Cambridge: Cambridge University Press.

Singer, J.D., Bremer, S. and Stuckey, J. (1972) 'Capability Distribution, Uncertainty and Major War', in B. Russett (ed.) *Peace, War and Numbers*, Beverly Hills, CA: Sage, 19–48.

Singer, J.P. (2002) *Die rechtlichen Vorgaben für die Beobachtung der Organisierten Kriminalität durch die Nachrichtendienste der Bundesrepublik Deutschland*, Aachen: Shaker Verlag.

Singh, V.K. (2007) *India's External Intelligence: Secrets of Research and Analysis Wing (R&AW)*, New Delhi: Manas Publications.

SIS (2012a) 'What We Do'. Online. Available: https://www.sis.gov.uk/about-us/what-we-do.html (accessed 26 June 2012).

SIS (2012b) 'About Us'. Online. Available: https://www.sis.gov.uk/about-us/faqs.html (accessed 26 June 2012).

Sisson, R. and Rose, L.E. (1990) *War and Succession: Pakistan, India and the Creation of Bangladesh*, Berkeley: University of California Press.

Skocpol, T. (1979) *States and Social Revolutions: A Comparative Analysis of France, Russia, & China*, New York: Cambridge University Press.

Slapper, G. and Tombs, S. (1999) *Corporate Crime*, Harlow, UK: Longman.

Smist, F., Jr (1994) *Congress Oversees the United States Intelligence Community, 1947– 1994*, 2nd edn, Lawrence: University Press of Kansas.

Smith, B. (1993) *The ULTRA-MAGIC Deals and the Most Secret Special Relationship, 1940–1946*, Novato, CA: Presidio Press.

Smith, B. (1996) *Sharing Secrets with Stalin: How the Allies Traded Intelligence, 1941–1945*, Lawrence: University of Kansas Press.

Smith, D.E. (1917) 'John Wallis as a Cryptographer', *Bulleting of the American Mathematical Society*, 24, 82–96.

Smith, R. (2005) *The Utility of Force: The Art of War in the Modern World*, London: Allen Lane.

Snyder, J.L. (1977) *The Soviet Strategic Culture: Implications for Limited Nuclear Operations*, Santa Monica, CA: Rand.

Sobelman, D. (2003) *New Rules of the Game: Israel and Hizbollah after the Withdrawal from Lebanon*, Tel Aviv: Jaffee Center for Strategic Studies.

SOCA (2006) Annual Plan 2006–7. Online. Available: http://www.soca.gov.uk (accessed 5 July 2013).

Soldatov, A. and Borogan, I. (2010) *The New Nobility: The Restoration of Russia's Security State and the Enduring Legacy of the KGB*, New York: Public Affairs.

Sontag, S. Drew, C. and Drew, A. (2000) *Blind Man's Bluff: The Untold Story of American Submarine Espionage*, New York: William Morrow Paperbacks.

Sovacool, B.K. and Brown, M.A. (2010) 'Competing Dimensions of Energy Security: An International Perspective', *Annual Review of Environment and Resources*, 35, 77–108.

Sovacool, B.K. (ed.) (2011) *The Routledge Handbook of Energy Security*, New York: Routledge.

Srivastava, L. and Rehman, I.H. (2006) 'Energy For Sustainable Development in India: Linkages and Strategic Direction', *Energy Policy*, 34, 643–654.

Steele, R.D. (1988–2012) All articles and chapters, briefings and lectures, books, videos, etcetera, easily accessed online. Online. Available: http://tinyurl.com/Steele2012 (accessed 19 June 2013).

Steele, R.D. (2002) *The New Craft of Intelligence: Personal, Public, & Political*, Oakton, VA: OSS International Press.

Stein, A. (1990) *Why Nations Cooperate*, Ithaca, NY: Cornell University Press.

Stein, J. (2012) 'CIA's Secret Fear: High-Tech Border Checks Will Blow Spies' Cover', *Wired Danger Room*, 12 April. Online. Available: http://www.wired.com/dangerroom/2012/04/cia-spies-biometric-tech/ (accessed 15 April 2012).

Stern, R. (2006) 'Oil Market Power and United States National Security', *Proceedings of the National Academy of Sciences of the United States of America*, 103(5), 1650–1655.

Stiglitz, J. (2002) *Globalisation and its Discontents*, New York: Norton.

Stock, J. (2009) 'Internationaler Terrorismus: Aktuelle Bedrohungslage und Gegenstrategien aus Sicht der deutschen Polizei', in T. Görgen *et al.* (eds) *Interdisziplinäre Kriminologie: Festschrift für Arthur Kreuzer zum 70. Geburtstag*, Frankfurt a.M.: Verlag für Polizeiwissenschaft, 819–832.

Stokes, D. (2007) 'Blood for Oil? Global Capital, Counter-insurgency and the Dual Logic of American Energy Security', *Review of International Studies*, 33, 245–264.

Stokes, M.A., Lin, J. and Hsiao, L.C.R. (2011) *The Chinese People's Liberation Army Signals Intelligence and Cyber Reconnaissance Infrastructure*, Project 2049 Institute.

Strachan, H. (2005) 'The Lost Meaning of Strategy', *Survival: Global Politics and Strategy*, 47(3), 33–54.

Strachan, H. (2007) *Carl von Clausewitz's 'On War': A Biography*, London: Atlantic.

Strange, S. (1988) *States and Markets*, London: Continuum.

Strategic Air Command (1973) *SAC Reconnaissance History: January 1968–June 1971*, 7 November, US Air Force Freedom of Information Act, Top Secret.

Strong, K. (1968) *Intelligence at the Top: The Recollections of an Intelligence Officer*, London: Cassell.

Stubbington, J. (2010) *Kept in the Dark*, Barnsley, UK: Pen and Sword.

Subramanian, K. (2005) 'Intelligence Bureau, Home Ministry and Indian Politics', *Economic and Political Weekly*, May, 40, 2147–2150.

Sullivan, J.P. (2008) 'Transnational Gangs: The Impact of Third Generation Gangs in Central America', *Air & Space Power Journal* (Spanish edn), Second Trimester. Online. Available: http://www.airpower.maxwell.af.mil/apjinternational/apj-s/2008/2tri08/sullivaneng.htm.

Sullivan, J.P. (2010) 'Explosive Escalation? Reflections on the Carbombing in Ciudad Juarez', *Small Wars Journal*, 21 July.

Sullivan, J.P. (2012) *From Drug Wars to Criminal Insurgency: Mexican Cartels, Criminal Enclaves and Criminal Insurgency in Mexico and Central America: Implications for Global Security*, Paris: Fondation Maison des sciences de l'homme, FMSH–WP–2012–09, April.

Sullivan, J.P. and Bunker, R.J. (2012) *Mexico's Criminal Insurgency: A Small Wars Journal-El Centro Anthology*, Bloomington: iUniverse.

Sun Tzu (1963) *The Art of War*, trans. S. Griffith, Oxford: Clarendon Press.

Sun Tzu (1971 [1963]) *The Art of War*, trans. and intro. S.B. Griffith, foreword by B.H. Liddell Hart, New York: Oxford University Press.

Sunday Morning Herald (2011) 11 February.

Sutton, B. (2006) 'Global Coverage, Looking Backward, Looking Forward', *Phi Beta Iota Public Intelligence Blog*, 24 December. Online. Available: http://tinyurl.com/Sutton-2006 (accessed 19 June 2013).

Swire, P. and Ahmad, K. (2011) '"Going Dark" Versus a "Golden Age for Surveillance"', Center for Democracy and Technology, 28 November. Online. Available: https://www.cdt.org/blogs/2811going-dark-versus-golden-age-surveillance (accessed 3 May 2012).

Swords, C. (2007) 'Evidence to the Standing Senate Committee on National Security and Defence', Senate of Canada, 1st Session 39th Parliament, 28 May.

Taibbi, M. (2010) *Griftopia: Bubble Machines, Vampire Squids and the Long Con That Is Breaking America*, New York: Spiegel & Grau.

Taigai Joho Kinou Kyouka ni Kansuru Kondankai (Committee of Enhancement of Overseas Intelligence) (n.d.) Press release. Online. Available: http://www.mofa.go.jp/mofaj/press/release/17/rls_0913a.html (accessed 5 July 2013).

Tamnes, R. (1991) *The United States and the Cold War in the High North*, Aldershot, UK: Dartmouth.

Tan Po Cheng Ming (1996) 'Communist China's Intelligence, External Affairs Research Organs' by [Hong Kong] 1 Sep 96 No 227, 28–31 (PRC: Analysis of CPC Intelligence, Other Organs FBIS–CHI-96–196, 1 Sep 1996).

Tanaka, J. (ed.) (1980) *Sengo Seiji Saiban Shiroku 2 (The History of Court after the Second World War, Vol. 2)*, Tokyo: Daiiichi Houki Shuppan.

Tankel, S. (2011) *Storming the World Stage: The Story of Lashkar-e-Taiba*, London: Hurst.

Tao, H. and Tzu, S. (1987) *The Art of War: Modern Chinese Interpretation*, New York: Sterling Pub Co Inc.

Taplin, W.L. (1989) 'Six General Principles of Intelligence', *International Journal of Intelligence and Counterintelligence*, 3(4), Winter, 475–491.

Taylor, J. and van Doren, P. (2008) 'The Energy Security Obsession', *Georgetown Journal of Law and Public Policy*, 6(2).

Taylor, S. and Buchanan, K. (2010) 'Treason: Tis Worse than Murder', in L. Johnson (ed.) *The Oxford Handbook of National Security Intelligence*, Oxford: Oxford University Press.

Taylor, S. and Snow, D. (1997) 'Cold War Spies: Why They Spied and How They Got Caught', *Intelligence and National Security*, 12, 101–125.

Tenet, G. with Harlow, B. (2007) *At the Center of the Storm: My Years at the CIA*, New York: HarperCollins.

Tessman, B. and Wolfe, W. (2011) 'Great Powers and Strategic Hedging: The Case of Chinese Energy Security Strategy', *International Studies Review*, 13(2), 214–240.

Tharakan, P.K.H. (2010) 'Spooks and Shadows', *Indian Express*, 8 February.

Thayer, C.A. (2008) 'Vietnam', in S. Farson *et al.* (eds) *PSI Handbook of Global Security and Intelligence*, Vol. 1, Westport, CT: Praeger Security International.

Thompson, D.H.N (2009) 'Meet Canada's Directorate of Geospatial Intelligence', *Pathfinder*, 7(2), 3–4.

Thucydides (1974) *History of the Peloponnesian War*, trans. Rex Warner, ed. and introduced by M.I. Finlay, London: Penguin.

Tilly, C. (1985) 'War Making and State Making as Organized Crime', in P. Evans *et al.* (eds) *Bringing the State Back In*, Cambridge: Cambridge University Press, 169–191.

Timm, T. and York, J.C. (2012) 'Surveillance Inc: How Western Tech Firms Are Helping Arab Dictators', *The Atlantic*. Online. Available: http://www.theatlantic.com/international/archive/2012/03/surveillance-inc-how-western-tech-firms-are-helping-arab-dictators/254008/ (accessed 5 July 2013).

Timmermans, S. and Mauck, A. (2005) 'The Promises and Pitfalls of Evidence-based Medicine', *Health Affairs*, 24, 18–28.

Tirosh, S. (2012) 'Technology in the Service of Intelligence', in A. Gilboa and E. Lapid (eds) *Israel's Silent Defender: An Inside Look at Sixty Years of Israeli Intelligence*, Jerusalem: Gefen, 187–196.

Titus, J. (2002) 'Review of "Henry L. Stimson: The First Wise Man" by David F. Schmitz', *Aerospace Power Journal*, XVI(2). Online. Available: http://www.airpower.maxwell.af.mil/airchronicles/apj/apj02/sum02.html.

Toohey, B. and Pinwell, W. (1989) *Oyster The Story of the Australian Secret Intelligence Service*, Melbourne: William Heinemann.

Tovey, M. (2008) *Collective Intelligence: Creating a Prosperous World at Peace*, Oakton, VA: Earth Intelligence Network.

Trend, B. (1967) Minute to Prime Minister Harold Wilson, 13 March. PREM 13/2688, London: National Archives.

Trend, B. (1973) Minute to Hunt, 1 June. CAB 163/212, London: National Archives.

Treverton, G. (2007) 'Risks and Riddles', *Smithsonian Magazine*, June. Online. Available: http://www.smithsonianmag.com/people-places/presence_puzzle.html?c=y&story=fullstory (accessed 22 April 2012).

Treverton, G., Jones, S.G., Boraz, S. and Lipscy, P. (eds) (2005) *Toward a Theory of Intelligence: Workshop Report*, Santa Monica, CA: RAND.

Treverton, G.F. (1986) 'Producer versus Consumer Outlooks', *Steele*, 2000, 48–49, cf. Figures 11–12.

Treverton, G.F. (1987) *Covert Action: The Limits of Intervention in the Postwar World*, New York: Basic Books.

Treverton, G.F. (2009) *Intelligence for an Age of Terror*, New York: Cambridge University Press.

Treverton, G.F. (2012) E-mail correspondence with the author, 25 June.

Treverton, G.R. (2001) *Reshaping National Intelligence in an Age of Information*, RAND Studies in Intelligence, Cambridge: Cambridge University Press.

Troy, T.F. (1991–92) 'The "Correct" Definition of Intelligence', *International Journal of Intelligence and Counterintelligence*, 5(4), 433–454.

Truman, H. (1963) 'Limit CIA Role to Intelligence', *Washington Post*, 22 December. Online. Available: http://tinyurl.com/Truman-CIA-63.

Tucker, J. (ed.) (2000) *Toxic Terror*, Cambridge, MA: MIT Press.

Turner, M.A. (2004) 'A Distinctive US Intelligence Culture', *International Journal of Intelligence and Counterintelligence*, 17, 42–61.

Turner, S. (1985) *Secrecy and Democracy: The CIA in Transition*, Boston, MA: Houghton Mifflin.

Uhrlau, E. (2009) 'Modernisierung und Zukunftsfähigkeit: Die Strukturreform des Bundesnachrichtendienstes', *Zeitschrift für Außen- und Sicherheitspolitik*, 2(4), 449–453.

UKUSA Communications Intelligence Agreement and Appendices Thereto (1951) 1 June. Online. Available: http://www.nsa.gov/public_info/declass/ukusa.shtml (accessed December 2012).

Ulizio, A. (2012) 'Former CIA Director Talks American Cyber Security', *The Review*, 20 March. Online. Available: http://www.udreview.com/former-cia-director-talks-american-cyber-security-1.2822499 (accessed 10 April 2012).

Umbach, F. (2010) 'Global Energy Security and the Implications for the EU', *Energy Policy*, 38, 1229–1240.

United Nations (1948) *UN Declaration of Human Rights*. United Nations, Online. Available: http://www.un.org/en/documents/udhr/

United Nations (2004) *A More Secure World: Our Shared Responsibility, High-Level Panel on Threats, Challenge and Change*, New York: United Nations.

United Nations Convention Against Transnational Organized Crime (2000) Online. Available: http://www.unodc.org/unodc/en/treaties/CTOC/index.html.

United Nations Security Council (UNSC) (2007) 'Security Council Holds First-ever Debate on Impact of Climate Change, on Peace, Security, Hearing Over 50 Speakers', SC/9000. United Nations Security Council, Online. Available: http://www.un.org/News/Press/docs/2007/sc9000.doc.htm

US (Brown-Aspin) (1996) 'Commission on the Roles and Capabilities of the United States Intelligence Community (1996) Preparing for the 21st Century: An Appraisal of US Intelligence', Washington, DC: US Government Printing Office.

US Air Force: Department of the Air Force (1984) *3400th Technical Training Wing, 3454th School Squadron, Study Guide and Workbook, Introduction to Detection Systems*, 18 October. For official use only, US Air Force Freedom of Information Act.

US Army (1985) *Military History and Professional Development*, US Army Command and General Staff College, Fort Leavenworth, Kansas: Combat Studies Institute, 85-CSI-21 85.

US Army (2004) *US Army Field Manual: Intelligence 2–0*. Online. Available: http://www.cgsc.edu/CARL/docrepository/FM%202_0_2004.pdf

US Army Air Corps (1940) *FM1–40 Intelligence Procedure in Aviation Units*, Washington: US Government Printing Office.

US Department of Defense (2010) *Quadrennial Defense Review 2010*, Washington, DC. Online. Available: http://www.defense.gov/qdr/images/QDR_as_of_12Feb10_1000.pdf (accessed 5 July 2013).

US Department of Defense (US DoD) Joint Chiefs of Staff (2004) *Joint and National Intelligence Support to Military Operations JP 2–01*, Washington, DC.

US Director of National Intelligence (2008) Vision 2015, July. Online. Available: http://www.dni.gov/Vision_2015.pdf (accessed 24 June 2012).

US House of Representatives (1996) Permanent Select Committee on Intelligence, *IC21: Intelligence Community in the 21st Century*, Permanent Select Committee on Intelligence, IC21 104th Congress, 9 April, unclassified.

US Joint Chiefs of Staff (1986) *Dictionary of Military and Associated Terms*, JCS Publication 1, 1 January.

US Joint Chiefs of Staff (2010) *Dictionary of Military and Associated Terms*, Joint Publication 1–02, 8 November, as amended through 15 April 2012. Online. Available: http://www.dtic.mil/doctrine/dod_dictionary/ (accessed 16 June 2012).

US Joint Chiefs of Staff (2011) *Joint Publication 1-02: Dictionary of Military and Associated Terms*. Online. Available: http://ra.defense.gov/documents/rtm/jp1_02.pdf (accessed 2nd July 2013)

US Navy (1985) OPNAVINST, *Submarine Surveillance Equipment Program (SSEP), Training and Support Program Management Plan*, 9 August, US Navy Freedom of Information Act, Secret.

US Office of the Director of National Intelligence (2006) 'Exploring the Doctrinal Principle of Integration'. Proceedings of a workshop in Washington, DC, 12 October.

US War Department (1940) *Basic Field Manual FM 30–5 ('Military Intelligence')*, US War Department, Online. Available: http://www.cgsc.edu/CARL/docrepository/FM30_5_1951.pdf

Ushakov, V. (2006) *FSB Rossii. Nauchno-prakticheski kommentarii [Russia's FSB. A Scientific-Practical Commentary]*, Moscow: Eksmo.

Valero, L. (2000) 'The American Joint Intelligence Committee and Estimates of the Soviet Union, 1945–7', *CIA Studies in Intelligence*, Summer.

Van der Oye, D.S. (1998) 'Tsarist Codebreaking Some Background and Some Examples', *Cryptologia*, 22(4), 342–353.

Van Duyne, P. (1997) 'Organized Crime, Corruption and Power', *Crime, Law and Social Change*, 26, 201–238.

Vanhecke, N. (2012) 'Belgische spionnen online te vinden', *De Standaard*, 26 November.

Vaughan-Williams, N. (2009) *Border Politics: The Limits of Sovereign Power*, Edinburgh: Edinburgh University Press.

Vaughan-Williams, N. (2011) 'The Border', in S. Legg (eds) *Geographies of the Nomos: Schmitt, Spatiality, and Sovereignty*, London: Routledge.

Vaughn, B. (1993) 'The Use and Abuse of Intelligence Services in India', *Intelligence and National Security*, 8(1), 1–22.

Verghese, B.G. (2010) *First Draft: Witness to Making of Modern India*, New Delhi: Tranquebar.

Verkaik, R. and Morris, N. (2008) 'Exclusive: Storm over Big Brother Database', *Independent*, 15 October.

Vickers, C.G. (1943) *Centralised Intelligence*, CAB 163/6, London: National Archives.

Von Lampe, K. (2009) 'Human Capital and Social Capital in Criminal Networks: Introduction to the Special Issue on the 7th Blankensee Colloquium, *Trends in Organized Crime*, 12, 93–100.

Walker, B. (2011) *Independent National Security Legislation Monitor (INSLM): Annual Report*, Canberra: Commonwealth of Australia, passim.

Waller, M.J. (1994) *Secret Empire: The KGB in Russia Today*, Oxford: Westview Press.

Walsh, J.I. (2010) *International Politics of Intelligence Sharing*, New York: Columbia University Press.

War Office (1930) *Memorandum by the General Staff on Industrial Intelligence in Foreign Countries*, 14 February. CAB 48/3, London.

War Office (1931) *Report by the War Office on the Trial Scheme for the Study of Industrial Intelligence in the USSR Carried Out During the Months July–December 1930*, 17 March. CAB 48/3, London: National Archives.

Wardlaw, G. (1989) *Political Terrorism: Theory, Tactics and Counter-Measures*, Cambridge: Cambridge University Press.

Wark, W.K. (1985) *The Ultimate Enemy: British Intelligence and Nazi Germany, 1933–39*, New York: Cornell University Press.

Wark, W.K. (1989) 'The Evolution of Military Intelligence in Canada', *Armed Forces & Society*, 16(1), 77–98.

Wark, W.K. (1993) 'Introduction: The Study of Espionage: Past, Present, Future?', *Intelligence and National Security*, 8.

Wark, W.K. (ed.) (1994) *Espionage: Past, Present, Future?* Ilford, UK: Frank Cass.

Wark, W.K. (2003) 'Introduction: Learning to Live with Intelligence', *Intelligence and National Security*, 18(4).

Warner, M. (2002) 'Wanted: A Definition of Intelligence', *Studies in Intelligence*, 46. Online. Available: https://www.cia.gov/library/center-for-the-study-of-intelligence/csi-publications/csi-studies/studies/vol46no3/article02.html (accessed 20 June 2012).

Warner, M. (2004) 'Intelligence Transformation and Intelligence Liaison', *SAIS Review*, 24(1), 77–89.

Warner, M. (2006) 'The Divine Skein: Sun Tzu on Intelligence', *Intelligence and National Security*, 21(4), 483–492.

Warner, M. (2007) 'Sources and Methods For The Study Of Intelligence', in L. Johnson (ed.) *Handbook of Intelligence Studies*, London: Routledge, 17–27.

Warner, M. (2008) 'Intelligence as Risk Shifting', in Peter R. Gill, Mark Phythian, and Stephen Marrin (eds) *Intelligence Theory: Key Questions and Debates,* London: Routledge.

Warner, M. (2009a) 'Building a Theory of Intelligence Systems', in G.F. Treverton and W. Agrell (eds) *National Intelligence Systems: Current Research and Future Prospects*, New York: Cambridge University Press.

Warner, M. (2009b) 'Intelligence as Risk Shifting', in P. Gill, S. Marrin and M. Phythian (eds) *Intelligence Theory: Key Questions and Debates*, London: Routledge, 16–32.

Warner, M. (2009c) Review of Farson, Gill, Phythian and Shpiro (eds) *PSI Handbook of Global Security and Intelligence: National Approaches, Studies in Intelligence*, 53. Online. Available: https://www.cia.gov/library/center-for-the-study-of-intelligence/csi-publications/csi-studies/studies/vol53no2/handbook-of-global-security-and-intelligence.html (accessed 5 July 2013).

Warner, M. (2012) 'Fragile and Provocative: Notes on Secrecy and Intelligence', *Intelligence and National Security*, 27(2).

Warner, M. (2012) 'Intelligence and Reflexivity: An Invitation to a Dialogue', *Intelligence and National Security*, 27(2).

Warner, M. (2012) 'Reflections on Technology and Intelligence Systems', *Intelligence and National Security*, February, 27(1), 133–153.

Warner, M. (2012) 'The Past and Future of the Intelligence Cycle'. Unpublished paper presented to the International Studies Association convention, San Diego, April.

Watts, M. (2004) 'Resource Curse? Governmentality, Oil and Power in the Niger Delta, Nigeria', *Geopolitics*, 9(1), 50–80.

Weapons of Mass Destruction Report (2005) *Report to the President*, The Commission on the Intelligence Capabilities of the United States Regarding Weapons of Mass Destruction, 31 March.

Weaver, M. (2008) 'India Admits Intelligence Failure in Run-up to Mumbai Attacks', *Guardian*, 5 December.

Webster, F. (2006) *Theories of the Information Society*, 3rd edn, London: Routledge.

Weigley, R.F. (1973) *The American Way of War: A History of United States Military Strategy and Policy*, Bloomington, IN: Indiana University Press.

Weinberger, D. (2012) *Too Big to Know: Rethinking Knowledge Now that the Facts Aren't the Facts, Experts are Everywhere and the Smartest Person in the Room is the Room*, New York: Basic Books.

Weiner, T. (2008) *Legacy of Ashes: The History of the CIA*, London: Penguin. Online. Available: http://www.nytimes.com/1996/05/29/world/gun-running-in-the-balkans-cia-and-diplomats-collide.html (accessed 5 July 2013).

Weiner, T. and Bonner, R. (1996) 'Gun-Running in the Balkans', *New York Times*, 26 May.

Weinstein, A. (2007) 'Civic Education: Lighting the Path to the Future', *Prologue Magazine*, 39(1). Online. Available: http://www.archives.gov/publications/prologue/2007/spring/archivist.html (accessed 5 July 2013).

Weir, G.E. (1961) 'The American Sound Surveillance System: Using the Ocean to Hunt Soviet Submarines, 1950–1961', *International Journal of Naval History*, 5(2), August 2006.

Weissman, S.R. (2010) 'An Extraordinary Rendition', *Intelligence and National Security*, 25, April, 198–222.

Wellesley, V. (1930) *A Proposal for the Establishment of a Politico-Economic Intelligence Department in the Foreign Office*, 1 December. FO 371/14939, London: National Archives.

Wendt, A. (1992) 'Anarchy is What States Make of It: The Social Construction of Power Politics', *International Organization*, 46(2), 391–425.

West, N. and Tsarev, O. (1999) *The Crown Jewels: The British Secrets Exposed by the KGB Archives*, London: HarperCollins.

West, N. and Tsarev, O. (2009) *Triplex: Secrets from the Cambridge Spies*, London: Yale University Press.

Westerfield, H.B. (ed.) (1995) *Inside CIA's Private World: Declassified Articles from the Agency's Internal Journal, 1955–1992*, New Haven, CT: Yale University Press.

Westerfield, H.B. (1996) 'America and the World of Intelligence Liaison', *Intelligence and National Security*, 11(3), 523–560.

Whaley, B. (2002) 'Conditions Making for Success and Failure of Denial and Deception: Authoritarian and Transition Regimes', in R. Godson and J.J. Wirtz (eds) *Strategic Denial and Deception: The Twenty-First Century Challenge*, New Brunswick, NJ: Transaction Publishers.

Wheaton, K.J. (2012) Blog. Online. Available: http://sourcesandmethods.blogspot.com/2011/05/part-4-traditional-intelligence-cycle.html (accessed 27 February 2012).

Wheaton, K.J. and Beerbower, M.T. (2006) 'Towards a New Definition of Intelligence', *Stanford Law & Policy Review*, 17(2).

White House, the (2011) *National Strategy for Counterterrorism*, Washington, DC: The White House.

Whymat, R. (2006) *Stalin's Spy: Richard Sorge and the Tokyo Espionage Ring*, New York: Palgrave Macmillan.

Wiebes, C. (2003) *Intelligence and the War in Bosnia: 1992–1995*, The Hague: Lit Verlag.

Wilensky, H.L. (1967) *Organizational Intelligence: Knowledge and Policy in Government and Industry*, New York: Basic Books.

Wilkie, A. (2004) *Axis of Deceit*, Melbourne: Black Inc.

Williams, P. and Godson, R. (2002) 'Anticipating Organized and Transnational Crime', *Crime, Law & Social Change*, 37, 311–355.

Williams, R. (2009) 'The Analysis of Culture', in J. Storey (ed.) *Cultural Theory and Popular Culture: A Reader*, 4th edn, Harlow, UK: Pearson.

Willrich, M. (1976) 'Energy Independence for America', *International Affairs*, 52(1), 53–66.

Wilson, E.O. (1999) *Consilience: The Unity of Knowledge*, New York: Vintage.

Wink, R.W. (1987) *Cloak & Gown: Scholars in the Secret War, 1939–1961*, New York: Morrow.

Winterbotham, F.W. (1975) *The ULTRA Secret*, New York: Dell.

Wirtz, J. and Sullivan, J.P. (2009) 'Global Metropolitan Policing: An Emerging Trend in Intelligence Sharing', *Homeland Security Affairs*, 5(2), May. Online. Available: http://www.hsaj.org/?article=5.2.4 (accessed 5 July 2013).

Wirtz, J.J. (1989) The Intelligence Paradigm, *Intelligence and National Security*, 4(4).

Wirtz, J.J. (1993) 'Constraints on Intelligence Collaboration: The Domestic Dimension', *International Journal of Intelligence and Counterintelligence*, 6(1), 85–99.

Wirtz, J.J. (2007) 'The American Approach to Intelligence Studies', in L.K. Johnson (ed.) *Handbook of Intelligence Studies*, London: Routledge.

Wirtz, J.J. (2008) 'Hiding in Plain Sight: Denial, Deception and the Non-State Actor', *SAIS Review of International Affairs*, 28, 55–63.

Wise, D. (1988) *The Spy Who Got Away: The Inside Story of Edward Lee Howard*, New York: Random House.

Wise, D. (1992) *Nightmover*, New York: Random House.

Wise, D. and Ross, T. (1964) *The Invisible Government*, New York: Random House.

Witt, J., Poneman, D. and Gallucci, R. (2005) *Going Critical*, Washington, DC: Brookings.

Wohlsetter, R. (1962) *Pearl Harbor: Warning and Decision*, Stanford, CA: Stanford University Press.

Wolf, M. (1997) *Man Without a Face: The Memoirs of a Spymaster*, London: Jonathan Cape.

Wolf, M. (2004) *Why Globalisation Works*. New Haven, CT: Yale University Press.

Wolfers, A. (1962) 'The Goals of Foreign Policy', in A. Wolfers (ed.) *Discord and Collaboration. Essays on International Politics*, Baltimore, MD: Johns Hopkins Press, 67–80.

Woodiwiss, M. (2001) *Organized Crime and American Power*, Toronto: University of Toronto Press.

Woodiwiss, M. (2003) 'Transnational Organized Crime: The Strange Career of an American Concept', in

M.E. Bearse (ed.) *Critical Reflections on Transnational Organized Crime, Money Laundering and Corruption*, Toronto: University of Toronto Press.

Woodward, B. (1987) *Veil: The Secret Wars of the CIA, 1981–1987*, New York: Simon & Schuster.

Woodward, B. (2004) *Plan of Attack*, New York: Simon & Schuster.

Wright, A. (2006) *Organised Crime*, Cullompton, UK: Willan Publishing.

Wright, A. (2011) 'Fit for Purpose? Accountability Challenges and Paradoxes of Domestic Inquiries', in H. Born, I. Leigh and A. Will (eds) *International Intelligence Cooperation and Accountability*, London: Routledge, 170–198.

Wright, L. (2007) *The Looming Tower: Al-Qaeda and the Road to 9/11*, New York: Vintage Books.

Wright, R. (2001) *Nonzero: The Logic of Human Destiny*, New York: Vintage.

Yardley, H.O. (1931) *The American Black Chamber*, Indianapolis, IN: Bobbs-Merrill.

Yergin, D. (2006) 'Energy Security', *Foreign Affairs*, 85(2), 69–82.

Zabetakis, S.G. and Peterson, J.F. (1964) 'The Diyarbakir Radar', *Studies in Intelligence*, RG-263, Entry 27, Box 15, College Park, Maryland: National Archives.

Zamir, Z. (2012) *With Open Eyes*, Or Yehuda: Kinneret, Zmora-Bitan, Dvir (Hebrew).

Zegart, A. (2009) *Spying Blind: The CIA, the FBI and the Origins of 9/11*, Princeton, NJ: Princeton University Press.

Zegart, A. (2011) *Eyes on Spies: Congress and the United States Intelligence Community*, Stanford, CA: Hoover Inst. Press Publication.

Zegart, A.B. (1999) *Flawed By Design: The Evolution of the CIA, JCS and NSC*, Stanford, CA: Stanford University Press.

Zegart, A.B. (2005) 'Cloaks, Daggers and Ivory Towers: Why Academics Don't Study US Intelligence', in L.K. Johnson (ed.) *Strategic Intelligence: Understanding the Hidden Side of Government*, Vol. 1, Westport, CT: Praeger: 21–34.

Zegart, A.B. (2007) *Spying Blind: The CIA, the FBI and the Origins of 9/11*, Princeton, NJ: Princeton University Press.

Zeiler, T.W. (1990) 'Kennedy, Oil Imports and the Fair Trade Doctrine', *Business History Review*, 64(2), 286–310.

Zhang, Z., Lohr, L., Escalante, C. and Wetzstein, M. (2010) 'Food versus Fuel: What Do Prices Tell Us?', *Energy Policy*, 38(1), 445–451.

INDEX

9/11 6, 12, 46–7, 55, 61, 65, 69–70, 102–3, 120,
    154–5, 157, 162, 166, 168, 221, 223–5, 246,
    248–9, 251, 253–4, 265–6, 286, 309–11, 314,
    338
    National Commission on Terrorist
        Attacks Upon the United States (9/11
        Commission) 253, 308, 311

Abwehr 97, 99, 308
accountability 2, 9, 12, 16–18, 82, 96, 1076, 142,
    152, 268, 271–3, 305, 307, 309–10
'actionable intelligence' 78, 222, 274–5, 280–2
Aldrich, Ames 98–9, 101–2, 177
Aldrich, Richard 303
Al Qaeda 18, 43, 46–7, 55–6, 64, 92, 94, 102–3,
    204, 245–6, 252–3, 314
    in the Arabian Peninsula (AQAP) 246, 252
    in the Islamic Maghreb (AQIM) 181
Aman (MI, ISR) 209–17
American Political Science Association (APSA) 18
analysis 3–4, 7, 9–12, 16–18, 20, 29, 33–4,
    39–41, 43, 45–6, 51, 59–62, 65–6, 69–71, 73,
    111–12, 115, 120, 125–6, 128–30, 257–60,
    262, 268–92, 294–6, 302, 315–19
    in Australia 163, 167, 172
    in Britain 135, 139–41, 143
    in Canada 154–7, 159
    in China 191–4, 196–9
    comparative analysis 35–6, 38
    and counterterrorism 247, 249–50, 254
    'four levels' of 35–7
    in Germany 220, 224, 226
    in Israel 211, 215–17
    in Japan 201–2
    in Russia 230, 233
    in Spain 236, 238–41
    'target centric' 67

in the United States 147–53
    Video Content Analysis (VCA) 303
    and weapons of mass destruction 274, 276, 280
Andrew, Christopher 3, 6, 20, 25, 103
Arab Spring 177, 214, 217, 270, 298, 300–1
Arendt, Hannah 50
Armed Forces Intelligence Centre (CIFAS,
    SPN) 238
Assessments Staff (UK) 139–41
assets 11, 28, 54, 56, 65, 96, 119, 139, 195, 214,
    258, 260, 292
Australian Secret Intelligence Service (ASIS)
    161–4, 169
Australian Security and Intelligence Organization
    (ASIO) 161–2, 165–9
Aviation Research Centre (ARC, IND) 186

Baker, Stewart 149
Barrett, David M. 5, 20
Bay of Pigs invasion 38
Betts, Richard K. 3, 19–20, 53, 69, 188, 206
Bin Laden, Osama 43, 94, 125, 159, 266
BlackBerry Messenger (BBM) 299–300
Board of National Estimates (BNE, US) 43
Bolshevism 39
Bosnia 37, 44, 56
Bozeman, Adda 5, 26, 71
Breakspear, Alan 27
Bundesnachrichtendienst (BND, GER) 218–26
Bush, George W. 9, 18, 19, 58, 166, 286, 310
business intelligence 73, 269
Butler Review (Review of Intelligence on
    Weapons of Mass Destruction) 6, 60, 135–6,
    138–40, 142, 157, 303

Cabinet Intelligence Research Office (CIRO,
    JPN) 201–6

Canadian Forces Information Operations Group (CFIOG) 156
Canadian Security and Intelligence Service (CSIS) 154, 157–60
Centre of Intelligence against Organized Crime (CICO, SPN) 241
Center for the Study of Intelligence (CSI, CIA) 8, 19
Central Intelligence Agency (CIA) 4–5, 8, 12, 16–7, 19, 40, 44, 59, 63–4, 68, 73, 91, 96–9, 102–3, 106, 112, 114, 119, 125, 127, 147–8, 162, 164, 168, 184, 186–7, 203, 205, 219, 230, 259, 266, 270–3, 306–7, 309–10
Cheka 39
Chilcot Inquiry 6, 303
China Institute for International Strategic Studies (CIISS) 198
civil liberties 148, 151–2, 159, 224, 268
civil society 71, 231, 264–5, 268, 271, 273
Clausewitz, Carl von 50–8
climate change 75, 266–7, 283–4, 286–7
Clinton, Bill 44, 127, 187, 262
closed circuit television cameras (CCTV) 303
Clough, Chris 293
Cold War 11–12, 25–6, 30–1, 33, 43, 64–5, 68, 90–2, 94, 96–105, 107–9, 111, 114, 117–9, 124–5, 130, 143, 147–8, 150, 154–5, 159–63, 165–6, 169–70, 183, 186, 201–3, 206–7, 218, 222, 227, 246–8, 264–7, 270–1, 276, 286, 289–90, 298, 313
collection 3–4, 9–11, 16–19, 26, 29, 43, 46–7, 59–73, 89, 92, 111, 115–22, 124–5, 127–8, 135–40, 142, 147–50, 152, 154–6, 159, 161, 163, 170, 172, 184, 188, 191–9, 2001–2, 204, 208–15, 220–2, 238, 240, 247, 249–50, 255, 257–62, 269, 272, 274, 276, 291–2, 294–7, 301–4, 317
Commercial Intelligence 73, 241
Commonwealth Investigation Service (CIS) 161
Communication Capabilities Development Programme (CCDP, UK) 303
communications intelligence (COMINT) 37, 90–1, 164, 211–3, 220–1
Communications Security Establishment Canada (CSEC) 155–9
Communist Party of the Soviet Union (CPSU) 329, 231, 233
competitive intelligence 73
corruption 36, 38, 50, 72–4, 76, 78, 178, 231, 265, 267, 289, 291, 317, 319
Council of Europe (CoE) 272, 309–10
counterespionage 54, 98–9, 136, 162, 172, 178–9, 195–6, 214, 259, 271
counterintelligence (CI) 3–11, 16–20, 27, 31, 54, 65, 71, 74–5, 79, 98, 150, 162, 193–4, 196, 203, 207–10, 219–21, 228, 230–2, 236–7, 241, 260, 268, 318

counterterrorism (CT) 10, 65, 102, 124, 149–50, 153, 155–6, 158, 172, 1766, 188, 214, 223–5, 231, 234, 240–1, 245–9, 251–4, 258, 266, 268, 271, 273, 318
covert action 3–4, 9–10, 12, 17–18, 28, 35, 41, 44, 65, 71, 73, 193, 267–8, 270
Criminal Intelligence Service of Canada (CISC) 156
critical energy infrastructure protection (CEIP) 286
cryptography 164, 269
Cuban Missile Crisis 43–4, 91. 98, 144, 187
Cyber Command (CYBERCOM, US) 93
cyberspace 63, 137, 193, 251, 256–62
and cyber security 128, 226
and cyberterrorism 250, 252, 254, 258

Dandeker, Christopher 29
data 11, 15–16, 20, 26, 31, 59–60, 64–5, 69, 72–3, 77, 93, 112, 114, 116, 120–1, 124, 126, 169, 186, 192–3, 195, 198–9, 224–5, 237, 249–50, 252, 254, 257–62, 269, 272, 282–3, 296–8, 301, 303, 312, 316, 319
Data Communications Bill (UK) 93
deep penetration agents (moles) 11, 17, 54, 98–100, 103, 187
Defence Imagery and Geo-spatial Organisation (DIGO, AUS) 161, 165, 169
Defense Intelligence Agency (DIA, US) 4, 45, 115, 119–20, 125, 148, 197–8
Defense Intelligence Headquarters (DIH, JPN) 201–2
Defence Intelligence Organisation (DIO, AUS) 163–4
Defence Intelligence Staff (DIS, UK) 109, 139
Defence Signals Directorate (DSD, AUS) 161, 163–4
democracy 16, 36, 48, 100, 138, 145, 149, 151, 194, 210, 232, 297, 306
denial and deception (D&D) 47, 276–82
Department of Defense (DoD) 51, 91, 93, 126, 284
Department of Homeland Security (DHS, US) 150, 242, 253, 318
Der Derian, James 28–30
Diaz, Milton 27
'digital debris' 261
Direction Centrale des Renseignements Généraux (RG, FRA) 172, 179
Direction Centrale du Renseignement Intérieur (DCRI, FRA) 172, 178–80
Direction de la Protection et de la Sécurité de la Défense (DPSD, FRA) 172
Direction du renseignement militaire (DRM, FRA) 172
Direction de la Surveillance du Territoire (DST, FRA) 172, 178

Direction Générale de la Sécurité Extérieure (DGSE, FRA) 172, 174, 176, 178–81
Director of Central Intelligence (DCI) 5, 9, 44–5, 102, 119–20, 126, 149, 183
Director of National Intelligence (DNI) 3, 25, 29, 149, 173, 180, 246, 252
Directorate of Economic Intelligence (DEI, UK) 109
dissemination 9–11, 13, 17–18, 20, 29, 39, 59–61, 63–5, 67, 69–71, 124, 135–6, 139–41, 183, 197, 236, 240, 259
double agents 98, 101
Duffield, Mark 265
Dulles, Allen 125–6, 162

Economic Intelligence Department (EID, UK) 108
Ehrman, John 29, 31
electronic intelligence (ELINT) 90–2, 173, 177, 211–12
encryption 88, 90, 257, 262, 268–9, 299
energy security 143, 283–8
espionage 4, 6, 8–9, 12–13, 16, 25, 27 31, 51, 56, 73, 88, 96–104, 138–9, 143, 149, 169, 171, 177, 184, 191–4, 198–200, 202, 208, 258, 271
European Court of Human Rights (ECtHR) 308
European Parliament (EP) 273, 288, 302
European Police Office (EUROPOL) 318
European Union (EU) 237, 288, 302
Evans, Johnathan 65, 245, 254, 302, 312
Evidence-Based Intelligence Studies (EBIS) 12
exceptionalism 35, 40, 147
extraordinary rendition 17, 167–8, 180, 268, 27–3, 305, 308–10

Facebook 68, 129, 214, 300
Federal Bureau of Investigation (FBI, US) 16, 59, 61, 98, 124, 139, 149, 180, 203, 223, 230, 234, 271, 305
Federal Criminal Police Office (BKA, GER) 220–1, 223, 226
Federalnaya Sluzhba Bezopasnosti (FSB, RUS) 228–9, 231–4
Ferris, John 5, 7, 52, 89–90
Financial Transactions Reports Analysis Centre (FINTRAC, CA) 156, 158–9
food security 283–4, 288–9
Foreign Affairs Committee (FAC, UK) 6
Foreign Broadcast Information Service (FBIS, US) 68, 124
foreign intelligence liaison 9
foreign intelligence services 6, 8, 124, 196, 236, 238, 272, 293, 318
Fuchs, Klaus 100
'fusion centres' 64, 150, 318

Gemeinsames Terrorismusabwehrzentrum (GTAZ, GER) 224–6
geophysical intelligence 121
geospatial intelligence 16, 68, 156–7, 165
Gill, Peter 6–7, 26, 29, 31
Global Game 73, 75
globalization 71, 93, 130, 246, 249, 252, 254, 260, 263–9, 271, 273
Global South 265–7, 270
Google 124, 251
Gordievsky, Oleg 99, 101, 103
Government Codes and Cyphers School (GCCS, UK) 89–90
Government Communications Headquarters (GCHQ, UK) 7, 91–2, 94, 96, 135, 138–9, 180, 269, 299, 308
Government Delegate Commission for Intelligence Affairs (CDGAI, SPN) 235, 237–8
Gulf War 45, 54, 174, 275, 278, 289

Hague, William 305
Halliday, Fred 37–8
Handel, Michael 5, 52–3, 55, 57
Hanssen, Robert 98–9, 177
Hastedt, Glenn 5, 30, 35
Hayden, Gen. Michael 53, 270, 272
Herman, Michael 4, 6–7, 20, 28, 78
Hezbollah (Hizb'allah) 213, 246
Hoffman, John 37
Holloway, David 101
'honey traps' 101
House Permanent Select Committee on Intelligence (HPSCI, US) 307, 310
human intelligence (HUMINT) 9–12, 55–7, 68–9, 87, 89, 91–2, 94, 96–7, 115, 127, 130, 143, 155, 157, 177, 186, 193, 196–8, 204, 208, 211, 213–15, 220, 226, 259, 261, 267
human rights 36, 166–8, 192, 268, 270, 273, 289, 291, 296, 303, 306–7, 314, 319
Hussein, Saddam 43, 53, 275–6

ideology 38–9, 52, 71, 77, 99, 176, 247–8, 265
imagery intelligence (IMINT) 46, 64, 68, 89, 94, 115, 198, 201, 205, 221–2, 226
Immerman, Richard H. 12, 56, 260
Indian Intelligence Bureau (IB) 182
indicators and warnings (I&W's) 127
Industrial Intelligence Centre (IIC, UK) 107
information communication technology (ICT) 123–4, 129–30
information pathologies 79
information sharing 75, 77, 80, 150, 205, 254, 258–9, 302, 318
Inspector-General of Intelligence and Security (IGIS, AUS) 166, 168
Institute for Intelligence and Special Operations (Mossad, ISR) 209–11, 214–17

Integrated Terrorism Assessment Centre (ITAC, CA) 157
Intelligence and Research Bureau (INR, US) 4
Intelligence and Security Committee (ISC, UK) 6, 127, 142, 308
'intelligence brokers' 69
Intelligence Community (IC) 5, 12, 39, 44, 51, 58–60, 63, 65–9, 72, 79, 94, 113–16, 119–20, 126–8, 130, 135–6, 138, 141–3, 148–9, 153–4, 158–61, 163, 166, 169, 172–3, 178–80, 201–3, 206–11, 214, 218, 226, 235, 237, 245, 248, 250, 252–4, 257, 260, 276, 278, 286, 305, 309–10, 317
intelligence cycle 9, 11–12, 20, 35, 39, 59, 60–7, 70, 128, 137, 142, 184, 206, 219, 256–7
intelligence failures 16, 39, 43, 49, 53, 96, 103, 120, 182–3, 188, 253
intelligence objectives 112, 200, 236
intelligence product 45, 60, 64, 69, 94, 115, 126–7, 156–7, 219–20
Intelligence Reform and Terrorism Prevention Act (IRTPA) 149
intelligence studies 4–9, 12–21, 24–5, 33–4, 36–7, 70, 105, 242, 274, 283–4, 289, 313–4
International Assessments Staff (CA) 157
International Energy Agency (IEA) 287
international political economy (IPE) 287, 319
Internet 9, 64, 78, 80–1, 93, 97, 123–4, 128–9, 155, 224, 246, 250, 256, 258–9, 261–2, 268–9, 272, 299–303, 312
Iran 37–8, 44, 71, 75, 103, 211–12, 214–15, 217, 220, 246, 260, 275, 289, 314; Iran-*contra* scandal 12
Iraq 5, 12, 18, 37, 56, 89, 194, 213, 217, 246, 303, 314; 2003 invasion of 38, 45, 53, 57, 69–71, 102–3, 120, 135, 142, 165, 167, 180, 254, 266, 271, 278, 289; Operation DESERT STORM 54, 97, 115, 213, 216
Israeli Defense Force (IDF) 209–14, 216–17

Jervis, Robert 5, 53, 189
Johnson, Loch K. 5, 30–2
Joint Chiefs of Staff (JCS, US) 26, 126
Joint Intelligence Committee (JIC, UK) 7, 28, 60, 63, 68, 106–12, 136–43, 184–5, 187–8, 205–6
Joint Terrorism Analysis Centre (JTAC, UK) 140, 224
Jomini, Antonie-Henri 50–3, 56
Just War theory 28

Kaldor, Mary 265, 289
Kant, Immanuel 101, 104
Kennan, George 125
Kent, Sherman 4, 43–4, 63, 70, 73, 184
Khrushchev, Nikita 43, 210, 230
Kim Jung Il 44

Komitet Gosudarstvennoi Bezopasnosti (KGB, RUS) 12, 56, 98–103, 119, 207, 227–34
Kommando Strategische Aufklärung (KSA, GER) 219, 221, 226
Kosovo 37, 222

Lander, Stephen 270, 317
Laqueur, Walter 5, 26, 105, 112
Lefebvre, Stéphane 154–5, 293
liberal institutionalism 48–9, 293–5
liberty 40, 76, 130, 148, 152, 272
Libya 37, 181, 300 308

Machiavelli, Nico 3, 51–2
materials intelligence 121
McConnell, Mike 25, 246
measurement and signature intelligence (MASINT) 68, 113–16, 118–20
Militärischer Abschirmdienst (MAD, GER) 219, 221, 226
military intelligence (MI) 9–10, 13, 18, 26, 61, 65, 96–8, 108, 111, 139, 162, 184–5, 194, 196–9, 202, 208–9, 219, 221–2, 226, 228, 230–1, 238, 313
Military Intelligence Department (MID, CHN) 196
Military Intelligence Directorate (MI, IND) 184
Ministry for Economic Warfare (UK) 106–7
Ministry of Defence (MoD) 105, 139, 141, 184, 301, 308
Ministry of Foreign Affairs (MOFA, JPN) 201–5, 207
Ministry of Intelligence and National Security (VEVAK, Iran) 38
Ministry of Public Security (MPS, China) 194, 196
Ministry of State Security (MSS, China) 194–6, 199
Morgan, Richard 149
multiplayer online games (MMOGs) 251

Naím, Moisés 267
National Centre for Critical Infrastructure Protection (CNPIC, SPN) 241
National Counterterrorism Coordination Centre (CNCA, SPN) 240–1
National Crime Agency (NCA, UK) 313, 318
National Geo-spatial Agency (NGA, US) 16
National Intelligence Centre (CNI, SPN) 235–42
National Intelligence Council (CNR, FRA) 173
National Intelligence Estimate (NIE) 60, 142, 206, 210, 253
National Intelligence Strategy 25
National Intelligence Topics (NIT's) 68
National Intelligence University (US) 4
National Police Agency (NPA, JPN) 201, 203–5, 208

National Reconnaissance Office (NRO, US) 16
national security 3, 8, 10–11, 19–20, 36, 40, 53,
    67, 92, 137–8, 146–8, 152, 156, 164–5, 169,
    194, 199, 210, 236, 254, 262, 285–6, 289, 306,
    308, 310, 312–13
National Security Act (US) 58, 147
National Security Agency (NSA, US) 5, 16, 20,
    53–4, 90–4, 1176, 164, 180, 188–9, 269–70,
    272, 308
National Security Council (NSC, US) 147–8
National Security Council (NSC, UK) 137
'new terrorism' 264, 266, 268
New York Police Department (NYPD) 249
Nolte, William 5, 19–20
North Atlantic Treaty Organization (NATO) 48,
    62, 100, 109, 125, 154, 219, 227, 237, 286, 289
North Korea 44, 118, 203–4, 208, 220, 270
nuclear intelligence (NUCINT) 114, 122

O'Connell, Kevin 30–1
objectivity 44–5, 48
Office of National Assessments (ONA, AUS) 161,
    163–5
Office of Strategic Services (OSS, US) 26
Omand, Sir David 7, 19–20, 28
Open Source Center (OSC, US) 124, 129
open source intelligence (OSINT) 9–11, 17, 42,
    68, 72–3, 76, 78–9, 81–2, 123–30, 140–1,
    143, 186, 192, 198–99, 201, 203–4, 250, 254,
    258–9, 268, 273, 292, 302, 319
optical intelligence (OPINT) 117–8, 120–1
organised crime 220, 223–5, 232, 239, 241, 249,
    267, 270–1, 313–9
Organization of Arab Petroleum Exporting
    Countries (OAPEC) 285
Ott, Marvin 306
Overseas Economic Intelligence Committee
    (OEIC, UK) 112
oversight 10, 33–5, 38–41, 47, 49, 119, 141–2,
    151, 189, 226, 230–3, 237–8, 261, 268, 272–3,
    304–12, 317, 319

paramilitary operations 3, 64, 193, 209, 211, 278
Parlamentarisches Kontrollgremium (PKGr,
    GER) 307
Parliamentary Joint Committee on Intelligence
    and Security (PJCIS, AUS) 166
Penkovsky, Oleg 97–99, 102
Peoples Liberation Army (PLA, CHN) 93, 196
Philby, Kim 98–100, 102–3, 177
Phythian, Mark 7, 21, 29, 30–1, 126, 275
policy-making 105, 109, 126, 136–7, 142, 145,
    147–9, 153, 189, 193, 202, 204–6, 208, 233
politicization 13, 45, 70, 178
Powell, Colin 57
privacy 9, 93, 124, 155, 178, 238, 250, 262, 269,
    277, 297–8, 302–3, 306

Privacy International (NGO) 297
private security agencies 271, 310–11
propaganda 3, 8, 79, 101, 124, 251, 278–9
protected information (PROTINT) 69
Provisional Irish Republican Army (IRA) 102
Public Security Intelligence Agency (PSIA,
    JPN) 201–4, 208
Putin, Vladimir 36, 228–9, 231–4

radar intelligence (RADINT) 118, 121
radio frequency (RF) intelligence 115, 121
Raghavan, Srinath 184, 189
realism 28, 36–7, 48
'Real Intelligence Cycle' 66
Research and Analysis Wing (R&AW, IND) 182,
    185–8, 190
research and development (R&D) 262, 276,
    278–9, 281
Reveron, Derek 293
Review of Intelligence on Weapons of Mass
    Destruction see *Butler Review*
Richelson, Jeffrey T. 5, 120
Rumsfeld, Donald 57

Schelling, Thomas 55–6
Schindler, John R. 54
Secret Intelligence Service (SIS, UK) 4, 90, 138,
    183, 230, 308
'security dilemma' 48, 49, 91
Security Intelligence Review Committee (SIRC,
    CA) 155
Senate Select Committee on Intelligence (SSCI,
    US) 307, 309–10
Security Service (MI5, UK) 98, 138–40, 182,
    202, 245, 266, 307
Serious Organised Crime Agency (SOCA,
    UK) 140, 317–8
Shabak (ISR) 210, 214, 216–17
short message service (SMS) 78, 129, 259, 299
Sims, Jennifer E. 25, 28
Skocpol, Theda 38–9
Skype 269, 299
Sluzhba Vneshnei Razvedki (SVR, RUS) 99,
    228, 231–3
Smart Nation 72–3
Socialist Unity Party of Germany (SED) 39
social media intelligence (SOCMINT) 68
social networking 93, 124, 129, 251, 254, 297,
    301–2
Soviet Union 37–8, 92, 100, 105, 163, 166, 183,
    194, 202, 229–30, 248, 270
special forces 181, 268–9, 271
Strachan, Hew 50, 52–3
strategic analytic model 75–6
strategic intelligence 4, 30, 1, 53, 107, 163, 175,
    184, 200, 210, 218–19, 226, 241, 248
strategic studies 7, 34, 36, 198

strategy 29, 31, 34, 44–7, 49–52, 54–5, 58, 67, 82, 106, 108, 137, 156, 160, 191, 194, 199, 201, 218, 226, 235, 241–2, 245–7, 276–8, 281, 309, 317
Straw, Jack 308
Sullivan, William 176, 305
surveillance 11, 29, 36, 65, 90, 93, 114, 117–18, 139, 153–4, 156, 159, 161–2, 166,177, 189, 231, 239–40, 250–1, 258, 261–2, 272. 297–9, 304, 306, 308

'talent spotter' 102
'target centric analysis' 67
technical intelligence (TECHINT) 9–11, 124, 130, 186, 221
Tehrik-e-Taliban Pakistan (TTP) 246
Tenet, George 102
terrorism 10, 54, 57, 65, 69, 75, 78, 93–4, 102, 125, 136–41, 149–50, 153, 155–9, 163, 166–7, 169, 172, 176, 188, 190, 194, 203, 211, 214–15, 220, 223–6, 232–4, 239–41, 245–54, 257–8264–8, 270–1, 273, 303, 309, 313, 316, 318
Terrorism Early Warning group (TEW, US) 249
tradecraft 9, 98, 103, 129, 193, 198, 250, 254, 261
'traffic analysis' 92
trafficking 37, 148, 172, 233, 240, 246, 265, 270, 317–19
'transmission' 46
Treverton, Gregory 5, 19, 64
Turner, Michael 5, 35
Twitter 68, 129, 214, 300
Tzu, Sun 3, 28, 31, 50–8, 87, 96, 191

UK-USA Communications Intelligence Agreement 154

Unified Command of State Security Forces and Corps (CEMU, SPN) 239–40
United Nations (UN) 20, 74, 269, 273, 283–4, 286–7, 314
  Food and Agriculture Organization (FAO) 288
  Office for Drugs and Crime (UNODC) 315
  Security Council (UNSC) 219, 233, 284, 288
United States Constitution 76, 105, 145–7, 152

Varash (ISR) 210
Verfassungsschutz (BfV/LfV, GER) 210 219, 221–2
Viet Minh 56
visual intelligence (VISINT) 210, 212, 214–15

'walk-ins' 102
Warner, Michael 5, 33–5, 37, 42, 256, 315
Watergate scandal 4
War of Attrition 212–14, 216
'War on Terror' 54, 166, 225, 249, 266, 271, 305
weapons of mass destruction (WMD) 6, 43, 97, 102, 120, 139, 169, 220, 223, 240, 246, 252–3, 274–82
Weinberger, David 75
Whaley, Barton 278
Wikileaks 97, 123–4, 204, 258, 261, 301
Williams, Raymond 33–4, 316
'window of opportunity' 275, 278–80, 282
'window of vulnerability' 275–8, 281
Wolf, Markus 102
World Brain 72–3, 75

Yeltsin, Boris 231, 233
Yom Kippur War 210, 213–16

Zegart, Amy 9, 308

44626277R00215

Made in the USA
San Bernardino, CA
19 January 2017